Fathoms Deep But Not Forgotten:
Wisconsin's Lost Ships

Volume I: Kenosha to Port Washington

Brendon Baillod

A Complete Reference to the Ships & Shipwrecks of Southeastern Wisconsin

A Wisconsin Underwater Archeology Association Publication
with support from the
Great Lakes Shipwreck Research Foundation

Fathoms Deep But Not Forgotten: Wisconsin's Lost Ships
Volume I: Kenosha to Port Washington

Copyright © 2010 by the Wisconsin Underwater Archeology Association. All rights reserved. No part of this publication may be reproduced or transmitted in any form or by any means, electronic or mechanical, including photocopying, recording or any information storage and retrieval system, without permission in writing from the publisher. Persons or organizations wishing to reprint text or images contained in this volume should contact the author for permission. All images used in this volume are from the Author's personal collection unless otherwise noted.

First printing, January 2010

Inquiries concerning corrections to this volume, obtaining retail copies of this volume or further information about specific vessels may be addressed to the author via email at: brendon@baillod.com.

Inquiries about reproduction rights should be addressed to the publisher:

Wisconsin Underwater Archeology Association
P.O. Box 6081
Madison, Wisconsin 53716

DESIGN: Brendon Baillod & Betsy True
EDITING: Pam Grill
PHOTO RESEARCH: Brendon Baillod
PRINTING: Omnipress, Inc. Madison, Wisconsin

ISBN 978-0-9842919-1-5

Library of Congress Control Number: 2010922832

Cover Photo: An original woodcut engraving of Milwaukee Harbor in 1880 from Harper's Illustrated Magazine - taken from an original in the Author's Collection.

Table of Contents

Introduction 1

Part I – Subject Overview

Shipwrecks & Archeology 4
Lake Michigan Maritime History Overview 7
Great Lakes Shipwreck Research Methods 9
Searching for Great Lakes Shipwrecks 15
Shipwreck Discoveries, Locations & Laws 21
Great Lakes Shipwreck Conservation 25
Methodology & Explanation of Terms 28

Part II – Wisconsin's Lost Ships – Kenosha to Port Washington

Kenosha Shipwrecks 34
Ships Built at Kenosha 57
Racine Shipwrecks 60
Ships Built at Racine 86
Milwaukee Shipwrecks 1800-1875 92
Milwaukee Shipwrecks 1876–1900 113
Milwaukee Shipwrecks 1901-1925 128
Milwaukee Shipwrecks 1926-2000 142
Unidentified Milwaukee Wreck Sites 156
Ships Built at Milwaukee 161
Port Washington Shipwrecks 194

Part III – Wisconsin Shipwreck Stories

Lake Michigan's Lost *Mistress* – 1941 219
The Harrowing Loss of the Schooner *Jo Vilas* – 1876 222
The Last Run of the *Velocipede* – 1877 223
Captain Krumer's Close Call on the *Reliable* – 1913 227
The Brig *Mahoning* Joins Wisconsin's Sunken Fleet – 1864 229
The Schooner *Maine* Comes Ashore – 1887 233
Chopped out of the Steamer *H.A. Root* – 1907 235
The Yacht *Idler*: 20 Hours of Hard Work – 1895 236
The Schooner *Snowdrop*: Beaten to Pieces on the Rocks – 1892 237
The Loss of the Schooner *Edna* – 1887 238
The Scow *Hunter* Overturns – 1887 239
The *Toboggan* Founders – 1887 239
The Fireboat *M.F.D. No. 23* Meets a Fiery End – 1929 240
The Schooner *Alma* Goes on the Rocks – 1892 244
The Schooner *Monguagon* Goes to the Bottom – 1888 245
The Grave of the Steamer *M.H. Stuart* – 1948 247
The Wreck of the *Lady Elgin* – 1860 253

Bibliography 262
Vessel Index 268
About the WUAA 278
About the Author 280

*This book is dedicated to my father, Bob Baillod,
who introduced me to the Great Lakes.*

Introduction

Lake Michigan is statistically the most treacherous of the Great Lakes. She has hosted more shipwrecks that any of her four sisters and sees some of the most violent weather. It should not be surprising that her beaches are lined with the bones of thousands of 19th century sailing ships. 100 years ago, the Great Lakes were the equivalent of today's interstate freeway system. They carried nearly all the raw materials and commerce of the fast growing region known today as the rust belt. On a summer day in 1870, nearly 100 ships might pass a given point on Lake Michigan, and each of Wisconsin's port cities had a substantial maritime community and culture. Schooner masts bristled like forests in Wisconsin harbors, and thousands of young men worked on the docks and on the boats. Nearly all the industries of eastern Wisconsin were geared toward or dependent on Lake commerce, and people of that day followed the movement of Lake vessels the way people today follow professional sports.

In the passing of a century, our proud and vibrant maritime culture has all but disappeared. Wisconsin still has her ports, but they are now filled with pleasure boats and marinas. The arrival of a big ore boat or cement boat now attracts a small crowd, much the same way the arrival of old Lake schooner did in the 1920s. Today, the primary vestiges of our Wisconsin maritime history are our lighthouses, life saving stations and shipwrecks. Shipwrecks, in particular, hold a special fascination for many people. Their tragic and heroic stories have yielded countless books and movies and their remains have inspired generations of treasure hunters, sport divers and archeologists.

As society has become more technological and generic, many people and port towns have sought to rediscover and reconnect with the maritime past that defined their communities and shaped the lives of their ancestors. Few historical resources provide as tangible and compelling a connection to a community's past as the physical remains of an actual 19th century shipwreck. The story of the ship's career, the people that built and sailed her, the story of her loss and of her discovery and documentation, all provide an important link to our maritime past and enrich the character and identity of our communities.

It is consequently, appropriate that Wisconsin has taken a leading role among state governments in preserving and documenting our maritime past. The Wisconsin Historical Society has supported a maritime archeology program for over twenty years and Wisconsin now leads all Great Lakes states in nominating historic shipwrecks to the National Register of Historic Places. The Wisconsin Historical Society's maritime archeology program gave birth to the Wisconsin Underwater Archeology Association, a non-profit community volunteer group, which assists the State program in documenting and preserving our Wisconsin shipwrecks.

The result has been a tangible benefit to our communities and to our historical resources. Our waterfronts have become regentrified and play host to maritime museums and interpretive displays, and a vibrant tourism exists among divers who travel to our port cities to visit our many shipwreck sites. A code of honor now exists among most divers who "take only pictures and leave only bubbles," recognizing that our historic wrecks belong to all Wisconsinites, and should be preserved for the future.

Despite the significance of Wisconsin's historical ships and shipwrecks, no comprehensive inventory of them has ever been published. It is noteworthy that Wisconsin waters likely contain about 1000 historic vessels, making the task of creating a comprehensive inventory nearly impossible. However, the emergence of the electronic age has made the task much less daunting than it had been even ten years ago.

I began collecting accounts of historic shipwrecks in Wisconsin waters over 20 years ago with the intent of creating a comprehensive database and I soon discovered that a number of other researchers were doing likewise. Through my affiliation with the Association for Great Lakes Maritime History (AGLMH), I was able to collaborate with many other researchers and historians, including the Wisconsin Historical Society, to build a comprehensive collection of historic Wisconsin shipwreck accounts taken from original primary source material.

I also worked with the Wisconsin Marine Historical Society at Milwaukee Public Library to transcribe the vessel index cards of legendary marine historian Herman Runge and to place their 50,000 vessel enrollment database online. Through these efforts, I developed a familiarity with 19th century Lake vessels and I built a significant collection of original 19th century Great Lakes books, registers, charts and photos, including full runs of many 19th century Great Lakes marine registers.

In the development of my shipwreck data, I must acknowledge the vessel enrollment databases of Dr. Charles E. Feltner and Walter Lewis as particularly important to this effort, as well as the collections and resources of C. Patrick Labadie, Dave Swayze and Bill McNeil. My own newspaper microfilm research was conducted over many years and relied primarily on the Milwaukee Sentinel, the Racine Advocate and the Chicago Inter-Ocean, although I located and fleshed out many accounts through the work of other local researchers including former Wisconsin Underwater Archeologist David Cooper, the late Walter Hirthe of Milwaukee, Bob Jaeck of Racine, Steve Radovan and the late Jim Jetzer of Sheboygan and Rick Smith of Port Washington. The Wisconsin marine newspaper transcriptions of Russ Leitz also proved extremely important.

It was my initial intention to present a purely historical account of area ships and shipwrecks, but with the frequency of new shipwreck discoveries and many unidentified area wreck sites still requiring investigation, I felt that discussion of physical remains and site locations was important and would be beneficial to future investigators. It is noteworthy that the Great Lakes wreck hunting community is rapidly graying and few young people are entering the ranks. As such, it seemed that this publication would be a good opportunity to record and preserve the accounts of discovery for many obscure and otherwise unknown wreck sites. Along these lines, I approached and interviewed a number of local historians and wreck hunters who were most gracious in sharing their remembrances with me. Among these were Jerry Guyer, Bob Jaeck, Rick Smith, Paul Ehorn, Steve Radovan, Harry Zych, Dr. Richard Boyd, Dan Johnson, the late Bill Prince, Kent Bellrichard, Butch Klopp, Roger Chapman and John Steele.

I must also note here the substantial contributions of Keith Meverden and Tamara Thomsen of the Wisconsin Historical Society's Maritime Archeology Program. Like their predecessors, they have worked tirelessly to document new and existing wreck sites in Wisconsin waters and have been particularly innovative in recording wreck sites both historically and physically. They have continued to forge a strong relationship with the sport diving community and to share their fieldwork with Wisconsin's port communities. Keith and Tammy have personally visited most of the discovered remains mentioned in this book and have documented many of them photographically and historically.

Given the above pool of resources and expertise, it may seem likely that I've captured every ship lost in the area of inquiry. Unfortunately, I know from experience that this volume has likely overlooked as many as 10% of the area's losses. Many early wrecks were not recorded in newspapers, insurance records or government registers, and many vessels simply vanished on the Lake and could lie anywhere. I am never surprised when a new wreck is discovered many miles from where it was reported to have gone down. New historical resources are also constantly becoming available, such as Google Books, which frequently reveal new sources for maritime research. It is consequently, likely that new historical wreck accounts will be located and corrections to existing accounts will emerge. I would consequently, welcome corrections and additions to the material in this book by readers.

Readers will note that most of the wreck and ship accounts in this book are quite short. As a rule, I attempted to limit each account to no more than a paragraph in the interest of space and time. With well over 300 historical wrecks detailed, it would be prohibitive to include a full overview of each. Indeed, many of the wrecks herein have had entire books written about them. As such, I have attempted to give only the central facts about each shipwreck and I have provided only the most primary reference and photo. In nearly every case, I have a complete file on the vessel, often with multiple news accounts, career info and photos. For some vessels however, I included detailed historical overviews in a separate section. I did so in instances where I had previously published my research into a given wreck event. Most of these pieces were previously published in Soundings, the quarterly publication of the Wisconsin Marine Historical Society, Inland Seas, the quarterly journal of the Great Lakes Historical Society, Anchor News, the quarterly publication of the Wisconsin Maritime Museum and Underwater Heritage, the WUAA publication.

I must also acknowledge the generous cooperation of several public research collections and institutions. Although the entries in this book are almost exclusively the result of original research by myself and my colleagues, I did make use of the files of the Historical Collections of the Great Lakes at Bowling Green State University, the Wisconsin Marine Historical Society at the Milwaukee Public Library, the C. Patrick Labadie Collection at the George N. Fletcher Library in Alpena, Michigan, the Wisconsin Maritime Museum Collection at Manitowoc, the Door County Maritime Museum at Sturgeon Bay, the Tri-Cities Historical Museum at Grand Haven, Michigan and the Collections of the State Historical Society of Wisconsin at Madison. Kevin Cullen and Chris Winters at Milwaukee's Discovery World Museum also provided valuable graphical material and insight.

It is noteworthy that every marine collection and historical society around the Lakes agreed to waive image usage fees for this book. I am extremely grateful to these organizations, as this book would not have been possible without their generosity. In particularly, the Great Lakes Marine Collection at the Milwaukee Public Library, the Historical Collections of the Great Lakes at Bowling Green State University and the Thunder Bay NMS C. Patrick Labadie Collection at Alpena's George N. Fletcher Library were most helpful in making their vessel images available. The Wisconsin Historical Society, the Kenosha Historical Society, the Tri-Cities Historical Museum at Grand Haven, MI, the Wisconsin Maritime Museum and the Door County Maritime Museum were also most generous. In instances where I have credited an image to the "Author's Collection," it is because I personally own a verifiable archival original of the image, such as an antique stereo-opticon, carte-de-viste or antique nautical/harbor chart. I believe strongly in recognizing the provenance of historical images and I believe that crediting images correctly to our community historical groups helps publicize their collections and supports their ongoing work.

I would also like to acknowledge the support of the Wisconsin Underwater Archeology Association. This book is a benefit for the WUAA and all proceeds from sales will serve to support their mission of documenting and preserving underwater historic sites. Two years ago, WUAA approached me with the suggestion of publishing my Wisconsin shipwreck database serially in their publication, Underwater Heritage. Each quarter, for the last two years, I authored a new article detailing the wrecks of a different port, with Milwaukee requiring four articles. WUAA then offered to publish the articles as the first in a series of books. I would like to offer my sincere thanks to Danny Aerts, the editor of Underwater Heritage, Besty True and to WUAA directors Dr. Richard Boyd, Greg Kent and Janet Defnet for their support and encouragement.

Lastly, and in particular, I would like to thank my mother, Pam Grill, who proofread this manuscript, created the index, performed much of the layout and provided substantial editorial guidance. Without her diligent but tedious work, this book would not have been possible. I hope to publish the remainder of my database in a series of books over the coming years. Readers are advised to check the Wisconsin Underwater Archeology Association website, www.wuaa.org, for information about the availability of other titles. Readers who wish to contact me, may do so via email at brendon@ship-wreck.com. I would be pleased to hear from readers and I welcome corrections, additions and feedback.

Brendon Baillod
January 2010

Part I: Subject Overview

Archeology and Shipwrecks

I am often asked why I use the term "underwater archeology" to describe the work we do on Great Lakes shipwrecks. In most cases, the wrecks we study are under 200 years old. In many cases, they are under 100 years old. By European standards, Great Lakes wrecks hardly qualify as historic. Indeed, many people consider Great Lakes shipwrecks to be industrial waste from a recent era.

The main reason that Great Lakes shipwrecks attract attention is that they occurred during a time of rapid technological change. In 1840, people could not conceive of something like an airplane or an automobile. In fact, the people who founded Milwaukee would have scoffed at the idea of an electric light and would have considered cell phones and personal computers to be pure science fiction. So, although Great Lakes shipwrecks may not be particularly "old," they represent a tangible example of the technology of a time completely alien to ours. Most ships of the 19th century were built of wood with hand tools and were sailed by men from an entirely different culture than that of today.

In recent years, the field of Industrial Archeology has grown in popularity to the extent that many universities offer formal programs in it. Technological change has happened so quickly that the technology of even 100 years ago is now considered esoteric and interesting. There is a tremendous desire on the part of historically minded people to know more about the culture, technology and society of these relatively recent but culturally and technologically different times.

The discovery of a new historic shipwreck off one of our lakeshore communities consequently, fires the imagination of local citizens and attracts considerable attention precisely because of this desire to reconnect with a simple but more demanding way of life. It is for these reasons that we search for shipwrecks and we respond to inquiries from land owners who have found wreck debris on their beach. Our first task is generally to identify the remains in question in order to provide some context and community connection for the wrecksite.

Most people are not particularly interested on anonymous wrecks with no identity or story. A case in point in the Alvin Clark, raised from Green Bay in the early 1970s. Once she was again above the water, her owners billed her as "the mystery ship" even though it was very clear what her name was. She was presented with no tangible connection to the community and little interpretation was done to explain her role in our regional history. It is consequently, not surprising that people lost interest fairly quickly and she never lived up to her potential as a teaching tool for Great Lakes regional and community history.

It is for this reason that we spend a great deal of time and effort documenting and interpreting historic shipwrecks in Wisconsin. Our State Underwater Archeology program has examined, documented and published information on nearly every historic shipwreck discovered in Wisconsin waters. However, the State lacks the resources to locate new shipwrecks or to respond to every new shipwreck discovery. This book alone includes information on dozens of unidentified wrecksites that would benefit from further study and interpretation.

New discoveries are made every year and each new site has a story to tell. The key to preserving a site is getting the community to identify with it and to take ownership of it. For example, Sheboygan has very strong community ties to the wreck of the steamer Phoenix, as it played a large part in the settlement of their area and many families lost ancestors in the wreck. Likewise, Milwaukee has strong ties to the Prinz Willem V because is generates a vibrant dive tourism and because of its local lore. The Wisconsin Historical Society's Maritime Trails project represents a successful effort connect communities with their maritime history through shipwrecks and other historic maritime sites in this way.

However, many historic wrecksites have not received the attention they deserve and the result has been theft, damage and a failure to recognize truly historic resources and learn from them. An example is the schooner Gallinipper. She was built in 1832 as the fur trade schooner Nancy Dousman and is a relic of the years when all Lake Michigan was a wilderness. Her nearly intact remains were located in 1994 off Sheboygan, but were not publicized for nearly ten years until someone removed important artifacts from the wreck. Because nobody took the initiative to promptly research the site, identify the wreck and tell its story, its substantial historical significance was missed and very few people are even now aware of this tremendous historical and archeological bridge to Wisconsin's fur trade era.

To prevent these situations, Wisconsin has tried diligently to promote the study of shipwrecks as archeological sites. Some of the most interesting historical mysteries in Wisconsin waters still remain to be solved and are open to avocational historians and divers for their study and attention. Groups like the Wisconsin Underwater Archeology Association offer classroom and underwater training to people who are interested in learning how to research and tell the story of a wrecksite as well as how to document and interpret the physical remains of a shipwreck. WUAA works closely with the State Underwater Archeology program to share information and resources.

One of the most interesting archeological tasks associated with shipwreck sites is identifying a ship whose remains we have located. Shipwreck identification is a fascinating forensic pursuit and is similar in many ways to solving a crime. By examining the physical remains as well as the historical record, it is usually possible to make a reasonably certain identification of an historic wrecksite. It is also often a thrilling task to reconstruct the career of an historic vessel and to tell the story of how she wrecked, who her crew were and what their lives were like. In many cases, it is possible to connect a wrecksite directly to a community through living descendents or direct impact on the community. An obvious case in point is the wreck of the steamer Lady Elgin, which orphaned nearly 1000 children in Milwaukee and decimated her Irish community.

An equally interesting pursuit is documenting the physical remains of a wrecksite. We know that Great Lakes shipwrecks are a perishable resource. Even the biggest, deepest steel shipwrecks will someday crumble into nothing and old wood shipwrecks eventually collapse. With the arrival of invasive Zebra and Quagga Mussels adding weight to old wooden wrecks, it is more vital than ever that we begin to locate and document our historic shipwrecks while they are still recognizable. By recording the remains as we have found them, it allows future researchers to learn from the remains and perhaps to re-interpret the site. In my research, I routinely find it necessary to correct and update the work of previous researchers. This is largely due to the amazing amount of new information available from electronic sources. It now takes only minutes to pull together vast amounts of information that once would have taken years to collect. It is easier to see the "bigger picture" with respect to a historical event's significance and to give it a meaningful historical context. As such, the breadth and depth of our knowledge concerning our own community and regional history has grown exponentially in just the past ten years.

I can only imagine that a researcher twenty or fifty years from now might look back and our work and find ample opportunities to correct and enhance it. But, these researchers will not have the ability that we currently enjoy to see the physical remains of wrecksites in their present condition. Indeed, many wrecksites that we documented in the 1980s may not be present at all in 50 years. For these reasons, we spend a great deal of time and effort doing scale drawings, photo mosaics and sonar studies of wrecksites to record their condition and contents for future investigators.

We nominate our wrecksites to the State and National Registers of Historic Places not only to protect them, but also to make a lasting record of the fact that the historic resource exists and is significant to our area. It is a legacy that we leave for future generations who will be further removed in time than we are from our nautical heritage.

The study of Great Lakes shipwrecks may seem like relatively esoteric knowledge, akin to studying the mating habits of the blind cave fish. However, in the final analysis, it is important for us as historians to tell the stories of the sacrifices and endeavors of those who built the society we live in and to explain how modern midwestern metropolises such as Milwaukee and Chicago came into being through the Great Lakes maritime highway. A knowledge of how our maritime history shaped our culture and society is important for understanding many of the challenges we face today, such as global warming, economic instability and international trade issues. Cities grew here *because* of the Lakes. Had Lake Michigan been a large prairie or a forest, it is unlikely that Milwaukee or Chicago would exist. As the rate of technological change continues to accelerate, we will doubtless continue to face challenges and experience the continued need to adapt. A record of how we did so in the past is available in the technology that our ancestors left behind and serves to inform our decisions as we move forward.

Lake Michigan Maritime History Overview

The area around southeastern Wisconsin is rich in maritime history. Milwaukee was the chief grain port on the Lakes in the 1850s and saw a great deal of shipbuilding activity. To give the reader an historical context, one must note that Lake Michigan was almost entirely a wilderness prior to 1830. Chicago, Milwaukee, St. Joseph and Fort Howard (now Green Bay) were small settlements, and perhaps only a few dozen vessels visited even the largest ports on the Lake annually at that time. Prior to the 1830s, Lake Michigan was still largely unknown to easterners. Her primary visitors were military vessels, explorers and fur traders.

The Lake had been known since Jean Nicolet first entered her waters in 1634 in search of a route to China. He didn't find China, but succeeded in establishing trade relations with the Winnebago Indians and claimed the land for France. In 1673, Father Jacques Marquette and explorer Louis Joliet visited the Lake on their way to the the Mississippi River. Father Marquette returned in 1675 to minister to the Illinois Indians and died during his return voyage on the East coast of the Lake. The location of his death is still widely debated but is generally believed to have been just north of the entrance to Ludington or possibly at the mouth of the Betsie River. Marquette's bones were later removed by his Indian parishioners and buried in his mission at St. Ignace. Lake Michigan was again visited by French explorer and fur trader Rene-Robert Cavalier, Sieur de LaSalle in September of 1679 on his famous, ill-fated bark *Griffon*, which vanished in a gale on its return voyage from Green Bay. The *Griffon* was the first decked vessel on the western Great Lakes and has become the Lakes' most sought shipwreck. Original accounts of the *Griffon* loss are difficult to interpret and have spawned many claims as to the ship's final resting place. She is thought to lay somewhere in northern Lake Michigan.

Aside from possible visits by small French bateaux in the 1750s, there is no further record of significant decked vessel traffic on the Lake until about 1761 when the British gained control of Fort St. Joseph (now St. Joseph, Michigan) from the French. British control of the Lake was met with great resistance by the native Indian tribes. In 1763, Indians, with French encouragement, attacked the small forts on Lake Michigan, taking all but Green Bay. The forts were reclaimed by the British within a year, but control of the Lake remained uncertain. During the 1770s, small British sloops such as HMS *Felicity*, *Welcome* and *Archangel* regularly visited Lake Michigan to bring troops and supplies to the Forts and to manage relations with fur traders and Indian villages. These were likely the first decked vessels since LaSalle's *Griffon* to sail the Lake. Preserved in the log book of the HMS *Felicity*, is a visit to Milwaukee Bay by Captain Samuel Robertson in the Fall of 1779. She was the first decked vessel to call at the future port. By 1781, it appeared that the fledgling United States would inherit the Lake from the recently defeated British, but the opportunistic Spanish had other ideas. In January of that year, a Spanish expedition left St. Louis bound for Fort St. Joseph near Lake Michigan. Upon arrival, the small fort was quickly taken and the Spanish flag was raised over Lake Michigan. The Lake's Spanish period was very short-lived however, as negotiations in Europe between the US, Britain, France and Spain quickly resolved the matter, handing formal ownership to the fledgling US. By 1783, the United States had assumed ownership of Lake Michigan, but the British refused to remove their garrisons and allow free passage to US vessels until 1796. It wasn't until the establishment of Fort Dearborn (now Chicago) in 1803 that US vessels from the East began to traverse Lake Michigan. Pioneer settlers reported that only 2 or 3 vessels a year called at Fort Dearborn before 1812.

The last territorial warfare on Lake Michigan occurred during the War of 1812. The British had been encouraging unrest among the Lake Michigan Indian Tribes since the 1780s and saw the Tribes as a valuable ally in their efforts to retake the colonies. British and Indian forces moved on Fort Michilimackinac in the spring of 1812, taking it with little effort. When word of the British victory reached Fort Dearborn, the local tribes attacked, massacring many of the garrison and their families. War raged on the Great Lakes until the end of 1814, with many battles and skirmishes being fought in present-day Michigan and Wisconsin. By 1815 all hostilities had ceased and the Lakes were firmly and permanently under US control.

Traffic on the Lake grew slowly between 1815 and 1830. During this period, a small fleet of coastal trading schooners made occasional trips to the Lake, running mostly out of Detroit and Mackinac, but very few commercial vessels if any called a Lake Michigan port home. Nearly all traffic was associated with the fur trade or provisioning the forts. In 1817 the schooner *Heartless* became the Lake's first verified wreck when she stranded during an attempt to enter the Chicago River near the recently reconstructed Fort Dearborn. On October 3, 1818 the first verifiable fatal wreck occurred when the schooner *Hercules* was blown down and driven ashore just south of Fort Dearborn. Her entire crew perished, their remains reportedly being mauled by wild animals. The first steamer to enter Lake Michigan was the *Walk-in-the-Water*. In August of 1820, she took a group of excursionists, soldiers and dignitaries to the wilderness port of Fort Howard (now Green Bay.) The native Winnebago Indians had never seen a powered vessel and were very frightened of the ship, which they were told was propelled by sturgeons.

By 1835, the US had begun rapid westward expansion into the territories. Michigan, Wisconsin and Illinois began to receive thousands of immigrants and land speculators via schooners and steamers from the East. As cities grew up around the Lakes, vessel traffic further increased. In 1837, over 100 vessels called at St. Joseph, Michigan, and in 1838, over 400 vessels called at Chicago. In 1839, the grain trade was initiated with the East when the brig *Osceola* departed Chicago with the first load of wheat bound for Oswego, New York. By 1840, several newspapers existed around Lake Michigan and civilization was rapidly growing around the Lake. The population of cities such as Chicago and Milwaukee began to skyrocket and lumber was needed to build structures. The 1840s and 50s saw the emergence of many lumber ports on the Michigan coast. The rivers of the Michigan coast opened into large inland lakes before emptying into Lake Michigan, making them ideal sites for logging operations and sawmills. The ports of the Wisconsin coast were well situated for the grain trade and also served as busy shipbuilding centers.

In June of 1857, the first foreign flagged vessel entered Lake Michigan. The schooner *Madiera Pet* of Liverpool, England astonished Chicagoans of the day when she anchored off the harbor flying the Union Jack. She was the first of a growing surge of foreign vessels to visit the western Lakes by way of the newly enlarged Welland Canal. Throughout the remainder of the 1800s, the ports of the Michigan coast would provide most of the lumber used to build the cities of Milwaukee and Chicago. In 1858, over 800 different vessels called at the Port of Chicago and by the close of the Civil War, Lake Michigan was no longer a wilderness area, with well over 1000 different vessels crossing her waters annually. The later part of the 19th century saw the rise of the iron ore trade between Escanaba, Michigan and the steel mills of Chicago and later, Gary, Indiana. By the turn of the century, sailing vessels began to disappear from the Lakes, being replaced with much larger steamers, and by 1930 commercial sailing vessels had disappeared from the Lake entirely.

The first half of the 20th century saw the lumber trade and eventually the grain trade on the Lake replaced with carferries, iron ore, cement, manufactured goods and many commercial fishing vessels. In 1959, the St. Lawrence Seaway was opened, allowing large foreign flagged merchant vessels to trade with Lake Michigan ports. By the 1970s, huge, 1000-foot ships plowed through the waters of Lake Michigan, passing silently over the broken remains of their wooden predecessors, and carrying more cargo in one trip than the entire Great Lakes fleet of 1850 carried in a whole season. Today, Lake Michigan shipping has ebbed from a rushing torrent to a small trickle, primarily due to the changing nature of the US economy and international trade. The only tangible reminders of our rich and dramatic maritime history are the bones of vessels that met their end trying to make port during the many eras of Lake Michigan's past.

Great Lakes Shipwreck Research Methods

One of the most interesting aspects of wreck diving is learning the story of a vessel and its subsequent accident before diving it. Sometimes this involves reading a book or talking with a dive charter captain to learn a little about the wreck's history. However, so many wrecks litter the Great Lakes that divers often find little or no information about many of the wrecks they visit. Very few Great Lakes marine accidents were widely known prior to the publication of contemporary Great Lakes marine history books by Dwight Boyer and Dana Thomas Bowen in the 1950s and 60s. Prior to their books, most Great Lakes shipwrecks were little more than the faded memories of old-timers. Recently, numerous authors and divers have begun researching and publishing accounts of obscure Great Lakes shipwrecks. Uncovering the stories behind Great Lakes ships and their accidents has become an exciting and fascinating avocation for many Great Lakes divers and new wrecks are being found every year by divers who spend time in the library as well as in the water.

Two terms shipwreck researchers should be familiar with are "primary" and "secondary" resources. Primary historical resources are usually first or second hand reports of an accident which were gathered or published at the time of the accident, while secondary resources are generally the published work of researchers who have collected data from primary resources. Secondary resources are often a good starting point for establishing the existence of a wreck or accident. Primary resources however, are essential for discovering new historical wrecks or fleshing out fragmentary information on existing wrecks. Before turning to primary resources, it is a good idea to check all secondary resources to make sure you are not conducting redundant research.

Many primary and secondary resources for Great Lakes shipwreck research are listed in Chuck and Jeri Feltner's 1982 book **Great Lakes Maritime History: Bibliography and Sources of Information**. Their book is an important guide for Great Lakes shipwreck researchers and lists nearly all the important works and major repositories for Great Lakes nautical history up to 1982. Another very important secondary resource is the ongoing research of historian David Swayze. His 1991 book **Shipwreck!** lists data on almost 4000 Great Lakes shipwrecks, and his ongoing research has since grown to include perhaps twice that number. Any wrecks that are not in David Swayze's Wrecklist are truly obscure. Other important resources are the collections of research libraries such as the Milwaukee Pubic Library's Herman Runge Collection, the Canal Park Museum at Duluth, the Institute for Great Lakes Research at Perrysburg, Ohio and Detroit's Dossin Great Lakes Museum. These libraries boast massive indices and catalogs containing photos and history on many thousands of Great Lakes vessels. Many of these indices are now computerized for quick research and a few are even available on-line via the internet. Other important secondary resources are books by local and regional authors. Aside from the obvious books about Great Lakes shipwrecks, many obscure, self published books on local history list excellent shipwreck information. County, city and regional historical societies are also excellent resources for information on obscure local vessels.

Other very important sources for Great Lakes shipwreck information are the various vessel registers and directories produced in the latter 1800s by insurers and the government. In 1867 the Treasury Department began producing a yearly directory of **US Merchant Vessels**. These directories, which are still produced today in electronic form, list various info, depending on the year, including tonnage, year built, builder, year built and lost and many other demographics for Great Lakes vessels. Another important directory is the **Inland Lloyds Register**. Inland Lloyds cataloged insured vessels and published a yearly listing of all Great Lakes vessels that were insured beginning in 1856. These directories also list many demographics and often contain information on obscure vessels that can be found nowhere else. Other important registers which list information on Great Lakes vessels are the **Beeson's Marine Directory** (1887 - 1921), **Green's Marine Directory** (1908 - 1954) and **Polks Marine Directory** (1880s, 1890s). Many other directories exist for Great Lakes vessels of the early 1900s and are mentioned in Feltner's Bibliography.

The best primary resources for information on Great Lakes shipwrecks are commercial and sport fishermen. They know where their nets and lines snag and often keep GPS or LORAN numbers on notorious snags. More wrecks have been found through the reports of fishermen than by any other means. The second best primary resources are newspapers. As early as the 1820s, newspapers ran columns devoted exclusively to Great Lakes marine news. These papers carried word of all known accidents, regardless of severity and usually reported all salvage work on wrecks as well as vessel movements in and out of major ports. Many of these papers have been preserved on microfilm as far back as the 1820s and are now extremely valuable sources for archival information. Among those papers which reveal the most information on Great Lakes wrecks are the **Milwaukee Sentinel**, **Racine Advocate**, **Door County Advocate, Manitowoc Herald,** the **Lake Superior Journal**, the **Duluth Minnesotian**, the **Marquette Mining Journal**, the **Chicago Inter-Ocean, Cleveland Plain Dealer, Buffalo Morning Express, Oswego Herald** and the **Detroit Free Press**. Numerous other community newspapers also carried news of shipwrecks if they occurred in the area. Today, the repositories for these newspaper microfilms are local and regional libraries. Researchers who wish to make use of newspapers must however, know at least the year, and preferably the date of an accident. Without a date, researchers have the thankless task of reading through months and even years of newspapers in order to find perhaps one cryptic entry. However, researchers who have been forced to do this are often rewarded by finding accounts of other previously unknown wrecks.

Early Great Lakes Directories and Coast Pilots – Author's Collection

Perhaps we know only the name of a vessel and have no idea when she wrecked. We have checked all known secondary resources and they don't list her. We might then look at the vessel's "enrollment" records. Sometimes referred to as a registry or certificate, a vessel's enrollment certificate is like a birth certificate. Beginning around 1812, all American merchant vessels on the Great Lakes were required to carry a Certificate of Enrollment issued by customs houses at major ports. Beginning in 1867, all merchant vessels were also assigned an "official number" when they were enrolled. An official number is like a fingerprint which stayed with a vessel throughout her life even if her name changed. Official numbers are particularly useful in identifying the many vessels which changed names multiple times and in identifying multiple vessels with common names such as the many vessels named "Mary" or "Ann."

When a vessel was first launched, she was given an enrollment certificate and had to surrender it and get a new one any time she changed tonnage, dimensions, rig, owners, captains, home ports, or was wrecked. Certificates of Enrollment give a tremendous amount of information about a vessel. They list her owner, master, builder, gross and net tonnage, official number (before 1867), dimensions, rig, year and place built, type of stem and stern, date and place of current and previous registry and reason for surrender of certificate. These vessel enrollments have been preserved by the National Archives and are available on microfilm at several research libraries in the midwest. It is through vessel enrollment certificates that we know the names of many historic Lake captains as well as the dimensions and description of many historic vessels.

The enrollments for many Great Lakes ports have been compiled into chronological indices which list dates and places of subsequent enrollments as well as the reasons for subsequent surrendering of certificates. Using these indices it is possible to trace the entire career of a Great Lakes vessel. We can find each time she was sold and to whom, who all her captains were, when and if she was rebuilt or rerigged, if she changed home ports or names, and most importantly, when and if she wrecked. Finding a vessel enrollment that was surrendered as "vessel lost," "abandoned" or "wrecked" indicates that the vessel probably never sailed again. It also gives us an idea of the year and possibly the month that the vessel was lost. However, some owners and captains waited months and even years to surrender a vessel's papers, while holding out hope for salvage. Subsequently, surrendered enrollments can give only an estimate of when the vessel wrecked, but they also provide a great deal of vessel information and can save a good deal of time searching through newspapers.

Another important primary resource for information on Great Lakes shipwrecks is the US Lifesaving service. In 1874 the US Government established many Lifesaving Stations on the Great Lakes in response to the appalling loss of life caused by shipwrecks. Staffed by well trained and fearless crews, these stations kept regular watches and responded to any reports of marine accidents regardless of the weather. Using only small surfboats, these "storm warriors" often lost their own lives trying to save those of shipwrecked sailors. The harrowing accounts of their daring rescues have been preserved by the National Archives and are both fascinating and dramatic. The Station Keepers were responsible for recording the handwritten accounts of each call the crew went out on, and these are now available at selected research libraries in the midwest. Abbreviated versions of these accounts are also available in the printed hardcover **Annual Report of the US Lifesaving Service**, which runs from 1876 - 1914.

Often overlooked as primary resources for shipwreck information, archival and modern maps and charts commonly show the location of shipwreck remains. Many old ships were abandoned in harbors and waterways without a second thought and their identities have since faded into history. Their remains however, sometimes offer unparalleled wreckdiving and excellent opportunities for archeological investigation. Older charts in particular are likely to show the location of long forgotten wrecks and many research libraries have map collections dating back to the early 1800s.

Probably the most important historical work ever written about the Great Lakes was John Brandt Mansfield's 1899 epic **History of the Great Lakes**. This rare two volume series is simply unbelievable in the amount and scope of information it contains. Mansfield attempted to list every vessel that ever sailed the Lakes before 1899, as well as every shipwreck. The result was a massive index which preserved historical information on many obscure vessels that would have otherwise been lost. These volumes have become standard research tools for Great Lakes historians and aside from vessel enrollments, are one of the best sources for information on Great Lakes vessels of the 1800s.

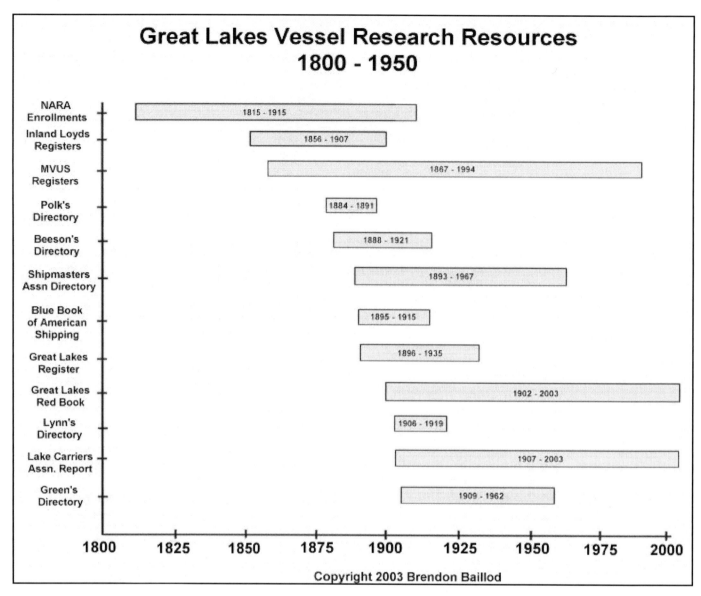

When conducting research into shipwrecks it is also important to contact other divers. More than a few divers have spent long hours searching for a "virgin" wreck only to find that local divers had been visiting it for years. Divers today are increasingly willing to share wreck locations with other responsible divers. In this regard, it may be valuable to attend some of the annual meetings and conferences where Great Lakes wreckdivers and historians gather. The annual Gales of November Conference at Duluth, Minnesota is a great place to network with other divers, as are Chicago's annual Our World Underwater Conference and Detroit's Great Lakes Shipwreck Festival. The premier event of this sort is probably the Ghost Ships Festival hosted annually by the Great Lakes Shipwreck Research Foundation in Milwaukee. It has been held for over 10 years and attracts thousand of divers and researchers each year. It is also very helpful to become involved with one of the many volunteer organizations for Great Lakes wreckdivers. Such organizations have developed to assist State and Provincial Underwater Archeology efforts and to maintain and monitor underwater preserves. The Wisconsin Underwater Archeology Association, the Underwater Archeology Society of Chicago, Great Lakes Shipwreck Research Foundation, Save Ontario Shipwrecks and the Great Lakes Shipwreck Preservation Society are examples of active organizations involved in research and preservation of submerged historic and cultural resources. They offer many opportunities for divers to receive training in Underwater Archeological survey methods and to network with other divers and historians.

The internet has also become an excellent resource for Great Lakes shipwreck divers and historians. Many websites are available that list locational and historical information on wrecks. The Great Lakes Shipwreck Research Website is an important hub for researchers seeking a central starting point. Some research facilities have also placed their catalogs online in searchable databases. Another online database that is interesting is the NOAA Submerged Obstruction Database, which contains LON/LAT coords for many unknown obstructions. This database however, is rather difficult to use and contains a good deal of inaccurate information. The Marine Museum of the Great Lakes at Kingston has placed several databases online including its file on Canadian vessel enrollments. Save Ontario Shipwrecks has also placed several large databases online in its Marine Heritage Database. The following sites are some of the most useful on the internet at the time of this publication:

Searchable Relational Vessel Databases

Hosted by Brendon Baillod's Great Lakes Shipwreck Research website
- Charles E. Feltner Great Lakes Vessel Enrollment Abstract Database (1810-1868, c. 25000 entries) - http://www.ship-wreck.com/shipwreck/feltner/
- WMHS Great Lakes Vessel Enrollment Database (1815-1915 c. 44,000 entries) – http://www.ship-wreck.com/shipwreck/wmhs/
- David Swayze Great Lakes Shipwreck Database (c. 5000 entries) – http://www.ship-wreck.com/shipwreck/swayze/
- The Association for Great Lakes Maritime History research portal - http://www.ship-wreck.com/shipwreck/links/aglmhlinks.php
- Brendon Baillod Great Lakes Vessel Accident Database (1840 – 1900, c. 30000 entries) – http://www.ship-wreck.com/shipwreck/wreckdb/
- Milwaukee Public Library Online Vessel Data Search Engine (c. 8000 entries) – http://www.ship-wreck.com/shipwreck/runge/
- Mansfield's History of the Great Lakes Vessel Accident Database – http://www.ship-wreck.com/shipwreck/hgldb/

Hosted by Walter Lewis' Maritime History of the Great Lakes website
- Maritime History of the Great Lakes Vessel Enrollment Database (1815 – 1861, 8000 entries) - http://www.maritimehistoryofthegreatlakes.ca/Enrolment/default.htm
- Maritime History of the Great Lakes Marine Accident News Database (c. 25000 entries) - http://www.hhpl.on.ca/GreatLakes/Wrecks/search.asp
- Maritime History of the Great Lakes Vessel News Database - http://www.hhpl.on.ca/GreatLakes/Extracts/search.asp
- Maritime History of the Great Lakes Vessel Renamings Database - http://www.hhpl.on.ca/GreatLakes/rename/search.asp

Hosted by the Historical Collections of the Great Lakes
- HCGL Vessel Database (c. 8000 entries) - http://ul.bgsu.edu/cgi-bin/xvsl2.cgi
- HCGL Maritime Personnel Database - http://ul.bgsu.edu/cgi-bin/mpi_pub.cgi

Hosted by Alpena George N. Fletcher Library
- TBNMS C. Patrick Labadie Vessel Database (c. 14000 entries) - http://www.greatlakesships.org/

Hosted by the Marine Museum of the Great Lakes at Kingston
- The Mills Canadian Steamship List Database (c. 6000 entries) - http://db.library.queensu.ca/marmus/mills/index.html
- The Canadian Great Lakes Vessel Registry Database – http://db.library.queensu.ca/marmus/registry/index.html

Hosted by University of Detroit – Mercy
- The Father Dowling Great Lakes Vessel Image Database – http://www.dalnet.lib.mi.us/gsdl/cgi-bin/library?p=about&c=shipping

Hosted by NOAA Fisheries Department
- Current US Merchant Vessels Database – http://www.st.nmfs.noaa.gov/st1/CoastGuard/VesselByName.html

Hosted by the State Historical Society of Wisconsin
- The SHSW Wis Maritime Newspaper Index – http://www.wisconsinshipwrecks.org/tools_newspapers.cfm
- The SHSW Wisconsin Shipwrecks Database – http://www.maritimetrails.org/research.cfm

Searchable Digital Image and OCR Book Collections

Hosted by Google
- Google Books – Specific Great Lakes resources linked on AGLMH Portal - http://books.google.com/advanced_book_search

Hosted by the Library of Congress
- American Memory Collection - http://memory.loc.gov/ammem/index.html

Hosted by National Archives of Canada
- Early Canadiana Online - http://www.canadiana.org/eco/index.html

Hosted by the State Historical Society of Wisconsin
- The SHSW Great Lakes Maritime History Database - http://digicoll.library.wisc.edu/WI/subcollections/GreatLakesAbout.html
- The SHSW Local History and Biography Online Database - http://www.wisconsinhistory.org/wlhba/articleSearchAdv.asp

- The SHSW Digital Collections – http://www.wisconsinhistory.org/libraryarchives/collections/digital.asp
- Wisconsin 1830s Land Survey Images – http://digicoll.library.wisc.edu/SurveyNotes/Search.html

Hosted by Walter Lewis' Maritime History of the Great Lakes website
- Great Lakes Newspaper Transcription Database – http://www.hhpl.on.ca/GreatLakes/news.asp
- Great Lakes Vessel Image Database – http://www.hhpl.on.ca/GreatLakes/GLImages/search.asp
- Online Vessel Registers and Documents – http://www.hhpl.on.ca/GreatLakes/scripts/shiplists.asp
  http://www.hhpl.on.ca/GreatLakes/scripts/documents.asp

Hosted by the Archives of Michigan
Archives of Michigan Digital Collections - http://haldigitalcollections.cdmhost.com/

Hosted by the University of Michigan
University of Michigan Digital Collections - http://quod.lib.umich.edu/cgi/t/text/text-idx?page=home

Hosted by Ancestry.com (Subscription Site)
- US Census Online Databases and Images - http://www.ancestry.com/search/rectype/census/usfedcen/default.aspx
- Searchable Online Newspaper Database – http://www.ancestry.com/search/rectype/default.aspx?rt=38

Hosted by NewspaperArchive.com (Subscription Site)
OCR Searchable Newspaper Archive (c. 3000 titles) - http://www.newspaperarchive.com/

New York Times Online OCR News Archive (Subscription Site)
OCR Searchable Newspaper Archive (excellent Great Lakes shipwreck material) - http://query.nytimes.com/search/query?srchst=p#top

Satellite/Map Database

Online mapping tools have become extremely detailed and accurate. They can now be used to locate historic shallow-water shipwrecks.

Microsoft Maps – http://maps.live.com

Google Maps – http://maps.googe.com

Offline Electronic Resources

The following digitized and searchable electronic resources have been created but are not available online. They must be accessed through the holding organization/s.

- The J.W. Hall Marine History News Scrapbook (1876-1883) – Pat Labadie, HCGL
- The Herman Runge Vessel Index Card Database (c. 25000 entries) – Milwaukee Public Library
- The MVUS Digital Archive (1866 – 1884) – Mike Spears, Brendon Baillod, HCGL
- The USLSS Log Lake Michigan Digital Archive (1876-1915) – Brendon Baillod
- The WMHS Project Shipshape Database – Milwaukee Public Library
- The BLU/Inland Lloyds/Vessel List Database (1816-1907, c. 20000 entries) – Brendon Baillod

Electronic Reference Finding Aids

The following resources may be used to locate specific archival reference material for Great Lakes maritime history. Many references have not been digitized by can be obtained from a source repository. These finding aids are generally library and collection online catalogs. The most important of these follow.

- Google – http://www.google.com
- Milwaukee Public Library Online Catalog – http://www.ship-wreck.com/shipwreck/runge
- Bowling Green State University Online Catalog – http://maurice.bgsu.edu/search/X
- University of Michigan Online Catalog – http://mirlyn.lib.umich.edu/F/?func=file&file_name=find-b
- University of Wisconsin Online Catalog – http://madcat.library.wisc.edu/cgi-bin/Pwebrecon.cgi?DB=local&PAGE=hbSearch
- State Historical Society of Wisconsin Archive Catalog – http://arcat.library.wisc.edu/cgi-bin/Pwebrecon.cgi?DB=local&PAGE=sbSearch
- Library of Congress Catalog – http://catalog.loc.gov/
- US National Archives Search Tools – http://www.archives.gov/research/tools/index.html
- Canadian National Archives Search – http://search-recherche.collectionscanada.ca/archives/search.jsp?Language=eng

Searching for Great Lakes Shipwrecks
Reprinted from WUAA Underwater Heritage

For the last 200 years, ships have regularly gone down on the Great Lakes. I would conservatively estimate that about 8000 commercial ships have been lost on the Lakes and of those, perhaps 2000 foundered in open water. That is to say, they probably have physical remains which still lie on the bottom of the Lakes and have been or could be found. Of these, about 1000 have been located, leaving about 1000 historic Great Lakes shipwrecks that have yet to be found. It is consequently, not surprising that wreck hunting has become an avocation among many Great Lakes divers and historians. Discovery of an historic shipwreck on the Lakes provides a number of exciting opportunities. Among these are the chance to see a time capsule of daily life in the 1800s, the opportunity to study the construction techniques and handiwork of a bygone era, the ability to solve the mystery of a lost ship and the chance to document a new historic site. Unfortunately, for some, the finding of a new wreck also represents an opportunity for souvenir collecting, financial gain and personal glory. This destructive minority has given rise to the adage "a wreck found is a wreck lost" among historians and has contributed to an unfortunate negative perception of avocational wreck hunting.

Despite these facts there remain a substantial number of historically important undiscovered wrecks as well as a large number of people enthusiastic about finding them. The intent of this short article is to suggest some logical pointers for locating undiscovered shipwrecks on the Great Lakes using historical records as well as common sense. I hope to explore a few general guidelines and suggestions for finding historic wrecks based on personal experience as well as the experiences of others.

A central concept that is important to our discussion is that of a search grid. A search grid can be thought of as a geographical area in which the remains of the vessel in question are believed to lie. The result of any serious historical research aimed at finding an undiscovered wreck is usually a search grid. At its simplest, a search grid is a box drawn on a map that shows a best guess as to a lost vessel's location. It is usually based on an analysis of many factors, but always represents an estimate.

A search grid is extremely important given the time and money involved in staging a search. Experienced wreck hunters are all too aware of the short search windows afforded by weather conditions on the Lakes. Added to this limitation are the money and effort required to bring together the necessary equipment and personnel. Wrangling a boat, side scan sonar, magnetometer, ROV, drop camera and crew is in itself, a daunting task. Coupled with the above barriers to entry, arranging time away from family, work commitments and opportunity cost keep most people from ever doing serious wreck hunting. The cost for a weekend of searching can range well into the thousands of dollars and a bad weather forecast can scrap an expedition that took weeks and even months to plan. As such, few people will venture out on a wreck hunting expedition without a VERY good search grid in mind and lots of research under their belt. There are those who are fortunate to live near urban ports or on major shipping lanes where the wreck density is high. In these areas it is still possible to simply "mow the lawn" in hope of running something over and make an occasional find. However, in most parts of the Lakes, it's a good idea to have a target or targets in mind and a good deal of preparation under one's belt.

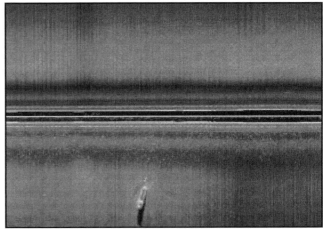

A shipwreck (in this case the EMBA) as it appears on sidescan at 300 meter range - Jerry Guyer

When laying out a Great Lakes shipwreck search grid there are ten parameters that should always be factored into the mix. They may be derived from historical data, present observations, logical deduction, outright speculation or a combination thereof. The following examples are intended to show the use of each parameter based on real-world cases.

Last Known Position (LKP) is one of the most important concepts in search theory and is usually the first factor considered. For our purposes, LKP is equivalent to the point at which the vessel was definitively last known to be. LKP is the base point from which all other analyses are made. In historical shipwreck research, LKP is usually a very rough figure. Depending on the technology of the day and the reporter's frame of reference, a given LKP may have significant error. A good case study in this regard is the big carferry *Pere Marquette 18*. She went down in plain view of two other carferries in 1910 on Lake Michigan. She is commonly reported to have gone down 19 miles East of Sheboygan. Given the implied accuracy of her position (19 miles, not 20 miles), we might assume that she'd be easy to locate. However, contextual information suggests that her LKP is probably not known with the accuracy implied. The run of the PM18 was not her usual (she had been bound Ludington to Milwaukee, but turned to run for Sheboygan) and her master likely had only a general idea of his distance from Sheboygan. Likewise, the technology of the day did not allow for accurate position estimation. In 1910 position was still largely estimated by speed over time on a given course. As such, the *PM18's* LKP is likely only known to within +/- 5 miles N/S and E/W. A plot of her course using modern techniques based on the reports of survivors strongly suggests that she is significantly south of Sheboygan, and not directly east as commonly stated. Beginning in the 1920s and 30s, Radio Direction Finders were placed in many Great Lakes vessels enabling them to more accurately fix a position, but few captains could be expected to triangulate a position if their ship was in peril. Consequently, even the resting place of the freighter *Jennifer*, lost 30 mi NE of Milwaukee in 1974, can only be gridded to within +/- 5 miles based on the LKP given in her USCG investigation file. Her crew was rescued by Helicopter as another vessel stood by, but locational technology was still relatively primitive even in the 1970s. Following the inception of LORAN-C on the Lakes in 1980, pinpointing locations over water become much more realistic.

Loss of the *PM 18* from an original postcard in the Author's Collection

Known or probable course is also an important concept in search grid construction. In the case of many wrecks, we know the course the vessel was on with great accuracy. In other cases, it can be strongly inferred. Vessels on the Lakes lost money when they were overdue and masters were particularly conscious of taking the shortest route between two points. Navigational charts and "Coast Pilot" books for the Lakes have shown the courses for these routes since the 1850s and most captains didn't deviate significantly from them without good reason. As such, if we know where a vessel was bound to and from, we can often find the given courses for the day and plot the ship's path with relative accuracy. A good case in point is the steamer *L.R. Doty*, lost in 1898 on Lake Michigan. She was bound from South Chicago for the Straits of Mackinac by way of the Manitou Passage and would have certainly used the conventional steamer lanes of the day, which called for a course line to Point Betsie. As such, we have a relatively good idea of her course. We have an LKP from her consort, the *Olive Jeanette*, whom she cut loose just north of Milwaukee. Based on the steamer lanes of the day and the position reported by the *Olive Jeanette*, we can plot a fairly pragmatic search grid, placing the *Doty* about midlake off Milwaukee.

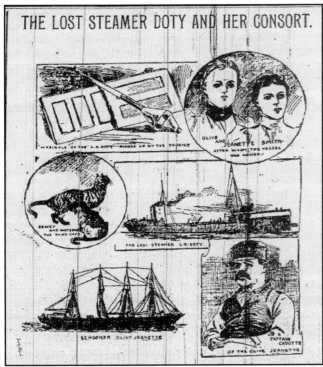

L.R. Doty news illustration – Milwaukee Sentinel (from microfilm)

Time/distance analysis is used to predict where a vessel might have been at a given time, given a particular speed. This concept has been used to grid vessels that went missing in storms. It is also necessary when plotting a grid for the *Pere Marquette 18*. We know the *PM18* traveled at about 12 mph under good conditions. She left Ludington at almost exactly midnight. At 3:30 her flooded flicker was discovered and she was turned due south for 40 minutes to keep the waves from a following sea off her stern. She was then turned due west and ran until she foundered at 7:30 AM, her speed decaying as she went. Based on the above data, one can make some logical inferences about the resting place of the PM18. Time/distance analysis is seldom used as a sole determinant. It is usually employed in conjunction with other data, including debris reports and wind/wave conditions.

Debris Scatter - Nearly all vessels that went down on the Lakes left some kind of debris. This is particularly true of the wooden vessels of the 19th century. In most cases the newspaper reports of the day related a good deal of information about the location of debris and bodies from shipwrecks. In many cases, wrecks have been located through careful analysis of debris patterns in conjunction with knowledge about current and weather patterns. A good example is the wreck of the *Kamloops* on Lake Superior. A good deal of debris from the wreck had washed up on the beach at Twelve O'Clock Point on Isle Royale. More importantly, the mate and stewardess had made it to shore alive in a fierce blizzard with temperatures of 20 below zero. The mate was found frozen in an upright position sitting on a log and the stewardess was found in a makeshift lean-to near the remains of a small fire. Clearly, the wreck had to be within a few miles at most of the ill-fated survivors. The location and condition of the bodies was well known, but it wasn't until 50 years after the accident that researchers deducted her location from these obvious clues. The wreck was indeed found within a few hundred yards of the location of the crews' bodies. Another case in Point is the *L.R. Doty* disappearance in 1898. She was last seen about midlake, just north of Milwaukee. Forty hours later, her debris was found 25 miles off Kenosha. Wind direction and intensity during the storm that sank her are well known. Given her LKP, the location of her debris, the wind direction and the elapsed time, we can make some substantive predictions about her final resting place.

Weather, wind and wave conditions are important parameters to consider in conjunction with time/distance analysis. These factors have a great effect on the reliability of sighting reports, distance traveled over time and probable point of foundering. An important fact to consider in analyzing any Great Lakes shipwreck is the dominant wind pattern. On the Lakes, the wind moves from west to east over 80% of the time. Wind out of an easterly direction is quite rare on the Lakes. However, to know the specific direction and velocity of wind during an historical wreck, it is best to consult archival news accounts. A very fortunate instance of unusual wind conditions on the Lakes occurred during the *Lady Elgin* disaster. On September 8, 1860, the *Lady Elgin* was struck by the schooner *Augusta*, about 8 miles off Winnetka, IL. She broke up as she went down, casting over 600 people in the Lake. Had the wind followed its customary pattern, nearly all of them would have surely died. However, a rare northeast wind drove the *Elgin's* wreckage toward shore where some 160 people were saved. Sadly, at least 450 people died in the surf between Evanston and Winnetka. When the *Lady Elgin* was found, she had been driven exactly as one would have expected, given the wind and waves at the time. She was found just 3 miles from shore and considerably south of the point of the collision. In fact, one can draw a straight line in the direction of the wind between the point where the *Elgin's* stern had come ashore and the point where the wreck was discovered.

Original *Lady Elgin* ticket courtesy of Harry Zych

Identical ticket shown in 1892 Milwaukee Sentinel retrospective

The Visibility when a ship foundered is often very important in making an accurate analysis. Any locational references given to or from the ship should be filtered considering this criterion. If a vessel went down at night, any distance or identification information gleaned from physical observation must be given a significant margin of error. Likewise, any observations made in towering seas, fog, haze, smoke, etc. must be given a wide berth. In December of 1864, the brig *Mahoning* was reported to have foundered "nearly opposite the Ulao Pier." However, the brig went down at night in rain and sleet. They could probably see the light on the end of the Ulao Pier, but few other light sources would have existed along the shore to show its contour and distance. Not surprisingly, the *Mahoning's* remains proved to be significantly north of the position given in the first hand reports.

Current - Often overlooked on the Lakes, is the effect of current. The Lakes all rotate in a known specific direction, and general maps of Lake currents have been made. In the absence of opposing wind and waves, it is possible to predict the direction that current will carry an object on the Lakes. All three of the western lakes have a pronounced counter-clockwise rotation, which is more noticeable near shore. Islands and peninsulas also effect the direction and intensity of the currents. Many local currents are particularly well known and hazardous on the Lakes. The Keweenaw Current on Lake Superior is an unusually shallow, fast moving current and was responsible for the loss of the Coast Guard Cutter *Mesquite* in 1989. The vessel was doing precision maneuvers at night and did not compensate for the dramatic current, which laid her on a reef. Likewise, many of the islands in northern Lake Michigan have erratic and strong surrounding currents. These currents must be taken into consideration for any debris scatter analysis.

Depth of Water – The depth of water is an important factor to consider from a number of perspectives. In the case of the *Pere Marquette 18*, a foundering depth of 400 ft was reported at the time of her loss. Given the era of her foundering, the presence of other company vessels at the site and subsequent speculation about raising her, the depth of 400 ft may well have resulted from a lead line sounding at the site. The depth also fits well with her search grid. Depth must also be considered in terms of schooner masts. Often news reports mention the mastheads of a sunken vessel breaking the surface. In such cases, we can estimate the depth with relative accuracy if we know the vessel's length. Such is the case with the schooner *Garden City*, lost off Little Sable Point in 1858. The *Garden City* was 132 ft long and consequently, would have had a main top mast between 125 and 140 ft above her keel. We can say with relative certainty that the *Garden City* lies in 115 to 125 ft of water, based upon the news reports of the day. Just as often however, depths given in historical shipwreck accounts have proven to be wildly speculative. In general, I tend to discount newspaper reports of 19th century Great Lakes shipwreck depths unless they are less than 100 ft or are bolstered with specific explanation, such as visible masts breaking the surface.

Vessel Characteristics should be factored in when thinking about a ship's resting place. The main factors to consider here are the sailing characteristics of schooners versus steamers. Powered commercial vessels generally took the shortest route between two points, whereas sailing vessels were at the mercy of the wind. As such, when plotting a sailing vessel's location, one MUST consider wind direction and speed as well as the need to tack when sailing against the wind. Likewise, it might be useful to determine a steamer's likely cruising speed based on its engine characteristics and its size. Cargo is another interesting factor to consider. Shifting grain cargos have been responsible for the loss of many Lake vessels. The loss of the schooner *Louis Meeker* is a good case in point. In August of 1873, she found herself becalmed off Little Sable Point, whilst bound for Buffalo with grain. A vicious squall swept down upon her from the west, but she was able to drop all her canvas before it hit. Despite being under bare poles, she was pushed over at 45 degrees and her grain shifted, pulling her over completely and filling her with water. She sank with her masts out of sight and has never been found. Likewise, lumber cargoes often served to keep an overturned schooner afloat by increasing its buoyancy, sometimes permitting the vessel to drift great distances before sinking. Conversely, iron ore cargoes, while preventing vessels from capsizing, also sent them to the bottom rather directly in the presence of a substantial leak.

Credibility of Information is probably the most important factor that can be considered in our analysis. All historical data must be considered suspect to some degree. This is particularly true of first person reports. People's interpretation of events is often clouded during times of great emotion, such as shipwreck, and their memory of events may be influenced by subsequent reports. Reporters of the 19th century often played fast and loose with the facts and shipping companies often suppressed unfavorable information. An example is the loss of the *Lady Elgin*. The death toll from the disaster is commonly given as 297. However, at least 450 persons have been verified lost by modern research and the count continues to rise. Then as now, many vessels were lost purposefully and information was often intentionally obfuscated by captain and crew. Likewise, many ships were reported "dashed to pieces" our "foundered in deep water" and somehow managed to be put back in service. As any researcher of Great Lakes shipwrecks can attest, the meaning of the terms "dashed to pieces" and "foundered in deep water" must have changed considerably since the 19th century! The use of secondary sources for research introduces many additional problems. The researcher making use of secondary sources is forced to rely on the original researcher's skill and integrity. MANY published works on Great Lakes shipwrecks contain highly dubious accounts and outright fabrications. Too often, these accounts are promulgated by authors who rely only on secondary sources and repeat the errors. The literature is consequently, littered with many wrecks that never happened. The most famous of these is the French ship *Le Jean Florin*, reported lost off Barcelona, NY in 1721 with a payroll of gold coins. Her loss appears in several books, databases and charts of Great Lakes wrecks, despite the well known fact that no decked vessels were on the western Lakes between 1679 and at least 1750, and Barcelona, NY didn't exist until almost 100 years later. The myth seems to have originated in 1964 from Adrian Lonsdale's Guide to Sunken Ships in American Waters, and is a reinvention of an actual shipwreck off Barcelona, Spain. It probably hasn't seen its last published repetition.

Many additional factors could be considered, but most will fall under one of the above categories. As a general rule, all of the above areas should be explored at some level when plotting a search grid. After carefully considering all of the above areas of inquiry, one might base the size and shape of the search grid on the perceived margin of error for the data considered. As an example, the search grid for the schooner *Edna*, lost off Kenosha in 1887, was quite small. First person accounts from the US Lifesaving Service who rescued her crew, placed her directly off Kenosha harbor and her mast protrusion and sighted location suggested a depth of about 45 ft. Her subsequent grid was less than a mile square. Conversely, the search grid for the *L.R. Doty* is nearly 10 x 20 miles. The main factor of uncertainty in her case is whether or not she turned back to pick up the *Olive Jeanette*. In any event, her wreckage was found approximately 40 miles south of her LKP, about 40 hours after she was last seen. This suggests, but does not prove, that she foundered soon after she was last seen, and consequently leaves us with a fairly large search grid.

Above all, logic and common sense should be applied to the analysis of historical data for the development of a search grid. Many clues can be found by scanning the news microfilms, reading court transcripts, ordering investigation files, reviewing local histories and browsing original periodicals and reports. However, it is the researcher's task to assemble those clues into a logical, coherent picture that represents the most likely scenario and provides a grid with the highest chance of containing the search target.

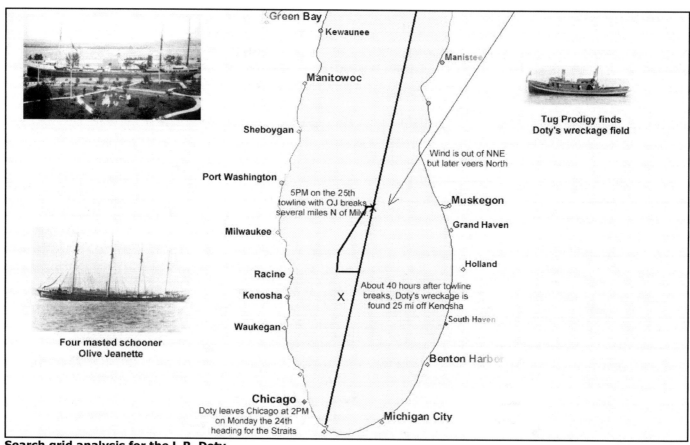

Search grid analysis for the L.R. Doty

Shipwreck Discoveries, Locations & Laws

Beginning with the widespread availability of scuba in the 1950s, a subculture developed in the Great Lakes maritime history community with a focus on treasure hunting. Many early divers developed extensive collections of brass shipwreck artifacts, dishes and glassware, while others made furniture from large wooden shipwreck timbers. By the 1970s, advanced remote sensing technology made the discovery of deep wrecks possible and hundreds of legendary Great Lakes wrecks gave up the secret of their location. Despite the large number of wrecks located, none of the early divers-turned-wreckhunters ever realized any significant income from their finds. Eventually, most of them donated their artifact collections to museums.

In recent years, several Great Lakes shipwreck artifact collections have been sold at online auction sites. In most cases, the artifacts no longer had any context and could not be attributed to any particular vessel. Without exception, these artifacts fetched a fraction of the hoped for price. Even in the case of large artifacts that could be attributed, the items sold for hundreds, not thousands. Most artifacts taken from Great Lakes wrecks quickly deteriorate and all but the most valuable eventually find their way to the landfill, discarded by wives and children who don't have room for Dad's shipwreck stuff. Indeed, most families find that today's museums don't have the funds to buy artifacts and private collectors won't pay much for them.

Despite the folly of Great Lakes "treasure hunting," there was for years, a persistent culture of secrecy and competitiveness among those who searched for historic sites on the Lakes. The location of historic wreck sites was a closely guarded secret and was seldom released until divers had taken what they could. The matter of who discovered a given wreck was often the subject of great contention and wreck discoveries by individuals were tallied as notches in one's belt. This culture of finders-keepers functioned well until 1987 when the Federal Government passed the Abandoned Shipwreck Act (ASA). This law had the effect of awarding ownership of all **abandoned, historic wrecks in the Lakes' bottomlands** to the States. The States then proceeded to pass statutes protecting the wrecks in their waters.

With those laws, the entire landscape of Great Lakes wreck hunting and diving changed forever. The ASA was written with Spanish galleons in mind and did little to define the vagaries of Great Lakes wrecks. It was left to the courts to interpret on a case by case basis, which wrecks were historic, which were abandoned and which were in the bottomlands of the States. The ASA provides the guideline that for a wreck to be historic, it must be **deemed eligible** for inclusion in the National Register of Historic Places. The NRHP provides a general guideline that a site be older than 50 years to be "historic." A central question is whether the site must have already been formally evaluated for NRHP inclusion to be deemed historic or if a wreck is inherently historic without the need for prior evaluation to establish its historic significance. Beyond those criteria, a general principle has been observed that a wreck is abandoned if the owners have made no attempt to recover it, despite being technically feasible to do so. However, this principle has proven to have exceptions. The question of embeddedness has also been interpreted differently in specific court cases, but for practical purposes, all Great Lakes wrecks could be said to be embedded, as their entire keel is nearly always below the mud-line. However, not all courts have agreed with this position.

Following these precepts, the Lake States have asserted that nearly all wrecks in the Lakes, discovered or undiscovered, are state owned and the burden of proving otherwise falls on would-be salvors. State law follows this principle and you will consequently be arrested if you are caught removing anything from a Great Lakes shipwreck that you don't already explicitly own or have a State archeological recovery permit for. Salvors of course, believe that wrecks should generally be available for claim and the burden of proving otherwise should fall on the States. A number of court cases have tested this question and have shown that the state's position is not fool proof. Although very few salvors have sought outright to own a historic wreck, several have challenged State ownership as a means of avoiding legal charges after being caught removing material from a wreck without proper permission from the State. These instances have resulted in a few successful challenges to the ASA, resulting in the private ownership some historic wrecks. However, the cost to wage a challenge is prohibitive. In general, challengers have spent in excess of $100,000 to own a pile of boards (and to avoid charges). Even then, law enforcement has done little to protect these privately owned wreck sites from theft. If you would like to remove something from a Great Lakes shipwreck, most States have a formal process for requesting permission. However, it is generally an expensive process and must be done under the supervision of an archeologist.

As the wreck hunters of the 1970s have retired, they have been replaced by a mixture of technical divers and underwater archeologists. This new breed of explorer is much less concerned with collecting artifacts or discovery credit and is much more interested in documenting the sites and sharing them with others. Events such as Milwaukee's Ghost Ships Festival draw several hundred visitors each year to see video of the latest wreck discoveries and to learn about maritime history. Today, the story of how a wreck was located is far more important and interesting than who is credited with discovering it. As it is, most wrecks are "discovered" by more than one person over several years and often a team is involved. An historian researched the wreck and publicized its existence, perhaps in a book. A person supplied the boat, another supplied the sidescan sonar. Perhaps a commercial fisherman snagged the wreck and gave a general location. Perhaps an historian or underwater archeologist identified the remains. One of the divers was the first person on the wreck site. Someone was the first to see the wreck image crawl across the sidescan paper. Another called the local newspaper to announce the find. Someone else may be the person who shot the first video and shared it with the public. Yet another may release the coordinates. Which of these found the wreck? Does it really matter?

It seems far more important to tell the story of the ship, the wreck event and the discovery accurately and completely. Stories of discovery are important from an archeological and a cultural perspective and are one of the most interesting aspects of a shipwreck's history. However, giving credit to one person for finding an historic site is at best, an oversimplification and tends to bring out the worst in people.

Before planning to search for a wreck, people should consider the substantial responsibility that comes with a find. Shipwrecks are an important part of our community and regional history, and are irreplaceable and perishable as well as vulnerable to theft and damage. Prospective shipwreck hunters should have a management plan in place before they leave the dock and should have general agreement among search participants as to the plan of action if a discovery is made. A badly managed discovery can result in the destruction of a wreck site and theft of artifacts. At the very least a badly managed find can result in the failure to recognize a historically significant site and can cause hard feelings among the discoverers.

The main questions associated with a discovery are usually centered around a few points. Should the find be shared? If so, when, by whom and to whom? I believe that the best course is to contact the State Underwater Archeologist and ask for their guidance, particularly on a find of substantial significance or with many portable artifacts. Sites should, at a minimum, be filmed and historically documented prior to publicizing the find. Wreck sites are most vulnerable to theft and damage immediately after discovery.

Given that the primary value of most wrecks is for community and regional history, it only makes sense to share these finds with the public through local, state and regional historical groups. In Wisconsin, groups such as the Wisconsin Historical Society, the Wisconsin Underwater Archeology Association and the Great Lakes Shipwreck Research Foundation are all active in documenting, preserving and sharing information about Great Lakes shipwrecks.

As an incentive for divers, I was encouraged to include GPS coordinates for all "discovered" shipwrecks in this volume. I had some initial misgivings about doing this because one of the chief criticisms of similar books is inaccurate coordinates. I am not an avid scuba diver and as such, have never made it my business to record accurate wreck locations. I consequently, relied heavily on my wreckhunting and dive charter friends and on the NOAA AWOIS system.

There are a few caveats that should be noted about all numbers in this book. First, many GPS systems in the 1990s did not record LAT/LON to thousandths of decimal minutes due to the US government's Selective Availability policy and the limitations of the technology at the time. This means that a LAT of 42.36.344 would have registered as 42.36.34 back in the mid 90s, and many of the coordinates in this book are only expressed to that precision. The numbers in the book are in decimal minutes unless otherwise noted. I make no guarantee on the numbers in this book, as in all but a few cases, I did not take them onsite myself. Divers who attempt to visit the wrecks for which I give locations do so at their own risk and are responsible for having adequate experience, equipment and training. I did sanity check all the numbers given in this book. If they plotted to the other end of the Lake or to a farm-field, I did not include them. For known sport diving wrecks, the numbers are probably quite accurate, and in most cases can also be obtained on the internet or in dive guides. For lesser known wrecks, shallow sites and AWOIS entries, the numbers are likely to be accurate, as they plot correctly, but it may require some work to find the site.

In several cases, I took numbers from the NOAA AWOIS system. AWOIS is NOAA's marine obstruction database, in which they attempt to record every obstruction or shipwreck shown on their nautical charts. There are a few problems with the AWOIS. In the 1980s, the database became watered down with many theoretical obstructions when NOAA staff decided to add many historical wrecks that were known to have occurred but had never actually been located. As such, the database includes entries for ships such as the legendary "treasure ship" Westmoreland in the Sleeping Bear area of Michigan, which has never been found, and the long sought steamer *Water Witch* in Saginaw Bay. In other instances, the database includes entries for "phantom wrecks," which were reported by boaters or divers and charted, but didn't actually exist anywhere near the given coordinates. Over the last 20 years, NOAA staff have attempted to verify all the major wrecks and obstructions in the database, and entries were updated to reflect wreck sites that could not be found in the area of the stated coordinates. However, the entries themselves have not been removed. As such, it is necessary to wade through a great deal of spurious information in the AWOIS database in order to find a few good entries. It is possible to filter by obstruction type and area as well as accuracy, which makes the resource much more usable if you are technically adept.

In our area, the AWOIS database includes a few wrecks that are likely to be decent dive targets, but have not been relocated. The site alleged to be the fish tug *Ole* near Kenosha and the burned fiberglass yacht off Kenosha are both accurate reports of wrecks that have been verified in the past. However, the AWOIS system's numbers for the sites are extrapolated from chart positions. It would likely be necessary to relocate the sites with sidescan sonar, but given the coordinates stated in the database, it would likely be a quick search. It should also be noted that the AWOIS system is only meant to list charted wrecks. Very few wrecks are charted, and as such, the AWOIS database includes only a small percentage of the known wrecks in a given area. However, the wrecks listed in AWOIS are often obscure, little known sites that local divers may not have visited.

In the case of shallow or beach wrecks, I have sometimes extrapolated the numbers from charts. In these cases, the positions given should have a margin of error +/- 50 yards. Wrecks in this category would include the schooner *Guiding Star*, which is under the bluff at Virmond Park and the schooner Persia, which Bob Jaeck located in the shallows north of Wind Point.

There are several wreck sites given in this book which remain unidentified. In most cases, I have given likely candidates for the targets. These include the unidentified barges located by Jerry Guyer off Milwaukee as well as a few fisherman snags that have been verified to be wrecks but have never been dived. Part of the reason these sites were included is to make a concrete record of their existence. Too often, wreck sites have been located and kept so secret that they were lost and never relocated. Many wrecks with only LORAN TDs to locate them are likely to suffer this fate when NOAA decommissions the LORAN system in the coming year. It is hoped that these sites can be visited and identified by divers in the future. A case in point is the deep wreck reported to Jerry Guyer in 330 ft of water 17 miles off Oak Creek. This site has been graphed and is almost certainly a large shipwreck. However, due to distance it has never been investigated.

I was also strongly encouraged to include maps showing the relative positions of historic shipwreck sites. With significant misgiving, I agreed to do this. In many cases, the location of a wreck is not known with any degree of accuracy. It seemed to me, a bit misleading to put an "X" on the map and claim it to be the resting place of an undiscovered historic ship. The maps are meant only to show the general area of an historic wreck and in many cases, are probably completely inaccurate. Still, the maps do help visualize the wreck density hotspots of a given port and reveal some interesting historical locations, such as the Milwaukee ship boneyards.

I would welcome additional accounts of wrecks from divers, historians and beachcombers. It is my hope to add additional wrecks in future printings of this book. As such, if you find an old keel and ribs on the beach or in the shallows, I want to hear about it. I can be contacted at brendon@ship-wreck.com.

Great Lakes Shipwreck Conservation

Ever since the loss of LaSalle's *Griffon* in 1679, the Great Lakes have continued to claim ships. There are literally thousands of shipwrecks littering the floor of the five Great Lakes and tributary waters. What often distinguishes these wrecks from others is their excellent state of preservation. Because the Great Lakes are so cold and because of the relative scarcity of marine life, many wrecks remain intact and undiscovered for hundreds of years. Great Lakes divers can attest to the presence of intact bodies in 50 to 100 year old wrecks. Others have seen three masted wooden schooners lying on the bottom in such good shape that they could easily be refloated. Still others have found readable books and logs, and tables still set for a meal that was to be served 100 years ago.

It is conservatively estimated that the Great Lakes have hosted 8,000 significant shipwrecks. Of these, perhaps 80% have extant remains and about 2,000 are now considered dive targets. The large number of wrecks in the Great Lakes is due primarily to the difficulties of navigating in relatively confined bodies of water which bristle with shoals. Waves on the lakes tend to be shorter in period than ocean waves and are comparatively much steeper. These pounding waves have conspired to weaken and breach many hulls. Weather patterns on the lakes are particularly notorious for creating dive targets. In the Midwest, November often brings violent storms which sweep over the lakes with amazing speed and fury. Prior to the age of weather radar, boats were often lured to their death by the large financial incentives for November cargo deliveries. Violent gales in November of 1869 for example, caused the loss of over 100 merchant vessels and countless lives on the lakes.

In terms of historical significance, Great Lakes wrecks are unparalleled. One would have to search for a long time to find a 150 year old wooden structure on land, let alone one that still contains all of its contents just as they were left 150 years ago. Great Lakes shipwrecks are time capsules of a kind that can be found nowhere on land. In addition to giving us a look into the society, technology, culture and artifacts of a bygone century, many of these vessels give an eerie picture of the horrific and desperate last moments of a ship and crew who knew they were likely to die. It is a startling realization that a short 150 to 200 feet under nearby waters lay many remarkable archeological resources which are largely undiscovered. Many Great Lakes communities are now recognizing the shipwrecks in their area as part of the community's cultural history. Some communities have put up historical markers, interpretive plaques and even maritime museums to showcase their rich maritime history. These communities recognize the importance of their historical shipwrecks and many have become involved in preservation activities by preventing the destruction of historic vessel remains in their harbors and on their beaches.

The Gallinipper May 2003 vs. May 2005 - Bob & Charlie Tom, Bob Epsom & Bob Broten, respectively

Because the widespread availability of SCUBA is a relatively recent phenomenon, many historic and legendary vessels have yet to be discovered or disturbed. Most shallow wrecks that are easily accessible have already been damaged by waves, ice, zebra mussels and souvenir hunters. Vessels deeper than 100 feet, however, are likely to be in excellent shape and are less likely to be found without an intensive search. Thus, many divers have taken up wreck hunting and new historical wrecks are being found every year. As sport divers become more comfortable in the 200 to 400 foot depth range, more and more discoveries will be made. The increasing availability of technology such as side scan sonar and the growing popularity of technical diving also insure that more wrecks will give up the secret of their locations.

The *Alvin Clark* awaits the bulldozer c. 1990
Author's Collection

The discovery of new wrecks is perhaps a positive and unavoidable eventuality. However, what happens to discovered wrecks is not. Experienced divers always relate stories of what a fantastic dive a wreck was "before she was stripped." In fact, just about every wreck that has been found in the Great Lakes has a collateral story of some artifacts that were stolen from it. Consequently, the adage "a wreck discovered is a wreck lost" has come into general parlance among Great Lakes divers. Too often, naive divers are lured with stories of "treasure" to damage wrecks. The hard truth is that most Great Lakes wrecks contain nothing even remotely resembling gold or silver. Divers find only "semi-precious" artifacts of an historical nature which they remove from the wreck site and stick in the corner of their garage where no one else can view them. Wooden artifacts soon begin to rot no matter how much care is taken with them. This was the case with the 150 year old schooner *Alvin Clark* that was raised from Green Bay in 1969. She was destroyed after her wood decayed and her metal parts cracked. She rotted into the ground and was eventually bulldozed and hauled to a landfill. History has clearly shown the futility of removing structural artifacts from Great Lakes shipwrecks. Further, because the removal of artifacts from Great Lakes shipwrecks is in most cases illegal, many of these items are never seen again and rarely find their way to museums for proper archeological conservation.

As the diving community in the Great Lakes has grown, many people have become staunch advocates of wreck conservation. The State of Michigan took a leading role when it established the Underwater Preserve system. These preserves ensure that wreck stripping and plundering will be kept to a minimum and that violators will receive harsh penalties. Organizations such as the Great Lakes Shipwreck Research Foundation, Save Ontario Shipwrecks, the Wisconsin Underwater Archeology Association, the Underwater Archeology Society of Chicago and others take an active role in conservation by regularly inspecting local wrecks to insure proper conservation. Other divers ensure conservation simply by letting their diving friends know that they will not dive with looters.

Many divers now believe that there is questionable validity in bringing artifacts to the surface for display in museums. Many name boards have been taken off the sterns of wrecks and are now on the walls of museums and restaurants. Chadburns, binnacles, capstans, wheels, propellers and rudders have all been removed and placed in foreign environments where they look awkward and tell us little about their vessels. On land, these items often appear to be rusty and rotted pieces of junk. Aboard the ship however, these items have a great significance. They convey a greater sense of the vessel's historical nature and give clues as to its final moments and ultimate demise. Artifacts are also likely to last longer in the cold waters of the Great Lakes than anywhere else. There are already enough shipwreck artifacts in museums and displays to sate the appetite of the non-diving public. With the exception of sites threatened by theft or natural forces, the artifacts of new shipwreck discoveries should be left in state for those interested enough to don a wetsuit.

Several years ago, the Alger Underwater Preserve sank an old harbor tug within its waters as a dive attraction. This tug which wouldn't have garnered a snapshot from even the most ardent marine historian now brings hundreds of divers to Munising each year, generating thousands of tourism dollars. However, on dry land one of the oldest and most historic wrecks on the Great Lakes, the *Alvin Clark*, couldn't even generate enough interest to keep her from the bulldozer. Clearly, these facts speak for themselves.

For these reasons divers in the Great Lakes region have taken action to further establish and maintain bottomland preserves and conservation organizations in all five Great Lakes and surrounding states and provinces. Many divers have even returned artifacts taken many years ago to their original wreck sites. Despite these efforts, there remains a small but active contingent of Great Lakes divers who still visit wrecks with crobars, saws and lift bags. Because of this, most Great Lakes divers continue to remain vigilant with respect to protecting wrecks and many wrecks are inspected regularly to insure that they are not damaged. Fines and confiscation of boats and equipment have already occurred in several cases where divers were discovered to be souvenir hunting.

Because of the changes in state laws and diver attitudes, the destruction of our historic Great Lakes wrecks has been slowed but not stopped. In an informal survey, almost all Great Lakes divers questioned admitted that at some point they had removed an artifact from a Great Lakes shipwreck. Because the number of Great Lakes wreck divers continues to grow, it is important for all of us to practice what we preach. The next time we're on an obscure wreck and we see a brass porthole still in the hull, rather than take it because "someone else will if we don't," why not be part of the solution rather than part of the problem. Many divers who have been faced with this dilemma have placed interpretive plaques on such wrecks to help divers enjoy them, and to let divers know that the wreck is being monitored. Other divers have responded to this dilemma by lobbying to include the wreck in a state underwater preserve. Still others have chosen to map the wreck site and publish information about it in books and articles. These are all important ways to let divers know that people care about a particular wreck and that it should not be disturbed.

Hopefully, all historic Great Lakes wrecks will eventually be "adopted" by groups of divers who take responsibility for ensuring that the wreck is properly conserved and respected. Organizations such as Save Ontario Shipwrecks, the Wisconsin Underwater Archeology Association, the Great Lakes Shipwreck Research Foundation and the Underwater Archeological Society of Chicago continue to generate action and enthusiasm among sport divers for this type of cost effective wreck stewardship. With any luck, the momentum of such efforts will continue to grow until every Great Lakes wreck can be taken off the endangered resources list.

Methodology and Explanation of Terms

Methodology

In researching the wrecks that appear in this book, I followed a basic methodology, which is worth recounting for readers and researchers.

In about 1990, when I began work on my initial Lake Michigan wreck database, the many internet databases for Great Lakes vessel research had not yet been created. It was much more time consuming to conduct original research prior to about 1998 because of the lack of computerized data, online or otherwise. Locating and compiling wreck accounts was a manual process of scanning thousands of pages of tiny, sometimes hand-written text, looking for the words "Lake Michigan" and "total loss."

I began by scanning all the common/popular published books and other secondary sources in order to extract any accounts of total loss shipwrecks in Lake Michigan waters. I collected hundreds of local and regional history books and charts of varying quality and comprehensiveness, which I sifted for information. I then surveyed the more comprehensive and authoritative resources and extracted all Lake Michigan wreck accounts. Among the most time consuming and useful were the Herman Runge Wreck List, the Herman Runge Index Card File, the accident lists of the Board of Lake Underwriters (1856 – 1880), the Annual Reports of the US Lifesaving Service, Loss and Abandonment Lists in the Annual List of Merchant Vessels of the United States, Loss Lists in Beeson's Marine Directory, Frederickson's Lake Michigan Wreck Charts, Wreck Reports from the various Great Lakes Customs Houses, Great Lakes Vessel Enrollment Master Abstracts (causes of surrender), the Milwaukee Sentinel Index Cardfile and US Coast Guard Casualty Reports.

From these, I built a comprehensive, but skeletal list of losses. For each entry in the list, I then conclusively identified the vessel in question and verified that it was a total loss or abandonment through the use of vessel enrollment certificates, entries in the Annual List of US Merchant Vessels, insurance records from the Board of Lake Underwriters/Inland Lloyds/ABS Registers and news microfilm accounts. Over the years, I worked with several other researchers to untangle the various vessels of the same name that were lost in Wisconsin water such as the many schooners Challenge, Union, Eagle, Dolphin, etc. In all cases, I was able to locate conclusive evidence from the historical record to identify a specific vessel.

After identifying the vessel, I confirmed its build year and place, builder, official number (if available), tonnage, dimensions, rebuilds/renaming and career details to the extent possible. I compiled these into the database and then began to collect detailed information on the vessel's loss/abandonment event. In most cases, this was done through the use of newspaper microfilms, but archival local history books, Life Saving Service reports, marine insurance and court documents also yielded valuable, detailed information. In some instances, I also used data from the US Census and vital records to identify people involved in specific accidents and to verify a death or survival.

After constructing a brief account of the loss and its circumstances, I tried to ascertain the final location of the vessel's remains and the likelihood of locating them. I assigned each vessel to a series of categories based on the type of loss and likelihood of having intact physical remains and the degree of accuracy with which the location is known. This designation allowed me to quickly generate lists of findable wrecks and those with a high probability of having physical remains. The categories are as follows:

Type of Loss (Foundering, Stranding, Abandonment)
- Foundering is used for any vessel that sank, whether from burning, collision or capsizing.
- Stranding is used for any vessel that went aground or ashore and stayed there.
- Abandonment is used for any vessel that was intentionally abandoned, whether in

the harbor, on the beach or out in the Lake.
- Other causes may appear for vessels that were not total losses

Depth (Buried, Surfline, Shallow, Deep, Very Deep)
- Buried means the wreck is mostly buried and by definition, shallow or on land.
- Surfline means the wreck is either on the beach or just off the beach in less than 5 ft of water.
- Shallow = 5 to 50 ft.
- Deep = 50 to 200 ft.
- Very Deep = over 200 ft.

Remains (Removed, Probably Removed, Possibly Removed, Probably Present, Definitely Present) – This category is used to gauge the likelihood of a wreck having extant remains.
- Removed indicates that I found a confirmed account of the wreck's removal.
- Probably Removed indicates that removal is likely given the location or that a search of the location failed to locate any remains.
- Possibly Removed indicates that a wreck has the potential to have been removed due to its location, but still has some chance of having extant remains.
- Probably Present indicates that a wreck has some potential to have been removed, but probably was not removed due to location or circumstances.
- Definitely Present indicates that a wreck has no potential to have been removed due to depth or circumstances.
- Located means the site has been found and positively identified with reasonable certainty.

Accuracy (¼ mile, 1 mile, 5 miles, 10 miles, 20 miles) – This category gives the relative accuracy with which the wreck's resting place is known based on historical accounts and/or field investigation.
- Coordinates are given for identified sites.
- ¼ Mile means the wreck site probably lies within a grid ¼ mile square.
- 1 Mile means the wreck site probably lies within a grid 1 mile square.
- 5 Miles means the wreck site probably lies within a grid 5 miles square.
- 10 Miles means the wreck site probably lies within a grid 10 miles square.
- 20 Miles means the wreck site probably lies within a grid 20 miles square.

The above classification system allows me to quickly generate lists of vessels that fit a given pattern. For example, using the database, I can quickly generate a list of all deep and very deep, undiscovered wrecks off Racine/Kenosha that have a 5 square mile grid. The wrecks with the best potential for discovery by wreckhunters are Founderings in Deep or Very Deep water with remains Definitly Present and an accuracy of 5 or 10 miles.

Readers will note that some of the vessels included in this book were not total losses. I included several non-total loss shipwrecks in each section for purposes of clarification. While constructing my database, I came across many accounts of "total losses" that upon deeper investigation proved to have been recovered. If a vessel was incorrectly stated to have been a total loss in any primary or secondary source, or if a significant loss of life was involved, I included it in the database. In these instances, I verified the recovery and the final disposition of the vessel.

Once I had developed the basic entries for the full Lake Michigan database, I found that they numbered well over 2000 entries. By 1998, I had completed the initial database and had added about 70% of its current content. I then began the task of conducting original research to locate new losses that were not in any of the initial sources. For the most part, I located these by transcribing data from archival wreck and accident lists and placing the data into relational databases for quick and easy searching. This enabled me to find over 100 new total loss Lake Michigan shipwrecks within a short period of time. I also found many new wreck accounts simply by reading through marine columns in newspaper microfilms and by asking my colleagues to keep an eye out for any obscure looking Lake Michigan wreck accounts during their research.

For the first several years, I added new historic wrecks to the database at the rate of about one per week and I shared these research finds with many colleagues. In recent years, my rate of new historic Lake Michigan wreck discoveries has slowed to less then one per month, but I still find new Lake

Michigan vessel loss accounts regularly and I continue to add them. Most of the new losses I now find are early 20th century losses to commercial fish tugs and abandonments of vessels in the 1930s and 40s.

A similar methodology was followed in developing the lists of vessels built at each port. However, these lists were created specifically for this book and initially involved a great deal of electronic database merging. In addition to querying existing databases, I also added many area builds by manually scanning through the MVUS and other registers. After the basic build lists were compiled in spreadsheet form, I individually researched each vessel in the various enrollment databases and in the MVUS to build a complete account of its career and final disposition. This was a rather lengthy task, requiring hundreds of hours, but it resulted in the discovery of several previously unknown area wrecks and abandonments. It was also very interesting to see how far many area vessels traveled from their place of build and to see some of the very early area builds that are still in service. An example is the steel Barge M. 2, built at Milwaukee in 1910. This vessel is still registered and in use by Rausch Construction in Broaview, Illnois. She is the oldest Milwaukee built vessel still in service, now entering her 100th year.

Explanation of Terms

A general explanation of terms is presented here to aid the layperson in understanding some of the nautical and vessel terminology of the 19th century:

Official Number: In order to keep better vessel records, the US Government began to require that vessels carry an official number in 1866. The number stayed with a vessel even if her name changed or she was rebuilt. Prior to 1867, vessels did not always have official numbers and were difficult to follow through name changes. The start of official numbering coincides roughly with the first publication of the Annual List of Merchant Vessels of the United States (MVUS) in 1867.

Tonnage: All modern vessels carry two different tonnage measures, gross tonnage (gt.) and net tonnage (nt.). Generally, gross tonnage does not refer to a vessel's weight, but rather refers to a vessel's carrying volume. Gross tonnage is a measurement of the total carrying volume of a vessel, including crew quarters, engine space, etc. Net tonnage is generally obtained by deducting non-freight carrying spaces such as crew quarters, engine space, etc. from the gross tonnage. Tonnages were historically given in 95^{ths} rather than 100^{ths}. Consequently a 19th century tonnage of 320.34 in this book should be read as 320 34/95ths tons.

Builders Old Measure (BOM): The tonnage of vessels prior to 1864 was determined using the "Builders Old Measure" system of measurement. This system determined the capacity of a vessel based only on the vessel's length, beam and depth. This resulted in an over-estimation of the vessel's tonnage. In 1864, the United States began to implement the Moorsom Rule for determining tonnage. This new measurement system used additional dimensions to calculate tonnage and was consequently much more accurate. Readers will note that all tonnages in this book are expressed as BOM for Builders Old Measure or gt. for the gross tonnage of the Moorsom system.

Enrollment: Beginning in about 1812, United States merchant vessels were required to have several types of documents on file at customs houses. In the Great Lakes region approximately a dozen customs houses kept builders certificates, certificates of enrollments, certificates of register and other official documents related to merchant vessels. New certificates of enrollment were required to be filed any time a vessel was built, changed owners, captains, rig, name or home port. The certificate listed the vessel's year and place of build, owner(s), captain, dimensions, physical description, etc. and can be used to track a vessel's career from her build to her loss. The majority of Great Lakes customs house documents were microfilmed by the National Archives and are today available for most Great Lakes customs houses. Much of the historical information about the appearance and careers of vessels in the book comes from vessel enrollment certificates.

Inland Lloyds: From 1856 to 1907, the Board of Lake Underwriters (a cartel of marine insurance companies on the Great Lakes, later called the Inland Lloyds) published a directory of every insured vessel on the Great Lakes for both Canadian and US vessels. These registers are commonly referred to as "Inland Lloyds" registers and provide descriptive, condition and rebuild information on the majority of vessels active on the Lakes in a given year. Similar marine directories were published by Harvey C. Beeson, R.L. Polk & Co. and others from the 1880s through the present day. Grading hull condition and establishing insurance value was the main purpose of the Inland Lloyds register. Hull ratings were given based on construction quality and the observed degree of hull rot. Vessels rated A, AE or B were considered in good condition and were permitted to carry grain cargoes. Vessels rated C or I were fit only for lumber and vessels rated O were considered unseaworthy.

Vessel Description Terms: Enrollment papers often provided physical descriptions of a vessel's construction. Generally, a vessel's stern was described as either square (for schooners) or round (for most steamers). The vessel's stem or bow was described in terms of its ornamentation. A plain stem had no ornamentation. A scroll stem had ornamental scroll work carved into the bow just below the bowsprit. A figurehead stem had an ornamental figure, usually a serpent or a human figure, carved into the bow. Particularly in the early days on the Lakes (1812 to 1860), vessels had very elaborate figures, some of which survive on deeper wrecks to this day. A vessel noted as having a gallery sported a raised stern with windows built into the transom. This was sometimes referred to as a poop deck which was atop a poop cabin. Nearly all vessels considered in this volume had 1 deck, although many large Great Lakes steamers had 2 or more.

Measurement: Vessel measurements in this book are given in feet and tenths of feet unless otherwise noted. Dimensions are of the form Length x Beam x Depth. Unless otherwise noted, a dimension of 100.8 x 23.4 x 8.5 should subsequently be read as 100 ft. 110 inches x 23 ft. 3 inches x 8 ft. 6 inches.

Vessel Types: 19th century Great Lakes vessels came in a limited range of types. Great Lakes commercial vessels were grouped into broad categories by vessel men of the day and fine distinctions in rigging were seldom made. For our purposes, the following vessel types and descriptions apply:

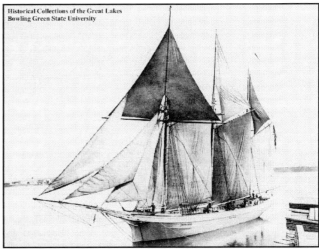

Rouse Simmons in typical Great Lakes schooner rig - Historical Collections of the Great Lakes

- *Schooner* – A wooden hulled sailing vessel having two or more masts, and triangular, fore & aft aligned sails. There were many rig variations among Lake schooners and the types and sizes of sails varied greatly over the 1800s. By far the most common type of vessel ever to sail the Lakes, nearly all schooners had disappeared from active use on the Lakes by 1930.

Scow Schooner R.H. Becker at Sheboygan - Historical Collections of the Great Lakes

- *Scow Schooner* – A wooden hulled sailing vessel having two or more masts and a sharp turn at the bilge, stern and bow. Scow schooners often had a boxy appearance, with flat sides rather than the graceful curves of schooner hulls. Scow schooners first appeared on the Lakes in the 1830s and became quite popular in the lumber trade from 1860 – 1900. There were some early scow brigs and scow sloops as well.

Sloop Hummingbird built Detroit 1871 - Historical Collections of the Great Lakes

- *Sloop* – A wooden hulled sailing vessel having one mast with triangular, fore & aft rigged sails.

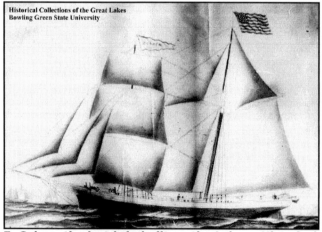

E. Cohen, the last brig built on the Lakes - Historical Collections of the Great Lakes

- *Brig or Brigantine* – A wooden hulled sailing vessel with two masts and square sails oriented with the beam of the ship on the main mast and usually on the foremast as well. Usually there were two or more flights or yards of sail per mast. This type of vessel was common on the Lakes between the 1830s and 1860s and had disappeared by the 1870s. For Great Lakes purposes, the terms Brig and Brigantine were almost always synonymous. Some early brigs were referred to as Hermaphrodite Brigs because they sported some triangular sail on their main mast. Very few Great Lakes vessels were true brigs, sporting all square sails on their fore and main and almost none had more than three yards of sail.

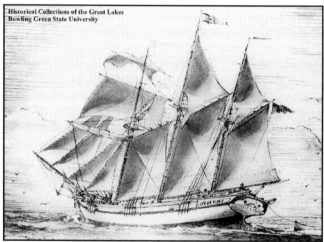

Bark Ocean Wave - Loudon G. Wilson illustration courtesy of Historical Collections of the Great Lakes

- *Bark or Barque* – A wooden hulled sailing vessel with three or more masts, having square sails on her foremast and triangular, fore & aft oriented sails on her remaining masts. Barks were common on the Lakes between 1840 and 1870 and were usually three masted and larger than schooners. The development of large steam cargo vessels hastened their demise. The terms Bark, Barque and Barkentine were used synonymously on the Lakes.

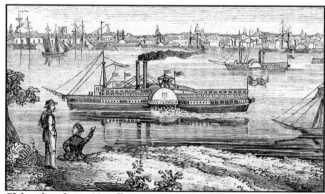

Sidewheeler Mayflower 1852 from an original woodcut in the Author's Collection

32

- *Steamer/Sidewheeler* – Prior to about 1870, the term steamer always referred to a sidewheel steamer. After about 1870, a distinction was always made between sidewheel steamers and propeller steamers. With very few exceptions, all self propelled 19th century Great Lakes vessels were steamers. Gas engines didn't become common on boats until the early 1900s. The first US steamer appeared in the Lakes in 1818. Steam engines fell out of general commercial use on the Lakes in the 1960s. Nearly all sidewheel steamers were made of wood, but some of the larger, passenger sidewheelers of the late 1800s and early 1900s were steel hulled.

1880s, steel overtook both wood and iron as the preferred hull material and by 1890, most commercial vessels being built were steel propellers. Wood hulls continued to be used until the early 1900s, but by 1910, wood was only being used for small steamers and tugs.

E.G. Maxwell - typical Great Lakes work tug

Propeller Ontonagon at Milwaukee c. 1870 - from an original stereoview in the Author's collection

- *Propeller* – Propeller driven ships appeared on the Lakes in 1841 and didn't overtake sidewheelers as the preferred propulsion type until the 1870s. Iron hulled propellers began to appear in the 1860s, and propellers became common as tugs and package freight ships. By the mid

- *Tug* – With few exceptions, all tugs on the Lakes were propeller driven. In the 1870s, many tugs were built with iron hulls and later with steel hulls, but most had wooden hulls. Many types of tugs were used on the Lakes, including towing tugs, wrecking tugs, fish tugs and work boats. Some large wrecking tugs were over 100 ft. in length, while some commercial fish tugs were only 20 ft. in length. They varied widely in their hull design and appearance. Before 1900 nearly all tugs were steam powered. Beginning in about 1900, fish tugs began to use gas or naphtha engines and later they used diesel engines. The diesels were often referred to as Oil Screws, abbreviated as Ol.s.

Part II: Lake Michigan's Shipwrecks Kenosha to Port Washington

Kenosha Shipwrecks

From her humble beginnings as a shallow, wilderness river mouth, Kenosha Harbor has grown into a busy modern Lake Port with a rich and varied history.

Southport – October 1844 – Wisconsin Historical Society

The native Winnebago Indians called both the creek and the river at the site Kenosha, which means Pike, as the waters were well populated with the fish. In June of 1835, a group settlers from Hannibal, New York led by John Bullen picked the spot as a permanent settlement and established a small community known as Pike on the south side of Pike Creek. Vessels could not enter the shallow entrance and had to anchor off shore while small boats ferried people and cargo ashore. In 1835 no steamers visited at Pike Creek and only three schooners anchored off the small port, ferrying their good to shore. In 1836, Pike Creek was visited by her first steamer, the *Detroit*, which anchored ½ mile off shore and ferried her goods and passengers in. In 1837, the community's name was changed to Southport, it being the southernmost Lake settlement in the Wisconsin Territory. Traffic to the small settlement began to increase, and in 1837 the port was visited by 61 steamboats, 80 schooners and two brigs. In 1838, 72 steamboats and 88 schooners called, and in 1839 102 steamboats, 47 schooners, 3 brigs and one fully rigged ship anchored off the Harbor. Kenosha hosted the first pier ever built on Lake Michigan. B.P. Cahoon reportedly constructed and maintained a pier near the mouth of Pike Creek between 1840 and 1842. Vessel captains thought the pier would wash away with the first storm, but it was reportedly quite sturdy and greatly aided the landing of goods and passengers.

Original 1836 Land Survey Plat of Pike River and Pike Creek – Wisconsin Historical Society

The mouths of Pike Creek and Pike River just to the north were both surveyed by the US Government as possible harbor sites in 1837 and 1839, and considerable conflict arose among the communities of Southport and Pike River over which would be the site of the harbor. Several years passed before the question of the harbor site was resolved and at length, Southport was chosen to receive the federal harbor appropriation. Harbor work began in 1845 and by 1846 vessels could enter the new Harbor safely. Southport immediately became an important port for vessels trying to shelter from storms and for settlers and lumber shipments. In 1847, the first permanent lighthouse was built at

Southport, replacing a crude makeshift beacon that had served since 1837 and shipments of grain began to be sent east by area farmers. By 1850, the newly renamed Kenosha was a major grain exporting site on Lake Michigan and traffic included several vessels each day.

In 1866, the present, historic light tower was erected. Kenosha served as an active lumber, grain and merchandise port for the remainder of the 1800s and the Goodrich steamboat line added a passenger stop at Kenosha. By 1879, vessel traffic had increased to the extent that the US Lifesaving Service erected a station at Kenosha. These "storm warriors" as they were called, played an important role in Kenosha's shipwrecks and their accounts tell us a great deal about Kenosha's marine accidents.

Kenosha Breakwater Light c. 1900 – Author's Collection

Shipping at Kenosha began to decline in the 1880s and by 1900 commercial vessel traffic was minimal. However, a significant fleet of commercial fishing boats developed and continued to fish out of Kenosha for most of the 20th century.

The last 100 years has seen Kenosha Harbor's commerce change dramatically. Large steel ships called at Kenosha in the first half of the 20th century loading cargoes of automobiles. The second half of the 20th century has seen most traffic in the form of pleasure craft, including fishing charters and sailboats, but occasional large foreign flagged cargo ships entered the harbor until the mid 1970s. Kenosha's shipwrecks represent all eras of her maritime past and many have extant remains that can be viewed or explored. These wrecks are now an important part of the community's culture and history.

The waters of Kenosha County now host a large number of potential historic shipwreck sites per square mile due to its location between the two major shipping centers of Milwaukee and Chicago. A tremendous volume of 19th century vessel traffic passed through this area, leaving a rich array of historic vessel remains.

Pleasure Boats in Kenosha Harbor 1961 Author's Collection

Beginning in the 1960s, divers and historians started actively searching for historic shipwrecks in the Great Lakes with the result that several hundred historic wrecks were located on Lake Michigan alone. Kenosha waters now hold six discovered shipwrecks, two of which, remain unidentified. A barge filled with rocks lies just south of Kenosha in 35 ft. of water and was probably abandoned in the 20th century and another unknown hull lies in the shallows just north of Kenosha. Both are shown on nautical charts of the area. A few area wrecks are now popular dive sites, including the steamer *Wisconsin* and yacht *Rosinco*. Shallow remains have been located that are attributed to the historic steamer *Detroit*, the schooner *T.P. Handy* as well as a handful of others, and at least two schooner hull beds were reportedly removed during harbor improvements in the 20th century. At least ten other historic shipwrecks thought to lie in Kenosha waters remain undiscovered. Most Great Lakes shipwrecks are now protected by State and Federal law from unauthorized salvage and souvenir hunting. Consequently, the main motivations for locating these historic vessels are now mostly recreational and academic.

The following accounts present a fairly complete survey of Kenosha's historic marine disasters, although additional historic losses will likely turn up by future research.

Although Kenosha waters have seen several deadly losses to pleasure craft and small aircraft in the past 40 years, I chose not to include details of these accidents because they are relatively recent and do not have historically significant remains. Some of these modern losses also have yet to be located and are still under investigation. As such their inclusion seemed inappropriate. There were many vessels that simply disappeared on Lake Michigan as well. It is certainly possible that any of these many vessels that went missing could lie in Kenosha waters. As such, the accounts below may be considered a preliminary survey and I would definitely welcome additions and corrections to them.

Sidewheel Steamer *Detroit* – from an 1837 lithograph of Detroit in the Author's Collection

Remains attributed to the *Detroit* – Dan Joyce, Kenosha Historical Museum

Sidewheel Steamer *Detroit* (predates registry numbering) – Built 1833 at Swan Creek, Michigan - 125.6 x 17.6 x 6.6 ft. – 137.66 gt. – The steamer *Detroit* was driven ashore and abandoned at Southport on October 25, 1837 while bound from Chicago to Milwaukee with passengers a package freight. She is believed to have stranded just north of the present harbor mouth. Her upper deck and houses were removed and used by local merchants and her engines were removed and later used in the steamers *G.W. Dole* and *Columbia*. Local residents reported her remains buried in 8 ft of sand in the 1930s and remains attributed to her were removed by the Corps of Engineers on September 14, 1953 to deepen the harbor channel. Additional vessel remains were unearthed by construction on Simmons Island in 1995 but could belong to several different vessels. (Milwaukee Sentinel – October 31, 1837) Type: Stranding, Depth: Buried, Remains: Probably Present, Accuracy: ¼ Mile.

> **A CARD.**
>
> The undersigned, citizens of the village of Southport, and passengers on board the Steamboat Detroit, during her passage from Chicago to this place, on the 22d and 23d inst., which unfortunately resulted in the vessel's being beached at this village; deem it an act of justice to Capt. Jno. Crawford, Commander, to state in this public manner, that during the passage, he placed the passengers under peculiar obligations to him, for his uniform kindness; and that from the time the vessel left Chicago, until she was driven on the beach, he done all that an accomplished and prudent seaman could do, to avoid the accident that occurred; and displayed a degree of courage and self-possession during the voyage, that reflects the *highest* *credit* upon him as the commanding officer.—Southport, Oct. 26, 1837.
>
> Davis Divine,   G. Kimball,
> F. S. Lovell,   J. A. Noonan,
> R. H. Deming,   Jared Lake,
> Lysander Baldwin,   Samuel Holmes,
> Sam'l. Hale, Jr.,   J. Ressiquie,
> William Bullen,   Roswell C. Otis,
> John Cogswell,   J. Bullen, Jr.,
> A. D. Northway,   Reasin Bell,
> Elisha M. Kinney,   R. B. Winsor,
> F. Moore,   David Walker, Jr.,
> Nathan Dye,   D. Gilman Smith,
> N. R. Allen,   Cha's Durkee,
> G. W. Thomas.

Note of support for the captain of the Detroit from early Southport citizens - Milwaukee Sentinel - 10/31/1837

Woodcut of the brig *Osceola* from Andreas History of Chicago

Brig *Osceola* (predates registry numbering) – Built 1839 at Silver Creek, NY by John Vail, 88.0 x 24.2 x 9.2 ft., 171.37 gt. BOM, Scroll head, 2 masts, no gallery. The brig *Osceola* went ashore at Southport on November 18, 1843 bound Chicago to Buffalo with 6000 bushels of wheat and was reported a total loss. She was pulled free and towed to Chicago on November 26th by the steamer *Champion* for a rebuild. She sailed until 10/7/1851 when she was lost off Fairport, Ohio. She had carried the first cargo of grain from Chicago to the east in 1839. (Milwaukee Sentinel – December 2, 1843) Type: Stranding, Depth: Shallow, Remains: Definitely Removed, Accuracy: 1 Mile.

Brig *H.H. Sizer* (predates registry numbering) – Built 1845 at Pillar Point, NY, 114.0 x 24.3 x 9.6 ft., 240.06 gt. BOM. - The brig *H.H. Sizer* was bound from Chicago to Racine with several passengers when she capsized about ten miles south of Southport on June 19, 1846. Seven member of the Bevins family drowned before the schooner *A.V. Knickerbocker* took the survivors off the hull. The *Sizer* was towed to Chicago and rebuilt. In 1855, she was rebuilt and launched as the brig *Ocean Eagle*. She sailed until 10/23/1862 when she was lost at Sheboygan, WI. (Buffalo Courier – July 3, 1846) Type: Capsizing, Depth: n/a, Remains: Definitely Removed, Accuracy: 1 Mile.

Schooner *Baltic* (predates registry numbering) – Built 1842 at Burtchville, MI by Jonathan Burtch - 80.4 x 19.8 x 6.9 ft. - 96.04 gt. BOM, 2 masts, plain stem, no gallery – The schooner *Baltic* was bound for Chicago in ballast on May 19th, 1852 when she was blown down midway between Kenosha and Waukegan. The schooner *Elbe* tried to rescue her 7 crew to no avail. She was last seen stern up, floating about 7 miles off Southport (now Kenosha). (Milwaukee Sentinel – May 25, 1852) Type: Foundering, Depth: Deep, Remains: Probably Present, Accuracy: 10 Miles.

Schooner *Lamira* (predates registry numbering) – Built 1851 at Manitowoc, WI by C. Sorenson, 68.0 x 21.2 x 7.0 ft., 89.67 gt. BOM, 2 masts, last enrolled Chicago, 4/6/1852 – Bound for Chicago with lumber, the *Lamira* was driven ashore south of the harbor piers on November 11, 1852 while trying to enter the harbor and broke up. She was owned by K.K. Jones of Manitowoc. (Milwaukee Sentinel – January 5, 1853) Type: Stranding, Depth: Buried, Remains: Probably Present, Accuracy: 1 Mile.

Scow Schooners at Kenosha 1868 – from an original Samuel Truesdell stereoview – Author's Collection

Sloop *Lady Ann* (predates registry numbering) – Built 1849 at Kenosha, WI, 48 x 17 x 5.7 ft., 30.37 gt. BOM, 1 deck, 1 mast, plain stem, scow bottom, owned by David Youngs. – The little sloop *Lady Ann* was driven ashore on a sandbar on the north side of the harbor entrance at Kenosha on September 18, 1855 due to the entrance light being out. Her crew were able to jump onto the pier but she was reportedly left to break up just off the north pier. (Chicago Democrat – 9/23/1855) Type: Stranding, Depth: Shallow, Remains: Possibly Removed, Accuracy: ¼ Mile.

Kenosha Harbor 1857 – Kenosha County Historical Society

Kenosha Lighthouse c. 1895– Author's Collection

Schooner *George Hanson* (predates registry numbering) – Built 1851 at St. Joseph, MI, 53.0 x 14.9 x 5.5 ft., 37.81 gt. BOM, 2 masts, last enrolled Chicago 7/17/1855. – The *George Hanson* was a small coastal schooner that was lost on March 30, 1857 after leaving Racine with a cargo of wood and most of the Nichols family who owned her. A gale blew up and the vessel was feared lost. Her mastheads were later found breaking the surface a few miles off shore near Kenosha. This vessel has not been located and contrary to some reports, she did not strand in the shallows. She is likely to have significant remains. (Milwaukee Sentinel – April 17, 1857) Type: Foundering, Depth: Shallow, Remains: Probably Present, Accuracy: 1 Mile.

Schooner *Arkansas* (predates registry numbering) – built 1849 at Sherwins Bay, NY, 107 x 23.9 x 9.9 ft. - 240.43 gt. BOM, one deck, two masts, scroll head. – The schooner *Arkansas* was lost in June of 1858 when she missed the harbor entrance at Kenosha, grounding on the bar on the north side of the piers. She broke up and became a total loss, valued at $2000, but her lumber cargo was saved. (Board of Lake Underwriters Casualty List – January 15, 1859) Type: Stranding, Depth: Buried, Remains: Probably Present, Accuracy: ¼ Mile.

Schooner *T.P. Handy* (predates registry numbering) – Built 1849 at Black River, Ohio by William Jones, 116.10 x 23.11 x 9.1 ft., 234.41 gt. BOM, 2 masts, scroll head, square stern. – Went ashore "a few rods" south of the piers at Kenosha on October 14, 1860 when she missed the harbor entrance. She was reportedly in ballast inbound for a cargo of wheat when lost. Remains attributed to her in the 1980s were referred to as the "wagon wheel wreck" because wagon wheels were found amidst the debris. The ID was never confirmed. (Milwaukee Sentinel – October 15, 1860) Type: Stranding, Depth: Buried, Remains: Probably Present, Accuracy: ¼ Mile.

Scow Sloop *Coquette* (5057) – Built 1858 at Perry, Ohio by A. & D. Bailey, 87.8 x 20.0 x 9.0 ft., 95.91 gt., 2 masts, last enrolled Milwaukee, 6/2/1866 – The sloop *Coquette* capsized and foundered on July 17, 1866 while bound for Chicago from Manitowoc with a cargo of pig iron. She reportedly went to the bottom about 30 miles ENE of Kenosha with her 4 crew. She had been a US Survey vessel and had at one time been schooner rigged. She is sometimes confused with a larger Canadian vessel of the same name. She is thought to lie in deep water. (Milwaukee Sentinel – July 24, 1866) Type: Foundering, Depth: Very Deep, Remains: Definitely Present, Accuracy: 10 Miles.

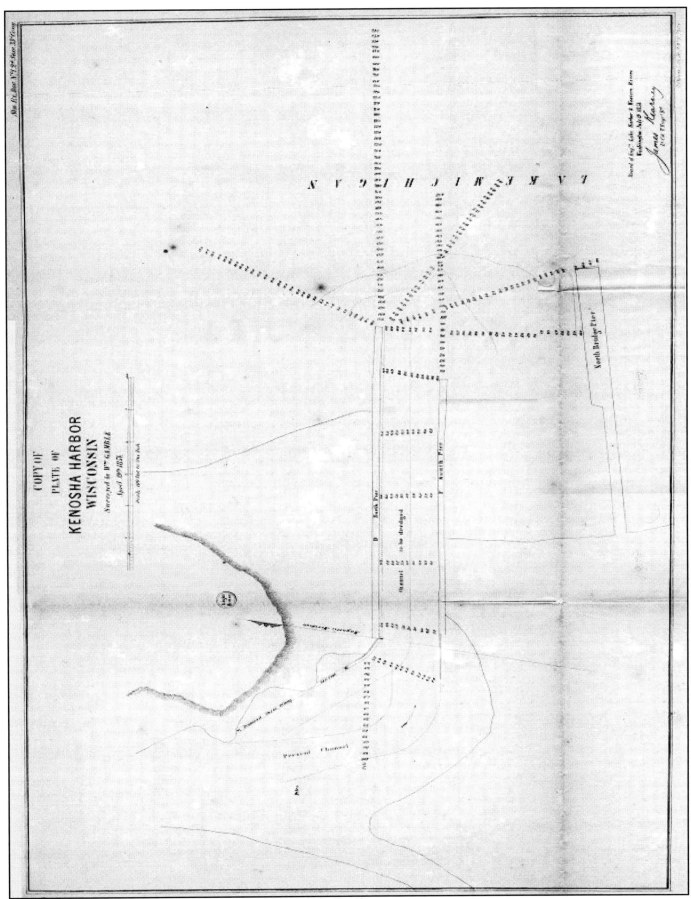

Kenosha Harbor Survey 1853 – Original in Author's Collection

Kenosha Harbor in 1856 showing schooner C. Harrison (foreground) – From a very early photographic engraving – Kenosha County Historical Society

Schooner *Elizabeth* (predates registry numbering) – Built 1863 at Milwaukee - 40.5 x 12.8 x 4.6 ft. - 20.32 gt., 2 masts - The little schooner *Elizabeth* was lost on August 11, 1866 bound Chicago to Kenosha with lumber when she missed the harbor entrance and stranded just north of the piers. Her lumber cargo was removed, but the vessel became embedded deeply in sand and proved a total loss. This is some confusion as to the identity of this vessel. Some original news reports state this was the 66 gt. schooner *Elizabeth* built 1850 at Kingston, Ontario, enrolled out of Oswego. In either case, the vessels disappear after 1866 and the Milwaukee vessel seems more likely. (Milwaukee Sentinel – August 21, 1866) Type: Stranding, Depth: Surfline, Remains: Possibly Present, Accuracy: ¼ Mile.

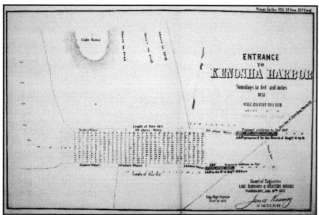

Kenosha Harbor 1853 showing the relative position of the shoreline over time – Author's Collection

Schooner *E.M. Peck* (7490) – Built 1857 at Cleveland, OH by Peck and Masters, 111.3 x 26.1 x 8.8 ft., 228.00 gt. BOM, last document surrendered at Grand Haven, 6/30/1870 – "vessel wrecked" – The schooner *E.M. Peck* was bound light from Chicago to Pentwater for lumber when she capsized off Kenosha on April 13, 1868. Her hull was found capsized 7 miles off the port with no sign of her crew. An attempt to tow the Peck to Milwaukee was unsuccessful as she fetched up on the bottom. The Peck was so badly damaged that it was agreed she must have hit Racine Reef. On 5/4/1868 she was freed and towed to Chicago where she was abandoned in the harbor. Her lifeboat with three lifeless crewmen eventually came ashore on the Michigan side. (Milwaukee Sentinel – April 18, 1868) Type: Capsizing, Depth: n/a, Remains: Definitely Removed, Accuracy: 1 Mile.

Schooner *Scottish Chief* (23744) – Built 1867 at Detroit, MI by Turner & Leithard, 72.4 x 19.4 x 5.9 ft., 54.96 gt., square stem, scow bottom, 2 masts. – The scow schooner *Scottish Chief* became waterlogged between Racine and Kenosha on August 8, 1871, and floated partly submerged for 3 days until her crew abandoned her in their yawl. The crew rowed to Chicago and the hull was towed in to Kenosha by the schooner *Robert Campbell* on 8/14/1871. Eventually the hull was towed to Chicago and abandoned outside the harbor, a total loss. (Milwaukee Sentinel – August 1871) Type: Waterlogged, Depth: n/a, Remains: Removed, Accuracy: 5 Miles.

Schooner *M. Courtright* (16393) – Built 1856 at Erie, PA by DeWolf, 135.8 x 28.7 x 11.25 ft., 276.44 gt., 2 masts, last document surrendered 12/30/1871 at Milwaukee – "total loss" – The *M. Courtright's* crew abandoned her off Racine on November 7, 1871 when she became waterlogged. The ship was driven ashore 1.5 miles north of Kenosha in badly damaged condition with 225,000 ft of lumber cargo. The revenue cutter *Andrew Johnson* tried to pull her off to no avail and she was left in the surf. (Kenosha Telegraph – November 16, 1871) Type: Stranding, Depth: Surfline, Remains: Probably Present, Accuracy: ¼ Mile.

Remains attributed to the *Hutchinson* in 1938 – Kenosha Telegraph – 1/15/1938

Schooner *C.J. Hutchinson* (4360) – Built 1846 at Milwaukee by Samuel Farmin, 136.0 x 26.1 x 10.4 ft., 341.0 gt., 2 masts, figurehead, built as a brig for Champion J. Hutchinson of Southport, WI – The *C..J. Hutchinson* was lost on November 12, 1871 while trying to enter the harbor in ballast. She struck the pier and swung around to the outside of the north pier where the waves broker her keel. She was later dragged into the shallows. In 1938, WPA workers unearthed remains attributed to the *Hutchinson* under the Kenosha municipal beach on Simmons Island. The identity of the remains was never confirmed. (Kenosha Telegraph – November 1871) Type: Stranding, Depth: Buried, Remains: Probably Present, Accuracy: ¼ Mile.

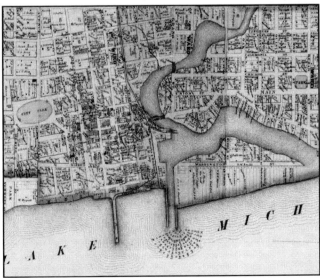

Kenosha Harbor 1857 – Author's Collection

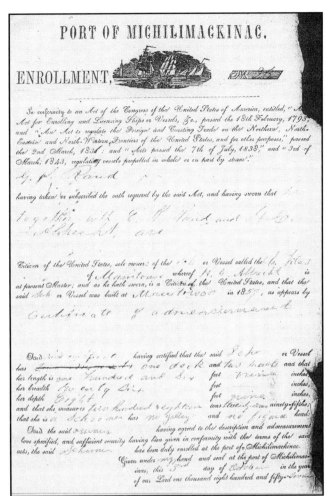

First certificate of Enrollment for the schooner *Jo Vilas* 1857 – National Archives

Schooner *Jo Vilas* (12767) – Built 1857 at Manitowoc, WI by G.S. Rand, 106.75 x 26.0 x 8.75 ft., 149 gt., 2 masts, plain stem – The *Jo Vilas* was bound from White Lake, Michigan to Chicago with lumber on October 9, 1876 when she began to break up about midlake. Her crew was taken off her debris by the schooner *Andrew Jackson*, but the *Vilas'* hull went to the bottom. She is believed to lie in deep water well offshore between Kenosha and Racine. (Milwaukee Sentinel – October 11, 1876) Type: Foundering, Depth: Very Deep, Remains: Definitely Present, Accuracy: 20 Miles. (See detailed account in Part 3)

Schooners drying sails at Kenosha 1868 from an original Samuel Truesdell stereoview in the Author's Collection

Bark *Northwest* (18102) – Built 1862 at Cleveland, Ohio by Peck & Masters, 167.65 x 31.0 x 12.7 ft., 458.54 gt., last document surrendered at Chicago, 12/30/1876 – "total loss" – The big bark *Northwest* was sunk by a collision with the propeeler steam tug *F.L. Danforth* on October 24, 1876. The *Northwest* was bound from Chicago to Buffalo with a cargo of grain when she was struck about 4 AM and sent rapidly to the bottom while off Kenosha. Upon settling, her mastheads were breaking surface. This wreck is believed to lie within sport diving depths somewhere off Kenosha. She has been actively searched for but contrary to reports, has never been identified. (Milwaukee Sentinel – October 26, 1876) Type: Foundering, Depth: Deep, Remains: Definitely Present, Accuracy: 5 Miles.

Kenosha Pierheads – 1872 – Author's Collection

Schooner *Hans Crocker* (11174) – Built 1856 at Milwaukee by James M. Jones, 139.0 x 32.75 x 11.5 ft., 335.03 gt., built as a bark, last document surrendered at Chicago 12/30/1876 as "lost" – The schooner *Hans Crocker* was lost November 29, 1876 while bound from Sturgeon Bay to Chicago with lumber and shingles. She became waterlogged and tried to enter the harbor at Kenosha, but overshot the piers, driving ashore just south of the entrance. She was badly broken and abandoned in the shallows just off the beach. Her remains were purchased but most of her hull was never removed. The *Hans Crocker* had been the queen of the Milwaukee grain fleet and the finest bark on the Lakes when launched. (Milwaukee Sentinel – December 1, 1876) Type: Stranding, Depth: Buried, Remains: Probably Present, Accuracy: ¼ Mile.

Schooner *Velocipede* (25848) – Built 1869 at Menominee, MI by James Dickie, 39.6 x 11.0 x 4.3 ft., 10.12 gt., built as a sloop, later had a second mast added – The little schooner *Velocipede* was lost April 28, 1877 after leaving Racine for Muskegon in ballast. A storm hit and the *Velocipede* was later found with her side stove in off Kenosha. Her two crew were missing. She was towed in near the Kenosha piers where she sank and was abandoned. (Milwaukee Sentinel – May 2, 1877) Type: Stranding, Depth: Shallow, Remains: Probably Present, Accuracy: 1 Mile. (See detailed account in Part 3)

Steamer *City of Madison* – C. Patrick Labadie

Steamer *City of Madison* (4350) – Built 1857 at Buffalo, NY by Van Slyke and Notter, 144.0 x 26.0 x 11.5 ft., 487 gt., rebuilt as a bulk freighter in 1874 – The *City of Madison* was bound light from Chicago to Ludington on August 17, 1877 when she was found to be on fire. Her crew abandoned her in their yawl while the Madison reportedly burned to the water line. She reportedly did not sink for several hours and is commonly reported to have sunk about 35 miles off Kenosha. Wreckhunter Paul Ehorn believes he may have located the ship's remains in about 250 ft of water off Waukegan, Illinois. The remains are reportedly skeletal and disarticulated. (Milwaukee Sentinel – August 18, 1877) Type: Foundering, Depth: Very Deep, Remains: Definitely Present, Accuracy: 10 Miles.

Customs House Wreck Report for the *City of Madison* National Archives

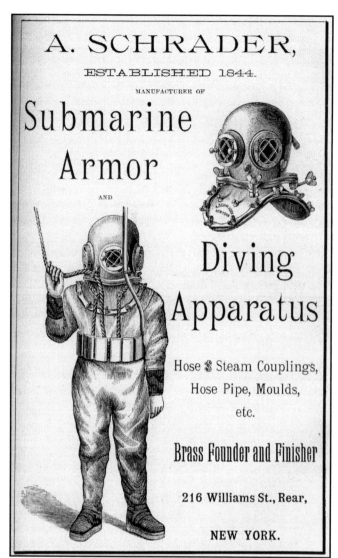

Polk's Marine Directory 1884 – Author's Collection

Schooner *Hippogriff* (11143) – Built 1863 at Buffalo, NY by William Crosthwaite, 137.0 x 26.3 x 12.0 ft., 295.24 gt. – The *Hippogriff* was lost September 27, 1877 bound Chicago to Buffalo with 28,000 bushels of oats when she collided with the schooner *Emma L. Coyne*. The captains of the vessels were brothers and were reportedly playing chicken. The *Hippogriff* sank immediately by the bow. She was reportedly about 20 miles off Kenosha when lost, but one source states she was in 30 fathoms of water. (Chicago Tribune – September 28, 1877) Type: Foundering, Depth: Very Deep, Remains: Definitely Present, Accuracy: 10 Miles.

Scow Schooner *Marion Dixon* (16629) – Built 1864 at Fairport, Ohio by Roswell Hayes, 88.3 x 20.2 x 4.6 ft., 68.67 gt., 2 masts, scow stem, flat bottom – The *Marion Dixon* was lost June 14, 1880 when she capsized about 10 miles from shore midway between Racine and Kenosha with a cargo of tan bark. She later came ashore a few miles south of Kenosha where she was abandoned in the shallows. (Milwaukee Sentinel – June 16, 1880) Type: Stranding, Depth: Surfline, Remains: Probably Present, Accuracy: 1 Mile.

C. Patrick Labadie Collection, Thunder Bay National Marine Sanctuary

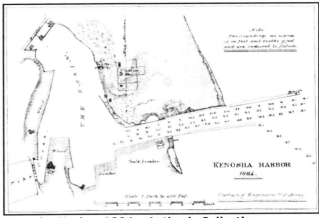

Kenosha Harbor 1884 – Author's Collection

Sidewheel Steamer *Alpena* (404) – Built 1866 at Marine City, MI by Thomas Arnold, 197.0 x 26.8 x 12.0 ft., 653 gt., 2 decks, 24 ft wheels. – The disappearance of the Goodrich steamer *Alpena* on October 16, 1880 remains one of the great unsolved mysteries of the Lakes. She left Grand Haven, MI bound for Chicago with about 80 passengers & crew on October 15 at 9:30 PM during pleasant "Indian Summer" weather. Several hours later, one of the worst storms of the century swept Lake Michigan from the southwest, bringing 70 mph winds and snow squalls. The *Alpena* was seen several times between 6AM and noon struggling toward Kenosha with a severe list. Captain Gilbert Nelson of the bark *S.A. Irish* last reported seeing the *Alpena* at around noon, ten miles off Kenosha, visibly listing in the trough of the sea, but still under steam, heading for Kenosha. She is often reported as being lost off Holland, MI as that is where much of her debris came ashore. However, authorities of the day believed she foundered off Kenosha, as the wind soon blew due east and it took several days for debris to make landfall over a 20 mile stretch of coast around Holland. Some news accounts contended that she became disabled and blew across the Lake, closer to the Michigan shore before foundering. However, based on debris scatter and last sighting, it is more likely that she capsized and foundered catastrophically soon after she was last seen. (Chicago Inter-Ocean – October 20, 1880, Lake Michigan Passenger Steamers - Hilton) Type: Foundering, Depth: Very Deep, Remains: Definitely Present, Accuracy: 30 Miles.

Schooner *Arab* (311) - Built 1854 at Buffalo, NY by Lavayea, 100.0 x 23.9 x 9.4 ft. – 158 gt., 2 masts owned out of Milwaukee – The schooner *Arab* was lost on November 13, 1883 while being towed by the tug Protection from St. Joseph, MI, where she had stranded, to Milwaukee for repairs. She was reportedly about midway between Kenosha and Racine and about 25 miles out then she rolled and sank. One life was lost when her captain was crushed by a steam engine during the accident. Some erroneous reports place her close to shore, but she is believed to lie in very deep water and has not been the subject of any search efforts. (Chicago Tribune – November 14, 1883) Type: Foundering, Depth: Very Deep, Remains: Definitely Present, Accuracy: 20 Miles.

Image taken on the wreck of the yacht *Greyhound* in Kenosha Harbor 1884 – Kenosha County Historical Society

Yacht *Greyhound* (unregistered) – Built c. 1880 – c. 50 ft. – The yacht *Greyhound* was owned by James H. Howe, an attorney for the Chicago & Northwestern Railroad at Kenosha. Sometime in 1884, the *Greyhound* sank in

Kenosha Harbor. She is believed to have been a total loss, but her remains were likely removed. (Kenosha County Historical Society, Louis Milton Thiers Image) Type: Abandonment, Depth: Shallow, Remains: Probably Removed, Accuracy: ¼ Mile.

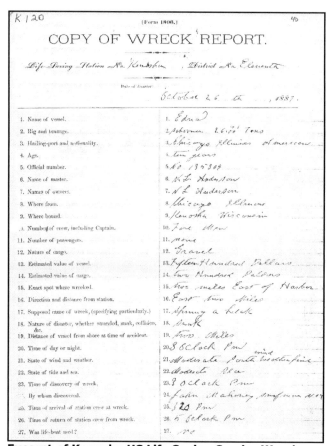

Excerpt of Kenosha US Life Saving Service Wreck Report for Schooner Edna – National Archives

Schooner *Edna* (135309) – Built 1877 at Chicago, IL by N.L. Anderson, 62.1 x 17.2 x 5.2 ft., 38.32 gt., 1 deck, 2 masts, plain stem, square stern – The *Edna* was a small coastal schooner engaged in the gravel trade. She foundered suddenly on October 26, 1887 in calm water bound Chicago to Kenosha. Her crew were rescued from their small yawl by the Kenosha Lifesavers but the *Edna* was left on the bottom with her masts breaking the surface. The vessel reportedly went down 3 miles from shore just south of the Kenosha Lifesaving Station in 45 ft of water. The *Edna* was been reported found by the Author and Harry Zych in 1999 but her remains have not yet been positively identified at this time. (USLSS Wreck Reports – Kenosha Station) Type: Foundering, Depth: Shallow, Remains: Tentatively Identified, Accuracy: N42.34.44 / W87.45.56. (See detailed account in Part 3)

Schooners unloading Tan Bark at Kenosha c. 1900 – Kenosha County Historical Society

Steamer *Solon H. Johnson* (6887) – Built 1875 at Clayton, NY by A. Cook, 106.5 x 21.5 x 8.1 ft., 128.78 gt., built as passenger steamer Dolphin at Clayton, NY by A. Cook, rebuilt 1879 and renamed, last document surrendered at Chicago, 11/27/1888 – "vessel lost" – The steamer *Solon H. Johnson* was lost November 24, 1887 while towing a barge loaded with bricks. She fouled the towline in her prop during a storm and drifted ashore 9 miles south of Kenosha, fetching up 600 ft from shore. Much of the brick was tossed overboard and the barge was freed, but the Johnson was abandoned. The Kenosha Lifesavers rescued her crew. Her wreck site could be located with a little effort. (Kenosha USLSS Station Wreck Report) Type: Stranding, Depth: Shallow, Remains: Definitely Present, Accuracy: 1 Mile.

Kenosha US Life Saving Station – Author's Collection

Scow Schooner *Lenzena* (48566) – Built 1882 at Charlevoix, MI, 42.0 x 13.0 x 4.8 ft., 12.60 gt., owned out of Chicago, 2 masts, built as an unmasted barge, last enrolled Chicago, 2/25/1889. – The little scow schooner *Lenzena* was lost on May 29, 1890 while bound for Chicago with gravel. She stranded in the shallows at Kenosha, but the exact location remains a mystery. (Chicago Tribune – June 4, 1890) Type: Stranding, Depth: Surfline, Remains: Probably Present, Accuracy: 5 Miles.

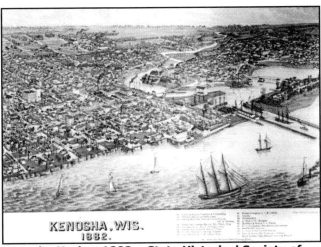
Kenosha Harbor 1882 – State Historical Society of Wisconsin

Schooner *Eliza* (8248) – Built 1868 at Spring Lake, Michigan by. H.C. Pierson, 53.2 x 14.9 x 6.0 ft., 30.03 gt., 2 masts – The little schooner *Eliza* left Chicago for Milwaukee with a cargo of sand and two crewmen under Captain John Hansen at the end of June 1890. A fierce storm raged for days after she left and she was never heard from again. No debris was ever found to suggest a location, but she is thought to lie off the Wisconsin coast based on the storm trajectory. (Herman Runge Wreck List) Type: Foundering, Depth: Deep, Remains: Definitely Present, Accuracy: 40 Miles.

Schooner *R.B. Hayes* (110338) – Built 1877 at Gibraltar, MI by Linn & Craig, 177.5 x 34.0 x 14.2 ft., 668.86 gt., built as a 3 masted schooner, later cut down to a sch. barge – The Hayes was a large schooner barge being towed by the steamer *A.P. Wright* from Chicago with lumber when she began to founder a few hours after leaving Chicago on April 20, 1893. The *Wright* cut both her consorts free and their crews were taken off, but the *Hayes* was seen still afloat several hours later. Her towmate *F.L. Danforth* was cast ashore at Chicago, but some reports state that the *Hayes* foundered 15 miles SE of Kenosha. The *Hayes* is most likely in Illinois waters well off shore and has not been the target of search efforts to date. (Chicago Tribune – April 21, 1893) Type: Foundering, Depth: Very Deep: Remains: Definitely Present, Accuracy: 20 Miles.

Schooner *Lem Ellsworth* (140062) – Built 1874 at Milwaukee by Wolf & Davidson, 138.6 x 26.2 x 11.8 ft., 340.14 gt., 3 masted canal schooner – This big canal schooner was last seen clearing the Straits on May 16, 1894. Her battered yawl was found a few days later midlake off Kenosha. She was hauling sandstone blocks from Jacobsville, MI to Chicago when she went missing. A 1929 Racine newspaper article relates a claim by a man who states he saw the *Ellsworth* founder several miles off Racine. This wreck has not been specifically searched for as she has a rather large search grid. She could potentially lie anywhere in the Lake, but most accounts place her off Kenosha due to the lifeboat discovery. (Chicago Tribune – May 23, 1894) Type: Foundering, Depth: Very Deep: Remains: Definitely Present, Accuracy: 20 Miles.

Schooner *Lem Ellsworth* – Historical Collections of the Great Lakes

Racine Man Sheds Light On Lake Mystery of 35 Years

Simeon Dutton Saw Lem Ellsworth Sink, Belief; Tells Story Today.

After the elapse of 35 years it has become known with a considerable degree of definiteness that the schooner Lem Ellsworth and her crew of seven men went down in Lake Michigan about five or six miles off this port. She disappeared in the terrific blow of May 18, 1894, and it was always supposed that she sank off Evanston or Waukegan. A yawl boat with her name painted on the bow was picked up by fishermen off Waukegan several days after the storm, but her fate was wrapped in mystery.

Today, a signed statement issued by Simeon Dutton, 2931 Washington avenue, is believed to shed the first definite ray of light on that mystery of the inland sea. He is believed to have been the only eye witness to the sinking of the Lem Ellsworth view, so one can see that I must understand Lake Michigan after seeing it in all of its stages. I have been up and down this lake in all kinds of weather a great many times. While at home on May 18, 1894, there was a terrible storm on the lake. The wind was blowing a gale from the northeast, and a tremendous sea was running. After dinner, at 1:30 p.m., the folks went into the living room on the second floor. Mother was sitting in her chair at the north window facing the lake. Sister Jennie was sitting at the south window facing the lake. Father was taking his afternoon nap on the sofa. I was reading a Chicago newspaper, I think it was the Tribune. I stood up close to the south window and looking out saw the seas running high. I stepped into the hall and took my marine glass, a telescope glass, and went out onto the front porch. I focused the glass and looked out onto the lake. Looking over Wind Point, I saw a square-rigged sailing vessel headed south up the lake, some distance north and well out into the lake. I moved my glass along the horizon south up the lake, and my eyes caught another

Racine Journal – November 6, 1929

Scow Schooner *Contest* (4525) – Built 1863 at Holland, MI by Hopkins, 76.2 x 20.5 x 5.8 ft., 97 gt., lengthened 1872 at Kenosha to 101.0 x 21.4 x 6.5 ft., later had 3 masts - The *Contest* missed the Kenosha harbor entrance was driven ashore and wrecked 100 ft. south of the harbor on April 16, 1897. She was later towed to Milwaukee and abandoned at an unknown location. (Door County Advocate – April 24, 1897) Type: Stranding, Depth: Buried, Remains: Possibly Present, Accuracy: 5 Miles.

Contest stranded off Kenosha, April 1897 – Louis Thiers Collection, Kenosha County Historical Society

Original painting of the *L.R. Doty* – C. Patrick Labadie Collection, TBNMS

Steamer *L.R. Doty* (141272) – Built 1893 at West Bay City, MI by F.W. Wheeler, 291.0 x 41.0 x 19.8 ft., 2056.0 gt., wooden bulk freight steamer – The *Doty* is one of the largest vessels still missing on the Great Lakes. She vanished in a tremendous gale on October 24, 1898 while towing the barge *Olive Jeanette* from South Chicago to Midland, Ontario with corn. The *Jeanette* survived and her captain was the last person to see the *Doty*. The *Doty* is generally reported to lie off Kenosha, as that is where her debris was found. However, analysis of her last known position and debris scatter suggest she was lost far offshore, perhaps as far north as Milwaukee. The propeller *Saranac* claimed to have struck the wreck of the *Doty* off Racine in 1903, prompting an investigation, but it turned out to be a new section of Racine Reef. This vessel has not specifically been searched for but at least one wreck hunter claims to have imaged her hull. Rumors of her discovery in shallow water near Kenosha have been reported in the past, but are untrue. A target that may well be the *Doty* was snagged by commercial fishermen in 1983 and reported to Jerry Guyer, who located the site with a fish finder prior to getting sidescan. Guyer reported what appeared to be a large wreck on the bottom about 17 miles SE of Milwaukee in 330 ft of water at N42.55.50 / W87.27.50. Nobody has ever been back to check the target to due its distance. The Author believes the *Doty* is the most likely candidate. (Milwaukee Sentinel – October 26, 1898) Type: Foundering, Depth: Deep: Remains: Definitely Present, Accuracy: 20 Miles.

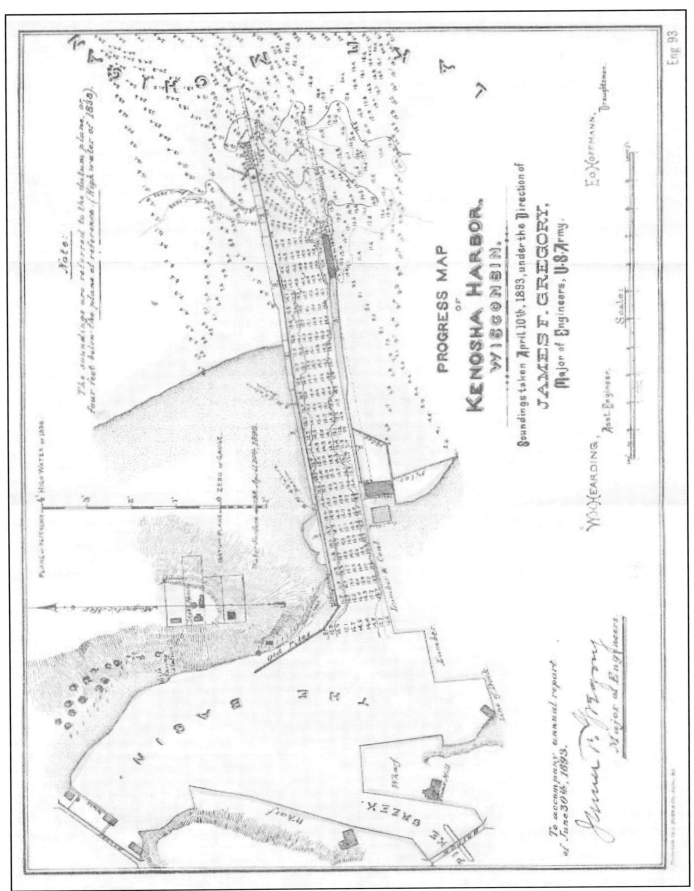
Kenosha Harbor 1893 – Author's Collection

Kenosha's original pierhead lights c. 1900 – Author's Collection

Schooner *Idler* (unregistered) – Built 1893 at Marinette, WI by Ole Peterson, c. 40 ft., 25 gt. – On November 1, 1905, this yacht stranded 100 ft. off shore at present day Illinois Beach State Park. The Kenosha Lifesavers attempted to release her, but pulled her bow out. She was abandoned where she lay. (Kenosha USLSS Wreck Report) Type: Stranding, Depth: Shallow, Remains: Definitely Present, Accuracy: ¼ Mile. (See detailed account in Part 3)

Steamer *H.A. Root* sunk at Kenosha 1907 – John Kane Collection, Milwaukee Public Library

Steamer *H.A. Root* (95885) – Built 1886 at Saugatuck, MI by James Elliott, 114.0 x 24.6 x 9.2 ft., 198.0 gt., rabbit steamer, later sold Canadian with number C126195. – The steamer *H.A. Root*'s boiler exploded at Kenosha on September 3, 1907, destroying the ship's upper works. Later while moored at the dock during the night, she sank, killing 2 crew. She was rebuilt and sailed until 1912 when she was abandoned in Canadian waters. (Kenosha USLSS Wreck Report) Type: Explosion, Depth: n/a, Remains: Recovered, Accuracy: ¼ Mile. (See detailed account in story section)

Ships in Kenosha Harbor c. 1900 – Author's Collection

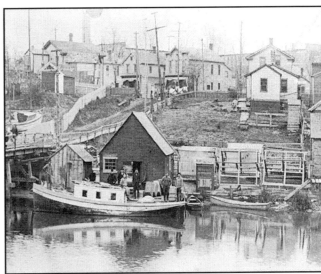
Fish Tug *Mischief* 1905 at Kenosha – Louis Milton Thiers Collection, Kenosha County Historical Society

Remains of the *Mischief* 1909 - Louis Milton Thiers Collection, Kenosha County Historical Society

Fish Tug *Mischief* (unregistered) – Built Kenosha c. 1900, c. 30 ft. – The *Mischief* was a small unregistered fish tug that ran out of Kenosha. She was completely destroyed by spring storms at Kenosha in 1909. Her shattered remains were driven high up on the beach south of the city. She was owned by Joseph Borkenhagen, and Fred Joernt. The scene was captured by Kenosha photographer Louis Milton Thiers, whose important glass plate negative collection is at the Kenosha County Historical Society. (Louis Milton Thiers Collection) Type: Stranding, Depth: n/a, Remains: Definitely Removed, Accuracy: ¼ Mile.

The fish tug *Forelle* – Milwaukee County Historical Society

Steel Fish Tug *Forelle* (205777) – Built 1908 at Ferrysburg, MI by Johnston Bros, 54.6 x 15.8 x 7.5 ft., 46 gt., steam powered – The fish tug *Forelle* went missing on September 20, 1923 bound from Benton Harbor, MI to Milwaukee with a cargo of fruit and 5 crew. She was last seen about midlake. Debris from the wreck was located several miles off Kenosha. The *Forelle* is has been a search target for decades but has never been reported found. Accounts state that she foundered very near the location where the Rosinco was later lost. (Herman Runge Wreck List) Type: Foundering, Depth: Very Deep, Remains: Definitely Present, Accuracy: 10 Miles.

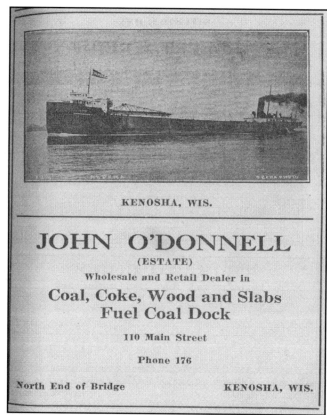

John O'Donnell Coal Dock – Kenosha – Lynn's Marine Directory 1918 – Author's Collection

A busy Kenosha Harbor about 1890 - Louis Milton Thiers Collection - Kenosha County Historical Society

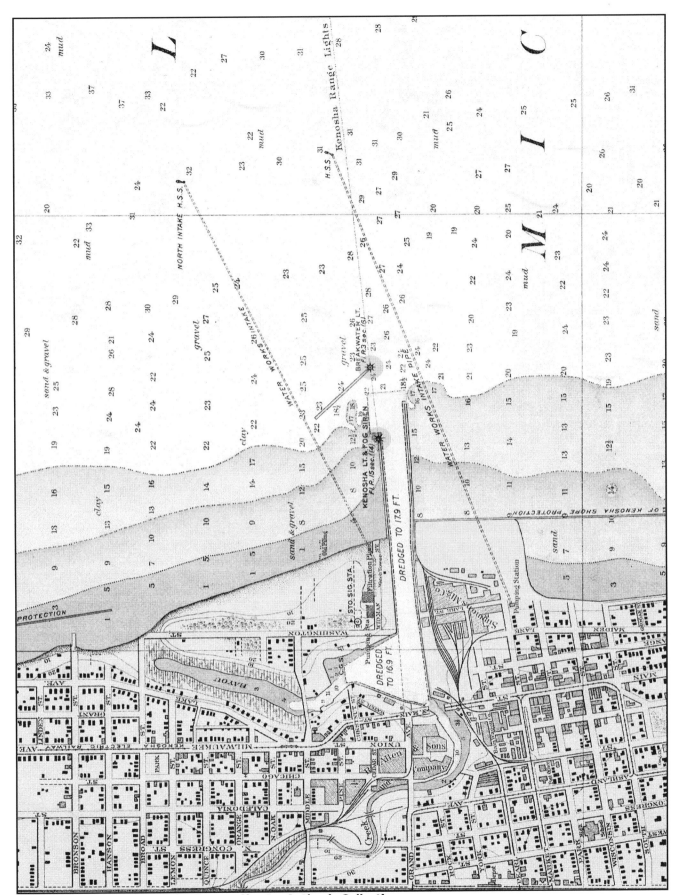

Kenosha Harbor 1921 – Lake Survey Chart – Author's Collection

Steamer *Charles McVea* – Author's Collection

Steamer *Charles McVea* (126517) – Built 1888 at Saugatuck, MI by R.C. Brittain, 123.0 x 24.1 x 10.0 ft., 331.0 gt., passenger and package freight steamer. - The *Charles McVea* was owned by the Hill Steamboat Line of Kenosha when she was laid up just below the bridge in Kenosha Harbor aside the *City of Marquette* in 1922. She was cut down about 1923 and her hull was used as a floating drydock for small yachts. Her final document was surrendered at Milwaukee on 2/28/1928 endorsed "dismantled and abandoned," but the final disposition of her hull is unknown. It may still lie on the bottom of the harbor. (Milwaukee Public Library Marine Collection Vessel File) Type: Abandonment, Depth: Shallow, Remains: Probably Removed, Accuracy: 1 Mile.

Rosinco as the *Whitemarsh* c. 1920 – Wisconsin Historical Society

Steel Yacht *Rosinco* (214160) - Built 1916 at Wilmington, Delaware by Harlan & Hollingsworth Corp., 88.0 x 15.0 x 7.8 ft., 91.0 gt. Built as the gas yacht *Georgiana III*, renamed *Whitemarsh* in 1919, and later *Rosinco* in 1925, later converted to diesel. - The luxury yacht *Rosinco* was bound from Milwaukee to Chicago in the early morning hours of April 18, 1928 when she struck floating debris and began rapidly taking on water. Her seven occupants abandoned to a small motor tender and yawl, but the *Rosinco* went to the bottom 185 ft below in ten minutes. The *Rosinco's* resting place was found in 1961 when she was snagged by commercial fishermen who shared the location with Milwaukee wreckhunter Kent Bellrichard. The *Rosinco* has been placed on the National Register of Historic Places and was the subject of a detailed investigation by the Wisconsin Historical Society, which has placed an excellent history of the vessel and the wrecksite on their website. (Wisconsin Historical Society Website) Type: Foundering, Depth: 185 ft., Remains: Located, Accuracy: N42° 37.30' / W87° 37.74'.

The *Wisconsin* in ice c. 1890 – C. Patrick Labadie Collection, TBNMS

Steel Steamer *Wisconsin* (80861) – Built 1881 at Wyandotte, Michigan by Detroit Dry Dock Co., 203.9 x 40.0 x 24.6 ft., 1181.66 gt., built as *Wisconsin*, renamed *Naomi* 1899, *E.G. Crosby* 1910, *Gen. Robt. M. O'Reilly* 1918, *Pilgrim* 1920, *Wisconsin* 1924. – The Goodrich steamer foundered off Kenosha on October 29, 1929 with cargo of autos, iron castings, boxed freight and 9 lives, a total loss. She had burned 5/21/1907 in midlake with the loss of 5 lives but was rebuilt. She was one of four major ships lost on the Lakes in October 1929, the others being the *Senator*, the carferry *Milwaukee* and the *Andaste*. She is one of the most popular dive sites on Lake Michigan and was recently placed on the National Register of Historic Places by the Wisconsin Historical

Society. The wreck was salvaged in the 1930s by Chicago salvor Frank Hefling who passed the location to salvor Dick Race. Race relocated the site in the 1960s. (Milwaukee Sentinel – November 1929) Type: Foundering, Depth: 130 ft., Remains: Located, Accuracy: N42° 31.80' / W087° 42.55'.

Fish Tug Cheerio – Historical Collections of the Great Lakes

Steel Fish Tug *Cheerio* (237885) – Built 1935 at Sturgeon Bay, Wisconsin by Sturgeon Bay Shipbuilding Co., 36.8 x 12.5 x 5.1 ft., 21 gt., Oil screw, later lengthened to 36.8 x 12.5 x 5.1., renamed *Resolute* in 1977. The *Cheerio* sank in ice floes off Kenosha harbor on January 17, 1936, while trying to make it into the harbor during a severe northeast blow. The sinking took the lives of her 3 crew, including her captain. She was later raised and returned to fishing on Lake Michigan in 1939. Remarkably, she is still in service, fishing out of Tampa, Florida as of 2009, entering her 75th season. (Herman Runge Wreck List) Type: Foundering, Depth: n/a, Remains: Recovered, Accuracy: 1 Mile.

***Hoegh Cliff* in service c. 1966 – Author's Collection**

The *Hoegh Cliff* sunk at Kenosha – Racine Journal, October 14, 1965

Steamer *Hoegh Cliff* (IMO 5152195) – Built 1956 at Hamburg by Deutsche Werft AG, 495.9 x 64.1 x 26.5 ft., 9194 gt, 5274 nt., powered by a 7-cylinder Burmeister & Wain Diesel, 740 x 1600 mm - The steel Norwegian freighter *Hoegh Cliff*, owned by Lief Hoegh Lines of Oslo, Norway and under charter to Waterman Steamship Line of NY was nearly lost at Kenosha in the evening hours of October 13, 1965. She was bound from Chicago with flour and wheat being shipped under the US Foreign Aid Program. She planned to load 200 tons of flour and some Nash Ramblers at Kenosha when she struck the Kenosha north pier tearing a 44 ft gash in her hull and creating a dramatic shower of sparks. She was to go to Duluth and Buffalo before going to the Mediterranean. The General Salvage Company left their unsuccessful project to raise the *Prinz Willem V* at Milwaukee to work on the ship, and divers from the Kenosha Aqua Club were hired to inspect her hull. It was found that her frames were broken below the waterline and a temporary patch was welded in place. Her cargo was lightered and the vessel raised, but she sank again a few days later. She was eventually raised and towed to Chicago for repairs. The *Hoegh Cliff* had a long career, renamed *Eastern Cliff* in 1967 and *Bihua* in 1972. In 1979 she was sold Chinese and renamed *HONG QI 134*. She sailed until being mothballed in China in 2005 and was abandoned there in 2007. The *Hoegh Cliff* wasn't the first "salty" to wreck at Kenosha. In June of 1962, the Swiss freighter *Castagnola* ran aground at the harbor entrance, in April 1960 the *Marco Martinoli* pulled up 63 ft of city water main and in May of 1962, the *La Loma* once again pulled up the water main. (Kenosha News, October 1965) Type: Stranding, Depth: n/a, Remains: Recovered, Accuracy: ¼ Mile.

Vessels at Kenosha c. 1910 - Author's Collection

Simmons plant & Kenosha Waterfront 1918

Rock Barge (unknown) – In August of 1975, the USCG charted a large rock filled scow barge in 32 ft of water south of Kenosha. An attempt to remove the wreck in May of 1976 failed and Kenosha dive shop owner Jim Watters reported that the wreck was still there in the early 90s. This is probably a commercial barge used for shoreline reinforcement work in the 1960s that foundered while under tow. Type: Foundering, Depth: Shallow, Remains: Located, Accuracy: N42.38.4299 / W87.47.2896.

Kenosha International Harbor 1966 - Author's Collection

Burned Fiberglass Yacht (unknown) – The AWOIS database and diver reports confirm that a 40 ft. fiberglass yacht burned and sank in about 45 ft of water south of Kenosha in 1981. The site has reportedly been dived but hasn't been relocated in recent years. At least one attempt to locate the remains at the reported location was unsuccessful. Foundering, Depth: 45 ft., Remains: Located, Accuracy: N42.34.24 / W87.45.42.

Vessels Built at Kenosha

Although Kenosha has never been known as a center of shipbuilding, she has seen the launch of a number of historically significant vessels. A few schooners were launched from the beach on Simmons Island and several fish tugs were constructed in the harbor. The list below comprises all the registered vessels attributed to Kenosha in government records.

Schooner *Lewis C. Irwin* (14664) – Blt. 1847 by Emerson – 85 gt. – 84.5x21.0x7.25 – Ashore and wrecked 11/1869 near Ludington, MI

Brig *Sam Hale* (22345) - Blt. 1847 by Samuel Farmin – 279.31 gt. BOM, 225.96 gt. NM – 117.6x24.3x10.6 – Renamed *Redick*, 1867 – Lost on Whaleback Shoal, Green Bay, 9/22/1868

Sloop *Lady Ann* (none) - Blt. 1849 – 30.37 gt. - 48.0x17.0x5.7, Driven ashore and wrecked at Kenosha, 9/18/1855

Scow Schooner *L.B. Nichols* (48195) – Blt. 1854 by Jason Lathrop – 64 gt. – 73.0x21.0x6.0 – Went ashore and broke up north of Sheboygan Harbor, 11/30/1868 with cargo of wood and cedar posts.

Tug Fred Engel at Kenosha - C. Patrick Labadie Collection, TBNMS

Tug *Fred Engle* (120206) – Blt. 1875 by James & Nathan Brooks – 21 gt., 14 nt. – 51.7x13.1x5.5 – Later P.W. Arthur – Abandoned Escanaba, MI, 3/31/1920

Schooner *Cleopatra* (none) - Blt. c. 1880 – 104 gt., no data

Sloop Yacht *Rambler* (110705) – Blt. 1880 by Horace G. Cole – 13 gt. – 37.0x14.6x4.5, last enrolled 7/9/1901, Chicago

Gas Launch *Vixen* (208032) – Blt. 1906 – 8 gt. – 39.0 x 8.3x3.5 - Sold Canadian 1913

Steel Gas Fish Tug *Liberty* (219163) - Blt. 1916 by Richard Julien – 12 gt. – 35.2x9.0x4.0 – Dismantled 1951

Gas Launch *Hugh B* (220568) – Blt. 1920 by E.J. Hamilton – 12 gt. – 38.8x10.1x4.2 – Abandoned 12/1938

Tug W.W. Hill at Bayfield, WI, 1948 - Courtesy of Harvey Hadland

Diesel Fish Tug *W.W. Hill* (227094) – Blt. 1927 by W.W. Hill – 37 gt. – 49.6x14.0x5.2 – Dismantled 1954 at Duluth, MN

Gas Fish Tug *Vernon* (231734) – Blt. 1932 – 13 gt. – 32.9 x 10.3 x 4.4 – Struck *Str. Harry Colby* and foundered off Grand Marais, MI 8/5/1950

Gas Fish Tug *Christy* (232743) - Blt. 1933 by W.W. Hill – 13 gt. – 31.5 x 9.2 x 3.8 ft. – Abandoned 1956

Fish Tug Energy in early days Courtesy Steve Ceskowski

Steel Fish Tug *Energy* (233896) – Blt. 1934 by Kenosha Boiler & Structural Co. – 36 gt. – 44.0x13.8x5.5 ft. – Still in commission on Lake Superior, owned by Cecil Peterson on the Keweenaw Waterway

Gas Fish Tug *Judith C* (234935) – Blt. 1936 – 21 gt. – 41.7x11.3x4.6 – Abandoned 1955

Steel Yacht *Anna Z* (547576) – Blt. 1973 – 16gt., 15, nt. – 42.0x12.8x6.2 ft., blt. by Matthew M. Putra, 85 hp, owned out of Genoa, IL in 1999.

Steel Yacht *Ramunda* (579542) – Blt. 1976 by Oldrich Fencl, 75 gt., 66nt., 64.6x17.6x8.0 ft., 225 hp. Out of Florida in 1999.

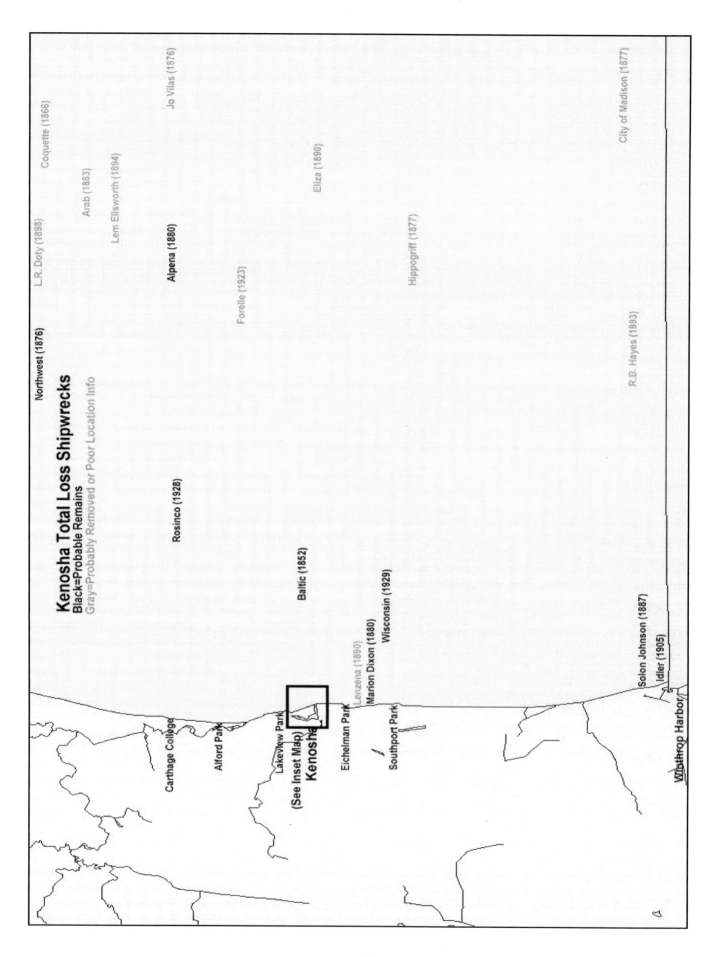

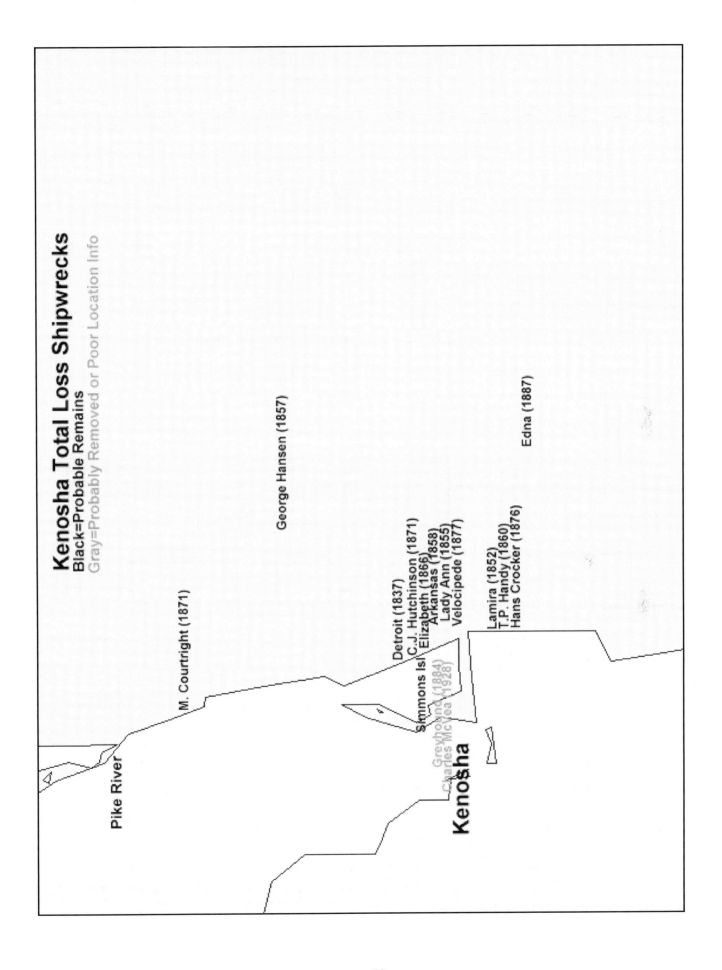

Racine Shipwrecks

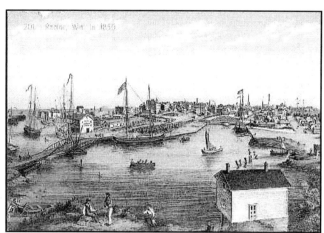

Artist's Conception of Racine Harbor 1850 - Author's Collection

Local Racine Historian Bob Jaeck is one of the leading experts on the maritime history of Racine. He has spent his life researching Racine's ships and shipwrecks, and has amassed a substantial collection of original Racine maritime news accounts. He has been an invaluable friend and colleague, and I consequently, asked him to write a brief Racine maritime history as the introduction to the Racine Shipwrecks section of this book.

Racine's Maritime History
By Bob Jaeck

The name "Racine" in French means "root", as the harbor of Racine is formed by the Root River, which empties into Lake Michigan. The Root River watershed flows from New Berlin in Waukesha County, though parts of Milwaukee County. A small branch flows north from Kenosha County with the larger branches flowing though Racine County into the City of Racine forming the Racine Harbor. The Root River has also been known in the past by other names such as Chippecotton, Chipperooton, Kipikawi, Ot-chee-beek, and the Racine River.

On October 10, 1699 a group of French explorers in eight canoes led by Henry de Tonty, Francois Morgan de Vincennes and Father Jean François Buisson de St. Cosme entered the Root River seeking a route to the Fox River. These men are believed to be the first recorded Europeans to visit Racine County. They ventured several miles up the river before turning back and continuing on to present day Chicago. It is likely that Henri de Tonty had seen the river before. He had been with Lasalle's ill-fated Griffon expedition twenty years early and almost certainly had encamped there while traveling down the west shore of Lake Michigan in October 1679.

In 1828, Captain Gilbert Knapp of the United States Revenue Cutter Service, in command of the J. A. Dallas, was on a cruise north along the west shore of Lake Michigan. He had his vessel anchored off the Root River and then went ashore to look over the area. This was when he first laid his eyes on the small natural harbor formed by the mouth Root River. This part of the country was still in the hands of the Native Americans. Later that year, Captain Knapp retired from the Cutter service, but he would not forget the pretty little harbor.

On September 26, 1833 the second Treaty of Chicago was signed and on February 21, 1835 it was ratified. But just after the Treaty was signed, some significant events were placed in motion. The Native Americans were given $100,000 and a reservation of equal size on the Missouri River. In exchange, they ceded 5,000,000 acres and all tribal lands west of Lake Michigan to the United States. Some Native Americans fled to Canada, while others slowly headed west of the Mississippi. Many in Wisconsin, including the Racine area, went to Milwaukee where the government hired drivers for wagon trains. They were taken by wagon, with their first stop at De Moines, Iowa. Even though it was not legal until three years after the signing, settlers in small numbers began to enter the yet Indian land. When retired Captain Knapp learned of the Treaty being signed, he remembered the Root River along the Wisconsin west shore.

In the early summer of 1834, Captain Knapp visited the Racine area by horse with an Indian guide for a second time. He stayed couple days looking over the region and planning a harbor. In November of 1834, Knapp returned for a third time to the mouth of the Root River, this time with three helpers and building supplies for a cabin. After the cabin was constructed Knapp left, but the three men stayed behind to hold his claim.

Early in 1835, Knapp, with two other investors, filed a claim for 140.98 acres around the mouth of the Root River and established "Port Gilbert," named after Captain Knapp. Knapp is regarded as the first settler of Port Gilbert because of his accepted claim. On November 3, 1836, one of the two investors with Captain Knapp, Mr. Gurdon S. Hubbard, renamed the certificate of title to his section of land as Racine. This new name "Racine" was accepted legally and officially.

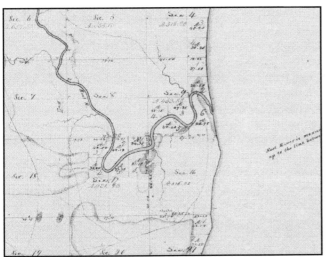

Root River 1835 – Original Survey Plat – Wisconsin Historical Society

In 1835 and 1836, settlers arrived in small numbers. The sailors were fearful of the still present Native Americans, so when vessels arrived off the shore of Port Gilbert, they anchored near shore. The sailors took the settlers and their belongings close to shore in yawl boats where they were off loaded by either by wading ashore or being carried ashore on the men's shoulders. Supplies were also off loaded using this method. Wood was taken back out to the steamers for fuel and bagged wheat was also transported to the waiting vessels for sale back east. Soon small boats and scows were also used powered by oars, to help with the process of moving passengers and goods. If weather conditions were good, the schooners would be run onto the beach to help with the process.

A large sand bar at the mouth of the Root River created shallow water that prevented vessels from entering the protection of the river. Early citizens dug a small channel in the beach for small scows and boats. Then using oxen and shovels they started to dig a straight channel to form a shallow entrance into the Root River. However, the wind and waves would bring in sand that soon reformed a sand bar across the opening. The need for a harbor was soon obvious to all the citizens. In 1839 the first government lighthouse in Racine went into operation, called the Root River Lighthouse. This lighthouse was located just south of the harbor entrance.

In 1836 the citizens paid $100 for a harbor survey and on March 16, 1843 voters decided to build a harbor. Each citizen contributed with two days of pay or the equivalent in labor. Later that month, the territorial legislature issued a 15% tax on the people of Racine, Rock and Walworth Counties, and on April 22, 1843, a special tax was voted for Racine to secure $5000 to further fund the building of a harbor. It was in 1840 that the first effort to build piers for a harbor entrance took place. Two piers were first constructed. Then, the beach and river materials between the piers were slowly removed, first by shovel and oxen, later by a steam dredge arrived from Chicago to speed the job along. The goal was to obtain a channel depth of 15'. Other taxes followed, but the harbor was needed to bring in the arriving immigrants and to ship out the goods produced. No federal government money helped with this early effort to establish Racine's first harbor. By late 1843 a shallow artificial channel and harbor piers were built allowing larger schooners to enter the river.

Amidst all the funding and building, a schooner finally was able to cross the sand bar in March of 1842, and for the first time a vessel stayed in the safety of the Root River. It was July 26, 1843 that the first steamboat, the little C.C. Trowbridge from Milwaukee, under the command of Captain Lane, succeeded in crossing the sand bar to enter the Root River. This caused great enthusiasm for the citizens of Racine. Even though the work on the harbor was incomplete, it allowed them to see that their hard work in building the harbor would soon be rewarded.

In July of 1844, the Racine Harbor was nearing completion and would soon be declared open to lake commerce. Sunday morning, July 14, 1844, Captain Kelsey brought the steamer Chesapeake through the narrow piers and into the Racine Harbor. As the vessel entered, a cannon was fired from shore to let all in the city know the steamer had arrived. The Chesapeake is recognized as the first vessel to enter the Racine Harbor, and the first vessel to enter a man made harbor in Wisconsin. The harbor was now declared open for commercial use.

In the mid 1840s, local business men built two narrow piers just south of the harbor entrance out from the shore. This was done to assist in the loading and unloading of vessels when weather permitted. This method however, resulted in many vessels being blown ashore, although most vessels were recovered. Also the harbor channel was narrow. This was a challenge for the vessels of the wind, and even some steam ships found it thrilling to enter during times of unfavorable weather. In 1849 the government added a small lighthouse to the outmost end of the north pier. This Lighthouse was in service until December 3, 1859 when a schooner collided with the pier and swept away the lighthouse.

In 1846 the first schooner "Diamond," was built in Racine by Captain Bailey. Over the years over a hundred vessels were constructed at Racine. Most of the schooner building took place between 1850 and 1880, although vessels of many types were constructed at Racine and were considered to be of high quality. Scows, schooners, and barges were the specialty of the Racine builders. In 1878 the Racine Hardware Manufacturing Company became the first to built pleasure boats. Over the years, there were a variety of different boat building companies at Racine constructing canoes, launches, and yachts, the last closing in 1926.

By 1848, Racine Harbor was one of the busiest harbors on the Great Lakes in terms of tonnage. In the 1850s, harbor traffic continued to grow, bringing in immigrants, settlers, passengers and their supplies, while shipping out grain and lumber. By mid 1854 the first steam locomotive arrived at the docks on a lake steamer. This small wood burning engine was called the "Tiger." Later in the day, a second locomotive arrived on the railroad tracks and was called the "Beloit." With its large supply of lumber, Racine became a terminal point for both lake vessels and railroads, as both used wood to fuel the early steam engines. It was not until the Civil War that the government provided more substantial funding for further widening of the harbor entrance and dredging of the river.

During the 1860s, the harbor was a busy place with steam ships and a large number of schooners hauling cargoes of wheat, crops, wool, leather, flour, ship knees, and lumber. Wheat was largest export, and was brought to Racine by wagons or railcars, then to the grain warehouses and elevators located along the river. The grain was then loaded into lake schooners for shipment to the eastern ports. By 1860, Racine was the third largest grain port on Lake Michigan behind Milwaukee and Chicago. It was during Racine's grain boom that Mr. George A. Thomson purchased the first tug boat for Racine. As reported on May 16, 1866, the little tug boat named Daisy Lee arrived from Buffalo New York and was to provide a much needed service in Racine. Many other tugboats arrived in the coming years and would provide service to Racine for many decades to come. The tugboats would assist vessels into and out of the harbor during times of calm weather and foul weather and increased the safety and efficiency of the harbor operations. The tugboats would also assist vessels passing the harbor with a tow, release grounded vessels, help with light salvage work, serve as fishing vessels and provide lifesaving service to crew and vessels. The government discontinued service of the Root River Lighthouse on September 10, 1865. The light's Fresnel lens was removed and placed in the new Racine Harbor Lighthouse, which went into operation on September 19, 1866.

By 1875 the peak of the great shipping era for Racine Harbor had passed, and a long slow decline in activity would begin. Racine Harbor did have some hazards for the mariners of the sweet waters to contend with. Several miles to the north, near Wind Point, there are three rock-like dolomite reefs, which come near to the surface. Today, two of these reefs are marked with buoys by the US Coast Guard. Another reef about ½ mile north of the Wind Point Lighthouse, reaching out about 800' from shore, still claims recreational vessels. However, years ago over 50 vessels stranded or wrecked on this reef.

To the east and slightly south of the harbor entrance is the most treacherous reef along this part of the western shore of Lake

Michigan, the famous Racine Reef. Between the early 1840s and 1906, over 46 vessels' hull bottoms found the rocks of this reef. Most were released with assistance, but many were total losses to their owners. From the 1850s to the present time, there has been a buoy marking the reef in some capacity. Today, there are still occasional calls for assistance from recreational boaters in distress that have stranded on the Racine Reef.

Racine's most famous wreck was on the evening of October 6, 1875. The steam driven propeller Merchant was on its return run from Chicago, Illinois to Buffalo, New York as it had done for 13 seasons. The first mate was at the helm when the Merchant was driven hard aground on the Racine Reef. This collision was due to the fact that a reef buoy was over 1000 ft. out of position. The Merchant was built in 1862 at Buffalo and was the first commercial vessel on the American side constructed with an iron hull and marked a turning point for shipbuilding on the Lakes. The wreck was visible for years from shore as the salvagers and divers feasted on the scrap iron for profit.

Due to the large number of shipwrecks at Racine, the US Lifesaving Service established a station here in 1876, The Racine lifesavers rescued many ships from peril and included a lifesaver and salvor named John Harms who would become one of Racine's best known hard hat divers. Harms later became a Racine police officer before his untimely death. The Racine USLSS station was transferred to the Coast Guard in 1915 and decommissioned in 1971.

During the 1880s, the decline in shipping continued. The decline was brought on by less lumber coming from the north by ship and less wheat being grown locally, as farmer switched from wheat to dairy, along with the impact of railroads. On May 2, 1882, a large fire along the waterfront burned the large grain warehouse, elevator, forty buildings, and over ten million feet of lumber. The fire ended wheat as an export from the Racine Harbor. On the morning of October 28, 1882, the most well known tugboat ever to operate in Racine, the Rudolph Wetzel, exploded her boiler killing all three men aboard. The accident took place to the north off Oak Creek. Captain Frank Lovell was admired by all that knew him and was greatly missed.

Three miles to the north, construction was finished on the Wind Point Lighthouse. This lighthouse went into service on November 15, 1880, and is still in service to this day. Also a second beam of a red light was cast towards the south end of Racine Reef to help warn vessel away. This red light never worked as intended due to being three miles away where fog, rain and other elements could obstruct the beam. This red beam was taken out of service January 27, 1907.

Racine's North Point Light c. 1907 - Author's Collection

The decline of the harbor continued through the 1890s, as fewer schooners operated from Racine and elsewhere. By the end of the 1890s, there was a increase in coal shipping and commercial fishing was still a viable industry that employed many. In 1899, a red Pintsch gas light tower structure was finished and put into service on the Racine Reef.

By the 1900s, even fewer schooners sailed out of Racine, but fishing vessels could still be seen doing their work. The coal boats went about their business bring in this important fuel. By the fall of 1906, the Racine Reef Lighthouse was finished and went into operation. It was built on the east end of the reef with a small crew of 4 men living out there for days at a time, tending the fog horn and light. After this new reef lighthouse went in service, the red Pintsch gas light was taken out of service on October 6, 1906.

Racine Reef Light c. 1900 – Author's Collection

In June of 1914, the last schooner owned and operated out of Racine, the J.B. Newland, was sold off to a Canadian group. This was the end of what was once a large and proud fleet of vessels that sailed out the Racine. Many old timers felt a loss, but they understood that times change. Schooners would still come to Racine until the late 1920s, but by the early 1930s the last of them would disappear from the Great Lakes forever. In 1916, Congress approved funding for the arrowhead piers, with construction being finished around 1923. Though the 1920s, coal boats, occasional oil tankers, barges, passenger boats and fishing vessels were still part of the harbor traffic.

By 1930, commercial shipping at Racine was finished. In 1933, the passenger service that had been a part of Racine's history since the beginning of the first settler's arrival came to an end. The early 1940s brought a revival in shipping due to World War II. Supplies were being sent out to aid the massive war effort. After the war ended, shipping declined sharply. By the 1950s, only the coal boats, barges, oil tankers, and fishing vessels were working in the harbor. This trend continued into the 1960s, when the growth of recreational boating started to fill the void left by the decline of commercial shipping. In 1954, the Racine Reef Lighthouse was taken out of service, and dismantled in 1961. A white skeleton tower was put in its place with a light and fog horn on the large concrete base of the old lighthouse.

By the 1970s, even the coal boats' cargo was no longer needed, and almost all commercial shipping ceased in Racine Harbor. Just a few ships arrived, along with barges bringing in salt for the streets and rocks for shore protection, along with the commercial fishing vessels, yachts, sport fishing boats, and recreational boats. However, the activity from these smaller boats was increasing. The Army Corps of Engineers ended Racine's classification as a commercial harbor in 1981. During the 1980s, pleasure boating and fishing continued to grow, as did the number of slips and yacht clubs. By 1987 a large new marina was opened. This brought in many out of town visitors. Also, some shipwrecks from long ago were discovered off the shores of Racine. It became a common site to see divers heading out of the harbor for a quick dive one of these old vessels.

The 1990s saw a continued growth in sport fishing, pleasure boating, SCUBA diving and yachting. By 2009 this trend had leveled off, but Racine's great harbor has been able to change with the times and continues serve many people. It will continue to be the centerpiece of Racine's waterfront for centuries to come.

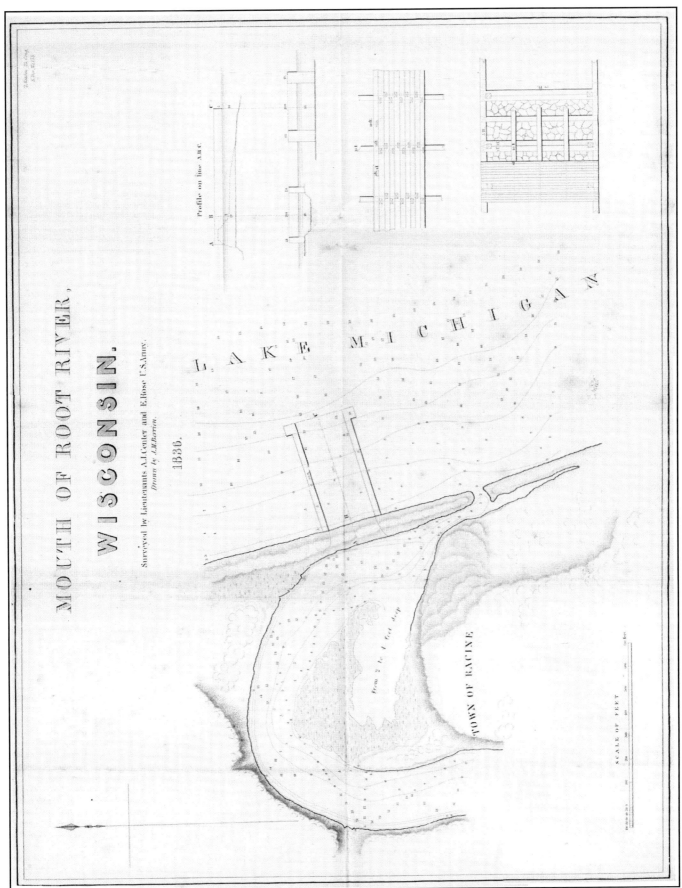

Racine's First Harbor Survey 1836 – Original in Author's Collection – Clearly shows why early vessels had difficulty entering the shallow, narrow river mouth – the piers shown were planned for the new harbor entrance, but would not be built for several years.

Schooner *McFarlane* (predates registry numbering) – Built about 1840 – size unknown – December 1, 1841 – A schooner by this name is reported in news accounts to have gone ashore near Racine and been lost. No record of this vessel exists in any vessel list or government document, but numerous news accounts reported the wreck in specific detail. The most likely candidate is the schooner *Harriet Farlin* (often seen as *H. Farlin*), 106 gt., built 1837 at Dexter, NY. (Milwaukee Sentinel – December 19, 1841) Type: Stranding, Depth: Buried, Remains: Possibly Present, Accuracy: 5 Miles.

Schooner *Wave* (predates registry numbering) – Built 1835 at Swan Creek, Michigan by Samuel Sutherland, 54.3 x 17.6 x 5.6 ft., 44.30 gt. BOM, Enrolled Detroit 10/31/1836, 7/26/1841, 2 masts, figurehead, no gallery. - The schooner *Wave* is commonly reported to have been lost at Racine when she capsized and went ashore in a gale on March 17, 1844. However, she was released and lost a few weeks later when she foundered in a gale ten miles SSW of the Kalamazoo River mouth at present-day Saugatuck, MI. Her masts were breaking the surface, but all her crew perished. Her remains have never been located. (Buffalo Commercial Advertiser – April 5, 1844) Type: Stranding, Depth: n/a, Remains: Definitely Recovered, Accuracy: 5 Miles.

Schooner *Savannah* (predates registry numbering) – Built 1845 at Milwaukee by Hubbell, 61.0 x 15.5 x 4.4 ft., 36.38 gt. BOM, enrolled Detroit 8/26/1845, one deck, 2 masts, plain stem. - On April 7th, 1845, the schooner *Savannah*, under Capt. McComber, stranded on the bar at the mouth of Racine Harbor during a snow storm. Her cargo of lumber was saved; but the Savannah was reported a total loss at $2500. She had been the first vessel ever to enter Racine Harbor. Despite initial reports, she was pulled free and repaired the next spring and went on to strand multiple times the next year, finally becoming a total loss in a standing on the Michigan shore in December 1846. (Racine Advocate – April 15, 1845). Type: Stranding, Depth: n/a: Remains: Recovered Accuracy: ¼ Mile.

Schooner *Black Hawk* (predates registry numbering) – Built 1832 at Fairport, OH by R.W. Skinner, 60.0 x 17.2 x 5.85 ft., 51.30 gt. BOM – October 15, 1847 - The schooner *Black Hawk* stranded at Racine on October 10, but was freed and departed for Manistee the same week under Captain Green. She was never heard from again and was declared a total loss in March 1848. (Racine Advocate – November 24, 1847) Type: Foundering, Depth: Very Deep, Remains: Definitely Present, Accuracy: 20 Miles.

Schooner *Bolivar* (predates registry numbering) – Built 1842 at Chicago, IL, 60.0 x 15.0 x 5.9 ft., 46.28 gt. BOM, 1 deck, 2 masts, plain stem – November 21, 1847 – Bound Milwaukee to Chicago, this small schooner was blown ashore in a gale three miles north of Racine. She broke up over the winter, a total loss for her owner, J.P. Allen of Chicago. (Milwaukee Sentinel – November 25, 1847) Type: Stranding, Depth: Buried: Remains: Possibly Present, Accuracy: 1 Mile.

Schooner *A.H. Newbold* (predates registry numbering) – Built 1848 at China, Michigan by J.S. Andrews, 93 x 21.9 x 8.4 ft., 152.60 gt. BOM, 2 masts, scroll head. – The *Newbold* went ashore on the north side of Wind Point on December 3, 1848 and was reported a total loss with her cargo. However, she was recovered the next spring and later lost at Buffalo, NY in November 1852. (Milwaukee Sentinel – December 1848) Type: Stranding, Depth: n/a, Remains: Definitely Recovered, Accuracy: 5 Miles.

Schooner *LaSalle* (predates registry numbering) – Built 1835 at Huron, OH by Burton Parson, 83.0 x 24.0 x 9.8 ft., 167.46 gt. BOM, scroll stem – September 23, 1849 – Bound Chicago to Buffalo, the *LaSalle* capsized and was last seen on her beam ends about 12 miles off Racine. 8 of her crew were lost and 1 was rescued. Sources suggest that her hull was towed in, but she never sailed again. (Milwaukee Sentinel – September 25, 1849) Type: Abandonment, Depth: Shallow, Remains: Possibly Present, Accuracy: 1 Mile.

Brig *Theodore W. Maurice* (predates registry numbering) – Built 1831 at Fairport, OH, 52.3 x 17.10 x 5.2 ft., 45.54 gt. BOM, plain stem – August 30, 1850 – The brig *T.W. Maurice* became waterlogged off Ahnapee (present-day Algoma, WI) while bound to Chicago with oak planks. She was driven south and fetched up off Wind Point, where she broke up completely. Her cargo was scattered down the beach all the way to Racine. (Milwaukee Sentinel – September 3, 1850) Type: Stranding, Depth: Shallow, Remains: Possibly Present, Accuracy: 1 Mile.

Schooner *Chas Howard* (predates registry numbering) – Built 1845 at Huron, Ohio, 99.9 x 21.1 x 8.0 ft., 103.94 gt. BOM, 2 masts, 1 deck, scroll head. - The *Chas Howard* went ashore and was declared a total loss at Racine on 9/1/1850, but was later released and repaired. She was lost by going ashore five miles north of Chicago in December of 1856. (Milwaukee Sentinel – September 3, 1850) Type: Stranding, Depth: n/a, Remains: Definitely Recovered, Accuracy: 5 Miles.

Schooner *Sylvanus Marvin* (predates registry numbering) – Built 1842 at Milwaukee, WI by Samuel Farmin, 65.0 x 18.9 x 6.1 ft., 64.63 gt. BOM, plain stem – May 22, 1851 – This schooner, also seen as *Sylvester Marvin* is reported to have foundered off Racine. She was lost with 8 crew and her captain W.P. Denton. She ran out of Milwaukee primarily in the lumber trade. Sources also place this loss off Grand Haven, MI, but it likely occurred at mid-lake. (Milwaukee Public Library – Runge File) Type: Foundering, Depth: Very Deep, Remains: Definitely Present, Accuracy: 20 Miles.

Schooner *Mary Ann Larned* (predates registry numbering) – Built 1846 at Newport, MI, 73.0 x 17.8 x 6.9 ft., 79.33 gt. BOM. – May 23, 1851 – This schooner was driven through Waterman's Bridge Pier at Racine and blown upon the beach about 800 ft south of the harbor entrance with a lumber cargo. She was reportedly pulled off the beach, but at $1300 her loss was likely total. (Milwaukee Sentinel – May 27, 1851) Type: Stranding, Depth: Shallow, Remains: Possibly Present, Accuracy: 1 Mile.

Schooner *Flying Cloud* (predates registry numbering) – Built 1852 at Racine, Wisconsin, 85.7 x 23.2 x 7.0 ft., 122.35 gt. BOM, 2 masts, last enrolled Milw. 7/29/1853. - The *Flying Cloud* capsized off Racine on September 20, 1853 and was believed to have foundered until the schooner *New Hampshire* found her capsized hull and towed her into Muskegon nearly three weeks later. Her crew had perished and the vessel never sailed again. She is easily confused with two other schooners of the same name active at the same time on the eastern Lakes. (Milwaukee Sentinel – September 22, 1853) Type: Stranding, Depth: n/a, Remains: Definitely Removed, Accuracy: 5 Miles.

Schooner *Homer Ramsdell* (predates registry numbering) – Built 1853 at Buffalo, New York, 119 x 26 x 9.9 ft., 275.91 gt. BOM, 2 masts, plain stem, square stern – The *Ramsdell* was noted to have broke loose from Dutton's pier and to have been driven against Waterman's Pier on May 10, 1855 at Racine. She was noted to have been "half full of water, will probably go to pieces." Despite being reported lost, she was recovered and quickly repaired. She was lost in October of 1856 while under tow from a stranding at South Manitou Island. She foundered off Two Rivers, WI in deep water with a steam pump on board and was a total loss. (Chicago Press – May 12, 1855) Type: Stranding, Depth: n/a, Remains: Definitely Removed, Accuracy: 5 Miles.

Schooner *Young America* (predates registry numbering) – Built 1854 at Oswego, NY by Rogers and Crockett, about 139 x 29 x 10 ft., 331.43 gt. BOM. – September 23, 1855 – The big, new schooner *Young America* was bound from Chicago to Oswego with corn when she was run down by the schooner *Black Hawk* several miles northeast of Racine. She went down in deep water, a total loss. A brig of the same name was built in 1853 at Buffalo and is often confused with this schooner. This wreck has never been found. (Milwaukee Sentinel – September 25, 1855) Type: Foundering, Depth: Deep: Remains: Definitely Present, Accuracy: 10 Miles.

Schooner *Dean Richmond* (predates registry numbering) – Built 1855 at Cleveland, OH, about 140 ft., 362.73 gt. BOM – October 21, 1855 – The big, new schooner *Dean Richmond* was lost only three weeks after her launch when she went on the Rocks five miles north of Racine with a cargo of coal and lumber, bound for Chicago. Her bow was high out of the water and her stern submerged, but she could not be pulled free and broke up over the winter. Another schooner of the same name was launched the following year. This site probably has extant remains but has yet to be located. (Milwaukee Sentinel – October 24, 1855) Type: Stranding, Depth: Shallow, Remains: Probably Present, Accuracy: 1 Mile.

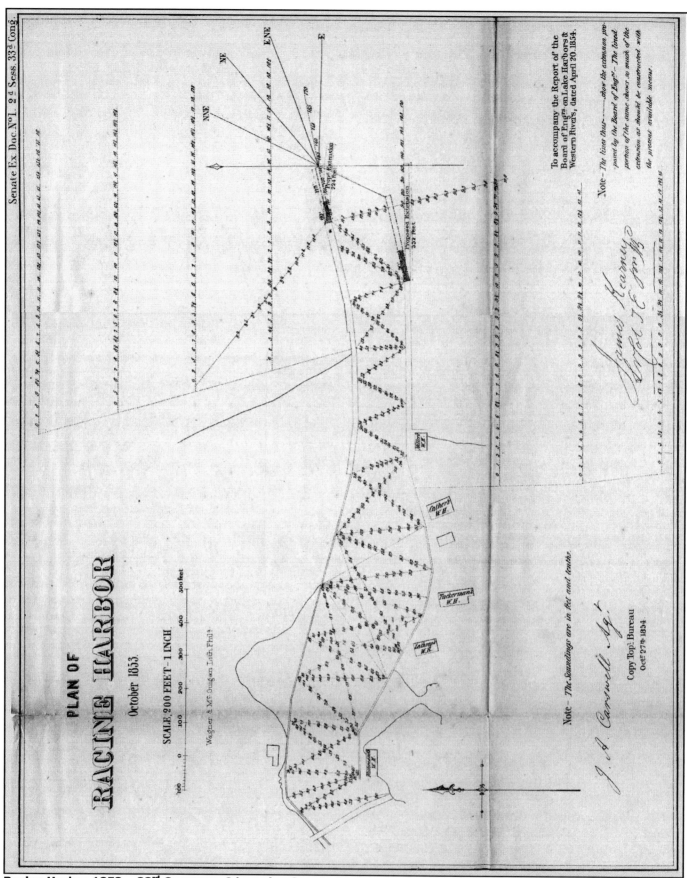

Racine Harbor 1853 – 33rd Congress, 2d session Senate Ex. Doc. No.1 – Original in Author's Collection

Schooner *W.B. Hibbard* (26234) – Built 1856 at Buffalo, New York by F.N. Jones, 119.3 x 26.1 x 10.2 ft., 214 gt. - The *W.B. Hibbard* was driven on the beach on December 5, 1856, five miles north of Racine with a cargo of iron ore. The papers declared her a total loss, but she was pulled free the next April and sailed until November 1867 when she stranded and was lost at Southampton, Ontario. (Board of Lake Underwriters Wreck List 1856) Type: Stranding, Depth: n/a, Remains: Definitely Removed, Accuracy: 1 Mile.

Schooner *Temperance* (predates registry numbering) – Built 1847 at St. Joseph, MI by J. Randall, 108.6 x 22.4 x 7 ft., 156.57 gt. BOM, plain stem. - The schooner *Temperance* was under tow by the tug *McQueen* with a lumber cargo on April 1, 1857 when she broke free in a gale and drove ashore a few miles north of Racine. She was declared a total loss at $3000. However, she appears in the Lake Underwriters registers until 1864 and there is a September 1867 account of the loss of a schooner *Temperance* on Lake Michigan. It is possible that this schooner was recovered from her Racine stranding. (Milwaukee Sentinel – April 4, 1857) Type: Stranding, Depth: Buried, Remains: Possibly Present, Accuracy: 1 Mile.

Schooner *Peter Doling* (predates registry numbering) – Built 1848 at Conneautville, PA by Girard, 78.6 x 14.6 x 5.8 ft., 60.57 gt. BOM – September 11, 1857 – This schooner went ashore on the point just south of the Racine Lighthouse with a cargo of lumber and fruit. She was pulled free but sank in the harbor where she was abandoned. (Milwaukee Sentinel – September 16, 1857) Type: Abandonment, Depth: Shallow, Remains: Possibly Present, Accuracy: 1 Mile.

Schooner *Henry Clay* (predates registry numbering) – Built 1842 at Presque Isle, MI, 73.25 x 15.5 x 5.75 ft., 59.40 gt. BOM – October 15, 1857 – The schooner *Henry Clay* of Milwaukee was driven ashore about seven miles north of Racine in an October storm. She reportedly broke up as a total loss, although insurance damages were placed at only $300. She disappears from news accounts and enrollments after this accident. (Milwaukee Sentinel – October 20, 1857) Type: Stranding, Depth: Surfline, Remains: Possibly Present, Accuracy: 1 Mile.

Scow Schooner *Rocky Mountain* (predates registry numbering) – Built 1852 at Black River, OH, 76.5 x 23.5 x 6.25 ft., 123.47 gt. BOM – October 21, 1857 – This scow schooner was driven ashore with a lumber cargo a few miles north of Racine in a Fall storm. She was a total loss at $3200. (Milwaukee Sentinel – October 23, 1857) Type: Stranding, Depth: Surfline, Remains: Possibly Present, Accuracy: 5 Miles.

Schooner *William Foster* (predates registry numbering) – Built 1842 at Cleveland, OH by William Foster, 47.1 x 14.5 x 5.4 ft., 30.07 gt. BOM, scroll stem - June 1858 – This little schooner was reported capsized with the loss of two lives ten miles off Racine and later towed in to the harbor. She disappears from enrollments and news accounts after this accident and was probably a total loss, but several sources place the mishap at Chicago and not at Racine. (Mansfield's History of the Great Lakes, Chicago Tribune – June 30, 1858) Type: Abandonment, Depth: Shallow, Remains: Probably Removed, Location ¼ Mile.

Bark *Colorado* (predates registry numbering) – Built 1857 at Cleveland, OH by Peck & Masters, 147.9 x 30.5 x 12.1 ft., 503.44 gt. BOM, three masts – December 30, 1863 – The big bark *Colorado* went on the reef off Wind Point on October 28th with a coal cargo. She was abandoned in place in November and was sold at auction before she broke up completely on December 30th. Another bark *Colorado* was built the next year. This wreck may have extant remains but has never been found. (Milwaukee Sentinel – January 4, 1864) Type: Stranding, Depth: Shallow, Remains: Definitely Present, Accuracy: 1 Mile.

Schooner *Mary S. Scott* (predates registry numbering) – Built 1856 at Cleveland, OH by George W. Jones, 135.8 x 25.11 x 11 ft., 358.58 gt. BOM, figurehead stem, figure on stern, hard been in ocean service to Germany – September 20, 1866 – The *M.S. Scott* was being towed out of the harbor with 7000 bushels of wheat for Buffalo by the tug *Daisy Lee* when the *Scott's* tiller chains broke and she became unmanageable. The tug cut her loose and she was driven aground just north of the Racine harbor entrance. Part of her wheat cargo was removed but efforts by the tugs *Muir* and *Leviathan* to remove her were unsuccessful and the ship was abandoned to the underwriters where she lay. Although initially believed salvageable, Fall storms broke her spine and she ended her days on the beach. (Racine Advocate – September 26, 1866) Type: Stranding, Depth: Shallow, Remains: Possibly Present, Accuracy: 5 Miles.

Bark *Great West* (10149) – Built 1854 at Buffalo, NY by S.R & G.S. Weeks, 175 x 34 x 15 ft., 554.87 gt., three masts – October 10, 1866 – The big bark *Great West* was bound for Chicago with 800 tons of coal when she struck Racine Reef, holing herself badly. She was run ashore south of Racine to prevent her from foundering. She was stripped and abandoned to the elements where she lay. She probably has extant remains but she has yet to be located. (Milwaukee Sentinel – October 12, 1866) Type: Stranding, Depth: Shallow, Remains: Definitely Present, Accuracy: 1 Mile.

Propeller *F.W. Backus* (predates registry numbering) – Built 1846 at Malden Centre, Ontario by Bates as the *Earl Cathcart*, 133 x 25 x 9.4 ft., 289.78 gt. BOM – November 25, 1866 – The steamer *F.W. Backus* was bound from Kenosha to Racine with passengers and livestock when she was found to be on fire. She was run into the shallows about ¾ mile south of Racine where she burned to the water's edge. It is possible that a significant portion of the wreck remains and could be located. (Milwaukee Sentinel – November 26, 1866) Type: Stranding, Depth: Surfline, Remains: Probably Present, Accuracy: 1 Mile.

Schooner *H.L. Whitman* (11187) – Built 1856 at Milan, OH by Salmon Ruggles, 120.9 x 24.9 x 10.3 ft., 208.43 gt. – October 11, 1869 – The schooner *H.L. Whitman* was bound for Chicago with a lumber cargo when she struck a rock off Racine's North Point and immediately sank. She was abandoned where she lay and is believed to have been located. Based on measurements, she is most likely the keel and ribs under Wind Point at N42.46.50 / W87.45.80, (Milwaukee Sentinel – October 13, 1869) Type: Stranding, Depth: Shallow, Remains: Definitely Present, Accuracy: 1 Mile.

Scow Schooner *Flora Temple* (9302) – Built 1866 at St. Joseph, MI, about 30 ft., 6.5 gt. – July 26, 1870 – The little scow schooner *Flora Temple* was driven ashore nine miles north of Racine by a sudden squall. She is one of the smallest registered commercial vessels known to have wrecked in Wisconsin waters. (Milwaukee Sentinel – July 29, 1870) Type: Stranding, Depth: Surfline, Remains: Possibly Present, Accuracy: 1 Mile.

Racine Harbor 1872 – Author's Collection

Schooner *Anna Henry* (1801) – Built 1867 at Erie, PA, 214 gt. – October 4, 1870 – The *Anna Henry* departed Chicago for Hamilton, Ontario with a load of pig iron, but was found to be leaking off Little Sable Point. She was run to Racine, repaired and set out again, but foundered about 20 miles off Racine. 8 of her crew were rescued by the schooner *George Steele*. She probably lies in very deep water. (Toronto Globe – October 13, 1870) Type: Foundering, Depth: Very Deep, Remains: Definitely Present, Accuracy: 10 Miles.

Racine Harbor in 1874 - Wisconsin Historical Society

Sloop *North Star* (18165) – Built 1867 at Holland, MI, c. 30 ft., 15.55 gt. – The little sloop *North Star* of Holland, MI was driven high on the beach at Racine in September of 1871 and was reported a total loss. However, she was pulled free in the spring by the tug *American Eagle* and is listed on registers until 1879. (Herman Runge Wreck List) Type: Stranding, Depth: n/a, Remains: Definitely Removed, Accuracy: 5 Miles.

A Trip Through the Lakes 1865 Ed. – John Disturnell
Author's Collection

The *Lac La Belle* at Port Huron c. 1867 – C. Patrick Labadie Collection, TBNMS

Propeller *Lac La Belle* (15803) – Built 1864 at Cleveland, OH by Ira Lafrinier, 218 x 36 x 12 ft., 1187.19 gt. – October 13, 1872 – The steamer *Lac La Belle* sprang a leak and foundered in heavy en route from Milwaukee to Grand Haven with a grain cargo. She had left Milwaukee at 9 PM and began leaking about midnight when 25 miles off Racine. About that time, she shipped a heavy sea, which put out her boiler fires and she was driven before the gale which was out of the north. About 5 AM, the ship was abandoned, with lifeboats making shore about 6 miles south of Racine 12 hours later. 8 crew died when one of the lifeboats capsized. The *Lac La Belle* had been a passenger steamer but was rebuilt as a bulk carrier. Wreckhunter Bill Prince had reported scanning a deep target off Racine, but claims that it might be this vessel are probably premature. (Milwaukee Sentinel – October 14, 1872) Type: Foundering, Depth: Very Deep, Remains: Definitely Present, Accuracy: 10 Miles.

Schooner *Enterprise* (7296) – Built 1854 at Sheboygan, Wisconsin by Michael Lynch, 94.0 x 20.0 x 8.0 ft., 101.28 gt., 142.3 BOM, last enrolled Chicago, 2/20/1873, scroll head, 2 masts, square stern - On June 8, 1874, the schooner *Enterprise* was bound for Racine with a cargo of wood when she became waterlogged and unmanageable. The tug *Wetzel* went to her aid, but she capsized ¼ mile from the piers while under tow. She was declared a total loss. However, she was towed into the harbor and repaired. In 1876, she was one of four Racine vessels that made trans-Atlantic crossings to Europe, the others being the brig Mechanic, schooner Challenge and schooner City of Manitowoc. The *Enterprise* never returned to the Lakes, wrecking off the coast of Scotland. She is often confused with a schooner of the same name active on the eastern Lakes as the same time. (Milwaukee Sentinel – June 10, 1874, Bob Jaeck Collection) Type: Stranding, Depth: n/a, Remains: Definitely Removed, Accuracy: ¼ Mile.

THE PROVIDENCE CAPSTAN WINDLASS,

—WITH—

T. J. SOUTHARD'S

MESSENGER CHAIN ATTACHMENT.

Patented Feb. 17, 1874, March 21, April 18, 1876, March 27, Nov. 13 and 27, 1877, June 25, Dec. 3 and 17, 1878, June 1, 1880, Feb. 8 and 15, 1881.

The above arrangement is the simplest and best yet devised for driving a Capstan Windlass by endless chain from a donkey engine.

AMERICAN SHIP WINDLASS CO.

Are the exclusive builders under the patents.

Barnet's Coast Pilot 1881 – Author's Collection

The iron propeller *Merchant* in ice off Buffalo 1868 - from an original Stereoview – Author's Collection

Racine Harbor in the 1870s – from History of Racine & Kenosha Counties 1879

Propeller *Merchant* (16332) – Built 1862 at Buffalo, NY by David Bell, 200.0 x 29.0 x 14.0 ft., 1009 gt., rebuilt & lengthened in 1873 to 220.6' x 29.4' x 12.9', 1068 gross tons, passenger cabins removed – The *Merchant* was the first iron propeller on the Lakes and is one of the most historic vessels lost in Wisconsin waters. She blundered onto Racine Reef with a large cargo of bulk corn, barreled flour and flax on October 6, 1875. She stranded in about 13 ft of water where she holed her hull and settled onto the reef. Although initially thought salvageable, she was given up as a loss by the 13th and stripped. By November 1st, the vessel had started breaking up. She had been insured for $100,000 and was the worst loss of the season. In the summer of 1877, Knapp and Gillen removed her engines and significant scrap, and by 1880 she was no longer visible above the waterline. In the ensuing years, she was dynamited and salvaged by various groups. She was all but forgotten until some of her remains were found on the reef during the 1990s by Bob Jaeck. Only minor fragments of the vessel remain and are widely scattered. In 2007 the author located and purchased two previously unknown original photos of her and made them available. (Buffalo Commercial Advertiser – October 8, 1875) Type: Stranding, Depth: Shallow, Remains: Identified, Accuracy: Withheld by request.

Bark *Thomas Clark Street* (C74372) – Built 1869 at St. Catherines, Ontario by Louis Schickluna, 138.4 x 25.6 x 11.5 ft., 343 gt., 3 masts, plain stem - The big Canadian bark *T.C. Street* was bound for Chicago with 21,000 bushels of barley on November 29, 1875 when she became iced up and was in danger of capsizing. She became unmanageable and was driven on Wind Point where she sustained significant hull damage and was declared a total loss. However, she was recovered the next season and sailed until 1902 when she was wrecked at Point Peter on Lake Ontario. (Racine County Argus – December 2, 1875) Type: Stranding, Depth: n/a, Remains: Definitely Removed, Accuracy: 5 Miles.

Schooner *Whirlwind* (26226) – Built 1848 at Racine, WI by Justice Bailey, 99.9 x 21.1 x 8.0 ft., 111.45 gt., plain stem - September 9, 1876 – The *Whirlwind* was bound for Chicago with 100,000 ft of lumber when she was driven into the shallows near Racine and stranded. Captain Henry Wilson ordered the yawl launched and the men made it to shore. The vessel reportedly wrecked off a large ravine just south of Senator Doolittle's residence. Research indicates that this house was near present day Sixth St and Park Drive. It may be possible to locate the vessel's remains. (Milwaukee Sentinel – September 11, 1876) Type: Stranding, Depth: Shallow, Remains: Possibly Present, Accuracy: ¼ Mile.

Racine Dredge – Polk's marine Directory 1888 – Author's Collection

Schooner *Dolphin* (6132) – Built 1854 at Port Dover, Ontario by A.M. Shaw, 91.2 x 22.9 x 7.8 ft., 154.27 gt., scow bottom - The schooner *Dolphin* lost at Racine was one of three vessels active in 1876 by that name. She was bound Chicago to White Lake with lumber when she was driven ashore at the foot of 11th Street and thrown upon the breakwall during a gale on September 7, 1876. Her last enrollment was surrendered at Chicago on 9/30/1876 as a total loss. She should not be confused with the vessel of the same name built at Racine. (Racine Daily Journal – September 13, 1876) Type: Stranding, Depth: Buried, Remains: Possibly Present, Accuracy: ¼ Mile.

Scow Schooner *Home* (42215) – Built 1867 at Milwaukee by Ellsworth & Davidson, 84.9 x 23.2 x 6.3 ft., 91.77 gt. - The scow schooner *Home* was bound for Chicago with lumber on November 13, 1876 when her steering gear broke. She was driven ashore near the Racine Lighthouse pier. Her cargo was salvaged but she proved a total loss. (Evening Wisconsin – November 15, 1876) Type: Stranding, Depth: Shallow, Remains: Probably Removed, Accuracy: 1 Mile.

Customs House Wreck Report for Scow Schooner *Home* – National Archives

Original 1877 painting of the *Grace Channon* – Courtesy of Elizabeth Cave, granddaughter of Grace Channon

Schooner *Grace Channon* (85309) – Built 1873 at East Saginaw, Michigan by W.S. Ellinwood, 141 x 26 x 12 ft., 265.99 gt. – The schooner *Grace Channon* was bound from Buffalo to Chicago with 600 tons of coal on August 2, 1877 when she was struck by the propeller favorite north of Racine. She sank immediately, taking the owner's 7 year old son with her. Her remains were located in 1985 by Kent Bellrichard and she is now a popular divesite in 205 ft of water. (Milwaukee Sentinel – August 4, 1877) Type: Foundering, Depth: 185 ft., Remains: Identified, Accuracy: N42°55.765' / W87°36.120'.

Schooner *Alice* (105020) – Built 1871 at Holland, MI, 45.0 x 13.7 x 3.9 ft., 14 gt. – The little lumber hooker *Alice* was lost with a load of Christmas trees for Chicago when she blundered onto Wind Point on December 10, 1877. She was a total loss. There is some question as to the identity of this vessel. There were two other small hookers named *Alice* active on Lake Michigan at the time. (Racine Journal – December 12, 1877) Type: Stranding, Depth: Shallow, Remains: Possibly Present, Accuracy: 1 Mile.

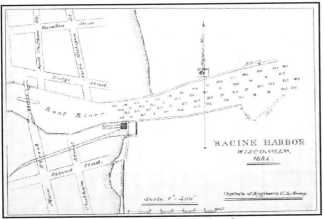
Racine Harbor 1884 – Author's Collection

Scow Schooner *Eagle* (135158) – Built 1870 at Green Bay WI by Chas LeClair, 71.6 x 19.4 x 4.2 ft., 40 gt. – The scow schooner *Eagle* was trying to enter the harbor with 20 cords of wood on March 28, 1878 when she missed the pier and was thrown against the pier at the end of Second St. Her crew escaped but she was smashed to pieces. (Racine Journal – April 3, 1878) Type: Stranding, Depth: Shallow, Remains: Possibly Present, Accuracy: ¼ Mile.

Yacht *Undine* (unregistered) – A large locally built steam yacht – April 16, 1881 – A spring flood of the Root River swept the schooner *Belle* and scow *Frost* down the river and into the Yacht *Undine*, completely destroying her. (Weather Bureau Chief Signal Officer Wreck List - 1882) Type: Foundering, Depth: Shallow, Remains: Probably Removed, Accuracy: ¼ Mile.

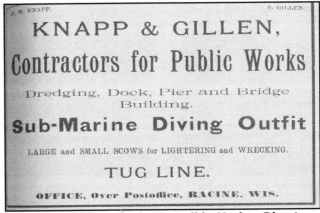
Knapp & Gillen – Racine – Polk's Marine Directory 1884 – Author's Collection

Schooner *Thomas C. Wilson* (24579) – Built 1868 at Black River, Ohio by Thomas C. Wilson, 50.0 x 13.0 x 6.0 ft., 24.44 gt., 2 masts, rebuilt 1880 to 58.5 x 15.7 x 5.0 30.87 gt. – The *T.C. Wilson* was off Racine on July 29, 1882 when she was run down by the steam barge Gordon Campbell about 7 miles off Racine, sending her to the bottom. Although reported as a total loss and clearly in deep water, the Wilson was raised and refloated. It would be interesting to find an account of her salvage. She survived until going ashore at Egg Harbor, WI in November of 1902. (Chicago Tribune – August 1, 1882) Type: Foundering, Depth: n/a, Remains: Definitely Recovered, Accuracy: 5 Miles.

Schooner *Speed* (22357) – Built 1848 at Madison Dock, OH by Lockwood, 97.3 x 20.8 x 7.85 gt., 104.44 gt. – The venerable old schooner *Speed* stranded on Racine's north beach on April 18, 1883 while bound from Pentwater, MI to Racine with a cargo of shingles. She was being towed in by the tug Sill, when the line parted and she was driven aground on her side. Her crew were rescued by the USLSS via breeches buoy. Efforts to free her failed and she had completely broken up within a week. (Racine Daily Journal – April 21, 1883) Type: Stranding, Depth: Buried, Remains: Possibly Present, Accuracy: 1 Mile.

Schooner *Capella* (4578) – Built 1850 at Algonac, Michigan by Halver Nelson, 51.3 x 15.5 x 5.6 ft., 24.65 gt. - This schooner stranded four miles north of Racine Harbor on May 9, 1883 with a cargo of wood slabs. She was pulled off after several days, but rolled on her beam ends twice while being towed. Her three crew were rescued, but she was declared a total loss. She was towed up the river above the Mead St. Bridge where she was abandoned after attempts to haul her out for rebuild failed. By the end of the summer, however, salvors had managed to raise and repair her. She was put back in service and lost only a few months later on December 17, 1883 when she went ashore at Waukegan, IL. (Racine Daily Journal – June 13, 1883) Type: Stranding, Depth: n/a, Remains: Definitely Recovered, Accuracy: 1 Mile.

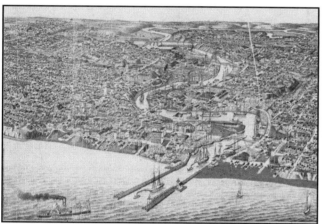
Racine Harbor 1883 – Wisconsin Historical Society

Schooner *Elizabeth Jones* (8193) – Built 1867 at Buffalo, NY by Mason & Bidwell – 184 x 23 x 13 ft. – 636.47 gt. - November 11, 1883 – The big schooner *Elizabeth Jones* stranded on the south side of Racine Reef while bound from Chicago to Buffalo with corn. Her bottom was badly damaged and she could not be refloated. Her cargo was partially salvaged and she was allowed to break up over the winter. Her hull-bed has reportedly been located just south of the old Racine Reef Light by divers but the identification has not been confirmed. (Milwaukee Sentinel – November 12, 1883) Type: Stranding, Depth: Shallow, Remains: Probably Present, Accuracy: 1 Mile.

The *Commerce* at Duluth c. 1870 while still brig rigged – Historical Collections of the Great Lakes

Schooner *Commerce* (4363) – Built 1857 at Sandusky, Ohio by David Dibble, 141.5 x 31.8 x 10.8 ft., 327.43 gt., originally built as a brig – The big schooner *Commerce* was bound from Chicago to Sarnia, Ont. with 39,000 bushels of oats on 11/6/1887 when she stove in her hull on Racine Reef. She began sinking rapidly but was quickly towed in by the tug Sill and sunk aside the Racine piers. She was initially reported a total loss, and much of her cargo was damaged, but she was refloated and repaired. She was lost in 1909 off Sheboygan, WI. (Racine Daily Journal – November 7, 1887) Type: Stranding, Depth: n/a, Remains: Definitely Recovered, Accuracy: 1 Mile.

Racine Pier and Pierhead Lighthouses c. 1895
Author's Collection

Scow Schooner *Laura Johnson* (140527) – Built 1882 at South Haven, MI by L.D. LaFountaine, 50 ft., 34.23 gt. – July 17, 1890 – The little gravel scow *Laura Johnson* was loading gravel off Racine's North Point when a storm blew up and drove her ashore. She was a total loss of $700. (Racine Daily Journal – July 18, 1890) Type: Stranding, Depth: Surfline, Remains: Possibly Present, Accuracy: 1 Mile.

Schooner *Persia* (19672) – Built 1855 at Chicago, IL by D. Barrett – 95.5 x 21.1 x 6.8 ft. – 96.69 gt. – June 2, 1892 – The old schooner *Persia* stranded 3 miles north of Wind point while bound from Menominee, MI to Racine with a lumber cargo. The crew reached shore in their yawl, but the ship broke up rapidly, scattering lumber down the beach where area farmers scavenged it. Her remains were located just off the beach by Bob Jaeck in the 1990s. (Racine Evening Times – June 2, 1892) Type: Stranding, Depth: 5-10 ft., Remains: Tentatively Identified, Accuracy: N42.49.048 / W87.48.242.

Schooner *Evra Fuller* (15956) – Built 1873 at Fort Howard, WI by Soren Anderson as the *Lena Johnson* - 132.6 x 26.3 x 9.9 ft. – 228.87 gt. – 3 masts – renamed 1882 – October 8, 1893 – The schooner *Evra Fuller* was bound from Menominee, MI to Chicago with lumber when she went on Racine Reef while trying to enter the harbor in a dense fog. She broke in two just forward of her deck cabin and was a total loss. Her remains have been located 450 east of the Racine Harbor entrance and are broken up. (Racine Daily Journal – October 18, 1893) Type: Stranding, Depth: 30 ft., Remains: Tentatively Identified, Accuracy: N42.44.15 / W87.46.05.

Propeller *Thomas H. Smith* (145284) – Built 1881 at Manitowoc, WI by Rand & Burger, 130.5 x 27.6 x 11.1 ft., 281.11 gt. – The steamer *Thomas H. Smith* was bound from Chicago to Menominee, MI in heavy fog for a lumber cargo on November 10, 1893 when she was nearly cut in two by the steamer Arthur Orr. She sank immediately, her crew jumping onto the Orr. As the Smith settled, water hit her boiler and it exploded, further destroying the ship. Reports place the disaster between 4 and 5 miles off Wind Point, but despite intensive searches, the Smith's remains have never been found. She is thought to lie in deeper water than was reported at the time. (Racine Daily Journal – November 15, 1893) Type: Foundering, Depth: Very Deep, Remains: Definitely Present, Accuracy: 5 Miles.

Propeller *Thomas H. Smith* Door County Maritime Museum

Customs House Wreck Report for the Steamer *Thomas H. Smith* – National Archives

Customs House Wreck Report for the schooner *Dreadnaught* – National Archives

Scow Schooner *Dreadnaught* (35270) – Built 1867 at Detroit, Michigan by Charles E. Luff, 66.4 x 18.8 x 6.6 ft., 59.41 gt., originally 41.7 x 17.5 x 4.2 ft, 34 gt., enlarged 1881 & 1889, gunwale built, cross planked scow, 2 masts. - A confused report exists of the big canal schooner *Dreadnaught* (6130) having wrecked off Racine in December 1893. *Dreadnaught* 6130 was actually abandoned at Cleveland in 1879. The smaller scow schooner *Dreadnaught* (35270) was bound from Washington Island to Milwaukee with 45 cords of wood on November 28, 1893 when she became heavily ice up off Milwaukee. Her two man crew could not manage her and she drifted out into the Lake. The next day, the vessel was sighted by the steamer Syracuse about 30 miles off Racine with her two crew literally frozen to the decks. The men were chopped free from the ice and rescued, but the Dreadnaught came ashore at Saugatuck, MI where she completely broke up. Her papers were surrendered at Milwaukee as a total loss. The *Dreadnaught* is also incorrectly reported to have come ashore at Sturgeon Bay and at Seul Choix Point after this accident. (Milwaukee Customs House Wreck Report) Type: Iced up, Depth: n/a, Remains: Definitely Removed Accuracy: 5 Miles.

Granddaughter of Captain Hartley Hatch poses with *Kate Kelly* artifacts at Lockwood Scuba Diving Museum, Loves Park, IL – Courtesy of Dan Johnson

Schooner *Kate Kelly* (14031) – Built 1867 at Tonawanda, NY by J. Martel, 126.3 x 25.8 x 10.4 ft., 280.93 gt., 3 masts – The schooner *Kate Kelly* struck Racine Reef on May 13, 1895 while bound from Sheboygan to Chicago with a load of Hemlock railroad ties. She foundered shortly after striking the reef in 50 ft of water, taking her crew with her. The wreck was located by Dan Johnson in 1983 is a popular dive site. She has been surveyed by the State Historical Society of Wisconsin and is listed on the National Register of Historic Places (Racine Daily Journal – May 15, 1895) Type: Foundering, Depth: Shallow, Remains: Identified, Accuracy: N42° 46.684', W87° 43.509', 55 ft.

Schooner *Mount Vernon* sunk in the Root River at Racine, sch. *Kewaunee* is afloat next to her – Historical Collections of the Great Lakes

Schooner *Mount Vernon* (17745) – Built 1855 at South Black River, Michigan by Henry Smith, 72.8 x 16.9 x 4.9 ft., 53.35 gt. BOM, 2 masts, reblt. 1863 to 77.9 x 17.2 x 5.5 ft., 59.84 gt. BOM,, square stern, plain stem. - The schooner *Mount Vernon* sank in the river at Mitchell & Lewis Dock in July of 1893 due to poor condition. Later that year, she was raised & abandoned along river bank near W. 6th Street Bridge and her papers were surrendered at Milwaukee on 8/11/1894 as "abandoned." Finally, on July 4, 1895, she was towed into Lake Michigan & blown up as a Fourth of July spectacle. The exact location was not recorded. (Milwaukee Public Library Marine Collection) Type: Abandonment, Depth: Shallow, Remains: Probably Present, Accuracy: 5 Miles.

Racine Harbor Scene 1914 – Author's Collection

Schooner *George Barber* (10191) – Built 1857 at Milwaukee by George Barber, 92.5 x 24.1 x 7.95 ft., 98.71 gt., 2 masts – March 1, 1895 – The schooner *George Barber* sank in the river at Racine and was pumped out, towed out into the Lake and pushed on the beach at the site of the former Racine College for use as a breakwall. (Door County Advocate – March 2, 1895) Type: Abandonment, Depth: Surfline, Remains: Possibly Present, Accuracy: ¼ Mile.

The end of the schooner *Sunrise* – illustration from the Chicago Chronicle – 5/23/1896

Schooner *Sunrise* (22349) – Built 1862 at Cleveland, OH by Peck & Masters as a bark - 159.0 x 30.5 x 12.41 ft. - 439.33 gt. - 3 masts – May 21, 1896 – The big schooner *Sunrise* was running in ballast in heavy fog bound from Chicago for the Straits when she fouled a towline between the steamer *William H. Gratwick* and her consort, whaleback barge 133. The barge struck the *Sunrise* taking off 15 ft of her bow and sending her directly to the bottom about midlake off Racine. Her 8 crew escaped. (Chicago Tribune – May 23, 1896) Type: Foundering, Depth: Very Deep, Remains: Definitely Present, Accuracy: 10 Miles.

Racine Breakwater Light c. 1910 – US Coast Guard

Barge *A* (30189) – Built 1895 at Peshtigo, WI as an unrigged barge - 135.2 x 35.0 x 9.5 ft. – 410 gt. – May 15, 1900 – The barge *A* sank in the river at Racine with 150 cords of stone on board, just east of the Main Street Bridge. The tug *Sydney Smith* tore out her side and bow trying to move her as she completely blocked the river. Her cargo was removed by divers and her hull was towed out and beached outside the harbor. (Racine Daily Journal – May 18, 1900) Type: Abandoned, Depth: Shallow, Remains: Probably Present, Accuracy: 1 Mile.

Schooner *Caledonia* (4384) – Built 1861 at Saugeen, Ontario, Canada by Alfred Hackett, 66.0 x 18.2 x 7.9 ft., 54.17 gt., Canadian registry C71186, sold US in 1867, lengthened 1886 to 70.4 x 18.3 x 6.7 ft. – The old schooner *Caledonia* was owned out of Racine for over 25 years, beginning in 1874. After a long career, she was abandoned in the Root River in September of 1901. However, her hulk was sold to Hans Peterson of Kenosha who raised and refitted her. The *Caledonia* was lost only a few months later when she departed Boyne City, MI for Racine with a cargo of potatoes and Christmas trees on November 27, 1901. She began to founder a few hours out and the men took to the yawl. They were eventually rescued but the *Caledonia* came ashore at Glen Haven, MI near Sleeping Bear Point and broke up, a total loss. Her remains are not in the Root River as sometimes stated. (Herman Runge Wreck List)

Schooner *H. Rand* (11185) – Built 1856 at Manitowoc, Wisconsin by Rand & Brothers, 86.8 x 23.5 x 7.6 ft., 134.23 gt. - This schooner capsized off Manitowoc while bound Coyne, MI to Milwaukee with lumber on May 24, 1901. The captain, his daughter and two crew perished, and the ship floated as a derelict before fetching up on Racine Reef. She was then towed to the beach at the foot of Texas Ave in Milwaukee where she was dynamited. In June of 1959, dredging in the area uncovered some of her remains. (Milwaukee Sentinel, 6/10/1959, Door County Advocate, 6/1/1901) (See account in Milwaukee Section)

The *Caledonia* in winter layup at Racine c. 1890 – C. Patrick Labadie Collection – TBNMS

Whaleback steamer *Christopher Columbus* entering Racine Harbor c. 1896 – Author's Collection

Schooner *John Eggers* (76714) – Built 1887 at Milwaukee by John Eggers - 58.7 x 14.0 x 3.4 ft. – 25 gt. – 2 masts – May 26, 1906 – The little gravel scow *John Eggers* was collecting gravel off Wind Point when she was driven ashore and was a total loss. (US Merchant Vessel List – 1906) Type: Stranding, Depth: Surfline, Remains: Probably Removed, Accuracy: 1 Mile.

Racine US Life Saving Station 1900 - Author's Collection

Gas Yacht *Scorpion* (116447) – Built 1891 at Chicago - 35.3 x 12.0 x 4.7 ft. – 10 gt. – built as a sail yacht – September 11, 1912 – The yacht *Scorpion* was sunk and abandoned at Racine. The accident location is still unknown but may have been in the river. (Herman Runge Wrecklist, Beeson's Marine Directory 1913) Type: Abandonment, Depth: Shallow, Remains: Probably Removed, Accuracy: 1 Mile.

William Rudolph laid up at Racine - Bob Jaeck Collection

Steamer *William Rudolph* (80762) – Built 1880 at Mt. Clemens, MI by R.J. Kandt - 145 x 23.5 x 9.0 ft. – 267.89 gt. – October 23, 1913 – The wooden steambarge *William Rudolph* had outlived her usefulness and was abandoned in the surf near Racine as shore protection from erosion. Her anchor and one of her lifeboat are now displayed on shore at a private residence. (Historical Collections of the Great Lakes Vessel File) Type: Abandonment, Depth: Surfline, Remains: Probably Present, Accuracy: 1 Mile.

J.V. Taylor under sail c. 1900 – Historical Collections of the Great Lakes

Schooner *J.V. Taylor* abandoned at Racine c. 1920 Bob Jaeck Collection

Schooner *J.V. Taylor* (13874) – Built 1867 at Winneconne, WI by Gilson, 125.0 x 26.2 x 8.9, 199.94 gt. - The *J.V. Taylor* was abandoned in 1915 above the Mead Street Bridge after a long career in the Lake Michigan lumber trade, running mostly out of Chicago. Her remains were visible in the river until the 1950s and were relocated in the 1990s by Bob Jaeck and Brad Friend. (Milwaukee Public Library Marine Collection, Bob Jaeck) Type: Abandonment, Depth: 8 ft., Remains: Located, Accuracy: See map next page.

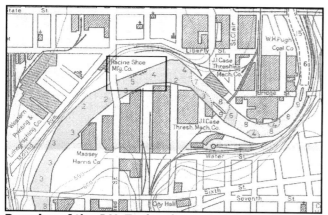
Remains of the *J.V. Taylor* shown just below the Mead St. Bridge where they can still be found – Lake Survey Chart 1935 – Bob Jaeck

The remains of the *E.M. Peck* explosion, June 1913 – Author's Collection

Steamer *E.M. Peck* (135983) – Built 1888 at Detroit, MI by the Detroit Dry Dock Co., 252.6 x 40.2 x 18.6 ft., 1809 gt. – The steamer *E.M. Peck* was moored at Racine on June 11, 1913 when her boiler exploded in one of the worst Great Lakes boiler explosion disasters of the 20th century. Seven men were killed when the boiler exploded, showering the harbor with debris and completely destroying the ship's upper works. The Peck was rebuilt in 1914 as the Canadian steamer Malton. She sailed until 1935 when she was dismantled on Lake Ontario. (Racine Advocate – June 1913) Type: Explosion, Depth: n/a, Remains: Recovered, Accuracy: 1 Mile.

Racine Pierhead Light c. 1900 – Author's Collection

Steam Fish Tug *Ole* (207918) – Built 1900 at Milwaukee as the fishing sloop Paul Jones, 27.4 x 8.8 x 2.8 ft., 8 gt. Rebuilt as small steamer and renamed *Ole* in 1910 for the City of Chicago, IL. Sold to Fred Bishop of Cairo, IL, who lost her south of Racine in 1914. The wreck was located by the USCG Survey prior to 1990 and listed in the AWOIS database. She is shown on NOAA charts at N42.40.05/W87.47.68 and lies in 24 ft of water. She was verified present in 1994 but is reportedly difficult to locate. The identification is per the NOAA AWOIS database, but should be considered tentative. (AWOIS Database) Depth: Shallow: Remains: Tentatively Identified, Accuracy: N42.40.05/W87.47.68, 24ft.

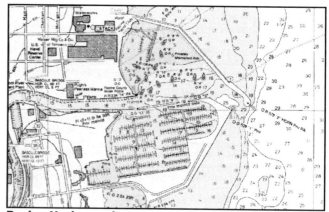
Racine Harbor as it now appears - NOAA Chart

Unidentified Racine Wreck Sites

South Racine Schooner
A charted wreck obstruction between Racine and Kenosha has appeared on NOAA charts for about 30 years. The AWOIS database attributes this site to the schooner Arab, lost in the November 1883 storm. This identification is almost certainly an error. The site has not been relocated in recent years. Accuracy: N42.38.70 / W87.47.49, 35 ft. (AWOIS Database)

Wind Point Schooner
The hull bed of a large schooner lies in the shallows just below Wind Point and can be seen from the air. There are several possibilities for this vessel's identity, but the most likely is the schooner *H.L. Whitman*, lost 1869. The hull bed is reportedly well over 100 ft in length. Accuracy: N42.46.50 / W87.45.80, 12 ft. (Jerry Guyer, Bob Jaeck)

Racine Reef Schooner
Divers have reported a substantial hull bed resting in 30 ft of water off the south side of Racine Reef, just south of the old Racine Reef Light structure. This wreck site is reportedly difficult to find and is mostly likely the remains of the big schooner *Elizabeth Jones*, lost in 1883. (Jerry Guyer, Bob Jaeck)

Racine Reef Iron Barge
Historian Bob Jaeck located a large flat bottom barge laden with railroad iron not far from the reported site of the Racine Reef Schooner (above). The barge is approximately 80 x 20 ft and appears to have been used in salvage work on the steamer Merchant. (Bob Jaeck)

Ice built up to a height of 30 ft on Racine Reef Light, March 1912 – Author's Collection

Racine pier, light and lifesaving station c. 1905 – Author's Collection

Racine USLSS station and keepers dwelling today – Author's Collection

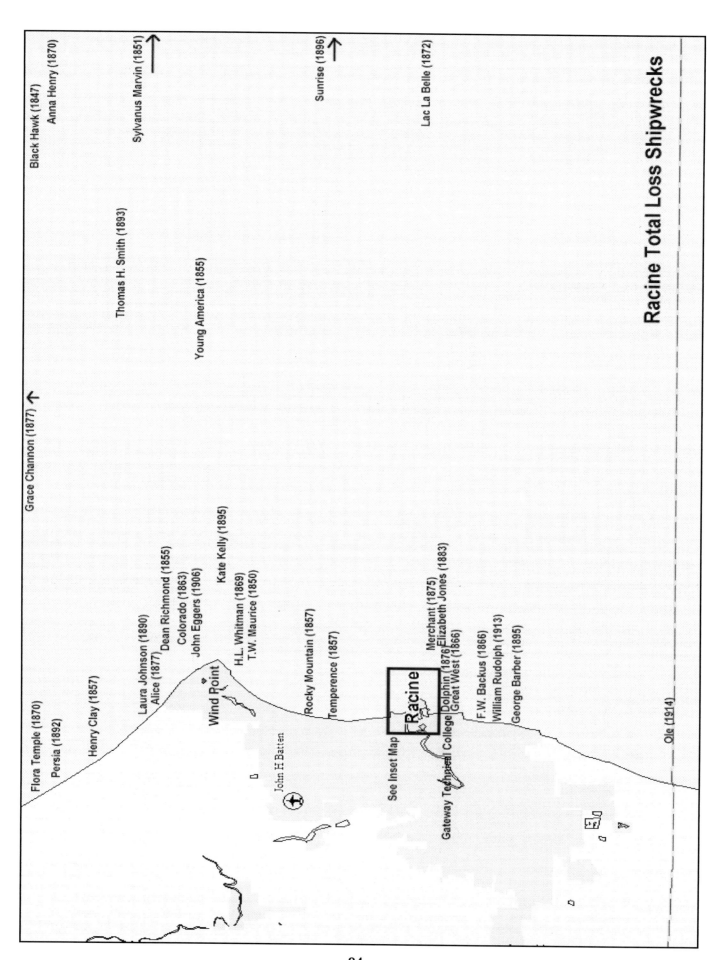

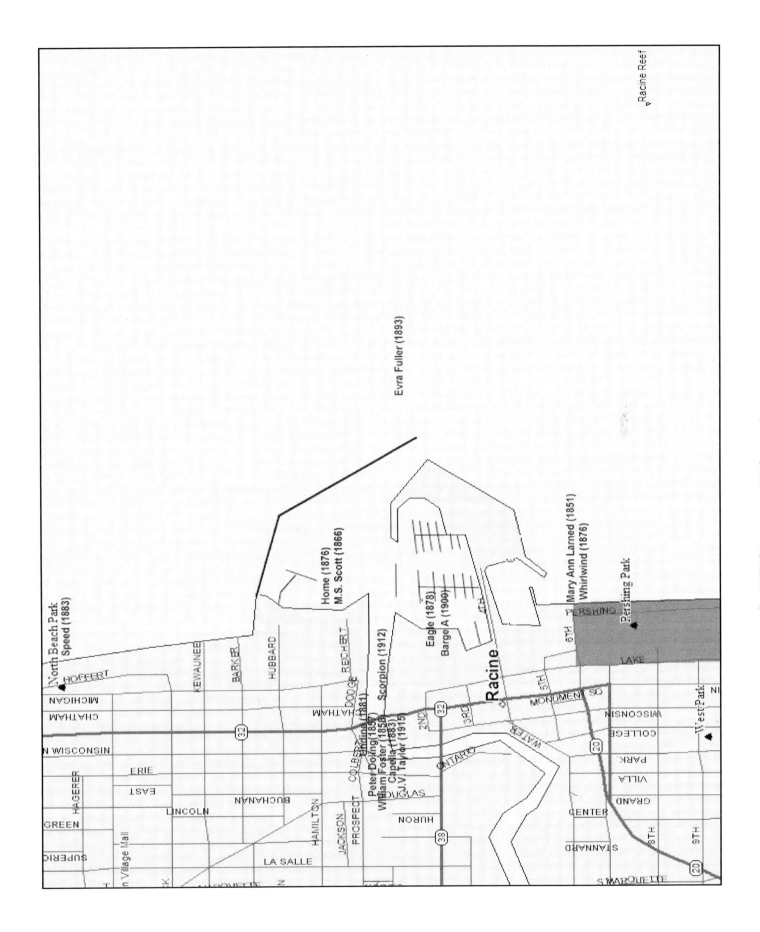

Vessels Built at Racine

The following list includes all the registered vessels known to have been built at Racine as well as a significant number of smaller unregistered steam yachts. The list is drawn primarily from the various Great Lakes vessel enrollment databases and from my collection of marine registers and boat company ads. The list is almost certainly incomplete, as many substantial Racine built vessels were likely not registered and therefore, would not appear in any marine registers. This is particularly true of the many yachts built in the 1890s by the Racine Boat Manufacturing Company. The company turned out well over 100 significant yachts from the Racine yard, but most of these were never registered. The marine salvage and construction business of Knapp & Gillen also built several scows at Racine, most of which were not registered.

Racine saw several periods of vessel construction, the first being from the yards of Racine shipbuilders Justice Bailey, Edward M. Beckwith, Daniel Putney and Alfred Gilson & Co. who built vessels at Racine in the 1840s and 50s. Several small builders worked out of Racine in the 1860s and 70s, but large scale vessel construction didn't resume until the 1880s when the Racine Hardware Company began building yachts under owner Thomas Kane. In the 1890s, they recruited yacht designer Fred W. Martin and began to turn out larger yachts to a wider audience under the name Racine Boat Manufacturing Co. They continued to turn out high quality boats until the 1930s but moved most operations to Muskegon, Michigan in the early 1900s. The Racine Boat Manufacturing Company was planning to expand to automobile manufacturing in 1903 when a disastrous fire destroyed much of the Racine yard. Fred Martin also parted ways with the company, relocating to Chicago in the early 1900s, but his designs became relatively influential and he achieved significant regional notariety as a yacht designer. Many of his design plans survive and were published by the Racine Historical Society. The last Racine built vessels were the steel fish tugs built by Peter Mayer in the 1950s and 60s.

SHIPPING, OWNED WHOLLY, OR IN PART, AT RACINE:		Tonnage	Value
Propeller James Wood	owned by W. T. Richmond	300	$12,000
Brig Mohegan	Norton and Durand	255	8,000
Brig Sam Strong	Norton and Durand	245	7,500
Brig Cherokee	Durand and Hill	204	7,500
Brig Iroquois	W. T. Richmond	310	7,500
Brig Olive Richmond	W. T. Richmond	250	5,000
Brig Ontonagon	Isaac Taylor	230	6,000
Brig Anne Winslow	F. A. McHenry	200	3,000
Brig Ontario	N. Pendleton and Co.	160	2,500
Schooner Mount Vernon	W. T. Richmond	240	7,500
Schooner Whirlwind	Canfield and Co.	190	5,000
Schooner Newbold	John G. Conroe	180	4,000
Schooner Lewis C. Ervin	Canfield and Co.	170	4,000
Schooner Charles Howard	Messrs. Raymond	160	2,500
Schooner Union	H. Denton	100	2,500
Schooner Colonel Benton	W. T. Richmond	160	2,000
Schooner Rocky Mountains	Coleman and Linn	135	1,500
Schooner Seventy-Six	George D. Fellows	85	1,800
Schooner Glynachor	J. W. Jones and others	78	1,600
Schooner Erie	John Gallien	70	1,400
Schooner Mariner	E. M. Beckwith	80	1,200
Schooner Asa Wilcox	Harvey, Francis, and others	125	1,200
Schooner Dolphin	James M. Sprague	90	1,200
Schooner Liberty	Miller and Peters	80	1,200
Schooner Amelia	Mrs. Clark	85	800
Schooner on the stocks	Alexander C. Stebbins	130	4,000
Sloop Wunx	A. D. Eveland	60	1,200
Sloop Lady Ann	David Youngs	60	600
		4,372	104,200

Whole number of Vessels owned, in whole or in part, at Racine, 28.

Ships owned at Racine 1851 – Transactions of the Wisconsin Agricultural Society 1852

Schooner *Colonel Benton* - Built 1846, 159.15 gt. BOM, a substantial rebuild of sch. blt. 1835 at Richmond, OH, lost 1850, Canadian shore of Lake Erie

Schooner *Diamond* - Built 1847, 68.10 gt. BOM, sold off lakes 1850, went to New Orleans via Il canals.

Schooner *Tempest* (24150) - Built 1848 by Gilson and Co., 196.30 gt., 106.0 x 26.0 x 8.0 ft., scuttled off Chicago 1896

Schooner *Union* - Built 1848, 87.90 gt., 82.4 x 17.5 x 6.6 ft., lost 1864 at Milwaukee

Schooner *Whirlwind* (26226) - Built 1848 by Justice Bailey, 111.45 gt., 101.8 x 22.0 x 7.9 ft., lost 1876 at Racine

Schooner *Cherokee* - Built 1849 by Gilson, 203.85 gt., 103.0 x 24.0 x 9.0 ft., lost 1856 near Manistee, MI

Schooner *Glynn Acor* - Built 1849 by Justice Bailey, 65.02 gt., 64.9 x 17.6 x 6 ft., wrecked Chicago 1853

Sloop *Ranger* - Built 1849, 22.06 gt.

Schooner *Racine* Clipper - Built 1851, 11 gt., 41.0 x 9.0 x 3.4 ft., last enrolled Milwaukee 1853.

Schooner *Seventy Six* - Built 1851, 76.39 gt., last enrolled 1858 Chicago.

Sloop *Wunx* - Built 1851, 41.30 gt., 59.8 x 17.0 x 4.8 ft., lost November 1857 at Saugatuck, MI.

Schooner *Flying Cloud* - Built 1852, 122.35 gt., 85.7 x 23.2 x 7.0 ft., lost 1853, LM

Scow Schooner *Active* (363) - Built 1853 by Justice Bailey, 84.27 gt., abandoned Chicago c. 1880.

Schooner *Belle City* (2153) - Built 1853 by E.M. Beckwith, 168.04 gt., 97.5 x 22.25 x 8.5 ft., burned 1869, Detroit River

Schooner *Falcon* (9190) - Built 1853 by Bailey, 126.22 gt., 97.0 x 25.0 x 8.5 ft., sunk 1876 Detroit

Propeller *Pacific* - Built 1853 by E.M. Beckwith, 113.68 gt., 93.5 x 18 x 7.2 ft., last listed 1860.

Brig *Racine* (21183) - Built 1853 by J. Bailey, 213.81 gt., 106.4 x 26.2 x 9.2 ft. lost 1868, Point Aux Barques, LM

Schooner *Sovereign of the Seas* - built 1853, 226 gt., 104.0 x 26.1 x 9.3 ft., lost 1853 Beaver Island

Schooner *Curlew* (4339) - Built 1854 by D. Putney, 192.26 gt., 117.0 x 26.0 x 10.0 ft., abandoned c. 1880 at Chicago

Schooner *Gilbert Knapp* (10337) - Built 1854 by E.M. Beckwith, 186.09 gt., 100.0 x 26.0 x 8.5 ft., lost 1896, LM

Schooner *Pacific* - Built 1854 by E.M. Beckwith, 122.33 gt., 95.0 x 18.0 x 7.75 ft., lost 1857 east coast of Lake Michigan.

Schooner *Telegraph* (24232) - Built 1854 by E.M. Beckwith, 81.77 gt., 79.5 x 12.9 x 6.8 ft., lost 1867 at Muskegon, MI

Scow Schooner *Three Bells* (24643) - Built 1854 by N. Griswold, 60 gt., 76.0 x 20.0 x 6.0 ft., still in commission in 1901 at Chicago.

Schooner *John W. Sargent* (12773) - Built 1855 by E.M. Beckwith, 98 gt., 96.5 x 22.0 x 7.7 ft., wrecked 1872, Lake Erie

Schooner *A. P. Dutton* (376) - Built 1856 by Edward M. Beckwith, 43.62 gt., 60.5 x 14.6 x 5.5 ft., foundered 1869, LM

Schooner *Daniel Slawson* - Built 1857 by A. Gilson, 273.91 gt., 115.5 x 27.5 x 9.6 ft., wrecked 1863, Pilot Island LM

Steamer *Colonel M. Steeves* - Built 1860, 44.06 gt., 75.0 x 16.0 x 4.0 ft., abandoned 1862.

Schooner *Lydia Case* (14800) - Built 1862 by G.S. Rand, 246 gt., 122.3 x 25.6 x 10.2 ft., lost 1872, Pilot Island, LM

Steam Tug Robert Emmett - Historical Collections of the Great Lakes

Steam Tug *Robert Emmett* (21304) - Built 1863 by Lemuel H. Brown, 32 gt., 58.5 x 13.0 x 6.3 ft., abandoned 1909

Schooner *Neshoto* (18104) - Built 1864 by G.S. Rand, 392 gt., 127.6 x 28.3 x 11.11 ft., sunk 1872 Lake Huron. Also listed as built Neshoto (Manitowoc County)

Scow Schooner *Hurrah Boys* (95341) - Built 1872 by Anthony Beffol, 13 gt., 37.1 x 13.0 x 3.6 ft., wrecked 1874, Milwaukee

Schooner *Swan* (115352) - Built 1872, 5 gt., sold off lakes 1884

Scow Schooner *Two Katies* (24980) - Built 1873 by Henry Roisay, 73 gt., 88.2 x 18.4 x 6.0 ft., wrecked 1878 at Bailey's Harbor, WI

Steam Tug *Fred Wild* (120381) - Built 1879 by F. C. Viele, 13.81 gt., 49.0 x 10.0 x 3.4 ft., sold off Lakes 1884, listed at New Orleans, out of doc by 1885.

Scow No. 2 (163489) - Built 1883, 84 gt., burned 1918 at Duluth

Scow No. 1 (163492) - Built 1884, 90 gt., burned 1918 at Duluth

Early Racine Boat Ad - Steam Yachts & Launches 1887

Steam Yacht *Lillian* (unregistered) - Built 1885 by Racine Boat Manufacturing Co

Steam Yacht *Patience* (unregistered) - Built 1885 by Racine Boat Manufacturing Co

Steam Yacht *Pemberwick* (unregistered) - Built 1886 by Racine Boat Manufacturing Co

Steam Yacht *Whistler* (unregistered) - Built 1886 by Racine Boat Manufacturing Co., 5 gt., listed Beesons 1896

Steam Yacht *Sarama* (C90575) - Built 1886, 25.6 x 5.5 x 1.8 ft., Out of documentation 1910

Steam Yacht *Ventner* (unregistered) - Built 1886 by Racine Boat Manufacturing Co

Steam Yacht *Iroquois* (unregistered) - Built 1887 by Racine Boat Manufacturing Co., 2 gt., listed Beesons 1896

Steam Yacht *Thomas Kane* (unregistered) - Built 1887 by Racine Boat Manufacturing Co., 4 gt., listed Beesons 1896

Steam Yacht *Lizzie L.* (unregistered) - Built 1887 by Racine Boat Manufacturing Co

Steam Yacht *Mamie Ellar* (unregistered) - Built 1887 by Racine Boat Manufacturing Co

Steam Yacht *Mignon* (unregistered) - Built 1887 by Racine Boat Manufacturing Co

Steam Yacht *Speranza* (unregistered) - Built 1888 by Racine Boat Manufacturing Co., 3 gt., listed Beesons 1896

Steam Yacht *Venus* (unregistered) - Built 1888 by Racine Boat Manufacturing Co., 1 gt., listed Beesons 1896

Steam Yacht *Franklin* (unregistered) - Built 1888 by Racine Boat Manufacturing Co., 2 gt., listed Beesons 1896

Steam Yacht *Pilgrim* (unregistered) - Built 1889 by Racine Boat Manufacturing Co., 3 gt., listed Beesons 1896

Racine Hardware – Polk's Marine Directory 1888 – Author's Collection

Steam Yacht *Mollie D.* (unregistered) - Built 1891 by Racine Boat Manufacturing Co., 3 gt., listed Beesons 1896

Steam Yacht *Marguerite* (unregistered) - Built 1892 by Racine Boat Manufacturing Co., 2 gt., listed Beesons 1896

Steam Yacht *Me Too* (unregistered) - Built 1893 by Racine Boat Manufacturing Co., 3 gt., listed Beesons 1896

Steam Yacht *Southern Cross* (116639) - Built 1894 by Racine Boat Co., 25 gt., 56.6 x 14.0 x 5.0ft., abandoned 1921

Steam Yacht *Lena B.* (not enrolled) - Built 1894 by Racine Boat Manufacturing Co., 3 gt., listed Beesons 1896.

Sloop Yacht *Mayme* (unregistered) – Built 1894 by Fred W. Martin for Racine Boat Mfg., 36 ft.

Sloop Yacht *Valiant* (161741) - Built 1894 by Racine Boat Manufacturing Co., 9 gt., 38.0 x 12.0 x 4.4 ft.

Steam Yacht *Comrade* (not enrolled) – Built 1895 by Racine Boat Manufacuring Co., 5 gt., burned at Erie, PA, 7/19/1896.

Steam Yacht *Nancy E.* (not enrolled) - Built 1895 by Racine Boat Manufacturing Co., 1 gt., listed Beesons 1896.

Steam Yacht *Annie B.* (not enrolled) - Built 1895 by Racine Boat Manufacturing Co., 2 gt., listed Beesons 1896.

Steam Yacht *Lulu M.* (not enrolled) - Built 1895 by Racine Boat Manufacturing Co., 3 gt., listed Beesons 1896.

Sloop Yacht *Puritana* (150698) - Built 1895 by Racine Boat Works, 23 gt., 58.0 x 14.0 x 6.3 ft., Out of doc. 1940

Steam Yacht *Redfield* (111420) - Built 1895 by Racine Boat Manufacturing Co., 10 gt., 31.5 x 11.5 x 3.0 ft.

Steamer *Pathfinder* (150730) - Built 1896 by Racine Boat Manufacturing Co., 168 gt., 136.0 x 18.3 x 10.0 ft., sold off lakes 1918

Schooner Yacht *Schlitz Globe* (116747) - Built 1896 by H.W. Moffatt, 20 gt., 34.0 x 10.9 x 4.4 ft.

Sloop Yacht *Siren* (116721) - Built 1896 by Racine Boat Manufacturing Co., 16 gt., 50.3 x 12.6 x 5.4 ft., last documented 1916

Fred W. Martin – Racine Yacht Designer – Beeson's Marine Directory – 1897 – Author's Collection

Sloop Yacht *Vanenna* (161774) - Built 1896 by Racine Boat Manufacturing Co., 19 gt., 49.0 x 13.0 x 4.9 ft., last documented 1924

Sloop Yacht *Vencedor* (161773) - Built 1896 by Racine Boat Manufacturing Co., 18 gt., 49.5 x 12.3 x 4.9 ft., wrecked 1911, Charlevoix, MI

Schooner Yacht *Glad Tidings* (86390) - Built 1897 by Racine Boat & Launch Co., 9 gt., 38.0 x 11.0 x 4.0 ft., sank 1916, Chicago

Steam Yacht *Hathor* (unregistered) - Built 1898 by Racine Boat Manufacturing Co

Steam Yacht *Olivette* (unregistered) - Built 1898 by Racine Boat Manufacturing Co

Gas Yacht *Mae* (93049) - Built 1899 by Racine Boat Manufacturing Co, 15 gt., 45.0 x 8.2 x 3.5 ft.

Gas Launch *Pandour* (171933) - Built c. 1900 by Racine Boat Manufacturing Co, 12 gt., 46.4 x 9.5 x 3.5 ft.

Gas Launch *Canuck* (107808) - Built 1900 by Racine Boat Manufacturing Co, 16.3 x 4.3 x 1.8 ft.

Motor Sail *Cynthia* (107896) - Built 1900 by Racine Boat Manufacturing Co, 18.0 x 4.5 x 2.0 ft., abandoned 1930

Steamer *Derry Carne* (107422) - Built 1900 by Racine Boat Manufacturing Co, 15.5 x 4.5 x 2.8 ft.

Gas Yacht *Kid* (161163) - Built 1900 by Racine Boat Manufacturing Co, 17 gt., 49.2 x 10.0 x 3.0 ft.

Steam Fish Tug *Major* (93079) - Built 1900 by W.E. Collins, 12 gt., 37.3 x 10.0 x 4.7 ft., abandoned 1922

Motor Sail *Bessie* (111589) - Built 1901 by Racine Boat Manufacturing Co, 18.3 x 4.3 x 2.3 ft.

Steam Yacht *Doozie* (157649) - Built 1901 by Racine Boat Mfg. Co., 47 gt., 80.0 x 13.0 x 3.6 ft., abandoned 1921

Burning of the Racine Boat Company yard 1903 - History of Racine County

Steamer *Hepburn* (C111921) - Built 1901 by Racine Boat Manufacturing Co, 15 gt., 55.0 x 8.6 x 4.2 ft.

Gas Yacht *Idle Hour* (100738) - Built 1901 by Racine Boat Manufacturing Co, 10 gt., 43.6 x 9.3 x 3.0 ft.

Gas Launch *Roseneath* (C111660) - Built 1901 by Racine Boat Manufacturing Co, 20.0 x 5.5 x 2.6 ft., abandoned 1919

Racine Boat Mfg Co. Motors 1902 - Author's Collection

Gas Launch *Little Jap* (121702) - Built 1902 by Racine Boat Manufacturing Co, 22.5 x 5.6 x 2.0 ft.

Motor Sail *Margota* (122262) - Built 1902 by Racine Boat Manufacturing Co, 10 gt., 38.4 x 8.0 x 4.0 ft.

Steamer *Stanley* (C112046) - Built 1902 by Racine Boat Manufacturing Co, 16.2 x 5.2 x 3.8 ft., abandoned 1910

Gas Launch *Dolphin* (206126) - Built 1903 by Carl Benson, 11 gt., 32.5 x 10.7 x 4.3 ft., last documented 1930

Scow *M. J. Gillen* (162469) - Built 1903 by Edward Gillen, 613 gt., 189.0 x 37.4 x 11.6 ft.

Steam Yacht *Roxana* (200436) - Built 1903 by Racine Boat Mfg. Co., 99 gt., 97.0 x 17.0 x 4.9 ft., abandoned 1942

Gas Launch *Florence* (207494) - Built 1905 by Racine Boat Manufacturing Co, 6 gt., 40.0 x 8.0 x 4.0 ft.

Gas Yacht *Bella Jane* (210606) - Built 1906 by Racine Boat Manufacturing Co., 22 gt., 46.5 x 10.4 x 5.2 ft., abandoned 1946

Gas Launch *Globe* (213448) - Built 1906 by Racine Boat Company, 11 gt., 30.5 x 9.5 x 3.8 ft., renamed J.B. Flaherty, 1916, abandoned 1933

Gas Yacht *Morris* (unregistered) – Built 1907 by Racine Boat Mfg Co., 46 ft.,

Gas Yacht *Loretta* (212049) - Built 1907 by Racine Boat Manufacturing Co, 22 gt.

Gas Launch *Neptune* (204747) - Built 1907 by P.M. Gadske, 11 gt., 34.0 x 11.7 x 3.6 ft., abandoned 1956

Gas Yacht *Isabella* (unregistered) – Built 1908 by Racine Boat Mfg Co., 52 ft.

Gas Launch *Lyle D*. (206510) - Built 1908, 11 gt., 37.7 x 9.7 x 2.5 ft., burned 1922, Lake Superior

Racine Boat Mfg – 1908 – Author's Collection

Gas Launch *Florence* (206399) - Built 1909 by Erwing W. Schoeppe, 10 gt., 31.2 x 8.6 x 3.6 ft., sold off lakes, 1921

Gas Yacht *Philistina* (206678) - Built 1909 by Racine Boat Company, 12 gt., 38.0 x 8.8 x 4.3 ft.

Gas Yacht *Falcon* (209161) - Built 1911 by H.S. Hurlbut, 7 gt., 26.5 x 9.6 x 3.7 ft., abandoned 1931

Gas Yacht *Montana* (210911) - Built 1911 by Racine Boat Co., 36 gt., 55.5 x 13.0 x 8.0 ft., abandoned 1931

Steamer *Nemadji* (C156861) - Built 1912 by Racine Boat Co., 64.1 x 16.6 x 7.2 ft.

Gas Launch *Sterling* (209915) - Built 1912 by Racine Boat Co., 13 gt., 38.7 x 10.0 x 4.9 ft

Gas Yacht *Raboco* (211353) - Built 1913 by Racine Boat Co., 39 gt., 58.1 x 14.0 x 6.4 ft., burned 1932, Chicago River

Gas Launch *Seminole* (221126) - Built 1913, 9 gt., 34.5 x 10.7 x 4.6 ft., lost by collision at Chicago, 1928

Gas Launch *Argyle* (232071) - Built 1914, 9 gt., 38.0 x 9.0 x 4.0 ft., abandoned 1957

Fish Tug *W. H. Pugh* (213950) - Built 1916 by Heming Larsen, 39 gt., 53.5 x 14.3 x 6.5 ft., dismantled 1946

Gas Yacht *Annella* (215477) - Built 1917, 36 gt., 62.6 x 12.0 x 3.9 ft., burned Lake Erie 1921

Gas Yacht *Ethel Louis* (217169) - Built 1918, 19 gt., 41.4 x 11.1 x 3.9 ft., abandoned 1933

Gas Launch *Elizabeth* (217398) - Built 1918, 14 gt., 37.3 x 9.4 x 4.7 ft., abandoned 1932

Gas Launch *Marco II* (C153136) - Built c. 1920, 18 gt., 46.2 x 9.5 x 4.9 ft.

Gas Launch *Beaulah L* (227522) - Built 1920, 15 gt., 46.6 x 10.8 x 4.4 ft., abandoned 1930

Gas Launch *Glenroy* (237050) - Built 1921, 10 gt.

Gas Launch *Sea Bird* (237429) - Built 1925, 9 gt., 38.1 x 9.6 x 4.3 ft., out of documentation 1957

Gas Yacht *Ahana* (266250) - Built 1933, 12 gt., 36.3 x 9.7 x 4.3 ft.

Steel Fish Tug *Chief* (D275653) - Built 1957 by Peter L. Mayer Boat Co., 16 gt., 33.8 x 9.9 x 4.9 ft.

Racine built Fish Tug *Kathy* – Harvey Hadland

Steel Fish Tug *Kathy* (D277442) - Built 1958 by Peter L. Mayer Boat Co., 32 gt., 42.7 x 13.10 x 5.2 ft.

Steel Yacht *Valkyrie* (D283514) - Built 1960 by Peter L. Mayer Boat Co., 27 gt., 43.1 x 14.1 x 7.1 ft.

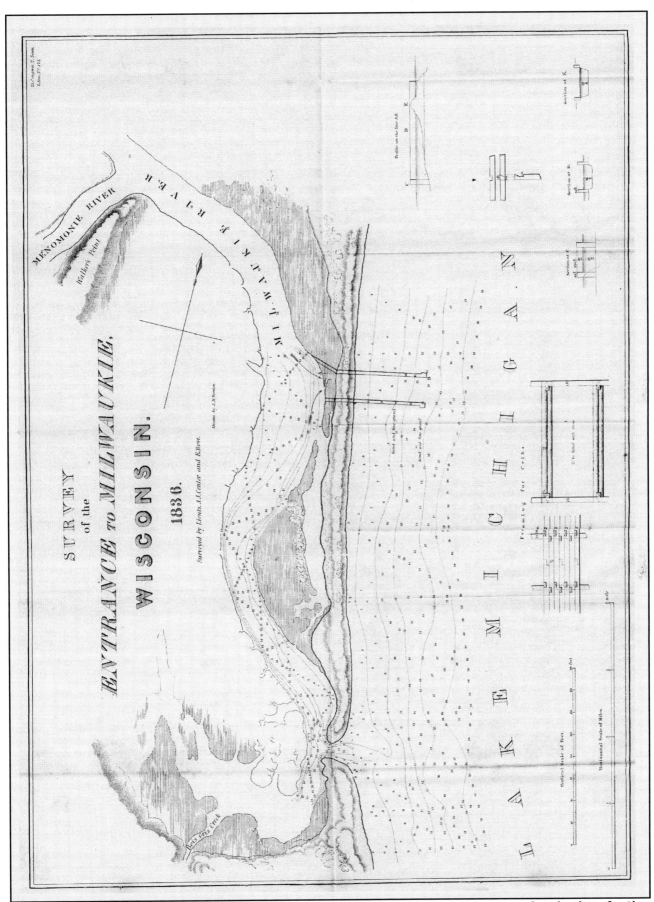

Milwaukee's first detailed Harbor survey, 1836, showing the narrow river entrance and early plans for the straight cut - Report from the Secretary of War, 25th Congress, 2d Session – Original in Author's Collection

Milwaukee Shipwrecks 1825-1875

The area now occupied by Milwaukee harbor has a long history of human habitation and was one of the first points on the southern end of the Lake to be visited by Europeans. The area's natural geography made it a logical place for a city. Native Americans had established a large village at Milwaukee which had been occupied for hundreds of years by the Fox, Sauk, Winnebago, Menomonee and Pottawatomie Indians. The site was formed by the confluence of three rivers, the Milwaukee, the Menominee and Kinnickinnic. The rivers formed a huge marshland hosting vast quantities of wild rice, which in turn, attracted a great deal of waterfowl. Indian trade routes converged in the area and later evolved into the area's plank roads. Even before the arrival of the familiar woodland Indians, the area had hosted other civilizations. Dozens of effigy mounds dotted the shores of Milwaukee's rivers as testament to a substantial earlier period of occupation.

The first European to visit the site of Milwaukee was probably Father Jacques Marquette, who camped on the east shore of the Milwaukee River from November 23 to 27, 1674 while on his expedition to found a mission at Kaskaskia, among the Illinois Indians. Father Marquette would die on his return from this expedition at present-day Ludington, Michigan the next year. Europeans again visited Milwaukee in 1679 when the LaSalle expedition passed through the area after leaving their ill-fated ship Griffon at Door County. Father Hennepin relates a harrowing adventure full of storms and privation traveling down the western shore of Lake Michigan. After passing present-day Sheboygan, the group paddled for over a week down a rugged shore with high bluffs and little game. The men were weak from starvation when on October 16, 1679, the bluffs receded and they came upon a fair and temperate area with an abundance of deer and fowl, which their hunters easily took. This was Milwaukee Bay, at which the party camped for some days to regain their strength before arriving at the foot of Lake Michigan at the present-day Illinois-Indiana border on October 28th, 1679. From there, the group set out on their first abortive effort to reach the Gulf of Mexico via the Mississippi. The last early European visitors to Milwaukee were a group of French explorers in eight canoes led by Henry de Tonty, Francois Morgan de Vincennes and Father Jean François Buisson de St. Cosme. On November 10, 1699, St. Cosme notes that they sheltered in the Milwaukee River for two days to wait out a storm. The group was searching for a river route from Wisconsin to the Mississippi.

Between 1700 and about 1750, French fur traders from Green Bay and Michilimackinac visited periodically and had summer trading posts at the river mouth. After the French and Indian War, formal control of the area passed to the British, who first noted the Indian village at Milwaukee in 1762 when the British trader Alexander Henry visited Milwaukee. British commandant DePeyster at Michilimackinac sent the first vessel to Milwaukee on November 4, 1779 when he dispatched Captain Samuel Robertson on board the sloop HMS Felicity to try winning over the troublesome Milwaukee Indians to the British cause. He plied them with liquor and tobacco, but the village maintained a strong allegiance with the new American traders that had begun to influence the area following the Revolutionary War. Robertson found two permanent French residents at Milwaukee, a trader named Moreau and another named St. Pierre. The logbook of the HMS Felicity has been preserved and provides interesting insight into the early navigation of the Lake.

In 1795, the American Fur Company set up a permanent post at Milwaukee under the direction of Jacques Vieau, although Vieau himself did not reside at the post year-round. It wouldn't be until the arrival of Solomon Juneau on September 24, 1818 that Milwaukee would receive her first permanent European resident. Juneau was a French fur trader and the successor to Jacques Vieau. He is rightly credited as the founder of Milwaukee as a city, having been involved in every aspect of the area's early development. Juneau spent nearly 20 years managing the trading post at Milwaukee with only infrequent visits from other traders. However, he very quickly began to make his mark on the place. In 1823, Juneau brought the first US commercial vessel to call at Milwaukee when he chartered the 30 ton schooner Chicago Packet under Captain Brittan with goods from Detroit and Michilimackinac. The schooner landed off the river mouth with trade goods that were ferried in by canoe. The same year, the small schooners Virginia and Aurora called at Milwaukee from Michilimackinac and Green Bay with goods for Juneau, the Virginia being the first vessel to successfully enter the shallow river mouth.

In 1831 and 1833, the Menomonee and Pottawatomie Indians ceded their lands around Milwaukee to the US government by treaty, and the conclusion of the Blackhawk War ended hostilities with the region's Sauk Indians. This opened up a wave of immigration from the east that brought notable Milwaukee settlers Byron Kilbourn and Col. George H. Walker.

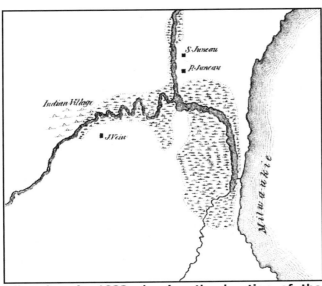

Milwaukee in 1833 showing the location of the Indian Village and various traders - Pioneer History of Milwaukee, vol. 1

In 1835, Juneau, Walker and Kilbourn each platted towns at their respective locations; Juneau platting the east side of the Milwaukee River, Kilbourn platting the west side and Walker platting the south side near present-day Walker's Point. The men had no idea that the entire area would someday become an urban metropolis, and introduced a generation of civic conflict due to the fact that none of their platted streets lined up with the other's. This prompted the "bridge wars" of 1845, in which backers of Kilbourn and Juneau each tore down each others bridges, culminating in a cannon being aimed at Byron Kilbourn's residence by Juneau's backers. Eventually, the dispute was settled in 1846 by combining the two towns into the City of Milwaukee.

Milwaukee vessel traffic in August 1837 - Milwaukee Sentinel - 8/22/1837

Also in 1835, Milwaukee received her first steamboat when the sidewheel steamer United States dropped anchor of the harbor. 1836 saw 314 commercial vessels call at the port, as thousands of new settlers streamed in. The 1830s also saw significant efforts to drain the large marsh in order to create habitable land. Drainage systems were built and fill was added throughout the area and by the 1850s, the huge marsh had all but disappeared.

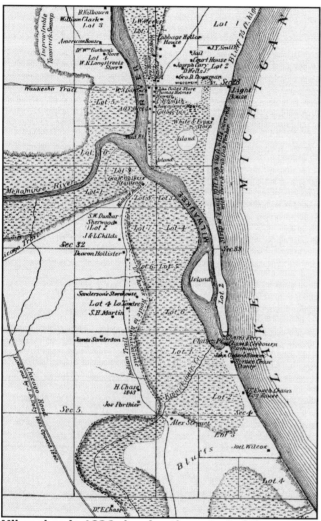

Milwaukee in 1836 showing the extent of the original marsh, Milwaukee County Historical Society

1836 saw requests from Kilbourn and Walker for government funds to improve the harbor at Milwaukee and a survey (shown on p. 91) was undertaken which suggested that the straight cut be built. Unfortunately, twenty years and dozens of shipwrecks would come to pass before the government finally built the straight cut. Regular dredging of the sand bar at the old river mouth began about 1836, rendering the harbor enterable by small sloops and by 1837, shallow draft schooners could enter the river and navigate as far as the wharves at Kilbourn town and Juneau town. In 1838, a crude lighthouse was built a mile north of the river mouth to guide ships in at night and in 1842 a large pier was built at the river mouth, upon which ships could moor in fair weather. The 1840s also saw the establishment of small shipyards along the rivers and several small schooners were built. Byron Kilbourn had two small steam lighters, the Badger and Menomonee, built for the purpose of bringing in freight from the large steamers that could not enter the shallow river mouth.

Milwaukee's first lighthouse built 1838 - Pioneer History of Milwaukee, vol. 2

In 1838, George Dousman set up a warehouse at Milwaukee. Dousman was the son of prominent Mackinaw fur trader Michael Dousman and the brother of Talbot Dousman (founder of Dousman, Wisconsin) and Hercules Dousman, Wisconsin's first multi-millionaire. George Dousman started Milwaukee's grain trade and became the town's first and largest grain merchant. He would play a large role in the development of Milwaukee's harbor and port facilities during the 1840s, 50s and 60s. In 1841, Dousman shipped the first grain cargo from Milwaukee on the schooner Illinois, beginning a trade that would culminate in

1862 with Milwaukee's exports exceeding Chicago's, making her the largest grain port in the world.

Milwaukee Harbor 1862 showing both harbor entrances in use - Wisconsin Historical Society

Despite Milwaukee's great promise as a grain port, residents had tremendous difficulty securing government funding for harbor improvements. Milwaukee repeatedly petitioned the federal government for funds and held many meetings to discuss the impasse. Government surveyors ignored Milwaukee's plans for the straight cut and instead made only small appropriations for keeping the old river mouth clear of sand. This greatly hampered Milwaukee's economic growth, as large vessels had difficulty entering and caused many shipwrecks. In 1853 alone, 1,483 vessels entered Milwaukee Harbor. It would not be until 1857, well into Milwaukee's grain boom, that the government finally completed the straight cut entrance originally suggested in 1836. Also in 1857, the first grain elevator was constructed at Milwaukee allowing vessels to easily load with minimal manual labor. The increase in traffic also demonstrated the need for a better lighthouse that could be seen from a distance. In 1851, congress approved funding for the North Point Lighthouse to replace the crude 30 ft tower constructed in 1838. Completed in 1855, it would be the tallest light on the Lakes. Although reconstructed in 1888 and again in 1912, the light station is still in place and is a striking reminder of Milwaukee's maritime past.

North Point Light circa 1910 - Author's Collection

The Harbor funding problem was of particular concern to Wisconsin lay-scientist Increase Lapham, who created detailed lists of area shipwrecks in 1843 in order to demonstrate the need for a harbor. Lapham eventually used his Milwaukee shipwreck data in 1869 to request the creation of the US Weather Bureau, which proved instrumental in preventing shipwrecks and saving lives. Following the financial downturn caused by the Panic of 1857 and the Civil War, Milwaukee commerce once again boomed, with a significant trade in grain, lumber, tanned leather and finished goods. The 1870s saw a dramatic increase in Milwaukee shipbuilding spawned by a renewed grain boom. Large Milwaukee built three masted grain schooners like the Moonlight and Porter were considered the finest on the Lakes and cemented Milwaukee's reputation as a leading shipbuilding port.

Milwaukee 1856 north of the harbor - Wisconsin Historical Society

In 1869, Milwaukee planners were badly in need of additional dock space and plans were made to drain the flooded swampland of the Menomonee River Valley. This large wetland, shown on the 1862 chart was a source of mosquitoes and massassauga rattlesnakes, and was seen as the potential site of a canal system. As such, during the 1870s, the area was drained and the South Menomonee Canal, the Burnham Canal and the Kneeland Slip were all constructed.

Milwaukee Harbor 1872 showing flooded Menomonee River - Wisconsin Historical Society

The 1870s saw the inception of the US Lifesaving Service as a direct result of the tremendous loss of life on the Great Lakes by shipwreck. Stations were established at regular intervals on the coasts of Lakes beginning in 1875. Milwaukee hosted one of the first stations on Lake Michigan, being constructed in 1875. It was initially located at McKinley Park and staged many rescues over its long career. In 1885, the station was relocated to Jones Island and was taken over by the Coast Guard in 1915 when the USLSS was absorbed. A new Coast Guard station was built in 1916 at McKinley Park and was demolished in 2008 having been abandoned since 1970. The hand written logs from the Milwaukee USLSS station have been preserved by the National Archives and are available in facsimile from the Milwaukee Public Library. They make for fascinating reading and could easily be used to fill a book solely about the exploits and rescues of the Milwaukee "storm warriors."

USLSS Station Milwaukee c. 1900 - Author's Collection

By the 1880s, the volume of vessel traffic and the long, unprotected stretches of Lake Michigan had shown the need for a harbor of refuge at Milwaukee. Beginning in 1881, funding was appropriated for the construction of a breakwall system that would span the north side of the harbor, providing protection from the northeast. The first section completed would be the north breakwall arm, which was in place by 1884 (see map on p. 111). The remainder of the breakwall was completed over many years, with the majority of the enclosing north structure completed before 1900. However, storms frequently washed away sections of the breakwall. By 1912, the north enclosure was completed by it wouldn't be until the 1930s that the south enclosure was completed.

Milwaukee Harbor piers 1883 showing the original wooden pierhead light - Author's Collection

Depression era construction funding allowed the remaining portions of the breakwall to be completed, along with a tremendous land reclamation project that created many acres of new property at Jones Island and at the present-day Summerfest grounds.

Milwaukee Harbor 1912 showing the north breakwall enclosure at the time - Author's Collection

By 1935, new land had been created on both sides of the straight cut. To the south a new wastewater treatment plan was built and to the north an airstrip called Maitland field was created. At this time, the inner and outer harbor facilities were also planned and construction begun. With the increasing size of Lake vessels, Milwaukee was badly in need of slips and several new, large slips were developed in the outer harbor once the south breakwall was completed. This massive effort dramatically altered the shoreline in many of the historic coastal areas where famous wrecks had occurred. It is likely that several wrecks were buried or removed during this effort. The KK and Menomonee Rivers were also widened and turning basins were added, removing the old boneyards and scuttled vessels from along their shores.

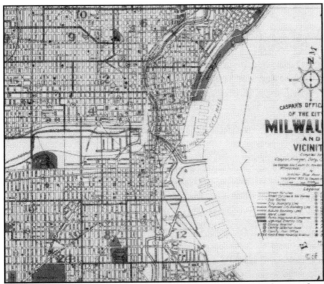
Milwaukee Harbor in 1930 showing the work on the south breakwall and the planned outer slip areas then being created - AGS Collection, UW-Milwaukee

Since the 1860s, a community of Polish fisherman had existed on Jones Island. The Kaszubes, as they were called, were evicted from the island in the 1930s to make way for the construction efforts. Today, only a small park remains in testament to this bustling community, which existed for nearly 80 years.

Milwaukee Breakwater Light c. 1910 - Author's Collection

Milwaukee has had several lighthouses over the years, including the 1838 and current North Point Light, the old and new breakwater lights, and the old and new pierhead light. In 1907, Milwaukee's original square, wooden pierhead light (shown in the 1883 image on the previous page) was replaced with the cylindrical light tower shown below. This tower is still in place on the north inner pier.

Milwaukee Pierhead Light c. 1910 - Author's Collection

In 1912, Milwaukee received a lightship to guide vessels out on the Lake to her harbor. Anchored three miles out in the Lake, Lightship No. 95 was built in 1912 at Muskegon, Michigan. She was 108.5 x 23.0 x 11.6 ft. and 368 gt. She sported a large electric lamp on a tall mast that could be seen for several miles. She was moored on station even in the foulest weather and had a hull designed to take massive waves. She was the last vessel ever to sight the ill-fated carferry Milwaukee as she sailed into oblivion in 1929. The Milwaukee Lightship service was discontinued in 1932 and the vessel was sent to the east coast. She was decommissioned and donated as a museum ship in 1966, but her final disposition is unknown.

Milwaukee Lightship No. 95 - C.Patrick Labadie Collection, TBNMS

In 1926, Milwaukee received her current breakwater lighthouse. It was constructed with a fourth order Fresnel lens, which is still in use today. The light was automated in 1966.

Current Milwaukee breakwater light c. 1930 - Milwaukee Public Library

Since the development of the outer harbor area in the 1930s, the Milwaukee lakefront has undergone nearly constant change. World War II saw Milwaukee once again become a major shipbuilding center, turning out the largest vessels ever constructed in the area from the Froemming Brothers shipyard on the KK River. Following the War, Milwaukee's main exports switched from grain to manufactured goods and her import traffic increased as her factories turned out machinery. By the 1950s, development of the St. Lawrence Seaway was underway and its opening in 1959 dramatically changed the vessel traffic at Milwaukee. A large number of foreign flagged ships began to call at the harbor and Milwaukee became a major international port. The 1960s saw continued waterfront development, including a massive land reclamation project that would create McKinley Marina.

The modern era has brought additional dramatic waterfront changes to Milwaukee, including the creation of the Summerfest Grounds area, the creation of the South Shore Marina and the regentrification the urban waterfront. Riverwalks have been added along Milwaukee's rivers and her waterfront now boasts impressive structures like the Milwaukee Art Museum and Discovery World Museum. Milwaukee's waterfront is now one of the most picturesque on the Great Lakes and is the gem of Lake Michigan.

In her 175 years, Milwaukee has been transformed from a wilderness to a modern urban city and her waterfront has reflected this transformation. The waterfront has also preserved a great deal of Milwaukee's history, much of which still lies undiscovered in the depths of Lake Michigan. The following accounts include every commercial vessel that was reported lost in the Milwaukee area. In addition to telling the story of each ship, these accounts also paint a picture of Milwaukee's history and growth, reflecting changes in commerce, technology and the people who call Milwaukee home.

Schooner *Sea Serpent* (predates registry numbering) – Built 1821 at Cleveland, OH by Captain D. Tyler for John Burtis – 26 gt. BOM, – Fall 1837 – The schooner *Sea Serpent* was a small, early Lake Michigan coastal schooner that had been brought from Lake Erie where she had been named *Lake Serpent*. She had been wrecked on the eastern Lakes in 1829, but rebuilt as the *Sea Serpent*. She was wrecked and rebuilt at Michigan City in June 1836, but was lost when she went ashore on the bar at Milwaukee in the Fall of 1837. (Increase Lapham, Losses on Lake Michigan 1834 - 1841, Senate Document 186, 27th Congress) Type: Stranding, Depth: Shallow, Remains: Probably Removed, Accuracy: 1/4 Mile.

Steamer *Dewitt Clinton* (predates registry numbering) – Built 1836 at Huron, Ohio, Fairbanks Church, 147.0 x 27.2 x 11.0 ft., 413.00 gt. BOM, 2 decks, 2 masts, scroll stem. This steamer is erroneously stated in several sources to have been lost off Milwaukee in 1839. On 10/11/1839, her yawl capsized while ferrying passengers in to the harbor, drowning five. The event was presented as evidence of the need for an improved harbor at Milwaukee. The *Clinton* was wrecked at Dunkirk, NY in May 1851, after which she was rebuilt as a freighter. She was dismantled in June 1869. (Milwaukee Sentinel – October 1839)

Schooner *H. Marsh* (predates registry numbering) – Built 1838 at Cleveland, OH by H.H. Trebout – 47.92 gt. BOM, 54.9 x 16.2 x 6.3 ft., last enrolled Cleveland, 1840 – 11/20/1840 – The schooner *H. Marsh* was lost trying to enter the harbor in a Fall gale. She was driven hard aground at the river mouth and broke up. She was a total loss with her cargo. (Milwaukee Sentinel – November 24, 1840, Increase Lapham, Losses on Lake Michigan 1834 - 1841, Senate Document 186, 27th Congress) Type: Stranding, Depth: Shallow, Remains: Probably Removed, Accuracy: 1/4 Mile.

Steam Ferry *Badger* (predates registry numbering) – Launched 7/4/1837 – 60 gt. BOM, 64 x 12 ft - owned by Byron Kilbourn – Fall 1840 – The steam lighter *Badger* had been used to ferry in passengers and freight from steamers. Her cabins could seat about 100 persons and she was the first steam vessel built at Milwaukee. She had been wrecked on the bar in 1837 but was salvaged. She was abandoned inside the harbor, after it was enlarged in the Fall of 1840. Her remains were almost certainly removed. (Pioneer History of Milwaukee I – p. 116, Milwaukee Sentinel – July 8, 1837) Type: Abandoned, Depth: Shallow, Remains: Probably Removed, Accuracy: 1 Mile.

Schooner *Cincinnati* (predates registry numbering) – Built 1828 at Lower Sandusky, Ohio, 61.6 x 18.2 x 5.6 ft., 53.57 gt. BOM – The schooner *Cincinnati* was brought to Milwaukee from Buffalo in the 1830s and wrecked in the Fall of 1840. She was afterwards towed to the corner of Reed and S. Water Street where she was abandoned. Her remains were still buried there in the mud in 1890. (Pioneer History of Milwaukee, Vol. 1, p. 108) Type: Abandoned, Depth: Shallow, Remains: Probably Removed, Accuracy: ¼ Mile.

Sloop *Clarissa* (predates registry numbering) – Built 1836 at Chicago – Fall 1840 – The sloop *Clarissa* was the first vessel built at Chicago. She was never enrolled and was probably a small coastal trader. She was lost in the Fall of 1840 when she was driven ashore at Milwaukee. (Increase Lapham, Losses on Lake Michigan 1834 - 1841, Senate Document 186, 27th Congress) Type: Stranding, Depth: Shallow, Remains: Probably Removed, Accuracy: 5 Miles.

Sloop *Wenonah* (predates registry numbering) – Built 1836 at Milwaukee by George Barber – 30 gt. BOM – 11/25/1841 – The sloop *Wenonah* was a small, unregistered vessel, built as a lighter. She had been started after the schooner Solomon Juneau but was launched first, making her the first vessel launched at Milwaukee. She went ashore at Milwaukee in a gale on 11/25/1841 and disappears from all records, probably a total loss. (Lapham List, Milwaukee Sentinel – December 1, 1841) Type: Stranding, Depth: Shallow, Remains: Probably Removed, Accuracy: 5 Miles.

The Milwaukie - Early American Steamers, vol. VI - Erik Heyl

Steamer *Milwaukie* (predates registry numbering) - Built 1837 at Grand Island, NY by Peter Hotaling - 401.40 gt. BOM, 172.0 x 24.0 x 10.1 ft. - July 1841 - The steamer Milwaukie was purchased by Solomon Juneau and George Walker as a means of competing with Byron Kilbourn. Both men had overspent on the ambitious plan and the Milwaukie sale was tied up in litigation while the vessel remained in layup at Buffalo. Incensed, Juneau sent a group of men to Buffalo who seized the ship on July 4, 1841 and absconded with it to Milwaukee. On July 9, the Milwaukie arrived, but fetched up on the bar at the river mouth. She was initially feared unsalvageable and she lay there all summer until Juneau and Walker could free her and take her up river. Litigation kept the Milwaukie out of operation until November 1842 when Juneau sold her at a substantial loss. Her new owner, Oliver Newberry lost the Milwaukee on her first trip when she fetch up off shore two miles north of present-day Saugatuck, MI on November 17, 1842. Several crew froze to death and the vessel was a total loss. Newberry was later able to salvage the wreck and towed her to Cleveland for scrapping. Her machinery ended up in the steamer Nile, which also wrecked at Milwaukee. (Erik Heyl - Early American Steamers, vol. VI) Type: Stranding, Depth: N/A, Remains: Definitely Removed, Accuracy: N/A.

Steamer *C.C. Trowbridge* (predates registry numbering) – Built 1838 at Saugatuck, MI by William Wilkin – 42.72 gt. BOM, 73.0 x 16.0 x 4.6 ft. – 12/5/1842 – The *C.C. Trowbridge* was a small steamer brought to Milwaukee as a harbor ferry and lighter. She was wrecked on 12/5/1842 when she went ashore off North Point. She was condemned and her engines removed. Her hull was later recovered and lengthened in 1843. She was still at Milwaukee in 1846 and participated in the recovery of the machinery of the steamer Boston. She may have lasted as late at 1871, but was not enrolled. (Lytle-Holdcamper List, Kit Lane-Built on the Banks of the Kalamazoo) Type: Stranding, Depth: Shallow, Remains: Definitely Removed, Accuracy: 1 Mile.

Sidewheel Steamer *Boston* (predates registry numbering) – Built 1846 at Detroit by John Robinson – 757.80 gt. BOM, 205.0 x 30.0 x 12.10 ft. – 11/24/1846 – The *Boston* was Milwaukee's first major shipwreck. She lost her smoke stack while trying to depart during a gale and was driven broadside into shallows just south of the old harbor piers. She was badly damaged and was salvaged in place. Her hull was left where it lay and may still have buried remains offshore. (Milwaukee Sentinel – November 26, 1846) Type: Stranding, Depth: Buried, Remains: Possibly Removed, Accuracy: 1 Mile.

Schooner *Solomon Juneau* (predates registry numbering) – Built 1837 at Milwaukee by George Barber – 86.14 gt. BOM, 72.6 x 19.2 x 7.0 ft. – 11/1846 – The *Solomon Juneau* was the first vessel ever built at Milwaukee. She had numerous mishaps and strandings before being driven ashore at the foot of Chicago St. (off the present-day Summerfest grounds) in November of 1846. She was abandoned after spending the winter on the beach. (Pioneer History of Milwaukee IV, p. 143) Type: Stranding, Depth: Shallow, Remains: Probably Removed, Accuracy: 1/4 Mile.

The Steamer *Nile* – Historical Collections of the Great Lakes

Sidewheel Steamer *Nile* (predates registry numbering) – Built 1843 at Detroit by B.F. Goodsell – 642.64 gt. BOM, 183.0 x 26.9 x 13.8 ft. – 9/6/1850 – The *Nile* stranded at Milwaukee on November 3, 1849 at the foot of Huron St. and was released after spending the winter. She was towed to Sweet's Warehouse dock near the Jones Shipyard to be rebuilt, when on 9/6/1850, an arsonist burned the warehouse, also burning the ship's upper works. The ship's engines were salvaged and she was abandoned in the mud until November 1860, when Milwaukee ship owner Caleb Harrison announced he would raise the hull and rebuild on it. It is unknown if he succeeded. (Lytle-Holdcamper List, Milwaukee Sentinel – November 10, 1860) Type: Stranding, Depth: Shallow, Remains: Probably Removed, Accuracy: 1/4 Mile.

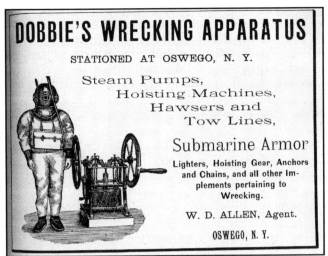

Polk's Marine Directory 1884 – Author's Collection

Bark *Buckeye State* (predates registry numbering) – Built 1852 at Black River, OH by Amos Hubbard – 309.85 gt. BOM, 132.5 x 25.1 x 10.0 ft. – 11/5/1852 – The 3 masted bark *Buckeye State* was brand new when she stranded off South Point with a cargo of railroad iron for the Milwaukee-Mississippi Railroad. She was released and under tow when she beached again near the old river mouth (at the South end of present-day Jones Island) where she went to pieces. (Walter Hirthe Wreck List, Milwaukee Sentinel November 13, 1852) Type: Stranding, Depth: Shallow, Remains: Possibly Removed, Accuracy: 1/4 Mile.

Schooner *Mary Margaret* (predates registry numbering) – Built 1852 at Chicago, IL – 38.80 gt. BOM, 50.8 x 17.6 x 5.3 ft. – 11/9/1854 – The schooner *Mary Margaret*, sporting an ornate figurehead and bound Milwaukee to Chicago with lumber capsized about 20 miles ESE of Milwaukee on 11/9/1854. Her crew clung for hours to the overturned hull before being rescued by the sch. *Magic*. (Buffalo Democracy – November 15, 1854) Type: Foundering, Depth: Very Deep, Remains: Definitely Present, Accuracy: 20 Miles.

Sidewheel Steamer *Sebastopol* (predates registry numbering) – Built 1855 at Cleveland by Luther Moses – 863.00 gt. BOM, 245.0 x 37.8 x 12.6 ft. – 9/20/1855 – The big, new steamer *Sebastopol* as lost when she went ashore 500 ft from shore, 3 miles south of the Government Pier (south of the present-day South Shore Yacht Club) with a cargo of merchandise and passengers for Chicago. She missed the harbor entrance, as its lights were extinguished and mistook the lights of the stranded schooner *Rockwell* for the piers. She was driven broadside to the waves and quickly taken apart. Seven persons died, despite gallant rescue efforts. The ship's remains were located in 1976 and were the subject of an avocational archeology survey. (Milwaukee Sentinel – September 1855) Type: Stranding, Depth: Shallow, Remains: Identified, Accuracy: Located.

Schooner *Active* (predates registry numbering) – Built 1845 at Green Bay, Wisconsin, 26.62 gt. BOM, last enrolled Milwaukee 3/21/1854 – The little schooner *Active* under Captain A. Rogers was bound from Manitowoc to Chicago with shingles when she capsized off Port Washington on October 10, 1855. Her crew were rescued after two days by the schooner Thornton, but the hull drifted south, last seen 15 miles off Milwaukee by the steamer *Sciota*. (Milwaukee Sentinel – October 12, 1855) Type: Foundering, Depth: Very Deep, Remains: Definitely Present, Accuracy: 20 Miles.

Brig *Orleans* (predates registry numbering) – Built 1846 at Clayton, NY – 173.55 gt. BOM, 100.75 x 20.0 x 8.5 ft. – 10/21/1855 – The brig *Orleans* was bound with lumber for Chicago when she was driven aground just south of the Government Pier at Milwaukee. Citizens staged a gallant rescue of the crew but the captain and mate perished. Vessel and cargo were a total loss. (Milwaukee Sentinel – October 23, 1855) Type: Stranding, Depth: Shallow, Remains: Probably Removed, Accuracy: 1/4 Mile.

Schooner *J. Steinhart* (predates registry numbering) – Built 1853 at Milwaukee – 68.64 gt. BOM, 72.83 x 18.67 x 5.67 ft. – 10/21/1855 – The schooner *J. Steinhart* was bound from Green Bay to Chicago with lumber when she became waterlogged and capsized 6 miles north of Milwaukee on the same day the *Orleans* wrecked. Her mate and cook perished. (Erie Weekly Gazette – November 1, 1855) Type: Foundering, Depth: Deep, Remains: Definitely Present, Accuracy: 5 Miles

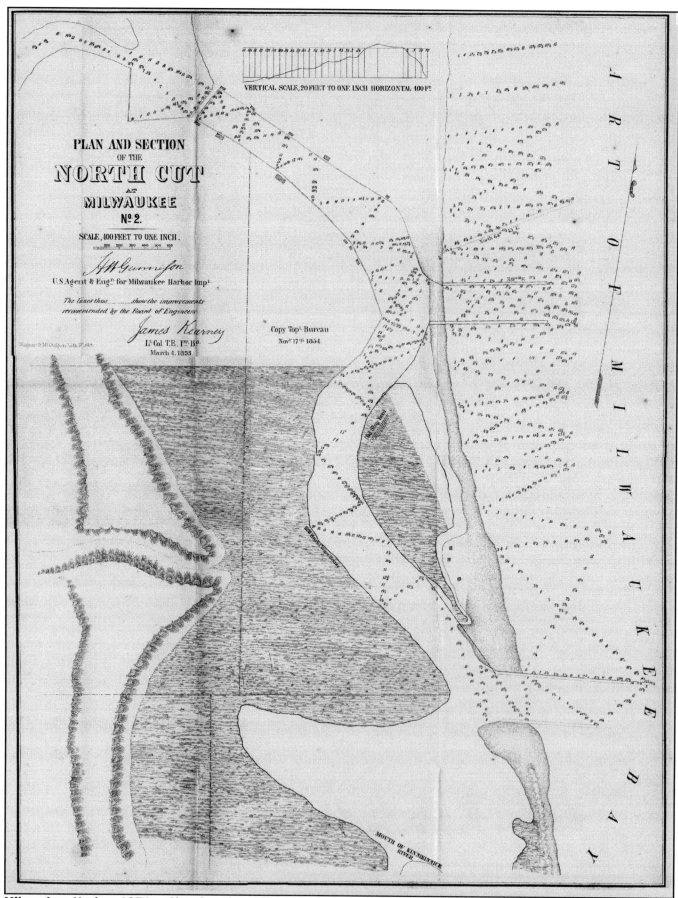

Milwaukee Harbor 1854 – Showing the old harbor entrance (site of many early wrecks) and the long planned straight cut entrance – House Ex. Doc. No. 1, 2nd Session, 33rd Congress – Original in Author's Collection

Schooner *John F. Porter* (predates registry numbering) – Built 1842 at Buffalo, NY on hull of steamer Cincinnati – 124.49 gt. BOM, 87.8 x 21 x 7.6 ft. – 10/22/1855 – The schooner Porter was bound from Chicago with provisions for the lumber camps when she capsized 3 miles off North Point. All but one of her crew made it ashore in the yawl, but the vessel was a total loss. She drifted into the shallows where she broke up. (Daily Wisconsin – October 23, 1855) Type: Stranding, Depth: Shallow, Remains: Possibly Present, Accuracy: 1 Mile.

Sidewheel Steamer *Alleghany* (predates registry numbering) – Built 1849 at Cleveland by Luther Moses – 468.02 gt. BOM, 177.2 x 25.0 x 10.11 ft. – 10/24/1855 – Only a month after the *Sebastopol* loss, another big sidewheeler was unable to find the unlighted harbor entrance and was driven aground just north of the *Sebastopol* wreck. The Alleghany was bound from Buffalo to Chicago with heavy merchandise when, failing to find the harbor piers, she anchored off shore. The storm felled her stack and she dragged ashore, fetching up barely 100 ft. from shore. Reports that her remains have been located are unsubstantiated. (Milwaukee Sentinel – October 22, 1855) Type: Stranding, Depth: Shallow, Remains: Possibly Present, Accuracy: 1 Mile.

Schooner *Rover* (predates registry numbering) – Built 1854 at Manitowoc, WI, 35.74 gt. BOM, 2 masts. – The little schooner Rover went ashore near the south pier in October of 1855 and spent the entire winter on the beach. Although feared lost, she was repaired and put back in service, only to be sunk with only her mastheads showing on September 12, 1856 off South Point. She was carrying brick and was reported a total loss. Despite her difficult circumstances, she was raised and put back in service by her owner, J.H. Meyer of Milwaukee. She was lost in October 1858 north of Manistee Michigan. (Milwaukee News – October 13, 1856) Type: Foundering, Depth: Shallow, Remains: Definitely Recovered, Accuracy: 1 Mile.

Milwaukee Harbor 1854 - Wisconsin Historical Society

Brig *Nebraska* (predates registry numbering) – Built 1849 at Milwaukee by Hubbell – 240.71 gt. BOM, 121.3 x 23.9 x 9.0 ft. – 10/19/1856 – The *Nebraska* was run down by the propeller *Oriental* off Racine and began sinking with her cargo of brick. She tried to run for Milwaukee harbor but fetched up very near the *Sebastopol* wreck where she broke up. The *Oriental* was libeled for her value of $5,500. (Milwaukee Sentinel – October 25, 1856) Type: Stranding, Depth: Shallow, Remains: Possibly Present, Accuracy: 1/4 Mile.

Schooner *Storm King* (predates registry numbering) – Built 1856 at Buffalo, New York by B.B. Jones, 130.0 x 28.3 x 11.0 ft., 375 gt. BOM – The schooner Storm King was dismasted and badly damaged in a gale near the Manitous in November of 1856. Her captain had her towed to Milwaukee where she sank in the harbor and was declared a total loss. After spending the winter on the bottom of the harbor, she was raised and rebuilt at the Jones Shipyard. She was lost off the Manitous in a June 1861 collision with the steamer *Michigan*. (Milwaukee Sentinel – April 26, 1857) Type: Foundering, Depth: Shallow, Remains: Definitely Recovered, Accuracy: 1 Mile.

Schooner *Emily* (predates registry numbering) – Built 1853 at Milwaukee by J.M. Jones – 69 gt. BOM, 65.0 x 19.25 x 6.5 ft. – April 1857 – The little schooner Emily vanished on a trip from Milwaukee to Sand Bay, Door County with 5 crew, including the captain's wife. She left on April 16th and was never seen again. A storm struck soon after she departed. (Milwaukee Sentinel – April 27, 1857) Type: Foundering, Depth: Very Deep, Remains: Definitely Present, Accuracy: 40 Miles.

Brig *Cumberland* (predates registry numbering) – Built 1844 at Cleveland by S.W. Turner – 195.87 gt. BOM, 100.6 x 23.6 x 9.2 ft. – 10/20/1859 – The *Cumberland* was moored near the end of the south pier of the new straight cut when she was struck astern by the schooner *Curlew*. Her stern settled and the waves pounded her against the pier until she broke up. She was carrying lumber from Oconto to Chicago. (Milwaukee Sentinel – October 21, 1859, November 5, 1859) Type: Foundering, Depth: Shallow, Remains: Probably Removed, Accuracy: 1/4 Mile.

Schooner *Twin Brothers* (predates registry numbering) – Built 1848 at Milwaukee by George Barber – 143.40 gt. BOM, 90.5 x 21.5 x 8.2 ft. – 3/11/1860 – The *Twin Brothers* had departed for Sheboygan when she was found to be leaking. She ran back inside the piers and was pounded on the south pier until she stove a hole in her hull. She capsized and sank broadside in the channel, a total loss. (Milwaukee Sentinel – March 13, 1860) Type: Foundering, Depth: Shallow, Remains: Probably Removed, Accuracy: 1/4 Mile.

Schooner *Champion* (predates registry numbering) – Built 1844 at Milwaukee by Samuel Farmin, 205.73 gt. BOM. – The schooner *Champion* was an early Milwaukee build. She was lost on September 13, 1860 when she capsized and sank five miles south of Milwaukee. Her crew of 8 was rescued by the propeller *Plymouth* but the *Champion* was a total loss. (C. Patrick Labadie Vessel File, 1860 Underwriters Accident List) Type: Foundering, Depth: Shallow, Remains: Probably Present, Accuracy: 5 Miles.

Brig *Algomah* (predates registry numbering) – Built 1845 at Cape Vincent, New York by L. Goler, 114.9 x 25.9 x 10 ft., 269.14 gt. BOM, fully rigged brig, 1 deck, 2 masts, square stern, plain stem - This brig was stranded and reported lost at Milwaukee in March 1856 and again in July 1861. However, she was last enrolled at Chicago in September 1862 and appeared in news reports and registers as late as 1866. Her ultimate fate is unknown, but she survived her Milwaukee strandings. (Herman Runge Wreck List)

Scow Schooner *Angelique* (29299) – Built 1855 at Detroit, MI, 43.0 gt. BOM, 66.7 x 18.4 x 4.0 ft., sometimes seen as *Angeline*. - The scow schooner *Angelique* capsized off North Point and fetched up 200 ft. from shore on Milwaukee's North Point bound Chicago to St. Joseph, MI with a cargo of shingles on November 18, 1863. Her crew was rescued by the schooner Norway, but her captain perished. Her hull lay off the beach midway between the hospital and the lighthouse. The vessel was recovered in spring and sailed for many more years, her last enrollment being April 1887 at Detroit. (Miilwaukee Sentinel – May 1866, Customs House Wreck Index) Type: Stranding, Depth: Shallow, Remains: Definitely Recovered, Accuracy: 1 Mile.

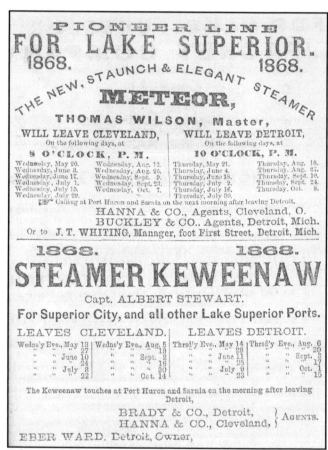

Trip Through the Great Lakes 1868 Ed. – John Disturnell - Author's Collection

Bark *Emily A. Roelofson* (predates registry numbering) – Built 1854 at Buffalo, NY by George S. Weeks – 385.23 gt. BOM, 138.0 x 26.0 x 11.5 ft. – 11/18/1863 – This 3 masted bark had been wrecked on a reef near Eagle Harbor in Green Bay in 9/1855. She was freed and towed to Milwaukee for rebuild, but was abandoned in the Milwaukee River. (SHSW Wisconsin Shipwreck Database) Type: Abandonment, Depth: Shallow, Remains: Probably Removed, Accuracy: 1 Mile.

Schooner *Union* (predates registry numbering) – Built 1848 at Racine, WI, 87.90 gt. BOM - The schooner *Union* of Racine was reported lost when she drove ashore at South Milwaukee on 5/11/1864. She disappears from all lists and enrollments following this accident and is believed to have been a total loss. (Erik Heyl Wreck List, Herman Runge Wreck List) Type: Stranding, Depth: Surfline, Remains: Possibly Present, Accuracy: 1 Mile.

Steamer *May Queen* – Early American Steamers, Erik Heyl

Sidewheel Steamer *May Queen* (b.1853) – Built 1853 at Trenton, Michigan by Eli Bates, 220 x 30 x 13 ft., 688 gt. BOM, later 527 gt. – The Goodrich steamer *May Queen* burned and sank during winter layup at Jones Island on January 15, 1866 and was declared a total loss. The hull was raised in June 1866 and the engines put in the steamer *Manitowoc*. The hull was sold for $600 and rebuilt as the barge *May Queen*. The barge broke up in a gale while under tow and foundered off Saugatuck, MI on 10/31/1868. (Early American Steamers – Erik Heyl) Type: Burning, Depth: Shallow, Remains: Definitely Recovered, Accuracy: 1/4 Mile.

Looking South at Milwaukee Harbor 1860s from an original stereoview – Author's Collection

Schooner *Elizabeth* (predates registry numbering) – Built 1863 at Milwaukee, Wisconsin, 40.5 x 12.8 x 4.6 ft., 20.32 gt. BOM, 2 masts - Listed as crushed by ice at Milwaukee in 1864 on the SHSW database, this vessel was actually recovered and lost at Kenosha on 8/11/1866. Although several schooners *Elizabeth* were active on the Lakes at this time, only one was active on Lake Michigan. (Milwaukee Sentinel – August 21, 1866) Type: Foundering, Depth: Shallow, Remains: Definitely Recovered, Accuracy: 1/4 Mile.

Schooner *Free Mason* (predates registry numbering) – Built 1854 at Green Bay, WI – 26.96 gt., 51.9 x 14.5 x 5.6 ft. – 4/2/1866 – The *Free Mason* was bound Chicago to Milwaukee when she was swept from her moorings below Walker's Point Bridge and out through the straight cut into the Lake. She was towed in by the tug *Davidson* and made fast to the south pier where she lay a total wreck. Her remains were almost certainly removed. (Milwaukee Sentinel – April 3, 1866) Type: Foundering, Depth: Shallow, Remains: Probably Removed, Accuracy: 1/4 Mile.

Scow Schooner *Tempest* (predates registry numbering) – Built 1854 at Fairport, OH – 60.21 gt. BOM, 80.25 x 18.84 x 4.93 ft. – 11/24/1867 – The *Tempest* was riding out a storm with a cargo of lumber for Chicago when she dragged her anchor and went aground off South Point. She broke her keel and was abandoned where she lay. (Milwaukee Sentinel – November 27, 1867) Type: Stranding, Depth: Surfline, Remains: Possibly Present, Accuracy: 1/4 Mile.

Scow Schooner at Milwaukee c. 1870 from an original stereoview – Author's Collection

Scow Schooner *Sunshine* (23057) – Built 1856 at Mt. Clemens, MI by Jerris Deprees – 60.21 gt. BOM, 97.0 x 24.0 x 6.2 ft. – 9/29/1869 – The *Sunshine* was bound from White Lake, MI to Milwaukee with lumber when she became waterlogged and stranded on North Point. She broke up and became a total loss. (Milwaukee Sentinel – October 5, 1869) Type: Stranding, Depth: Shallow, Remains: Possibly Present, Accuracy: 1 Mile.

Sidewheel Tug *Traffic* (24506) – Built 1853 at St. Clair, Michigan by O.V. Kellferich, 75 x 16 x 5 ft., 50 gt. - This vessel is reported by several sources, including an original Milwaukee Sentinel news account, to have burned at Milwaukee on October 11, 1869. However, she actually burned on the Saginaw River in Michigan where she was owned and most reliable sources place the loss there. (Milwaukee Sentinel – October 16, 1869)

Milwaukee Harbor 1874 - Wisconsin Historical Society

Schooner *Adell* (predates registry numbering) – Built 1860 at Milwaukee – 19.03 gt. BOM, 48 x 12 x 4.7 ft. – 11/16/1869 – The little schooner *Adell* was out in the disastrous gale of 1869 and was driven ashore at the south pier, 1 mile below the Bay View pier where she reportedly completely broke up. (Milwaukee Sentinel – December 8, 1869) Type: Stranding, Depth: Buried, Remains: Possibly Present, Accuracy: 1/4 Mile.

Schooner *A.B. Ward* (383) – Built 1854 at Philadelphia, PA as a tug – 32 gt. – 4/25/1870 – The *A.B. Ward* was bound Pentwater to Milwaukee with a cargo of potatoes and shingles when she was blown over by a squall 20 mi NE of Milwaukee. Her three crew perished but her hull was towed in by the scow *D.R. Owen* and abandoned at Milwaukee. She was a total loss. (Milwaukee Sentinel – April 27, 1870, Annual List of US Merchant Vessels) Type: Abandonment, Depth: Shallow, Remains: Probably Removed, Accuracy: 5 Miles.

The Milwaukee River in the 1860s from an original stereoview – Author's Collection

Schooner *Liberty* (14805) – Built 1835 at Avon, OH by Hawley Reed – 54.49 gt., 54.6 x 17.5 x 5.8 ft. – 4/6/1872 – The *Liberty* was by far the oldest ship on the Lakes when she was smashed against the Milwaukee pierheads and sank while trying to enter during a gale. One of her crew perished. She had been a pioneer Lake Erie vessel and may have been built on the bed of the original schooner *Liberty*, built by Hawley Reed at Buffalo in 1818. The venerable schooner refused to die, as in 1898, a storm brought up her remains and dashed them against the pierhead light once again. (Milwaukee Sentinel – April 16, 1872) Type: Foundering, Depth: Shallow, Remains: Probably Removed, Accuracy: 1/4 Mile.

Schooner *Challenge* (4574) – Built 1853 at Youngstown, New York by H.N. Throop at John Oades Yard, 96.0 x 20.8 x 8.75 ft., 99.31 gt., 2 masts, last enrolled Milw, 6/17/1876 – The three schooners *Challenge* on Lake Michigan have always presented a challenge to researchers. This schooner *Challenge* (4574) wrecked at Milwaukee on 11/11/1873 and was declared a total loss. However, she was recovered and taken overseas by Captain Kelly of Racine. She was engaged in the British coal trade and never returned to the Lakes. Two other Challenges also existed. The famous clipper built at Manitowoc in 1852 (4349) was lost near Sheboygan in 1910, the other (4386), built at Vermilion OH in 1852 was lost at Muskegon, MI in October of 1872. However, none of them were lost at Milwaukee as often reported. (Detroit Free Press – August 10, 1878, J.W. Hall Wrecklist 1872)

Milwaukee Harbor 1874 – Wisconsin Historical Society

Schooner *St. Peter* (23516) – Built 1868 at New Baltimore, MI by Peter Perry – 119.66 gt., 90.0 x 23.8 x 8.5 ft. - 5/5/1874 – Bound Chicago to Buffalo with 8000 bu of corn, the St. Peter was found to be leaking, which soon overwhelmed her pumps and sent her to the bottom. Her crew reported that they rowed the yawl 35 miles in a SW direction to reach Milwaukee (Milwaukee Sentinel – May 7 & 9, 1874) Type: Foundering, Depth: Very Deep, Remains: Definitely Present, Accuracy: 20 Miles.

Milwaukee River in the 1870s from an original woodcut – Author's Collection

Schooner *Union* (25045) – Built 1861 at Menekaunee, WI by N. Saunders – 17.94 gt., 54.0 x 18.0 x 5.5 ft. – 6/15/1874 – Many schooners Union plied the Lakes in the 1800s, but this one verifiably went ashore at South Milwaukee, a total loss. She was owned out of Manitowoc and disappears from lists and enrollments after 1874. (Milwaukee Public Library – Runge Card) Type: Stranding, Depth: Surfline, Remains: Possibly Present, Accuracy: 1 Mile.

Tug *Ida H. Lee* (100058) – Built 1865 at Buffalo, NY by Hingston Bros. – 35.66 gt., 44.8 x 10.0 x 5.0 ft. - 4/23/1874 – The *Ida H. Lee* was towing the schooner Ida 2 miles NE of the harbor entrance when the schooner struck her stern, holing her. She took on water, capsized and foundered in 50 ft. of water, a total loss, with one life. Remains attributed to her have been reported in 50 ft of water north of the Milwaukee Harbor entrance but have not been substantiated to date. (Milwaukee Sentinel – September 15, 1875, Port Huron Daily Times – April 25, 1874, Runge Wrecklist) Type: Foundering, Depth: Shallow, Remains: Located, Accuracy: Identified.

Scow Sloop *Hurrah Boys* (95341) – Built 1872 at Racine, WI by Anthony Beffol – 13.68 gt., 37.1 x 13.0 x 3.6 ft. – 7/23/1874 – The *Hurrah Boys* was carrying stone for the water works cribs when she was driven ashore off Milwaukee's Third Ward. She was initially thought salvageable, but was dismantled and abandoned where she lay. (Milwaukee Sentinel – August 1, 1874) Type: Abandonment, Depth: Surfline, Remains: Probably Removed, Accuracy: 1/4 Mile.

Looking south on the Kinnickinnic River 1876 at the Dr. Enoch Chase Farm - Author's Collection

The Bark *Tanner* - Historical Collections of the Great Lakes

Bark *Tanner* (24236) – Built 1863 at Milwaukee by Ellsworth & Davidson – 434.95 gt., 157.9 x 32.3 x 13.2 ft. – 9/9/1875 – The big bark *Tanner* with a full cargo of wheat from Chicago to Buffalo was under tow into the harbor, when the line parted. The ship was driven south past the straight cut and fetch up on the old harbor piers where she sank with her decks submerged. Her back soon broke and her spars fell. She was declared a total loss. (Milwaukee Sentinel – September 11, 1875) Type: Foundering, Depth: Shallow, Remains: Possibly Present, Accuracy: 1/4 Mile.

Schooner *Buena Vista* (none) – Built 1847 at Chicago, Illinois by Francis Jordan, 174.03 gt. BOM, 104.3x23.3x7.9 ft., 1 deck, 2 masts, scroll stem – The schooner *Buena Vista* is listed on the SHSW database as lost at Milwaukee in August of 1875. This accident actually occurred at Perry's Pier near Manistee, Michigan and the ship was recovered. There were two schooners *Buena Vista* on Lake Michigan. The one shown above was lost in December of 1857 a few miles south of Sheboygan. Another slightly larger schooner *Buena Vista* (2241) built 1847 at Cleveland, OH was involved in many Lake Michigan accidents from which she was declared a total loss. However, she ended her days in 1887 in the Milwaukee River Bone Yard. (Milwaukee Sentinel – August 12, 1875)

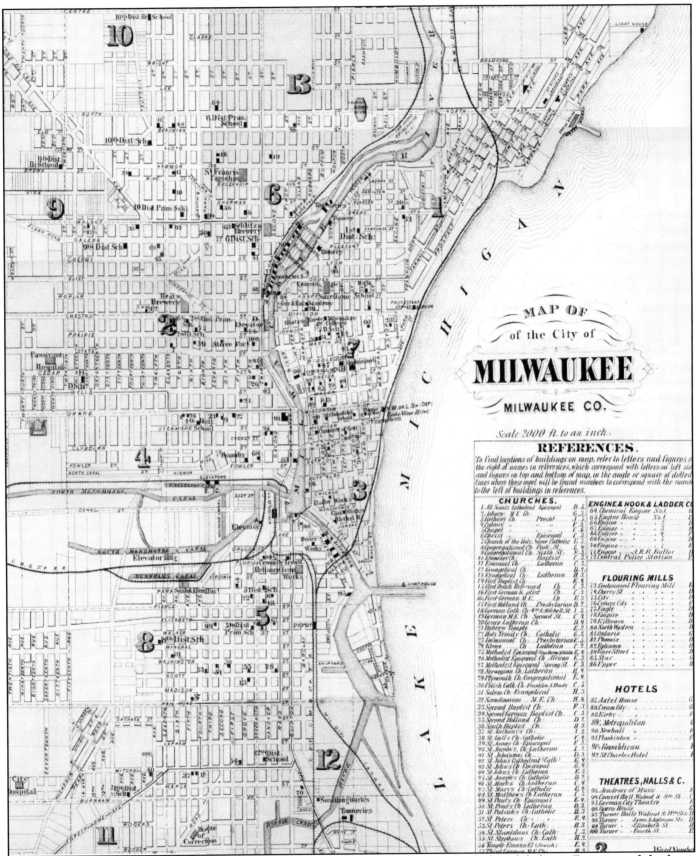

Milwaukee 1877 showing both harbor entrances, the canal system and major industrial sites - From an original in the Author's Collection

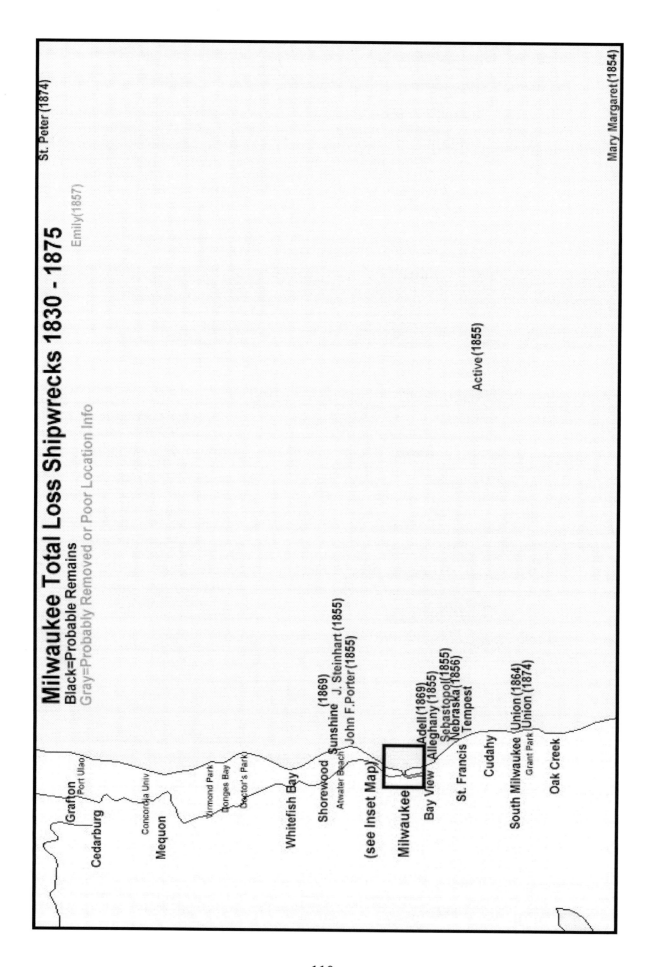

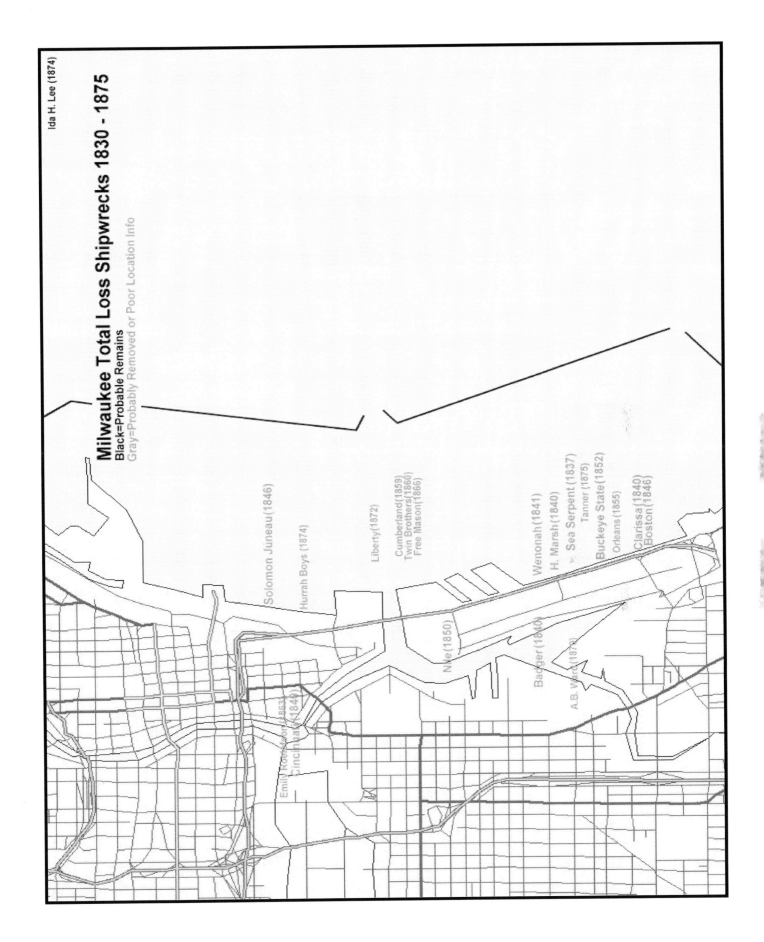

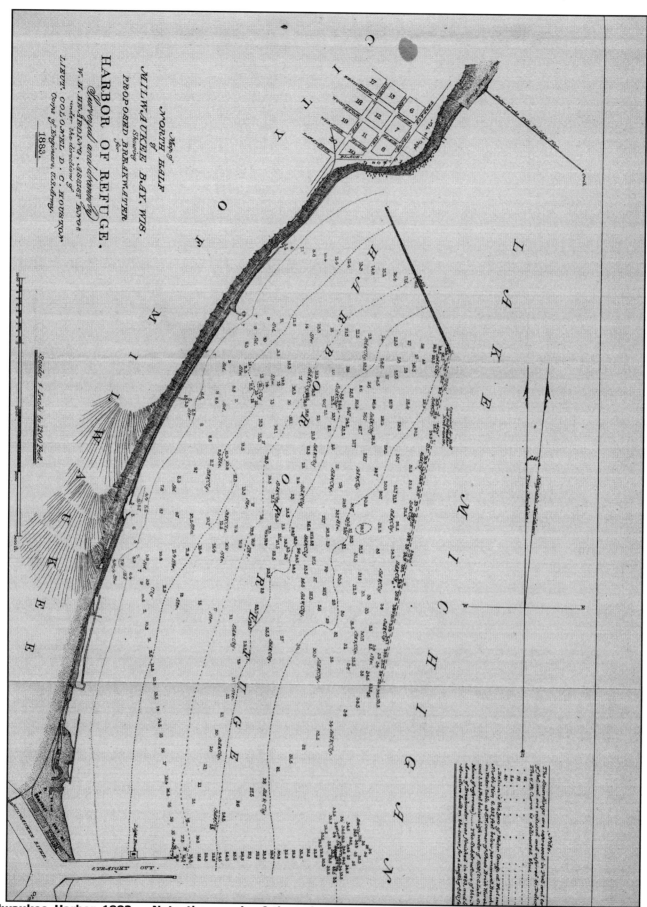

Milwaukee Harbor 1883 – Note the wreck of the schooner *Thomas A. Scott* off the straight cut – Author's Collection

Milwaukee Shipwrecks 1875-1900

By 1875, Milwaukee had become one of the leading port cities of the Lakes and become the center of the grain trade. Large three and four masted schooners pulled up to the grain elevators daily and hundreds of vessels traversed Milwaukee's waters each day. This period saw the industrialization of the city and the modernization of Milwaukee's waterfront. It also saw the dominant trade on the Lakes change from wooden sail to giant steel bulk freighters. The following list details all the historic total loss shipwrecks known in Milwaukee County from 1875 to 1900. It is likely that some qualifying wrecks were missed in this listing due to sparse reporting and scant records, but this lists probably comprises the vast majority. A significant number of vessels were also scuttled and abandoned in and outside the harbor during this period without any media reports. Many of these vessels will consequently, not appear in this list, and many hulls and keels litter the bottom off Milwaukee that are difficult to identify because they are not the result of an accident.

Milwaukee Pierheads 1880 from an original woodcut – Author's Collection

Schooner *St. Lawrence* (22584) – Built 1842 at Clayton, NY by George Barber – 92.8 x 19.8 x 8.0 ft., 110.76 gt., scroll stem – 4/30/1878 – The schooner *St. Lawrence* was under way with a lumber cargo 25 miles ESE of Milwaukee when a kettle of sealing pitch on her stove spilled, lighting her cabin on fire. The crew launched the yawl, which capsized, drowning Captain Larkin and a passenger. The crew were taken off by the schooner *Granada*, but the *St. Lawrence* burned and foundered. (Milwaukee Sentinel – May 2, 1878) Type: Foundering, Depth: Very Deep, Remains: Definitely Present, Accuracy: 10 Miles.

Schooner *Swallow* (57280) – Built 1860 at Gibraltar, MI by D. Brown – 84.0 x 20.5 x 6.7 ft., 89 gt., 2 masts – 12/31/1878 – According to marine historian Herman Runge, this lumber schooner was driven aground at South Milwaukee with a load of lumber late in the 1878 season. She was a total loss and disappears from the Annual Lists of US Merchant Vessels after 1878. (Runge Card, MVUS) Type: Stranding, Depth: Surfline, Remains: Possibly Removed, Accuracy: 1 Mile.

Schooner *Liberty* (14672) – Built 1861 at Cottrellville, MI by L. Larned – 81.44 gt., 2 masts – 12/16/1879 – The schooner *Liberty* became badly iced up and unmanageable off Milwaukee's South Point. She was driven ashore on the extreme end of the point and was broken in two by a northeast sea the following day. (Chicago Tribune – December 18, 1879) Type: Stranding, Depth: Shallow, Remains: Possibly Removed, Accuracy: 1 Mile.

Schooners *Honest John*, *Elbe* and *Buena Vista* in the Menomonee River Boneyard c. 1888 – Milwaukee Public Library Marine Collection

Schooner *Honest John* (11180) – Built 1849 at Oak Creek, WI by David Clow – 98 gt., 89.3 x 21.9 x 7.1 ft., 2 masts – 4/2/1880 – The old schooner *Honest John* was abandoned in the corner of the slip near the Chicago, Milwaukee & St. Paul elevator A. There, she was later joined the schooners *Lewis Ludington* (14804), *Buena Vista* (2241) and *Elbe* (7519), to start the Milwaukee ship boneyard. The remains are thought to have been removed by harbor improvements. (MPL – Runge Card, Hirthe – Schooner Days in Door County) Type: Abandonment, Depth: Shallow, Remains: Definitely Removed, Accuracy: 1/4 Mile.

Bay View Rolling Mills just south of the harbor, 1910 – Author's Collection

Scow Schooner *Evergreen* (8301) – Built 1868 at Holland, MI – 67.75 gt., 71.3 x 20.0 x 6.2 ft. – 4/16/1880 – Bound Muskegon to Racine with lumber, the *Evergreen* was driven aground in a gale between Milwaukee's south pier and the Bay View rolling mill docks. Her crew was rescued by bystanders, but the ship went to pieces. (Chicago Inter-Ocean – April 17, 1880) Type: Stranding, Depth: Surfline, Remains: Possibly Removed, Accuracy: 1 Mile.

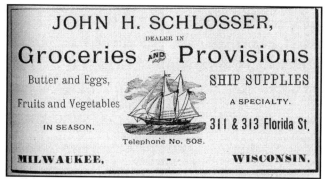
Polk's Marine Directory 1884 – Author's Collection

Schooner *Kearsarge* (14042) – Built 1865 at Clayton, OH by John Oades – 153.65 gt. – 10/12/1880 – The schooner *Kearsarge* was bound from Traverse Bay to Chicago with lumber when she fetch up on Racine Reef in fog. The US Lifesaving Service rescued her crew and the schooner was pulled free. However, she capsized when pulled off and was towed to Milwaukee on her beam ends. She fetched up offshore south of Milwaukee and broke up. (Chicago Inter-Ocean October 20, 1880, USLSS Annual Report 1881) Type: Stranding, Depth: Shallow, Remains: Probably Present, Accuracy: 5 Miles.

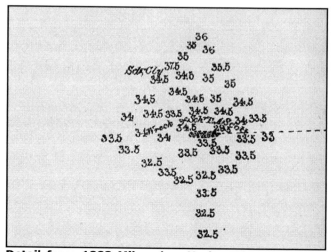
Detail from 1883 Milwaukee Harbor Chart showing the wreck of the schooner *Thomas A. Scott* off the Straight Cut – Author's Collection

Schooner Barge *Thomas A. Scott* (24785) – Built 1869 at Buffalo, NY by Hitchcock & Gibson as a steamer – 740 gt., 207.0 x 33.0 x 13.0 ft., 4 masts – 10/29/1880 – The *Thomas A. Scott* had been built as one of the largest steamers on the Lakes, but was refitted as a giant 4-masted grain barge in 1877. She was at anchor 3/4 mile off the harbor entrance with a corn cargo when she was struck by the steamer *Avon* and sunk in approximately 30 ft of water. Plan to raise her were never carried out and she was salvaged by divers where she lay. She remained a hazard to shipping for years. Fragments of her giant hull-bed were located by Jerry Guyer, but her hull has been completely disarticulated by dredging in the area. (Milwaukee Sentinel – March 24, 1881) Type: Foundering, Depth: Shallow, Remains: Located, Accuracy: Identified.

Artist rendering of the *E.M. Carrington* new – Milwaukee Public Library Marine Collection

Schooner *E.M. Carrington* (8104) – Built 1866 at Port Huron, MI by A.S. Stewart – 121.15 gt., 88.0 x 22.4 x 8.4 ft., 2 masts – 11/5/1880 – Bound Muskegon to Milwaukee with lumber, the *Carrington* became waterlogged and began to sink about 25 miles SE of Milwaukee. Vessels in the area didn't realize she was in distress and she soon capsized drowning her four crew. Although most sources state she was a total loss, at least one account claims she was towed in and salvaged. She does appear in MVUS until 1882. (Milwaukee Sentinel – November 20, 1880, David Swayze) Type: Foundering, Depth: Very Deep, Remains: Possibly Removed, Accuracy: 10 Miles.

The steamer *St. Albans* at Milwaukee c. 1880 – courtesy of the Historical Collections of the Great Lakes

Propeller *St. Albans* (23514) – Built 1868 at Cleveland, OH by Ira Lafrienier – 435.75 gt., 135 x 26 x 11 ft. – 1/30/1881 – Bound Milwaukee to Ludington with 27 passengers and crew, the Northern Transportation Co. steamer St. Albans was about 15 miles NE of Milwaukee when she holed herself below the waterline on an ice cake. She foundered slowly, allowing the passengers and crew to escape in the lifeboats, but the ship foundered in 160 ft of water. Her remains were located in 1976 by Kent Bellrichard and Richard Zaleski and are now a popular dive site. (Milwaukee Sentinel – January 31, 1881) Type: Foundering, Depth: Deep, Remains: Located, Accuracy: Identified.

Milwaukee River 1879 – Wisconsin Historical Society

Schooner *J.P. DeCoudres* (75530) – Built 1873 at Saugatuck, MI by Thomas Yandis on the hull of the sch. Appleton (1551) – 146.16 gt., 119.5 x 22.8 x 6.6 ft., 3 masts – 6/3/1882 – Bound Charlevoix to Milwaukee with cordwood, the *DeCoudres'* steering gear became disabled in heavy seas and the vessel stranded just off the beach and next to the breakwall, 1 mile north of the lifesaving station at the foot of Juneau St. The lifesavers rescued the 7 crew by breeches-buoy and the schooner broke up completely within a few days. (Chicago Inter-Ocean – June 5, 1882, USLSS Annual Report 1883) Type: Stranding, Depth: Surfline, Remains: Probably Removed, Accuracy: 1/4 Mile.

Tug *Rudolph Wetzel* c. 1880 – courtesy C. Patrick Labadie Collection, Thunder Bay National Marine Sanctuary

Customs House Wreck Report for the Rudolph Wetzel – National Archives

Steam Tug *Rudolph Wetzel* (21944) – Built 1870 at Buffalo, NY by George Notter – 23.25 gt., 56.4 x 14.0 x 6.6 ft. – 10/28/1882 – The tug *Rudolph Wetzel* was racing the tug *Henry S Sill* about 3 miles off Oak Creek in competition for a tow when she exploded her boiler. The blast was extremely powerful, killing her 3 crew and completely destroying the *Wetzel* above deck, but her hull reportedly sank in 7 fathoms. Despite many searches and a well known location, her remains have yet to be identified. (Chicago Inter-Ocean – October 30, 1882) Type: Foundering, Depth: Shallow, Remains: Possibly Removed, Accuracy: 1 Mile.

Schooner *Collingwood* (4344) – Built 1855 at Buffalo, NY by F.N. Jones – 258.17 gt., 131.8 x 28.4 x 11.1 ft., 2 masts, scroll stem – 11/23/1882 – The *Collingwood* was bound from St Helena Island in the Straits for Chicago with a load of cedar shingles when she became waterlogged, eventually capsizing about 15 mi NE of Milwaukee and about 15 miles from shore. 3 of hr 8 crew were rescued in the yawl after a harrowing 31 hours adrift. Her hull was initially attributed to a wreck that later proved to be the *Tennie & Laura*. At least one account states that her hull later came ashore. (Door County Advocate – November 30, 1882) Type: Foundering, Depth: Very Deep, Remains: Possibly Removed, Accuracy: 10 Miles.

Propeller *R.G. Peters* (110424) – Built 1880 at Milwaukee by Milwaukee Shipyard – 386.04 gt., 175.4 x 31.0 x 10.5 ft. – 12/1/1882 – Bound Chicago to Manistee in a gale with consort schooner *A.W. Luckey*, the *Peters* was found to be on fire about 3 AM. She burned so quickly that none of the 14 crew could escape. She reportedly burned to the water's edge and sank 20-25 miles SE of Milwaukee in deep water. (Chicago Inter-Ocean – December 4, 1882) Type: Foundering, Depth: Very Deep, Remains: Definitely Present, Accuracy: 10 Miles.

Scow Schooner *Midge* (16643) – Built 1866 at Green Bay, WI by S.C. Fowler – 23.83 gt., 53.0 x 13.6 x 6.0 ft., 2 masts – 5/9/1883 – The little scow *Midge* was bound from White Lake, MI to Milwaukee with 40 tons of lumber when she dropped her anchors in an attempt to ride out a gale. Her hooks dragged and she stranded about 8 miles south of the harbor entrance. She proved a total loss (Milwaukee Customs House Wreck Report – May 12, 1883). Type: Stranding, Depth: Surfline, Remains: Probably Present, Accuracy: 1 Mile.

Milwaukee Harbor and Environs 1881 from Flower's History of Milwaukee - Wisconsin Historical Society

Milwaukee Shipyard 1880s – from an original stereoview – Author's Collection

Scow Schooner *Sailor Boy* (23105) – Built 1866 at Algonac, MI by C.E. Owen – 76.00 gt., 75.0 x 21.0 x 6.7 ft., 2 masts – 5/21/1883 – Bound from Pierport, MI to Milwaukee with lumber, the *Sailor Boy* was trying to ride out a storm at anchor when her chains parted, casting her upon the beach 2 miles south of the harbor entrance at Bay View. The crew made it ashore with the help of local citizens and the ship went to pieces within days. (USLSS Annual Report - 1883) Type: Stranding, Depth: Surfline, Remains: Probably Removed, Accuracy: 1/4 Mile.

Polk's Marine Directory 1884 – Author's Collection

Scow Schooner *Sea Bird* (23390) – Built 1855 at Conneaut, OH by M. Woodworth – 139.84 gt., 99.6 x 23.3 x 6.6 ft., 2 masts – 7/21/1883 – The *Sea Bird* was bound Muskegon to Chicago with lumber when she capsized in a gale about midlake. Her hull was found floating about 30 miles off Milwaukee with the yawl gone and no sign of the 10 crew and passengers, who all perished. The hull was later seen 20 miles off Milwaukee and is believe to have foundered in deep water somewhere off Milwaukee after three weeks afloat. (Milwaukee Sentinel – July 25, 1883) Type: Foundering, Depth: Very Deep, Remains: Definitely Present, Accuracy: 10 Miles.

Polk's Marine Directory 1884 – Author's Collection

Schooner *Ashtabula* (367) – Built 1852 at Ashtabula, OH by G. Thayer – 95.31 gt., 89.6 x 21.0 x 7.38 ft., 2 masts, scroll stem – 11/11/1883 – Bound Chicago to Escanaba with barreled salt, tar and sundries, the *Ashtabula* was found to be leaking when about 15 miles north of Milwaukee. She turned about to run for the harbor, but reportedly capsized three miles off North Point. The crew made it into the yawl before the schooner settled to the bottom, reportedly with only 4 ft of her topmasts breaking the surface. A diver visited the site shortly after to assess the possibility of recovering the vessel, but due to her age she was probably left on the bottom. Despite many searches of the area, the *Ashtabula's* remains have never been positively identified but divers claim to have located and dived this wreck in the 1970s. (Milwaukee Sentinel – November 13, 1883) Type: Foundering, Depth: Deep, Remains: Probably Present, Accuracy: 5 Miles.

Schooner *Elbe* (7519) – Built 1853 at Chicago by Doolittle & Miller, 78.9 x 18.0 x 6.9 ft., 67 gt. – The old schooner *Elbe* stranded at Whitefish Bay in June 1883. She was pulled free and abandoned in the Milwaukee River boneyard near St. Paul Elevator A. Her final enrollment was surrendered in 1889 and her remains have likely been removed. (US Life Saving Service Annual Report – 1883) Type: Abandonment, Depth: Shallow, Remains: Definitely Removed, Accuracy: 1/4 Mile.

Scow *Toboggan* (unregistered) – Built 1886 at Milwaukee by Milwaukee Shipyard – Not enrolled – believe to be about 150 x 30 ft. – Carried a steam hoist for loading and unloading - 7/12/1887 – Described in news accounts as an "Ark," the *Toboggan* was a big unregistered flat barge meant to be towed in the harbor. She was overloaded and being towed from Manistee to Milwaukee by the steamer *Marshall F. Butters* with a cargo of barreled salt and lumber, when she began leaking and capsized, going to the bottom about 15 miles off Milwaukee. Her crew escaped in a yawl. Paul Ehorn reports that he and John Steele may have dived this site in the early 1980s in 250 ft of water off Milwaukee. Paul noted that it had an A-frame unloading apparatus on the deck. (Milwaukee Sentinel – July 13, 1887) Type: Foundering, Depth: Very Deep, Remains: Definitely Present, Accuracy: 5 Miles. (See detailed account in Part 3)

Scow Schooner *Hunter* (11301) – Built 1855 at Milan, OH by Smith, Kelly & Lockwood – 131,75 gt., 100.75 x 24.3 x 7.1, 2 masts – 17/12/1887 – The Milwaukee Tug Co's sand scow *Hunter* was unloading between the East Water Street and Broadway Bridges when she became unbalanced and capsized, going to the bottom upside-down in 15 ft of water. Her steam gear thrust upward through the bottom of her hull, ending her career. (Milwaukee Sentinel – July 13, 1887) Type: Foundering, Depth: Shallow, Remains: Possibly Present, Accuracy: 1/4 Miles. (See detailed account in Part 3)

Schooner *Maine* (16402) – Built 1852 at Black River, OH by W.B. Linn – 102.8 x 25.3 x 6.7 ft., 151.77 gt., 2 masts, scroll stem - 10/23/1887 – The old schooner *Maine* was bound from White Lake, MI for Chicago with a cargo of railroad ties when she parted the line from the tug towing her into shelter at Milwaukee harbor. She dragged ashore stern first, 250 yards south of the harbor piers, 150 ft from shore, where the lifesavers took off her 6 crew in a daring rescue. The old schooner quickly broke up and her cargo floated around the Lakes for months, a menace to navigation. (Milwaukee Sentinel – October 24, 1887) Type: Stranding, Depth: Surfline, Remains: Probably Removed, Accuracy: 1/4 Miles. (See detailed account in Part 3)

Steambarge *Josephine* (75763) – Built 1874 at Milwaukee by Allen, McLelland & Co – 99 x 25 x 6 ft., 146 gt., - 4/14/1888 – The barge *Josephine* was steaming up Whitefish Bay with a cargo of sand under the command of her first mate when she strayed too close to shore and struck a rock, holing her hull and settling to the bottom in the shallows 2 miles north of the North Point Light. Debris off Atwater Beach formerly ascribed to her is actually part of the Appomattox. The *Josephine's* remains have yet to be identified and may have been removed. (Milwaukee Customs House Wreck Report – April 17, 1888) Type: Stranding, Depth: Shallow, Remains: Probably Removed, Accuracy: 1 Mile.

Tug *A.W. Lawrence* (105948) – Built 1880 at Sturgeon Bay, WI by John Gregory – 72 x 16 x 9 ft., 48.41 gt., - 10/30/1888 – The tug *A.W. Lawrence* was off about 3 miles off North Point awaiting sailing vessels in need of a tow when she exploded her boiler killing 4 of her 6 occupants. The tug *J.B. Merrill* rescued the survivors but the *Lawrence* went to the bottom. Jerry Guyer believes he may have located her remains in 2005. (Milwaukee Customs House Wreck Report – November 7, 1888) Type: Foundering, Depth: Deep, Remains: Definitely Present, Accuracy: 5 Miles.

Schooner *Union* (25046) – Built 1867 at Sheboygan, WI by Arne Johnson – 55.6 x 16.5 x 6.2 ft., 41.0 gt., 2 masts - 11/5/1888 – The schooner *Union* capsized and went ashore at Milwaukee in a November storm. Specifics on the exact location have yet to be determined, but the vessel was abandoned as a total loss. (Runge Card, C. Patrick Labadie Collection) Type: Stranding, Depth: Shallow, Remains: Possibly Present, Accuracy: 10 Miles.

Tug *Starke Brothers* in action c. 1880 – courtesy C. Patrick Labadie Collection, Thunder Bay National Marine Sanctuary

Tug *Starke Brothers* (115226) – Built 1872 at Buffalo, NY by George Notter – 61.4 x 15.4 x 8.0 ft., 35.0 gt, - 1889 – The harbor tug *Starke Brothers* was abandoned in 1889 at Milwaukee. Whether she was sunk in the Harbor or scuttled offshore is unknown. (Herman Runge Index Card) Type: Abandonment, Depth: Shallow, Remains: Possibly Present, Accuracy: 10 Miles.

Tug *Dexter* (6804) – Built 1873 at Milwaukee by Nathan Brooks – 58.0 x 12.4 x 7.0 ft., 23.67 gt, - 1889 – The harbor tug *Dexter* was abandoned in 1889 at Milwaukee. Her engine was removed and she was scuttled. Whether she was sunk in the Harbor of offshore is unknown. (Herman Runge Index Card) Type: Abandonment, Depth: Shallow, Remains: Possibly Present, Accuracy: 10 Miles.

Propeller *Monitor* (90163) – Built 1870 at Detroit by Campbell & Owen – 92.5 x 23.0 x 7.6 ft., 128.19 gt, - 8/19/1890 – The rabbit steamer *Monitor* was bound from Pierport, MI to Milwaukee with tan bark when she began leaking and foundered about 20 mi NE of Racine in a fierce NW gale. The crew barely escaped and were rescued by a passing schooner. The *Monitor* had a single cylinder steam engine of 14x16" and a single tubular steam boiler of 5x12'. (Port Huron Daily Times – August 20, 1890) Type: Foundering, Depth: Very Deep, Remains: Definitely Present, Accuracy: 5 Miles.

Wreck Report for the schooner *Dawn* - National Archives

Schooner *Dawn* (6127) – Built 1858 at Clayton, New York by John Oades, 87.37 x 19.1 x 7.5 ft., 82.24 gt., 2 masts, enrollment surrendered Milwaukee 4/13/1892, total loss. - The schooner *Dawn* capsized in heavy seas off Port Washington on August 23, 1891 with 100,000 ft. of Maple lumber in her hold and on her deck. Her crew was rescued by the steamer *John Schroeder* but her hull later drifted ashore near Fox Point where it broke up in the surf. (Milwaukee Sentinel – August 24, 1891) Type: Stranding, Depth: Surfline, Remains: Possibly Present, Accuracy: 1 Mile.

Schooner *M.C. Springer* (91936) – Built 1887 at Red River, WI by A.S. Tibbetts – 32.0 x 11.5 x 4.9 ft., 10.38 gt, - 10/8/1892 – The little schooner *M.C. Springer* was bound light for Menominee, MI when she struck a sunken hulk off Oak Creek, knocking a hole in her hull. The crew was able to get the *Springer* into Milwaukee Harbor before she sank, a total loss. (Milwaukee Customs House Wreck Report – August 25, 1894) Type: Foundering, Depth: Shallow, Remains: Possibly Present, Accuracy: 5 Miles.

Schooner *Snow Drop* (22377) – Built 1853 at Conneaut, OH by J.W. Lent – 125.8 x 24.8 x 7.8 ft., 190.38 gt, - 4/30/1892 – The old schooner *Snow Drop* was attempting to enter the harbor in a storm with a cargo of cedar posts from Ford River when her rigging became fouled and she was driven on the rocks just off the North Point Lighthouse. After an unsuccessful rescue attempt by the tug *Coe*, the tug *Starke*, with lifesavers in tow, rescued the drenched crew from the roof of the schooner's cabin. In the late 1970s a keel and ribs ascribed to the *Snow Drop* were located off the old North Point pumping station known as Love Rock. Subsequent efforts to relocate the remains have been unsuccessful. (Milwaukee Sentinel – May 1, 1892) Type: Stranding, Depth: Shallow, Remains: Probably Present, Accuracy: 1 Mile. (See detailed account in Part 3)

Beeson's Marine Directory 1902 - Author's Collection

Scow Schooner *Alma* (106517) – Built 1887 at Milwaukee by Henry S. Downer – 57.4 x 15.9 x 3.0 ft., 25.10 gt, - 5/18/1892 – Less than a month after the *Snow Drop* loss, the little gravel scow *Alma* stranded only a few hundred yards away when she sprang a leak and drifted onto the rocks off North Point. Her crew were rescued by the fishing schooner *Prince*, but the ship proved total loss. (Milwaukee Sentinel – May 19, 1892) Type: Stranding, Depth: Shallow, Remains: Probably Present, Accuracy: 1 Mile. (See detailed account in Part 3)

Propeller *Alice E. Wilds* – Tri-Cities Historical Museum, Grand Haven, MI

Propeller *Alice E. Wilds* (106170) – Built 1883 at Detroit, MI by John Oades – 136.0 x 28.3 x 10.8 ft., 292.86 gt, - 5/28/1892 – The *Alice E. Wilds* was a small lumber steamer bound from Chicago to Escanaba in dense fog when she was struck by the steamer *Douglas* about 18 miles off Milwaukee at 11 PM. The *Wilds* sank in less than 5 minutes but all crew were rescued by the *Douglas*. The *Douglas* was eventually found to be at fault. A few deep targets have been found with sonar off Milwaukee in 300+ ft of water that are claimed to be the *Wilds*. One target of note was snagged by fishermen in 1983 in 330 ft of water, about 17 miles SE of Milwaukee. Jerry Guyer went to the site and marked a very large object on the bottom. Nobody has ever been back with a sidescan to very the find. It is thought to be too far south to be the Wilds, but may well be the *L.R. Doty*. (Milwaukee Sentinel – October 19, 1892) Type: Foundering, Depth: Very Deep, Remains: Definitely Present, Accuracy: 5 Miles.

Customs House Wreck Report for the Schooner *Lumberman* – National Archives

Scow Schooner *Laurina* at Racine c. 1890 – C. Patrick Labadie Collection, TBNMS

Schooner *Lumberman* (14828) – Built 1862 at Blendon's Landing, MI by Hilyne Litchfield – 126.5 x 23.5 x 7.1 ft., 160 gt, 3 masts - 4/7/1893 – The *Lumberman* was bound light from Chicago to Kewaunee on her first trip of the season when she was blown down by a squall about 8 mi NW of Wind Point. Captain Orian Vose was pulled down when the ship foundered and barely managed to untangle himself from the rigging. The vessel settled in 65 ft of water and the crew were rescued from the rigging by the steamer *Menominee*. The wreck was located by Dan Johnson in 1983 and is now a popular dive site. She was surveyed by the State Historical Society of Wisconsin and is listed on the National Register of Historic Places. (Milwaukee Customs House Wreck Report – April 12, 1893) Type: Foundering, Depth: 65 ft., Remains: Located, Accuracy: N42° 52.06' W87° 45.45'.

Scow Schooner *Laurina* (15875) – Built 1873 at Chicago, IL – 71.1 x 17.7 x 4.0 ft., 37.59 gt, - 4/20/1893 – The *Laurina* was bound from Manistee to Racine with lumber when she entered Milwaukee Harbor to shelter from a gale. 50 ft of the pier breakwall was push over by a storm, allowing heavy seas into the inner harbor, which caused the *Laurina* to drag her anchor and go ashore at the foot of Knapp St. near Juneau Park. She proved a total loss for Captain Samuel Martin, her owner. (Milwaukee Customs House Wreck Report – August 1, 1893) Type: Stranding, Depth: Surfline, Remains: Probably Removed, Accuracy: 1/4 Mile.

Beeson's Marine Directory 1891 – Author's Collection

Schooner *M.J. Cummings* – C. Patrick Labadie Collection, TBNMS

This old view of Winter layup at Sheboygan Harbor around 1890 shows both the schooners *Island City* (left) and *Dawn* (right) – Author's Collection

Schooner *M.J. Cummings* (90592) – Built 1874 at Oswego, NY by Goble & McFarland – 137.9 x 26.0 x 11.8 ft., 330.12 gt, - 5/18/1894 – The canaller *M.J. Cummings* was bound Buffalo to Chicago with coal to pick up a grain cargo in one of the worst storms recorded on Lake Michigan. She arrived off Milwaukee in leaking condition and was driven aground about 1/2 mile off the Bay View Rolling Mill dock in 18 ft of water. Her crew took to the rigging, lashing the woman cook to the crosstrees. Several valiant attempts were made to rescue the crew, who one by one, dropped into the Lake. Only 2 of 6 people were finally rescued, the rest, including the cook, froze to death in the rigging. Kimm Stabelfeldt reports seeing the outline of a wreck from the air that matches the location of the Cummings. It has yet to be located. (Milwaukee Sentinel – May 20, 1894) Type: Stranding, Depth: Shallow, Remains: Probably Present, Accuracy: 1 Mile.

Scow *Saint Ignace* (57924) – Built 1882 at Sturgeon Bay, WI – 238 gt, - 11/10/1894 – The unrigged scow *Saint Ignace* was under tow from Milwaukee to Grand Haven with bricks when she began leaking and foundered about mid-lake off Milwaukee. Crewman Frank Leland was drowned when the scow foundered. (Manitowoc Pilot – November 15, 1894) Type: Foundering, Depth: Very Deep, Remains: Definitely Present, Accuracy: 10 Miles.

Schooner *Island City* (12084) – Built 1859 at Harsen's Island, MI by Peter Perry – 80.9x17.9x6.0 ft., 46.55 gt, - 4/8/1894 – The *Island City* was bound from Ludington to Milwaukee with lumber when she sprang a leak during a heavy NW gale about 14 miles from Milwaukee and foundered. Her captain was the only survivor, drifting ashore unconscious in the yawl near Port Washington. The wreck lies in 135 ft of water and is badly broken for its depth with a good deal of tangled fishnet. It is seldom dived and was located in the 1982 by Butch Klopp and Steve Borsse from a snag by Miller Fisheries. When found, the wreck had collected a mile long train of gillnet with tons of rotting fish, which Klopp and Borsse removed. (Evening Wisconsin – May 7, 1894) Type: Foundering, Depth: 135 ft., Remains: Located, Accuracy: N43°14.390' W87°50.730'.

Scow #1 (unregistered) – No data – probably an unregistered scow - 9/22/1895 – The unrigged scow *#1* went ashore at the foot of Wisconsin St. and was abandoned in the shallows. The scow was a total loss at $2000 but half her lumber cargo was saved. (David Swayze Wreck Database) Type: Stranding, Depth: Surfline, Remains: Probably Removed, Accuracy: 1/4 Mile.

Schooner Cuba in the KK River boneyard c. 1894 – C. Patrick Labadie Collection, TBNMS

Schooner *Cuba* (4576) – Built 1856 at Milan, OH by E. Bates – 119.2x24.6x9.6 ft., 190 gt, - 1894 – The old schooner *Cuba* had been stranded at Kenosha in 1889 and lay in the KK River boneyard until 1894 when she was towed out into the Lake and scuttled. The location of her sinking is unknown but at least one deep schooner hull was reportedly located in 200+ ft of water far off Milwaukee. (HCGL Vessel Database) Type: Abandonment, Depth: Deep, Remains: Definitely Present, Accuracy: 10 Miles.

Sumatra ashore at Marquette 1883 – C. Patrick Labadie Collection, TBNMS

Schooner *Sumatra* (115240) – Built 1874 at Black River, OH by Quelos & Peck – 204.1 x 34.0 x 14.2 ft., 845.34 gt, - 9/30/1896 – The big schooner *Sumatra* was bound from Chicago to Milwaukee with a load of railroad iron under tow of the steamer *B.W. Arnold* and had been taking on water for several hours when she began to founder off South Point. The *Arnold* signaled for a tug but the *Sumatra* foundered just as it arrived. The tug rescued the cook and the mate and the lifesaving service succeeded in getting the captain ashore, but 4 other crew drowned. The *Sumatra* went down 1.5 miles SE of the harbor entrance. Her remains were located by Jerry Guyer in the early 1980s. (USLSS Annual Report - 1897) Type: Stranding, Depth: 35 ft., Remains: Located, Accuracy: 43.01.42 / 87.53.00.

Steam Yacht *Edna* (none) – Built 1886 at Milwaukee, c. 40 gt., a locally built, unregistered steam yacht of about 40 ft. – The *Edna* was moored at the straight cut pier when she was struck by the tug *S.S. Coe* and sunk on September 21, 1897. She was reportedly a total loss, but her damages were place at only $700. She was almost certainly recovered. (Herman Runge Wreck List) Type: Foundering, Depth: Shallow, Remains: Probably Removed, Accuracy: ¼ Mile.

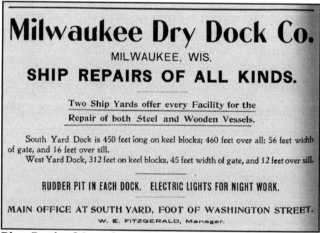

Blue Book of American Shipping 1898 - Author's Collection

Schooner *Lavinda* (14673) – Built 1863 at Allegan, Michigan by St. Germain, 100.0 x 20.5 x 6.9 ft., 125.64 gt. – The old schooner *Lavinda* was abandoned in the KK River boneyard in 1897 due to age and condition. Her remains were removed along with those of the other ships in the KK boneyard. (Runge Vessel File – Milwaukee Public Library) Type: Abandonment, Depth: Shallow, Remains: Definitely Removed, Accuracy: 1 Mile.

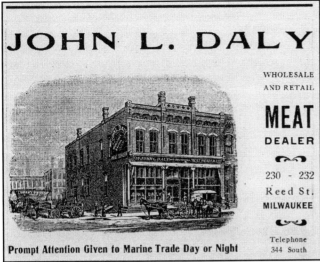
Shipmasters Association Directory 1900 - Author's Collection

Schooner *L.W. Perry* (15654) – Built 1870 at Port Huron, MI by Fitzgerald – 128 x 26 x 11 ft., 253.92 gt, - 1897 – The old schooner *L.W. Perry* was reported abandoned in the KK River boneyard along with the schooner Lavinda (14673) in 1897. These, and other abandoned schooners were subsequently removed and were scuttled off the harbor or abandoned along the beach. (C. Patrick Labadie Collection) Type: Abandonment, Depth: Shallow, Remains: Definitely Removed, Accuracy: 1 Mile.

Schooner Barbarian wrecked at Milwaukee - Milwaukee Sentinel – 10/26/1898

Schooner *Barbarian* (2137) – Built 1855 at Oswego, NY by A. Miller – 136.1 x 25.8 x 10.8 ft., 297.58 gt, - 10/25/1898 – The *Barbarian* was bound from Bark River, MI to Chicago with Hemlock ties when she was caught in the tremendous storm of 1898. She attempted to anchor 1/2 mi NE of the harbor piers when she was dismasted and began to founder. The lifesaving service went to her rescue and with great difficulty succeeded in taking off her 7 crew. She was driven on the breakwall 1 mi NE of the harbor, a total loss. (USLSS Annual Report - 1899) Type: Stranding, Depth: Shallow, Remains: Probably Present, Accuracy: 1 Mile.

US Life Saving Station Milwaukee c.1895 - Author's Collection

Tug *Leo* (140827) – Built 1886 at Chicago, IL – 67.6 x 15.3 x 6.0 ft., 34.98 gt, - 10/12/1898 – The big fishing tug *Leo* was bound for Milwaukee to have a leak repaired when a gale drove her ashore between St. Francis and South Milwaukee. She was a total loss at $2,500. Her engine was later used in the tug *A.C. Tessler*, but her boiler was scrapped. (Walter Hirthe Wreck List) Type: Stranding, Depth: Surfline, Remains: Possibly Removed, Accuracy: 1 Mile.

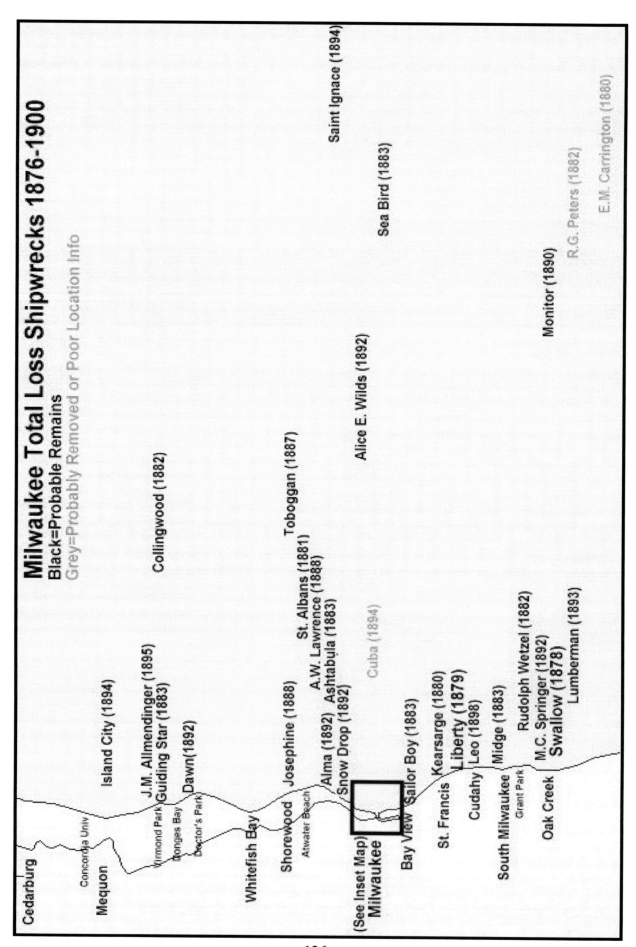

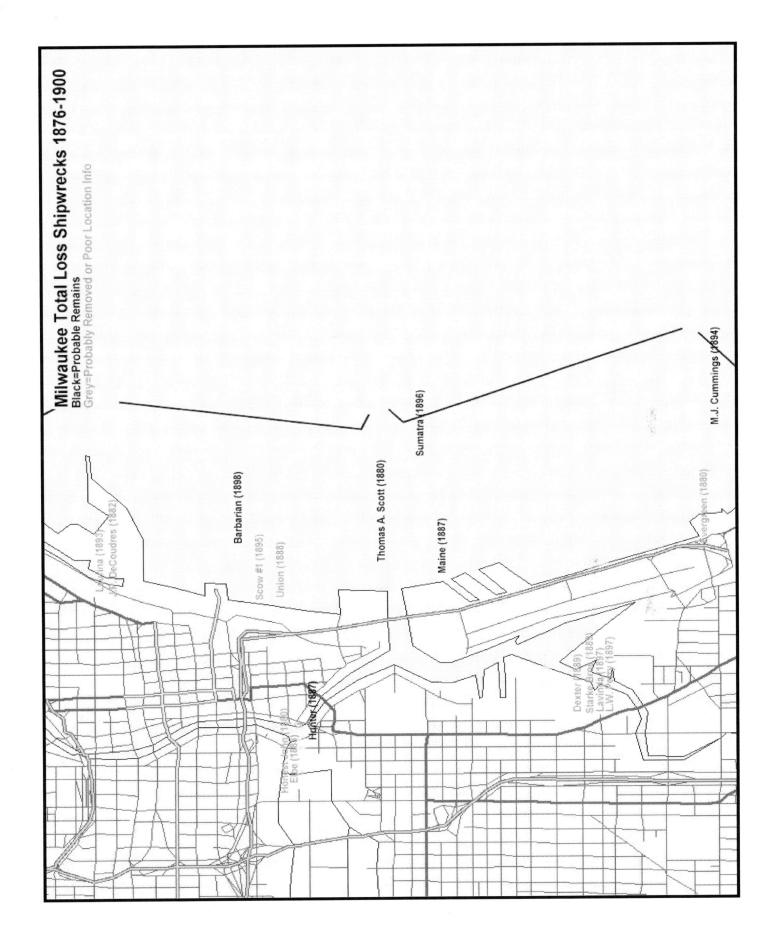

Milwaukee Shipwrecks 1900-1925

By 1900, Milwaukee's Lake trade had begun to change from grain to manufactured goods and fewer schooners were seen. Most vessel traffic was in the form of large, modern lake steamers, which began to dominate the bulk freight trade. Milwaukee's waterfront started to look much like it does today, with the modern straight-cut into the harbor and many of the buildings seen today along the waterfront. The period 1900 – 1925 saw a surge in abandonments and scuttlings as the old sail and small steam vessels of the 1800s were replaced by giant bulk freighters and gas powered boats. Environmental laws did not prohibit the sinking of derelicts until well after WWII and many vessels were simply disposed of in the depths. The following list details all the historic total loss shipwrecks and hulls known in Milwaukee County from 1900 to 1925. This list includes only registered commercial vessels. Countless small, unregistered pleasure boats grace the bottom off Milwaukee but these are outside the scope of this article.

Schooner *H. Rand* at Milwaukee c. 1890 – Milwaukee Public Library Marine Collection

Schooner *H. Rand* (11185) – Built 1856 at Manitowoc, Wisconsin by Rand & Brothers, 86.8 x 23.5 x 7.6 ft., 134.23 gt. - This schooner capsized off Manitowoc while bound Coyne, MI to Milwaukee with lumber on May 24, 1901. The captain, his daughter and two crew perished, and the ship floated as a derelict before fetching up on Racine Reef. She was then towed to the beach at the foot of Texas Ave in Milwaukee where she was dynamited. In June of 1959, dredging in the area uncovered some of her possible remains. (Milwaukee Sentinel - June 10, 1959, Door County Advocate - June 1, 1901) Type: Abandonment, Depth: Surfline, Remains: Possibly Removed, Accuracy: 1/4 Mile.

Schooner *G. Ellen* – Milwaukee Public Library Marine Collection

Schooner *G. Ellen* (10194) – Built 1854 at Detroit, MI by Daniel Meisel - 78.6 x 21.3 x 5.0 ft., 71.41 gt. BOM., rebuilt c. 1865 by Hicks - 92.6 x 21.9 x 6.4 ft., 85.88 gt. – The schooner *G. Ellen* was bound from Pine Lake, MI to Racine when she became waterlogged 20 miles off Milwaukee with a cargo of wood on September 15, 1901. Her crew was taken off by the steamer *Nyack* and the *G. Ellen* eventually drifted ashore on the Michigan coast near Grand Haven where she was abandoned. She is often incorrectly stated to be a Milwaukee wreck. (Racine Daily Advocate – September 20, 1901) Type: Stranding, Depth: Surfline, Remains: N/A, Accuracy: 1 Mile.

Beeson's Marine Directory 1905 – Author's Collection

Wooden Fish Tug *Alvah Eaton* (105470) - Built 1872 at Milwaukee by J.W. and Nathan Brooks, 14.81 gt., 49.0 x 12.0 x 4.0 ft. - The Alvah Eaton was the first steam-driven fish tug built in Milwaukee. She sailed for many seasons out of Milwaukee and Port Washington before being abandoned at Jones Island in 1901. Her hull was likely removed and scuttled outside the harbor during improvement work in the 1920s. Her remains have yet to be identified. (Milwaukee Public Library Vessel File) Type: Abandonment, Depth: Shallow, Remains: Possibly Present, Accuracy: 5 Miles.

Schooner *A.B.C.F.M.* (12978) – Built 1854 at Milwaukee, Wisconsin by George Barber as the J & A Stronach - 109.9 x 23.9 x 2.0 ft., 143 gt. – This schooner was renamed for the American Baptist Council Foreign Mission in October 1881, serving briefly as a floating bethel. After a long career as a lumber carrier, she was abandoned in the KK River in July 1900. She was towed out and scuttled off Milwaukee in the summer of 1902. Her remains have yet to be found. (MPL – Runge Index Card) Type: Abandonment, Depth: Deep, Remains: Definitely Present, Accuracy: 10 Miles.

Schooner *Ella Ellinwood* – C. Patrick Labadie Collection, TBNMS

Schooner *A.B.C.F.M.* in drydock – Thunder Bay National marine Sanctuary C Patrick Labadie Collection

Schooner *Ella Ellinwood* (8604) – Built 1869 at East Saginaw, Michigan by Dixon - 106.0 x 26.0 x 9.0 ft., 163.17 gt., 3 masts – The *Ellinwood* went aground north of Fox Point, 14 miles north of the Milwaukee harbor entrance on September 21, 1901 with a cargo of tan bark due to smoke from the city. Her crew escaped in their yawl, which capsized nearly drowning them. The schooner broke up on the 24th. Her remains are likely still in the area but have never been identified. (1902 US Lifesaving Service Report) Type: Stranding, Depth: Surfline, Remains: Possibly Present, Accuracy: 1 Mile.

An unidentified derelict ashore at Bay View – Milwaukee Sentinel - August 5, 1903

Schooner *Dale* (?) – The Milwaukee Sentinel of July 17, 1903 reported that "the derelict schooner Dale, which sank in the river at the foot of Hanover St. two years ago, has been dragged into the lake by the board of public works to a spot near the rolling mills where it will no longer impede navigation." This derelict reportedly later washed ashore in a gale at the foot of Oklahoma Ave. as reported in the Sentinel on August 5, 1903. The article reports the hull as that of a substantial three masted schooner, but no schooner existed on the Lakes with 'Dale' anywhere in her name. The derelict towed out of the harbor was likely the hull of the schooner *Annie Dall* or *Lincoln Dall*, both of which were reported lost by stranding a few years earlier and could have been towed to Milwaukee and abandoned, but no definitive record exists. The vessel that washed ashore may well have been the bow of the schooner *M.J. Cummings*, as she matches the general description given in the August 5th article. Jerry Guyer attributed an unidentified wreck near the South Shore Yacht Club to this ship. (Milwaukee Sentinel - August 5, 1903) Type: Abandonment, Depth: 10 ft., Remains: Identification speculative, Accuracy: N42°59.220' W87°52.170'.

Small scow schooner possibly the *Rough and Ready* at Beaver Island c. 1890 – Beaver Island Historical Society

Schooner *Rough and Ready* (110686) – Built 1885 at St. James, Michigan - 41.0 x 14.7 x 4.3 ft., 12.0 gt. - The little coastal schooner *Rough and Ready* was lost when she was driven aground near Milwaukee on November 10, 1904. Further research would be needed to determine the exact location. (Walter Hirthe Wreck List) Type: Stranded, Depth: shallow Remains: Possibly Removed, Accuracy: 5 miles.

The *J.V. Jones* lies a derelict in Milwaukee Harbor, 1905 – Milwaukee Public Library Marine Collection

The deck of the *J.V. Jones* showing the tremendous damage done by the gale – Milwaukee Public Library Marine Collection

Schooner *John V. Jones* (75766) – Built 1875 at Manitowoc, Wisconsin by G.S. Rand - 125.2 x 27.0 x 8.6 ft., 236.02 gt., 3 masts. Bound Traverse Bay to Milwaukee with lumber, the old *J.V. Jones* became waterlogged and capsized on October 20, 1905 about midlake. The *Pere Marquette 18* took her crew off, but two had died of exposure. The hull was recovered by the revenue cutter *Tuscarora* and towed to

Milwaukee where it was unloaded at the Milwaukee Dry Dock Co. and deemed a total loss. She was scuttled at an unknown location. Researchers Walter and Mary Hirthe located original photos of Jones' battered remains and wrote a detailed account of her loss in WMHS Soundings. (Milwaukee Sentinel – 10/26/1905, WMHS Soundings, Vol. 27, No. 1) Type: Abandonment, Depth: Deep, Remains: Probably Present, Accuracy: 10 miles.

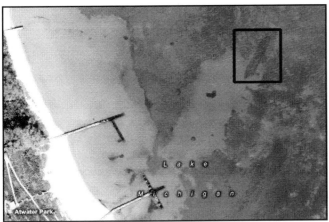
Wreck of the Appomattox from satellite - Courtesy of Microsoft Corporation under Fair Use Doctrine

Steamer *Appomattox* c. 1900 – courtesy Historical Collections of the Great Lakes

Wooden Steamer *Appomattox* (107236) – Built 1896 at West Bay City, Michigan by James Davidson - 319.8 x 42.0 x 23.0 ft., 2643.0 gt. – The steamer *Appomattox* was the largest wooden steamer ever built on the Lakes. She was lost November 2, 1905 when she went aground with a coal cargo just off present-day Atwater Beach due to smoke from the city. Her machinery was salvaged but her massive hullbed is now a popular dive site. The wreck was the subject of a survey by the State Historical Society of Wisconsin and she is now listed on the National Register of Historic Places. (Milwaukee Sentinel – 11/5/2005) Type: Stranding, Depth: 20 ft., Remains: Definitely Present, Accuracy: 43° 05.35N / 087° 52.24W.

The Bond as she appears on the bottom - Sidescan image courtesy of Jerry Guyer

Wooden Steamer *Hiram R. Bond* (95966) – Built 1888 at Milwaukee, Wisconsin by Milwaukee Ship Yard Co. - 113.0 x 26.0 x 7.7 ft., 230.53 gt. The *Hiram R. Bond* was built as a steamer but later cut down to an unrigged scow and used as a sandsucker. She was returning to port in dense fog with a load of sand on May 29, 1905 when she was hit by the *Pere Marquette 20* just outside the harbor piers and sent to the bottom. Accounts state she was dynamited and the site dredged, but a site located by Jerry Guyer is attributed to her. The site is exactly where reports placed the collision and includes a large boiler. (Walter Hirthe Wrecklist, Buffalo Evening News) Type: Foundered, Depth: 40 ft., Remains: Definitely Present, Accuracy: 43.02.12N / 87.52.23W.

Shipmasters Association Directory 1905 - Author's Collection

Schooner *Cape Horn* (4345) – Built 1857 at Huron, Ohio by William Barker - 121.4 x 25.4 x 9.7 ft., 267 gt. – The *Cape Horn* had a long career before being abandoned at Milwaukee. She ended her career as a garbage scow before being loaded with rocks, towed out by a fire tug and scuttled 100 ft. off Iron St. on September 16, 1910. This places her right off the South Shore Yacht Club. The AWOIS database showed a wreck here for years, but the area has been the site of much shoreline alteration. Her remains have likely been removed. (Walter Hirthe Wrecklist) Type: Abandoned, Depth: 10 ft., Remains: Probably Removed, Accuracy: Given in AWOIS as LAT 42-59-58.6N, LONG 87-53-04W.

Commercial Fishermen at Jones Island c. 1910 - Jim Baye Collection

Fish Tug *Dan Costello* (6854) – Built 1874 at Milwaukee, Wisconsin by Nathan Brooks - 48.0 x 12.8 x 6.3 ft., 22 gt., later 27.92 gt. – The *Dan Costello* was a large steam fish tug that ran out of the Jones Island Fisheries. She was scuttled and abandoned near Jones Island on November 8, 1913. The exact location is unknown. (Herman Runge Card File) Type: Abandonment, Depth: Shallow, Remains: Probably Present, Accuracy: 5 miles.

Schooner *Kate Howard* wrecked at Milwaukee 5/1/1911 – Author's Collection

Schooner *Black Hawk* – Loudon Wilson photo, courtesy C. Patrick Labadie Collection, TBNMS

Schooner *Kate Howard* (14169) – Built 1867 at Holland, MI by Waring – 97.3x21.9x6.4 ft., 96 gt., 2 masts – The schooner *Kate Howard* capsized 13 miles north of Milwaukee with a lumber cargo on May 1, 1911. She was recovered and towed to Milwaukee where her lumber was removed. She was then towed to Bay View, beached and abandoned (see photo). Her remains may still lie in the area, but have not been identified. (1912 US Lifesaving Service Annual Report) Type: Stranded, Depth: Shallow, Remains: Possibly Present, Accuracy: 1 mile.

Schooner *Black Hawk* (2140) – Launched May 14, 1861 at East Saginaw, Michigan by Thos. A. Estes - 98.6 x 24.4 x 8.3 ft., 178 gt., rebuilt 1891 to 122 x 24 x 8.1 ft. – After a long career, the *Black Hawk* lay for many years in the KK River bone yard until October 13, 1913 when she was towed out and burned as a spectacle for the Perry Centennial Celebration. Her remains have never been identified but she is definitely on the bottom off Milwaukee. (Vessels Built on the Saginaw) Type: Abandoned, Depth: Deep, Remains: Definitely Present, Accuracy: 5 miles.

Great Lakes Shipmasters Association Directory 1910
Author's Collection

Steamer *Reliable* (110435) – Built 1880 at Detroit, Michigan by Thomas Davis - 91 x 23 x 6 ft., 97 gt., built as a schooner barge, converted to a sand sucker c. 1890. Size also given as 87.0 x 21.9 x 5.6 ft., 69 gt. Captain Wm Krumer and his two young sons almost died when the sand-sucker *Reliable* capsized and exploded 2.5 miles south of the harbor entrance on August 16, 1913. They were taken off by a passing steamer, but the *Reliable* was reduced to kindling. Her remains may be one of the debris fields located by Jerry Guyer. (WMHS Soundings – vol. 41 no. 4) (See article in Section III of this book) Type: Foundered, Depth: Shallow, Remains: Definitely Present, Accuracy: 1 mile.

Steamer *Volunteer* c. 1890 – C. Patrick Labadie Collection, TBNMS

Wooden Steamer *Volunteer* (161592) – Built 1888 at Trenton, Michigan by John Craig & Son - 270.8 x 41.6 x 20.4 ft., 1944.76 gt., later 2316 gt. – The big wooden steamer *Volunteer* was part of a fleet consisting of several aged wooden steamers that was laid up at Milwaukee after 1910. Most were converted to barges or scrapped, but the *Volunteer* burned and was scuttled about a mile south of the present day South Shore Yacht Club on August 16, 1914. Her substantial remains are now a popular dive target inside the south breakwall. She was the subject of a survey by the GLSRF. (MPL - Vessel File) Type: Abandoned, Depth: 10 ft., Remains: Identified, Accuracy: 42.58.87N / 087.51.72W.

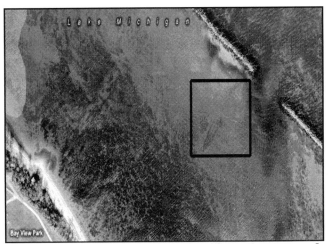

Wreck of the Volunteer from satellite - Courtesy of Microsoft Corporation under Fair Use Doctrine

Tug similar to the Welderine, Beeson's Marine Directory 1905 - Author's Collection

Tug *Welderine No. 2* (90004) - Built 1869 at Tonawanda, New York by F.N. Jones - 72.0 x 16.0 x 8.0 ft., 53.47 gt., built as *Mollie*

Spencer, renamed in 1913 – This large tug was abandoned at Milwaukee in 1911. On November 12, 1914, she was towed out into the Lake and intentionally burned and sunk. Her remains have yet to be identified. (Herman Runge Card File) Type: Abandoned, Depth: Deep, Remains: Definitely Present, Accuracy: 5 Miles.

Tug *Mae Martel* – courtesy of the Historical Collections of the Great Lakes

Tug *Mae Martel* (92678) – Built 1895 at Saugatuck, MI by Brittain - 71.2 x 14.5 x 6.4 ft., 38.0 gt. – The big wooden tug *Mae Martel* was laid up at Milwaukee on June 15, 1915 and abandoned after a long career in the lumber industry, serving mostly with the Nau Tug Line of Green Bay. The exact location is unknown. (Runge Card File) Type: Abandoned, Depth: Shallow, Remains: Probably Present, Accuracy: 5 Miles.

Tug *Sioux* at Sault Ste. Marie, c. 1900 – courtesy of the Historical Collections of the Great Lakes

Tug *Sioux* (95759) – Built 1883 at Green Bay, Wisconsin by P.F. Thrall at Johnson Yard - 71.6 x 16.5 x 8.6 ft., 52 gt., built as the *Henry Marshall*, renamed *Jesse Spaulding* in 1884, renamed *Sioux* 1900 – The *Sioux* was a wooden harbor work tug that had outlived her usefulness. In the summer of 1918 she was stripped and towed to a point behind the north breakwall near the old city garbage disposal plant and scuttled next to the remains of the tug *Golden*. The site has never been located and may have been cleared by subsequent harbor work. (Herman Runge Wrecklist) Type: Abandoned, Depth: Shallow, Remains: Possibly Present, Accuracy: 5 Miles.

Tug *Golden* - courtesy of the Historical Collections of the Great Lakes

Tug *Golden* (86194) – Built 1892 at Milwaukee, Wisconsin by Wolf & Davidson - 63.9 x 17.6 x 8.0 ft., 44.0 gt. The wooden tug *Golden* was a harbor work tug that was abandoned for old age. In the summer of 1918 she was stripped and towed to a point behind the north breakwall near the old city garbage disposal plant and scuttled next to the remains of the tug *Sioux*. The site has never been located and may have been cleared by subsequent harbor work. (Herman Runge Wrecklist) Type: Abandoned, Depth: Deep, Remains: Possibly Present, Accuracy: 5 Miles.

Schooner *Westcott* in her prime - courtesy of the Historical Collections of the Great Lakes

Schooner *George W. Westcott* (10335) – Built 1863 at Sacketts Harbor, NY by S. Reed Jr. - 81.66 x 24 x 9.16; 111.69 gt., rebuilt 1876 at Milwaukee, 111.5 x 24.66 x 7.66, 122.87 gt. – The old schooner *George W. Westcott* was intentionally beached and stripped just north of Bay View in 1918. Her remains are likely to have been removed. (Herman Runge Card File) Type: Abandoned, Depth: Surfline, Remains: Probably Removed, Accuracy: 1 Mile.

Ship remains on the beach north of Milwaukee c. 1900 – Author's Collection

Tug *S.S. Coe* early in her career - courtesy of the Historical Collections of the Great Lakes

Tug *S.S. Coe* (23450) – Launched May 16, 1868 at Buffalo, New York by George H. Notter - 66.3 x 15.0 x 6.8 ft., 31.45 gt. – The old wooden tug *S.S. Coe* was abandoned at Milwaukee in 1917. In the summer of 1919, she was towed out off Milwaukee and scuttled in deep water. Her remains have yet to be identified, but her dimensions are similar to the small tug located by Jerry Guyer near the *Hiram Bond*. (Herman Runge Wrecklist) Type: Abandoned, Depth: Deep, Remains: Probably Present, Accuracy: 5 Miles.

Tug *Starke* c. 1900 – C. Patrick Labadie Collection, TBNMS

Tug *Starke* (116269) – Built 1889 at Sheboygan, Wisconsin by Rieboldt & Wolter - 65.3 x 19.1 x 7.7 ft., 49.24 gt. – The wooden steam tug *Starke* had a long career at Milwaukee before being laid up some time after 1910. On November 12, 1919, she was sunk in Milwaukee Harbor in front of the Chase Bag Company. (Herman Runge Card File) Type: Abandoned, Depth: Shallow, Remains: Probably Removed, Accuracy: 1/4 Mile.

Steamer *John D. Dewar* c. 1910 - C. Patrick Labadie Collection, TBNMS

Schooner *Rosa Belle* at Benton Harbor c. 1910 - courtesy of the Historical Collections of the Great Lakes

Steamer *John D. Dewar* (76571) – Built 1885 at Ludington, Michigan by A. Betters - 72.0 x 15.5 x 7.0 ft., 52.0 gt. – On September 19, 1921, the little passenger steamer *John D. Dewar* was being towed from Chicago to Sturgeon Bay for a rebuild by the steamer *Silver Spray* when she sprang a leak and sank behind the Milwaukee breakwall. She was abandoned in place with her engines and boilers being salvaged. Her upper works were burned in 1923. Her location has not been found. (Herman Runge Wrecklist) Type: Foundered, Depth: Shallow, Remains: Possibly Present, Accuracy: 5 Miles.

Schooner *Rosa Belle* (21302) – Buit 1863 at Milwaukee, Wisconsin by Leonard H. Boole - 100.1 x 26.3 x 7.1 ft., 132 gt., 2 masts, later 115 gt., owned by House of David sect. – On October 30, 1921, the schooner *Rosa Belle* was bound from High Island to Benton Harbor, MI when she capsized in a gale about midlake off Milwaukee. When she was discovered by the passing steamer *Ann Arbor #4*, all her crew of 11 had vanished. Her hull was towed to Racine, stripped and beached north of the Racine Lighthouse. She is often incorrectly stated as a Milwaukee area wreck. (Racine Journal – October 20, 1921) Type: Abandoned, Depth: Surfline, Remains: Probably Removed, Accuracy: 1 Mile.

South Shore Yacht Club at her mooring c. 1916 - Milwaukee Public Library Marine Collection

South Shore Yacht Club smolders in 1922 - Milwaukee Public Library Marine Collection

The Norlond as she now appears - Jerry Guyer

Schooner *South Shore Yacht Club* (15872) - Built 1869 at Manitowoc, WI by Jasper Hanson as the *Louisa McDonald*, renamed *Lillie E.*, 6/1883, renamed *South Shore Yacht Club*, 1915 - 123.6 x 25.6 x 8.0 ft., 191.59 gt. - The lumber schooner Lillie E. was purchased in 1915 by the South Shore Yacht Club after lying derelict at Sturgeon Bay. She was rebuilt as a clubhouse vessel and moored at the present day South Shore Yacht Club. By 1920, she had started to leak and storms in the spring of 1921 settled her on the Lake bottom. The club agonized over what to do, but finally decided to burn and scuttle the hull. In the following years, the city covered her with fill and in 1936 the present SSYC building was constructed over her remains. In May of 1883, she had wrecked at Milwaukee harbor and was nearly a total loss. She was recovered at great expense and rebuilt. (WMHS Soundings, Vol. 22, No. 4 1982) Type: Abandoned, Depth: Buried, Remains: Definitely Present, Accuracy: 1/4 Mile.

Steamer *Norlond* (136131) – Built 1890 at Manitowoc, Wisconsin by Burger - 126.5 x 25.0 x 9.5 ft., 407.56 gt. as the *Eugene C. Hart*, renamed *Norlond* 1919. – On November 13, 1922, the passenger steamer *Norlond* was bound for Milwaukee in a storm when she sprang a serious leak. She ran for shore, but foundered just over a mile out. Her 19 crew and passengers escaped. Her wreck was found in 1958 by John Steele, his first wreck discovery. (MPL – Runge Vessel File) Type: Foundered, Depth: 65 ft., Remains: Identified, Accuracy: 42°58.434/87°48.672.

M.F.D. No. 23 – courtesy of the Milwaukee Fire Department

Steamer *Norlond* at Milwaukee c.1920 – C. Patrick Labadie Collection, TBNMS

Steamer *M.F.D. No. 23* (130711) – Built 1896 at Sturgeon Bay by Rieboldt & Wolter as the *August F. Janssen*, renamed in 1903 - 100.5 x 24.7 x 10.2 ft., 133 gt. – The *MFD #23* had a long career protecting the Milwaukee waterfront from fire before outlasting her usefulness in 1922. On July 27, 1923, she was towed out and scuttled directly off the straight cut. Her likely remains were located by Jerry Guyer in January 2005 and were the subject of an archeological survey by the WUAA, GLSRF and SHSW. Her sister, the

MFD 17 remains to be identified. (Runge Card File) (See detailed account in Part 3) Type: Abandoned, Depth: 75 ft., Remains: Identified, Accuracy: 43°00.94/87°48.18.

Photo-mosaic of the MFD No. 23 wrecksite by Tamara Thomsen - Wisconsin Historical Society

Transfer as the *William McGregor*, 1904 – Andrew Young photo – courtesy C. Patrick Labadie Collection, TBNMS

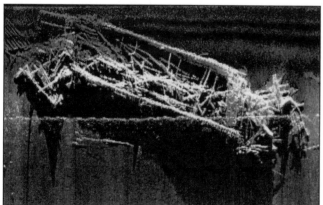
Sidescan image of the Transfer as she now appears - courtesy of Jerry Guyer

Barge Transfer goes to the bottom off Milwaukee - Courtesy of Jerry Guyer

Barge *Transfer* (80268) – Built 1872 at Gibraltar, Michigan by Linn & Craig as sch. bge. *William McGregor* - 200.0 x 33.9 x 13.7 ft., 732 gt., rebuilt as barge *Transfer* at Milwaukee, 1910. - The big barge *Transfer* had been owned by the Milwaukee Western Fuel Co, who abandoned her in 1910. After many years, she was towed out into the lake and intentionally sunk on December 6, 1923. Her unloading machinery was removed prior to her scuttling and placed in the EMBA. Her remains were located by Jerry Guyer in 110 ft of water on April 6, 2005. (Runge Card File, Jerry Guyer) Type: Abandonment, Depth: 110 ft., Remains: Identified, Accuracy: 43.01.09N / 087.45.85W.

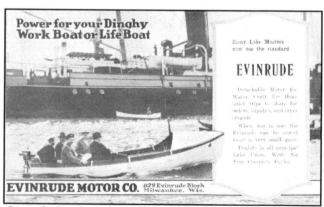
Green's Marine Directory 1920 – Author's Collection

Gas Fish Tug *Mayflower* (213449) – Built 1915 at Detroit Harbor, Wisconsin by John Ellefson - 33.5 x 9.4 x 3.9 ft., 12 gt. – Three lives were lost when the fish tug *Mayflower* burned about 8 mi. off Milwaukee on June 11, 1924. 2 burned bodies were found on raft about 8 miles east of Port Washington, but the vessel had gone to the bottom. (Herman Runge Wrecklist) Type: Foundered, Depth: Very Deep, Remains: Definitely Present, Accuracy: 5 Miles.

Sandsucker Ellen off Kenosha c. 1910 – Louis Milton Thiers Collection Kenosha County Historical Society

Lightship No. 57 – courtesy Historical Collections of the Great Lakes

Steamer *Lightship No. 57* (not commercially registered) - Built 1891 at Toledo, OH by Craig Shipbuilding Co. - 90 x 20 x 8 ft., 130 gt. – This venerable Great Lakes lightship was owned by the District 12 US Lighthouse Board and had served as the Grays Reef Lightship for many years. She was abandoned in Milwaukee Harbor in 1924 after being sold to the South Shore Yacht Club as a clubhouse vessel. Her remains were scuttled and lay on the bottom for years before being covered with gravel during the deep tunnel project. The wreck was surveyed by the State Historical Society of Wisconsin in 1990/91 prior to the construction of the marina, which completely buried the wreck. She was listed on the National Register of Historic Places in December of 1991 and reportedly lies at N42.59.97 / W87.53.07, although she is now buried. (SHSW Shipwreck Database) Type: Abandoned, Depth: Buried, Remains: Identified, Accuracy: N42.59.97 / W87.53.07.

Ellen abandoned in the Milwaukee River c. 1930 – WMHS Soundings

Sand Sucker *Ellen* (136358) – Built 1893 at Milwaukee, Wisconsin by Milwaukee Dry Dock Co. as a scow - 121.0 x 30.6 x 8.0 ft., 350 gt.- The sand sucker *Ellen* was abandoned at the foot of Lyon St. in the east branch of the Milwaukee River in 1924 due to age and condition. Her remains were removed and scrapped in the summer of 1931 by Great Lakes Dredge & Dock Co. It is possible that her hull was scuttled off Milwaukee after she was scrapped. (WMHS - Soundings) Type: Abandoned, Depth: N/A, Remains: Definitely Removed, Accuracy: N/A.

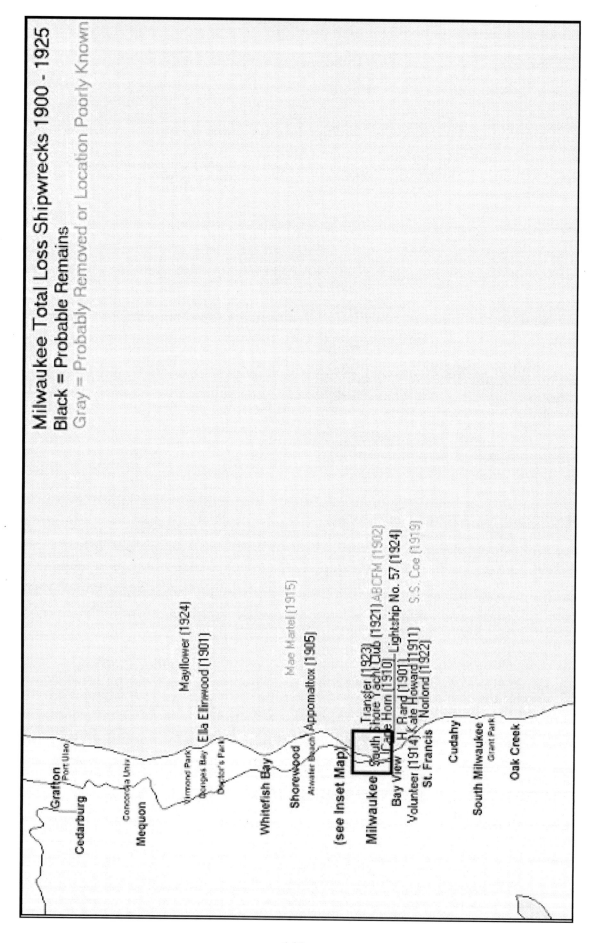

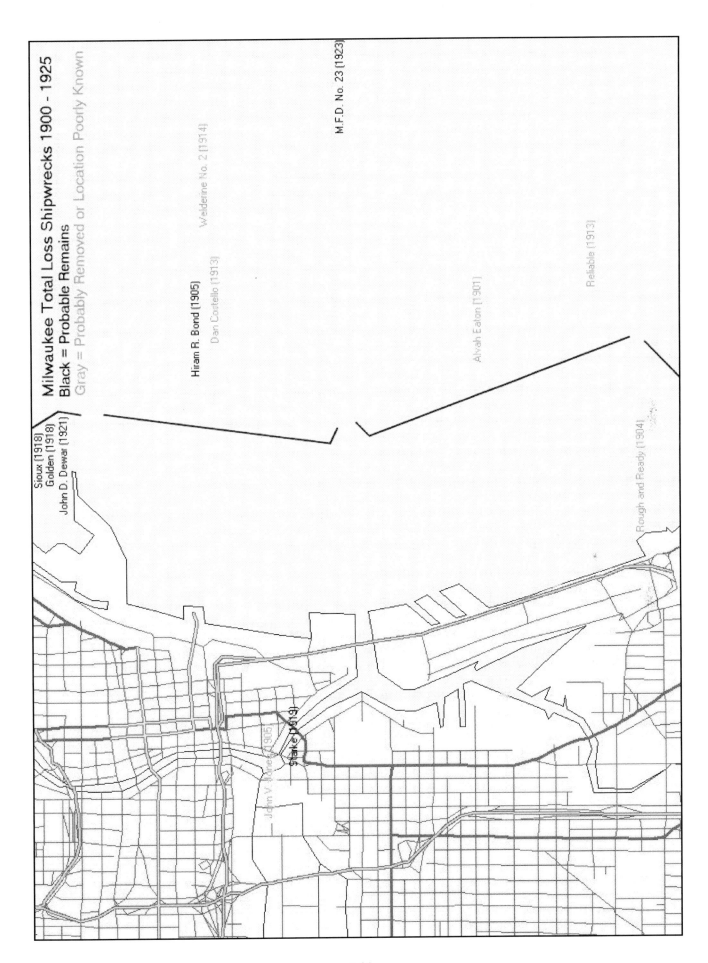

Milwaukee Shipwrecks 1925 -Present

By 1925, Milwaukee's Lake trade had begun to change from grain to manufactured goods and commercial schooners had become so rare that an arrival in the harbor would attract a crowd. Most vessel traffic was in the form of large, modern lake steamers, which began to dominate the bulk freight trade. Milwaukee's waterfront started to look much like it does today, with many of the buildings seen today along the waterfront.

Steamers on the Menomonee River c. 1910 - Author's Collection

The period after 1925 saw a large number of hull abandonments and scuttlings as steam powered vessels were replaced by diesel and old sailing vessel hulls were laid to rest. Environmental laws did not prohibit the sinking of derelicts until well after WWII and many vessels were simply disposed of in the depths. The following list details all the historic total loss shipwrecks and hulls known in Milwaukee County after 1925. This list includes only registered commercial vessels. Countless small, unregistered pleasure boats grace the bottom off Milwaukee but these are outside the scope of this article.

Wooden Gas Yacht *Tuna III* (213207) – built 1915 at Port Inglis, Florida, 26 gt., 43.5 x 11.5 x 6.3 ft. – The gas yacht *Tuna III* had come to the Lakes from Florida when she stranded and burned on November 2, 1926 at St. Francis. Her remains have never been located and it is doubtful if any identifiable remains survive. (Herman Runge Index Card) Type: Stranded, Depth: Surfline, Remains: Probably Removed, Accuracy: 1 Mile.

Tug Knight Templar - Milwaukee Public Library, marine Collection

Tug *Knight Templar* (14495) – Built 1890 at Milwaukee, Wisconsin by Wolf & Davidson, probably on the bed of the tug *F.C. Maxon*, 62.1 x 16.7 x 7.4 ft, 38.69 gt. – The old wooden harbor tug *Knight Templar* was abandoned at Milwaukee in 1925 and taken off the books in 1929. She had been owned by the Gillen Towing Company. Accounts relate that she was abandoned in the Kinnickinnic River. Her hull is thought to have lain next to the remains of the Edward Gillen near First and Becher, and is believed to have been removed. (Herman Runge Index Card, WMHS Vessel File, Tugboat Edward E. Gillen – DNR Study by Mark Dudzik) Type: Abandoned, Depth: Shallow, Remains: Probably Removed, Accuracy: 1/4 Mile.

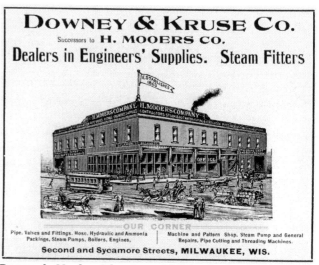
Beeson's Marine Directory 1905 – Author's Collection

Barge *Progress* c. 1920 – C. Patrick Labadie Collection, TBNMS

Wooden Barge *Progress* (150205) - built 1880 at Milwaukee, Wisconsin by Wolf & Davidson as a steamer, 255.2 x 37.0 x 19.8 ft., 1596.20 gt. Rebuilt as a barge at Manitowoc in 1908, 844 gt., 248.0 x 37.6 x 14.0 ft. – The big wooden barge *Progress* was abandoned off Milwaukee Harbor on July 13, 1927. She had outlived her usefulness and was scuttled, probably a few miles off the straight cut. Her owner, Edward Gillen removed her engine before scuttling her. No hull of her size has been located off Milwaukee to date, and her remains may have been removed or disarticulated by dredging. (Pat Labadie Collection, Herman Runge Index Card) Type: Stranded, Depth: Deep, Remains: Possibly Removed, Accuracy: 5 Miles.

Jones Island Fishing Community c. 1910 - Author's Collection

Wooden Steamer *Raymond* (208205) – built 1910 at Erie, Pennsylvania as a fish tug by Parch Bros., 52.8 x 15.4 x 6.0 ft., 27.00 gt. - The big wooden steam fish tug *Raymond* sailed out of the Jones Island fisheries before being abandoned and scuttled at Milwaukee just west of the Clinton St. Bridge on August 15, 1929. (Herman Runge Index Card and Wrecklist) Type: Abandoned, Depth: Shallow, Remains: Probably Removed, Accuracy: 1/4 Mile.

The carferry *Milwaukee* new as the MM&N#1 – Historical Collections of the Great Lakes

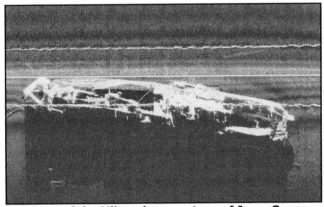
Sidescan of the Milwaukee courtesy of Jerry Guyer

Steel Car Ferry *Milwaukee* (93363) – built 1903 at Cleveland, Ohio by the American Shipbuilding Co. as *Manistique, Marquette & Northern #1*, renamed *Milwaukee* in 1909, 338.1 x 56.0 x 19.5 ft., 2933 gt. – The big steel car ferry *Milwaukee* foundered on October 22, 1929 in one of the Lakes' worst and best known disasters. She was bound Milwaukee to Grand Haven in a tremendous gale when she disappeared, leaving only a short message and a sea of debris. Her loss was a mystery until she was found by John Steele and Kent Bellrichard in 120 ft of water off Whitefish Bay in May of 1972. The site is now a popular dive target, but the wreck has begun to deteriorate significantly from age. She was featured on the History Channel's Deep Sea Detectives series in 2007. (Milwaukee Public Library – Vessel File) Type: Foundered, Depth: 120 ft., Remains: Identified, Accuracy: 43°08.177/87°49.925.

The Grave of the Car Ferry Milwaukee

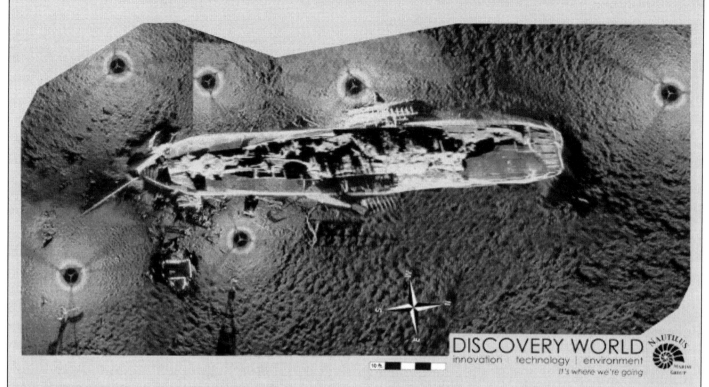

When the car ferry Milwaukee vanished on October 22, 1929, few realized that she lay only three miles off Whitefish Bay. Bound from Milwaukee to Grand Haven, she had turned back and nearly made it. Her fate remained a mystery until May of 1972 when John Steele and Kent Bellrichard found her lying upright and intact on the bottom. Over the years, she has begun to fall apart due to natural forces and there has been an increased urgency to document and record her condition.

The History Channel's Deep Sea Detectives series investigated her in 2007, concluding that the watertight hatchways on her car deck were only covered by grates, which allowed water to flood her lower compartments, contributing to her sinking. Additional efforts have been made to record her condition, but due to her massive size and relatively deep resting place, she has been difficult to document.

In 2009, staff from Milwaukee's Discovery World Museum teamed up with Underwater Archeologists from Nautilus Marine Group to create an innovative three dimensional sonar map of the vessel's remains. Using radial sector scanning sonar towers, a detailed map was made of the entire hull of the giant ship. Discovery World staff then superimposed detail from a side scan sonar image over the top of the sector scan mosaic to create a 3D rendering, completely mapped using acoustic imaging.

The image shows the large debris field around the wreck, including the pilothouse, shown just under the ship's bow. Discovery World staff continue to examine the wreck of the Milwaukee as well as other area wrecks using Remote Operated Vehicles, sidescan sonar and 3 dimensional hi definition camera systems. The Museum frequently leads remote sensing expeditions to area wreck sites from the Denis Sullivan, a replica of a 19th century Great Lakes schooner.

Image courtesy of Kevin Cullen, Discovery World Museum and David Thompson, Nautilus Marine Group

MFD No 17 at a Milwaukee warehouse fire c. 1900 – Historical Collections of the Great Lakes

Steam Fireboat *M.F.D. No. 17* (130654) – built 1893 at Sheboygan by Rieboldt & Wolter as the *James Foley*, 99.0 x 24.4 x 10.2 ft., 136 gt., name changed in 1901. – The *M.F.D. No. 17* was the City of Milwaukee's second fireboat, permanently posted in the harbor at the foot of Water Street. Fireboats wore out quickly from the need to keep their boilers fired at all times and the *No. 17* was laid up in December 1922. She was scuttled with her machinery 5 miles NE of the harbor piers on May 12, 1930. The *No. 17* has yet to be located and probably has findable remains. (Milwaukee Public Library Vessel File) Type: Abandoned, Depth: Deep, Remains: Definitely Present, Accuracy: 5 Miles.

North Shore when new in 1930 – Historical Collections of the Great Lakes

Steel Gas Launch *North Shore* (230121) – built 1930 at Milwaukee, Wisconsin by Mertes & Miller Co., 60.7 x 20.0 x 7.0 ft., 63 gt. – This steel vessel was welded together on the corner of Barclay and Lapham Streets in Milwaukee. She was lost on September 30, 1930 during her maiden season on a run from St. Joseph, MI to Milwaukee with a cargo of grapes and six crew, including the captain and his new wife. She is believed to have gone down closer to the Wisconsin shore but her remains have never been found. (Milwaukee Public Library Vessel File) Type: Foundered, Depth: Very Deep, Remains: Definitely Present Accuracy: 20 Miles.

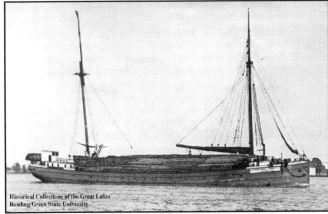
EMBA as the A.C. Tuxbury c. 1910 – Louis Pesha Photo – Historical Collections of the Great Lakes

Unloading machinery on the EMBA c. 1925 - Courtesy of Jerry Guyer

Schooner *EMBA* (106706) – built 1890 at West Bay City, Michigan by F.W. Wheeler as the *A.C. Tuxbury*, 181.0 x 35.0 x 13.1 ft., 679.51 gt., renamed *Cotton Blossom* 1920, *EMBA* 1924 – The big schooner barge *EMBA* was scuttled well off Milwaukee in 165 ft of water on December 10, 1932. Her remains were located by Kent Bellrichard and Richard Zaleski in December 1975 and she is now a popular dive target with her substantial A frame hoist still on her deck. (Kimm Stabelfeldt - Explore Great Lakes Shipwrecks, Vol. 1) Type: Abandoned, Depth: 165 ft., Remains: Identified, Location: N43°03.910' W87°44.950'.

The burned hulk of the *Nomad* 1933 – Milwaukee Public Library Marine Collection

Sandoval after conversion to a yacht – C. Patrick Labadie Collection, TBNMS

Wooden Sidewheel Steamer *Sandoval*
(220423) – built 1895 at Clydebank, Scotland by Clyde Shipbuilding & Eng. Co., 108.0 x 15.5 x 9.2 ft., 93 gt. – The wooden steamer *Sandoval* was built for the Spanish government as a gunboat, and in 1898 she was captured by the US near Havana becoming part of U. S. Navy. In 1921, she was converted to yacht at Milwaukee and in 1927 she was refitted as a package freighter, running in the fruit trade from Saugatauk to Milwaukee. In June of 1933, she was abandoned in the Kinnickinnic River. Her remains are believed to have been removed. (C. Patrick Labadie Collection) Type: Abandoned, Depth: Shallow, Remains: Probably Removed, Accuracy: 1/4 Mile.

Gas Yacht *Nomad* (209909) – built 1912 at New York, New York by Chas. L. Seabury Co., 69.7 x 12.0 x 5.9 ft., 33 gt. Built as *Mary II*, renamed *Gul* 1917, renamed *Althea II* 1920, *Nomad* 1922. On July 2, 1933 she burned to the water's edge and sank at the Milwaukee Yacht Club. A young girl was seriously burned in the accident. The wreck was sold for $25 and towed to South Shore Park a few days later. Although the hull remained on the books for a few years, she is believed to have been abandoned. It is speculated that she may have been removed for inland use. (Milwaukee Public Library Vessel File) Type: Burned, Depth: Shallow, Remains: Definitely Removed, Accuracy: 1/4 Mile.

Green's Marine Directory 1926 – Author's Collection

Wooden Gas Propeller *Lois Pearl* (92651) – built 1895 at Chicago, IL, 61.0 x 14.4 x 7.8 ft., 33 gt. - This wooden vessel was purchased by Captain George Lawrie of Milwaukee in 1924 for the passenger and package freight trade. She was sunk and abandoned in 1935 at the foot of the Kilbourn Street Bridge. She was dropped from registry in 1941. It is unknown if her remains are still in the area. (Bay View Compass – November 2008) Type: Abandoned, Depth: Shallow, Remains: Probably Removed, Accuracy: 1/4 Mile.

Tug *Grayling* sunk at Sheboygan c. 1935 – C. Patrick Labadie Collection, TBNMS

The *Grayling* earlier in her career – Milwaukee Public Library Marine Collection

Wooden Fish Tug *Grayling* (85444) – built 1876 at Buffalo, New York by Carroll Bros., 54.0 x 13.5 x 5.0 ft., 17.25 gt. Steam powered wooden fish tug. On May 30, 1936, the big fish tug *Grayling* was towed to Milwaukee from Sheboygan where she had been sunk in the shallows of the Sheboygan River. She soon sank near the Holton St. Bridge. On September 20, 1936, she was towed off Milwaukee by the Coast Guard and scuttled. Her remains have not been identified. (C. Patrick Labadie Collection, Milwaukee Public Library Vessel File) Type: Abandoned, Depth: Deep, Remains: Definitely Present, Accuracy: 5 Miles.

Scow No. 10 (168606) – built 1914 at Seneca Falls, New York as a deck scow with 1 deck and no masts, 120.0 x 32.0 x 7.5 ft., 229 gt. – This unrigged scow was abandoned at Milwaukee and scuttled in December 1937. Her remains may be one of the barges found by Jerry Guyer around the Prinz Willem wrecksite. (Herman Runge Index Card) Type: Abandoned, Depth: Deep, Remains: Definitely Present, Accuracy: 5 Miles.

The *Pinta* is raised by Gillen Co, May 1939 – Milwaukee Public Library Marine Collection

Gas Yacht *Pinta* (150651) – built 1893 at Essex, Massachusetts as a schooner, 92.6 x 24.4 x 9.8 ft., 100 gt. Rebuilt as a gas yacht in 1920s. The *Pinta* was brought to Milwaukee from Manitowoc 11/1933. She sank in a storm at the entrance to the Milwaukee Yacht Club piers on November 5, 1938. She was raised by Edward E. Gillen in May of 1939, towed out 10 mi NE of the piers and scuttled. Her remains have never been located. (Milwaukee Public Library Vessel File, Runge Card) Type: Abandoned, Depth: Very Deep, Remains: Definitely Present, Accuracy: 5 Miles.

Fish Tug *Two Brothers* sunk at Jones Island 1940 - Milwaukee Public Library Marine Collection

Fish Tug *Mistress* – courtesy of Bud Stenberg, Pentwater, Michigan

Wooden Fish Tug *Two Brothers* (145600) – built 1891 at Sheboygan, Wisconsin by Rieboldt & Wolter, 54.0 x 14.0 x 6.6 ft., 37.90 gt. - This big fish tug was owned by brothers John and Ole Hansen of Milwaukee, who abandoned her for age and condition at Milwaukee in October of 1940. Her final disposition is unknown, but her hull was not likely permitted to remain in the harbor. (C. Patrick Labadie Collection) Type: Abandoned, Depth: Deep, Remains: Probably Present, Accuracy: 5 Miles.

Wooden Fish Tug *Mistress* (222610) – built 1922 at Manitowoc, Wisconsin by Burger Boat Co., 38.7 x 10.5 x 4.0 ft., 15.0 gt. – The fish tug *Mistress* vanished off Milwaukee on March 3, 1941, while bound across the lake from Pentwater. She had just been purchased by new owners in Milwaukee who temporarily put a Buick auto engine in her for the trip and lashed their trailer to her roof. Some felt she may have iced up and rolled, but conventional wisdom holds that she exploded due to the hastily installed engine. Her remains are unlikely to be found. (WMHS Soundings – article by author) (See detailed account in Part 3) Type: Foundered, Depth: Very Deep, Remains: Definitely Present, Accuracy: 20 Miles.

Mayflower, Jr on the Fox River c. 1925 – Author's Collection

Wooden Steamer *Mayflower Jr*. (211304) – built 1913 at Oshkosh, Wisconsin by George D. Ryan, 85.6 x 15.0 x 5.2 ft., 94.0 gt. – The little wooden river steamer *Mayflower, Jr.* was abandoned at Milwaukee near 1st and Becher Streets in August 1940 by her owner George Lawrie, due to poor condition. Her remains were probably removed as this area has been dredged. (Milwaukee Public Library Vessel File) Type: Abandoned, Depth: N/A, Remains: Probably Removed, Accuracy: 1/4 Mile.

The burned hull of the *Oh Lou* – Milwaukee Public Library Marine Collection

Wooden Gas Yacht *Oh Lou* (207580) – built 1910 at Detroit, Michigan as the *E.E.E.E.*, 79.8 x 13.6 x 6.4 ft., 57.0 gt. Renamed *Alquinot* 1929, *Oh Lou* 1931. The *Oh Lou* was laid up for the winter at the foot of 25th Street at the

Milwaukee Gas Light Company dock when she burned to her decks on Feb. 23, 1942, possibly due to the overheating of a Kerosene heater left near her generator. Her documents were surrendered in 1943, but her final disposition remains unknown. She may have been scuttled out in the lake. (Milwaukee Public Library Vessel File) Type: Burned, Depth: Deep, Remains: Possibly Present, Accuracy: 5 Miles.

Tug *Fearless* c. 1900 – Historical Collections of the Great Lakes

Wooden Fish Tug *Fearless* (120943) – built 1893 at Manitowoc, Wisconsin by Burger & Burger, 59.2 x 14.6 x 6.8 ft., 28 gt. – The big fish tug *Fearless* sailed for years out of Jones Island before being abandoned at Milwaukee near the St. Paul Railroad Bridge in 1943 due to her extreme age. Her remains were shown on harbor charts for years and were confirmed by Jerry Guyer with sidescan imagery in 1990. She lies in 15 ft. of water with a portion of the riverwalk built over her. (Milwaukee Public Library Vessel File) Type: Abandonment, Depth: 15 ft., Remains: Located, Accuracy: 43.01.92N / 087.54.54W.

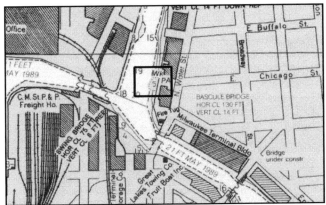

The Fearless show on modern NOAA charts at the foot of Chicago St. - Author's Collection

Wooden Gas Fish Tug *Freddie* (237558) – built 1901 at Manitowoc, Wisconsin by Burger Boat Co. for George Heitl, 32.1 x 9.4 x 3.2 ft., 8 gt., - The wooden fish tug *Freddie*, owned by John Scheffler of Milwaukee, was abandoned at Milwaukee in the harbor in 1945. Her remains were likely removed. (MVUS - 1945) Type: Abandoned, Depth: Deep, Remains: Possibly Present, Accuracy: 5 Miles.

Tug *Satisfaction* c. 1940 – Historical Collections of the Great Lakes

Wooden Fish Tug *Satisfaction* (116628) – built 1894 at Sheboygan, Wisconsin by Rieboldt & Wolter, 64.0 x 16.0 x 8.0 ft., 47.75 gt. - The tug *Satisfaction* had been rebuilt as a fish tug after serving for many years as a harbor tug. She was abandoned at Milwaukee in 1946, but later taken to Green Bay where she was dismantled in 1947. She is incorrectly stated in some sources to have been abandoned off Milwaukee. (C. Patrick Labadie Collection) Type: Abandoned, Depth: N/A, Remains: Definitely Removed, Accuracy: N/A.

USS *Wolverine* c. 1944 – courtesy C. Patrick Labadie Collection, TBNMS

USS Wolverine being scrapped at Milwaukee - Milwaukee Public Library, Marine Collection

Steel Steamer *Wolverine* (211085) - built 1913 at Wyandotte, Michigan by Detroit Shipbuilding Co. as the passenger ship *Seeandbee*, 484.5 x 58.1 x 24.0 ft., 6381 gt. – After a notable career, the famous and massive passenger steamer *Seeandbee* was converted in 1942 to a Navy aircraft carrier trainer called *Wolverine* based at Chicago, Illinois. During her career as an aircraft carrier, the *Wolverine* saw over 70,000 takeoffs and landings before being purchased by the A.F. Wagner Iron Works at Milwaukee for scrap. The *Wolverine* was dismantled at Milwaukee over 1947. (C. Patrick Labadie Collection) Type: Dismantled, Depth: N/A, Remains: Definitely Removed, Accuracy: N/A.

The *M.H. Stuart* headed to a watery grave – June 1948 – Milwaukee Public Library Marine Collection

Wooden Steamer *M.H. Stuart* (221409) – built 1921 at Sturgeon Bay, Wisconsin by Wolter & O'Boyle, 104.5 x 25.5 x 8.7 ft. 192.0 gt. Lumber steamer with 1 deck and 1 mast. – The *M.H. Stuart* was burned and scuttled at Milwaukee on June 10, 1948. She was then towed out into the lake and sunk 8 miles off the Harbor. Her remains were identified by the author in September of 2009 when divers Jitka Hanakova and John Janzen filmed the wreck. It had been located in 1981 by Jerry Guyer on a tip from a commercial fisherman. (Herman Runge Wrecklist) (See expanded article in Stories section) Type: Abandoned, Depth: 210 ft., Remains: Identified, Accuracy: N43.03.80 / W87.43.40.

M.F.D. No. 29 – courtesy of Milwaukee Fire Department

Steel Steamer *M.F.D. No. 29* (203072) – built 1906 at Manitowoc, Wisconsin by Manitowoc Shipbuilding Co., 88.0 x 25.6 x 13.0 ft., 171 gt. Later 137.38 gt., 96.0 x 25.8 x 11.6 ft. – The *M.F.D No. 29* was one of Milwaukee's longest serving fireboats. She was sold for scrap on June 28, 1948 and dismantled at Milwaukee on October 1, 1948. Her hull was likely cut up and melted down. (Milwaukee Public Library Vessel File) Type: Dismantled, Depth: N/A, Remains: Definitely Removed, Accuracy: N/A.

Dredge *G.G. Meade* – Historical Collections of the Great Lakes

Steel Dredge *General George G. Meade* – built 1904 at Sparrows Point, Maryland by Maryland Steel Co. for US Army Corp. of Engineers as *General Gillespie*, renamed in 1909. The big steel dredge *General Meade* was scrapped at Milwaukee in 1950. She was almost certainly cut up and melted down. (Milwaukee Public Library Vessel File) Type: Dismantled, Depth: N/A, Remains: Definitely Removed, Accuracy: N/A.

Prins Willem V – courtesy C. Patrick Labadie Collection, TBNMS

The Prinz Willem V as she looks on the bottom - Sidescan courtesy of Jerry Guyer

Steel Freighter *Prins Willem V* – built 1948 Neder-Hardinxveld, Netherlands by Van Vlier Co., 258.0 x 42.1 x 14.7 ft., 2763 gt. Construction began in 1940 but she was scuttled to block Rotterdam Harbor during WWII. She was completed in 1949. – The *Prins Willem V* was inbound at Milwaukee with a cargo of miscellaneous fright on October 14, 1954 when she struck the tow line of the oil barge *Sinclair XII* in tow of the tug *Sinclair Chicago* off Milwaukee Harbor, tearing a 20 ft. hole in her starboard side. She foundered quickly, settling on her side in 70 ft of water. All crew were rescued by USCG Hollyhock.

The wreck is now the most heavily dived site on the Great Lakes (Jerry Guyer) Type: Foundered, Depth: 75 ft., Remains: Identified, Accuracy: 43°01.533/87°48.523.

Luckime as the Via-Water in 1923 – Hacker Boat Co Catalog, 1927

Gas Yacht *Luckime* (227790) - built 1923 at Detroit, Michigan by Hacker Boat Co. for James D. Mooney of New York as *Via-Water*, 48.0 x 10.0 x 5.1 ft., 16.0 gt. Renamed *Rose Marie* in 1937, *Luckime* in 1954, 220 hp gas engine. The yacht *Luckime* was built as a high performance speed boat. She was sunk at her dock at the Milwaukee Gas Light Company in 1955. She was a total loss. Her final disposition is unknown, but she was likely removed and not scuttled. (Herman Runge Wrecklist) Type: Foundered, Depth: Shallow, Remains: Probably Removed, Accuracy: 1/4 Mile.

Dredge 906 in action - courtesy of Jerry Guyer

Wooden Dredge *Dredge 906* (165186) – built 1912 at Green Bay, Wisconsin by Herman A. Greiling as the Crane Dredge *Defiance*, 120.0 x 39.6 x 11.4 ft., 742 gt. – The *Dredge 906* was in tow of the tug *E. James Fucik* when she capsized and foundered in rough weather off Milwaukee Harbor on May 23, 1956 with the loss of nine lives. She is now a popular

Milwaukee area sport diving site. (Jerry Guyer) Type: Foundered, Depth: 70 ft., Remains: Identified, Accuracy: 42°58.099/87°47.193.

Dredge 906 as she looks today - Sidescan image courtesy of Jerry Guyer

Crew is taken off the stranded *Photinia* by USCG helicopter – Photo courtesy of Steve Loreck

Steel Cargo Ship *Photinia* (BR187933) – built 1961 at South Shields, England by John Readhead & Sons. British motor bulk cargo carrier. – The British cargo ship *Photinia* grounded in a storm off St. Francis on May 13, 1978. The crew were rescued by USCG helicopter, but the vessel remained stranded for most of the year and was declared a total loss. She was purchased by Selvick Marine and towed to Sturgeon Bay where she was scrapped. (Milwaukee Public Library Vessel File, Steve Loreck) Type: Stranded, Depth: Shallow Remains: Definitely Removed, Accuracy: 1/4 Mile.

Tug Gillen's remains in 2005 – Photo by Author

Wooden Tug *Edward E. Gillen* (227538) – built 1928 at Sturgeon Bay, Wisconsin by Sturgeon Bay Shipbuilding Co., 73.0 x 19.1 x 9.3 ft., 68 gt. – The tug *Edward E. Gillen* was one of three vessels to bear this name. This vessel was used by the Gillen Towing Company until being sold in 1964 for scrap. She was abandoned in 1965 in the Kinnickinnic River between First St and Becher St. Her remains were removed by dredging after an archeological assessment in 2008. For years, she was thought to be the tug *Knight Templar*. (Mark Dudzik – DNR Report: The Tug Edward E. Gillen 2008) Type: Abandoned, Depth: Shallow Remains: Definitely Removed, Accuracy: 1/4 Mile.

The *E.M. Ford* lies sunk at Milwaukee 1979 – Milwaukee Public Library Marine Collection

Steel Bulk Freighter *E.M. Ford* (150786) – Built 1898 by Cleveland Shipbuilding Co at Lorain, OH as the *Presque Isle*, 407.0 x 50.0 x 24.5 ft., 4578 gt. - The venerable cement carrier *E.M. Ford* was planning to layup for the Winter at Milwaukee in December 1979 when she was temporarily berthed in South Slip No. 1, which was notoriously exposed during storms. On Christmas eve, a tremendous gale arose tossing 12 ft seas into the slip, which battered the Ford's aging hull. A skeleton crew of 5 which had remained to tend the ship could do little to save her as she pounded against the pier. Within hours, she had sunk to the bottom with her upper works exposed and her cement cargo rapidly hardening in her hull. On January 20, 1980, the ship was finally raised and the massive load of hardened cement was chipped out of her hull. She continued in service until November 2008 when she was towed to Sault Ste. Marie, Canada for scrapping, having served 110 years on the Great Lakes. (Milwaukee Journal) Type: Stranded, Depth: Shallow Remains: Definitely Removed, Accuracy: 1/4 Mile.

Steel Tug *Edward E. Gillen* (205312) – built 1908 at Buffalo, New York by Cowles Shipyard as the steamer *Erastus C. Knight*, 56.5 x 15.3 x 7.9 ft. 47 gt. Renamed *Aubrey* 1928, converted to gas. Renamed *Edward E. Gillen* 1958. - The Diesel tug *Edward E. Gillen* was conducting towing winch tests with the USCG *Westwind* off Milwaukee when she capsized and foundered 2 ½ miles east of the harbor on June 3, 1981. Her four crew were picked up by the *Westwind*, but the tug was a total loss. The tug is now a popular dive target, resting upright in 73 ft. of water. (Jerry Guyer) Type: Foundered, Depth: 73 ft., Remains: Identified, Accuracy: 43°01.639/87°49.138.

Tug Edward E. Gillen as she now appears on the bottom - Courtesy of Jerry Guyer

Tug *Gillen* c. 1975 – Milwaukee Public Library Marine Collection

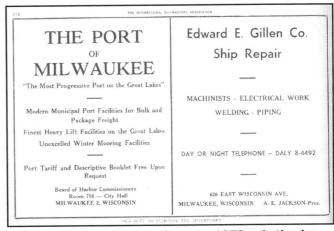

Shipmasters Association Directory 1952 - Author's Collection

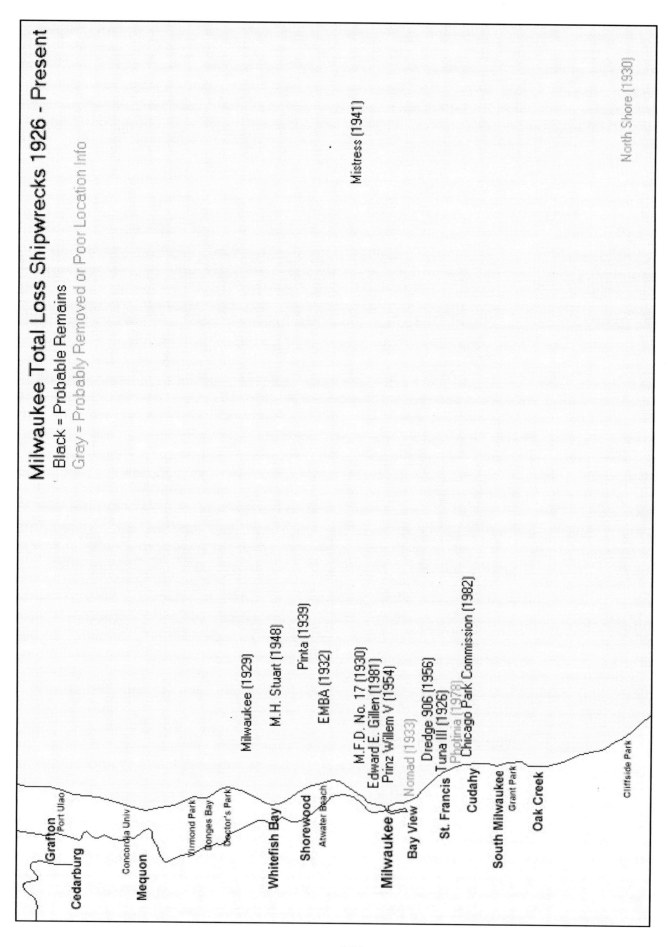

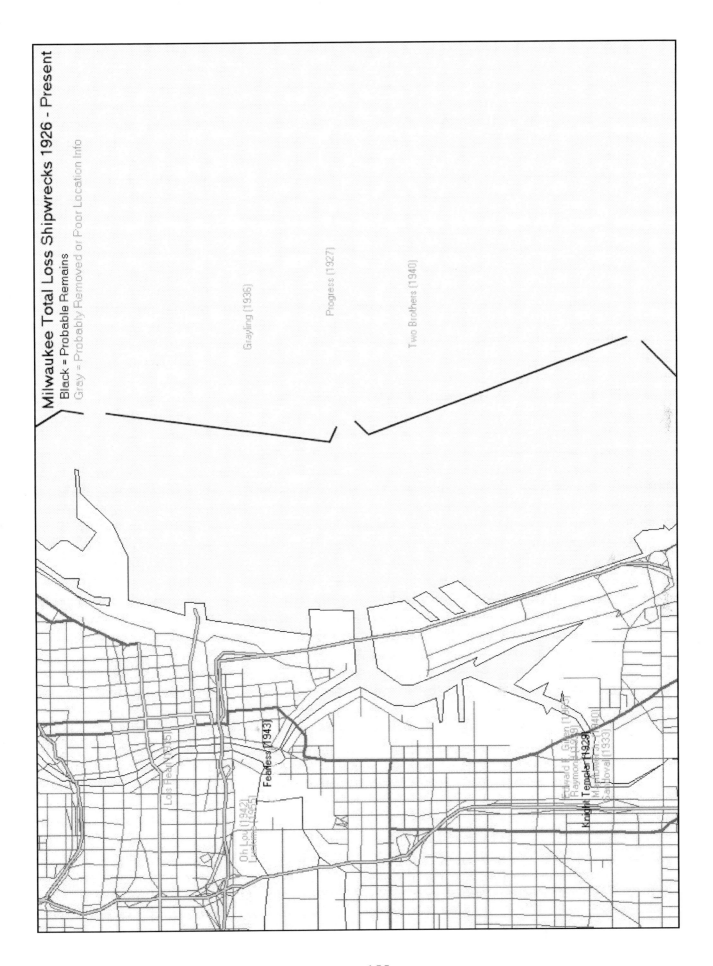

Unidentified Milwaukee Area Wreck Sites

Many wreck sites and debris fields grace the bottom off Milwaukee. Like any metropolitan area on the Lakes, the area off the harbor was, for many years, used as a dump. Many unusual and interesting items have been found on the bottom, including burial urns, pleasure boats and even a safe. Many tons of lead shot lie on the bottom off McKinley Marina due to the skeet shooting club that once existed in the area. The author once brought up several buckets full in a few minutes.

Prior to environmental protection laws, nearly any large object that needed to be discarded cheaply could simply be towed out and sunk. This was particularly true of old wooden ships. Many wooden hulls had been abandoned in the Harbor boneyards between 1880 and 1910. When major harbor improvements were made in the 1920s and 30s, most of these derelicts were simply towed out into the Lake and sunk. Today, their remains are targets for sport divers and wreck hunters. Many of these sunken derelicts remain to be found and many that have been found, have yet to be positively identified.

Considerable historical forensic work is required to positively identify a wreck site. If a vessel is relatively intact, hull measurements can be made, which often allow for an identification. Other helpful features that are often examined include engine and boiler remains. The size and configuration of engines and boilers were listed in turn of the century marine directories and can be diagnostic in making an identification. Sometimes, the ship's hardware, such as steering gears, windlass and capstan, are found on a wreck. These items can be used to date the time period in which the ship was built, as they often contain patent numbers and manufacturer information. For vessels after 1866, the ship's official number was required to be carved in one of the main beams. Placement of the number varied, but official numbers have occasionally been found on vessel debris and used for identification.

Unfortunately, many scuttled vessels contain little to aid in their identification, as they are stripped prior to abandonment and often burned. Many wooden barges, such as the Willie Barges, were of common sizes, making it difficult to identify them from measurements. It is generally possible to discern whether a vessel was a sailing vessel or a powered vessel. In the case of sailing vessels, it is often possible to determine how many masts the ship had because the mast steps are located in the main keel and are rarely destroyed. It is also useful to look for other features unique to sailing vessels, such as a centerboard trunk. Powered vessels will usually have an engine bed, often lined with brick to prevent boiler heat from charring the wooden hull. Large engine mounts area also often visible. Powered vessels can also be identified by the existence of a propeller shaft exit at the stern, if they are sufficiently intact.

Many brass steam fittings on wrecks also bear patent dates, which can help identify the era of a vessel, but these are often covered by zebra mussels and scale. It is generally not permissible for sport divers to remove zebra mussels or debris from wrecksites. Because most historic wrecks are public property (e.g. state owned), they are subject to Wisconsin archeological statute 44.47, which prohibits most physical contact with wreck remains (see Appendix).

The following Milwaukee area wreck sites remain unidentified and would benefit from additional efforts to identify them.

South Shore Yacht Club Wreck Debris - In about 1982, divers reported finding scattered wooden debris north of the Sebastopol wrecksite. The debris was fragmentary and has not been revisited in many years. It was originally referred to as the schooner "Dale" but is probably a hull fragment from the steamer Allegheny or Sebastopol. The debris was reported to lie in 10 ft. of water at N42°59.220' / W87°52.170'. (Jerry Guyer)

Unknown Steam Tug No. 2 - Jerry Guyer recently located the remains of a badly broken tug in 50 ft of water. It appears to have exploded and may be the remains of the Rudolph Wetzel. The remains are located at: N42.51.20 / W87.45.90. (Jerry Guyer)

Portion of Jerry's Wreck courtesy of Jerry Guyer

Jerry's Wreck - Jerry Guyer located a significant wreckage field with his Wesmar sidescan sonar on October 24, 1994, consisting of a broken wooden hull measuring 95 x 22 ft. with a large boiler, engine and towing stanchion just aft of the engine in 40 ft of water. This wreck is believed to be that of the sand sucker Reliable based on location, but the boiler is completely intact. This conflicts with the accounts of the violent Reliable boiler explosion, which was witnessed by dozens of people. As such, the identification remains tentative. The wreckage is located at: N43°00.870' / W87°52.530'. (Jerry Guyer)

Sidescan image of "Sandy's Wreck" courtesy of Jerry Guyer

Sandy's Wreck - Jerry Guyer was scanning with his wife Sandy just off the Milwaukee breakwall on November 9, 2004 when they located a broken wooden hull section in 35 ft of water measuring approximately 60 x 25 ft. The wreck appears to be the hull bed of a small schooner. It was only dived once and remains unidentified. It is reportedly located at 43.01.00 / 87.51.50. (Jerry Guyer)

Loves Rock Hull Debris - Divers have reported a wreck site north of the old Loves Rock water intake crib in 40 ft. of water. The wooden debris is scattered and consists of a keel and ribs. It has been speculated that this may be the remains of the exploded tug A.W. Lawrence, but divers have been unable to relocate this site in recent years. It is reported by Jerry Guyer to lie at: N43.03.720 / W87.51.450. (Jerry Guyer)

Small unknown tug sidescan courtesy of Jerry Guyer

Unknown Steam Tug No. 1 - Jerry Guyer located a 60 x 15 ft. wooden hull on August 5, 2003 while surveying around the Hiram Bond site with an underwater scooter. The hull contains a small single cylinder steam engine and lies in 40 ft of water. She is likely one of the many tugs that were abandoned and scuttled off the harbor, but the small engine suggests a fish tug rather than a harbor tug. She has been referred to as the "Ellen" in the past, but this identification is incorrect and was based on the large sandsucker Ellen, which was scrapped in 1931. The tug most closely matches the small harbor tug S.S. Coe, scuttled off Milwaukee in 1919, but this ID is tentative at best. She lies at: N43.02.12 / W87.52.23. (Jerry Guyer)

Boiler site courtesy of Jerry Guyer

Boiler - Jerry Guyer located a large 15 x 12 ft. boiler from a ship in 80 ft of water approximately one mile north of the Prinz Willem wrecksite. The site was located in the mid 1980s and only dived once. There was reportedly little visible wreckage at the site. It would be interesting to re-examine this location to determine if a wreck is nearby. It is located at: N43.02.70 / W87.48.20. (Jerry Guyer)

Oklahoma Avenue Wrecksite - The AWOIS database reported a dangerous submerged wreck off the foot of Oklahoma Avenue in 1984. This report was confirmed by Port Washington wreckhunter Butch Klopp in 1984 and again by the Coast Guard in 1993. This wrecksite has also been seen from the air by Kimm Stabelfeldt. To date, no area divers have reported diving the wreck, which remains unidentified. AWOIS gives its location as having been extrapolated from map data to: N42.59.51 / W87.51.25. A sidescan sonar may be required to relocate it. (AWOIS Database)

Pryor Avenue Wrecksite - The AWOIS database reports a wreck 200 ft off the end of E. Pryor Ave, just north of E. Iron St. in 12 ft of water. The wreck was added to AWOIS in 1977, verified in 1984 and 1993, and reportedly consisted of significant ribbing laying on a sand and gravel bottom. This wreck site is consistent with the location of the abandoned schooner Cape Horn and with the Lightship No. 57. This site may have been covered by the creation of the marina facilities in the 1990s. AWOIS extrapolated its location as N42.59.58. / W87.53.04. (AWOIS Database)

Single Engine Airplane - An unidentified airplane was found by Jerry on November 7, 1987 off North Point in 75 ft of water. It has not been visited since its discovery and reported lies at: N43°04.110' / W87°50.000'. It is noteworthy that many small, private aircraft have been found off southeastern Wisconsin, as the loss of small planes is a relatively frequent occurrence. Dozens of plane wrecks are known from Kenosha to Port Washington, but are outside the scope of this book. (Jerry Guyer)

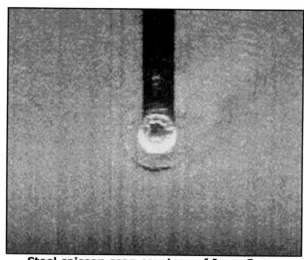
Steel caisson scan courtesy of Jerry Guyer

Steel Caisson - A large concrete filled steel caisson, 75 ft in diameter and 60 ft tall was located approximately 20 years ago off Milwaukee in 150 ft of water. It is believe to have been the scuttled remains of one of the old river bridges. It is seldom dived but is reportedly quite interesting. It is located at: N43.03.24 / W87.45.58 in 150 ft of water. (Jerry Guyer)

Sidescan image of Willie Barge I courtesy of Jerry Guyer

Willie Barge I - In 2005 and 2006, Jerry Guyer located four scuttled barges in the immediate area of the Prinz Willem V wreck soon after her acquired a high resolution Marine Sonic sidescan. All the barges appear to have been wooden stone barges used in the construction of the breakwall, which were scuttled once they outlived their usefulness. Willie Barge I was located on September 10, 2005 and lies in 70 ft of water. It measures approximately 80 x 29 ft and lies at N43.00.68 / W87.48.28. (Jerry Guyer)

Sidescan image of Willie Barge II courtesy of Jerry Guyer

Willie Barge II - Willie Barge II was located by Jerry Guyer on November 15, 2005 and lies in 75 ft of water. It measures approximately 125 x 35 ft and is located at N43.00.36 / W87.47.47. (Jerry Guyer)

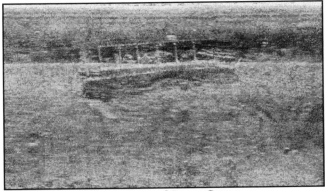
Willie Barge III courtesy of Jerry Guyer

Willie Barge III - Jerry Guyer located Willie Barge III on November 30, 2005 in 80 ft of water. It is very similar to Willie Barge II, also measuring approximately 125 x 35 ft. It is located at N43.00.81 / W87.47.19. (Jerry Guyer)

Willie Barge IV - Willie Barge IV was found by Jerry Guyer on September 15, 2006, while scanning east of the Prinz Willem V. She is of the same dimensions as Willie Barges II and III and lies in 101 ft of water. Her remains are located at: N43.01.828 / W87.47.033. (Jerry Guyer)

Bob's Barge - This barge was located by Jerry Guyer and Bob Schaefer on July 22, 2004. The barge is a small 40 x 20 ft wooden platform barge, probably used in construction of the nearby breakwall. It lies in 35 ft of water at N43.01.46 / W87.52.62. (Jerry Guyer)

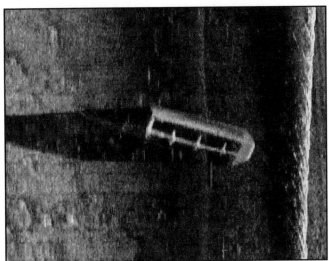
Large unknown object at the Dean's Wreckage site courtesy of Jerry Guyer

Dean's Wreckage - The site known as Dean's Wreckage was snagged by commercial fishermen in about 1990. The fishermen later reported the snag to diver Dean Moors who investigated the site with Jerry Guyer. the site consists of a series of unusual objects, which appear to be discarded wreckage. The object shown above is mostly concrete. The site is in 122 ft. of water and lies at: N43.02.58 / W87.46.60. Nearby, Jerry located another debris field on October 5, 2004, probably associated with a different wreck. It is also in 122 ft of water and located at: N43.02.67 / W87.46.56. (Jerry Guyer)

Unknown Hull near Willie Barge IV - On September 15, 2006, Jerry Guyer located what appeared to be a badly broken wooden hull just to the north of Willie Barge IV. The hull remains unidentified and lies in 101 ft of water at: N43.01.841 / W87.47.037. (Jerry Guyer)

Aluminum Launch *Maureen K.* (unknown) - 41 ft., an unidentified retired Coast Guard patrol boat owned by the Chicago Park District. The Maureen K was a retired USCG patrol boat that had been converted to a food concession vessel known as the "Lunch Boat" which traveled to southern Lake Michigan marinas in the summer. It was under tow off Racine when it foundered on September 1, 1982. A salvage attempt was made, after which she was scuttled off St. Francis. Her hull lies partially buried in sand in 40 ft of water at: 42.50.45 / 87.48.30. (Dan Johnson) Type: Foundered, Depth: 40 ft., Remains: Identified, Accuracy: 42.50.45/87.48.30

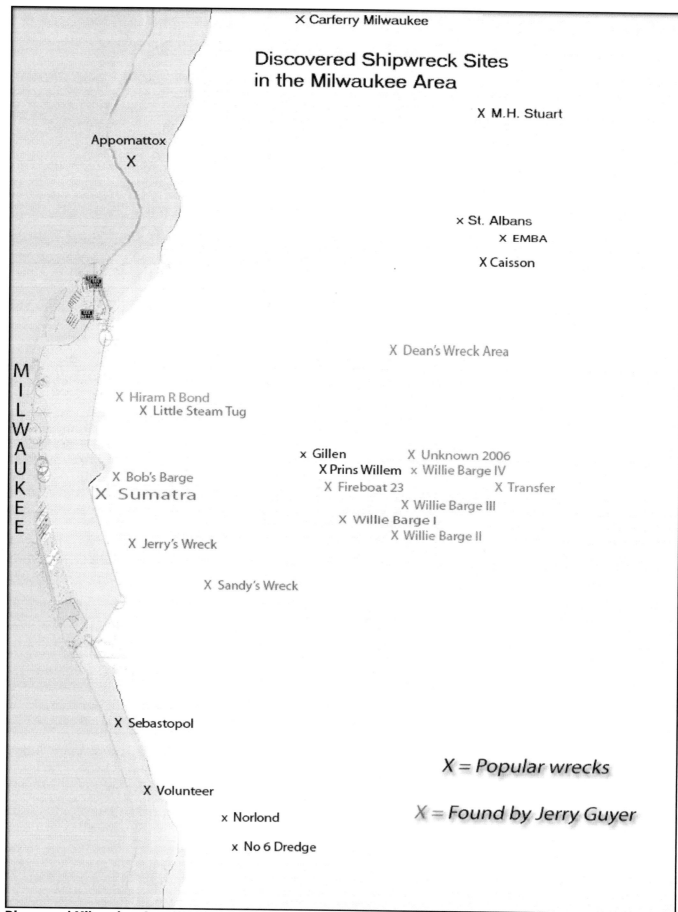

Discovered Milwaukee Area Wreck Sites - Courtesy of Jerry Guyer

Ships Built at Milwaukee

Milwaukee Harbor Scenes 1890 - Author's Collection

Milwaukee has probably seen well over 500 signficant vessels constructed in the area since the 1830s. Creating an accurate list of these builds is a difficult task. Many vessels were built at Milwaukee in the early years that were not enrolled, since Milwaukee's customs house didn't began enrollment until 1851. News accounts mention several small sloops and coastal trading schooners as part of the Milwaukee fleet for which no records have been preserved. A good example are the small vessels seen in the following article that appeared in the Milwaukee Sentinel on July 5, 1845:

THE MILWAUKEE FLEET
The first vessel was launched at Milwaukee in 1837, by Solomon Juneau, built by Capt. Barber. She was called the SOLOMON JUNEAU, of 90 tons; since which our commercial marine has been gradually on the increase, as will be seen from the following list:
Steamboat *C.C. TROWBRIDGE* 90 tons owner, G. Dousman & others.
Schr. *JOSEPH WARD* 260 tons Henderson, Sweet & Benedict.
Schr. *CHAMPION* 250 tons Higby, Furman & others.
Schr. *MICHAEL DOUSMAN* 160 tons G.D. Dousman.
Schr. *MARY G. BONESTEEL* 150 tons Hamble & Bonesteel.
Schr. *JESSE SMITH* 150 tons David Merrill.
Schr. *LESTER H. ROCKWELL* 120 tons C. Shepardson.
Schr. *BALTIMORE* 120 tons L.H. Cotton.
Schr. *ELIZABETH HENDERSON* 110 tons Henderson & Rudiman.
Schr. *ELIZA WARD* 90 tons Leavenworth & others.
Schr. *SOLOMON JUNEAU* 90 tons Payne & Van Alstyne.
Schr. *NANCY DOUSMAN* 90 tons J. & J.B. Smith.
Schr. *SYLVANIA MARVIN* 90 tons A. Gove.
Schr. *MAHALIA* 95 tons F. Southworth.
Schr. *MINT* 80 tons R. Caswell.
Schr. *OCEAN* 60 tons G.D. Dousman.
Schr. *SAVANNAH* 50 tons Powell & Ostrander.
Schr. *EAGLE* 50 tons Story Finch & others.
Schr. *LIBERTY* 50 tons Ward & others.
Schr. *D. WHITNEY* 50 tons G. Flemming.
Schr. *PILOT* 50 tons Powell & Ostrander.
Schr. *IRON SIDES* 50 tons C. Mears
Schr. *MISS DUFFY* 45 tons ---- Duffy
Schr. *MILWAUKIE* 30 tons Ludington & Co.
Schr. *ISABELLA* 20 tons Cook.
Sloop *RANGER* 30 tons C. Mears
Sloop *FLAT IRON* 25 tons John Fowle.
All these vessels are engaged directly in the trade of this city. In addition to the business transacted by this formidable fleet, (for a wilderness city,) all large class steamboats touch here weekly, on their upward and downward trips. - Milwaukee Sentinel, July 5, 1845

Although most of the vessels above are well known, the small sloops such as the *Flat Iron*, *Miss Duffy, Isabella, Iron Sides* and *Milwaukie* were probably locally built, but no official record exists of their existence.

In 1858, the State Historical Society published the following list of early Milwaukee built vessels compiled by George Barber. It gave the rough locations (by ward) of the various shipyards and proved to be rather accurate:

Name of Vessel	When Built	By Whom	Names of Owner	Wards	Tons
Sloop Wenona*	1836	Geo. Barber	William Brown	7	30
Schr. S. Juneau	1836		S. Juneau	7	90
Steamer Badger†	1837	Mr. Hubbell	Byron Kilbourn	2	50
Schr. Savannah‡	1837	"	"	2	55
" Bolivar§	1837	"	"	2	70
Steamer Menomonee	1838	"	"	2	75
Schr. Milwaukee	1840	Not known	R. Andrews	3	25
" Fur Trader ||	1842	B. B. Jones	William Brown	5	100
" S. Marvin	1842	S. Farmin	Merrill & Caswell	5	75
" M. Dousman	1843	"	Dousman, Merrill & Farmin	5	138
" Jo. Ward	1844	Geo. Barber	Barber & Sweet	7	217
" Champion	1844	S. Farmin	Farmin & Rathbun	5	205
" L. R. Rockwell	1845	Gelson	C. Sheperdson	3	105
" M. G. Bonesteel	1845	Geo. Barber	Geo. Humble	7	110
" E. Henderson	1845	"	J. Henderson	7	100
" Pilot	1845	"	G. Barber	7	40
Bark Utica	1846	Averell	Payson & Robb, Chicago	3	334
Brig C. J. Hutchinson	1846	S. Farmin	C. I. Hutchinson, Kenosha	5	341
Schr. E. Cramer	1847	Gelson	M. J. Clark	3	160
" J. Patton	1847	"	J. A. Helfenstein	3	260
Brig Helfenstein	1847	"	"	3	329
Schr. Traveler	1847	Geo. Barber	Geo. Barber	3	74
" Lawrence	1847	S. Farmin	Capt. Lawrence	5	284
Bark Nucleus	1848	"	Merrill, Farmin & Sweet	5	330
Schr. Muskegon	1848	"	Judge Newell, Kenosha	5	119
Bark Cherubusco	1848	Mr. Hubbell	Mr. Hubbell	7	255
Schr. Nebraska	1848	"	Luddington, King & Norris	2	241
" Twin Brothers	1848	Geo. Barber	John Thornson	4	144
" H. U. King	1848	"	G. D Dousman	4	100
" Geo. Ford	1852	"	Geo. Barber	4	132
" Kirk White	1852	"	James Porter	4	184
" D. Newhall	1852	J. M. Jones	D. Newhall	4	183
" Two Charlies	1852	"	D. Newhall & Hibbard	4	119
" Mariner	1853	Geo. Barber	William Porter	4	159
" Advance	1853	J. M. Jones	Meadowcroft & Co. Chicago	4	203
Bark Badger State	1853	"	Williams & Wheeler	4	496
Schr. Emma	1853	"	Bagnall & McVicker	4	169
" Emily	1853	"	Ben Phelps	4	69
Government Dredge	1853	"	United States	4	130
Schr. Kitty Grant	1853	Geo. Barber	S. B. Grant	5	85
" Wollin	1854	S. M. Jones	Mr. Wootsch	5	47
" J. Steinhart	1854	E. Euniac	C. Harrison	5	60
" C. Harrison	1854	"	"	7	187

*Built for a lighter. †Built for carrying passengers to and from steamboats in the Bay. ‡Old blue lighter. §Built for a steamer. \|\|Built for a steamer.

Name of Vessel.	When Built	By Whom.	Names of Owners.	Wards.	Tons.
Schr. Napoleon	1854	Geo. Barber	Geo. Barber	5	150
" J. Lawrence	1854	"	Lawrence & Saveland	5	110
" D. O. Dickinson	1854	J. M. Jones	D. Newhall	5	384
" Milwaukee Belle	1854	"	"	5	368
" Norway	1854	"	Norris & Thornson	5	230
" Fred Hill	1854	"	Davis & Hill	5	268
" North Cape	1855	"	J. Reinerson	5	107
" J. & A. Stronach	1855	Geo. Barber	J. & A. Stronach	5	149
" Fanny & Floy	1855	"	Smith & Sweet	5	143
" Adda	1855	J. M. Jones	Cook, Hall & Co	5	273
" Indus	1855	"	Humphrey & Hall	5	246
" May Queen	1855	"	Grant, Kellogg & Strong	5	246
" Undine	1855	"	J. M. Jones	5	100
" Odin	1855	"	John Thornson	5	173
" J. M. Jones	1855	"	A. Lanson	5	156
" Pauline	1856	Geo. Barber	Lawrence & Saveland	5	210
Bark Shanghai	1856	J. M. Jones	J. M. Jones	5	188
" Hans Crocker	1856	"	W. B. Hibbard	3	496
Propeller Alleghany	1856	"	Am. Transportation Co	3	593
Schr. Driver	1856	"	John Thornson	3	174
" Brilliant	1856	"	J. M. Jones	3	180
" Rose Dousman	1856	L. Cox	G. G. Dousman	5	133
" Wm. J. Whaling	1857	J. M. Jones	Bell & Whaling	3	374
" Geo. Barber	1857	Geo. Barber	Geo. Barber	5	157
Tug L. L. Boole	1858	L. H. Boole	P. Starkee	3	47

Beginning with the Annual List of US Merchant Vessels (MVUS) in 1867, a fairly good record exists for vessels built at Milwaukee. The area's builds were compiled each year from the MVUS by Milwaukee marine historian Herman Runge. However, upon Runge's death in 1958, the work of compiling the annual build data ceased. The MVUS registers are thick books, which grew to over 1000 pages by the 1980s, and are not available in any searchable form. As such, we may never have a complete record of the Milwaukee builds between 1958 and 1999. Beginning in 1999, the MVUS was released in a searchable, digital form. However, any vessel that was built at Milwaukee and went of out documentation between 1958 and 1999 is not likely to appear in this list unless it was a substantial commercial vessel.

The following 1892 excerpt concerning Milwaukee shipbuilding is seldom referenced and is extremely accurate concerning the early Milwaukee shipbuilders and yard locations. It is worth reprinting here in its entirety.

The Milwaukee Shipbuilding Industry by Louis Bleyer
Reprinted from Milwaukee's Great Industries, pps. 132-138, Louis Bleyer, 1892

SHIPBUILDING has been recognized as one of the prominent industries of Milwaukee ever since the earliest years of her history. Aside from a pressing necessity for its introduction, three navigable streams, with an abundance of oak in the dense forests which skirted their banks and extended for miles to the north, south and west, rendered this a suitable point for the exercise of mechanical skill in the construction of vessels, and the moneyed men of the early days were not slow in taking advantage of the situation. Iron was not only scarce and high, but also difficult to get, and it was therefore used to such a sparing extent that the hulls turned out lacked the substantiality which characterizes those built nowadays. The construction of vessels of the size then in use did not involve a heavy outlay of money. Oak cost very little, and manual labor constituted the chief item of expense. To show how low a value was placed upon ship-timber then, ancient mariners relate that in 1849 Capt. David Clow built at Oak Creek the schooner *Honest John*, whose hulk now lies buried just above St. Paul A Elevator, and appropriated nearly every foot of timber that entered into her construction from adjacent forests without the slightest protest from the owners of the land.

An urgent need of steam lighters to transfer passengers and their belongings, as well as freight, from the steamers arriving here which were unable to cross the bar at the mouth of the river and consequently had to anchor in the bay, led to the construction and equipment of two such boats in 1836. They were designed and built by a Mr. Hubbell on an island above Chestnut street bridge, and were named *Menomonee* and *Badger*. These were the first boats launched here, and to Mr. Hubbell belongs the credit of being the first ship-building contractor to locate in Milwaukee. Later on Mr. Hubbell built the schooner *Savannah* and scow *Churubusco* in the same locality.

Following closely after Mr. Hubbell came George Barber, whose building operations covered a period of twenty years. His first vessel, the schooner *Solomon Juneau*, was built during the winter of 1836-37, above Chestnut street bridge. Subsequently he built the schooner *Joe Ward* upon what was then a peninsula above Oneida street bridge, the schooners *Kirk White* and *Mary E. Bonesteel* near the Reliance Flouring Mills on West Water street, and the schooners *Kitty Grant* and *George Barber* near the site of the present Angus Smith Elevator A. The names given constitute only a partial list of the vessels constructed by Mr. Barber here, but they serve to show that the operations of our early-day builders were not confined to fixed sites.

The next builder in order was one Pangborne, who came here at the solicitation of William Brown, better known as "Indian" Brown because he dealt largely in Indian goods, to build for him a steam lighter to be operated in the interest of the East Side, which had been shown a cold shoulder by the owners of the other steamers engaged in the lightering business. The hull of this craft was started on the South Side, just west of Ferry street, but as it was nearing completion a halt had to be called because of the depletion of Mr. Brown's funds. Another builder named Samuel Farman was called in later to complete the craft as a sail vessel for Calvin Ripley and Benjamin Ackley. She was named the *Fur Trader*. Of this vessel it remains to be said that after a season or two on Lake Michigan she was transferred to Lake Superior by hauling her overland around the rapids of St. Mary river. She was either the second or third vessel thus put afloat on old Superior's waters, the schooner *Algonquin* having been the first. The dimensions of the *Fur Trader* attracted attention in her days. She had a length of 80 feet, and only 14 feet beam on a depth of 5 feet. After completing the *Fur Trader* Mr. Farman continued in business here until 1848, when he took a contract to build the schooner *Sam Hale* at Kenosha, and then removed to California and next to Portland, Oregon, where he built a number of steamers for the Columbia river trade. He is still a resident of Oregon. Among the Milwaukee vessels credited to Mr. Farman were the schooner *Sylvester Marvin*, built on the site from which the Fur Trader was launched; the schooners *Michael Dousman*, *Champion* and *C. I. Hutchinson* at the head of Barclay street; and the schooners *Muskegon* and *Lawrence* near the Angus Smith & Co. Elevator A. The *Muskegon* was built for a Kenosha lumberman who lost his life by the burning of the steamer *Phoenix* near Sheboygan, and the *Lawrence* for a retired whaling captain named Lawrence, then residing at Waukesha. The *Lawrence* was cut through by ice in the Straits and sunk, while downward-bound with a cargo of wheat, the property of Daniel Newhall, who also owned the vessel.

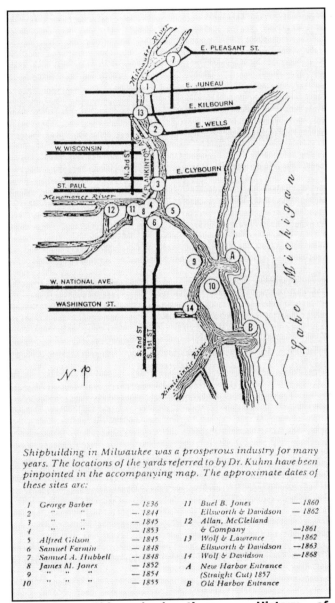

Milwaukee Shipyard locations — History of Milwaukee - John G. Gregory

Next on the list of builders comes one Gilson, who built the schooners *Eliphalet Cramer*, *Juniata Patton* and *J. A. Helfenstein* near the foot of Broadway. He then removed to Racine, where he built the schooner *Tempest* for James Slauson. Subsequently he undertook the construction of the schooner *Reuben Doud* on Wolf river for Reuben Doud and Capt. William Vance, of Racine, but decamped after the vessel had been got well under way, leaving the parties for whom she was being built considerably out of pocket. The barque *Utica* was built near Mann Brothers' blue warehouse, but the name of the builder cannot be remembered. G. D. Norris and others were the owners.

J. M. Jones, the next builder on the list, came to Milwaukee in the '50s. He located a yard near the west end of the present Western Transit Company dock, where he built the schooner *Dan Newhall* for Daniel Newhall, the schooner *Two Charlies* for William B. Hibbard, the bark *Badger State* for Thomas Williams, and the schooner *Advance* for Meadowcroft of Chicago; also the schooners *D. O. Dickinson* and *Fred Hill*. In the remarkably short period of forty-six days from the date of laying her keel the *Newhall* was launched and fitted out, ready for business. Mr. Jones next shifted to a point a little above the foot of Park street, where he built the schooners *May Queen*, *Milwaukee Belle*, *Shanghai* and *Tubal Cain* [not built Milwaukee]. He then bought a marine railway which Caleb Harrison had erected on Jones' Island, and established a shipyard there in connection with it. Among the vessels built on the island were the schooners *W. J. Whaling*, *Christie*, *Hans Crocker*, and steamer *Allegheny*. The *Christie* was built for Milwaukee parties, who subsequently sold her to parties residing in Toledo. From Toledo she was transferred to the Atlantic coast, where her light draught caused her to be employed in blockade running during the war of the rebellion. On one of her trips between a Southern port and the West Indies she was captured by a United States cruiser and destroyed. Failure closed the career of J. M. Jones in Milwaukee, but he was soon succeeded by B. B. Jones, of Buffalo, who raked up everything of value left in the Jones Island yard, bought and built a sectional dock, and established himself in business on the bank of the Menomonee river just north of St. Paul A Elevator. Simultaneously Wolf & Lawrence started a shipyard, with the adjunct of a sectional dock, on River street, above Oneida street bridge; and a little later twelve striking ship-carpenters, who were styled the "twelve apostles," established a cooperative yard on the south bank of the Menomonee river, near Sixth street bridge.

Wolf & Lawrence built the schooner *Dick Somers*, the co-operatives the schooner *Dolphin*, and, before transferring his business to Ellsworth & Davidson, B. B. Jones completed the barkentines *Constitution* and *Golden West*, and the schooner *Rosabelle*. Ellsworth & Davidson in turn built the barkentine *Tanner* and schooners *C. G. Breed*, *Waucoma* and *Hanover*—the latter expressly to cross the Atlantic—when they bought out Wolf & Lawrence and consolidated the two plants at the River street yard, where they built the barkentine *Nelson* and several other vessels. In 1867 Mr. Wolf returned to Milwaukee from Fort Howard, bought out Mr. Ellsworth, and established what will for years to come be known as the Wolf & Davidson yard at the foot of Washington street. In the meantime, also, the co-operative yard passed into the hands of Allan, McClelland & Co., who operated it until the death of Mr. McClelland, when Capt. John Fitzgerald purchased an interest and had the establishment converted into a joint stock corporation styled the Milwaukee Shipyard Company. Successive periods of prosperity for lake interests caused the business of these two yards to expand until they ranked among the largest and best equipped on the lakes, turning out first a fleet of sailing vessels, chiefly for Milwaukee owners, whose superiority in every respect was acknowledged along the entire chain of lakes, and next a fleet of steam vessels which for size, strength and carrying ability rank with anything in the shape of wood yet built either at Buffalo, Cleveland, Detroit, points on St. Clair river, or at West Bay City. The first Milwaukee-built sail vessel to attract general attention was the *Badger State*; then came the *Hans Crocker, Constitution, Golden West, Tanner, Nelson, John B. Merrill, Porter, Joseph Paige, Marengo, Alice B. Norris, Moonlight*, etc. Of steamers the *W. H. Wolf, Thomas Davidson, Fred Pabst, Ferdinand Schlesinger, Omaha, Topeka, John Rugee, Denver* and *Pueblo* may be pointed to as specimen craft. The last steamers built here, the *Schlesinger* and *Pueblo*, were launched in 1891.

Through the retirement of W. H. Wolf and Thomas Davidson the two yards have been merged under a single management known as the Milwaukee Dry Dock Company. The business is in the hands of men of wealth, but whether building will be carried on as energetically in the future as in the past is problematical. The fact that nearly all of the oak which enters into the construction of vessels here has now to be procured from Kentucky will explain their increased cost. Besides, steel is so rapidly supplanting wood as material for the construction of vessels that the old-time plants are threatened with speedy annihilation. Thus the only course left to Milwaukee ship-builders, should they desire to continue prominent in the ranks, is the establishment of a steel plant in common with those already in existence at other lake points. Whether they are prepared for such a step is an open question, but unless the determination is reached the ship-building days of the Cream City may be regarded as numbered, and she will be known hereafter only as possessing first class facilities for repair work.

I compiled the following Milwaukee build list from several sources. For the early builds, I decided not to rely initially on the work of earlier historians such as the George Barber List or the Herman Runge compilations. Instead, I first created a listing from the various electronic enrollment databases, the 1999 MVUS database and from the Johanson pre 1885 MVUS Index. I then extracted all the Milwaukee builds from the other various vessel databases such as the Labadie database, the HCGL database and the Runge Index Card Database. I then compared these lists, combining shared records and eliminating errors. The resulted in the addition of several previously unknown early Milwaukee builds, such as the schooners Manitowoc (1841), Mint (1843), Meteor (1845) and Astor (1847) and Mary (1853), as well as several others which are all well documented in the NARA enrollments.

It is noteworthy that the enrollment databases list MANY vessels as Milwaukee builds that were actually rebuilt at Milwaukee. It was a common practice to change the vessel's place of build if she was substantially enlarged or if a significant portion of her hull was replaced. This was the case with the schooners *Liberty* and *Gallinipper*, both of which appear as Milwaukee builds, but were actually built on earlier hulls.

I must also note with some annoyance the large number of small river steamers built at Mishiwauka, Indiana on the St. Joseph River that were attributed to Milwaukee. This seems to have been exclusively due to naïve transcribers, and it made research rather time consuming.

Wherever possible, I verified the build location of each vessel in multiple sources and I also checked the names of several of the early Milwaukee shipbuilders in the US Census schedules for 1840 and 1850. All tonnages and dimensions are from enrollment data unless otherwise noted. All final disposition data is from primary sources, such as news microfilms, enrollment surrenders or USLSS accounts. The following then, is the list of Milwaukee build commercial and registered vessels:

1830s & 1840s

Milwaukee's first wave of shipbuilding was primarily driven by the need of local merchants to bring in raw materials and finished goods from the older, eastern ports, but a significant number of early vessels were also built for the local coasting and lightering trades. Prior to the building of the straight cut in the 1850s, only shallow draft vessels could enter the harbor, and before the enlargement of the old river mouth in the early 1840s, no large lake going vessels could enter safely. As such, a number of early vessels were built for the expressed purpose of unloading larger vessels that were anchored out in the bay. Early builders such as Thomas Hubbell and George Barber built a number of small lighters and coastal trading schooners before starting to build larger trans-lake vessels. Most early Milwaukee built vessels were small, shallow draft schooners that ran between Milwaukee and Chicago, St. Joseph, MI, Green Bay and Mackinac. The vast majority of these small, early vessels ended their careers on Lake Michigan and two of them, the Gallinipper and Cherubusco, still have extant remains.

Sloop *Wenona* (none) - Built 1837 by George Barber, 30 BOM. Disposition - Ashore 11/1841 Milwaukee. Notes - Driven ashore near the harbor entrance.

Schooner *Solomon Juneau* (none) - Built 1837 by George Barber, 86.14 BOM, 72.6 x 19.2 x 7.0 ft. Disposition - Wrecked 11/01/1846 Milwaukee. Notes - Abandoned on the beach at the foot of Chicago St.

Steam Lighter *Badger* (none) - Built 1837 by Thomas Hubbell, 60 BOM, 64 x 12 x 4 ft. Disposition - Abandoned Fall 1840 Milwaukee. Notes - Abandoned inside the old harbor entrance.

Steam Lighter *Menomonee* (none) - Built 1838 by Thomas Hubbell, 75 BOM. Disposition - Abandoned c. 1845 Milwaukee. Notes - Not enrolled, steam engine used for many years in different lighters.

Schooner *Milwaukee* (none) - Built 1840 by Thomas Hubbell, 30 or 75 gt. BOM. Disposition - Ashore 1842 Lake Michigan. Notes - Not enrolled, owned by R. Andrews, Milwaukee, ashore 1840 & 1841 at Milwaukee per news micros.

Schooner *Manitowoc* (none) - Built 1841 by Benjamin Ackley, 52.22 BOM, 76.2 x 13.0 x 5.7 ft. Disposition - Unknown Before 1850 Lake Michigan. Notes - Last document surrendered Chicago 3/27/1849.

Schooner *Sylvanus Marvin* (none) - Built 1842 by Samuel Farman, 64.63 BOM, 65.0 x 18.9 x 6.1 ft. Disposition - Foundered 5/22/1851 Lake Michigan off Racine.

Schooner *Fur Trader* (none) - Built 1843 by B.B. Jones, 52.10 BOM, 80.0 x 14.6 x 4.11 ft. Disposition - Ashore 11/1852 Eagle Harbor, MI. Notes - Portaged to Lake Superior prior to the locks.

Schooner *Michael Dousman* (none) - Built 1843 by Samuel Farman, 137.11 BOM, 90.0 x 20.0 x 8.0 ft. Disposition - Ashore 12/7/1853 Point Abino, Lake Erie. Notes - Later 153.57 gt.

Schooner *Mint* (none) - Built 1843 by J.P. Allen, 43.64 BOM, 76.0 x 13.6 x 4.6 ft. Disposition - Ashore 8/1850 South of Chicago. Notes - Last enrolled Chicago, 5/12/1847.

Schooner *Champion* (none) - Built 1844 by Samuel Farman, 205.73 BOM, 102.0 x 23.9 x 9.3 ft. Disposition - Capsized & Sank 9/13/1860 South of Milwaukee. Notes - Last enrolled Chicago, 1854.

Schooner *Jo Ward* (none) - Built 1844 by George Barber, 216.04 BOM, 108.0 x 23.2 x 9.5 ft. Disposition - Ashore 8/4/1851 Buffalo.

Schooner *Liberty* (14805) - Built 1845 by George Barber, 54.42 BOM, 70.0 x 17.8 x 5.6 ft. Disposition - Wrecked 4/1872 Milwaukee. Notes - Rebuilt Milw. 1845 on earlier Liberty built 1835 at Avon, OH.

Schooner *Savannah* (none) - Built 1845 by Thomas Hubbell, 36.38 BOM, 61.0 x 15.5 x 4.4 ft. Disposition - Ashore 12/1846 East shore Lake Michigan.

Schooner *Elizabeth Henderson* (none) - Built 1845 by George Barber, 90.03 BOM, 88.0 x 18.0 x 6.8 ft. Disposition - Ashore 8/1861 At Waukegan, IL.

Schooner *Hiram Merrill* (none) - Built 1845 by David Merrill, 23.88 BOM, 51.0 x 11.5 x 4.6 ft. Disposition - Unknown 1851 Lake Michigan. Notes - Last enrolled Chicago, 3/23/1851.

Schooner *Lester R. Rockwell* (none) - Built 1845 by Alfred Gilson, 115.54 BOM, 84.0 x 19.6 x 7.8 ft. Disposition - Ashore 12/1855 Near Muskegon, MI. Notes - Last enrolled Chicago, 9/6/1847, also listed as built by Samuel Farman.

Schooner *Mary G. Bonesteel* (none) - Built 1845 by George Barber, 105.65 BOM, 85.8 x 18.9 x 7.2 ft. Disposition - Unknown 1864. Notes - Last listed by the BLU in 1864, Chicago.

Schooner *Meteor* (none) - Built 1845 by George Barber, 32.03 BOM, 50.7 x 15.6 x 4.9 ft. Disposition - Unknown Before 1860. Notes - Last enrolled Detroit, 4/22/1853, owned out of Detroit, went to eastern Lakes.

Schooner *Pilot* (none) - Built 1845 by George Barber, 46.30 BOM, 63.0 x 14. x 5.9 ft. Disposition - Ashore 12/1858 South of Sheboygan. Notes - Last enrolled Chicago, 10/16/1854.

Brig *C.J. Hutchinson* (4360) - Built 1846 by Samuel Farman, 253.87 gt., 341.42 BOM, 136.0 x 26.1 x 10.4 ft. Disposition - Aground 11/1871 Kenosha.

Schooner *Gallinipper* (none) - Built 1846 by Alfred Gilson, 144.89 BOM, 95.0 x 21.8 x 7.0 ft. Disposition - Foundered 7/7/1851 NE of Sheboygan. Notes - Rebuilt on hull of Nancy Dousman, blt. 1832, Black River, OH.

Bark *Utica* (none) - Built 1846 by James Averill, 334.33 BOM, 131.5 x 25.10 x 10.7 ft. Disposition - Stranded 11/1854 Buffalo Harbor.

Brig *J.A. Helfenstein* (11144) - Built 1847 by Alfred Gilson, 281 gt., 377.14 BOM, 130.2 x 26.3 x 10.5 ft. Disposition - Stranded 1877 Clay Banks, WI. Notes - Later a barge.

Schooner *Juniata Patton* (13458) - Built 1847 by Alfred Gilson, 195 gt., 260.75 BOM, 111 x 24.5 x 6.6 ft. Disposition - Collision 09/01/1868 Atlantic Coast. Notes - Off Lakes in 1860.

Schooner *Traveller* (24148) - Built 1847 by George Barber, 82 gt., 111.09 BOM, 86.8 x 18.9 x 7.4 ft. Disposition - Ashore 10/22/1868 S. Of Calumet Harbor, IL.

Schooner *Astor* (none) - Built 1847, 85.20 BOM. Disposition - Condemned 1855 Chicago. Notes - Built on hull of steamer Astor, built 1845, Green Bay, condemned 1855 at Chicago.

Schooner *Lawrence* (none) - Built 1847 by David Merrill, 284.50 BOM, 120.1 x 24.5 x 10.6 ft. Disposition - Sunk 4/10/1850 Straits of Mackinac.

Schooner *A.J. Vieau* (none) - Built 1847, 44.79 BOM, 67.0 x 15.0 x 4.10 ft. Disposition - Off Lakes 7/14/1853 Off Lakes. Notes - Sold off Lakes, last port illegible in abstracts. Built on hull of *A.J. Vieau*, blt. 1842, Green Bay.

Schooner *Alert* (none) - Built 1847 by A.Y. Birdsall, 24.50 BOM. Disposition - Off Lakes 3/30/1852 Off Lakes. Notes - Sold off Lakes, to New Orleans.

Schooner *Eliphalet Cramer* (none) - Built 1847 by Alfred Gilson, 160.78 BOM, 105 x 20.4 x 8.6 ft. Disposition - Ashore 1859 Chicago.

Bark *Cherubusco* (4329) - Built 1848 by Thomas Hubbell, 203 gt., 255.11 BOM, 114.0 x 26.9 x 9.3 ft. Disposition - Ashore 11/10/1872 Door County, WI.

Schooner *Muskegon* (16404) - Built 1848 by George Barber, 82.96 gt., 109.55 BOM, 88.4 x 19.8 x 6.11 ft. Disposition - Unknown Before 1870. Notes - Last enrolled Chicago, 1867.

Bark _Nucleus_ (18103) - Built 1848 by Farman & Merrill, 297 gt., 329.55 BOM, 137.8 x 25.8 x 11.3 ft. Disposition - Foundered 9/21/1869 Whitefish Point, Lake Superior.

Schooner _Henry U. King_ (none) - Built 1848 by George Barber, 99.20 BOM, 84.0 x 18.6 x 6.0 ft. Disposition - Unknown Before 1860. Notes - Last enrolled Detroit, 6/21/1855.

Schooner _Twin Brothers_ (none) - Built 1848 by George Barber, 143.40 BOM, 90.5 x 21.5 x 8.2 ft. Disposition - Ashore 3/11/1860 Milwaukee. Notes - Driven on Milwaukee breakwall.

Schooner _Honest John_ (11180) - Built 1849 by David Clow, 98.27 gt., 117.85 BOM, 89.3 x 21.9 x 7.1 ft. Disposition - Abandoned 4/2/1880 Milwaukee. Notes - Built Oak Creek.

Brig _Nebraska_ (none) - Built 1849 by Thomas Hubbell, 240.71 BOM, 121.25 x 23.75 x 9.0 ft. Disposition - Collision 10/19/1856 Milwaukee.

1850s

The 1850s saw the establishment of formal shipyards at Milwaukee, as the port was transformed from a wilderness into a bustling pioneer city. Shipbuilder James M. Jones came to Milwaukee from Ohio and was one of five shipbuilding sons of Connecticut shipwright Augustus Jones. The Jones family was largely responsible for bringing New England schooner construction practices and designs to the Lakes and had a profound effect on Lake shipbuilding. Brothers George W., Frederick N. Benjamin B, William and James M. Jones all established major yards around the Lakes and together, turned out over 200 Lake vessels from their yards. James M. Jones setup practice on an isthmus of land formed by the river, which was later named Jones Island. Although he left before 1860, he turned out many vessels and helped establish Milwaukee as a serious shipbuilding port before being replaced by his Brother Benjamin who relocated the yard across the river. Most of the Milwaukee built vessels of the 1850s were built for the grain and lumber trades. A few large barks such as the Nucleus, Badger State and Hans Crocker were built at Milwaukee during this period and were considered to be some of the largest and finest grain carriers on the Lakes. Milwaukee also turned out her first major steamer during this period, in the form of the sidewheeler Alleghany. She was built following the loss of another sidewheel steamer Alleghany at Milwaukee in 1855 and used the former's engines. The Panic of 1857 put a damper on Milwaukee's burgeoning shipbuilding industry and bankrupted the James M. Jones Shipyard. Milwaukee shipbuilding didn't fully recover until the end of the Civil War.

Schooner _Gazelle_ (10334) - Built 1850 by Edward Uniacke, 78.55 gt.,104.40 BOM, 88.0 x 22.0 x 6.5 ft. Disposition - Unknown Before 1880 Lake Michigan. Notes - Rebuilt on earlier schooner Gazelle (1835) and substantially enlarged.

Schooner _Daniel Newhall_ (6135) - Built 1852 by James M. Jones, 145.89 gt., 189. 88 BOM, 99.0 x 24.2 x 8.75 ft. Disposition - Foundered 10/1/1886 Off Michigan City, IN. Notes - Ranamed Ray S. Farr, 1882.

George W. Ford at Ontonagon, MI, 1864 - C. Patrick Labadie Collection, Thunder Bay National Marine Sanctuary

Schooner _George W. Ford_ (10322) - Built 1852 by George Barber, 127.13 BOM, 81.8 x 23.5 x 7.7 ft. Disposition - Sunk 8/12/1870 Eagle Harbor, Lake Superior. Notes - Portaged to Lake Superior prior to the locks.

Brig _Kirk White_ (14041) - Built 1852 by George Barber, 123 gt., 183.89 BOM, 102.0 x 24.5 x 8.2 ft. Disposition - Ashore 10/14/1869 Saginaw Bay.

Schooner _Two Charlies_ (24145) - Built 1852 by James M. Jones, 86 gt., 119.4 BOM, 83.2 x 20.58 x 6.5 ft. Disposition - Foundered 10/9/1876 At Grand Haven, MI.

Schooner _Juliana_ (none) - Built 1853 by David Clow, 11.33 BOM, 31.0 x 11.0 x 4.0 ft. Disposition - Unknown Before 1860 Lake Michigan. Notes - Built Oak Creek, last enrolled Milwaukee, 6/23/1855.

Schooner _Mary_ (none) - Built 1853, 16.63 BOM, 42.6 x 11.0 x 4.0 ft. Disposition - Unknown Before 1860 Lake Michigan. Notes - Enrolled Mackinac 1854, owned Green Bay.

Schooner _William Tell_ (none) - Built 1853 by Barney M. Eaton, 74.86 BOM, 97.72 BOM, 73.0 x 20.0 x 5.9 ft. Disposition - Unknown Before 1865 Lake Michigan. Notes - Built at Town of Lake, rebuilt 1854 at Holland, MI, listed BLU 1864, Chicago.

Schooner _Advance_ (365) - Built 1853 by James M. Jones, 179.92 gt., 268.40 BOM, 118.9 x 25.6 x 9.8 ft. Disposition - Foundered 9/8/1885 North of Port Washington.

Bark *Badger State* (2134) - Built 1853 by James M. Jones, 302.52 gt., 491.06 BOM, 150.5 x 28.4 x 12.3 ft. Disposition - Ashore 11/15/1870 At Sleeping Bear Point, MI.

Schooner *Emma* (7302) - Built 1853 by James M. Jones, 110.62 gt., 249.12 BOM, 99.8 x 24.9 x 7.1 ft. Disposition - Foundered 7/1883 Near Manitowoc.

Schooner *Kitty Grant* (14035) - Built 1853 by George Barber, 75 gt., 105.9 BOM, 78.0 x 21.95 x 7.1 ft. Disposition - Foundered 10/8/1884 Off Little Sable Point, MI.

Schooner *Mariner* (16401) - Built 1853 by George Barber, 112 gt., 159.63 BOM, 95.5 x 23.25 x 8.0 ft. Disposition - Ashore 11/11/1879 Horn's Pier, WI.

Schooner *Emily* (none) - Built 1853 by James M. Jones, 69.07 gt., 74 BOM, 70.0 x 19.0 x 6.0 ft. Disposition - Went Missing 5/1857 West coast Lake Michigan. Notes - Lost 1857, Lake Michigan.

Schooner *J. Steinhart* (none) - Built 1853 by Edward Uniacke, 68.64 BOM, 72 x 18 x 5 ft. Disposition - Foundered 10/21/1855 North of Milwaukee.

Schooner *C. Harrison* (4569) - Built 1854 by Edward Uniacke, 137.24 gt., 187.11 BOM, 96.0 x 24.25 x 9.0 ft. Disposition - Ashore 10/30/1898 Whitefish Bay, WI.

Schooner *D.O. Dickinson* (6133) - Built 1854 by James M. Jones, 241.82 gt., 333.83 BOM, 127.0 x 26.1 x 10.9 ft. Disposition - Stranded 10/8/1869 Strawberry Shoal, Green Bay.

Schooner *Josephine Lawrence* (12976) - Built 1854 by Barber & Farman, 88.13 gt., 110.26 BOM, 83.3 x 21.8 x 6.9 ft. Disposition - Ashore 10/16/1880 Baileys Harbor, WI.

Schooner *J. & A. Stronach* (12978) - Built 1854 by George Barber, 143.72 gt., 146.26 BOM, 109.9 x 23.9 x 2.0 ft. Disposition - Scuttled 1902 Off Milwaukee. Notes - Final enrollment surrendered at Milwaukee, WI, May 22, 1902 and endorsed "abandoned."

Schooner *Milwaukee Belle* (16642) - Built 1854 by James M. Jones, 242.69 gt., 368.06 BOM, 133.9 x 28.4 x 9.4 ft. Disposition - Foundered 11/18/1886 Straits of Mackinac.

Schooner *Norway* (18105) - Built 1854 by James M. Jones, 162.96 gt., 230.22 BOM, 108.1 x 26.0 x 9.0 ft. Disposition - Ashore 11/19/1870 Muskegon, MI.

Schooner *Napoleon* (18174) - Built 1854 by George Barber, 108.63 gt., 148.82 BOM, 88.0 x 22.0 x 8.0 ft. Disposition - Ashore 10/13/1887 South of Frankfort, MI. Notes - Stranded at Pierport, MI, Lake Michigan, on October 30, 1887; no lives lost.

Schooner *Souvenir* (22579) - Built 1854 by Barney M. Eaton, 87.42 gt., 51.50 BOM, 66.3 x 21.2 x 5.6 ft. Disposition - Ashore 11/1890 Tawas Bay, Lake Huron. Notes - Built at Town of Lake.

Schooner *Wollin* (26349) - Built 1854 by James M. Jones, 48.80 gt., 47.67 BOM, 84.0 x 18.8 x 5.3 ft. Disposition - Ashore 4/29/1897 North of Sheboygan.

Schooner *Fred Hill* (none) - Built 1854 by James M. Jones, 268.85 BOM, 119.11 x 26 x 9.5 ft. Disposition - Ashore 12/1863 North Manitou Island.

Schooner *Fanny & Floy* (9309) - Built 1855 by George Barber, 96.73 gt., 143.35 BOM, 88.7 x 23.5 x 7.1 ft. Disposition - Ashore 1874 Lake Michigan. Notes - Last enrolled Chicago, 1/22/1873.

Schooner *Odin* (18966) - Built 1855 by James M. Jones, 120.74 gt., 173.16 BOM, 94.3 x 25.2 x 7.5 ft. Disposition - Abandoned About 1890 Milwaukee. Notes - Last listed MVUS 1894.

Schooner *Adda* (none) - Built 1855 by James M. Jones, 274.39 BOM, 116.0 x 25.0 x 10.1 ft. Disposition - Foundered 12/4/1860 Atlantic Coast. Notes - Off Lakes in 1860.

Schooner *May Queen* (none) - Built 1855 by James M. Jones, 246.82 BOM, 108 x 25 x 9 ft. Disposition - Ashore 11/21/1859 South of Tawas Point, Lake Huron.

Schooner *Indus* (none) - Built 1855 by James M. Jones, 246.70 BOM, 114.1 x 25.9 x 9.1 ft. Disposition - Wrecked 1863 Atlantic Coast. Notes - To east coast, 1859.

Schooner *J.M. Jones* (none) - Built 1855 by James M. Jones, 156.53 BOM, 92 x 23 x 8 ft. Disposition - Foundered 9/2/1861 Off Manitowoc.

Schooner *North Cape* (none) - Built 1855 by James M. Jones, 102.73 BOM, 82.0 x 20.5 x 6.8 ft. Disposition - Ashore 11/1857 Grand Haven, MI.

Schooner *Undine* (none) - Built 1855 by James M. Jones, 71.61 gt., 100.05 BOM, 76.6 x 21.0 x 7.1 ft. Disposition - Unknown 6/1865 Lake Michigan. Notes - Last enrollment surrendered Chicago 6/20/1865 "Vessel Lost"

Alleghany at Manistique, MI c. 1890 after her rebuild - C. Patrick Labadie Collection, TBNMS

Steamer *Alleghany* (379) - Built 1856 by James M. Jones, 401.84 gt., 601.10 BOM, 167.2 x 28.3 x 10.5 ft. Disposition - Ashore 10/29/1896 Summer Island, Lake Michigan. Notes - Rebuilt as a bulk carrier in 1875, first major steamer built at Milwaukee.

Schooner *Barney Eaton* (2142) - Built 1856 by George Filkins, 104.31 gt., 166.84 BOM, 99.0 x 24.8 x 7.6 ft. Disposition - Foundered 9/13/1867 Union Pier north of New Buffalo, MI. Notes - Built Oak Creek.

Schooner *Driver* (6201) - Built 1856 by James M. Jones, 137.35 gt., 174.04 BOM, 105.6 x 26.3 x 7.0 ft. Disposition - Capsized 8/30/1901 Off Frankfort, MI. Notes - Became waterlogged and capsized off Frankfort, MI, Lake Michigan, on August 30, 1901, came ashore at Point Betsie.

Bark *Hans Crocker* (11174) - Built 1856 by James M. Jones, 335.03 gt., 473.16 BOM, 139 x 32 x 11 ft. Disposition - Ashore 11/29/1876 At Kenosha.

Schooner *Pauline* (19674) - Built 1856 by George Barber, 149.56 gt., 214.02 BOM, 122.9 x 26.9 x 9.0 ft. Disposition - Stranded 9/25/1921 Georgian Bay, Lake Huron. Notes - Later the *John Mee*, #76264, then renamed *Edward E. Skeele*, longest serving schooner on Lakes.

Schooner *Brilliant* (none) - Built 1856 by James M. Jones, 182.29 BOM, 100.0 x 26.8 x 7.8 ft. Disposition - Ashore 12/5/1857 South of Sheboygan.

Schooner *Rose Dousman* (none) - Built 1856 by Leander Cox, 96.14 gt., 133.26 BOM, 88.0 x 22.5 x 7.6 ft. Disposition - Ashore 4/4/1867 New Buffalo, Lake Michigan.

Bark *Shanghai* (none) - Built 1856 by James M. Jones, 188.34 BOM, 104.5 x 25.7 x 7.9 ft. Disposition - Unknown Before 1865 Lake Michigan. Notes - Last owned Chicago, listed BLU 1864, in Lake Michigan lumber trade.

Schooner *James Christie* (5991) - Built 1857 by James M. Jones, 146.84 gt., 100.9 x 25.5 x 7.7 ft. Disposition - Ashore 3/29/1882 Ludington, MI. Notes - Sold Canadian 1864 renamed *Mary Ellen*, Canadian #46243, used as a Civil War blockade runner, returned to Lakes and rebuilt 1869.

Schooner *George Barber* (10191) - Built 1857 by George Barber, 98.71 gt., 157.5 BOM, 92.5 x 24.1 x 7.95 ft. Disposition - Abandoned 3/2/1895 At Racine, WI.

Schooner *William J. Whaling* (26364) - Built 1857 by James M. Jones, 242.99 gt., 381.23 BOM, 138.0 x 25.9 x 11.4 ft. Disposition - Ashore 09/26/1873 Grand Haven, MI.

Steam Tug *L.H. Boole* (14809) - Built 1858 by Leonard H. Boole, 27.90 gt., 30.65 BOM, 46.0 x 12.6 x 6.25 ft. Disposition - Ashore 10/9/1872 South Haven, MI.

Scow Brig *Table Rock* (24146) - Built 1858 by James M. Jones, 179.33 gt., 226.2 BOM, 116.0 x 26.9 x 8.0 ft. Disposition - Ashore 9/29/1872 Tawas Bay, Lake Huron. Notes - Later a barge, no. 59044.

1860s

The 1860s was a time of decreased shipbuilding due to the Civil War and the reconstruction effort. However, most of Milwaukee's major shipbuilders arrived and set up yards during this period. Among these were B.B. Jones, Allen, McLelland & Co., Ellsworth and Davidson and William H. Wolf. These men later formed the core of the modern Milwaukee shipbuilding industry and most had labored as foremen or carpenters in the early yards of the 1850s. A few significant grain carrying barks were built during the period, including the barks Tanner, Cream City, Constitution, Nelson and Golden West, but most of Milwaukee's builds were small work tugs and scow schooners at this time. Notable among the builds of this decade was the brig Hanover, specifically built for overseas trade. She was one of several Milwaukee vessels to end their careers in Europe.

Steamer *Colonel M. Steeves* (none) - Built 1860, 44.06 BOM, 75.0 x 16.0 x 4.0 ft. Disposition - Abandoned 1862 Lake Michigan. Notes - Also stated built Racine.

Schooner *Adell* (none) - Built 1860, 19.03 gt., 24.7 BOM, 48.0 x 12.0 x 4.7 ft. Disposition - Ashore 11/16/1869 Bay View, WI.

Bark Constitution at the Soo Locks c. 1880 - Historical Collections of the Great Lakes

Bark *Constitution* (4568) - Built 1861 by B. B. Jones, 488.73 gt., 562.72 BOM, 148.0 x 32.3 x 13.2 ft. Disposition - Abandoned 9/20/1906 Kelleys Island, OH. Notes - Was overloaded and sank at west dock, Kelleys Island, OH, on September 20, 1906. Later had to be dynamited out.

Bark *Golden West* (10199) - Built 1861 by B.B. Jones, 456.63 gt., 616.33 BOM, 157.0 x 32.8 x 13.0 ft. Disposition - Ashore 10/21/1884 Snake Island, Georgian Bay.

Steam Tug *Zouave* (28021) - Built 1861 by B.B. Jones, 80.56 gt., 108.30 BOM, 84.0 x 17.6 x 8 ft. Disposition - Dismantled 5/24/1881 Windsor, Ontario. Notes - Sunk 1877 at Sombra, ONT, raised and dismantled in 1881 for engines.

Scow Schooner *Appleton* (1551) - Built 1862 by Buell B. Jones, 108.76 gt., 136.29 BOM, 96.0 x 23.2 x 6.8 ft. Disposition - Rebuilt 1873 Holland, MI. Notes - Rebuilt at Saugatuck, MI as scow *J.P. DeCoudres*, #75530.

Brig *C.G. Breed* (4577) - Built 1862 by Ellsworth & Davidson, 385.17 gt., 450.82 BOM, 140.1 x 26.3 x 13.1 ft. Disposition - Capsized 11/14/1879 Off Ashtabula, OH.

Schooner *Dolphin* (6205) - Built 1862 by Allan & McClelland, 233.99 gt., 322.40 BOM, 119.7 x 26.6 x 11.1 ft. Disposition - Collision, Sunk 7/6/1869 Waugoshance Reef, Straits of Mackinac.

Steam Tug *W.K. Muir* (26367) - Built 1862 by Leonard H. Boole, 66.37 gt., 66.8 x 14.3 x 7.4 ft. Disposition - Abandoned 10/1881 Jones Island. Notes - Abandoned in the KK River marsh.

Bark *Cream City* (none) - Built 1862 by B.B. Jones, 629.54 gt., 767.58 BOM, 173.6 x 34.0 x 14.0 ft. Disposition - Ashore 11/22/1869 Detour, MI. Notes - Build started at Shebygan, finished at Milwaukee.

Schooner *Erie* (none) - Built 1862, 60.22 gt., 86.21 BOM. Disposition - Ashore 4/2/1868 St. Joseph, MI. Notes - Last enrolled Chicago, 3/10/1868.

Brig *Hanover* (none) - Built 1862 by Ellsworth & Davidson, 427.61 BOM, 136 x 25.9 x 13.0 ft. Disposition - Off Lakes 5/20/1863 Germany. Notes - Built explicitly for foreign trade, she went overseas and was sold 10/1863 to owners in Hamburg, Germany.

Steam Yacht *Scotia* (none) - Built 1862, 4 gt. Disposition - Unknown Before 1867 Eastern Lakes. Notes - Not enrolled, out of Detroit & Cleveland 1864, owned Detroit by W.K. Muir.

Steam Tug *Continental* (4352) - Built 1863 by B.B. Jones, 41.3 gt., 72.54 BOM, 68.5 x 15.0 x 8.4 ft. Disposition - Off Lakes 1871 New Orleans. Notes - Abandoned 1889, Galveston, TX.

Schooner *Dick Somers* (6136) - Built 1863 by Wolf & Lawrence, 332.21 gt., 432.15 BOM, 137.6 x 26.1 x 12.9 ft. Disposition - Ashore 11/22/1877 Poverty Island, Lake Michigan.

Schooner *Elida* (7512) - Built 1863 by John McCollum, 192.12 gt., 275.27 BOM, 110.3 x 27.3 x 10.2 ft. Disposition - Abandoned 11/8/1912 Lake Michigan. Notes - Final enrollment surrendered at Milwauke, WI, on November 8, 1912, and endorsed "abandoned."

Schooner *Hattie* (11989) - Built 1863, 13.11 gt., 34.0 x 9.2 x 4.8 ft. Disposition - Unknown Before 1880 Lake Michigan. Notes - Owned Sheboygan, last listed MVUS 1878.

Schooner *Rosa Belle* (21302) - Built 1863 by Leonard H. Boole, 131.99 gt., 170.38 BOM, 100.1 x 26.3 x 7.1 ft. Disposition - Ashore & abandoned 11/30/1921 N. Harbor Pier, Racine. Notes - Capsized off Milwaukee, WI, Lake Michigan, October 31, 1921, hull beached at Racine.

Schooner *Trial* (24233) - Built 1863 by G.S. Rand, 35.54 gt., 67.4 x 16.4 x 5.2 ft. Disposition - Ashore 11/15/1883 Muskegon, MI. Notes - Rebuilt at Milwaukee as a schooner in 1863 on sloop *Trial*, built 1857, Manitowoc.

Bark *Tanner* (24236) - Built 1863 by Ellsworth & Davidson, 434.95 gt., 621.64 BOM, 157.9 x 32.3 x 13.2 ft. Disposition - Aground 09/09/1875 Milwaukee, WI.

Schooner *Waucoma* (26357) - Built 1863 by Ellsworth & Davidson, 361.01 gt., 438.72 BOM, 138.1 x 26.2 x 13.0 ft. Disposition - Off Lakes 10/1876 Ireland.

Schooner *Elizabeth* (none) - Built 1863, 20.32 BOM, Disposition - Unknown Before 1867 Lake Michigan. Notes - Owned Milwaukee by Wm Ahern, last enrolled 6/30/1863, Milwaukee.

Steam Tug *B.B. Jones* (2158) - Built 1864 by B. B. Jones, 108.92 gt., 171.55 BOM, 111.6 x 19.8 x 8.3 ft. Disposition - Explosion 5/25/1871 Port Huron, MI.

Steamer *Kate Ellis* (14152) - Built 1864, 54.82 gt. Disposition - Off Lakes 1864 Ohio River. Notes - Owned Covington, KY 1871, last listed MVUS 1880.

Scow Schooner *Flora* (9301) - Built 1866 by Allen McClelland & Co., 91.80 gt., 91.6 x 20.2 x 5.5 ft. Disposition - Ashore 11/16/1877 Grand Haven, MI.

Sloop *Mona* (16653) - Built 1866 by Edward Callow, 8.19 gt., 28.1 x 10.6 x 4.5 ft. Disposition - Unknown Before 1879 Lake Michigan. Notes - Last listed MVUS 1878.

Bark *Nelson* (18173) - Built 1866 by Ellsworth & Davidson, 462.79 gt., 503.55 BOM, 165.33 x 32.5 x 11.92 ft. Disposition - Foundered 5/11/1899 Off Grand Marais, MI, Lake Superior.

Steam Tug *William Goodnow* (26251) - Built 1866 by Louis Pahlow, 171.76 gt., 129.0 x 20.0 x 11.4 ft. Disposition - Abandoned 4/30/1885 Milwaukee. Notes - Dismantled and engine removed, abandoned.

Schooner *Jim* (75546) - Built 1866 by Ethel C. Penney, 10.74 gt., 38.1 x 10.7 x 3.6 ft. Disposition - Off Lakes 1877 New Orleans. Notes - Last listed 1879, Brashear, LA.

Schooner Ida breaking up in the surf near Frankfort, MI - C. Patrick Labadie Collection, TBNMS

Schooner *Ida* (12140) - Built 1867 by Allen McClelland & Co., 169.56 gt., 121.0 x 27.0 x 7.9 ft. Disposition - Capsized 9/29/1908 Frankfort, MI. Notes - Sprung a leak and capsized ten miles WNW of Frankfort, MI, Lake Michigan, September 29, 1908, with cargo of lumber.

Schooner *Apprentice Boy* (29604) - Built 1867 by George Barber, 208.91 gt., 122.1 x 27.2 x 9.9 ft. Disposition - Abandoned 1906 Chicago. Notes - Last listed MVUS 1905, American Bureau of Shipping 1906.

Scow Schooner *Home* (42215) - Built 1867 by Ellsworth & Davidson, 91.77 gt., 84.9 x 23.2 x 6.3 ft. Disposition - Ashore 11/10/1876 Racine, WI.

Scow Schooner *Milton* (50395) - Built 1867 by Ellsworth & Davidson, 130.35 gt., 101.75 x 24.08 x 6.5 ft. Disposition - Stranded 9/8/1885 Two Rivers, WI. Notes - Stranded at Two Rivers, WI, in September, 1885, a total loss. Final enrollment surrendered at Milwaukee, WI, September 30, 1885.

Scow Schooner *South Side* (57279) - Built 1867 by Herman Oertling, 139.75 gt., 101.5 x 25.3 x 5.8 ft. Disposition - Sunk 12/9/1893 Baileys Harbor, WI. Notes - Later rebuilt with no. 115334, last listed MVUS 1893.

Scow *Adventure* (none) - Built 1868, 8.55 gt. Disposition - Ashore 8/1869 Chicago. Notes - Last enrolled Milwaukee, 7/6/1869.

Steam Tug *B.W. Aldrich* (2701) - Built 1868 by Allen McClelland & Co., 49.24 gt., 65.16 x 15.08 x 6.58 ft. Disposition - Abandoned 8/1/1915 Canada. Notes - Sold Canadian, C116387, renamed *J.M. Diver*.

Schooner *C.H. Hackley* (5992) - Built 1868 by Allan McClelland & Co., 248.28 gt., 125.2 x 27.5 x 10.1 ft. Disposition - Off Lakes 4/1/1916 Atlantic Coast. Notes - Towed out to sea and sunk at Tampa, FL; abandoned 8/21/1933.

Schooner Rouse Simmons at Sheboygan, WI - C. Patrick Labadie Collection, TBNMS

Schooner *Rouse Simmons* (110024) - Built 1868 by Allan McClelland & Co., 205.26 gt., 124.2 x 27.6 x 10.1 ft. Disposition - Foundered 11/26/1912 Off Kewaunee, WI. Notes - Foundered off Kewaunee, WI, Lake Michigan with christmas trees on November 23, 1912 with all hands; eleven lives lost.

Scow Schooner *Emanuel* (8794) - Built 1869 by Gabriel Abrahamson, 38.97 gt., 54.5 x 15.7 x 4.9 ft. Disposition - Unknown Before 1890 Lake Superior. Notes - Last listed MVUS 1887, Marquette, MI.

1870s

The 1870s marked the high point of the golden age of sail on the Lakes and was the apex of Milwaukee's schooner building trade. Wolf & Davidson turned out a number of large, fast grain schooners, including the Moonlight, Marengo and Saveland, while Allen, McLelland & Co, turned out the bug schooner Porter, which would compete with Moonlight for the title of Queen of the Lakes. Milwaukee yards also began to turn out a significant number of small steamers from the yard of Nathan Brooks. The end of this decade saw an increase in steamer builds and foreshadowed changes in technology that would accelerate for the remainder of the 19th century.

Schooner *Skylark* (115024) - Built 1870 by Charles M. Downs, 16.65 gt., 44.7 x 12.4 x 4.6 ft. Disposition - Off Lakes 1876 Galveston, TX. Notes - Last listed MVUS 1886, Galveston, TX.

Steam Tug *Dick Davis* (6720) - Built 1871 by Nathan Brooks, 9.94 gt., 39.6 x 11.2 x 5.5 ft. Disposition - Collision, Sunk 10/6/1888 Manistee Lake, MI. Notes - Renamed *Joseph E. Rumbell, Jr.*, 1882.

Steam Tug *J.B. Merrill* (75363) - Built 1871 by Wolf & Davidson, 17.39 gt., 54.0 x 13.0 x 6.0 ft. Disposition - Abandoned 1914 Duluth, MN.

Schooner *Madonna* (90717) - Built 1871 by William Aylward, 76.66 gt., 79.66 x 24.5 x 6.16 ft. Disposition - Abandoned 5/27/1914 Detroit Harbor, WI.

Schooner *Angus Smith* (105030) - Built 1871 by Wolf & Davidson, 580.71 gt., 182.33 x 32.16 x 13.33 ft. Disposition - Abandoned 1910 Cleveland, OH. Notes - Final enrollment surrendered at Cleveland, OH, February 18, 1910, and endorsed "abandoned."

Barge *El Dorado* (135117) - Built 1871 by Wolf & Davidson, 487.23 gt., 189.0 x 31.7 x 11.0 ft. Disposition - Ashore 11/20/1880 Erie, PA. Notes - Built on hull of *Equator*, #7233.

Schooner *Penokee* (20468) - Built 1872 by Wolf & Davidson, 332.27 gt., 139.16 x 26.25 x 11.16 ft. Disposition - Off Lakes 1898 Atlantic Coast. Notes - Abandoned in 1923, last listed out of Boston, MA.

Schooner *Robbie Knapp* (21947) - Built 1872 by Wolf & Davidson, 15.25 gt., 50.0 x 13.3 x 4.5 ft. Disposition - Abandoned 1904 St. James, Beaver Island. Notes - Substantial rebuild of *Robbie Knapp*, built 1869 Bailey's Harbor, WI.

Schooner *Joseph Paige* (75593) - Built 1872 by Wolf & Davidson, 625.85 gt., 190.4 x 32.0 x 12.0 ft. Disposition - Stranded 12/1/1897 Vermillion Pt., Lake Superior. Notes - Stranded off Vermilion Point, Lake Superior, on December 1, 1897, while in tow of propeller *H.B. Tuttle*, and became total loss.

Steam Tug *James N. Brooks* (75718) - Built 1872 by Nathan Brooks, 10.15 gt., 41.1 x 11.5 x 4.8 ft. Disposition - Abandoned 1906 Kewaunee, WI. Notes - Early Lake Michigan Fish Tug.

Steam Fish Tug *Alvah Eaton* (105470) - Built 1872 by Nathan Brooks 14.81 gt., 49.0 x 12.0 x 4.0 ft. Disposition - Abandoned 1901 Milwaukee. Notes - Last listed MVUS 1901, owned by Tessler, Milwaukee.

Schooner *Alice B. Norris* (105471) - Built 1872 by Wolf & Davidson, 628.00 gt., 189.66 x 33 x 13.16 ft. Disposition - Abandoned 1932 Summer Island, Lake Michigan. Notes - Abandoned at Sturgeon Bay, WI, in 1927. Raised and towed to Summer Island by John Roen, then sunk as breakwater in 1932.

Steam Tug *Dexter* (6804) - Built 1873 by Nathan Brooks,, 23.67 gt., 52.2 x 14.0 x 6.2 ft. Disposition - Abandoned 1889 Milwaukee, WiI. Notes - Dismantled and engine removed, abandoned.

Schooner *Typo* (24981) - Built 1873 by Wolf & Davidson, 335.95 gt., 137.8 x 26.2 x 11.3 ft. Disposition - Collision, Sunk 10/14/1899 Off Presque Isle, Lake Huron.

Schooner *John B. Merrill* (75592) - Built 1873 by Allan McClelland & Co., 640.86 gt., 189.0 x 34.0 x 13.0 ft. Disposition - Foundered 10/14/1893 Off Drummond Island, Lake Huron.

Steam Fish Tug *J.W. Eviston* (75723) - Built 1873 by Allan McClelland & Co., 16.12 gt., 50.0 x 11.6 x 4.5 ft. Disposition - Burned 7/20/1897 Duluth, MN.

Schooner *George G. Houghton* (85374) - Built 1873 by Wolf & Davidson, 332.55 gt., 137.42 x 26.16 x 11.5 ft. Disposition - Foundered 9/10/1907 Bar Point, Lake Erie. Notes - Sprung a leak in heavy seas and sank when abreast of Bar Point Light, Lake Erie, on September 10, 1907.

Schooners Marengo, Itasca and Typo on the ways at Wolf and Davidson - Milwaukee Public Library Marine Collection

Schooner *Marengo* (90583) - Built 1873 by Wolf And Davidson, 648.25 gt., 189.0 x 32.0 x 13.4 ft. Disposition - Stranded 10/10/1912 Port Colborne, Lake Erie. Notes - Vessel sprung a leak and grounded on Morgans Point, five miles from Port Colborne, Ontario, Lake Erie, October 10, 1912, and went to pieces.

Steam Tug *H.F. Bues* (95346) - Built 1873 by Nathan Brooks, 23.70 gt., 46.5 x 13.6 x 6.0 ft. Disposition - Foundered 7/27/1910 Middle Ground, Lake Erie. Notes - Foundered, July 27, 1910, Middle Ground, Lake Erie.

Schooner *Itasca* (100108) - Built 1873 by Wolf & Davidson, 344.46 gt., 139.0 x 26.2 x 11.7 ft. Disposition - Collision, Sunk 10/7/1895 St. Clair Flats, St. Clair River.

Schooner *Saveland* (115227) - Built 1873 by Wolf & Davidson, 689.44 gt., 194.75 x 33.16 x 13.5 ft. Disposition - Stranded 10/22/1903 Grand Marais, MI, Lake Superior.

Steam Tug *General W.W. Belknap* (136032) - Built 1873 by Nathan Brooks, 20.21 gt., 45.2 x 15.5 x 6.0 ft. Disposition - Abandoned 1913 Milwaukee, WI. Notes - Built as Corp of Engineers tug, renamed *General A.A. Humphries*, 1879, sold private and renamed *Edward Watkins* 1889.

Steamer *Transfer* (none) - Built 1873, 90 gt. Disposition - Unknown Before 1900 Milwaukee, WI. Notes - Herman Runge notes this vessel - she appears in no other source, possibly an unregistered harbor barge.

Steam Fish Tug *Dan Costello* (6854) - Built 1874 by Nathan Brooks, 22.72 gt., 48.0 x 12.8 x 6.3 ft. Disposition - Abandoned 1913 Jones Island, Milwaukee.

Steam Scow *Josephine* (75763) - Built 1874 by Allan McClelland & Co., 146.00 gt., 99.0 x 25.0 x 6.0 ft. Disposition - Aground 4/14/1888 Whitefish Bay, North of Milwaukee.

Steam Fish Tug *G.R. Green* (85390) - Built 1874 by Ethel C. Penney, 18.16 gt., 48.2 x 11.4 x 4.9 ft. Disposition - Foundered 6/7/1915 Off Detour Light, Lake Huron.

Schooner *Moonlight* (90719) - Built 1874 by Wolf & Davidson, 777.01 gt., 205.75 x 33.5 x 14.16 ft. Disposition - Foundered 9/13/1903 Off Apostle Islands, WI. Notes - Foundered twelve miles off Michigan Island, Lake Superior, September 13, 1903.

Schooner *Myosotis* (90764) - Built 1874 by Milwaukee Shipyard Co., 333.22 gt., 137.6 x 26.2 x 11.5 ft. Disposition - Stranded 11/11/1887 St. Joseph, MI. Notes - Stranded 400 yards southwest of U.S. Life Saving Station, St. Joseph, MI, Lake Michigan, on November 11, 1887; crew of seven saved.

Steamer *Mystic* (93171) - Built 1874, 14.0 gt., 55.0 x 10.3 x 3.6 ft. Disposition - Abandoned 1904 Fox River, WI. Notes - Inland service, owned Neenah, WI 1902.

Schooner *Hattie Taylor* (95356) - Built 1874 by Ethel C. Penney, 84.84 gt., 84.1 x 22.6 x 8.1 ft. Disposition - Capsized, Sunk 8/26/1886 Off Sheboygan.

Steam Tug *F.C. Maxon* (120182) - Built 1874 by Nathan Brooks, 25.33 gt., 54.5 x 15.0 x 7.1 ft. Disposition - Dismantled 1890 Milwaukee.

Steam Tug *E.D. Holton* (135116) - Built 1874 by Wolf & Davidson, 24.70 gt., 58.66 x 14.5 x 6.48 ft. Disposition - Burned, Sank 8/31/1927 Dollar Bay, MI, Lake Superior. Notes - Burned to a total loss at Dollar Bay, MI, Lake Superior, on August 27, 1931.

Schooner *Lem Ellsworth* (140062) - Built 1874 by Wolf & Davidson, 340.14 138.6 x 26.2 x 11.8 ft. Disposition - Foundered 5/23/1894 Off Kenosha. Notes - Foundered with all hands during gale of May 23-24, 1894, on Lake Michigan; seven lives lost.

Schooner *Porter* (150012) - Built 1874 by Allan, McClelland & Co., 747.68 205.33 x 34.5 x 14 ft. Disposition - Off Lakes 1898 Gloucester, MA. Notes - Under charter, and in tow of propeller *Aragon*, along with schooners *David Wallace* and *San Diego*, broke tow line, December 3, 1898, 50 miles south of Cape Sable, N.S. Crew rescued by tug PROCYON, December 4, 1898, and vessel sank.

Steam Tug *Jennie Silkman* (none) - Built 1874 by Nathan Brooks, 36 gt., 60 x 12 x 3 ft. Disposition - Abandoned 1908 Torch Lake, Charlevoix, MI. Notes - Inland service on Torch and Clam Lakes, MI, unregistered.

Steam Fish Tug *Fred Engel* (120206) - Built 1875 by Nathan Brooks, 21.10 gt., 50.4 x 13.2 x 5.6 ft. Disposition - Abandoned 3/31/1920 Escanaba, MI. Notes - Renamed *P.W. Arthur*, 1904. Her hull was built at Kenosha, but she was powered and completed at Milwaukee.

Passenger Steamer *Flora* (120210) - Built 1875 by Wolf & Davidson, 531.73 gt., 174.25 x 27.58 x 10.5 ft. Disposition - Burned 12/2/1912 Chicago, IL. Notes - Burned at Chicago, IL, while being dismantled, December 2, 1912. Final enrollment surrendered at Port Huron, MI, March 28, 1913.

Steam Tug *James McGordon* (75867) - Built 1876 by Wolf & Davidson, 53.96 gt., 76.66 x 17.58 x 7.42 ft. Disposition - Abandoned 1914 Chicago, IL. Notes - Renamed *J.C. Evans*, 1898.

Steam Tug *Welcome* (80582) - Built 1876 by Wolf & Davidson, 56.65 gt., 82.0 x 17.0 x 8.0 ft. Disposition - Dismantled 1906 Cleveland, OH. Notes - Rebuilt 1906 at Cleveland as tug *George T. Nelles*, #202925, abandoned 1925.

Yacht Mary - C. Patrick Labadie Collection, TBNMS

Steam Yacht *Mary* (90910) - Built 1876 by Nathan Brooks, 50.12 gt., 71.0 x 13.0 x 5.6 ft. Disposition - Foundered 11/27/1910 Off Chicago, IL. Notes - Tug foundered fifteen miles east of Chicago, IL, Lake Michigan, on November 27, 1910; no lives lost. Final enrollment surrendered at Chicago, November 30, 1910, and endorsed "vessel & original lost."

Schooner *Starke* (115474) - Built 1876 by Allen & McClelland, 209.48 gt., 124.16 x 27.25 x 9 ft. Disposition - Off Lakes 1896 Louisiana. Notes - Stranded on Chandeleur Island, LA, on February 5, 1906.

Steam Tug *Hannah Sullivan* (95475) - Built 1877 by Ethel C. Penney, 28.55 gt., 59.0 x 14.2 x 6.0 ft. Disposition - Abandoned 1905 Waukegan, IL. Notes - Last listed MVUS 1905.

Schooner *Maria* (91096) - Built 1878 by J.R. Smith, 8.6 gt., 33.7 x 12.3 x 3.8 ft. Disposition - Abandoned 1899 East coast Lake Michigan. Notes - Last listed MVUS 1899, Beesons 1899, owned Pentwater, MI, wrecked 1895, Two Rivers Pt, recovered.

Steam Fish Tug *Alice* (106005) - Built 1878 by David Wilson, 8.93 gt. Disposition - Unknown Before 1885 Lake Michigan. Notes - Enrolled Chicago, 8/5/1881, owned Michigan City, 1884 (Polks), last listed MVUS 83, Chicago.

Propeller *Commerce* (125645) - Built 1878 by Wm. Aylward, 112.86 gt., 99.0 x 19.0 x 6.0 ft. Disposition - Abandoned 1931 Toledo, OH. Notes - Final enrollment surrendered at Toledo, OH, October 30, 1930, and endorsed "abandoned, propelling power removed; if used again, will be only in harbor."

Steam Tug *Johnny Hawkins* (none) - Built 1878 by Wolf & Davidson, 14.90 gt., 47.0 x 11.3 x 4.5 ft. Disposition - Unknown Before 1900 Inland Wisconsin. Notes - Built for service on Chippewa River, WI, owned Eau Claire, WI.

Passenger Steamer *Ariel* (105870) - Built 1879 by Philip O'Connor, 21.11 gt., 45.0 x 10.2 x 4.6 ft. Disposition - Off Lakes 1885 New Orleans. Notes - Last listed MVUS 1886.

Schooner *Resumption* (110384) - Built 1879 by Wolf & Davidson, 293.63 gt., 143.33 x 29 x 10.25 ft. Disposition - Stranded 11/7/1914 Plum Island, Door County.

Schooner Barge *Ford River* (120367) - Built 1879 by Wolf & Davidson, 299.36 gt., 143.2 x 29.0 x 10.4 ft. Disposition - Off Lakes 1917 Barbados. Notes - Sold Canadian, C122345 in 1907, sold Barbados 1917, scrapped 1919.

1880s

The 1880s marked the high point of Milwaukee's steamer building trade. Milwaukee Shipyard Company came into being through the merger of a few earlier builders and Wolf & Davidson switched their efforts from large schooners to steamers. Many of the gallant old barks and schooners were cut down to schooner barges and steam power clearly surpassed even the largest sailing ships for the ability to deliver grain cargoes. Large steamers like the *William H. Wolff* and *Thomas Davidson* were considered among the best on the Lakes, but were not the largest. By the 1880s, Milwaukee had been eclipsed as a shipbuilding center by the yards at Detroit, Cleveland and Bay City. Manitowoc was also rapidly becoming the center of Wisconsin shipbuilding activity. By the end of the 1880s, new builds of large vessels were becoming less common at Milwaukee and her yards began to shift their emphasis toward rebuild, repair and maintenance of vessels.

Steam Yacht *Barney* (3186) - Built 1880 by W. H. Wolf, 10.18 gt., 38.0 x 10.4 x 3.8 ft. Disposition - Unknown Before 1885 Lake Michigan. Notes - Last enrolled Chicago, 4/18/1882, last listed MVUS 1883, Chicago.

Propeller _Minnesota_ (91272) - Built 1880 by Wolf And Davidson, 1138.03 gt., 206.75 x 36.66 x 18.42 ft. Disposition - Burned 11/15/1903 Algonac, MI. Notes - Caught fire in engine room and burned off Walpole Island, St. Clair River, on November 17, 1903.

Propeller _R.G. Peters_ (110424) - Built 1880 by Milwaukee Shipyard Co., 386.04 gt., 175.4 x 31.0 x 10.5 ft. Disposition - Burned 12/02/1882 Off Milwaukee. Notes - Lost c. 30 miles off Milwaukee.

Steam Tug _Crawford_ (125799) - Built 1880 by Wolf and Davidson, 36.50 gt., 60.16 x 16.75 x 7.33 ft. Disposition - Scrapped 1908 Chicago. Notes - Destroyed by Great Lakes Towing Co., 1908.

Schooner Barge _Progress_ (150205) - Built 1880 by Wolf & Davidson, 1596.20 gt., 255.16 x 37 x 19.66 ft. Disposition - Scuttled 7/13/1927 Off Milwaukee.

Propeller Business - Historical Collections of the Great Lakes

Propeller _Business_ (3163) - Built 1881 by Wolf & Davidson, 985.63 gt., 191 x 34.58 x 17.58 ft. Disposition - Abandoned 1911 Lake Erie. Notes - Final enrollment surrendered at Erie, PA, June 24, 1912, and endorsed "abandoned."

Propeller _James H. Shrigley_ (76214) - Built 1881 by Milwaukee Shipyard Co., 459.92 gt., 171.5 x 31.16 x 11.5 ft. Disposition - Foundered 8/18/1920 Lake Ontario. Notes - Foundered off Braddock Point, Lake Ontario, August 18, 1920.

Steam Tug _W.H. Wolf_ (80821) - Built 1881 by Wolf & Davidson, 42.65 gt., 62.0 x 16.5 x 9.3 ft. Disposition - Abandoned 1911 Chicago. Notes - Rebuilt 1898 as _James A. Quinn_, last enrollment surrendered Chicago 5/15/1911.

Scow Schooner Helen - Historical Collections of the Great Lakes

Scow Schooner _Helen_ (95651) - Built 1881 by Wolf & Davidson, 119.60 gt., 90.2 x 23.2 x 7.4 ft. Disposition - Foundered 11/18/1886 Off Muskegon. Notes - Built on hull of scow _Ulster_, blt 1874.

Propeller _C.H. Starke_ (125945) - Built 1881 by Milwaukee Ship Yard Co., 317.98 gt., 149.42 x 30 x 9.58 ft. Disposition - Abandoned 10/10/1924 Cleveland, OH. Notes - Listed in MVUS 1925 as abandoned.

Steam Tug _Pearl Smith_ (150225) - Built 1881 by Wolf & Davidson, 21.59 gt., 49.4 x 13.7 x 5.9 ft. Disposition - Off Lakes 1887 New Orleans. Notes - Enrolled Milwaukee, 11/10/1881, last listed MVUS 1895, Shieldsboro, MS.

Steam Tug _Joseph Goldsmith_ (76317) - Built 1882 by Wolf And Davidson, 60.13 gt., 71.5 x 17.5 x 8.5 ft. Disposition - Foundered 7/26/1901 Toledo, OH. Notes - Final enrollment surrendered at Toledo, OH, May 4, 1903, and endorsed "abandoned."

Propeller _Marshall F. Butters_ (91408) - Built 1882 by Milwaukee Shipyard Co., 376.39 gt., 164 x 30.33 x 10.42 ft. Disposition - Foundered 10/20/1916 South East Shoal, Lake Erie. Notes - Foundered on October 20, 1916, ten miles southeast of Southeast Shoal, Lake Erie.

Steam Tug _Chicago_ (126009) - Built 1882 by Wolf & Davidson, 40.77 gt., 60.4 x 17.8 x 8.7 ft. Disposition - Abandoned 1915 Chicago, IL.

Propeller _Louis Pahlow_ (140559) - Built 1882 by Milwaukee Shipyard Co., 366.37 gt., 155.33 x 30.33 x 10.42 ft. Disposition - Abandoned 4/1938 Oswego, NY.

Steam Fish Tug _L.A. Schultz_ (140563) - Built 1882 by Wolf And Davidson, 31.81 gt., 58.3 x 15.5 x 7.0 ft. Disposition - Abandoned 1914 Milwaukee, WI. Notes - Last owned F.T. Shramm, Milwaukee, 1914.

Sloop *Thyra* (145551) - Built 1882, 8.45 gt., 33.5 x 10.9 x 3.8 ft. Disposition - Unknown Before 1900 Lake Michigan. Notes - Enrolled 7/11/1890, Chicago, last listed MVUS 1895, Chicago.

Steam Tug *Pilot* (150270) - Built 1882 by Wolf And Davidson, 30.83 gt., 55.0 x 16.6 x 7.9 ft. Disposition - Burned 7/29/1899 Menominee, MI.

Propeller Jim Sherriffs, Historical Collections of the Great Lakes

Propeller *Jim Sherriffs* (76392) - Built 1883 by Wolf & Davidson, 634.61 gt., 182.66 x 32 x 13.25 ft. Disposition - Burned 12/10/1922 Manistee River. Notes - Burned on Manistee Lake, December 10, 1922; one life lost. Final enrollment surrendered at Grand Haven, MI, March 28, 1923.

Propeller *George C. Markham* (85779) - Built 1883 by Milwaukee Shipyard Co., 309.23 gt., 141.33 x 28.16 x 10.42 ft. Disposition - Abandoned 12/6/1932 Detour, MI. Notes - Renamed *John W. Cullen*, 1920.

Schooner Barge *Menominee* (91551) - Built 1883 by Milwaukee Shipyard Co., 455.89 gt., 166.2 x 33.1 x 10.9 ft. Disposition - Sold Foreign 1917 Canada. Notes - Sold Canadian 1917, C138238, owned Sorel, Quebec, last listed 1935.

Sloop Yacht *Rambler* (110613) - Built 1883 by Milwaukee Shipyard Co., 43.83 gt., 61.0 x 16.8 x 2.2 ft. Disposition - Off Lakes 1886 New Orleans. Notes - Enrolled Milwaukee, 11/20/1883, last listed MVUS 1895, Tampa, FL.

Schooner Barge *Fred Carney* (120559) - Built 1883 by Milwaukee Shipyard Co., 361.0 gt., 152.2 x 30.4 x 10.5 ft. Disposition - Sold Foreign 1917 Canada. Notes - Sold Canadian 1917, #C138237, last listed Montreal, 1930.

Schooner *Norman* (130265) - Built 1883 by A. Peterson, 20.07 gt., 50.5 x 13.8 x 5.0 ft. Disposition - Unknown 1905 Cheboygan, MI. Notes - Last enrolled Milwaukee, 4/15/1897, last listed MVUS 1904, last listed Beesons 1909, out of Cheboygan, MI.

Schooner *James Mowatt* (76518) - Built 1884 by Wolf & Davidson, 523.17 gt., 166.4 x 33.1 x 13.0 ft. Disposition - Collision 10/10/1919 Alpena, MI. Notes - Collided with pier at Alpena, MI, on October 10, 1919, a total loss.

Steam Tug *John Evenson* (76523) - Built 1884 by J. Evenson, 32.73 gt., 54.2 x 13.8 x 7.1 ft. Disposition - Collision, Sunk 4/5/1895 Off Algoma, WI. Notes - Collided with str. *I. Watson Stephenson* and sunk in 300 ft.

Propeller *Joys* (76537) - Built 1884 by Milwaukee Shipyard Co., 268.07 gt., 131 x 28.16 x 9.75 ft. Disposition - Burned 12/25/1898 Sturgeon Bay, WI. Notes - Burned at Sturgeon Bay, WI, December 25, 1898. Final enrollment surrendered at Milwaukee, WI, December 31, 1898.

Scow Schooner *Cumberland* (126476) - Built 1884 by John Rehorst, 18.98 gt., 54.1 x 12.4 x 3.5 ft. Disposition - Unknown 1895 Lake Michigan. Notes - Enrolled 3/12/1888, Milwaukee, last listed MVUS 1894, owned M.J. Hansen, Manitowoc, WI.

Scow Schooner *J.I.C.* (76716) - Built 1885 by Michael Collins, 16.01 gt., 51.0 x 12.0 x 3.2 ft. Disposition - Unknown 1894 Lake Michigan. Notes - Built on the hull of schooner *Farmer*, #9454, laid up 1878, last owned Milwaukee 1894 by C. Gannus.

Steam Fish Tug *George R. West* (85879) - Built 1885 by Wolf & Davidson, 22.84 gt., 54.6 x 13.4 x 6.0 ft. Disposition - Abandoned 1925 Frankfort, MI. Notes - Last listed MVUS 1925, Henry F. Robertson, Frankfort, MI.

Scow Schooner *Hilda* (95944) - Built 1885 by Emil Robrahn, 14.48 gt., 49.0 x 12.0 x 3.0 ft. Disposition - Abandoned 1892 Milwaukee, WI. Notes - Sand & gravel scow, last enrolled Milwaukee, 6/12/1891, last listed MVUS 1891, Milwaukee, last owned O. Lietzke, Milwaukee, 1895 - Beesons.

Propeller *Susie Chipman* (116044) - Built 1885 by Milwaukee Shipyard Co., 216.10 gt., 122.0 x 26.1 x 9.4 ft. Disposition - Sold Foreign 1/18/1921 Canada. Notes - Last in commission in 1933. Removed from registration in 1955, but dismantled many years prior to that date.

Propeller *Josephine* (76618) - Built 1886 by Milwaukee Shipyard Co., 474.95 gt., 165.0 x 31.6 x 19.0 ft. Disposition - Collision, Sunk 9/27/1905 Off Mobile, AL. Notes - Left Lakes 1898 for east coast.

Steam Yacht *Edna* (unregistered) - Built 1886, builder unknown, 4 gt., listed Beesons 1886, owned Louis Sandrock, Milwaukee, WI. Notes – Believed wrecked 9/21/1897 at Milwaukee.

Propeller *W.J. Carter* (81112) - Built 1886 by Wolf & Davidson, 235.13 gt., 122.0 x 28.0 x 9.6 ft. Disposition - Foundered 7/28/1923 Off Point Petre, Lake Ontario.

Steam Fish Tug *Frederick Koehn* (120702) - Built 1886 by Wolf & Davidson, 39 gt., 54.6 x 13.4 x 6.0 ft. Disposition - Abandoned 1925 Sheboygan, WI. Notes - Owned Sheboygan, last listed MVUS 1924.

Propeller *Veronica* (161560) - Built 1886 by Milwaukee Shipyard Co., 1093.02 gt., 210.2 x 34.8 x 17.9 ft. Disposition - Sold Foreign 4/24/1918 Canada. Notes - Sold Canadian, 1918 as *Muriel W.*, #C138505, struck sunken crib in Welland Canal, at Port Weller, Ontario, on August 11, 1919; broke in two, four days later as a total loss.

Wooden Scow *Toboggan* (none) - Built 1886 by Milwaukee Shipyard Co., c. 200 gt., c. 100 x 25 ft. Disposition - Foundered 07/12/1887 Off Milwaukee. Notes - Capsized and sank c. 15 mi off Milwaukee under tow of *Marshall F. Butters*.

Scow Schooner *John Eggers* (76714) - Built 1887 by John Eggers, 25.49 gt., 58.7 x 14.0 x 3.4 ft. Disposition - Ashore 5/26/1906 Wind Point. Notes - Driven ashore north of Racine on Wind Point, 5/26/1906, a total loss.

Artist's conception of the *Wolf* - Author's Collection

Propeller *William H. Wolf* (81164) - Built 1887 by Wolf & Davidson, 2265.75 gt., 285 x 42.25 x 19.16 ft. Disposition - Burned 10/20/1921 Near Marine City. Notes - Burned on the St. Clair River on way to dry dock, wreck removed and sunk in deep water, 1925.

Launch of the William H. Wolf with Jones Island in the background - Milwaukee Public Library Marine Collection

Scow Schooner *Alma* (106517) - Built 1887 by Henry S. Downer, 26.42 gt., 57.4 x 15.9 x 3.0 ft. Disposition - Stranded 5/18/1892 Off North Point, Milwaukee.

Propeller *Roswell P. Flower* (110724) - Built 1887 by Wolf & Davidson, 1593.40 gt., 264.0 x 38.1 x 17.7 ft. Disposition - Stranded 7/3/1918 Drummond Island. Notes - Renamed *Agnes W.*, stranded on Drummond Island, MI, Lake Huron, in heavy weather on July 2, 1918; became a total loss.

Sloop *Elizabeth* (136004) - Built 1887 by Henry Schroeder, 9.23 gt., 39.7 x 12.3 x 3.0 ft. Disposition - Out of documentation 1899 South Haven, MI. Notes - Last listed MVUS 1898, last owned South Haven, MI.

Steam Yacht *Eva Hill* (unregistered) - Built 1887, builder unknown, 4 gt., listed Beesons 1886, owned George Steimel, Suttons Bay, MI. Notes - Final disposition unknown.

Propeller *Omaha* (155146) - Built 1887 by Milwaukee Shipyard Co., 1231.08 gt., 222.8 x 34.8 x 18.7 ft. Disposition - Scuttled 1925 Off Amherst Island, Lake Ontario. Notes - Sold Canadian 1914, #C134350, renamed *Maplegreen* 1920. Abandoned and scuttled in Lake Ontario in 1925.

Dredge *No. 2* (163076) - Built 1887 by Christopher H. Starke, 236 gt., 79.5 x 27.8 x 7.6 ft. Disposition - Abandoned 1926 Duluth, MN. Notes - Last owned Great Lakes Dredge & Dock, Duluth.

Propeller *John Rugee* (76753) - Built 1888 by Milwaukee Shipyard Co., 1216.81 gt., 216.42 x 35 x 18.58 ft. Disposition - Scrapped 6/1927 Ogdensburg, NY. Notes - Burned at Ogdensburg, NY, in lay-up, January 18, 1925. Broken up at Ogdensburg shortly afterwards.

Propeller *George H. Dyer* (86016) - Built 1888 by Wolf & Davidson, 1372.18 gt., 208.66 x 35 x 21.5 ft. Disposition - Foundered 8/18/1927 Off South Haven, MI. Notes - Renamed *Hennepin* 1898, first self unloader on Lakes.

Propeller *May Durr* (91998) - Built 1888 by Milwaukee Shipyard Co., 583.11 gt., 162 x 31.33 x 11.66 ft. Disposition - Ashore 9/27/1911 S. Manitou Island. Notes - Renamed *John Spry* 1892, *Three Brothers* 1903.

Scow Steamer *Hiram R. Bond* (95966) - Built 1888 by Milwaukee Ship Yard Co., 230.53 gt., 113.0 x 26.0 x 7.7 ft. Disposition - Collision, Sunk 5/29/1905 Off Milwaukee. Notes - Sunk by *Pere Marquette 20*, in sand & gravel trade.

Propeller *Arcadia* (106552) - Built 1888 by Milwaukee Ship Yard Co., 230.29 gt., 118.66 x 26.16 x 9 ft. Disposition - Foundered 4/15/1907 Off Ludington, MI. Notes - Foundered off Ludington, MI, Lake Michigan, on April 15, 1907, with all hands; fourteen lives lost.

Scow Schooner *Sunrise* (116219) - Built 1888 by George H. Thompson, 26.17 gt., 60.5 x 14.1 x 3.7 ft. Disposition - Out of documentation 1916 Milwaukee, WI. Notes - Last listed MVUS 1916, 1921 Beesons, owned Milwaukee by Herman Krones, in sand & gravel trade.

Scow Schooner *Pathfinder* (none) - Built 1888 by Thomas Eggers, c. 10 gt., c. 30 x 10 ft. Disposition - Ashore 1894 Michigan City, IN. Notes - In Milwaukee sand & gravel trade, unregistered but well documented in news accounts.

The Thomas Davidson drydocked at Buffalo - Historical Collections of the Great Lakes

Steamer _Thomas Davidson_ (145482) - Built 1888 by Wolf & Davidson, 2226.49 gt., 285.66 x 41.58 x 20.33 ft. Disposition - Abandoned 1933 River Rouge, MI. Notes - Abandoned in the Detroit River at River Rouge, hull removed and broken up in 1941 at Ecorse, MI.

Scow Schooner _Dawn_ (157211) - Built 1888 by Thomas Eggers, 26.17 gt., 60.5 x 14.1 x 3.7 ft. Disposition - Ashore 9/18/1903 Kewaunee, WI. Notes - Struck Kewaunee south pier and went ashore.

Steam Fish Tug _Arthur_ (106683) - Built 1889 by Wolf & Davidson, 36.79 gt., 55.7 x 14.1 x 7.4 ft. Disposition - Abandoned 1921 Cheboygan, MI. Notes - Last listed MVUS 1920, Cheboygan, MI, owned J.R. Hilborn.

Sloop _Rival_ (110985) - Built 1889, 11.43 gt., 37.5 x 12.9 x 3.2 ft. Disposition - Unknown Before 1900 Chicago, IL. Notes - Listed MVUS 1893 only, not in ABS or Shipmasters, listed Beesons to 1903, owned by Scott Ralter, Chicago, IL.

Steam Tug _Carl_ (126575) - Built 1889 by Milwaukee Ship Yard Co., 33.34 gt., 57.0 x 15.8 x 7.6 ft. Disposition - Scrapped 9/1920 Toronto, ONT. Notes - Sold Canadian 1914, renamed _Torsand_, #C134245.

Propeller _Topeka_ (145510) - Built 1889 by Milwaukee Shipyard Co., 1376.17 gt., 228.25 x 36 x 19.16 ft. Disposition - Collision, Sunk 8/15/1916 Detroit River, MI. Notes - Sunk in collision with propeller _Christopher_, August 15, 1916, abreast of Clark Street, Detroit, Detroit River; no lives lost. Wreck removed by dynamite on December 26, 1916, as menace to navigation.

Steam Scow _Two Henrys_ (145521) - Built 1889 by Henry Schraeder, 76.33 gt., 74.0 x 19.0 x 4.0 ft. Disposition - Unknown 1900 Chicago, IL. Notes - Sandsucker, last listed MVUS 1900, owned Chicago, IL by Frank Rann, listed Beesons to 1905.

Schooner Barge _Peshtigo_ (150474) - Built 1889 by Milwaukee Shipyard Co., 633.17 gt., 201.0 x 34.4 x 12.0 ft. Disposition - Abandoned 1935 Bay City, MI. Notes - Went aground August, 1928 off Harbor Beach, Lake Huron; towed to Bay City for repairs, declared a total loss, abandoned at Old Davidson Shipyard.

1890s

The 1890s started with a bang for Milwaukee shipbuilders. Some of the largest vessels ever built at Milwaukee were turned out by Wolf and Davidson and the Milwaukee Shipyard Company in 1890 and 1891, including the giant Ferdinand Schlesinger, the Fred Pabst, the Denver and the Pueblo. However, the Pueblo would be the last ship over 200 ft. to be constructed at Milwaukee for over 50 years. Technology had turned toward steel ship construction and the Milwaukee yards were not prepared to compete. Milwaukee shipyards would retool to focus primarily on maintenance of wooden vessels and the construction of smaller tugs, scows and pleasure boats. The big yards like Wolf & Davidson would not outlast the 19th century.

Steam Tug _Knight Templar_ (14495) - Built 1890 by Wolf And Davidson, 38.69 gt., 62.1 x 16.7 x 7.4 ft. Disposition - Abandoned 1929 KK River, Milwaukee. Notes - Laid up in KK River c. 1925.

Steam Yacht _Adele_ (106770) - Built 1890 by Robert Schultz, 36 gt., 76.9 x 14.0 x 4.0 ft. Disposition - Abandoned 1900 Lorain, OH. Notes - Built for Corps of Engineers, last listed 1900 MVUS Lorain, OH, last listed Beesons 1901, owned Arthur Moxham, Lorain, OH

Fred Pabst c. 1900 - note her unique arched stern house - Historical Collections of the Great Lakes

Propeller _Fred Pabst_ (120794) - Built 1890 by Wolf & Davidson, 2430.78 gt., 287.25 x 42.5 x 24 ft. Disposition - Collision, Sunk 10/11/1907 St. Clair River. Notes - Sunk 10/11/1907 in collision with steamer _Lake Shore_, raised 1908 and taken to Sarnia, 1920 made into a floating drydock at Port Huron, MI

Steam Tug _Leathem D. Smith_ (141055) - Built 1890 by Milwaukee Shipyard Co., 46.42 gt., 70.3 x 15.7 x 7.6 ft. Disposition - Dismantled 1911 Cleveland, OH. Notes - Last listed MVUS 1911, owned Great Lakes Towing Co.

Propeller _Denver_ (157268) - Built 1890 by Milwaukee Ship Yard Co., 1295.47 222.33 x 37 x 19 ft. Disposition - Sold Foreign 1911 Canada. Notes - Rebuilt as Canadian dredge _McMartin_, 1914, #C131008, abandoned in 1938, St. John, New Brunswick.

C.H. Starke Dredge at Milwaukee c. 1890 - Author's Collection

Dredge _No. 4_ (164057) - Built 1890 by Christopher H. Starke, 332 gt., 84.8 x 29.8 x 8.2 ft. Disposition - Abandoned 1928 Duluth, MN. Notes - Last listed MVUS 1927, owned Great Lakes Dredge & Dock, Duluth, MN.

Wooden Barge _Milwaukee_ (51332) - Built 1891, 131.55 gt. Disposition - Abandoned 1905 Duluth, MN. Notes - Last listed MVUS 1905, Duluth, MN.

Steam Fish Tug _G.M.A. Herrmann_ (86171) - Built 1891 by Wolf & Davidson, 34.46 gt., 61.6 x 14.6 x 6.5 ft. Disposition - Abandoned 1925 Sturgeon Bay, WI. Notes - Abandoned 1925, last owned Universal Shipbuilding, Sturgeon Bay, WI. Burned 1899 Port Washington, repaired

Propeller _Ferdinand Schlesinger_ (120841) - Built 1891 by Wolf & Davidson, 2607.70 gt., 305.58 x 43.33 x 20.58 ft. Disposition - Foundered 5/26/1919 Passage Island, Lake Superior. Notes - Foundered May 26, 1919, 5 miles SE x E1/4E from Passage Island, Lake Superior, with cargo of 3500 tons coal from Erie, PA, for Port Arthur, Ontario.

Propeller _Pueblo_ (150512) - Built 1891 by Milwaukee Shipyard Co., 1349.06 gt., 225.58 x 36.5 x 19.33 ft. Disposition - Burned 1/16/1926 Kingston, ONT. Notes - Sold Canadian 1913, #C133922, renamed _Richard W_ 1916, renamed _Palmbay_ 1923, hull removed and scuttled in 1937.

Steam Tug _Golden_ (86194) - Built 1892 by Wolf & Davidson, 44.18 gt., 63.9 x 17.6 x 8.0 ft. Disposition - Abandoned 7/1/1918 Milwaukee. Notes - Scuttled off Milwaukee, Summer 1918.

Steam Tug _Calumet_ (126838) - Built 1892 by Milwaukee Shipyard Co., 62.55 gt., 73 x 19.5 x 9 ft. Disposition - Abandoned 1931 Duluth, MN. Notes - Last listed MVUS 1930, Great Lakes Dredge & Dock, Duluth, MN.

Gas Launch _Casey_ (154779) - Built 1892, 14 gt., 44.1 x 10.2 x 4.5 ft. Disposition - Unknown Before 1920 Lake Michigan. Notes - Cannot find in any source, official# probably a typo, would welcome input, reference is from Runge Card.

Wooden Scow _No. 3_ (163490) - Built 1892 by Christopher H. Starke, 175 gt. Disposition - Burned 10/12/1918 Duluth, MN. Notes - Owned Great Lakes Dredge & Dock, Duluth, MN.

Steam Fish Tug _Henry Gust_ (96236) - Built 1893 by Wolf & Davidson, 37.50 gt., 60.9 x 15.9 x 6.9 ft. Disposition - Scuttled 8/1/1935 Two Rivers, WI. Notes - Burned and scuttled off Two Rivers as a 4th of July exhibition.

Sloop _Nina_ (130637) - Built 1893 by Adolph Frietach, 13.98 gt., 41.4 x 9.4 x 5.0 ft. Disposition - Off Lakes 1895 New York, NY. Notes - Later a schooner, last listed MVUS 1895, NYC.

Steam Sand Scow _Ellen_ (136358) - Built 1893 by Milwaukee Dry Dock Co., 349.95 gt., 121.0 x 30.6 x 8.0 ft. Disposition - Abandoned 1924 Milwaukee River. Notes - Hull removed and scrapped 1931.

Steam Tug _Mabel_ (211216) - Built 1893 by Milwaukee Dry Dock Co., 19 gt., 54.5 x 13.7 x 4.4 ft. Disposition - Abandoned 1923 Detroit. Notes - Last listed MVUS 1922, owned E.M. Emory, Detroit, MI.

Wooden Scow _No. 4_ (163491) - Built 1894 by Christopher H. Starke, 192 gt. Disposition - Burned 10/12/1918 Duluth, MN. Notes - Owned Great Lakes Dredge & Dock, Duluth, MN.

Dredge _R.M & S. Dredge No. 2_ (164214) - Built 1895 by Christopher H. Starke, 247 gt., 84.0 x 29.5 x 8.3 ft. Disposition - Dismantled 7/11/1913 Toronto, ONT. Notes - Sold Canadian 1912, #130317.

Wooden Scow _Scow No. 4_ (164215) - Built 1895 by Christopher H. Starke, 190 gt. Disposition - Out of documentation 1912 Buffalo, NY. Notes - Listed MVUS 1911 only, Buffalo, NY.

Wooden Scow _Scow No. 5_ (164216) - Built 1895 by Christopher H. Starke, 142 gt. Disposition - Out of documentation 1915 Duluth, MN. Notes - Last listed mvus 1914, Duluth, MN.

Wooden Scow _No. 14_ (164058) - Built 1896 by Adolph Bues, 181 gt., 111.2 x 24.0 x 8.4 ft. Disposition - Abandoned 1928 Duluth, MN. Notes - Owned Great Lakes Dredge & Dock, Duluth, 1927.

Schooner _Julia D_. (77303) - Built 1898, 11 gt., 29.0 x 11.8 x 3.8 ft. Disposition - Out of documentation 1901 Chicago, IL. Notes - Last enrolled 4/10/1899, Chicago, last listed MVUS 1900, Chicago, owned J.M. Dimmick, policeman.

Steam Fish Tug _A.A.C. Tessler_ (107409) - Built 1898 by George Benning, 30 gt., 58.7 x 13.9 x 7.4 ft. Disposition - Abandoned 1922 Port Washington, WI. Notes - Last listed MVUS 1921, John Hollander, Port Washington, WI.

Steam Fish Tug _Badger_ (207380) - Built 1899 by Louis Larson, 9 gt., 30.0 x 8.2 x 3.6 ft. Disposition - Abandoned 1915 Cleveland, OH. Notes - Final enrollment surrendered at Cleveland, OH, March 31, 1915, and endorsed "abandoned." Owned James Gordon, Ashtabula, OH, 1914.

Beeson's Marine Directory 1891 — Author's Collection

1900s

The 1900s saw a distinct change in Milwaukee shipbuilding, with a focus on scows, workboats and pleasure boats. Another interesting change was the inception of gas engines. Although steam would still dominate small vessels for another 20 years, many small launches began to be built with gas, kerosene or naphtha engines. Another interesting change was a dramatic decrease in the construction of sail vessels. Even small sail vessels were now relatively uncommon for new construction.

Wooden Scow No. 15 (164059) - Built 1900 by Adolph Bues, 258 gt., 120.0 x 27.9 x 10.0 ft. Disposition - Abandoned 1930 Duluth, MN. Notes - Owned Great Lakes Dredge & Dock, Duluth, 1927.

Wooden Scow No. 16 (164060) - Built 1900 by Adolph Bues, 258 gt., 120.0 x 27.9 x 10.0 ft. Disposition - Exempt 1935 Muskegon, MI. Notes - Last owned Roy Love Construction, Muskegon, MI.

Steam Fish Tug Paul Jones (207918) - Built 1900 by Louis Larson, 8 gt., 27.4 x 8.8 x 2.8 ft. Disposition - Sunk 1914 South of Racine, WI. Notes - Built as undocumented fishing sloop *Paul Jones*, rebuilt as fish tug *Ole*, 1911, last listed MVUS 1914, Cairo, IL.

Steam Fish Tug Esther (136938) - Built 1901 by George Benning, 15 gt., 38.6 x 10.0 x 4.0 ft. Disposition - Abandoned 4/19/1919 Port Washington, WI. Notes - Originally steam, converted to gas, last listed MVUS 1915, Milwaukee, last owned N.C. Perry, Port Washington, WI.

Wooden Scow No. 17 (164061) - Built 1901 by Adolph Bues, 289 gt., 122.0 x 29.4 x 10.2 ft. Disposition - Out of documentation 1915 Duluth, MN. Notes - Last listed MVUS 1914, Duluth, MN.

Gas Launch Endeavor (213601) - Built 1901 by William Barr, 6 gt., 23.5 x 8.4 x 3.6 ft. Disposition - Exempt - yacht 5/28/1921 Milwaukee, WI. Notes - Last listed MVUS 1920, Milwaukee.

Steam Fish Tug Mascot (93302) - Built 1902 by Louis Larson, 13 gt., 42.5 x 9.9 x 4.6 ft. Disposition - Abandoned 1927 Menominee, MI. Notes - Last enrolled 5/5/1913, Milwaukee, last listed MVUS1926, Frank Seidl, Menominee, MI.

Schooner Ida Caroline (100771) - Built 1902 by Charles F. Williams, 22 gt., 43.5 x 13.2 x 5.7 ft. Disposition - Stranded 10/11/1912 Beaver Island. Notes - Later a gas launch, last enrolled 8/13/1912, Marquette, MI, owned Hugh Campbell, St. Ignace, MI, listed in 1913 MVUS loss list, stranded Beaver Island.

Wooden Scow No. 18 (164062) - Built 1903 by Adolph Bues, 350 gt., 125.4 x 30.0 x 11.4 ft. Disposition - Abandoned 1930 Duluth, MN. Notes - Last listed MVUS 1929, owned Great Lakes Dredge & Dock, Duluth.

Wooden Scow No. 19 (164030) - Built 1903 by Adolph Bues, 382 gt., 125.0 x 30.0 x 11.4 ft. Disposition - Sold Foreign 10/1927 Cuba. Notes - Last listed MVUS 1926, owned Great Lakes Dredge & Dock, Duluth.

Steam Sand Scow Atlas (200815) - Built 1903 by Louis Pahlow, 232 gt., 186.4 x 30.0 x 4.0 ft. Disposition - Collision, Sunk 6/26/1907 Chicago River. Notes - Built as a twin screw, probably the largest sand sucker ever built, struck Clark St. Bridge abutment and sank.

Gas Yacht Itasca (221124) - Built 1903 by Charles Domanek, 7 gt., 32.8 x 8.5 x 3.5 ft. Disposition - Abandoned 1926 Milwaukee, WI. Notes - Last listed MVUS 1926, owned Jay Welshonse, Milwaukee.

Wooden Scow No. 21 (165280) - Built 1904 by W.H. Gillen, 297 gt., 125.8 x 33.3 x 8.4 ft. Disposition - Dismantled 12/1947 Milwaukee, WI. Notes - Last listed MVUS 1946, owned Waterways Engineering, Milwaukee.

Gas Launch Irene (203812) - Built 1905 by Louis Larson, 14 gt., 37.2 x 9.7 x 3.4 ft. Disposition - Abandoned 1937 Sheboygan, WI. Notes - Built on Park St., lauched in Burnham slip per Runge, last enrolled 1/23/1913, Milwaukee, last listed MVUS 1937, owned Robert Perl, Sheboygan.

Steam Fish Tug Viola (203892) - Built 1906 by Conrad Schulteis, 11 gt., 34.0 x 10.0 x 3.8 ft. Disposition - Abandoned 1927 Traverse City, MI. Notes - Last listed MVUS 1926, owned Burney Stites, Traverse City, MI.

Gas Launch Lydia (209173) - Built 1906 by Louis Larson, 8 gt., 30.0 x 11.5 x 2.0 ft. Disposition - Abandoned 3/31/1918 Manistee, MI. Notes - Last listed MVUS 1917, owned Christ Miller, Manistee, MI, Beesons 1914.

Steam Fish Tug Martin Treu (204474) - Built 1907 by George J. Benning, 18 gt., 44.0 x 12.4 x 4.4 ft. Disposition - Abandoned 1927 Menominee, MI. Notes - Last listed MVUS 1926, owned Frank Seidl, Menominee, MI.

Gas Launch Elsie Marie (204489) - Built 1907 by Chas. F. Williams, 15 gt., 35.5 x 10.3 x 5.6 ft. Disposition - Abandoned 1924 Gladstone, MI. Notes - Last listed MVUS 1923, Beesons 1921, owned Fred H. Lewis, Gladstone, MI.

Barge Barge No. 8 (166944) - Built 1908 by Bucyrus Co., 464 gt., 114.5 x 48.1 x 7.7 ft. Disposition - Out of documentation 1929 New York, NY. Notes - Built South Milwaukee, to east coast, 1925, renamed *Barclay*, last listed MVUS 1928, Standard Dredging, New York City.

Scow Schooner Wanda (205327) - Built 1908 by Louis Larson, 39 gt., 70.0 x 16.2 x 4.3 ft. Disposition - Abandoned 1931 Muskegon, MI. Notes - Last listed MVUS 1930, owned Otto F. Oswald, Muskegon, MI.

Steel Scow No. 24 (167385) - Built 1909 by Milwaukee Bridge Co., 336 gt., 122.0 x 30.0 x 10.0 ft. Disposition - Exempt 4/15/1919 Milwaukee, WI. Notes - Listed MVUS 1919 only, Milwaukee, a dump scow used only at Milwaukee.

Steam Fish Tug Martha (206883) - Built 1909 by Louis Larson, 15 gt., 35.8 x 11.2 x 3.9 ft. Disposition - Abandoned 2/1940 Milwaukee, WI. Notes - Last listed MVUS 1939, owned Steve Ceskowski, Milwaukee, WI.

Gas Launch Comet (206980) - Built 1909 by Louis Larson, 8 gt., 31.6 x 8.6 x 8.0 ft. Disposition - Abandoned 6/1936 Kenosha, WI. Notes - Last listed MVUS 1935, owned Theodore Muhlenbeck, Kenosha, WI.

1910s

The 1910s saw two very significant changes in Milwaukee shipbuilding. The first was the arrival of the Great Lakes Boat Building Company. Beginning in 1910, the Great Lakes Boat Building Company established a yard near First and Becher under president W.C. Morehead. The yard focused on turning out high quality wooden hulled gas launches, and by 1920, they were one of the leading manufacturers of cruisers in the country. During the period before WWI, many Great Lakes built cruisers were donated to the US Navy as part of the National Preparedness Movement. These vessels were painted gray and given the Navy designation "SP" as patrol boats. Most only saw inland duty and were returned to their owners after the War. Great Lakes also produced four sizeable sub chasers for the US Navy under contract. In addition to their standard designs, Great Lakes Boat Building turned out many custom luxury vessels for famous patrons, including Robert Ringling and Philip Wrigley. Some of their boats even featured a Victrola record player built in to the cabin. By 1925, the Great Lakes yard was moved to Chicago and became the Henry C. Grebe yard. Great Lakes yachts were some of the mostly highly sought status symbols of the roaring 20s and two are still known to be afloat, the Boss and the Pam.

Fabricated Shipbuilding yard 1919 - International Marine Engineering

The other major development of the 1910s was the inception of the Fabricated Shipbuilding Company. Fabricated Shipbuilding was created exclusively for the purpose of bidding on a lucrative WWI vessel building contract. At the start of WWI, Fabricated didn't even exist, but by 1919 the Newton Engineering company had teamed with Coddington Engineering as Fabricated Shipbuilding to design some of the largest steel vessels ever produced at Milwaukee. The yard was established on the isthmus formed by the Menomonee Valley canals, an ideal spot for side-launching ships. For two years, 1919 and 1920, Fabricated employed hundreds of Milwaukeeans in the shipbuilding trade, creating thirteen massive sub chaser vessels. Two of these became ferries in the Straits of Mackinaw and the rest went on to various ends. These were the largest vessels built at Milwaukee since 1891. By 1921, the massive operation was gone and the yard site was no more. Today, the former shipyard is occupied by the Chicago, Milwaukee, St. Paul & Pacific Railway yards.

Steel Barge *M. 2* (171434) - Built 1910 by C.H. Starke Dredge & Dock, 133 gt., 86.0 x 30.0 x 5.9 ft. Disposition - Still in service 2010 Broadview, IL. Notes - Renamed *No. 102*, 4/4/1936, later *RCC-01-SPUD*, oldest Milwaukee vessel still in service, owned Rausch Construction, Broadview, IL.

Steam Fish Tug *Imperial* (207168) - Built 1910 by George J. Benning, 35 gt., 54.0 x 15.6 x 5.4 ft. Disposition - Abandoned 1930 Chicago, IL. Notes - Last listed MVUS 1929, owned Construction Materials Corp, Chicago, IL.

Gas Yacht *Frolic* (209291) - Built 1910 by Great Lakes Boat Building Co., 16 gt., 45.0 x 19.0 x 4.5 ft. Disposition - Exempt - yacht 4/1940 Tampa, FL. Notes - Last listed MVUS 1939, owned John F. Webster, Tampa, FL.

Gas Launch *Seneca* (209323) - Built 1910 by Otto E. Scherbarth, 11 gt., 32.4 x 9.3 x 3.5 ft. Disposition - Abandoned 1931 St. Louis, MO. Notes - Last listed MVUS 1930, owned William Heuer, St. Louis, MO.

Gas Launch *Edna May* (213554) - Built 1910, 7 gt. Disposition - Unknown Before 1920 Lake Michigan. Notes - Listed only in MVUS Supplement 8/1914, probably exempted for size, not in Beesons or other directories.

Steel Barge *M. 3* (171435) - Built 1911 by C.H. Starke Dredge & Dock, 80 gt., 69 x 29.5 x 4.5 ft. Disposition - Out of documentation 5/31/2006 Holland, MI. Notes - Owned Duluth by Great Lakes Dredge & Dock, renamed *No. 103*, 4/3/1936, last owned by Lake Michigan Contractors, Holland, MI, 2006.

Gas Fish Tug *Sicilia* (210226) - Built 1911 by George Baarsen, 5 gt., 23.8 x 7.2 x 3.2 ft. Disposition - Abandoned 1945 Chicago, IL. Notes - Last listed MVUS 1944, owned Arthur Wallis, Chicago, IL.

Steel Scow *M. No. 4* (171438) - Built 1912 by C.H. Starke Dredge & Dock, 77 gt., 69.0 x 29.5 x 4.1 ft. Disposition - Out of documentation 1981 Buffalo, NY. Notes - Renamed *No. 104*, MVUS 1936, owned Great Lakes Dredge & Dock, Duluth, last listed MVUS 1980, owned by Donald Spencer, Buffalo, NY.

Gas Launch *Catharina* (210338) - Built 1912 by Richard Kuether, 18 gt., 45.0 x 9.2 x 4.2 ft. Disposition - Abandoned 1925 Milwaukee, WI. Notes - Last listed MVUS 1924, owned E. French Fuller, Milwaukee, WI.

Gas Launch *Amelia* (210628) - Built 1912 by George Baarsen, 5 gt., 23.0 x 7.4 x 3.5 ft. Disposition - Abandoned 2/1933 Milwaukee, WI. Notes - Last listed MVUS 1932, owned by the City of Milwaukee.

Steam Fish Tug *Eagle* (210709) - Built 1912 by George J. Benning, 40 gt., 51.0 x 15.5 x 7.0 ft. Disposition - Dismantled 1952 Sault Ste. Marie, MI. Notes - Last listed MVUS 1951, owned Earl Couture, Sault Ste. Marie, MI.

Gas Launch *Sylvia* (211458) - Built 1912 by Christian E. Sommer, 7 gt., 29.0 x 8.2 x 3.4 ft. Disposition - Abandoned 1922 Milwaukee, WI. Notes - Last listed MVUS 1921, owned Matthew Ferko, Milwaukee, WI, Beesons 1921.

Gas Launch *Red Wing* (216324) - Built 1912 by Herbert G. Zeibel, 11 gt., 30.5 x 10.5 x 4.5 ft. Disposition - Exempt - yacht 8/1936 Chicago, IL. Notes - Last listed MVUS 1935, owned Robert J. Miller, Chicago, IL.

Steel Scow *M. 5* (171436) - Built 1913 by C.H. Starke Dredge & Dock, 86 gt., 69 x 29.42 x 4.75 ft. Disposition - Scrapped 8/1969 Duluth, MN. Notes - Renamed *No. 105* in 1936, last listed MVUS 1968, owned by Great Lakes Dredge & Dock, Duluth, MN.

Dredge Kewaunee - Historical Collections of the Great Lakes

Dipper Dredge _Kewaunee_ (173993) - Built 1913 by C.H. Starke Dredge & Dock, 291 gt., 109.33 x 33.25 x 9.5 ft. Disposition - Dismantled 1960 Frankfort, MI. Notes - Corps of Engineers dredge based at Milwaukee, dredge apparatus built by Marion Crane Works, Marion, OH, renamed _No. 6_ in 1955, last listed MVUS 1959, owned Luedke Engineering, Frankfort, MI.

Gas Yacht _Penguin_ (211497) - Built 1913 by Great Lakes Boat Building Co., 31 gt., 51.0 x 12.2 x 5.8 ft. Disposition - Burned 10/13/1924 Monroe, LA. Notes - Last listed MVUS 1925, owned Thomas Wittmer, Philadelpha, PA.

Gas Launch _Esther_ (212469) - Built 1913 by William Caspari, 11 gt., 46.5 x 10.5 x 4.0 ft. Disposition - Burned, Sank 7/12/1925 Ferrysburg, MI. Notes - Renamed _Comet_, 1925, last listed MVUS 1925, last owned by A.R. Sadon, purser on the ill-fated carferry Milwaukee.

Steel Barge _No. M-1_ (171433) - Built 1914 by C.H. Starke Dredge & Dock, 129 gt., 85.6 x 30.0 x 6.5 ft. Disposition - Scrapped 1968 Duluth, MN. Notes - Renamed _No. 101_, 4/4/1936, last listed MVUS 1965, owned Great Lakes Dredge & Dock, Duluth, MN.

Steel Dredge _54_ (172258) - Built 1914 by C.H. Starke Dredge & Dock, 261 gt., 100.0 x 35.0 x 7.3 ft. Disposition - Dismantled 1954 Duluth, MN. Notes - Renamed Power Scow No. 6, 1943, last listed MVUS 1952, owned Great Lakes Dredge & Dock, Duluth, MN.

Wooden Scow _No. 7_ (173488) - Built 1915 by C.H. Starke Dredge & Dock, 12 gt., 38.6 x 16.0 x 2.6 ft. Disposition - Exempt 1958 Milwaukee, WI. Notes - Last listed MVUS 1957, owned Gillen Tug Co, Milwaukee, WI.

Steam Fish Tug _Myrtle_ (213681) - Built 1915 by Sommer Boat Bldg. Co., 10 gt., 31.0 x 9.3 x 4.1 ft. Disposition - Abandoned 12/1934 Milwaukee, WI. Notes - Last listed MVUS 1934, owned Herman Krones, Milwaukee.

Steam Tug _Chicago_ (232533) - Built 1916 by Great Lakes Boat Building Co., 68 gt., 75.33 x 15.5 x 9.25 ft. Disposition - Foundered 8/1974 Alexandria, VA. Notes - Corps of Engineers tug based at Chicago, went to east coast in 1958, final enrollment surrendered 2/1977, Washington DC.

Gas Yacht _Greyhound_ (SP-43) - Built 1916 by Great Lakes Boat Building Co., 10 gt., 40.0 x 9.0 x 2.3 ft. Disposition - To US Govt 1917 Florida. Notes - Built for Mrs. Ida W. Seybert of Key West, FL, chartered by USN as patrol boat USS SP-43, sold private 1919, never registered.

Terrier in sea trials off Milwaukee - US Naval Historical Center Photo

Gas Launch _Terrier_ (SP-960) - Built 1917 by Great Lakes Boat Building Co., 13 gt., 41 x 10 x 2 ft. - Built as a patrol boat for the National Preparedness Movement prior to WWI and turned over to the US Navy. Returned to civilian service 1919, final disposition unknown, unregistered.

Gas Yacht _Viroling_ (none) - Built 1917 by Great Lakes Boat Building Co., 14 gt., 43.0 x 10.0 x 2.0 ft. Disposition - To US Govt 1917 Florida. Notes - Speed yacht built for Robert Ringling, unregistered.

Gas Yacht _Hazelton_ (SP-1770) - Built 1917 by Great Lakes Boat Building Co., 10 gt., 40.0 x 9.8 x 4 ft. Disposition - To US Govt 1917 Hazelton, PA. Notes - Build for George Markle, Hazelton, PA, chartered by the US Navy as a dispatch boat USS _SP-1770_ at Newport, RI in 1918, returned to owner at end of WWI.

Great Lakes Boat Building Corporation Ad - Appeared in The Rudder, December 1921

Edith II underway c. 1918 - US Naval Historical Center Photo

Gas Yacht *Edith II* (SP-296) - Built 1917 by Great Lakes Boat Building Co., 33 gt., 50.0 x 12.0 x 4.6 ft. Disposition - To US Govt 1917 New Jersey. Notes - Built for Carnot M. Ward of Whippany, NJ, transferred to USN in 1917 as patrol vessel USS *SP-296*, returned to Ward in 1919, never registered, final disposition unknown.

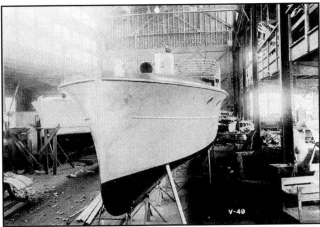
Sea Tag under construction at Great Lakes Boat Building - US Naval Historical Center Photo

Gas Yacht *Sea Tag* (SP-505) - Built 1917 by Great Lakes Boat Building Co., 20 gt., 51.0 x 10.3 x 2.5 ft. Disposition - To US Govt 1917 Detroit, MI. Notes - Chartered by USN as patrol boat USS *SP-505* from Donald Ryerson of Chicago, served at Detroit, returned 1919, never registered.

Gas Yacht *Sabot* (SP-213) - Built 1917 by Great Lakes Boat Building Co. 15 gt., 48.0 x 11.2 x 3.0 ft. Disposition - To US Govt 1917 Chicago, IL. Notes - Built for Mr. M.T. Clark of Winnetka, IL, chartered by the USN as patrol boat USS *SP-213*, never used as such, returned to owner 1919.

Gas Yacht *Rhebal* (SP-1195) - Built 1917 by Great Lakes Boat Building Co., 16 gt., 52.4 x 10.2 x 2.6 ft. Disposition - To US Govt 1917 Boston, MA. Notes - Chartered by USN as patrol boat *SP-1195* from A.R. Meyer, Boston, MA, returned to owner 1919, never registered.

Gas Yacht *Kumagin* (215919) - Built 1917 by Great Lakes Boat Building Co., 49 gt., 75.8 x 13.0 x 6.4 ft. Disposition - Abandoned 1946 New Jersey . Notes - Chartered by the USN as *SP-97* in 1917 but never used, renamed *Althea*, *Nick II*, *Spitfire II*, *Whiponong* 1928, last listed MVUS 1945, owned Reinauer Yacht Corp, New Jersey.

Gas Launch *Dreadnaught* (222281) - Built 1917 by Oscar M. Baarson 6 gt., 27.5 x 8.1 x 3.1 ft. Disposition - Abandoned 1931 Sturgeon Bay, WI. Notes - Last listed MVUS 1930, owned Frank Emmes, Brussels, WI.

Gas Yacht *Rosemary* (223384) - Built 1917 by Great Lakes Boat Building Co., 30 gt., 60.0 x 11.5 x 6.3 ft. Disposition - Burned 1/11/1925 New York, NY. Notes - Last listed MVUS 1927, owned Sound Motor Boat Service, New York, NY.

Gas Yacht *Quirl* (224915) - Built 1917 by Great Lakes Boat Building Co., 16 gt., 48.1 x 9.7 x 5.1 ft. Disposition - Abandoned 1959 Gloucester, MA. Notes - Last listed MVUS 1958, owned Robert S. Randall, Gloucester, MA.

Gas Launch *Paugus* (239887) - Built 1917 by Great Lakes Boat Building Co., 14 gt., 38.3 x 8.8 x 4.3 ft. Disposition - Exempt - yacht 1953 New York, NY. Notes - Last listed MVUS 1952, owned Gustav Ingold, New York, NY.

USN Sub Chaser *SC-328* (235624) - Built 1917 by Great Lakes Boat Building Co., 75 gt., 104.3 x 14.9 x 8.6 ft. Disposition - Foundered 1956 New Jersey Coast. Notes - Renamed *Sea Roamer* 1937, renamed *Katherine & Mary* 1948, last listed MVUS 1955, owned Trawler *Katherine & Mary*, Norfolk, VA.

USN Sub Chaser *SC-329* (222740) - Built 1917 by Great Lakes Boat Building Co., 89 gt., 104.3 x 14.9 x 8.3 ft. Disposition - Sold Foreign 8/1926 Panama. Notes - Renamed *Siwash III*, rebuilt as a gas yacht, went to east coast, 1923, sold foreign 1926, Panama.

SC 419 c. 1920 - Historical Collections of the Great Lakes

USN Sub Chaser *SC-419* (U.S. NAVY) - Built 1918 by Great Lakes Boat Building Co., 77 gt., 105 x 14.66 x 5.33 ft. Disposition - To Alaska 1927 Kodiak, AK. Notes - Sold to Alfred Lowengrund, Kodiak, AK, 1927, not in MVUS.

USN Sub Chaser *SC-420* (U.S. NAVY) - Built 1918 by Great Lakes Boat Building Co., 105 gt., 104.3 x 14.7 x 9.3 ft. Disposition - Sold Foreign 1921 Canada. Notes - Sold private as *Opco*, 1920, sold Canadian as *Mareuilendole*, 1921 #C138274, ran on Gulf of St. Lawrence in paper trade, owned by Robert McCormick, out before 1932.

Gas Launch _Nancy Winifred_ (228514) - Built 1918 by Great Lakes Boat Building Co., 17 gt., 37.0 x 9.5 x 4.5 ft. Disposition - Out of documentation 1951 Baton Rouge, LA. Notes - Renamed _Esso_ 1932, last listed MVUS 1950, owned Standard Oil Co, registered Baton Rouge, LA.

Yacht _Miss Liberty_ - Author's Collection

Gas Yacht _Miss Liberty_ (219148) - Built 1918 by Great Lakes Boat Building Co., 21 gt., 50.66 x 11 x 5 ft. Disposition - Burned 11/2/1969 Grand Rapids, MI. Notes - Last listed MVUS 1968, owned Ernest Vreeland, Muskegon, MI.

Gas Yacht _Vamp_ (218403) - Built 1919 by Great Lakes Boat Building Co., 21 gt., 47.3 x 10.7 x 5.5 ft. Disposition - Out of documentation 1945 New York, NY. Notes - Sold Canadian 1921 as #C138275, sold US 1943 as US218403, last listed MVUS 1944, owned Frederick Pfrommer, New York, NY.

Gas Yacht _Ranger_ (218641) - Built 1919 by Great Lakes Boat Building Co., 21 gt., 50.8 x 11.0 x 5.0 ft. Disposition - Burned 9/9/1939 Houston, TX. Notes - Burned in boathouse at Houston, TX, 9/9/1939, listed MVUS 1938, owned C.M. Dow, Houston, TX.

Gas Yacht _Nereid_ (219094) - Built 1919 by Great Lakes Boat Building Co., 23 gt., 53.9 x 11.0 x 4.9 ft. Disposition - Out of documentation 1960 Sault Ste. Marie, MI. Notes - Renamed _Nancy Ann II_, _Miss Liberty II_ 1937, last listed MVUS 1960, owned Richard Westrich, Sault Ste. Marie, MI.

Gas Yacht _Wild Goose II_ (219288) - Built 1919 by Great Lakes Boat Building Co., 21 gt., 50.8 x 11.0 x 5.0 ft. Disposition - Sold Foreign 1923 Argentina. Notes - To Missouri River, then sold foreign to Argentina.

Gas Yacht _Emma Belle III_ (219538) - Built 1919 by Great Lakes Boat Building Co., 27 gt., 62.0 x 12.5 x 5.0 ft. Disposition - Out of documentation 1955 St. Augustine, FL. Notes - Renamed _Kama_ 1920, _Mary_ 1930, _Wanda_ 1937 and _Thunderbird_ 1939, last listed MVUS 1954, owned Fred L. Munk, St. Augustine, FL.

Gas Launch _Mindora_ (222247) - Built 1919 by Christian E. Sommer, 14 gt., 47.8 x 12.0 x 4.8 ft. Disposition - Dismantled 1962 Milwaukee, WI. Notes - Runge notes she was a "booze boat" about 1923, last listed MVUS 1962, owned Willie Sommer, Milwaukee, WI.

US Navy Tug _No. 59_ (233306) - Built 1919 by Great Lakes Boat Building Co., 106 gt., 88.0 x 20.0 x 9.0 ft. Disposition - Dismantled 1951 New Haven, CT. Notes - Built for USN, to USCG renamed _Chautauqua_ 1920, sold private as _Edna May_ 1934, last listed MVUS 1950, New Haven Towing Co, New Haven, CT.

USCG Tug _No. 60_ (U.S. NAVY) - Built 1919 by Great Lakes Boat Building Co., 215 gt., 82.2 x 20 x 8.75 ft. Disposition - Dismantled 1941 Sturgeon Bay, WI. Notes - Built for USN, to USCG 1919 renamed _Chippewa_, sold private as _William Lloyd Greiling_ 1934, never enrolled, sank in slip, Sturgeon Bay, WI, c.1940; raised and dismantled.

Hull line layouts in the Fabricated Shipbuilding Mold Loft 1919 - International Marine Engineering

Mine Layer _General Rochester_ (222700) - Built 1919 by Fabricated Shipbuilding Co., 357 gt., 123.1 x 28.3 x 10.7 ft. Disposition - Scrapped 1961 Providence, RI. Notes - Built for US Army Quartermaster Corps, sold private to east coast, renamed _Michael J. Perkins_ 1923, last listed MVUS 1960, owned Harbor Construction Co, Providence, RI.

Mine Layer _Colonel Clayton_ (223237) - Built 1919 by Fabricated Shipbuilding Co., 364 gt., 122.6 x 28.5 x 10.3 ft. Disposition - Dismantled 1954 New York, NY. Notes - Built for US Army Quartermaster Corps, sold private 1924, last listed MVUS 1953, City of New York Dept of Docks, converted to a clubhouse, 1954 .

Mine Layer _Colonel Card_ (223692) - Built 1919 by Fabricated Shipbuilding Co., 429 gt., 172.5 x 28.0 x 10.7 ft. Disposition - Scrapped 1954 Keansburg, NJ. Notes - Built for US Army Quartermaster Corps as a minelayer, sold private 1923 as _Mackinaw City_, ran as ferry in the Straits, sold back to Army as _Brigadier General William E. Horton_ 1940, renamed _Mackinaw City_ 1947, sold for scrap 1952 at Keansburg, NJ, dropped from registry 1954.

Colonel Pond as the *Saint Ignace* c. 1950 - Historical Collections of the Great Lakes

Mine Layer *Colonel Pond* (223693) - Built 1919 by Fabricated Shipbuilding Co., 429 gt., 172.5 x 28.0 x 10.7 ft. Disposition - Scrapped 1954 Keansburg, NJ. Notes - Built for US Army Quartermaster Corps as a minelayer, sold private 1923 as *Sainte Ignace*, ran as ferry in the Straits, sold back to Army as *Brigadier General Arthur W. Yates* 1940, renamed *Sainte Ignace* 1947, sold for scrap 1952 at Keansburg, NJ, dropped from registry 1954.

The Bell on the ways at Milwaukee in 1919 - Historical Collections of the Great Lakes

Mine Layer *Gen. J. Franklin Bell* (U.S. ARMY) - Built 1919 by Fabricated Shipbuilding Co., 1130 gt., 172 x 32 x 17 ft. Disposition - Scrapped 1948 Boston, MA. Notes - Built as a minelayer, renamed *Brig. Gen. John J. Hayden*, sold commercial 1946, scrapped in 1948 by Boston Metals Co.

Gen. Absolom Baird in 1932 courtesy of Nick Tiberio

Mine Layer *Gen. Absolom Baird* (U.S. ARMY) - Built 1919 by Fabricated Shipbuilding Co., 1130 gt., 172 x 32 x 17 ft. Disposition - Scrapped 1954 Hoboken, NJ. Notes - Built as a minelayer, used at West Point as a training vessel, sold commercial 1946, repaired Hoboken 1952, scrapped NJ 1954.

Mine Layer Col. *George F.E. Harrison* (U.S. ARMY) - Built 1919 by Fabricated Shipbuilding Co., 1130 gt., 172 x 32 x 17 ft. Disposition - Captured 1942 Phillippines. Notes - Built as a minelayer, captured by Japanese in Philippines 1942, renamed *Harushima*, sunk at Yokosuka, 7/18/1945.

Launch of the Gen. John P. Story in the Menomonee River Canal - Milwaukee Public Library Marine Collection

Mine Layer *Gen. John P. Story* (WAGL-200) - Built 1919 by Fabricated Shipbuilding Co., 1130 gt., 172 x 32 x 17 ft. Disposition - Sunk in battle 3/15/1942 Caribbean Sea. Notes - Built as a minelayer, renamed *Acacia* 1924, went to USLHS, then USCG, sunk by German submarine U-161, on March 15, 1942, in Caribbean Sea.

Mine Layer *Gen. Edmund Kirby* (WAGL-222) - Built 1919 by Fabricated Shipbuilding Co., 1130 gt., 172 x 32 x 17 ft. Disposition - Beached, Burned 1948 Portland, ME. Notes - Built as a minelayer, to USCG renamed *Ilex*, to USLHS 1924, stationed South Portland, ME, decommissioned 1947.

Mine Layer *Gen. Wallace F. Randolph* (WAGL-230) - Built 1919 by Fabricated Shipbuilding Co., 1130 gt., 172 x 32 x 17 ft. Disposition - Sold Foreign 1947 Unknown. Notes - Built as a minelayer, to USCG renamed *Lupine* 1923, stationed in San Francisco, sold private 1947, not in MVUS, assumed sold foreign.

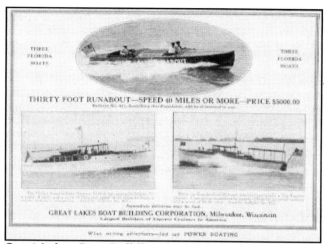

Great Lakes Boat Building Corp Ad - Power Boating 1923

1920s

The 1920s saw the end of WWI and along with it, the end of the Fabricated Shipbuilding yard. However, the Great Lakes Boat Building yard was going stronger than ever, turning out hundreds of luxury cruisers. It may never be known exactly how many significant yachts Great Lakes constructed, as many of them were never registered. The trade publications of the 1920s carried numerous articles about the speed of the Great Lakes yachts. Great Lakes was very active in the boat racing community and built several extremely fast gas yachts with advanced engines. These speed boats were built specially for racing and set several records during the 1920s. The 1920s also saw the emergence of the Gillen Tug Company, which began constructing barges at their yard on the KK River.

Mine Layer Col. Albert Todd (WAGL-229) - Built 1920 by Fabricated Shipbuilding Co., 1130 gt., 172 x 32 x 17 ft. Disposition - Sold Foreign 1946 Unknown. Notes - Built as a minelayer, to USCG renamed *Lotus* 1924 transferred to USLHS, served as a minelayer during WWII, last based Norfolk, VA, decommissioned 1946 and sold private, not in MVUS, assumed sold foreign.

Mine Layer Col. John V. White (WAGL-245) - Built 1920 by Fabricated Shipbuilding Co., 1130 gt., 172 x 32 x 17 ft. Disposition - Scrapped 1956 Jacksonville, FL. Notes - Built as a mine layer, to USCG renamed *Speedwell* 1920, sold private as *Santa Patricia* 1948, scrapped 1956, last owned Caribbean Fruit & SS Co.

Mine Layer Col. Garland N. Whistler (WAGL-246) - Built 1920 by Fabricated Shipbuilding Co., 1130 gt., 172 x 32 x 17 ft. Disposition - Abandoned Before 1950 South Carolina. Notes - Built as a minelayer, to USCG renamed *Spruce* 1923, stationed Staten Island as USLHS tender, decommissioned 1946, stored in South Carolina and offered for sale, further details not known.

Gas Yacht Eva (220358) - Built 1920 by Great Lakes Boat Building Co., 22 gt., 53.9 x 11.0 x 4.9 ft. Disposition - Burned 6/22/1933 Hyde Park, NY.

Gas Yacht Onyx (220399) - Built 1920 by Great Lakes Boat Building Co., 22 gt., 53.9 x 11.0 x 4.9 ft. Disposition - Burned 7/3/1937 Urbana, VA. Notes - Renamed *Wasp* 1922, *Roamer III* 1923.

Gas Yacht Olalen (220406) - Built 1920 by Great Lakes Boat Building Co., 22 gt., 53.9 x 11.0 x 4.9 ft. Disposition - Out of documentation 1954 Miami, FL. Notes - Renamed *Dea Maris* 1928, *Dorimar* 1931, *Norene II* 1937, last owned William Harben, Miama, FL.

Gas Yacht Suzanne (none) - Built 1920 by Great Lakes Boat Building Co., 45 gt., 76.6 x 13.9 x 6.0 ft. Disposition - Unknown Before WWII Unknown. Notes - Great Lakes Boat Building custom built speed yacht, pictured in The Rudder, May 1922.

Gas Yacht Frances (220433) - Built 1920 by Great Lakes Boat Building Co., 89 gt., 103.58 x 15 x 7.5 ft. Disposition - Dismantled 1957 Corpus Christi, TX. Notes - Renamed *Adroit II*, last owned Rockport Yacht & Supply, Corpus Christi, TX.

Gas Yacht Anna D. (220450) - Built 1920 by Great Lakes Boat Building Co., 22 gt., 53.9 x 11.0 x 4.9 ft. Disposition - Burned 10/8/1923 Hudson River.

Gas Yacht Miss Liberty II (220525) - Built 1920 by Great Lakes Boat Building Co., 33 gt., 61.8 x 12.0 x 5.8 ft. Disposition - Sold Foreign 2/1946 Britain. Notes - At Racine 1923, renamed *Renora II*, out of Buffalo, NY, renamed *Miss Liberty*, sold British 1946.

Gas Yacht Goodwill (220646) - Built 1920 by Great Lakes Boat Building Co., 22 gt., 63.0 x 11.0 x 4.0 ft. Disposition - Foundered 4/17/1964 Point Arena, CA. Notes - Shipped to Los Angeles in 1920, renamed *Goodwill Jr.*, later *Harmony*, 1926 out of San Francisco, last owned Coos Bay, OR.

Gas Yacht Sunshine (221028) - Built 1920 by Great Lakes Boat Building Co., 20 gt., 50.4 x 10.7 x 4.1 ft. Disposition - Dismantled 1959 New Orleans, LA. Notes - To New Orleans 1920, last owned Harvey Peltier, New Orleans, LA.

Gas Yacht Boss (none) - Built 1921 by Great Lakes Boat Building Co., 16 gt., 42.0 x 9.5 x 3.0 ft. Disposition - Still in service Cedarville, MI. Notes - Built for A.D. Goldman, St. Louis, MO, currently owned by Janet Carrington, Cedarville, MI.

Yacht *Pam* restored to pristine condition - courtesy of yacht's owners

Gas Yacht *Pam* (221234) - Built 1921 by Great Lakes Boat Building Co., 33 gt., 60.2 x 12.0 x 6.3 ft. Disposition - Still in service Newport, RI. Notes - Built as a hi speed rum runner for Detroit, MI owners of Hiram Walker Distillery, renamed *Apothecariana VI*, 1968, to Ft. Lauderdale, FL in 1980s and abandoned, restored at Newport, RI.

Gas Yacht *I.O.U*. (221235) - Built 1921 by Great Lakes Boat Building Co., 22 gt., 53.9 x 11.0 x 4.9 ft. Disposition - To US Govt 1945 Detroit, MI. Notes - Renamed *Thetis VII*, *Arabella* 1925, *Drieka* 1926, last owned George Naumann, Detroit, MI 1944, to US Maritime Commission 1945, disposition unknown.

Gas Yacht *Zodiac* (221261) - Built 1921 by Great Lakes Boat Building Co., 22 gt., 53.9 x 11.0 x 4.9 ft. Disposition - Out of documentation 1956 New York, NY. Notes - To New York City, 1921, renamed *Sazarac* 1923, *Restless* 1929, last owned Isabell Jeghers, NYC, 1955.

Gas Yacht *Mate O Mine* (221485) - Built 1921 by Great Lakes Boat Building Co., 22 gt., 53.9 x 11.0 x 4.9 ft. Disposition - Out of documentation 1971 Baltimore, MD. Notes - To Miami, FL, renamed *Julina II* 1928, *Bayforth II* 1929, *Far West* 1933, to Baltimore, MD, last owned John Francis, Baltimore, MD 1971.

Gas Yacht *Deedee* (221554) - Built 1921 by Great Lakes Boat Building Co., 18 gt., 48.0 x 10.0 x 4.5 ft. Disposition - Dismantled 1956 Miami, FL. Notes - Renamed *Messenger* 1923, to Miami, FL, last owned Oscar Christiansen, Miami, 1955.

Gas Launch *Dorethea III* (222242) - Built 1922 by Christian E. Sommer, 14 gt., 38.5 x 10.2 x 4.5 ft. Disposition - Exempt - yacht 1923 Milwaukee, WI. Notes - Last listed MVUS 1923, Milwaukee, WI.

Steel Dredge *Elizabeth Pfeil* (168841) - Built 1922 by Bucyrus Co., 378 gt., 145.0 x 40.0 x 7.0 ft. Disposition - Out of documentation 1970 Pittsburgh, PA. Notes - Built South Milwaukee for Iron City Sand & Gravel, Pittsburg, machinery built Midland, PA, last owned McDonough Company, Delaware, ported out of Pittsburgh.

Gas Yacht *Nereid* (222156) - Built 1922 by Great Lakes Boat Building Co., 17 gt., 43.1 x 10.0 x 5.5 ft. Disposition - Abandoned 4/1923 Off Palm Beach, FL. Notes - Listed MVUS 1922 home port Chicago, IL.

Gas Yacht *Roamer III* (222187) - Built 1922 by Great Lakes Boat Building Co., 22 gt., 52.0 x 11.0 x 4.9 ft. Disposition - Out of documentation 1981-1988 Cleveland, OH. Notes - To Seattle, WA, renamed *Hazel III* 1924, *Solace* 1925, *Amata* 1926, *Sally Ann II* 1927 to Lakes, last owned Ralph Harper, Cleveland, OH, MVUS 1981.

Gas Yacht *Uarco* (222267) - Built 1922 by Great Lakes Boat Building Co., 22 gt., 52.0 x 11.0 x 4.9 ft. Disposition - Out of documentation 1953 Chicago, IL. Notes - Renamed *Nanette* 1925, *Marlen* 1928, *Sea Esta* 1948, last owned John Hohenadel, Chicago, IL 1953.

Gas Yacht *Arrow* (222818) - Built 1923 by Great Lakes Boat Building Co., 22 gt., 52.0 x 11.0 x 4.9 ft. Disposition - Sold Foreign 1952 Mexico. Notes - To Los Angeles, CA 1923, converted to a fish tug, 1945 sold Mexican 1952, last owned, Lawrence Gibbons, Los Angeles, CA.

Gas Yacht *Wasp* (222978) - Built 1923 by Great Lakes Boat Building Co., 36 gt., 63.3 x 12.6 x 5.6 ft. Disposition - Out of documentation 1953 Chicago, IL. Notes - Built for Philip Wrigley of Chicago, renamed *Margaret M. II* 1936, last listed MVUS 1952, owned James C. Thompson, Chicago, IL.

Gas Yacht *Polly Lee* (223178) - Built 1923 by Great Lakes Boat Building Co., 36 gt., 63.3 x 12.6 x 5.6 ft. Disposition - To US Govt 1944 New York, NY. Notes - Built for Lee Rosenberg, NYC, renamed *Flash* 1927, *Dolphin* 1931, sold to US Maritime Commission 1944, last owned New York City, final disp unknown.

Gas Yacht *Elsie Fenimore* (223717) - Built 1923 by Great Lakes Boat Building Co., 22 gt., 52.0 x 11.0 x 4.9 ft. Disposition - Out of documentation 1970 Norfolk, VA. Notes - Renamed *See Bee* 1928, *Sea Bee* 1934, last listed MVUS 1970, owned Kenneth Meloney, Norfolk, VA.

Wooden Scow No. 12 (173491) - Built 1924 by Edward E. Gillen Co., 16 gt., 39.1 x 18.0 x 3.0 ft. Disposition - Dismantled 1957 Milwaukee, WI. Notes - First listed MVUS 1938, owned by Edward E. Gillen Co for entire career, last listed MVUS 1957, Milwaukee.

Gas Yacht *May B* (223728) - Built 1924 by Great Lakes Boat Building Co., 22 gt., 52.0 x 11.0 x 4.9 ft. Disposition - Forfeited 1932 New York, NY. Notes - To NYC, abandoned 1928, redocumented 1930 as a fish tug, forfeited 1932, owned James Murphy, NYC.

Gas Launch *Elizabeth* (223751) - Built 1924 by Great Lakes Boat Building Co., 8 gt., 30.6 x 8.5 x 5.1 ft. Disposition - Scrapped 1970 Newark, NJ. Notes - Built for John Crozer, Upland, PA, Exempt - yacht 1929, redocumented 1939, last listed MVUS 1970, owned Newark, NJ by Thomas A. Gordon.

Gas Yacht *Beth Anne* (223831) - Built 1924 by Great Lakes Boat Building Co., 23 gt., 54.7 x 11.0 x 5.1 ft. Disposition - To US Govt 1943 Miami, FL. Notes - Renamed *Nena* 1925, *J.I.M.* 1926, *Pepper* 1939, *Luzier II* 1940, sold to US Maritime Commission 1943, owned Thomas Luzier, Miami, FL, not in MVUS after 1943, final disp unknown.

Gas Yacht *Surdna III* (223832) - Built 1924 by Great Lakes Boat Building Co., 22 gt., 52.0 x 11.0 x 4.9 ft. Disposition - Burned 10/9/1949 Barnegat Bay, NJ. Notes - Renamed *Tech Jr*, later renamed *Snug*, last owned Perry T. Brown, New York City, MVUS 1949.

Gas Yacht *Solace III* (229969) - Built 1924 by Great Lakes Boat Building Co., 10 gt., 37.7 x 9.4 x 4.3 ft. Disposition - Exempt - tonnage 1934 Milwaukee, WI. Notes - Originally owned by Foster Stanfield, 1953 owned by Nathan Wilkinson of Milwaukee as undocumented vessel named 37-A-35.

Gas Yacht *Greyhound* (231517) - Built 1924 by Great Lakes Boat Building Co., 20 gt., 55.4 x 10.6 x 5.5 ft. Disposition - Out of documentation 1952 Los Angeles, CA. Notes - Renamed *Ting-A-Ling* 1936, last listed MVUS 1951 owned Irving J. Ulrich, Los Angeles, CA.

Gas Fish Tug *Wench* (253169) - Built 1924 by Great Lakes Boat Building Co., 9 gt., 34.4 x 10.0 x 3.6 ft. Disposition - Out of documentation 1950 Jacksonville, FL. Notes - Built as a gas yacht, not listed in MVUS until 1948, last listed MVUS 1949 owned by Harry J. Livingston, Jacksonville, FL.

Gas Yacht *Mistral* (224671) - Built 1925 by Great Lakes Boat Building Co., 22 gt., 52.0 x 11.0 x 4.9 ft. Disposition - Burned 7/19/1951 North River, NC. Notes - Renamed *Genevieve II* 1933, last listed MVUS 1952, Centre Motor Co, Norfolk, VA.

Gas Launch *Marshall E. Ross* (257559) - Built 1925 by Great Lakes Boat Building Co., 12 gt., 34.6 x 10.2 x 3.2 ft. Disposition - Out of documentation 1951 New York, NY. Notes - Last listed MVUS 1950, owned by Marshall E. Ross, NYC.

Gas Yacht *Priscilla* (225707) - Built 1926 by Great Lakes Boat Building Co., 37 gt., 57.0 x 13.5 x 5.1 ft. Disposition - Out of documentation 1965 Baltimore, MD. Notes - Built for Arthur E. Bendelari, Chicago, IL, owned Neenah, WI 1933, to east coast 1948, last listed MVUS 1965, Baltimore, MD.

Gas Yacht *Solace* (225610) - Built 1926 by Henry C. Grebe 53 gt., 69.3 x 14.5 x 6.2 ft. Disposition - Out of documentation 1981-1988 Pensacola, FL. Notes - Renamed *Alice Mary III* 1929, *Taneek* 1932, *Flohemia II* 1942, *Roamer II* 1946, to east coast, to Miami 1971 renamed *Vagabond*, last listed MVUS 1981 owned Patricia Ann Beck, Pensacola, FL.

Gas Fish Tug *Aquilon* (251025) - Built 1926 by Henry C. Grebe 15 gt., 39.4 x 10.6 x 5.1 ft. Disposition - Out of documentation 1980 Muskegon, MI. Notes - Renamed *Manda* 1957, last listed MVUS 1979, owned Ralph Matthews, Muskegon, MI.

Steel Scow *No. 11* (173490) - Built 1926 by Edward E. Gillen Co., 113 gt., 65.0 x 33.0 x 6.6 ft. Disposition - Exempt 1958 Milwaukee, WI. Notes - Built and owned by Edward E. Gillen, Co., Milwaukee, last listed MVUS 1957.

Steel Scow *No. 16* (173492) - Built 1926 by Edward E. Gillen Co., 106 gt., 70.1 x 34.1 x 5.0 ft. Disposition - Exempt 1958 Milwaukee, WI. Notes - Built and owned by Edward E. Gillen, Co., Milwaukee, last listed MVUS 1957.

Steel Scow *No. 17* (173493) - Built 1927 by Edward E. Gillen Co., 106 gt., 70.1 x 34.1 x 5.0 ft. Disposition - Exempt 1958 Milwaukee, WI. Notes - Built and owned by Edward E. Gillen, Co., Milwaukee, last listed MVUS 1957.

Steel Scow *No. 18* (173494) - Built 1927 by Edward E. Gillen Co., 106 gt., 70.1 x 34.1 x 5.0 ft. Disposition - Exempt 1958 Milwaukee, WI. Notes - Built and owned by Edward E. Gillen, Co., Milwaukee, last listed MVUS 1957.

Steel Barge Deck Scow *No. 16* (1026720) - Built 1929 by Edward E. Gillen Co., 119 gt., 70 x 34 x 6 ft. Disposition - Still in service 2010 Milwaukee, WI. Notes - Built and owned by Edward E.Gillen Co, Milwaukee, WI, possibly a re-documentation of scow *No. 16*, US173492.

Steel Barge Deck Scow *No. 18* (1026721) - Built 1929 by Edward E. Gillen Co., 119 gt., 70 x 34 x 6 ft. Disposition - Still in service 2010 Milwaukee, WI. Notes - Built and owned by Edward E.Gillen Co, Milwaukee, WI, possibly a re-documentation of scow *No. 18*, US173494.

Steel Barge Deck Scow *No. 23* (1026722) - Built 1929 by Edward E. Gillen Co., 119 gt., 70 x 34 x 6 ft. Disposition - Still in service 2010 Milwaukee, WI. Notes - Built and owned by Edward E.Gillen Co, Milwaukee, WI, possibly a re-documentation of scow *No. 23*, US173498, built Manitowoc, WI.

1930s

The 1930s was a very slow decade for Milwaukee ship building, mostly due to the depression, which hit Milwaukee quite hard. A few miscellaneous fish tugs and gas launches were built, but nothing on the scale of the previous decades.

Gas Launch *North Shore* (230121) - Built 1930 by Mertes Miller Co. 63 gt., 60.7 x 20.0 x 7.0 ft. Disposition - Foundered 9/26/1930 Off Racine, WI. Notes - Built corner of Barclay & Lapham, welded steel hull, owned W. J. Lawrie, Milwaukee.

Gas Launch *Alkco II* (239246) - Built 1930, 9 gt., 27.1 x 8.0 x 3.6 ft. Disposition - Out of documentation 1958 Milwaukee, WI. Notes - Owned by Albert Lester, Milwaukee, redocumented 1957, out of documentation 1958, Milwaukee, WI.

Fish Tug *Frank Braeger* (231087) - Built 1931 by Christian E. Sommer, 39 gt., 45.58 x 14.16 x 5.42 ft. Disposition - Out of documentation 1981 Chicago, IL. Notes - Built for Charles Braeger, Milwaukee, renamed *Majestic* 1974, last owned by Sandy Russell, Chicago, IL.

Gas Launch *Janet Virginia* (231862) - Built 1932 by A.J. Kaempfer, 17 gt., 44.2 x 10.5 x 4.6 ft. Disposition - Out of documentation 1951 Chicago, IL. Notes - Burned Chicago 7/21/1943 but redocumented as *Lobo* 1946, last listed MVUS 1950 owned Grace Braunsdorf, Chicago, IL.

Harry H at Manistee, MI c. 1950 - Historical Collections of the Great Lakes

Steel Fish Tug *Harry H.* (232597) - Built 1933 by Harry Hocks, 22 gt., 39.75 x 11.42 x 4.42 ft. Disposition - Still in service 2010 Muskegon, MI. Notes - Welded hull built at 27th St. for Eugene Hall, Grand Haven, rename *Bob Richard II* 1974, owned 2009 by Marine Mgt Ltd, Muskegon, MI.

Steel Fish Tug *H.W. Hocks* (234604) - Built 1935 by Harry Hocks, 34 gt., 47.2 x 13.0 x 6.0 ft. Disposition - Still in service 2010 Brimley, MI. Notes - Built at Burnham's slip, owned Milton Anderson, Algoma, WI 1970s, 80s, currently owned by Clifford Parrish, Brimley, MI.

Gas Launch *Segundo* (236400) - Built 1936, 11 gt., 34.4 x 9.3 x 4.3 ft. Disposition - Abandoned 1961 Key West, FL. Notes - To Florida, last listed MVUS 1961, owned Virgil Kidd, Key West, FL.

Gas Launch *Seafoam* (237699) - Built 1936, 12 gt., 34.8 x 10.0 x 4.2 ft. Disposition - Out of documentation 1976 Miami, FL. Notes - To Florida, last listed MVUS 1976, owned Benito National, Miami, FL.

Wooden Yacht *Wind Song* (525970) - Built 1936, 16 gt., 35.8 x 11.3 x 8 ft. Disposition - Out of documentation 1991 St. Croix, Virgin Islands. Notes - Last owned James R. Leblow, St. Croix, Virgin Islands, 1991.

Gas Yacht *Southern Belle* (263918) - Built 1938, 18 gt., 43.3 x 11.6 x 4.5 ft. Disposition - Out of documentation 1957 Tampa, FL. Notes - To Florida, last listed MVUS 1956 owned C.R. Naylor, St. Petersburg, FL.

1940s

The 1940s saw Milwaukee build the largest vessels ever turned out at the port. Milwaukee had always had a few small tug builders like Christian Sommer and Erich Slotty who operated small yards turning out a vessel each year. However, the onset of WWII brought another major push to turn out vessels with the Emergency Shipbuilding Program. Again, a government contract created a new shipyard in the form of Froemming Brothers on the north side of the KK River just west of South 1st St. Froemming Brothers had been a bridge construction business until 1942 when they decided to get into the ship building business. They teamed with Coddington Engineering again and in the space of three years, produce 27 massive steel ships. The contract began with 8 steel Navy V-4 tugs, each 185 ft. By 1944, Froemming employed over 1000 Milwaukee men and women, all engaged in building vessels for the War effort. A number of the Froemming tugs participated in the D-Day invasion at Normandy, while others went to the Pacific.

The Froemming yard also turned out four anti-sub frigates and 15 military cargo ships, many of which received decorations for their service. Some were sunk by enemy action and at least one was captured. With the end of the war, the Froemming Brothers yard was gone as quickly as it had been setup. Like the Fabricated yard before it, the facility had served its purpose and was abandoned. The Wagner Iron Works soon took over the site, which is now the site of Cramer Marine.

The Froemming Yard, Milwaukee Sentinel - April 17, 1944

Gas Yacht *Flying Cloud* (248784) - Built 1940, 23 gt., 46.9 x 15.6 x 6.3 ft. Disposition - Out of documentation 1994 Long Island City, NY. Notes - To east coast, last listed MVUS 1994 owned Michele Wolf, Long Island City, NY.

Steel Fish Tug *Loretta Mae* (241254) - Built 1941 by Erich H. Slotty, 26 gt., 41.0 x 12.3 x 5.4 ft. Disposition - Out of documentation 1994 East Point, FL. Notes - Last listed MVUS 1965, owned Seaman's Supply Co, Chicago, IL, out of doc., redocumented & rebuilt as *My Flower* 1974, to Florida renamed *Try Me II* 1989, last listed MVUS 1994 owned Bob Allen East Point, FL.

Gas Launch *Legionnaire* (264162) - Built 1941 by Christian E. Sommer, 9 gt., 43.2 x 9.7 x 3.3 ft. Disposition - Dismantled 1959 Milwaukee, WI. Notes - Last listed MVUS 1959 owned by Christian Sommer, Milwaukee, WI, probably rebuilt as *Legionnaire* #279829 at Milwaukee 1959.

Gas Fish Tug *Lorraine* (247699) - Built 1943 by Erich H. Slotty, 11 gt., 32.0 x 10.0 x 3.8 ft. Disposition - Out of documentation 1970 Chicago, IL. Notes - Last listed MVUS 1970, owned Chicago, IL by A.T. Rosenow.

Steel Tug *Point Loma* (243000) - Built 1943 by Froemming Brothers, Inc., 1117 gt., 185.5 x 37.6 x 17.8 ft. Disposition - Scrapped 1972 Unknown. Notes - Built as a US Maritime Commission V-4 tug, hull #1, delivered April 1943, scrapped 1972.

Steel Tug *Anacapa* (242999) - Built 1943 by Froemming Brothers, Inc., 1117 gt., 185.5 x 27.6 x 17.8 ft. Disposition - Scrapped 1971 Unknown. Notes - Built as a US Maritime Commission V-4 tug, hull #2, last listed MVUS 1971, owned US Secretary of Commerce.

Steel Tug *Point Vincente* (243246) - Built 1943 by Froemming Brothers, Inc., 1117 gt., 185.5 x 37.6 x 17.8 ft. Disposition - Sold Foreign 1969 Mexico. Notes - Built as a US Maritime Commission V-4 tug, hull #3, to Mexico 1969 as R 3, active as *Huitilopochtli* (A 51).

Steel Tug *Point Arguello* (243245) - Built 1943 by Froemming Brothers, Inc., 1117 gt., 185.5 x 37.6 x 17.8 ft. Disposition - Scrapped 1973 Unknown. Notes - Built as a US Maritime Commission V-4 tug, hull #4.

Steel Tug *Sankaty Head* (243387) - Built 1943 by Froemming Brothers, Inc., 1117 gt., 185.5 x 37.6 x 17.8 ft. Disposition - Scrapped 1978 Tacoma, WA. Notes - Built as a US Maritime Commission V-4 tug, hull #5, sold for scrapping to General Metals, Inc., at Tacoma, WA, in October, 1976; Scrapped July, 1978.

Steel Tug *Yaquina Head* (243389) - Built 1943 by Froemming Brothers, Inc., 1117 gt., 185.5 x 37.6 x 17.8 ft. Disposition - Scrapped 1971 Unknown. Notes - Built as a US Maritime Commission V-4 tug, hull #6, still in MVUS 1968, owned Secretary of Commerce, Milwaukee, WI, sold private 1971, scrapped.

Steel Tug *Bald Head* (243437) - Built 1943 by Froemming Brothers, Inc., 1117 gt., 185.5 x 37.6 x 17.8 ft. Disposition - Scrapped 1973 Unknown. Notes - Built as a US Maritime Commission V-4 tug, hull #7.

Steel Tug *Fire Island* (243531) - Built 1943 by Froemming Brothers, Inc., 1117 gt., 185.5 x 37.6 x 17.8 ft. Disposition - Scrapped 1975 Brownsville, TX. Notes - Built as a US Maritime Commission V-4 tug, hull #8, sold for scrapping in December, 1975, to Brownsville, TX.

Steel Fish Tug *Dela Elisa* (246807) - Built 1944 by Erich H. Slotty, 29 gt., 42.3 x 13.0 x 5.6 ft. Disposition - Out of documentation 10/31/2005 Buffalo, NY. Notes - Purchased by Falcon Marine, Chicago 1960, renamed *J G II*, documentation lapsed 1994 - 2004, renamed *Sea Mule* 2004, last listed 2005 at Erie, PA, owned Buffalo Industrial Diving Co.

Allentown in war colors - US Naval Historical Center Photo

Anti Sub Frigate *Allentown* (PF-52) - Built 1944 by Froemming Brothers, Inc., 1430 gt., 303.11 x 37.6 x 13.8 ft. Disposition - Scrapped 1971 Japan. Notes - Built as a USN Tacoma class patrol frigate, hull #9, to USSR 1945 as *EK-8*, to Japan 1953 as *Ume* (PF 289), scrapped 1971.

Launching of the USS Machias - US Naval Historical Center Photo

Anti Sub Frigate *Machias* (PF-53) - Built 1944 by Froemming Brothers, Inc., 1430 gt., 303.11 x 37.6 x 13.8 ft. Disposition - Scrapped 1969 Japan. Notes - Built as a USN Tacoma class patrol frigate, hull #10, to USSR 1945 as *EK-9*, to Japan 1953 as *Nara* (PF 282), scrapped 1969.

Anti Sub Frigate *Sandusky* (PF-54) - Built 1944 by Froemming Brothers, Inc., 1430 gt., 303.11 x 37.6 x 13.8 ft. Disposition - Scrapped 1970 Japan. Notes - Built as a USN Tacoma class patrol frigate, hull #11, to USSR 1945 as *EK-10*, to Japan 1953 as *Nire* (PF 287), scrapped 1970.

Launching of the USS Sandusky - US Naval Historical Center Photo

Anti Sub Frigate *Bath* (PF-55) - Built 1944 by Froemming Brothers, Inc., 1430 gt., 303.11 x 37.6 x 13.8 ft. Disposition - Scrapped 1966 Japan. Notes - Built as a USN Tacoma class patrol frigate, hull #12, to USSR 1945 as *EK-11*, to Japan 1953 as *Matsu* (PF 286), scrapped 1966.

Steel Cargo Ship *Charlevoix* (246354) - Built 1944 by Froemming Brothers, Inc., 3805 gt., 323.9 x 50.1 x 26.5 ft. Disposition - Scrapped 1970 Spain. Notes - Built as a USN Alamosa class cargo ship, hull #13, AK-168, sustained a fractured crankshaft in February, 1970; declared a constructive total loss. Arrived in tow at Castellon, Spain, on September 10, 1970, for scrapping.

Steel Cargo Ship *Chatham* (246561) - Built 1944 by Froemming Brothers, Inc., 3805 gt., 323.9 x 50.1 x 26.5 ft. Disposition - Foundered 1972 Off Puerto Rico. Notes - Built as a USN Alamosa class cargo ship, hull #14, AK-169, foundered in position 18.35N x 66.29W, twenty miles off Puerto Rico after suffering a rupture below the waterline on December 14, 1972; nineteen of twenty-four man crew lost. Was on voyage Santo Domingo for San Juan, Puerto Rico.

Steel Cargo Ship *Chicot* (246730) - Built 1944 by Froemming Brothers, Inc., 3805 gt., 323.9 x 50.1 x 26.5 ft. Disposition - Scrapped 1973 Taiwan. Notes - Built as a USN Alamosa class cargo ship, hull #15, AK-170.

Steel Cargo Ship *Claiborne* (AK-171) - Built 1944 by Froemming Brothers, Inc., 3805 gt., 323.9 x 50.1 x 26.5 ft. Disposition - Scrapped 1971 Spain. Notes - Built as a USN Alamosa class cargo ship, hull #16, AK-171.

The Clarion is launched into the KK River - Milwaukee Public Library Marine Collection

Steel Cargo Ship *Clarion* (AK-172) - Built 1944 by Froemming Brothers, Inc., 3805 gt., 323.9 x 50.1 x 26.5 ft. Disposition - Aground 1970 Peru. Notes - Built as a USN Alamosa class cargo ship, hull #17, AK-172, ran aground in fog about 560 miles north of Lima, Peru on April 26, 1970 and became a total loss.

Steel Cargo Ship *Coddington* (263025) - Built 1946 by Froemming Brothers, Inc., 3805 gt., 323.9 x 50.1 x 26.5 ft. Disposition - Scrapped 1973 Taiwan. Notes - Built as a USN Alamosa class cargo ship, hull #18, AK-173, sold foreign 1957, sustained minor damage at Phnom-Penh on November 11, 1972, and laid up at Singapore in January, 1973. Sold to Taiwan shipbreakers and arrived in tow at Kaohsiung for scrapping on January 14, 1974.

Colquitt during WWII - US Naval Historical Center Photo

Steel Cargo Ship *Colquitt* (AK-174) - Built 1945 by Froemming Brothers, Inc., 3805 gt., 323.9 x 50.1 x 26.5 ft. Disposition - Sold Foreign 1972 Phillippines. Notes - Built as a USN Alamosa class cargo ship, hull #19, AK-174, later USCG Cutter *Kukui*.

Steel Cargo Ship *Craighead* (AK-175) - Built 1945 by Froemming Brothers, Inc., 3805 gt., 323.9 x 50.1 x 26.5 ft. Disposition - Scrapped 1984 Turkey. Notes - Built as a USN Alamosa class cargo ship, hull #20, AK-175, decommissioned 1/18/1946, sold to Zeki Verel for scrapping in late 1983; arrived at Aliaga, Turkey, in January, 1984, for scrapping. Scrapping began on January 25, 1984, by Aydin Boru Endustrisi A.S.

The Doddridge as USCG Courier - Historical Collections of the Great Lakes

Steel Cargo Ship *Doddridge* (248685) - Built 1945 by Froemming Brothers, Inc., 3805 gt., 323.9 x 50.1 x 26.5 ft. Disposition - Scrapped 2008 US. Notes - Built as a USN Alamosa class cargo ship, hull #21, completed as Coastal Messenger, to USCG 1951 as *Courier* (WAGR 410), scrapped 2008

Steel Cargo Ship *Duval* (248687) - Built 1945 by Froemming Brothers, Inc., 3805 gt., 323.9 x 50.1 x 26.5 ft. Disposition - Scrapped 1975 Japan. Notes - Built as a USN Alamosa class cargo ship, hull #22, completed as Coastal Racer. Sold on March 3, 1975, by U.S. Dept. of Commerce to Umeya Trading Co., Ltd., Kobe, Japan, for $256,999, for scrapping.

Steel Cargo Ship *Knob Knot* (248121) - Built 1945 by Froemming Brothers, Inc., 3805 gt., 323.9 x 50.1 x 26.5 ft. Disposition - Scrapped 1971 Spain. Notes - Built as a USN Alamosa class cargo ship, hull #23.

Steel Cargo Ship *Salmon Knot* (248359) - Built 1945 by Froemming Brothers, Inc., 3805 gt., 323.9 x 50.1 x 26.5 ft. Disposition - Scrapped 1971 Spain. Notes - Built as a USN Alamosa class cargo ship, hull #24, arrived in tow, October 11, 1970, at Bilbao, Spain, for scrapping by Revalorizacion de Materiales, S.A.

Steel Cargo Ship *Yard Hitch* (248662) - Built 1945 by Froemming Brothers, Inc., 3805 gt., 323.9 x 50.1 x 26.5 ft. Disposition - Foundered 1967 Phillippines. Notes - Built as a USN Alamosa class cargo ship, hull #25, developed leaks and sank off the north coast of Luzon, Philippine Islands, in position 19.40N x 127.12E, on December 9, 1967; five lives lost.

Steel Cargo Ship *Taper Splice* (248879) - Built 1945 by Froemming Brothers, Inc., 3805 gt., 323.9 x 50.1 x 26.5 ft. Disposition - Scrapped Before 1980 Texas. Notes - Built as a USN Alamosa class cargo ship, hull #26, completed as Ben Froemming, sold private 1947, converted to drill ship *Goldrill 5* at Houston, TX, 1974.

Steel Fish Tug *A.E. Clifford* (249688) - Built 1946 by Milwaukee Shipbuilding Co, 33 gt., 40.5 x 13.42 x 5.58 ft. Disposition - Still in service 2010 Superior, WI. Notes - Still in service for Sivertson Fisheries, Superior, WI.

Steel Yacht *Namaycush* (250173) - Built 1946 by Sommer Boat Yard, 39 gt., 48 x 14 x 6.4 ft. Disposition - Still in service 2010 Leland, MI. Notes - Built at Sommer Boat Yard for Milton Anderson, renamed *Manitou Isle*, still in service, Leland, MI, owned Manitou Island Transit.

Steel Tug *Betty D*. (253177) - Built 1947 by Erich H. Slotty, 14 gt., 36.0 x 11.5 x 6.1 ft. Disposition - Out of documentation 1981-1988 Chicago, IL. Notes - Last owned by John Panzo, Chicago, IL, built for passenger service, later a fish tug.

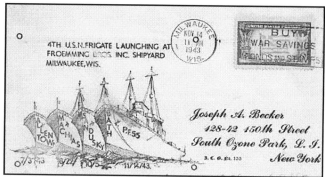
Envelope commemorating the launch of Froemming ships - Author's Collection

Tug Solomon Juneau in the Milwaukee River - Author's Collection

Steel Fish Tug *Kevin Bren* (254619) - Built 1947 by Erich H. Slotty, 42 gt., 50.9 x 15.1 x 7.0 ft. Disposition - Still in service 2010 Milwaukee, WI. Notes - Launched on the KK River as a fish tug, rebuilt by Milwaukee Shipbuilding as the tug *Solomon Juneau* in 1982, still in service, Milwaukee.

Wooden Yacht *Rainbow* (583710) - Built 1947 by Nimphius Boat Co., 9 gt., 36.7 x 9.8 x 5.5 ft. Disposition - Out of documentation 6/30/2005 Seaford, DE. Notes - Built at South Milwaukee.

Steel Fish Tug *Shirley K*. (255345) - Built 1948 by Erich Slotty, 22 gt., 34.6 x 11.3 x 4.2 ft. Disposition - Out of documentation 2/28/2001 Naubinway, MI. Notes - Owned by Kenwabikise Fisheries, cut of for scrap 2003 at Sault Ste Marie, MI.

1950s - 2000

Since the 1950s, Milwaukee has seen a number of small boat works come and go. The Sommer Boat Yard was one of Milwaukee's most enduring, lasting over 50 years. For a short time in the 1960s, a company called Island Yachts operated at Jones Island, building luxury yachts. In the 1970s and 80s, a number of local residents constructed vessels that were registered, including a relative of the author's, who built the yacht Liberty in 1973. Many of the vessels built at Milwaukee found their was to exotic locations, one even going as far as Hawaii. The last significant registered vessel built at Milwaukee was the replica schooner Denis Sullivan in 2000.

Wooden Yacht *Ann Patrice* (285041) - Built 1950 by F.M. Nimphius, 11 gt., 33 x 10.1 x 6.1 ft. Disposition - Out of documentation 12/31/1999 West Palm Beach, FL. Notes - Renamed *Dawntreader*.

Hanna-Kildahl on jacks at Milwaukee - Historical Collections of the Great Lakes

Propeller *Hanna-Kildahl* (264287) - Built 1952 by Sommer Boat Works, 45 gt., 61 x 16.42 x 6.25 ft. Disposition - Out of documentation 1981-1988 St. Louis, MO. Notes - To Missouri River, renamed *Zebulon Pike*, 1972.

Steel Tug *Leona B* (267897) - Built 1954 by Advance Boiler & Tank, 22 gt., 47.8 x 14 x 4.7 ft. Disposition - Still in service 2010 Franklin, WI. Notes - Built as *Advance No. 2*, still in service, Franklin, WI.

Wooden Yacht *Carolyn* (281865) - Built 1956 by Hoernke Boat Works, 15 gt., 38.0 x 12.7 x 5.3 ft. Disposition - Out of documentation 1981-1988 Ventura, CA. Notes - Renamed *Preceptor, Allison*, last listed 1980, Ventura, CA.

Steel Yacht *Vir-Bob-O* (274110) - Built 1957 by Robert W. Orth, 27 gt., 39.2 x 13.0 x 5.8 ft. Disposition - Out of documentation 1981-1988 Honolulu, HI. Notes - Renamed *Phyllis Ann, Lady Lorraine*, last listed MVUS 1980, Honolulu, HI.

Wooden Yacht *Rubaiyacht* (502675) - Built 1957 by Hoernke Boat Works, 15 gt., 37.8 x 12.9 x 7.1 ft. Disposition - Out of documentation 5/31/2003 Houston, TX.

Wooden Yacht *Legionnaire* (279829) - Built 1959 by Sommer Boat Works, 11 gt., 42.1 x 10.0 x 3.6 ft. Disposition - Out of documentation 1981-1988 Milwaukee, WI. Notes - Renamed *Elentari* 1971, owned by Christian Sommer, Milwaukee, WI, last listed MVUS 1981 owned Milwaukee, WI.

Wooden Yacht *Shenandoah* (284366) - Built 1959 by Hoernke Boat Works, 22 gt., 45.5 x 14 x 6.1 ft. Disposition - Out of documentation 10/31/2003 Chicago, IL. Notes - Last owned by Clipper Exxpress Co.

Wooden Yacht *Bobtail* (285988) - Built 1961 by Island Yachts, 8 gt., 33.4 x 9.5 x 4.8 ft. Disposition - Out of documentation 6/30/2003 Milwaukee, WI.

Wooden Yacht *Sea Hawk* (290175) - Built 1962 by Island Yachts, 33 gt., 47.9 x 14.9 x 7.2 ft. Disposition - Out of documentation 3/31/2004 Boca Raton, FL. Notes - Named *Max II* in 1976.

Wooden Yacht *Schatzie* (601274) - Built 1969 by Matthew Kornas, 13 gt., 34.8 x 9.1 x 8.8 ft. Disposition - Still in service 2010 Muskego, WI. Notes - Built South Milwaukee, still in service, Muskego, WI.

Wooden Yacht *Enchantress* (531813) - Built 1971 by Arthur L. Karnel, 13 gt., 36.6 x 12.1 x 6.2 ft. Disposition - Still in service 2010 Waukesha, WI. Notes - Renamed *High Seas Drifter*, sill in service, Waukesha, WI.

Wooden Yacht *Liberty* (559339) - Built 1973 by Howard Buretta, 11 gt., 35.5 x 11.7 x 5.3 ft. Disposition - Still in service 2010 Milwaukee, WI. Notes - Renamed *Spooner*, still in service, Milwaukee

Steel Pass *One More* (567955) - Built 1975 by Robert W. Orth, 15 gt., 28.1 x 11 x 4.8 ft. Disposition - Out of documentation 10/31/1994 Miami, FL. Notes - Built South Milwaukee.

Steel Yacht *Sails Call* (600631) - Built 1976 by Ron's Sales & Svc, 19 gt., 47.1 x 14.1 x 4.3 ft. Disposition - Still in service 2010 Racine, WI. Notes - Renamed *White Eagle, Romancing the Stone*, in service, Racine, WI.

Steel Yacht *La Rose* (612881) - Built 1979 by George Metzger, 26 gt., 56.8 x 10.1 x 9.1 ft. Disposition - Still in service 2010 Milwaukee, WI. Notes - In service, Milwaukee.

Plastic Yacht *Le Bote* (636151) - Built 1980 by Thomas Wahl, 8 gt., 26.5 x 9 x 7.5 ft. Disposition - Out of documentation 7/31/1997 South Milwaukee.

Steel Yacht *Gusty* (650104) - Built 1982 by Robert Boruta, 10 gt., 31.8 x 10.5 x 6.3 ft. Disposition - Still in service 2010 Milwaukee, WI. Notes - In service, Milwaukee.

Schooner Denis Sullivan - Author's Collection

Schooner *Denis Sullivan* (1100209) - Built 2000 by Wisconsin Lake Schooner, 99 gt., 85.8 x 22.8 x 10.6 ft. Disposition - Still in service 2010 Milwaukee, WI. Notes - In service, Milwaukee.

Port Washington Shipwrecks

Of the four port cities in this book, Port Washington has taken on the strongest maritime character. Even its name "*Port Washington*," suggests its nautical roots and reveals the intent of its early residents. Modern-day residents celebrate the town's maritime past with the annual Fish Days celebration, Maritime Heritage Festival and Pirate Festival. Smith Brothers Fisheries was for many years, a community landmark and the 1997 loss of the local fish tug *Linda E* reminded all of the community's cultural connections to Great Lakes shipwrecks.

The mouth of Sauk Creek was first settled in 1835 by a group led by Wooster Harrison, a clockmaker from the east coast. A small community was erected on the site but was abandoned after the 1837 land speculation collapse. Harrison returned in 1843 and continued development at the site. The settlers named the pioneer community Wisconsin City, but promptly renamed it Washington City after learning that the name had already been taken. At the time, the only access to the settlement was through the old Indian road between Milwaukee and Green Bay, so pioneer settler Solon Johnson quickly built a pier. Located at the foot of Jackson Street, the pier became known as the North Pier or Old Pier and remained in place until the 1870s. In 1844, the settlers made a conscious decision to emphasize the nautical nature of the town, renaming it Port Washington on a suggestion from pioneer George C. Daniells, and by 1847, the settlement had grown to a town with a brick yard, a saw mill and the grist mill driven by Sauk Creek.

1847 also saw the construction of the first pier at Port Ulao at the present day site of Kevich Light. Illinois investor James Gifford saw the need for a refueling station for wood-burning steamers and eventually built a 1000 foot pier at the foot of the bluffs. An elaborate system of chutes brought wood down from the bluff and nearly all large steamers bound up the coast called at the pier. During the 1850s, Port Ulao was known to vessel men from Chicago to Buffalo and rivaled Port Washington for vessel traffic. By the 1880s however, most Lake steamers had converted to coal and Ulao became a small fishing station. Ten miles north of Port Washington, a commercial pier was built at Rouksville and another was built twelve miles north at Amsterdam. These piers were built about 1860 and were active into the early 1900s.

Port Washington continued to gain popularity as a port of call, and the first lighthouse was erected in 1849 on a bluff overlooking the port, bringing 414 vessels to the piers that year. By 1853, lumberman Barnum Blake had built Blake's Pier at the foot of Pier Street, and that year 740 vessels called at the port. Soon after, Lyon Silverman built the South Pier at the site of the present-day south breakwall. The 1850s also saw the growth of the Wisconsin grain trade and Port Washington became a minor grain port. 1860 saw the construction of the present-day historic Port Washington Lighthouse to replace the crumbling 1849 structure. The 6th order Fresnel lense from the original light was placed in the tower and was eventually replaced with a larger 4rth order lense in 1870.

Schooner *E.R. Blake* on the stocks at Port Washington 1867 – Richard Smith

Port Washington was never known as a shipbuilding port, but two significant commercial vessels were built here. In July 1857, the steam tug *Ozaukee* was launched on the beach at Port Washington. She was an unusual sidewheel tug, serving across the Lakes before being lost on Lake Superior near Ashland in 1884. In 1867, the big three masted schooner *E.R. Blake* was side-launched from the beach just north of the harbor. She served across the Lakes until burning on Lake Huron in 1906

In 1869, a major plan was undertaken to improve the harbor, which was badly exposed to entering seas from the east and had already resulted in several accidents to vessels. Citizens raised $15,000 through a local property tax and work was begun in 1870. The massive harbor project resulted in the first entirely manmade harbor on the Lakes, as the mouth of Sauk Creek had never been navigable. The dredging contract was awarded to contractor Albert Conro and the specifications for the project were as follows:

"The present project for the improvement of the harbor, adopted in 1869 and modified in 1870 and 1876, was for the formation by dredging of two interior basins having a combined area of about 5 ¾ acres, with a depth of 12 ft and a channel of the same depth connecting them with the lake, the channel entrance to the basin to be north of the mouth of the Sauk River, enclosed between two piers so constructed that the flow of the river should be separated from the channel and that the debris brought down by freshets, instead of shoaling the channel should reinforce the south pier. The Channel at the mouth of the Sauk River was narrow and at the shoalest point had a depth of but one foot." – Annual Report of the War Dept, 1878

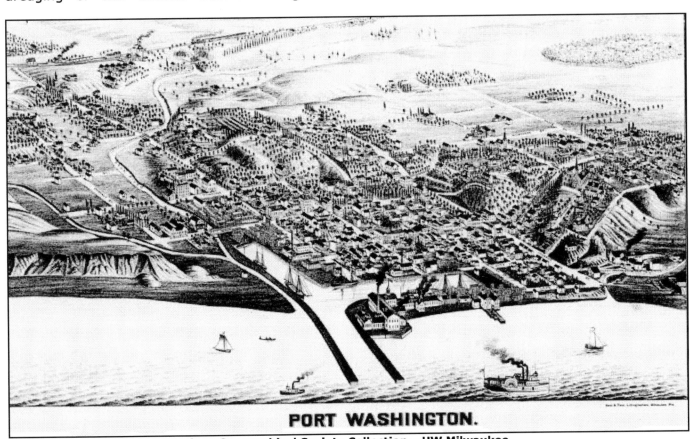

Port Washington 1883 – American Geographical Society Collection – UW Milwaukee

The dredging was completed and the north and south piers were in place by 1878, the north pier being 920 ft long and the south pier being 1226 ft long with a 400 foot revetment along the north bank of the Sauk River. The west slip built in 1870, proved to be very vulnerable to entering seas, prompting the 1876 construction of the north slip. Unfortunately, neither improvement completely solved the issue of entering seas and the harbor frequently required major maintenance after storms. In 1889, the Corps of Engineers erected a wooden pierhead light on the end of the north pier and placed a 6th order light in it to help guide vessels into the harbor, and vessel traffic continued to be brisk. Also in 1889, Port Washington businessmen formed the Wisconsin Chair Company, which would prove to be a mainstay of the city's economy for the next sixty years. The company accounted for much of the port's vessel traffic for the next 20 years and by 1893, the port saw 200 vessel arrivals and departures. As expected, the chief export was chairs, but exports also included barley, brick, leather, malt, lime and agricultural machinery. Imports included mostly coal, coke, tan bark, lumber and wheat. Despite the many harbor improvements, an 1893 survey still warned of many large boulders and the remains of a shipwreck (probably the schooner Bohemian) as hazards near the harbor's south pier.

1894 saw the emergence of the Gilson Manufacturing Company, which would later become the Bolens Company, making the Simplicity gasoline engine. By 1899, the chair company's buildings occupied most of the harbor area and were the victim of a disastrous fire, which burned a significant portion of the waterfront. The early years of the 1900s saw a drop in commercial vessel traffic, most arrivals and departures being furniture, lumber and produce carried on small steamers and schooners. The early 1900s also saw the emergence of Port Washington as a commercial fishing center with several commercial fish tugs calling the harbor home, including those of Smith Brothers Fisheries. Smith Brothers would go on to become one of the city's landmarks, operating Smith Brothers Fish Shanty restaurant and processing fish on the lakefront throughout the 20th century. Port Washington was the home of many commercial fishing families including the Bosslers, the Van Ells and the Ewigs, all of whom fished out of the port for much of the 20th century.

Schooners at Port Washington c. 1900 - Author's Collection

The 1930s saw dramatic reshaping of the city's south shoreline with the building of the Milwaukee Electric Railway & Light Company's new power plant. Initial construction was completed in 1935, and the plant radically extended the shoreline south of the piers, creating several acres of new land. Also in 1935 came the construction of Port Washington's current "art deco" pierhead light along with the current angled north breakwall. The 1940s saw the power plant enlarged with further shoreline alterations and frequent harbor improvements, but the basic harbor design of the north and west slip areas remained the same. The 1940s also saw the beginning of regular visits from large Great Lakes freighters carrying coal to the power plant. In 1959, the chair company buildings were demolished and the commercial fishing fleet began to decline, mostly due to the predation of invasive sea lampreys that almost completely eradicated the populations of Lake Michigan Lake Trout and Whitefish.

The 1960s saw the rise of scuba diving and many of the area's historic shipwrecks began to be located. Lake Michigan was restocked with non-native ocean fish that were resistant to the sea lamprey, including Chinook and Coho Salmon. The introduction of salmon to the Lake gave birth to a vibrant charter fishing industry, which continues to play a major role in Port Washington's summer tourism. In the 1970s, local diver Butch Klopp opened the Port Washington Sunken Treasures Maritime Museum to display his collection of area shipwreck artifacts and dive tourism became a small industry on the Great Lakes.

The 1980s saw laws passed outlawing the removal of artifacts from Great Lakes shipwrecks and also saw the creation of Port Washington's modern marina with its protective wave barriers. The 90s saw the loss of the venerable tug *Linda E* and her crew, bringing Port Washington's commercial fishing era to an end. The 21st century has seen further changes to the Port Washington waterfront, with the improvement of the modern marina, which finally provided full protection from waves entering the harbor and dramatically reshaped the north slip area. It also witnessed the removal of the iconic Smith Brothers Fisheries building, which had stood aside the harbor for nearly 100 years.

Port Washington in 2006 – City of Port Washington

Area marine historians Paul Weining, Linda Nenn and Rick Smith have researched and told the story of maritime Port Washington and took a leading role in preserving the 1860 Port Washington Lighthouse. Today, Port Washington has become a charming tourist destination with a harbor full of pleasure craft and charter boats. The waters off the harbor however, still hide the bones of many undiscovered shipwrecks and divers routinely set out from the harbor to dive the area's historic wrecks such as the *Niagara*, *Toledo*, *Northerner*, *Mahoning* and *Tennie and Laura*. The following accounts detail every commercial vessel known to have ended her career in Ozaukee County waters. Accounts are also given for vessels that were salvaged but had significant loss of life or were reported incorrectly as total losses. Locations shown on accompanying charts are approximate and in many cases are simply a best guess based on available historical info.

Hermaphrodite Brig reprinted from 1884 Annual US Merchant Vessels Register – Author's Collection

Brig *Illinois* (predates registry numbering) – built 1834 at Buffalo, New York by John Carrick, 99.0 x 25.2 x 9.5 ft., 209.31 gt. BOM, Enrolled Detroit 5/28/1839. Hermaphrodite Brig with 1 deck, 2 masts, and a figurehead. The Brig *Illinois* stranded and was nearly lost north of Port Washington in a November 1841 gale. She was released by salvors before the Winter set in and was repaired. She was lost November 4, 1847 when she stranded in a storm at Ahnapee (Algoma), Wisconsin. (Mansfield's History of the Great Lakes) Type: Stranding, Depth: Shallow, Remains: Definitely Removed, Accuracy: 5 Miles.

Schooner *W.G. Buckner* (predates registry numbering) – built 1837 at Irving, New York, 74.2 x 21.4 x 7 ft., 106.93 gt. BOM. Two masts, plain stem, square stern. Had gone ashore at Green Bay, 5/1849, released. The schooner *W.G. Buckner* sprang a leak and capsized 6 miles off Ozaukee with a lumber cargo bound from Bay de Noc to Chicago on September 28, 1849. The cargo owner, his wife and 5 children died. Survivors clung to wreckage for over 24 hours until they were taken off by the schooner *Erwin*. The *Buckner's* hull drifted ashore and was reportedly recovered but she disappears from all records after this accident. (Milwaukee Sentinel – October 4, 1849) Type: Stranding, Depth: Shallow, Remains: Possibly Present, Accuracy: 5 Miles.

Sidewheel Steamer *Lexington* (predates registry numbering) – built 1838 at Black River, Ohio by F.N. Jones, 152.0 x 20.6 x 11.1 ft., 353.53 gt. BOM, 1 deck, 2 masts, figurehead. Later 162.0 x 22.5 x 11.1 ft., 363.53 gt. BOM. The sidewheeler *Lexington* was driven aground and Stranded June 15, 1850 about 10 miles north of Port Washington in a rare June blow. Although she was reportedly pulled free, she never sailed again after this stranding and was condemned and dismantled. (Milwaukee Sentinel – June 18, 1850) Type: Stranding, Depth: Shallow, Remains: Probably Removed, Accuracy: 1 Mile.

Brig *Fashion* (9189) – built 1846 at Cleveland, OH by De Grote, 2 masts, eagle head, rebuilt 1864, 123.6 x 24.5 x 10.1 ft., 282.52 gt. BOM - The brig *Fashion* reportedly went ashore October 14, 1851 with a cargo of iron northeast of the Ulao Pier in the Fall of 1861. She was freed with $1500 damage before Winter set in and continued to sail until December of 1877, when she was wrecked at the mouth of the Kalamazoo River on the Michigan coast. (Mansfield's History of the Great Lakes, Buffalo Commercial Advertiser - Jan. 2, 1852) Type: Stranding, Depth: Shallow, Remains: Definitely Removed, Accuracy: ¼ Mile.

Schooner *A.V. Knickerbocker* (predates registry numbering) – built 1840 at Detroit, Michigan, 66.8 x 17.4 x 6.0 ft., 58.91 gt. BOM, 2 masts, plain stem - The schooner *A.V. Knickerbocker* Capsized and came ashore August 26, 1855 in a storm and washed ashore six miles North of Port Washington. The captain was lost trying to swim ashore, but the crew survived. The vessel was a total loss. She was abandoned in the surf and her remains are probably still buried under the beach. The remains of the *Knickerbocker* were reportedly visible on the beach as late as 1920, but their exact location is no longer known. (Milwaukee Sentinel - August 28, 1855) Type: Stranding, Depth: Shallow, Remains: Probably Present, Accuracy: ¼ Mile.

Brig rig typical on Great Lakes – Reprinted from 1884 US Merchant Vessels Register – Author's Collection

Brig *Racine* (21183) – built 1852 at Racine, Wisconsin by Justice Bailey, 1 deck, 2 masts, gallery, scroll stem, 106.5 x 26.2 x 9.2 ft., 229.05 gt. BOM - The brig *Racine* capsized in a storm, drifted for days and sank in shallow water off Ulao in October of 1855. Her master was Capt. Charles Cramer. The crew was rescued by the brig *Hutchinson*. The *Racine* was recovered with $8000 damage (a constructive total loss) and rebuilt as a schooner. She was lost for good on 10/30/1868 off Pt. Aux Barques in Lake Huron. (Buffalo Daily Republic - October 25, 1855, NARA Vessel Enrollment Data) Type: Stranding, Depth: Shallow, Remains: Definitely Removed Accuracy: 1 Mile.

Schooner *Active* (predates registry numbering) - built 1845 at Green Bay, Wisconsin, 25.62 gt. BOM, 1 deck, 2 masts, last enrolled 3/21/1854, Milwaukee - Bound Manitowoc for Chicago, the little schooner *Active* Capsized and foundered October 10, 1855 in a squall off Port Washington. Her crew clung to her upturned hull until rescued in a risky maneuver by the schooner *Thornton* on the 11th. She was last seen floating bottom-up by the prop *Sciota* on the 13th, 15 miles off Milwaukee. There is no record of her after this date. She had struck a bar and sunk off Manitowoc in June of the same year. Owned by Eslinger of Manitowoc. Vessel and cargo worth about $2500. (Milwaukee Sentinel – October 12, 1855) Type: Foundering, Depth: Very Deep, Remains: Definitely Present, Accuracy: 10 Miles.

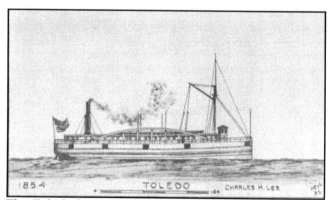

The *Toledo* from an Erik Heyl print in the Author's Collection

Propeller *Toledo* (predates registry numbering) – built 1854 at Buffalo, New York by B.B. Jones, 178.7 x 29.2 x 11.1 ft., 585.21 gt. BOM, 1 deck, 1 mast, square stern, plain stem. - About 40 people drowned when this vessel was driven ashore and broke up at Port Washington on October 22, 1856. Only 3 were saved. Merchandise was scattered for miles on the beach. The *Toledo* has just taken on a load of wood and departed when a severe gale blew up. The *Toledo* was unable to make headway and was being blown toward shore. The Captain consequently dropped the anchor, but it became fouled and the *Toledo* was blown into the shallows 100 yards north and 25 yards east of Port Washington's north pier where the waves took her apart. She was a total loss of over $100,000. Her broken and scattered remains reportedly uncover periodically on the sandy bottom in 20 ft of water. Remains displayed at Port Washington attributed to the *Toledo* are now believed, based on location, to be from the schooner *Bohemian* which wrecked at the same time. (Milwaukee Sentinel – 10/27/1856) Type: Stranding, Depth: Shallow, Remains: Identified, Accuracy: 43.23.430/87.51.671.

Lake Yields Wreck Relics

A drag which is excavating an intake channel for the new Port Washington power plant of the Electric Co. has been bringing up pieces of the hull and cargo of the steamer Toledo, which was lost with 78 lives in the summer of 1856. The picture shows the jagged lower timbers of the hull and the keel which pounded to pieces on the beach. Engineer F. W. Knapp is standing beside them, and behind him can be seen part of the drag which brought up the timbers. Other things recovered include 100 feet of anchor chain, a mast hoop, a car wheel with the date 1856 cast in it, and a boot of pre-Civil war style.

The remains brought up in October 1931 were attributed to the steamer *Toledo* because it was a well known area wreck. However, based on the nature of the cargo and its location these remains are now believed to be from the schooner *Bohemian*, which wrecked in the same storm as the *Toledo* (Milwaukee Sentinel – October 1, 1931)

Schooner *Bohemian* (predates registry numbering) built 1856 at Buffalo, NY, 137 x 26 x 11 ft., 372.54 gt. BOM, enrolled 7/3/1856, Oswego, NY. - The schooner *Bohemian* stranded at Port Washington in October 22, 1856 in the same gale that wrecked the *Toledo*. She was driven onto the south shore of Port Washington Harbor, 200 yards south of Silverman's Pier. She carried a mixed cargo of pig iron and railroad wheels. Her crew rescued by local citizens. The *Bohemian* was a brand new vessel and was launched only four months earlier in Buffalo, New York. Some of her cargo was found in 1930 when the harbor was dredged. It is now on display, misidentified as being from the steamer Toledo. The *Bohemian's* remains have never been positively identified. (Milwaukee Sentinel – 10/28/1856, Rick Smith) Type: Stranding, Depth: Shallow, Remains: Probably Present, Accuracy: ¼ Mile.

Steamer *Niagara* from a copy of an original lithograph – Author's Collection

Sidewheel Steamer *Niagara* (predates registry numbering) – built 1845 at Buffalo, New York by Bidwell & Banta, 245.0 x 33.6 x 14.0 ft., 1099 gt. BOM - The steamer *Niagara* burned and sank north of Port Washington on November 24, 1856, taking the lives of over 60 Dutch immigrants and crew. She was bound from Collingwood, Ontario to Chicago and carried some flammable cargo, which started the fire. The *Niagara* was run for shore when the fire was discovered, but this only fanned the flames and the ship's hull eventually burned through and she sank. The steamers *Traveler* and *Illinois* and a number of schooners including *Marble* and *Mary Grover* helped to rescue the survivors. Her approximate location was charted by the Lake Survey before WWII and was found with a fish finder about 1963 by Chicago dive shop owner Pat Delaney. John Jensen of the Wisconsin Historical Society did a detailed archeological survey of the site in the 1990s. The wreck is upright and partially intact in 50 ft of water. Her sidewheels are still present, but collapsed in the 1980s, boilers are a short distance from hull. (Milwaukee Sentinel – 11/28/1856) Type: Foundering, Depth: Shallow, Remains: Located, Accuracy: 43.29.100/87.46.581.

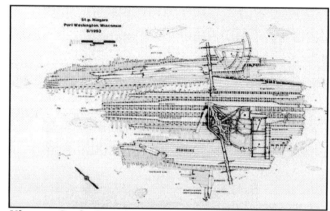
***Niagara* Scale Survey – Wisconsin Historical Society**

Schooner *Fair Play* (predates registry numbering) – built 1857 at Sheboygan, WI, 55.0 x 14.0 x 4.6 ft., 30.88 gt. BOM, last enrolled 11/7/1857, Milwaukee. 1 deck, 2 masts, square stern, plain stem, no gallery. The little schooner *Fair Play* reportedly foundered in November 1857 north of Port Washington in a late season gale with a cargo of supplies. She was a new vessel, having just been launched that spring at Sheboygan. She should not be confused with the other schooner *Fair Play* lost 1855 at Sheboygan. (Vessel Enrollment) Type: Foundering, Depth: Deep, Remains: Probably Present, Accuracy: 10 Miles.

Schooner *Mars* (predates registry numbering) – built 1855 at Michigan City, Indiana, 46.10 x 13.8 x 5.0 ft. 27.75 gt. BOM, 1 deck, 2 masts, square stern, plain stem, last enrolled 6/25/1857 - The small schooner *Mars* was lost in a gale on November 17, 1857 bound from Port Washington to Milwaukee. She was initially reported to have foundered, but her battered hull was found ashore two days later several miles south of Port Washington with no sign of her 4 crewmen. She was a total loss valued at $2000. (Milwaukee Sentinel – November 24, 1857) Type: Stranding, Depth: Surfline, Remains: Possibly Present, Accuracy: 5 Miles.

Schooner *Lavinia* (predates registry numbering) – built 1847 at Ohio City, Ohio by Sanford & Moses, 107.5 x 22.1 x 9.1 ft., 199.01 gt. BOM, deck, 2 masts, scroll stem, square stern, last enrolled Chicago 6/1/1857. - The Schooner *Lavinia* was blown ashore north of Port Washington in a storm on October 7, 1858 along with the schooner *Gazelle*. The *Gazelle* was freed, but the *Lavinia* proved a total loss. She was reportedly carrying a cargo of cobblestones and was valued at $2000. (Milwaukee Sentinel – 10/13/1858) Type: Stranding, Depth: Surfline, Remains: Possibly Present, Accuracy: 5 Miles.

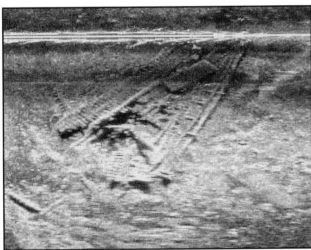
Sidescan image of the Mahoning's remains courtesy of Jerry Guyer

Brig *Mahoning* (predates registry numbering) – built 1847 at Black River, Ohio by William Jones, 119.1 x 25.5 x 9.8 ft., 259.42 gt. BOM, 2 masts, 1 deck, scroll stem, last enrolled Milwaukee, 4/23/1863. - The brig *Mahoning* capsized and sank a few miles off shore half way between Port Washington & Ulao. She was being towed to Milwaukee for repairs following a stranding at Sheboygan and had 2 large steam pumps running to keep her free of water. A heavy sea was running and the pumps began losing ground, causing the *Mahoning* to capsize and sink, taking the salvage captain and mate with her. The wrecking tug *Magnet* with a diver salvaged some of the pumps, blocks, anchors, chains and rigging in June 1865. The wreck was located by Paul Ehorn and Butch Klopp in 1999 on a tip from local fishermen. The wreck was located again by diver Brad Ingersoll in August 2005 and reported to the Wisconsin Historical Society. See expanded account in Section 3.

(Milwaukee Sentinel - 12/3/1864) Type: Foundering, Depth: 55 ft., Remains: Located, Accuracy: 43.20.438, 87.51.216.

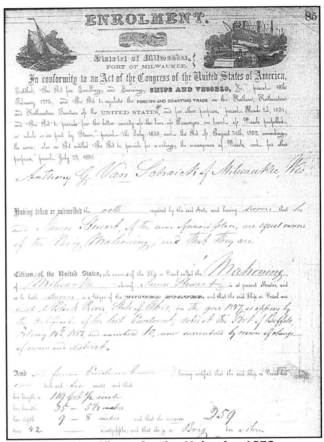
Enrollment Certificate for the *Mahoning* 1858 – National Archives RG41

Scow Schooner *Scud* (predates registry numbering) – Built 1854 at Detroit, Michigan by William Boulton, 63.8 x 17.4 x 3.4 ft., 32.37 gt. BOM, 2 masts, plain stem, no gallery, last enrolled 11/12/1859, Detroit. The little scow schooner *Scud* is reported to have been lost when she stranded south of Port Washington in 1866. She had stranded at Sheboygan the previous year, but was reportedly recovered. Supporting data for this loss is very fragmentary as a primary reference has never been located. However, the loss is plausible, as the *Scud* was still sailing in the area in the 1860s. (Frederickson's Wreck Charts) Type: Stranding, Depth: Surfline, Remains: Possibly Present, Accuracy: 5 Miles.

Brig *Alexander Mitchell* (predates registry numbering) – Built 1853 at Port Huron, Michigan by George Barber, 119.6 x 20.1 x 9.8 ft., 275.56 gt. BOM, 185.14 gt. (Moorsom), plain stem, 2 masts. The brig *Alexander Mitchell* was bound for Chicago with a cargo of lumber on October 24, 1866 when she capsized off Port Washington in an October squall. Her crew escaped in their yawl, but the *Mitchell* was driven across the lake and came ashore at White Lake, Michigan where she was abandoned as a total loss. (Milwaukee Sentinel-10/26/1866, 11/6/1866) Type: Stranding, Depth: Surfline, Remains: Definitely Removed, Accuracy: 5 Miles.

Sidescan of the Northerner - Jerry Guyer

Northerner figurehead - Courtesy of the Great Lakes Shipwreck Research Foundation

Schooner *Northerner* (18176) – Built 1851 at Clayton, New York by John Oades, 81.1 x 18.6 x 7.6 ft., 77 gt., 1 deck, 2 masts, figurehead. Rebuilt 1859 at Wells Island, NY. - The schooner *Northerner* damaged her hull on the lake bottom while loading at Amsterdam, WI. On November 29, 1868, while enroute to Milwaukee, she began to leak profusely and put into Port Washington. Later the prop *Cuyahoga* attempted to tow her to Milwaukee for repairs, but she capsized and foundered enroute. Her crew was rescued by the *Cuyahoga*. She was plotted on a trawl snag chart by Miller Fisheries who gave the chart to Port Washington diver Butch Klopp. Klopp and Roger Chapman located the wreck in 1976 with Chapman's Wesmar sonar. The wreck is very well preserved and intact. She sports a rare ram figurehead. The site was the subject of a video survey by the Wisconsin Historical Society in 2009. (Milwaukee Sentinel – 12/2/1868) Type: Foundering, Depth: 130 ft., Remains: Located, Accuracy: 43.19.00/87.49.41.

Scow *Supply* in the Milwaukee River c. 1883 – Milwaukee Public Library Marine Collection

Scow Schooner *Supply* (23497) – Built 1861 at Black River, Ohio by S.E. Field, 78.3 x 20.9 x 4.0 ft., 60.45 gt., rebuilt 1874 to 81.5 x 21.7 x 5.9 ft., 89 gt. - The scow schooner *Supply* was bound from Montague, MI for Chicago with a cargo shingles when she capsized off Port Washington on July 13, 1869. Her crew were rescued by the schooner *Len Higby* and taken to Sheboygan. The vessel was reported as a total loss, but was recovered and rebuilt. She sailed until 7/3/1890 when she capsized and foundered off Traverse City, Michigan. (Chicago Republican – July 14, 1869) Type: Foundering, Depth: Shallow, Remains: Definitely Removed, Accuracy: 5 Miles.

Steamer *Belle* - Historical Collections of the Great Lakes

Propeller *Belle* (2159) – Built 1859 at Port Huron, Michigan by B.M.Hagedorn, 90.5 x 9.6 x 7.5 ft., 120 gt. - The little passenger steamer *Belle* burned to the waterline and sank on November 20, 1869 off Port Washington with a cargo of lumber and 2 lives while bound from Manitowoc to Milwaukee. The fire originated around her smoke stack and spread rapidly. Two crew were lost, but the remainder made it to the life boat and rowed to Port Washington. The *Belle* foundered later the same day. In 1982, commercial fishermen on board the fish tug *Linda E* reportedly snagged a wreck in 360 ft. of water off Port Washington. Butch Klopp and Harry Zych imaged the wreck with Zych's Klein sidescan sonar in the 1990s and found it to be consistent with the *Belle's* description. (Milwaukee Sentinel – 12/8/1869) Type: Foundering, Depth: Very Deep, Remains: Definitely Present, Accuracy: 5 Miles.

Schooner *Eva M. Cone* (7522) – Built 1859 at Pensaukee, Wisconsin, 51.6 x 13.2 x 4.4 ft., 26.21 gt. BOM, 1 deck, 2 masts, no gallery, plain stem, enrolled Green Bay, last doc. surrendered as lost 4/20/1872. - The little schooner *Eva M. Cone* was making an early season run from Milwaukee to Port Washington for a lumber cargo. Just after leaving Port Washington she struck an ice flow and began to leak uncontrollably. Within minutes, she rolled over and her crew had to abandon her in the yawl. The crew rowed to Port Washington while the *Eva M. Cone* blew ashore three miles south of Port Ulao, where the waves took her apart. Wooden vessel remains have been reported just offshore in the area between Port Washington and Ulao, which may belong to this vessel. (Milwaukee Sentinel - April 24, 1872) Type: Stranding, Depth: Surfline, Remains: Probably Present, Accuracy: 1 Mile.

The scow schooner *Felicitous* – Great Lakes Historical Society

Scow Schooner *Felicitous* (120121) – Built 1873 at Manitowoc, Wisconsin by P. Larson, 126.0 x 26.6 x 7.8 ft., 198.78 gt., 3 masts, rebuilt 1888, 216.13 gt. - The scow schooner *Felicitous* was reported stranded and sunk in shallow water Southeast of Ulao in the fall of 1874 with a cargo of railroad ties. Details of the accident are sketchy, but the *Felicitous* was recovered and sailed until she was abandoned in 1924. A primary account of this accident has yet to be located, but it seems plausible, as the ship was trading in the area at that time. (Frederickson's Wreck Charts) Type: Stranding, Depth: Shallow, Remains: Definitely Removed, Accuracy: 5 Miles.

Scow Schooner *Mary Booth* (16392) – Built May 1857 at Buffalo, New York by Bidwell and Banta, 100.0 x 24.7 x 6.8 ft., 131.78 gt., 2 masts, used as a barge 1870, last enrolled Chicago, 8/15/1877, rated B2 1877, value $1,800, scow bottom. - The scow schooner *Mary Booth* was caught in a gale off Port Washington on November 6, 1877, when she began to leak. Her pumps were soon overwhelmed and she became waterlogged and subsequently capsized. Her crew escaped in yawl and blew across the lake to Montague, MI, but the *Mary Booth* is believed to have foundered southeast of Port Washington in deep water. A possible second target was reported by *Linda E.* searchers in the vicinity of the *Tennie & Laura*, which could be this vessel. (Detroit Free Press – November 9, 1877) Type: Foundering, Depth: Very Deep, Remains: Definitely Present, Accuracy: 5 Miles.

Schooner *Norma* (?) – Build info unknown, reported at 315 gt. – The US Life Saving Service index to wrecks and casualties on Lake Michigan records the total loss of the 315 gt. schooner *Norma* by going ashore 15 miles north of Milwaukee in September 1879 with a financial value of $1000. No vessel of matching name or tonnage appears to have sailed in US waters at this time. This may have been the little 18 gt. scow *Norma*, #18605, which was lost in 1900 near Egg Harbor, WI. (USLSS Wrecks and Casualties on the West Coast of Lake Michigan) Type: Stranding, Depth: n/a, Remains: Probably Recovered, Accuracy: 5 Miles.

Schooner *Narragansett* – Author's Collection

Schooner *Narragansett* (18110) – Built 1861 at Cleveland, Ohio by Quayle & Martin, 139.9 x 26.1 x 11.6 ft., 316 gt., 3 masts, used in the ocean trades, later in Michigan lumber trade. - On July 13, 1880 the big schooner *Narragansett* was run down by the schooner *Falmouth* off Port Washington, killing one crewman. The *Narragansett's* hull was cut 12 planks deep and several of her frames were shattered. She narrowly avoided foundering. Her grain cargo was damaged and she required major repairs at the Wolff and Davidson yard in Milwaukee. She continued service until 5/13/1901 when she foundered 50 miles off Port Sanilac, MI on Lake Huron. (Milwaukee Sentinel – July 15, 1880) Type: Collision, Depth: N/A, Remains: Definitely Removed, Accuracy: 5 Miles.

Scow Schooner *Pilot* (19667) – Built 1848 at Ashtabula, OH by G. Thayer, 180.82 gt. BOM, 98.7 x 24.9 x 8.7 ft., rebuilt 1861 at Depere, WI, 131.16 gt. - The scow schooner *Pilot* was bound from White Lake, MI to Chicago with shingles when she was run down by the upbound schooner *R. Halloran* 3 miles south and 5 miles off of Port Washington. The *Pilot* was struck on the starboard bow and cut nearly to her foremast. The crew abandoned ship to the *Halloran* and were landed at Manitowoc. The next day, the *Pilot* was found afloat and under sail 20 miles NE of Milwaukee and towed to port where she was rebuilt. She sailed until being abandoned in 1895. (Milwaukee Sentinel – September 28, 1883) Type: Collision, Depth: N/A, Remains: Definitely Removed, Accuracy: 1 Mile.

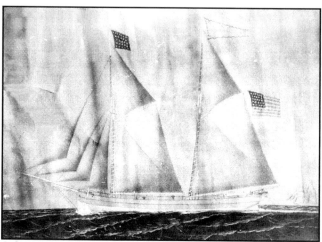

Schooner *Guiding Star* – Historical Collections of the Great Lakes

Schooner *Guiding Star* (85006) – Built 1869 at Oswego, New York by George Goble, 139 x 26 x 11 ft., 324 gt., 2 masts, enrollment surrendered Oswego 1/8/1884, vessel wrecked. - The schooner *Guiding Star* was driven ashore in a Fall gale on November 6, 1883 twelve miles North of Milwaukee with a cargo of 560 tons coal. 8 crew were rescued by Milwaukee Lifesaving Station crew and 2/3 of the cargo was recovered. The ship broke up a few weeks later. What are believed to be the ship's remains lie just south of parking lot of Virmond Park on the beach buried under the bluff with coal and a salvage cart buried near the keel. After storms, the wreckage is sometimes exposed. (Milwaukee Sentinel – November 7, 1883, USLSS Annual Report 1884) Type: Stranding, Depth: Buried, Remains: Located, Accuracy: 43.12.660 / 87.53.784. (Shown on Milwaukee Chart)

Remains attributed to the *Guiding Star* at Virmond Park c. 1994 – Bob Jaeck

Schooner *W.W. Brigham* (26363) – Built 1849 at Catteraugus, New York by Stevens, 90.3 x 24.8 x 7.2 ft., 93.71 gt., two masts, blt. as a brig with a scow stern, later 93.0 x 21.1 x 7.1 ft. - The schooner *W.W. Brigham* sprang a leak and capsized August 25, 1884 in a storm. She was found bottom up ENE of Port Washington, bound Muskegon to Chicago with a lumber cargo. The crew floated on a raft 3 days and 3 nights without food or sleep before rescue by the schooner *Walter Smith*. The floating wreck was located about midlake by the schooner *Tennie & Laura* and later towed to Grand Haven on 9/1/1884 where it was abandoned as a total loss. (Milwaukee Sentinel – September 1, 1884, Herman Runge Wreck List) Type: Capsizing, Depth: N/A, Remains: Definitely Removed, Accuracy: 10 Miles.

Schooner *Advance* (365) – Built 1853 at Milwaukee, Wisconsin by James M. Jones, 118.9 x 25.6 x 9.8 ft. , 268.40 gt. BOM, 179.92 gt. (Moorsom), 2 masts, gallery, plain stem. - The schooner *Advance* was bound Ahnapee to Chicago in a heavy sea and blinding rain with a lumber cargo on September 8, 1885 when she began to leak. Her captain launched the lifeboat and made for shore but it capsized in the breakers drowning all but one of the crew, including Captain Paulson and his son George. The *Advance* went down 2.5 miles from shore off Oostburg, about 10 miles north of Port Washington. She is very badly broken up for a wreck at her depth. Her hull is only partially intact. She was located in 1978 by Robert Vander Puy and Ray Larson. (Milwaukee Sentinel – September 9, 1885, Door County Advocate – September 17, 1885) Type: Foundering, Depth: 80 ft., Remains: Located, Accuracy: 43.36.75 / 87.43.00.

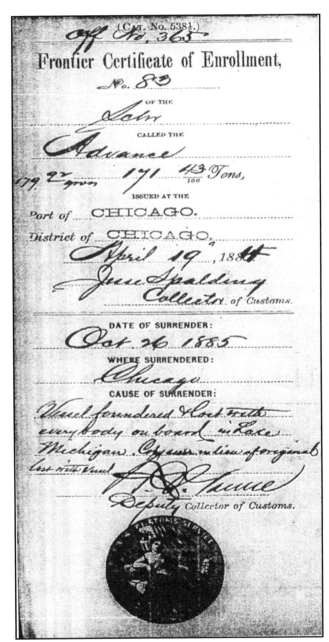

Surrender of Last Document for Schooner *Advance* – National Archives

Wreck Report for the Schooner *Gertie Wing* – National Archives

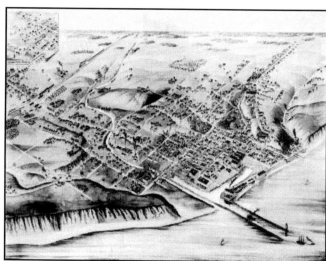

Port Washington 1893 – American Geographical Society Collection – UW Milwaukee

Schooner *Gertie Wing* (85665) – Built 1880 at Manistee, Michigan by James Burdick, 41.4 x 12.8 x 5.6 ft. 16.99 gt., last enrolled Milwaukee, 12/1885, 2 masts. - The little schooner *Gertie Wing* had just departed from Port Washington for Manitowoc in a heavy sea on September 25, 1886 with 5 tons apples when she became unmanageable. She dropped her anchor but the chain parted and she was driven aground ½ mile north of the Port Washington piers. By the time a tug arrived, she was firmly aground. Her Captain, William Burmaster of Manitowoc unloaded the apples and left the ship to break up. Her remains were still visible two years later. (Milwaukee Customs House Wreck Report – October 30, 1888) Type: Stranding, Depth: Surfline, Remains: Probably Present, Accuracy: ¼ Mile.

Schooner *Maggie Thompson* (16425) – Built 1867 at Whitehall, Michigan, 110.3 x 25.6 x 7.9 ft., 155.53 gt., last enrolled Milwaukee, 8/27/1888, 2 masts. - The schooner *Maggie Thompson* capsized off Port Washington in a gale on July 25, 1888 bound for Milwaukee with a cargo of tan bark. Her crew escaped and her upturned hull was located the next day and towed to Milwaukee where it was repaired. The schooner remained in service until November of 1900 when she was stripped and abandoned in the Jones Island boneyard at Milwaukee. (Chicago Inter-Ocean – July 25, 1888) Type: Capsizing, Depth: N/A, Remains: Definitely Removed, Accuracy: 10 Miles.

Schooner *Sophia Bonner* (115402) – Built 1875 at St. James, Michigan by John B. Connelly, 65.0 x 18.5 x 6.0 ft., 36.98 gt., Enrolled Milwaukee, 4/16/1888, built at Whiskey Point, Beaver Island. - The schooner *Sophia Bonner* had only recently been sold to new owners, John Watt & John Rooney of Ludington, MI at a Federal Marshall's debt sale when she capsized in a gale 18 miles northeast of Milwaukee on September 28, 1888. Her crew escaped, but the *Bonner* went to the bottom (Herman Runge Wreck List) Type: Foundering, Depth: Very Deep, Remains: Definitely Present, Accuracy: 5 Miles.

Schooner *Two Sisters* (145340) – Built 1883 Erin, Michigan by Whitmore Bros., 69.5 x 18.1 x 3.9 ft., 34 gt., 2 masts. - The schooner *Two Sisters* was sunk outside the harbor piers at Port Washington sometime in August of 1889. Her partially submerged hull was struck by the steamer *R.A. Seymour Jr.* on 9/3/1889, sinking the *Seymour*. The *Two Sisters* was later raised and lost in 1899 at Forest Bay on Lake Huron. (Out of the Past, Vol. 1 – Richard D. Smith) Type: Stranding, Depth: N/A, Remains: Definitely Removed, Accuracy: ¼ Mile.

Steamer *R.A. Seymour, Jr.* – Historical Collections of the Great Lakes

Propeller Steamer *R. A. Seymour Jr.* (110672) – Built 1876 at New Baltimore, MI by Saunders, 110 x 23 x 8 ft., 131.46 gt., built as *Lewis Gilbert*, rebuilt and renamed at Manitowoc 1882. - The steamer *R.A. Seymour* struck the wreck of the schooner *Two Sisters* just outside the Port Washington pierheads and foundered on September 3, 1889. She was raised by the tug *W.H. Simpson* and taken to Milwaukee where she was repaired. She sailed until 1925 when she was abandoned at Chicago. (Out of the Past, Vol. 1 – Richard D. Smith) Type: Collision, Depth: N/A, Remains: Definitely Removed, Accuracy: ¼ Mile.

Scow Schooner *Silver Cloud* (115025) – Built 1869 at Sheboygan, Wisconsin by Anton Kjelson, 79.4 x 21.9 x 6.3 ft., 96.94 gt., 2 masts, gunwale built, cross planked scow. - The scow schooner *Silver Cloud* was bound from Bailey's Harbor to Milwaukee with cedar posts when she capsized on July 7, 1891 in a rare July gale northeast of Port Washington. Captain Johnson had gone below decks to rescue his wife and child, and was drowned with them when the ship capsized. 3 of her crew were rescued from the debris by a fish tug. The vessel's hull came ashore two miles north of Port Washington where it was abandoned. She was valued at $3000. (Milwaukee Sentinel – July 8, 1891) Type: Stranding, Depth: Surfline, Remains: Possibly Present, Accuracy: 1 Mile.

Schooner *Starke* c. 1900 – Milwaukee Public Library Marine Collection

Schooner *Starke* (115474) – Built 1876 at Milwaukee, Wisconsin by R. Allen & G. McClelland, 124.2 x 27.3 x 9.0 ft., 209 gt., 3 masts, square stern, plain stem. - The schooner *Starke* was bound from Norwood, MI to Milwaukee with maple lumber when she was run down by the schooner *Charles E. Wyman* 16 miles off Port Washington on June 30, 1891. She began to sink and ran for Sheboygan but capsized 7 miles off Amsterdam, her crew escaping in the yawl. Her hull was located by the tug *Welcome* and towed to Sheboygan for repairs. She went to sea and was lost 2/5/1906 at Chandeleur Island, Louisiana by stranding. (Milwaukee Sentinel – July 1, 1891) Type: Collision, Depth: N/A, Remains: Definitely Removed, Accuracy: 1 Mile.

Sch. *J. Duvall*, tug *Imperial* and launch *Topaz* at Port Washington c. 1900 – Author's Collection

Stranding, Depth: Surfline, Remains: Definitely Recovered, Accuracy: 1 Mile.

Scow Schooner *Mary Ludwig* – C.Patrick Labadie Collection, TBNMS

Schooner *Knight Templar* (14110) – Built 1865 at Oswego, New York by George Goble, 136 x 26 x 11 ft., 289.74 gt., 3 masts. - The schooner *Knight Templar* was reported in Arthur & Lucy Frederickson's Lake Michigan shipwreck maps to have been lost in a storm south of Sheboygan, WI, approximately off present-day Harrington Beach State Park in 1893. This erroneous account is based on an actual stranding to the schooner *Knight Templar* in October 1893 south of Cheboygan, MI, but the error has been repeated enough that it has become a local oral tradition. Schooner remains were located in the surf about 1000 ft south of the old dock at the park and were attributed to the *Knight Templar*, but they remain unidentified. The *Knight Templar* was eventually lost in December of 1905 near Alpena, MI. (Out of the Past, Vol. 1 – Richard Smith)

Scow Schooner *Mary Ludwig* (90601) – Built 1874 at South Haven, MI by C.P. Ludwig, 2 masts, 81.5 x 19.7 x 6.0 ft. 68.84 gt. - The schooner *Mary Ludwig* stranded in a gale on a rock off Sucker Brook in September 1895. The crew's yawl overturned and they were rescued by a farmer and his horse. The *Ludwig* was later recovered and taken to Milwaukee for repairs, but her anchor, which was left at the site was located by divers in 1980 and recovered. The *Ludwig* sailed for many years until she was abandoned at Grand Haven, Michigan on 6/30/1919. (Out of the Past, Vol. 1 – Richard Smith) Type:

J.M. Allmendinger – Historical Collections of the Great Lakes

Wooden Steamer *J. M. Allmendinger* (76411) – Built 1883 at Benton Harbor, Michigan by G.H. Burgoyne, 104.0 x 24.4 x 10.0 ft., 230.64 gt., wooden bulk freight (lumber) propeller, rebuilt in 1888 to 183.17 gt., 104.6 x 24.0 x 9.4 ft. - The steamer *J.M. Allmendinger*, blinded by snow, went aground in a blizzard and gale just north of present-day Virmond Park on November 26, 1895 with a cargo of lumber. Her crew was rescued by the superhuman efforts of the Milwaukee Lifesaving Service, who rowed through the blizzard to the site. The lifesavers were frozen into the seats of their surfboat when they arrived, some having to be chopped out of the ice. The *Allmendinger* was quickly broken up by waves over the ensuing weeks and was a total loss. The wreck was charted by the Lake Survey and was salvaged by Max Nohl in the 1930s. She was dived by the Author and Bob Jaeck in 1998. A very large boiler with condenser is the most prominent artifact and is a hazard to navigation. The keel and ribs are also present. (US Lifesaving Service Annual Report 1895) Type: Stranding, Depth: 12 ft., Remains: Located, Accuracy: N43.13.024' / W87.53.631'. (Shown on Milwaukee Chart)

Scow Schooner *J.B. Prime* – Historical Collections of the Great Lakes

Scow Schooner *J.B. Prime* (13749) – Built 1865 at Fairport, Ohio by Roswell Hayes, 114.2 x 25.0 x 7.2 ft. 170.08 gt., 2 masts, later 148.38 gt. 115.4 x 25.5 x 6.5 ft. - The scow schooner *J.B. Prime* was abandoned at Port Washington in March of 1896 and was dismantled. She had been used as an unmasted scow and hauled brick from Port Washington to Milwaukee. She was renamed *'Noah's Ark'* in 1895. She had wrecked off Kewaunee on 9/25/1878 but was recovered. (Vessel Enrollment Certificate Surrendered 3/21/1896 endorsed "dismanted") Type: Abandonment, Depth: N/A, Remains: Definitely Removed, Accuracy: 1 Mile.

[Newspaper clipping:]

Tragedy of 1895 Is Seen in Wreck Off Fox Point

Fox Point has long been one of the sirens of Lake Michigan—a siren with boulder jaws and a shallow, treacherous reach into the lake—but meanest of all. Fox Point has always had a tendency in fog to trick the sailors and to loom ahead exactly where it shouldn't.

Plenty of ship ribs are strewn in the vicinity of the point and it is on one set of ribs that three Milwaukee boys, Max Nohl, Jack Browne and Verne Netzow, are now at work with raft, diving helmets and oxygen tanks. Young Nohl has had deep sea diving experience.

Possibility that the vessel on which the boys are working may be the J. M. Allmendinger, an old lumber carrier sunk in 1895, is seen by a former Milwaukee vessel owner and operator, Charles S. Neff, now of Cleveland, Ohio. He has an extensive collection of marine stories, photographs and records from the early days of mast and sail to the present. Some of his material is now being used in a history of the Great Lakes, being written by a Michigan man. After seeing an account of the diving operations in The Journal on July 15 Neff wrote Milwaukee relatives about the Allmendinger.

Known for Chime Whistle

"Old time lumber dealers will remember this sturdy little craft," he wrote. "She had a musical chime whistle and she was a familiar sight to Milwaukee, for she came puffing into the harbor three times a week on her run between Manistee, Mich. and Milwaukee. She had a big black sail and she carried timber on the deck. The lumber was loaded and unloaded with a timber boom, run by a steam winch."

The Allmendinger, old records show, was 120 feet long, had a 25-foot beam and 10-foot depth of hold. She had a fire box boiler and it was a door of a firebox that the young divers found in their search for a clew to the ship's identity. Benton Harbor, Mich., was the place where the Allmendinger was launched and 1883 was the date. The ship was bought in 1887 by Capt. Thomas Richardson and E. B. Simpson of Milwaukee. Simpson was sole owner when the vessel, which carried no insurance, was lost.

Grounded Four Times

Fox Point had a fatal attraction for the little Allmendinger. Four times in her career she ran aground, four times in the vicinity of North Point and Fox Point and each time in a pea soup fog. A desperate attempt was made to salvage the vessel. But the boulders gouged, the surf pounded and nothing afloat can stand that combination. Wrenched

***J.M. Allmendinger* salvage work - Milwaukee Sentinel – July 22, 1934**

The Scow Schooner *Tennie and Laura* – Wisconsin Maritime Museum

Scow Schooner *Tennie & Laura* (145115) – Built 1876 at Manitowoc, Wisconsin by Gunder Jorgenson, 73.0 x 19.0 x 5.6 ft., 56.69 gt., 2 masts. - The scow schooner *Tennie & Laura* was a frequent visitor to Port Washington.

She was lost on a trip from Muskegon to Milwaukee with a cargo of lumber when she capsized and sank 12 miles NE of Milwaukee on August 2, 1903. Her captain, John Sather, was picked up by the steamer *Mark Covell*, but her mate was lost. The vessel and her cargo were valued at $1000. The wreck was located in January 1999 in 310 ft of water by the USN *Defender* during the search for the *Linda E*. She was filmed using an ROV by the USCG *Acacia* and more recently has been visited and filmed by technical divers. She was surveyed by the Wisconsin Historical Society in 2005. (Door County Advocate – August 8, 1903) Type: Foundering, Depth: 310 ft., Remains: Located, Accuracy: 43.15.63 / 87.43.64.

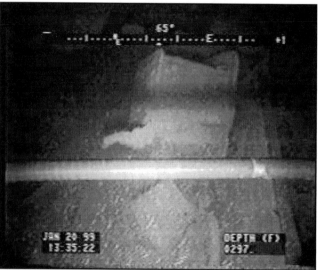
The galley stove of the *Tennie & Laura* before Quagga Messels covered it – US Coast Guard Video

D.C. Whitney aground north of Port Washington September 1905 – Richard Smith

Wooden Steamer *D.C. Whitney* (157075) – Built 1882 at St. Clair, Michigan by Simon Langell, 240 x 40 x 23 ft., 1490 gt., sold Canadian, renamed *Gargantua*, C122435, 1909; cut down in 1920 for use as a dock, 1920. - The steamer *D.C. Whitney* was driven ashore just north of Port Washington in the big storm of 1905 on September 3rd. Many other ships were lost across the Lakes in this storm. The *Whitney* was one of the lucky survivors. She was pulled free a few days later with minor damage. In 1913, she was beached on Beausoliel Isl., then used as a dry dock. Eventually she was abandoned in the Wingfield Basin, Georgian Bay. (Out of the Past, Vol. 1 – Richard Smith) Type: Stranding, Depth: N/A, Remains: Definitely Removed, Accuracy: 5 Miles.

Steamer *D.C. Whitney* – Historical Collections of the Great Lakes

Atlanta and sister ships in winter layup c. 1895 – St. Clair Collection, Great Lakes Historical Society

Wooden Passenger Steamer *Atlanta*
(106823) – Built 1891 at Cleveland, Ohio By: Cleveland Dry Dock Co., 200.1 x 32.2 x 13.6 ft. 1129.17 gt. - The steamer *Atlanta* was bound from Manitowoc to Chicago with passengers and a cargo of furniture on March 18, 1906 when she was found to be on fire just south of Sheboygan. The fish tug *Tessler* of Port Washington noticed the fire and proceeded to the *Atlanta* where nearly 70 passengers were taken aboard the *Tessler*. 1 life was lost during the rescue. The *Tessler* towed the burning *Atlanta* to the shallows and beached her at Amsterdam north of Port Washington. Today, her wreckage is broken but concentrated on sandy bottom with small artifacts in the sand. The vessel's hull outline can be clearly seen. (Milwaukee Journal – March 19, 1906) Type: Stranding, Depth: 12 ft., Remains: Located, Accuracy: 43.34.25' / 87.46.75'.

Yacht *Marguerite* burning at Port Washington – Milwaukee Public Library Marine Collection

Gas Yacht *Marguerite* (205420) – Built 1908 at Manitowoc, Wisconsin by Burger Boat Co., 54.0 x 12.8 x 6.1 ft., 32.0 gt., wooden hulled, last enrolled Chicago 6/9/1910. 50 hp engine. - The gas yacht *Marguerite* burned 8 miles off Port Washington on August 12, 1914 and was a total loss. She was towed in to Port Washington by the tug *Torrent*. Her hull was later towed to Sheboygan where she was scrapped. She had been owned out of Chicago. (Milwaukee Public Library – Runge Vessel File) Type: Burning, Depth: N/A, Remains: Definitely Removed, Accuracy: 5 Miles.

The *P. Reckinger* – Wisconsin Maritime Museum

Steam Fish Tug *P. Reckinger* (150577) – Built 1892 at Sheboygan, Wisconsin by Rieboldt & Wolter, 61.0 x 14.0 x 6.6 ft., 42.58 gt., steam fish tug. - The big fish tug *P. Reckinger* was abandoned at Port Washington sometime in 1917 due to age and condition. Her remains were likely removed. (Herman Runge Vessel Data Card – Milwaukee Public Library) Type: Abandonment, Depth: N/A, Remains: Definitely Removed, Accuracy: 5 Miles.

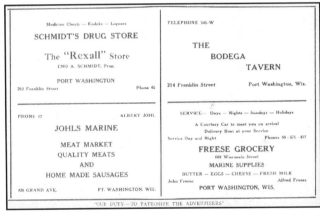

Port Washington Marine Ads – Shipmasters Association Directory – 1936 – Author's Collection

Wooden Fish Tug *Julia C. Hammel* (77076) – Built 1893 at Manitowoc, Wisconsin By: H.B. Burger Co., 55.2 x 14.5 x 6.0 ft. 28 gt., 19 nt., steam fish tug initially used as a harbor tug. - The fish tug *Julia C. Hammel* was built for E. Hammel, Sr. of Two Rivers but was brought to Port Washington in 1914 by John Heula. In 1917, she was bought by Arthur Breault, who was her last owner. She was abandoned at Port Washington on April 20, 1918 as "unfit for use". Her final resting place is unknown, but her remains are believed to have been removed. (Herman Runge Vessel Data Card – Milwaukee Public Library) Type: Abandonment, Depth: N/A, Remains: Definitely Removed, Accuracy: 5 Miles.

Smith Bros tug *Hope* about 1915 – Richard Smith

Wooden Fish Tug *Hope* (207087) – Built 1893 at Ashtabula, Ohio by J.G. Laird & Sons, 37.2 x 12.2 x 4.2 ft., 15 gt., rebuilt 1910 at Port Washington – The fish tug *Hope* was bought by the Smith Brothers in 1910 and rebuilt at Port Washington. She was used until 1918 when she was dismantled and her hull pulled up on the beach in the harbor. Her papers were surrendered on 2/14/1922, abandoned. Her remains were definitely removed. (Milwaukee Public Library Marine Collection) Type: Abandonment, Depth: N/A, Remains: Definitely Removed, Accuracy: 1 Mile.

The *Cambria* as a yacht c. 1910 - Neenah Public Library

Wooden Steamer *Cambria* (127100) – Built 1894 at Oshkosh, Wisconsin By: Ryan Brothers, 94.0 x 12.8 x 5.4 ft. 48.32 gt., twin screw steamer, sometimes referred to as a tug, originally a steam yacht; commercial use after 1910. - The steamer *Cambria* burst her boiler flue, sprang a leak and foundered in heavy weather 35 mi. NE of Milwaukee on September 21, 1921. 1 crewman was killed by steam, 6 others were rescued by the Coast Guard. She was bound from Pentwater to Milwaukee with a cargo of 300 barrels of apples. (Herman Runge Wreck List) Type: Foundering, Depth: Very Deep, Remains: Definitely Present, Accuracy: 10 Miles.

***Senator* with a deckload of cars c. 1929- Milwaukee Public Library Marine Collection**

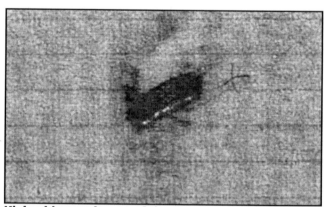

Klein sidescan image of the *Senator* at 400 meters courtesy of Paul Ehorn

Steel Steamer *Senator* (116725) – Built 1896 at Wyandotte, Michigan by Detroit Dry Dock Company, converted to an auto carrier in 1929, 410.0 x 45.4 x 23.9 ft., 4048.75 gt. - The steel steamer *Senator* was struck in fog by the str. Marquette 20 miles off Port Washington on October 31, 1929. She was bound for Milwaukee with cargo of 240 Nash autos. She sank in deep water and was a total loss with 10 lives. She had sunk on 8/22/1909 in the St. Mary's River, but was raised. The wreck was found on June 10, 2005 by Paul Ehorn and Rob Polich in over 400 ft of water off Port Washington. The sidescan stylus actually burned through the paper when the wreck was imaged and clearly showed a steel vessel over 400 ft in length. Subsequent passes with a fish finder showed that it rose nearly 40 ft off the bottom. (Milwaukee Sentinel – November 1, 1929) Type: Foundering, Depth: Very Deep, Remains: Located, Accuracy: Withheld by request.

Steamer *William B Pilkey* – Historical Collections of the Great Lakes

Tug *Evelyn C. Smith* as *Stella* - Milwaukee Public Library Marine Collection

***Evelyn C. Smith* sunk in the west slip May 1935 –** Richard Smith

Steel Fish Tug *Evelyn C. Smith* (226023) – Built 1926 at Manitowoc, Wisconsin by Burger Boat Co., 45.0 x 12.9 x 5.4 ft., 33 gt., renamed *Stella* 1945. First steel hull built by Burger Boat Co. Built as Ol.s, later converted to gas. - The steel fish tug *Evelyn C. Smith* sank at her dock in Port Washington on May 12, 1935 for unknown reasons. She was raised and returned to service. In 1945 she was renamed *Stella* and served on the Lakes until being retired in the 1980s. She was last owned by Ray Slupik of Chicago. (Out of the Past, Vol. 1 – Richard Smith) Type: Abandonment, Depth: N/A, Remains: Definitely Removed, Accuracy: 5 Miles.

Steamer *William B. Pilkey* (116732) – Built 1896 at Cleveland, Ohio by Globe Iron Works, 413.2 x 48.0 x 24.0 ft., 4344 gt., built as *Sir William Siemens*, renamed 1929; later the *Frank E. Vigor* 1941. The steamer *William B. Pilkey* was laden with coal when she ran aground 9 miles south of Port Washington in April of 1937, nearly ending her career. She was pulled off and her cargo was unloaded. She was lost 4/27/1944 when she collided with a vessel and sank 28.5 mi., 72 deg. from SE Shoal Lt., Lake Erie. She is now a popular Lake Erie dive target in 90 ft. of water. (Out of the Past, Vol. 1 – Richard Smith) Type: Stranding, Depth: N/A, Remains: Definitely Removed, Accuracy: 1 Mile.

Tug *Commoner* ashore and breaking up at Port Washington 1937 – Milwaukee Public Library, Marine Collection

Wooden Tug *Commoner* (211238) – Built 1913 at Manitowoc, Wisconsin by Burger Boat Co., 33.0 x 10.0 x 4.0 ft., 7.0 gt., gas engine. - The wooden tug *Commoner* was driven ashore in heavy weather at Port Washington on October 17, 1937. She was owned by salvager G.W. Falcon of Chicago, but she proved a total loss and was scrapped where she lay. (Milwaukee Public Library – Vessel File) Type: Stranding, Depth: Surfline, Remains: Probably Removed, Accuracy: ¼ Mile.

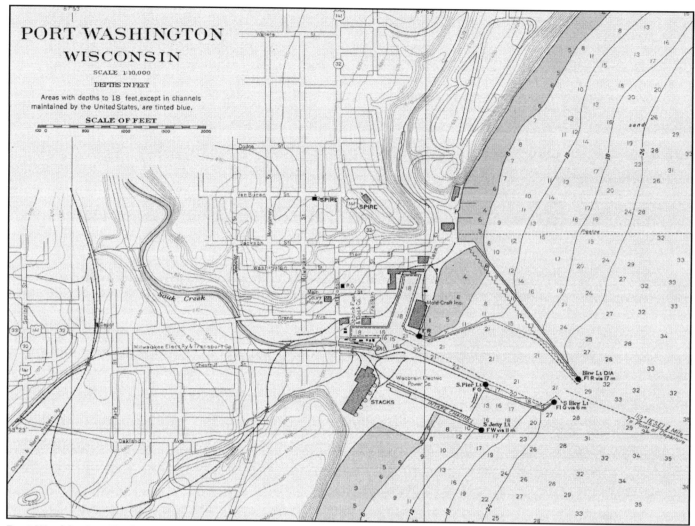

Port Washington Harbor 1957 – U.S. Lake Survey Chart – Author's Collection

Jennifer as the *Lorna P.* in 1973 - Author's Collection

Steel Steamer *Jennifer* (C313980) – Built 1964 at Lauzon, Quebec by George Davie Shipyard, 210 x 36 x 15 ft., 1092 gt., steel bulk package freight propeller. Built as *Cacouna* from halves of sister ships, renamed *Lorna P* in 1973. - The steamer *Jennifer* capsized and foundered in a storm c. 30 mi. NE of Milwaukee on December 1, 1974 when her cargo of steel plates shifted. Her crew was rescued by a USCG helicopter and the British frighter *Fortuna*. The vessel was a total loss, foundering in very deep water. (Milwaukee Journal – December 2, 1974) Type: Foundering, Depth: Very Deep, Remains: Definitely Present, Accuracy: 5 Miles.

Milwaukee Journal details the *Jennifer* sinking

Pleasure Boat *Submersion Excursion* - The recreational dive boat *Submersion Excursion* became waterlogged and was beached north of Port Washington in heavy weather on May 28, 1989. The boat was a charter dive boat that had been visiting the wreck of the steamer *Niagara*. She was a total loss. (Jerry Guyer)

The *Linda E* at Smith Bros Fisheries - Author's Collection

Steel Fish Tug *Linda E* (236906) – Built 1937 Manitowoc, Wisconsin by Burger Boat Co., 39.8 x 13.0 x 5.7 ft. 29 gt., 20 nt., built as the *Le Clair Bros*, later renamed, hull replated in 1996. - The fish tug *Linda E* vanished on December 11, 1998 with 3 crew in calm, clear weather, bound Milwaukee to Port Washington with a cargo of chubs. The crew had radio & cell phone, but got no call off and no debris was found. Her last known position was 9 mi. SE of Port Washington. She was located on 6/18/2000 in 260 ft. of water, 6 mi SE of Port Washington by the Navy Minesweeper USS *Defender*. Underwater films showed clear evidence of a collision. It was later determined that she had been run down by the British Petroleum tug/tanker combination *Michigan/Great Lakes*. The tug is now a grave-site for her crewmen, Captain Leif Weborg, Scott Matta and Warren Olson. (USCG Accident Investigation) Type: Foundering, Depth: Very Deep, Remains: Located, Accuracy: Withheld by request.

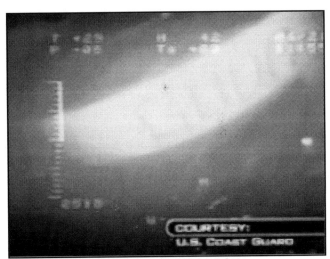

The *Linda E's* stern from the USCG ROV

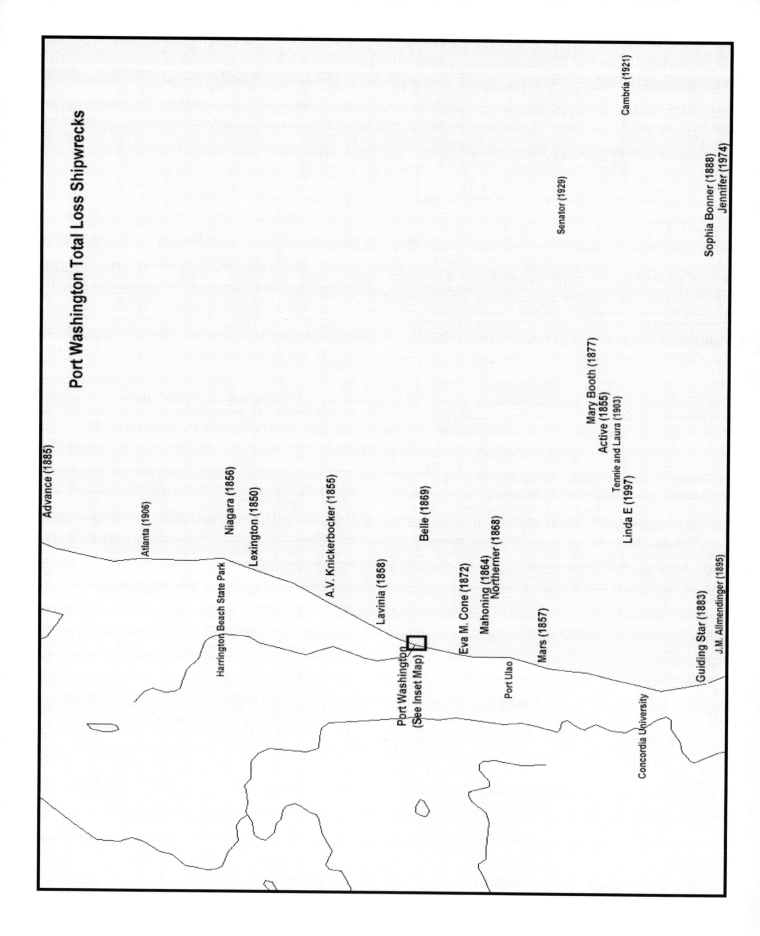

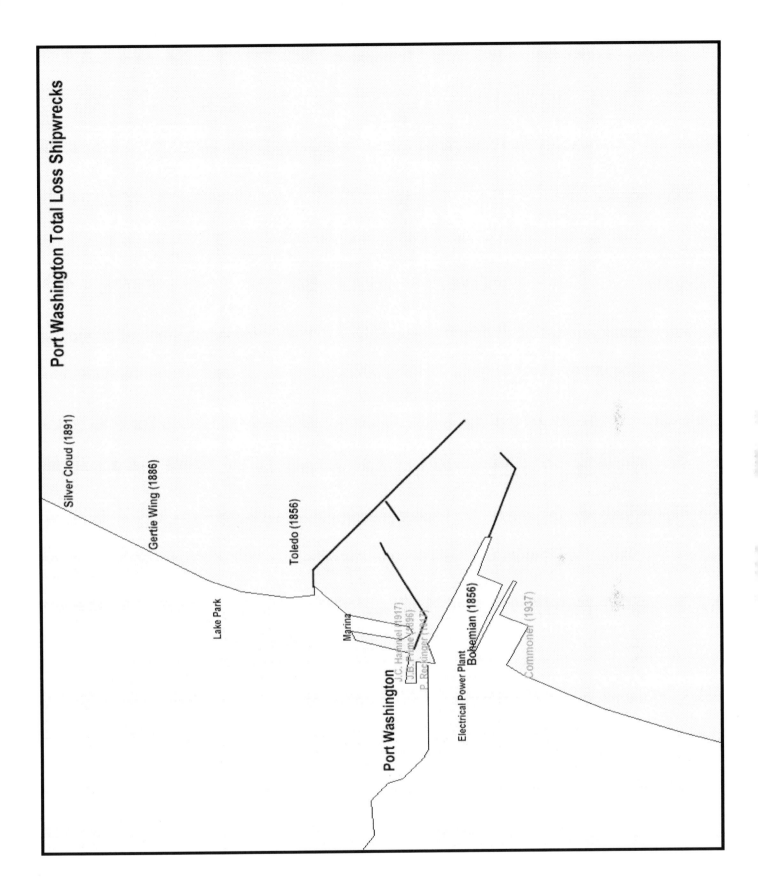

Providence Capstan Company Wooden Deck Windlass 1873 – Barnet's Coast Pilot for the Lakes – Author's Collection

Part III: Wisconsin Shipwreck Stories

In the course of many years of research, I wrote and published expanded accounts of many area wrecks in regional journals, magazines and newsletters. The following are several of the most interesting expanded accounts that I wrote over the years. These accounts give a unique insight into the variety of marine accidents that happened in the area, and paint a vivid picture of the dangers of Lake commerce during the 19th and early 20th centuries. Most of the articles appeared in Soundings, the quarterly publication of the Wisconsin Marine Historical Society. Others appeared in Inland Seas, the quarterly journal of the Great Lakes Historical Society. Some appeared in Anchor News, the quarterly publication of the Wisconsin Maritime Museum.

Lake Michigan's Lost *Mistress*

Reprinted from WMM Anchor News

Following the grisly wrecks of the 1940 Armistice Day Storm, better safety measures were adopted by commercial shippers around the Lakes. Radar soon became available to the big lakers and weather forecasting became much more reliable. These changes radically reduced the number of accidents in the latter half of the 20th century, but were little consolation to the fish tug *Mistress*. The *Mistresses* disappearance remains one of many unsolved "went missing" cases on Lake Michigan and was revisited by many researchers in 1997 in the wake of the disappearance of the fish tug *Linda E* off Port Washington, Wisconsin. The two accidents were superficially similar in that both vessels were Burger fish tugs with small crews that literally vanished without a trace on winter days. The *Linda E*, however disappeared on a clear, calm December afternoon, while the *Mistress* went missing on a blustery March day that raised concerns for a number of small craft that had been out. Unlike the Mistress, the *Linda E's* remains have since been located and the mystery of her loss has been solved. The *Linda E*. was run down by a massive tanker that was probably unaware of the impact, but the fate of the *Mistress* may never be known.

The *Mistress* was a very typical Great Lakes fish tug of her era and was one of several hundred built by the Burger Boat Company of Manitowoc, Wisconsin over the years. She was built in 1922 as a wooden fish tug of 38.7 x 10.5 x 4.0 ft. at a capacity of 15 gross tons with official number 222610. Burger boats were, and still are known as safe, sturdy craft that can handle most weather on the Lakes and the *Mistress* was no exception. Every year she ran well into the winter, after the big lakers had laid up and came out early in the spring, long before commercial shipping resumed. Her owner, John R. DeYoung of Pentwater used her in the Lake Trout and Whitefish fisheries on the north and east sides of Lake Michigan. At nineteen years of age, she was not a particularly old tug. Many tugs of her era lasted will into the 1960s and 70s. The *Mistress* was built as an Oil Screw with a 30/36 Kahlenburg diesel engine, but in the spring of 1941, her owner, John DeYoung, decided to remove the engine and place it in his new fish tug, *Mister*, which had just been built at Sturgeon Bay, Wisconsin. The *Mistress* was subsequently hauled out of the water at Ludington, Michigan where boat builder Elmer Gustafson removed the Kahlenburg. The *Mistress* was then towed back to Pentwater to await new owners.

The *Mistress* is shown on the ways at Elmer Gustafson's yard after her engine was removed – Elmer Gustafson

Within a few weeks, the DeYoung family sold the *Mistress* to prospective commercial fisherman Charles Jensen of Milwaukee and arrangements were made for the tug to make the trip across the Lake as soon as conditions permitted. Jensen and his assistant, H. Clair Graham, consequently drove from Milwaukee to Pentwater, pulling a trailer with a Buick automobile engine to repower the *Mistress*. Upon arriving, Jensen and Graham set to work installing the Buick engine in the *Mistress*. They quickly completed their work and for unknown reasons decided to fasten their trailer to the roof of the *Mistress* for the trip across the Lake. DeYoung and Gustafson were somewhat bemused by the novice fishermen's actions, but felt confident in the *Mistresses* ability to make the crossing. At six o'clock in the morning on Monday, March 3, 1941 Jensen piloted the *Mistress*, complete with her car-trailer headgear, between the snow-covered Pentwater piers and out into Lake Michigan. A moderate northeast gale was blowing and the temperatures ranged between 20 and 30 degrees out on the Lake. That was the last time the *Mistresses* whereabouts were known, as the gale quickly developed into storm conditions.

Tug Unreported in Lake Michigan – Former Pentwater Boat is One of Two Hunted by Coast Guardsmen – A former Pentwater fishtug which left there Monday for Milwaukee, Wis., was one of two fish tugs being sought by coast guards along the Wisconsin shore today. Reports at noon said one of the tugs had been located by guardsmen from the Chicago station, but officers here had no immediate word of which, if either, had been located. The Pentwater tug, the *Mistress*, formerly owned by William and Ray DeYoung of Pentwater, was recently sold and was being delivered Monday to Milwaukee in charge of Charles Jensen of Milwaukee and an assistant. Leaving Pentwater about 6 AM Monday, the tug was still unreported this morning. Ludington coast guard station, along with others on this shore, was notified to be ready for a search, but, due to the fact that strong northeast winds were blowing Monday, it was likely the search would be concentrated along the southwest end of the lake. Coast guard vessels from Chicago and other points in that region joined the search today. The second tug missing was reportedly from Kenosha, Wis. Coast guard authorities early this afternoon said the cutter Escanaba had left its base at Grand Haven to join the search for the *Mistress*, the tug being still unreported at that hour. In addition, a coast guard amphibian plane based at Traverse City had joined the hunt. The *Mistress*, well-known to commercial fishermen of this region, was a 40-foot boat. – Ludington Daily News, March 4, 1941

Concern was felt when the *Mistress* failed to arrive at Milwaukee by 5 PM that evening. The crossing should have taken no more than eight hours even in bad weather. By the next day, it became clear that the *Mistress* had foundered. A massive search was begun and speculation was rampant as to the vessel's fate. The weather was marginal, but certainly nothing the tug couldn't handle. Because she was heading across the lake in a following sea, the wind should have blown her ashore if her engine failed, but there wasn't a trace of her anywhere:

> Tug Unreported on Lake Michigan – Over Two Days Have Passed Since Boat Sailed from Pentwater Harbor – The fish tug *Mistress*, formerly of Pentwater, was still missing more than two days after it left Pentwater Harbor enroute to Milwaukee, Wis. A constant day and night coast guard search since late Monday night had failed, up until early this afternoon, to find any evidence of the 38 foot tug. The boat, sold recently by William and Ray DeYoung of Pentwater, its previous owners, was being delivered to Milwaukee when it disappeared. It left Pentwater early Monday morning in charge of Charles Jensen of Milwaukee and one assistant. Although a strong northeast wind was blowing at the time, mariners expressed the belief that the wind alone was not sufficient to engulf the tug. They expressed fears that a fire or explosion may have occurred. When the tug was still unreported Monday night, several hours after the tug should have reached Milwaukee, district Coast Guard officials at Chicago dispatched the cutter *Hollyhock* to make a search. The cutter cruised the southwest shore and adjoining region Monday night and Tuesday, being joined Tuesday by other coast guard patrols from the Wisconsin shore and by a coast guard plane from Traverse City. Coast guard headquarters at Chicago said the cutter *Escanaba* joined the search Tuesday but was forced to return to its base at Grand Haven early this morning because one of its crew was stricken with appendicitis. It was believed the *Escanaba* will resume the hunt after discharging the sick crewman. Coast patrols at Ludington, Pentwater and other points were given standby orders but had not been called out to date, due to the fact it was believed the northeast winds would have driven the tug to the Wisconsin Shore. – Ludington Daily News, March 5, 1941

The fish tug *Mistress* – Bob Grunst

By Thursday, March 6th, hopes for finding the tug were growing thin and news of the tug's engine swap had emerged, sparking speculation that there may have been a gasoline fire on the wooden boat.

> Hopes of Locating Missing Tug Wane – Hope of finding the fish tug *Mistress*, unreported since it set out from Pentwater Monday on a cross-lake trip to Milwaukee, Wis., was virtually abandoned today, as a constant coast guard search since Monday night failed to produce any evidence of the tug's whereabouts. The tug, sold recently by its former owners at Pentwater, was being delivered to Milwaukee in charge of two Milwaukee residents, Charles Jensen, about 45, a commercial fisherman who had purchased the tug, and Clair Graham, about 40, a diver. A coast guard plane, based at Traverse City flew over Ludington briefly Tuesday afternoon on a return flight from having searched the waters of Lake Michigan for the tug. Coast guard cutters, crews on the Wisconsin shore and the plane have been unable to date to find any evidence of the boat. – Ludington Daily News, March 6, 1941

Finally on Friday the 7th, the Coast Guard called off the search amid speculation that the tug had burned and foundered somewhere about mid-lake:

> Hope of Locating Tug is Abandoned – Hope of finding the missing tug *Mistress* was abandoned today after three days of searching Lake Michigan failed to locate the craft. Two coast guard ships and a coast guard plane from Traverse City returned to their bases without sighting any trace of the 38 foot tug or the two men who were aboard when it left Pentwater Monday morning for Milwaukee. Charles Jensen, 35 and H. Clair Graham, 40 both of Milwaukee had undertaken the crossing after purchasing the boat in Pentwater. A report that the *Mistress'* regular engine had been removed and replaced by a temporary gasoline motor for the crossing gave rise to the theory that the tug may have been destroyed by fire in mid-lake. Strong west winds whipped the lake Monday after the *Mistress* had put out but the craft was believed stout enough to withstand the heavy seas. – Ludington Daily News, March 7, 1941

The fate of the *Mistress* remains a mystery to this day. Many felt that the Mistress became top-heavy as the trailer on her roof accumulated ice, causing her to capsize and founder. Others felt that a fire erupted from the makeshift gasoline engine installation while the tug was far from shore. The strong winds and cold, dry air would have rapidly fed the flames, quickly engulfing the entire vessel and burning her to the waterline. The big waves would have conspired to send the remains of the disaster to the lake bottom in the cold, winter water, leaving little for searchers to find. Regardless of which story is believed, the hull of the *Mistress* now lies on the bottom of Lake Michigan in deep water somewhere on a line between Pentwater and Milwaukee, probably well offshore.

Stern view of the *Mistress* - Bob Grunst

In an interesting coincidence, the other missing fish tug referenced in the Ludington Daily News, the tug *Dornbos* out of Kenosha was finally located by a Coast Guard search plane five days after being reported missing. She was found one mile south of Beaver Island where she had run to shelter from the blow. She had her nets in the water and was actively engaged in fishing.

References : Milwaukee Public Library – Runge File, Runge Index Card, Herman Runge Wreck List, Ludington Daily News – March 1941, Bob Grunst, Burger Boat Company Archives

The Harrowing Loss of the Schooner *Jo Vilas*
Reprinted from GLHS Inland Seas

At one time the Great Lakes were the only major "freeway" in the midwest. Thousands of vessels once brought settlers, freight and merchandise through this vast inland waterway. Subsequently, it is not surprising that accidents were very commonplace. Today we are shocked to hear of a marine accident every few years. 120 years ago however, serious marine accidents were a daily occurrence. So many schooners and steamers were lost on the lakes that it is nearly impossible to chronicle each accident. The stories of many obscure vessel losses have subsequently faded into history. The following account details one of the many little known vessels that was swallowed whole by Lake Michigan.

The *Jo Vilas* was a typical two masted schooner of the Civil War era on the lakes. She was a coarse freighter that carried all manner of cargo between Lake Michigan ports. The *Jo Vilas* was built in the summer of 1857 at Manitowoc, Wisconsin by Rand & Brothers and was named for a member of Manitowoc's prominent Vilas family. Launched in September of 1857, she was an average sized schooner for her day. At 106.75 ft. long by 26 ft. wide by 8.75 ft. deep, she could hold 149 gross tons beneath her deck. She was initially owned by G.S. Rand, E.H. Rand and her first Captain, H.C. Albrecht of Manitowoc. On the third day of October, 1857, the Rand Brothers and Captain Albrecht sailed the *Jo Vilas* through the Straits of Mackinac and arrived at the frontier port of Michilimackinac where the *Vilas* was enrolled as a US merchant vessel. The *Vilas* had many owners during her 19 years on the lakes and was sold six times. When the assignment of enrollment numbers began, the *Vilas* received number 12767 and was eventually sold to George Wiegland of Chicago, Illinois where she held her last enrollment. She had previously sailed out of Manitowoc and Milwaukee and was a fairly well known vessel along the Wisconsin coast.

In her final years, the *Vilas* was used as a lumber vessel and could reportedly carry 150,000 feet of lumber above and below her deck. It was in this capacity that she arrived at the sawmills of White Lake, Michigan to take on a cargo of lumber which was badly needed to rebuild the fire charred city of Chicago, Illinois. On Sunday morning, October 8th, 1876, the *Vilas* finished loading and set out for Chicago on the other side of the lake.

Almost immediately, the *Vilas'* hull began to leak. Hull leakage was very common among old wooden schooners and the Vilas carried hand pumps to combat the slow, persistent flow of water into her hold. However, a fierce southwest gale blew up when she was in midlake, adding significant stress to her already tired hull. Water now began to pour in as her caulking started to give way. Every available crewman was put to the task of pumping as the cold water began to rise higher and higher in the *Vilas'* hold.

For Captain Richard Johnson and his crew of five, a race between the pumps and the rising water had begun. The men in turn kept up the grueling contest for 24 hours until they were exhausted. With the arrival of the dawn it became clear that the race was lost. Captain Johnson was now over half way to Chicago, but the weight of the water and a strong headwind made the *Vilas* sluggish as the heavy seas continued to build. Finally, at 8:00 AM on Monday the 9th, the water and wind conspired to lay the *Vilas* on her side. She quickly fell into the trough of the waves where the icy mountains of water washed clear over her waterlogged hull. In the freezing October gale, some 30 miles from the nearest land, the men had little chance for survival. The huge combing swells began to strip the deckload of lumber from the *Vilas*, sweeping her five man crew over the side with it.

In an amazing feat of endurance born of desperation, the five exhausted men in the water were able to gather together a quantity of floating lumber and lashed it together with a length of rope. Within minutes the *Vilas* began to settle in the water and Captain Johnson was forced to abandon her. The men on the raft were able to throw a rope to him and he leaped into the foaming surge, pulling himself along the line to the flimsy raft. For five minutes the crew watched as the *Vilas* struggled in the boiling sea. Then she slowly righted herself and paused as if bidding them farewell. The *Vilas* let out a deep sigh as her deck cabin blew off, then she ducked beneath the maelstrom into the serene silence, diving for the bottom some 70 fathoms below.

The six men were now totally alone in the middle of Lake Michigan in a howling October gale. As the whitecaps swept over them, pieces of their raft began to break free. The men occupied themselves trying to keep their precarious float from breaking up, but it seemed a futile task. The exhausted men had now been awake well over 24 hours and were waist deep in 50 degree water. It would be only a matter of time. For the next six hours the men endured the lashing spray and freezing surge. Then, in what must have seemed either an act of divine providence or a cruel mirage, the men saw what appeared to be the masts of a schooner through the waves and the spray. The odds of their little raft being spotted in the roiling tempest were almost nil and few vessels would be thirty miles out in such a storm. The men must then have thought it a miracle when the 126 ft. lumber schooner *Andrew Jackson* hove to alongside their makeshift raft.

The mens' troubles were still not over however. There remained the difficult task of getting them out of the water and into the pitching schooner. The men were too cold and exhausted to grasp and climb lines. The ropes had to be tied around the men who were then hoisted into the *Andrew Jackson*. Before half of the men were taken on board, the raft totally disintegrated. Had the *Andrew Jackson* arrived a few minutes later, the men would have undoubtedly perished. Before being hoisted aboard the *Andrew Jackson*, crewman William Cook smashed and broke his left hand and crewman Frank Folger broke one of his fingers, but remarkably, all six men were saved.

The gale remained so intense that the *Andrew Jackson* was unable to put into harbor until the next day. Tuesday afternoon, the men were landed at Racine and recounted their harrowing tale for reporters. "Their suffering was terrible," the Milwaukee Sentinel reported, "The waves were constantly breaking over them and at every moment they expected to go to the bottom." Another surreal fact came to light after the men reached port. The *Vilas* was lost on the 9th of October, 1876, the anniversary of the Chicago fire. Exactly five years before, during the conflagration, Captain Richard Johnson of the *Jo Vilas* had rescued the crew of the Brig *Hampton* which capsized under similar circumstances in almost the same spot - a remarkable coincidence. The Lakes however, had the last word. 25 years later, on September 7th, 1901 the *Andrew Jackson* met a tragic end. She was driven ashore in a gale and beaten to pieces at Pointe Aux Barques on Lake Huron.

In the end the *Vilas* amounted to a loss of $2000 for her owner, Mr. Wiegland. For Captain Richard Johnson, first mate John Minnig, and crewmen William Cook, Herman Klein, Frank Folger and Fred Schleiff the harrowing experience undoubtedly haunted them the rest of their lives. The *Vilas* went down about 30 miles off shore midway between Racine and Kenosha. She lies today in the cold inky darkness over 70 fathoms down and will probably never give up the secret of her location.

References:
The Herman G. Runge Wrecklist, Milwaukee Public Library, Marine Collection
Runge Index Cards, Milwaukee Public Library, Marine Collection
The Milwaukee Sentinel of October 11, 1876
Ports of Milwaukee & Chicago Vessel Enrollments, Master Index
Vilas Family Papers, State Historical Society of Wisconsin Collections
Port of Michilimackinac, Vessel Enrollments, National Archives
The David Swayze Wrecklist

THE PROVIDENCE MESSENGER CHAIN CAPSTAN WINDLASS.
Patented Feb. 17, 1874, March 21 and April 18, 1876, March 27 and Nov. 13, 1877, June 25, Dec. 3 and 17, 1878, June 1, 1880, Feb. 8 and 15, 1881.
American Ship Windlass Company, Providence, R. I.

Barnet's Coast Pilot for the Lakes 1881 – Author's Collection

The Last Run of the *Velocipede*

Reprinted from WMHS Soundings

Wisconsin's Lake Michigan coast has hosted countless marine accidents. Anyone who has looked out over the Lake on a windy day can easily see why. Severe storms blow in from the Great Plains without warning and quickly churn the Lake into a boiling torrent with giant waves that sweep the shoreline. The huge merchant vessels now on the Lakes have little to fear from most storms, but the small coastal trading schooners of the 1800s were often forced to brave weather that would be unthinkable for modern boats of the same size. Today, weather radar has made navigation on the Lake much safer, but in April of 1877 the crew of the tiny schooner *Velocipede* had no way of knowing that they were sailing into peril.

The *Velocipede* was built by master carpenter James Dickie at Menominee, Michigan in the Spring of 1869 for Captain Charles LaFontaine who was her first owner and master. She changed hands three times until being sold on September 1, 1874 to her final owner and master, Captain John Davis of Racine. One of the smallest merchant sailing vessels on the Lakes, she measured only 39.6 feet in length, 11.0 feet width, and 4.3 feet deep, carrying a mere 10.12 gross tons. Initially constructed as a single masted sloop, she had later been rebuilt as a schooner with two masts. She spent her entire career on Wisconsin's Lake Michigan shore, sailing mostly out of Racine, Wisconsin where she was used to transport both package and bulk freights. She carried official number 25848 and was considered a fast ship for her day, as evidenced by her title.

After a relatively short career, she found herself laid up at Racine over the Winter of 1877. She had been rebuilt only a year earlier at considerable cost, and Captain Davis was eager for a return on his investment. The ice in the harbor had only recently cleared when Captain Davis was seen searching for a yawl to replace the dilapidated old scow the *Velocipede* had carried as a lifeboat the previous year. Perhaps Lake Michigan's notorious reputation for April storms prompted his concern, as the captain was reluctant to sail without a good lifeboat. Captain Davis was apparently unsuccessful in his search, but the *Velocipede*'s departure could be delayed no longer. On the evening of Thursday, April 26, 1877 the *Velocipede* sailed light out of Racine Harbor, bound for Muskegon, Michigan where she was to take on a cargo.

Shortly after the *Velocipede* cleared the pierheads, the sky turned steel gray and a mixture of rain and sleet began to fall. A cold wind blew out of the north and began to whip the Lake's gentle swells into whitecaps. When the *Velocipede* was perhaps an hour out of Racine, a treacherous squall line appeared in the twilight and a violent gust swept at her from the northwest. Being light, the *Velocipede* would have had little or no ballast to hold her upright against the violent squall and she was probably pushed on her beam ends.

Throughout the night the gale increased in severity and persisted for the remainder of the week. Wave heights approaching twenty feet were reported the next day and all but the largest vessels ran for port. Concern was immediately felt for the little *Velocipede* which had failed to report in at Muskegon. By April 29th, the gale had abated enough that tugs were able to begin combing the waters off Racine and Kenosha in hopes that the *Velocipede's* crew had survived.

Then on Sunday afternoon, the fish tug *Engle* of Kenosha came upon a grisly scene about eight miles east-southeast of Kenosha Harbor. The mangled remains of a small vessel appeared on the horizon, which upon closer inspection were found to belong to the *Velocipede*. She was in sad shape, having been broken in two amidships with her sides smashed in and her decks washed away. She must have endured an incredible beating to have been so badly broken. Salvors were at a loss to explain how her hull and keel became smashed and broken. Some surmised that she could have been dashed upon the treacherous Racine Reef or hit a floating log after capsizing. Others suggested that during the storm she may have been run down by a larger vessel and left for dead. In either case, there was no sign of her crew, and salvors doubted that she had carried any lifeboat at all.

Lost were Captain John Davis and seaman John Hanley. The brothers of both men traveled to Kenosha where they chartered vessels to search for their loved ones, but nothing of the two men was ever found. Salvors were able to tow the wreckage of the *Velocipede* in near the Kenosha pier where she became waterlogged and was scuttled on the bottom. Only her masts and rigging were recovered, and her battered hull was subsequently abandoned in place.

Scuba divers have since reported the broken remains of a few small schooners on the bottom off Kenosha. Perhaps one of these debris fields is the 120 year old remains of the little schooner *Velocipede*.

References: Milwaukee Sentinel – May 2, 1877

Captain Krumer's Close Call on the *Reliable*
Reprinted from WMHS Soundings

1913 was a terrible year on the Lakes by any standard. The "Big Blow" of November 1913 ended the careers of many staunch vessels and caused tremendous damage to harbors and piers all around the Lakes. This great storm however, overshadowed a heart-rending disaster that befell a father and his two sons just off the Milwaukee Harbor entrance earlier that season. Perhaps it was providential that Captain William Krumer's career as master of the steamer *Reliable* came to an end in August of 1913, thereby sparing him the potential peril of being caught out in the rickety old vessel during the monster tempest that was to follow.

Krumer's little craft was built at Detroit in 1880 as a scow schooner by Thomas Davis. She was owned for most of her life by Detroit parties including her builder and John S. Quin. She sailed out of Detroit for most of her career and had been rebuilt a number of times. Launched at 69.47 gross tons with a length of 87 feet and a beam of 21.9 feet, in 1886 she was enlarged to 83.54 gross tons by a lengthening to 91 feet and a widening to 23 feet. Finally, in 1890, she was refitted with a steam power plant to be used as a sand sucker at 97.07 gross tons, 44 net tons.

In about 1910, at the ripe age of 30 years, the *Reliable* was brought to Lake Michigan to suction sand from the lake bottom for commercial use, and it was in this capacity that she met her end.

In July of 1913 the *Reliable* had been working the sand bottom south of Milwaukee when a stiff blow laid her on the beach. Unable to get up sufficient steam to make headway, she was hurled toward shore where she made a hard landfall. After several weeks in the shipyard she was thought to be in good enough shape to resume her duties, and on August 16, 1913, Captain William Krumer boarded the old steamer at Racine for a day of sand harvesting, after which, he would bring his cargo to Milwaukee for use in building materials. As it was a sunny August day, the Captain brought along his two young sons, Erwin, age 12, and William Jr., age 4. The two young boys doubtless enjoyed the excitement of running down the decks and watching their father harvest sand through the vessel's long suction tube. Also aboard the vessel were Deckhand Albert Boggs, Fireman Joseph Gay and Engineer Edward Leonard. The little six man crew was kept busy as the Captain and Boggs piloted the vessel and ran the sand apparatus, while Gay and Leonard fired the boiler and kept up steam to power the propeller and the sand apparatus. It was the vessel's first voyage after being rebuilt.

The morning of the 16th was spent about two miles off the shore of Wind Point, suctioning sand from the bottom, which was then poured into the vessel's hold. This activity continued until about two o'clock when 60 cubic feet of wet sand was loaded and the wind and waves began to pick up. Captain Krumer then decided to head for Milwaukee to unload, dock his vessel and take the boys home. All seemed to be going smoothly until about three o'clock when the vessel was a mile or two from South Milwaukee. The *Reliable* began to labor more heavily than usual in the building seas, and when Captain Krumer went below to inspect the hold, he found that the sand cargo had become a sea of mud. He immediately ordered all hands to the pumps in order to keep the vessel's bow above the building waves. The men pumped furiously for over two hours, but the water continued to rise ever faster. Finally, at five o'clock, the Captain ordered the exhausted men to begin dumping the heavy, wet sand overboard by the bucketful. Still, the vessel settled lower in the water and her engines became less effective at keeping her moving toward port.

Conditions continued to deteriorate, and by six o'clock, the Captain ordered the lifeboats made ready in case the worst should happen. The men were exhausted and the Captain's two sons were terrified. Despite the *Reliable's* worsening condition, the Captain stated his resolve to stay with the *Reliable* and refused to accept a position in the lifeboat. Fortunately for the *Reliable's* crew, the big Goodrich Steamer *Chicago* was passing through the area on her way from Chicago to Milwaukee. Just after six o'clock, she overtook the *Reliable* about 200 yards out. The *Chicago's* master, Captain Daniel J. McGarity clearly saw that the *Reliable* was in peril and trained his field glasses on the stricken vessel. He could see the frantic activity, but no request for help was made. He subsequently continued on toward the Milwaukee piers, which were now visible in the distance.

Amid the confusion, Captain Krumer looked up just long enough to see the *Chicago's* massive stern passing them by and promptly ordered Engineer Leonard to sound the steam whistle. Hearing the whistle, Captain McGarity of the *Chicago* immediately came about and raced toward the stricken steamer. As Captain McGarity neared the scene, he could see the crew of the sinking vessel putting off in the lifeboat. Three men and a boy leaped into the boat. On the deck, a man and another boy remained. The lad seemed to be trying to drag the man to the boat. Then the man gathered the little fellow in his arms and carrying him to the side, handed him down to one of the crew. It was twelve minutes after six and the *Reliable* was beginning to list heavily.

Captain McGarity could see tons of sand covering the upper deck where the crew had been trying to dump it overboard, and the sand appeared to be contributing to the vessel's extreme list. Within a minute, the man remaining on the vessel ordered the lifeboat away and at 6:15 PM, the vessel went over. Captain Krumer was last seen for a single moment standing near the deckhouse. He waved his hand and then disappeared as a big wave hid the foundering boat from view. The next instant the boilers exploded with such force that Captain McGarity nearly lost his footing several hundred yards away. A huge tidal wave swept shoreward, nearly swamping the little yawl containing the Captain's sons and the crew. Only frantic efforts on the part of the crew righted it, and a few moments later the *Chicago* hove alongside and threw a line.

The two boys, weeping frantically over the fate of their father who they supposed was lost, were drawn aboard the big steamer and taken to staterooms. Hours had passed and the sun began to set as the *Chicago* searched the debris field described as "matchwood." Believing Captain Krumer was lost, the Captain of the Chicago was about to give orders to get underway when he spied some motion about 100 yards from where the *Reliable* had gone down. It was Captain Krumer, waving his arms mechanically and trying to shout above the roaring waves.

In a few minutes the *Chicago's* crew had plucked the Captain from the floating beams to which he clung. He was exhausted and close to giving up when he was taken aboard, having been badly bruised and battered when struck by pieces of wreckage after the explosion. Captain Krumer was barely conscious when brought aboard the *Chicago* and was given stimulants to revive him, after which, he was reunited with his greatly relieved children.

The *Chicago* proceeded hurriedly to Milwaukee where Captain Krumer was taken for medical attention. After recovering overnight, the battered Captain told his story to reporters.

> "I did not think there was a chance for me to escape when the steamer *Reliable* sank after its boilers blew up outside the Milwaukee Harbor Saturday night," said Captain William Krumer on Sunday afternoon while resting from his perilous experience. "As soon as the boat started to list heavily, I thought it would sink and ordered my two boys and the crew to get in the lifeboat. It was a few minutes later that the ship turned turtle and the water which flooded the boiler room caused it to explode. The shock threw me about 15 feet into the water. I was probably stunned for several minutes for I do not remember anything that happened. When I came to I was resting on a small board which kept me floating until the *Chicago* came to my rescue."

The *Reliable* exploded and went to the bottom two and a half miles south of the Milwaukee Harbor entrance. Despite her well-known foundering point and close proximity to Milwaukee Harbor, her remains have never been found. She has been the subject of a number of searches, but her resting place continues to remain a mystery.

References:
Milwaukee Sentinel – August 16 & 17, 1913
Polks Marine Directory – 1884
Blue Book of American Shipping – 1903
Herman Runge Wrecklist
Lake Michigan Dive Chart – Paul Ackerman
Herman Runge Vessel Index Card File
Encyclopedia of American Shipwrecks – Bruce Berman
US Vessel Enrollment Certificates – Port of Detroit
Walter Hirthe Wrecklist

The Brig *Mahoning* Joins Wisconsin's Sunken Fleet

Reprinted from GLHS Inland Seas

Master carpenter William Jones stood on the bank of Ohio's Black River and watched as the vessel he had labored all Winter to construct slid down the ways into her destined element. It was April of 1847 and Jones was proud of his latest creation. She was a two masted brig of 119 ft. ½ in. by 25 ft. 5 ¼ in. by 9 ft. 8 in. She was christened *Mahoning* after the Mahoning River Valley which runs through eastern Ohio. She was an average sized vessel for her time with a capacity of 259 and 42/95ths gross tons of cargo and a hull depth that enabled her to enter the shallow river mouth harbors which predominated in the 1840s. She was definitely built with aesthetics in mind, sporting an ornate hand carved scroll on her stem and towering square sails which billowed overhead.

One of the most prominent shipbuilders on the lakes in the mid 1800s, William Jones came from a family of five shipbuilding brothers. His father, master shipwright Augustus Jones was descended from a long line of New England shipbuilders and not surprisingly, William's vessels came to be considered finely crafted and intricately designed works of nautical art. William's brother, George Washington Jones would become one of the most innovative builders on the lakes, contructing many large steamers. By contrast, William was a traditionalist who favored wind power. By the time he retired in 1863 William had built over 30 vessels and all but one would be windjammers. The *Mahoning* was unusual in that she would be one of the only brigs constructed by Jones. She would not be unusual however, in the place she ended her career. Two other of Jones' vessels, the *Meridian* and the *Winfield Scott* would also find a grave in Wisconsin's icy Lake Michigan waters.

As a brig, the *Mahoning* was not the most economical boat to operate on the Lakes. Because she was square rigged, her sailors had to go aloft to unfurl her topsails; a task for which they received a higher wage than schooner sailors. Her square rigging also made the *Mahoning* considerably less maneuverable than her fore and aft rigged counterparts. Although quite handy with the wind at her back, a brig such as the *Mahoning* would have found navigating the Lakes to be a demanding obstacle with fickle winds and frequent course changes. However, she more or less compensated for these shortcomings with a substantial advantage in speed and aesthetics. Still, the ease with which schooners could tack and jibe made them very popular in the tight confines of the Lakes and quickly decreased the popularity of the fast, elegant and graceful brigs. More amicable to ocean travel, within 20 years brigs had all but disappeared from the Lakes, mostly being converted to bark or schooner rigs. The *Mahoning* would be one of the few brigs never to fly a triangular sail on her masts.

On April 13, 1847, the *Mahoning* was delivered to her first owners, Charles Hickox, John F. Warren and John Jones who enrolled her at the Port of Cleveland, Ohio where her first master, Captain John Sims put her through her courses. The *Mahoning* was used extensively for the eastern lakes grain trade in her early career, running primarily between Cleveland, Buffalo and Oswego. She fared well on the long east - west stretches of Lakes Erie and Ontario, making quick times and paying for herself many times over.

She hadn't been out long when she tasted bottom for the first time. Late on the night of September 22, 1848, while downbound from Cleveland, Ohio with a load of wheat for Oswego, New York, the *Mahoning* was confronted by a rising gale from the west. Entering a harbor was a demanding task for a brig even in fair weather, and Captain Sims wanted to bring the *Mahoning* in before the blow intensified. Lining up as best he could between the Oswego Harbor piers, Sims drove the *Mahoning* under full canvas toward the harbor. Despite the efforts of Captain and crew, the ship was driven afoul and came to a grinding halt on a sand bar in the east harbor. Exposed to the fury of the gale, the brig was taking quite a pounding. Lines were thrown ashore and Captain Sims elected to raise sails to try pushing her off the bar. Luck was with the *Mahoning* that morning as she slowly ground her way over the bar and was back in deep water by ten o'clock the next morning. Despite spending a terrifying night at the gale's mercy, the staunchly built *Mahoning* required little repair and was back in service directly.

Like most Great Lakes vessels, the *Mahoning* changed hands and ports many times in her career. On May 14, 1852 she was sold to Robert Montgomery of Buffalo, New York where she continued in the grain trade under Captain Hugh Black. Soon western lakes ports began producing more grain than those in the east and the *Mahoning* was obliged to make the difficult journey up Lake Huron, through the Straits of Mackinac and down Lake Michigan to the new grain ports of Milwaukee and Chicago. By the late 1850s she was considered a bit undersized for the long hauls westward. Schooners and barks were now regularly being built to lengths of 160 ft. and could carry over twice as much grain as the little *Mahoning*. The rigors of many long trips had also put the *Mahoning* in need of a rebuild and her owners began looking to sell her.

It was on one of her trips to Milwaukee that the *Mahoning* was seen lying at dockside by Milwaukee marine men Captain James Stewart and Anthony G. Van Schaick. Van Schaick was in the process of building a fleet of vessels for the Lake Michigan lumber trade and on April 13, 1857 he and Captain Stewart purchased the *Mahoning* from Captain N. Gebhard of Buffalo for $6,000. Van Schaick also purchased the schooners *Virginia Purdy* and *Argo* that day and began running them to northern Lake Michigan lumber ports. The *Mahoning* would spend the rest of her years on the western lakes hauling lumber to build the fast growing cities of Milwaukee and Chicago.

On September 29, 1859, Captain Stewart bought out Van Schaick and became the sole owner and master of the *Mahoning*. By 1860 the brig's age and condition were beginning to show and the Board of Lake Underwriters awarded her only a C1 rating and a value of $3,800. Captain Stewart continued to sail her in the Green Bay lumber trade, but in March of 1861 he put her in dry dock for a badly needed rebuilding at Milwaukee's Wolf & Lawrence Shipyard from which she emerged as sound as ever. On April 23, 1863 Stewart sold the brig to her final owners, brothers Anson and Charles Bigelow of Chicago who placed her under the command of a new master, Captain William Vance, also of Chicago. Despite the difficulty of piloting a brig with a full deckload of lumber down Lake Michigan, the *Mahoning* seems to have been relatively accident free. She doubtless passed through Door County's notorious Death's Door many times without incident and escaped the teeth of such well known ship killers as Racine Reef and Manitou Passage.

The *Mahoning*'s luck changed on Thursday, November 4, 1864 when she left Chicago in ballast to pick up a load of Green Bay lumber. Unknown to Captain Vance, a roaring gale was waiting to unleash itself on the western lakes. That morning the wind freshened out of the northeast and by noon a massive surf was running. At Sheboygan the scow *Swallow* and the scow brig *Gladiator* were smashed against the pier by the driving wind receiving serious damage. At Manitowoc the schooner *Crudader* was driven ashore and badly mauled by the gale and at Two Rivers the brig *Oleander* was pitched upon the beach, a total wreck. The *Mahoning* had no sooner passed Milwaukee when the wind began to howl. Vance pressed on in hope of making Manitowoc, but the gale continued to build, lashing the crew with an icy, drenching spray that pounded over the starboard gunwale. As she neared Sheboygan, it became clear that the *Mahoning* would not last out in the open lake. Being light, she presented a high profile to the gusting wind and was becoming increasingly unmanageable. Vance elected to run for the shelter of Sheboygan Harbor, but in the cross wind was driven wide of the pierheads. Out of control, the *Mahoning* was at the mercy of a wild nor'easter. Her sails were in tatters and the crew prepared themselves for the worst by removing their boots in case they should need to swim for it. Fortunately, the staunch little brig held together until the wind and waves tossed her upon the beach 4 miles south of Sheboygan near the mouth of the Black River. Despite their wild ride, Captain Vance and his crew had no serious injuries and were able to walk the beach to Sheboygan where they were cared for by the local citizens.

The gale continued to blow for almost two weeks, sweeping the lake from different directions each day and Captain Vance was not able to make a serious attempt at freeing his vessel. Unfortunately, the gale had driven the *Mahoning* high on the beach and freeing her proved to be quite a task. The pounding surf had further weakened her hull and she had developed a seemingly unquenchable appetite for lake water. She was thus turned over to the underwriters as a total loss on November 14, 1864 and was placed under the command of a Captain Rierdon. As she was insured by Milwaukee's Columbia Insurance Company, they sent a well known salvor, Marine Inspector Captain William Tabberner, to try and recover the vessel.

Captains Tabberner, Rierdon and their crew labored for two weeks to patch and haul the *Mahoning* off the beach. With the help of the powerful tug *W.K. Muir* of Milwaukee they eventually released the brig from her sandy perch. For her part, the *Mahoning* continued to fill herself liberally with as much lake water as she could, forcing Captain Tabberner to fit a large steam pump on her deck and canvas patches under her bow to keep her afloat. Thus equipped, the *MUIR* began to slowly haul the *Mahoning* through the choppy November seas toward Milwaukee and the Davidson Shipyard where she was to be repaired.

The pair hadn't gone far when the steam pump began losing the battle to keep water out of the brig's hold. Seeing that the *Mahoning* was in danger of foundering, Tabberner headed for the nearest pier at Amsterdam, Wisconsin where he scuttled the brig in 9 ft. of water. Appearing happy to be under the waves, the *Mahoning* was left next to the dock while Captains Tabberner and Rierdon returned to Milwaukee for another steam pump. Returning two days later with a second pump procured from Captain J.B. Merrell, the crew soon had her hold free of water and placed another canvas sail beneath the brig's bow to patch her leaks. On Thursday, December 1st at 10:00 AM the *W.K. Muir* took the *Mahoning* in tow once again and headed slowly for Milwaukee some forty miles distant. She appeared to be riding well with both steam pumps running and plowed on through a freezing drizzle. By evening however, the lake began to kick up and the crippled brig's seams threatened to open further. By nightfall the water had once again begun to rise in the brig's hold and a fog settled in making conditions extremely hazardous. Still, Captain Tabberner pushed on. He could finally see the end of a long and thankless salvage job growing near and decided to press hard for Milwaukee.

By 11:00 PM the pair were midway between Port Washington and Port Ulao when the seas began to roll the *Mahoning* so badly that the pumps were in danger of going overboard. The whistle of the steam pumps soon signaled the tug to come alongside. The brig was leaking so badly that she could no longer be kept free of water and the waves threatened to capsize her. Part of the crew went aboard the tug, but Captain Tabberner still believed that the brig could be saved and would not abandon her. Captain Rierdon, mate Michael Gallivan, and four of her crew also remained on board the vessel, determined to stick by her to the last. The *Muir's* boilers were stoked and she headed for shore near the Ulao pier at full steam. Captain Tabberner hoped to once again scuttle the Mahoning in the shallows, but the pair were still about two miles out. As they raced shoreward the brig began rolling furiously and was filled with water nearly to her decks. Only a few minutes had passed when the steam pump boilers were seen to go overboard, followed in rapid succession by the capsizing of the *Mahoning*. Having already spent two nights underwater, the *Mahoning's* timbers had no more buoyancy. She wallowed briefly on her side as escaping air hissed out her holds and deckhouse. The *Muir* crew quickly chopped through the towing hawser as the brig righted herself, rapidly settling to the bottom with Captain Tabberner and mate Gallivan still below deck. Captain Rierdon, who was topside when she rolled, threw himself into the lake and was able to cling to the brig's mastheads along with the remaining crew. The *Muir* immediately wheeled around and took the men off the exposed spars but no trace could be found of Captain Tabberner or the mate. The *Muir* circled the area for hours in the darkness, fog and freezing drizzle but the men had disappeared in the churning vortex generated by the ship when she dove for the lake bottom.

Captain Tabberner was widely mourned by the Milwaukee maritime community. The Milwaukee Sentinel eulogized him as follows:

> "Captain Tabberner has been a resident of our city for a dozen years or more. He was a native of England and has followed the sea or the lakes ever since his boyhood. His life long experience had made him a skillful sailor, and his personal qualities made him an excellent

commander. During the time he has been a resident of this port he has sailed the schooners SACRAMENTO and DEWITT, the wrecking tug GEO. W. TIFFS, and afterwards the HENRY L. LANSING, the JESSE HOYT, and others, for aught we know. He has often shown great courage amounting apparently to perfect recklessness of his own life on occasions of shipwrecks on our coast. The wreck of the SEBASTOPOL off South Point, some ten years ago will be remembered by many. On this occasion Capt. Tabberner was foremost among the rescuers who brought off the passengers in a life boat at great risk of their own lives. His loss will be deeply felt by the maritime profession and by his fellow citizens generally. He leaves a wife and three children."

In June of the next year, the wrecking tug *Magnet* of Detroit was contracted by the Columbia Insurance Company to locate the wrecksite of the *Mahoning*. They hoped to recover the steam pumps which were quite valuable as well as any other items which might be saved. On June 16, 1865 the tugs *Magnet* and *Leviathan* located the wrecksite in 65 ft. of water about ¾ of a mile from shore just northeast of Ulao. Using a hard hat diver they were able to quickly recover one of the pumps, anchors, chains, blocks and most of the standing rigging. The salvage was accomplished surprisingly quickly, taking only half a day to complete. The salvaged items were taken to Detroit where they were sold by the insurance company for use on other lake vessels.

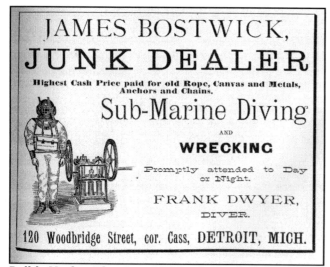

Polk's Marine Directory 1884 – Author's Collection

Because of her age and depth, recovering the *Mahoning* was prohibitively expensive and she was left in silent repose on the lake bottom. Today, 134 years later, she rests peacefully beneath the waves of Lake Michigan with her decks bathed in dim green light, another member of Wisconsin's historic sunken fleet.

References:
Runge Index Cards, The Herman G. Runge Collection, Milwaukee Public Library
James Jetzer Maritime Collection, Sheboygan Falls Historical Research Center
Richard Palmer Collection, Online Database
The David Swayze Wrecklist, Online Database
History of the Great Lakes, John Brandt Mansfield
Newspaper Microfilms: Milwaukee Sentinel, Daily Milwaukee News, Daily Wisconsin, Detroit Free Press,
Sheboygan Herald, Oswego Times
Inland Lloyds Register, 1860
Master Vessel Enrollment Indexes, Ports of Cleveland, Buffalo, Chicago & Milwaukee
Certificates of Vessel Enrollment, Ports of Cleveland, Buffalo, Chicago & Milwaukee
Schooner Meridian Wrecksite - National Register of Historic Places Nomination Form prepared by David Cooper and John Jensen of the State Historical Society of Wisconsin

The Schooner *Maine* Comes Ashore
Reprinted from WMHS Soundings

The schooner *Maine* was lost on October 23rd, 1887 in a dramatic accident that was witnessed by many Milwaukee residents. She was bound from Whitehall, Michigan to Chicago, Illinois with a load of railroad ties when she met with disaster in a powerful storm.

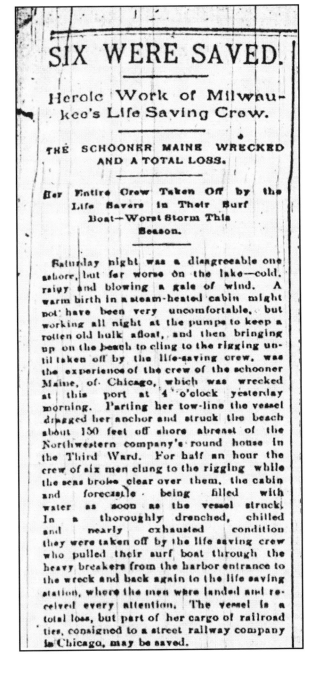

The *Maine* was a three masted wooden merchant scow schooner of 102.8 ft. x 25.3 ft. x 6.7 ft. and 151 gt., 144 nt., built in 1852 at Black River, Ohio by Lum, official number 16402. At the time of her loss she was owned and captained by Sam Christopherson of Chicago, Illinois. The Milwaukee Sentinel of October 24, 1887 carried the dramatic story.

Six Were Saved - Heroic Work of Milwaukee's Lifesaving Crew

Saturday night was a disagreeable one ashore, but far worse on the lake - cold, rainy and blowing a gale of wind. A warm birth in a steam heated cabin might not have been very uncomfortable, but working all night at the pumps to keep a rotten old hulk afloat, and then bringing up on the beach to cling to the rigging until taken off by the life saving crew was the experience of the crew of the schooner *Maine* of Chicago which wrecked at this port at 4 o'clock yesterday morning. Parting her tow line the vessel dragged her anchor and struck the beach about 150 ft. off shore abreast of the Northwestern company's round house in the Third Ward. For half an hour the crew of six men clung to the rigging while the seas broke clear over them, the cabin and forecastle being filled with water as soon as the vessel struck. In a thoroughly drenched, chilled and nearly exhausted condition they were taken off by the lifesaving crew who pulled their surf boat through the heavy breakers from the harbor entrance to the wreck and back again to the life saving station, where the men were landed and received every attention. The vessel is a total loss, but part of her cargo of railroad ties, consigned to a street railway company in Chicago may be saved.

The *Maine* was one of the oldest vessels on the lakes, having been built in 1852 at Black River, Ohio, and for thirty five seasons had been constantly in commission. She was a fore-and-after, of scow build and measured 144 tons. In the year she came out she was one of the largest vessels on the lakes, but her day had passed long ago, like all rotten old hulks, as time has made her. She was, however, kept in commission to bring earnings to the pockets of her owners at the risk of sacrificing the lives of her crew. But her fate was not to take the crew down to watery graves - only to give them such a narrow escape that they are not likely to forget it. Saturday morning the vessel left White Lake, Mich, bound for Chicago with 4,400 oak ties.

When in midlake Saturday evening the vessel commenced to make more water than usual. To prevent her filling and sacrificing the lives of her crew, all hands except the man at the wheel were set to work at the pumps. All night the men worked at the pumps, the water gradually gaining until she was half full when she arrived in the bay about 3 o'clock yesterday morning. Had she not been leaking she could have outridden the gale with other vessels at anchor to the south of the piers. But her captain was anxious to get her inside, and dropping his anchor to the north'ard of the pier, signaled for a tug. The tug *Morrill* went to her and taking her line - the best one she had - started in with her, the vessel dragging her anchor. As she got in the breakers just north of the pier the line parted. The tug was in danger of being swamped, the seas breaking entirely over her, forcing her into the harbor. The *Maine's* anchor found no holding ground and gradually she dragged ashore, striking the beach stern first about 250 yards north of the lighthouse piers. Clinging to the rigging while the seas broke clear over them, the crew watched longingly for the life saving crew, who, they knew must have discovered them.

Before the vessel had struck the beach the life saving crew were launching their surf boat in the river. The lookout having seen the vessel's danger, awakened Capt. Peterson and the others of the crew. Donning their cork jackets and oil skins, Capt. Peterson and his seven men pulled through the harbor entrance in their staunch little boat. No sooner had the boat got outside the piers than she was lifted by a breaker onto her end, throwing Capt. Peterson headlong into the boat. Several times this was repeated and the crew were obliged to await an opportunity between seas to catch the water with their oars. Pulling to abreast of the vessel, an anchor was dropped from the surf boat, which was then allowed to drift towards the beach with the sea, the line attached to the anchor being let go until 150 fathoms were out. Then the surf boat had reached the wreck. Here the sea was running very heavy and but for the line to the anchor it would have been hard work for the crew to keep the little boat from being carried up against the railway breakwater along the beach. But the line gave them better control of the boat, and dropping under the *Maine's* bow, they pulled up on the lee side of the vessel abreast the fore-rigging. Here there was less sea, but the crew had to keep the surf boat a few feet off the wreck, to avoid being swamped. Watching an opportunity between seas, the shipwrecked sailors jumped in the darkness into the surf boat, two at a time, and were caught by the life savers.

With thirteen men in the surf boat, it was pulled back through the breakers, a much more tedious job than reaching the wreck. The seas broke over them and half filled the surf boat, but there was no time for bailing. With their lower limbs in water to their knees and half blinded by the cold rain driven by the gale into their faces, the brave life savers pulled their human cargo into the harbor, making the same long circuit around the lighthouse piers. When the station was reached they were nearly worn out, and especially the shipwrecked crew, who had not a wink of sleep in twenty four hours, not a morsel of food or nourishment of any kind for twelve hours, were nearly exhausted. Stimulants were given them at the life saving station. The life saving crew stripped them of their thoroughly drenched clothing and provided all of them with dry clothing. Then they served breakfast for them and cared for them at the station all day. Capt. Christopherson, her master, went to Chicago on the 11 o'clock train to consult her other owners, and is expected back today. The others of the crew were Charles Anderson, Marcus Boyd, John Narum, Anton Reinholdson and Otto Hanson, all of Chicago. All of them were profuse in their praises of the work of Capt. Peterson and his brave crew for their heroic work. Hundreds of people visited the beach in the vicinity of the wreck during the day.

As soon as the vessel struck the beach she commenced to pound heavily and gradually worked into the sand until she was rail-to. The wind having shifted from southeast to southwest during the forenoon, the sea nearly all ran down and during the afternoon the lifesaving crewmade another trip to the wreck in their surf boat with a view to securing the crew's clothing from the forecastle and cabin, as the sailors had saved nothing from the wreck except what they wore. The cabin and forecastle were full of water and everything was afloat. Only a few articles were recovered. The vessel was so badly broken that the American flag which was in the cabin had floated out through her stern. She was found to be broken in two although her spars were still standing last night. Her deckload has washed off to the rail, some of the ties washing ashore while the others floated out in the lake. The cargo remaining aboard can be saved if the vessel holds together. Her cargo, consigned to one of the Chicago street railway companies was valued at $2200 and was uninsured. The vessel was valued at $1500 and was too old to insure. Capt. Christopherson owned three eighths, the other five eighths being owned by Swanson & Jorgenson, Chicago sail makers.

The *Maine* broke up on shore before any salvage could be made and her remains were removed for scrap. Much of her cargo of railroad ties drifted out into the lake and were an unqualified menace to navigation for the remainder of the season.

Historical sources for the wreck of the Maine include:
The Herman Runge Collection of the Milwaukee Public Library
The David Swayze Wrecklist
Mansfield's History of the Great Lakes
The Log of the Milwaukee Lifesaving Station
The Milwaukee Sentinel of October 24th, 1887

Chopped Out of the Steamer *H.A. Root*
Reprinted from WMHS Soundings

The little steamer *H.A. Root* was involved in two serious accidents at Kenosha, both of which cost the lives of some of her crew. The Root was a "rabbit steamer," having an aft pilothouse and a clear deck and was involved in the coarse freight trade hauling lumber, sand and gravel. She was built at Saugatuck, Michigan in 1886 by James Elliott for R.C. Brittain and Co. of Saugatuck. She had dimensions of 114.0 ft. x 24.6 ft. x 9.2 ft., 208 gross tons and was enrolled with number 95885. She had a long and varied career on the lakes, eventually being sold Canadian. The *H.A. Root* gained notoriety as one of the salvage vessels used in the 1897 raising of copper ingots from the steamer *Pewabic* which was sunk in Lake Huron in 1865. She was photographed at the site with a diving bell suspended over her deck on her forward cargo boom.

Steamer *H.A. Root* – Historical Collections of the Great Lakes

On September 3rd, 1907 the *H.A. Root* was hauling a load of sand from Milwaukee to Kenosha when her boiler exploded off Kenosha killing some of her crewmembers. She was taken in tow and brought into Kenosha Harbor where she was laid up undergoing repairs. One week later on the 10th while lying at her dock, the *Root* suddenly capsized. She had been slowly leaking for some time, no doubt a result of the boiler explosion and when the water got high enough, she rolled. Unfortunately, she went over at 3:30 in the morning and her captain and crew were asleep in their bunks.

Luckily, the accident was witnessed by surfmen Charles Olsen and Harry Hill at the Kenosha Lifesaving Station only 300 yards away and the crew sprang into action. Manning skiffs, the crew were at the wreck within five minutes and began looking for the eight crew members who were on board. They found four men floating in the water and got them into the skiffs, but four men were still unaccounted for. Moments later, Captain John Mooney and crewman W.R. Hunter poked their heads out of the side portholes. However, the men were still in danger because they couldn't get out through the portholes and were becoming exhausted. The lifesavers rushed back to the station and returned with axes. They then chopped the men out of the capsized hulk and continued searching the vessel until they found the drowned bodies of the two remaining crewmen. By 4:00 AM the six survivors were in the Lifesaving Station getting dry clothes and hot beverages.

The *Root* was valued at $12,000 and was worth the considerable effort to salvage her. Her cargo of sand was still on board but was a total loss of $110. The total damage to the *Root* amounted to $2000. When the final toll was taken, crewmen John Kebo and August Miller, both of Milwaukee had drowned. Captain John Mooney and crewmen W.R. Hunter, Robert Ryder, Frederick Zubly, William Hukman and Frederick Maukock were saved.

The *H.A. Root* was salvaged and continued in the Lake Michigan sand and gravel trade until she was sold to Captain E.J. Donohue of Detroit who sold her Canadian in 1910. She was bought by Samuel H. Braund and Charles W. Cadwell of Windsor, Ontario and enrolled with Canadian number 126195. By the next year the *Root* had disappeared entirely from the vessel rolls and may have foundered in the Straits.

Historical documentation for the Root's accident comes from the Wreck Reports of the Kenosha Lifesaving Station, Mansfield's History of the Great Lakes and the Herman Runge Collection of the Milwaukee Public Library.

The Yacht *Idler*: 20 Hours of Hard Work

Reprinted from WMHS Soundings

Historical information on the loss of the Idler comes from the Wreck Reports of the Kenosha Lifesaving Station and Arthur and Lucy Frederickson's Lake Michigan Shipwreck Charts.

On November 1st, 1895 at 8:30 AM the Kenosha Lifesaving Station received a telephone call from Waukegan, Illinois stating that "a little vessel was on the beach two miles north with one man aboard and wanting assistance." A fierce gale was blowing on the lake and the lifesavers were concerned for the crew's safety. They reported the following:

> We launched the life boat as it was blowing a gale from the northwest and after two and one half hours run we got to him. We found the man had got ashore and he asked to go with a tug and run a line to her. We ran a line and she was so rotten that the tug pulled her bow out and we gave it up as a total loss and retuned to Waukegan, the wind being ahead for us to sail home. We waited for the line boat who towed us back to Kenosha Station. Arrived to station at 4 PM, November 2nd after 20 hours hard work.

The little vessel the crew discovered on the beach was the 25 ton schooner *Idler* out of Marinette, Wisconsin. She was trying to return to Marinette from Chicago when Captain Ole Peterson ran her ashore just before dawn two miles north of Waukegan by present day Illinois Beach State Park. She was stranded 100 feet from shore and Captain Peterson was eager to get her off before the end of the shipping season. He immediately phoned for the lifesavers and a tug and by 11:00 AM both were at the scene of the wreck. Apparently the vessel's hull was weak and came apart under the stress of the tug's hawser.

The *Idler* was twelve years old and had probably been built at Marinette, Wisconsin. For unknown reasons, she was never enrolled and she may have been a pleasure craft rather than a commercial vessel. The Idler represented a loss of $200 to Captain Peterson and a loss of 20 hours to the crew at the Kenosha Lifesaving Station. She was a total loss, but was probably not left on the beach. She may have been rebuilt or scrapped and contemporary news accounts should be consulted to find what became of her.

Beaten to Pieces on the Rocks - The Schooner *Snowdrop*

Reprinted from WMHS Soundings

The *Snowdrop* was one of the oldest schooners on the lakes at the time of her loss. She was built in June of 1853 at Conneaut, Ohio by Lent and was enrolled with official number 22377. She was a good sized schooner for her day, with dimensions of 125.8 ft. x 24.8 ft. x 7.8 ft. and 190 gt. She carried three masts and sailed out of Chicago in the later part of her career. Among her many repairs were extensive refurbishings and recaulkings in 1866, 1868, 1887 and 1889. No doubt, it was due to these many repairs that she was able to sail the Great Lakes for 39 years before her tragic loss on April 30, 1892. The Milwaukee Sentinel reported her loss as follows:

> Ashore at North Point - Her Crew of Six Men Rescued Just in Time - After Two Perilous Trips to the Stranded Vessel the Life-Saving Crew Finally Succeeded in Taking Off Capt. Skipworth and his Sailors - Good Work of Capt. Driscoll of the Tug Starke - The Snowdrop an Old Timer
>
> One of the oldest schooners sailing the lakes, The *Snowdrop* of Chicago, drifted ashore on North Point opposite the light house yesterday afternoon. A heavy sea was rolling and the boat went to pieces on the rocks. The Snowdrop was headed for the harbor here when she struck upon the rocks. The crew was trying "to bring the vessel about" when a portion of her rigging gave way and she drifted on the reef. Distress signals were displayed and some one on shore telephoned to the office of the Independent Tug company for a tug. The Coe was immediately sent to assist the *Snowdrop*, but it was found impossible to aid the vessel as she had drifted too near the shore and the tug had not a line long enough to reach her. In attempting to assist the Snowdrop the *Coe* also struck upon the rocks but was not badly damaged. Finding that nothing could be done towards assisting the vessel the *Coe* returned to the city and the *Snowdrop* was left to pound to pieces. At a late hour last night a telephone message was received from the Lakeside club-house stating that the vessel was fast going to pieces and that before morning she would be a total wreck.
>
> A Perilous Rescue - Despite the terrible sea which was rolling the sailors remained by the *Snowdrop* until the sea which was rolling made it impossible for them to go ashore in the yawl. The Life Saving crew made an unsuccessful attempt to rescue the men early in the evening. When the Coe returned to the city, the Life Saving crew also came back with its boat. The sea was heavy and although in making the trip took the lives of himself and his crew in his hands, Capt. Driscoll of the Starke consented to tow the life boat to the scene of the wreck. The attempt proved a successful one and the members of the crew of the *Snowdrop* were all rescued and carried to the life saving station. When the life boat reached the *Snowdrop*, her crew were all huddled upon the roof of the cabin, and every wave which struck the boat washed over them. They were in the greatest peril about 9 o'clock when a series of squall struck the boat and for a few minutes the men feared that they would never see land again.
>
> The *Snowdrop* carried a crew of seven men. Capt. John Shipworth of Chicago, was her master, Nory Schwartz her mate. Charles Ericson, John Buss, Charles Ostburg, John Schaeppel and Martin Nelson composed her crew. They were all at the Life Saving Station this morning seemingly but little the worse for their exposure. They gave the highest praise to Capt. Driscoll and the Life Saving crew for their daring rescue. The life savers were in charge of Peter Nelson, Capt. Peterson being sick. Capt. Skipworth was very much downcast over his misfortune. He said he had cleared Friday from Ford River, near Green Bay, and that his voyage up to yesterday afternoon had been a fairly prosperous one. The boat, he said, was loaded with cedar posts and he placed the value of the cargo at $2000. There was no insurance on either boat or cargo.
>
> The *Snowdrop* was a Tub - For thirty-nine years the *Snowdrop* has plied the lakes, she having been built in 1853 at Conneaut. She was known at almost every port between Buffalo and Milwaukee. Her present load was cedar posts and she was bound for Chicago. Her object in trying to put in here is not known. The present owner of the boat is J. Tholer of Chicago. She is rated in the Inland vessel register as having a net tonnage of 181 tons and she was almost entirely rebuilt in 1887 and was recaulked in 1889. She was a three masted schooner and was valued at $3000. It is said that she was considered a particularly lucky boat as during her long service on the lakes she has suffered but few accidents.

The *Snowdrop* was abandoned on the rocks by North Point as eventually was flattened by year of ice and waves. What is thought to be her remains were located off the old North Point water pumping station in the early 1970s. This spine and ribs may also belong to the schooner *Alma*. Measurements would need to be taken to conclusively identify the remains.

Milwaukee Sentinel of May 1, 1892.

The Loss of the Schooner *Edna*

Reprinted from WMHS Soundings

At 3:00 PM on October 26th, 1887, surfman John Mahoney from the Kenosha Lifesaving Station witnessed the foundering of a schooner two miles off the Kenosha piers. He quickly dispatched a messenger to alert the lifesavers who sprung into action. Station Keeper Benjamin Cameron noted, "We launched the white hall boat and the surf boat in two minutes and were on the way to the rescue. When we got to the spot where she went down the crew of four men were on a little scow a drifting out into the lake. We got them aboard of the surf boat and pulled for the wreck and found she was the schooner *Edna* of Chicago, Ill. and loaded with gravel. She had sprung a leak and went down in five minutes. We stayed around the wreck for a while, and as we could not do anything and the crew was so cold we returned to the station where a good fire was burning. We gave the poor fellows some dry clothing and a good supper and they started for Chicago at 8:00 PM."

The *Edna* was built, owned and captained by N.L. Anderson of Chicago. She had been constructed and launched at Chicago in the summer of 1877 and was enrolled at the Port of Chicago on September 1, 1877. She was built as a two masted merchant schooner of 62.1 ft. x 17.2 ft. x 5.2 ft. and 38.32 gross tons, 36 net tons. Her official number was 135309 and she was rated A1 by Inland Lloyds at the time of her launch.

On her final voyage, the *Edna* had left Chicago early in the morning of October 26, 1887 with a cargo of gravel bound for Kenosha, but as she neared her destination, for unknown reasons she began to leak uncontrollably. Two miles off of Kenosha Harbor it became clear that the *Edna* would founder and the crew took to their life boat. Fortunately, there was only a moderate south wind and sea, and the *Edna's* crew were able to safely await the lifesavers. At 3:20 PM, with the help of the tug Kitty Smoke, the lifesavers arrived at the wreck scene and picked up Captain N.L. Anderson, Hans Offerson, Ole Holf and Peter Peterson, all of Chicago and by 5:00 PM they were all back at the Lifesaving Station having dinner.

Neither the *Edna* nor her cargo were insured and the lost cargo represented a financial loss of $200 to captain Anderson. There is no evidence that the *Edna* was ever recovered, and at only $1500 value she may not have been worth the effort to refloat. It is possible that Captain Anderson considered raising his vessel because he did not surrender her papers until June 4, 1888, over seven months after her loss. Although the location of her foundering is fairly well known, the remains of the *Edna* have never been positively identified and her loss has never been documented in any modern literature. Because she foundered in about 50 ft. of water, her masts would have shown above the surface. As such, she was probably a hazard to navigation since she was directly east of the harbor entrance. It is likely that the *Edna's* hull remained relatively intact because her gravel cargo would ballast her against wind, waves and ice, but it is certain that her masts were either removed or worked themselves free.

It is interesting to note that the modern NOAA chart of the Kenosha area shows a submerged wreck one mile south of the approximate location of the *Edna's* foundering. It would be interesting to compare the remains at this location with the historical dimensions of the *Edna*. According the the Lifesaver's report, the *Edna's* remains should be located in about 50 ft. of water, two miles due east of the old Kenosha Lifesaving Station, but any search should first involve checking the charted wreck just to the south at approximate LORAN coordinates: 33144 / 49597. Because the *Edna* only drew 5.2 ft. and has likely settled into the bottom, she will probably give a very weak signature on SONAR and sledding might necessary to find her.

Further research for this wreck would involve checking the Kenosha newspaper and Chicago Inter-Ocean microfilms. Historical information for the loss of the *Edna* comes from the Wreck Report of the Kenosha Lifesaving Station, Port of Chicago Vessel Enrollment Abstracts, the Milwaukee Sentinel, Inland Lloyds and the Herman G. Runge collection of the Milwaukee Public Library.

The Scow *Hunter* Overturns
From WMHS Soundings

The *Hunter* came to grief on July 12, 1887 while she was unloading sand in the Milwaukee River. She was a two masted wooden scow schooner of 100.75 ft. x 24.5 ft. x 7.35 ft. and 131 gt. She had been built in 1855 at Milan, Ohio by Smith, Kelley and Lockwood. Her official number was 11301. The July 13, 1887 Milwaukee Sentinel reported her loss:

> Bottom Side Up - Scow *Hunter* Meets with Disaster in the River - The Milwaukee Tug company's sand scow, *Hunter*, lies bottom side up and hard on her dumped cargo at the company's sand dock, between East Water street and Broadway bridges. After the steam shovel had about scooped out one of the forward pockets, the scow settled aft, and unnoticed began taking in water through her siphon. Not until she began to settle to one side was the inflow of water discovered and it was then too late to get steam on and pump her out. She settled gradually and the crew left her when her starboard rail was nearly even with the water. Hardly had they got on the dock when she careened over and a moment later came bottom side up dumping 150 yards of sand beneath her, on which she stuck fast. All attempts to right her were abandoned until today when dredges will be engaged. It is thought that the scow boiler has gone through the top of the house to the bottom of the river, and possibly the steampump too, although the latter was fastened to the deck. The damage and delay will amount to a considerable sum.

The *Hunter's* days of sailing were over as a result of this accident and her enrollment papers were surrendered as a total loss. Her remains were removed from the river and scrapped. Historical information for the loss of the *Hunter* comes from Arthur and Lucy Frederickson's Lake Michigan Wreck Chart, Mansfield's History of the Great Lakes, the Herman Runge Collection of the Milwaukee Pubic Library, Port of Milwaukee Vessel Enrollment Abstracts and the Milwaukee Sentinel of July 13, 1887.

The *Toboggan* Founders
From WMHS Soundings

The *Toboggan* was a big scow sometimes referred to as an ark because she likely carried no masts. She was built at Milwaukee in 1886, and because she was unpowered she was never enrolled. She was used for large bulk cargoes and was always towed behind the steamer *Marshall F. Butters*. Based on the size of the cargoes she carried, she was likely well over 100 ft. long and over 25 ft. wide. She was lost off Milwaukee in classic foundering which was reported in the Milwaukee Sentinel.

> Capsized and Sunk
>
> The steamer barge *Marshall F. Butters* arrived here last evening, bringing Capt. Cooney and crew of the Ark *Toboggan* which capsized and sunk about fifteen miles off Milwaukee yesterday afternoon. Yesterday morning the *Toboggan* left Manistee in tow of the *Butters*, the latter bound for Chicago. The *Toboggan's* cargo was for Milwaukee. She had 2000 barrels of salt in her hold, 250,000 feet of clear lumber and 100,000 feet of timber on deck, the timber being for use on the government breakwater. She was leaking somewhat and the crew was kept busy all the way shifting part of her deckload while she was siphoned out. Gradually she commenced to settle to port and when it became evident that there was no hope of saving her, the crew took to the small boat and pulled away for the *Butters*. In the meantime, the *Toboggan* settled over on her side, dumped part of her deck load and went to the bottom. Overloading is very likely the direct cause of the disaster, although what water she had in her hold with the weight of the salt, assisted materially. The *Toboggan* was a clumsy, big flat scow, capable of carrying a big load, and was rigged with steam hoisting machinery to unload. She came out only last spring, having been built at the Milwaukee shipyard during the winter, and was valued at $15,000, which with her cargo will make the loss exceed $20,000. She was owned by M.F. Butters of Manistee.

The *Toboggan* went to the bottom in over 200 feet of water, taking her cargo with her. She is at best an obscure wreck and her remains have subsequently never been located. Because the location of her foundering is documented, she may yet be found as her hoisting machinery would provide a decent signature on sonar. She is a very deep wreck however, and lies on the edge of being divable. - Milwaukee Sentinel of July 13, 1887

The Milwaukee Fireboat Number 23 Meets a Fiery End

Reprinted from WUAA Underwater Heritage

Milwaukee Fire Department *Fireboat Number 23*
Milwaukee Fire Department Photo

On January 10, 2005, Milwaukee dive charter captain Jerry Guyer was doing some routine sidescanning with his recently acquired Marine Sonic 900 kHz sonar when he encountered an unexpected surprise. Guyer was covering an area he had covered many times before, just to the south of the *Prinz Willem* wreck site, when the image of a previously unknown wreck crawled across his screen. The image showed a small (around 100 ft.) wooden hull with a big boiler on it, sitting in around 70 ft of water.

A few chilly dives quickly revealed that this was a new wreck site. A call to the author to compare notes confirmed Guyer's suspicions that the hull was most likely one of the Milwaukee Fire Department's early 20th century fireboats. The heavy boiler, the hull dimensions, the appearance of char on the hull and the condition all pointed toward the Milwaukee *Fireboat Number 23* as the leading candidate.

Two of Milwaukee's fireboats are known to litter the bottom off Milwaukee Harbor. The boats, known among historians as *MFD 23* and *MFD 17*, respectively, have been targets for area wreckhunters for about 30 years. The ships, although sunk intentionally, are considered valuable pieces of Milwaukee community history and would be popular dive targets. As such, the possible discovery of one of the fireboats generated considerable interest in the Milwaukee community as well as among the Milwaukee Fire Department.

Fireboat #23 was built at Sturgeon Bay, Wisconsin in 1896 by the yard of Ribeoldt & Wolter as the August F. Janssen. Competition had been stiff for the construction of Milwaukee's fireboat, and Riebolt and Wolter were eager to win the contract, having just transferred their shipbuilding operations from Sheboygan to Sturgeon Bay. When the contract was won on July 18, 1896, it was a big boost for Riebolt & Wolter, the Janssen being the first vessel they would build at Sturgeon Bay. The fireboat was named after the Milwaukee Fire Department's assistant chief, who had died along with eight other firemen in one of Milwaukee's most tragic blazes when the Davidson Theater burned on April 9, 1894. She was built at a hull cost of $32,800 and slid down the ways on November 14, 1896. She measured 100.5 x 24.7 x 10.2 ft. and 133 gross tons. Her enrollment paper states she had an 84.48 ton capacity under deck, plus a 48.96 ton capacity above deck. Subtracting 42.70 tons for non cargo deckhouse space gave her a net tonnage of 90 tons. She was described as a screw steamer with one deck, no mast, a plain head and round stern. Her official number was 130711 and she was put into service on April 1, 1897. Her launch was recorded as follows:

> Launch of the Milwaukee Fire Tug – Milwaukee's fine fire tug *A.F. Janssen* was launched at the shipyard of Riebolt, Wolter & Co, Wednesday noon with all the pomp and glory incident to such an occasion. The train, which arrived at 11 o'clock had on board a delegation of Milwaukee's citizens, who were met at the depot by Mayor George Nelson and John Conrad, the designer of the boat. Following is a list of the visitors: Chief Foley, Commissioners of Public Works Benzenberg and Brockman, Assemblyman Woller, Alderman Geo E. Hill, Constable Corcoran, Thos. F. Ramsey, Patrick H. Connelly, O.T. Renning, Henry J. Kuntz, L.C. Caufy, Ernest H. Doerfner, Peter A. Stamm, Dietrich Thiele, Herman Buth, Robt. L. Rudolph, Teter Pawinski, Elias Stellenwerk, A.J. Andreszewski, S. Hanisecki, George Thuering, S.J. Schmidt, Mathias Berg, George Glasser, superintendent of fire alarm, C.F. Elmes of the Elmes Engineering works, who furnished the machinery, Chas Nimmer and G.W. Steneve. Busses were in waiting and the visitors were driven directly to the shipyard where the fire

tug with colors flying made a handsome appearance. After looing over the craft the aldermen were lined on her starboard side and a photograph taken. While this was going on ship carpendters were completing the preparations for the send off. Before the props were removed from the tug's sides, all the aldermen, with the exceptions of Kuntz and Thuering, scrambled to terra firma. Charles Elmes and John Conrad also remained on the tug for the initial bath. Nine of the townspeople also remained on board, making in a ll a total of just thirteen persons – a lucky omen in marine circles. At precisely 12 o'clock noon the rope was cut that held the craft on the ways and Alderman Rudolph cracked a bottle of "Milwaukee's Best" on her bow with the words: "In the name of the City of Milwaukee, I christen thee *August F. Janssen*. It shall be thy duty to protect the city in times of danger and distress." With the last words, the magnificent craft was moving down the ways, which performance was accompanied by the shrieking whistles of several tugs. Without a hitch to mar the occasion the fine craft slid into the bay like an eel, her stern sinking deep into the water, driving a mess of foam and waves before it. And then the handsome tug straightened up with the grace of a swan amid the cheers of the hundreds of people who had assembled to witness the launch. Exclamations of delight and admiration were heard from all sides on the beauty of the tug's lines and the fine appearance she made in the water, and it was the verdict of all present that the city of Milwaukee had a fire tug it could well feel proud of. After the launch, the aldermen were served with refreshments by the dry-dock people, after which they had an hour or more in which to look about the city. They all returned home on the afternoon train. The *Janssen* left for Milwaukee on Thursday afternoon in tow of the tug *Sydney Smith*. – Door County Advocate, November 14, 1896

MFD 23's machinery was purchased at a cost of $30,000 and designed by the Elmes Engineering Works of Chicago. Charles F. Elmes specialized in fireboat machinery and had designed the power plants for both Milwaukee's and Chicago's previous fireboats. Elmes designed *MFD 23's* plant to pump 4,500 gallons per minute, delivered from two brass water cannons, mounted atop the deckhouse and bow, respectively. Elmes designed her with a double high pressure engine with a cylinder of 18 inches diameter and a 20 inch stroke. The engine was powered by a single firebox boiler of 9 ft by 16 ft. The 23's power plant was identical to the 17's in every respect except that the 17's cylinder had a diameter of 18 ¼ inches.

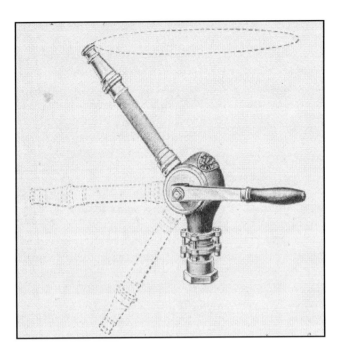

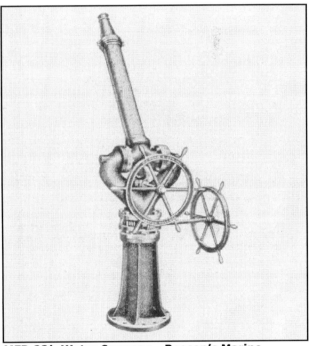

***MFD 23's* Water Cannons – Beeson's Marine Directory 1903**

The *MFD 23* was Milwaukee's third fireboat, built as a twin for Milwaukee's second fireboat, the *James Foley*. The *Foley* (later *MFD 17*), had been put in service in December 1893 and had proved a remarkable success, as had Milwaukee's first fireboat, the *Cataract*, placed in service in October 1889. These fireboats were part of a trend in firefighting to use fireboats in cities on rivers and lakes. The fireboats proved particularly useful for bringing large amounts of water to places where hydrants weren't available. Without fireboats, water had to be hauled by horse-drawn wagon, and was quickly used up. Fireboats however, permitted water to be pumped directly from a lake or river, and delivered great distances by powerful pumps. Fireboats revolutionized firefighting in waterfront areas and saved thousands of warehouses, grain silos, tanneries and other flammable waterfront buildings.

The *MFD 23* was initially used only in Milwaukee Harbor, and as such, didn't carry a certificate of enrollment with the customs house for several years. However, she did receive the usual inspections according steam vessels of the day. She was considered quite a fine fireboat and was looked over by the City of Duluth, which wished to purchase a similar vessel:

> The fire tug August F. Janssen, which was built at this port by Riebolt, Wolter and Co. for the city of Milwaukee has been inspected at that port by the board of fire commissioners of Duluth, who are desirous of buying fire boat. The Janssen engines were put in operation and one 2 inch stream and one 3 ½ inch stream were thrown high in the air for half an hour. The boat was then run up and down the river, affording the visitors a good view of the territory covered by the boats and showing their plan of operation. The people of Duluth are anxious to buy a fireboat and the commissioners expressed themselves a much pleased with the operations of the Janssen and the method employed in that city of utilizing the boats and pipe lines. The prospects are that the shipyard people will have another firetug to build. – Door County Advocate, March 13, 1897

MFD 23 had a long and successful career with the Milwaukee Fire Department, extinguishing many vessel fires and saving numerous waterfront businesses. In 1901, her name was officially changed to *No. 23 M.F.D.* This change was made to reflect the engine company which manned the specific boats. The *August F. Janssen* was manned by Engine Company 23, while the *James Foley* was manned by Engine Company 17. From May 1897 to June 1906, the *23* was stationed at the Cherry Street Bridge where she shared firefighting duties with the *James Foley* and *Cataract*. Following the *Cataract's* retirement, the *MFD 23* was moved to the Menomonee River Dock just west of 6th Street, where she remained stationed for the rest of her career.

She carried the following certificates of enrollment at the Port of Milwaukee during her career:

- No. 43: 3/19/1903 – H.G. Giddings, Master – David Rose, Owner – surrendered 4/18/1906 – Managing officer change
- No. 87: 4/18/1906 – H.G. Giddings, Master – Sherburn M. Becker, Owner - surrendered 4/22/1908 – Managing officer change
- No. 75: 4/22/1908 – Adolph J. May, Master – David Rose, Owner – surrendered 4/22/1910 – Managing officer change
- No. 87: 4/22/1910 – Adolph J. May, Master – Emil Seidel, Owner – surrendered 4/20/1912 – Managing officer change
- No. 124: 4/20/1912 – Adolph J. May, Master – T.A. Clancy, Managing Owner – surrendered 4/21/1914 – New form issued
- No. 245: April 21, 1914 – Adolph J. May, Master – T.A. Clancy, Managing Owner – surrendered 10/8/1923 – Dismantled & abandoned

It is interesting to note that the fireboat's first four owners were generally recorded as the Mayor of Milwaukee at the time, and that the tug's ownership followed the two year Mayoral election cycle. Following the 1912 election, the Fire Department began to record the Milwaukee Fire Department's Chief Engineer Clancy as the Managing Owner. This relieved the need for re-enrollment every two years. The *MFD 23* had two captains for most of her career, Adolph J. May serving the majority of her career as her master. Other firemen who crewed the 23, included Tom Rutherford, John Koster, Dan Ruppert, Timothy J. O'Donahue and Frank Etzel.

On April 30, 1906, the *23* was involved in a dramatic rescue, for which her captain, Harris G. Giddings, along with firemen Lawrence A. Hanlon and Peter Lancaster, were awarded gold Carnegie Medals. The citation read as follows:

> Harris G. Giddings, aged forty-five, captain of city fireboat, helped to save Jacob Flyter, aged thirty, labor foreman, from drowning, Milwaukee, Wis., April 30, 1906. Giddings and two other men descended a fifty five foot shaft and rescued Flyter, who was imprisoned in an air-chamber of a tunnel under the Milwaukee River, into which water was leaking.

By 1920, the Milwaukee Fire Department had two newer fireboats, the *MFD 15* and the *MFD 29*, as well as the *MFD 17*, which was still in service. With the aging *MFD 23* as the fourth fireboat, her days were numbered when the decision to order a new, modern fireboat was made in 1922. The MFD's new fireboat, to be named *Torrent*, would have nearly three times the pumping capacity of the aging *23*. As such, the *23* was stripped of all her major equipment in December of 1922. Her parts were removed for use as spares on the aging *MFD 17* and her engine was removed for scrap. On July 27, 1923, she was towed out into deep water off Milwaukee, set ablaze as a public spectacle and allowed to sink. It was an unceremonious end for a vessel that had fulfilled her duty "to protect the city in times of danger and distress."

The *MFD 17* would follow in the *23's* wake, being scuttled on May 12, 1930 with her engine and machinery reportedly still on board. Her remains have yet to be located, but are believed to lie further northeast.

Sidescan of the MFD No. 23 as she appears on the bottom - Courtesy of Jerry Guyer

The *MFD 23* is today in a fairly concentrated debris field in about 70 ft of water just south of the site of the Prinz Willem. Her main hull bed is relatively intact and features her massive boiler and condenser as well as her very substantial propeller, which is still standing upright beneath her sternpost. One of the WUAA's summer fieldwork projects has been to map and record the remains of the *MFD 23*. The site was initially filmed by Tamara Thompsen of the State Historical Society of Wisconsin, which revealed many interesting features. The WUAA fieldwork has been led by Kimm Stabelfeldt of the Great Lakes Shipwreck Research Foundation in conjunction with Jerry Guyer of LenDer Charters.

References:

Cyclopedia of Fire Prevention and Insurance, American Technical Society, Chicago, 1912

Carnegie Hero Fund Commission Report - 1907
Fireboats – Paul Ditzel
Fireboats in Milwaukee – James Moher, John Sutschek – Inland Seas, Spring 1962
Firefighting Ships – Herbert W. Dosey – Inland Seas, Fall 1961
WMHS Soundings – Vol. 31, No. 2
Evolution of Powered Workboats – James Barry – Inland Seas, Fall 2001
Annual Report of the Steamboat Inspection Service – 1897 – 1902
Beeson's Marine Directory – 1897 – 1903
Annual Lists of US Merchant Vessels – 1896 – 1930
Port of Milwaukee Customs House Vessel Enrollment Certificates
Milwaukee Public Library – Vessel File
Milwaukee Fire Department File – James Ley, Historian
Tamara Thompsen – State Historical Society of Wisconsin
Kimm Stabelfeldt – Great Lakes Shipwreck Research Foundation

The Schooner *Alma* Goes on the Rocks
From WMHS Soundings

The *Alma* was a wooden merchant scow schooner launched in 1887 at Milwaukee. She was originally built owned and captained by Henry S. Downer of Milwaukee. The *Alma* was a small two master of 57.4 ft. x 15.9 ft. x 3.0 ft and 26.42 gt, 25.10 nt. with a plain stem and square stern. She was enrolled at the Port of Milwaukee on December 28, 1887 with official number 106517 and in her short five year career she was sold a remarkable five times. She was lost under the command of Captain August Rosenow on Wednesday, May 18, 1892 when she capsized in heavy weather off Milwaukee with a cargo of gravel. Her enrollment was surrendered at the Port of Milwaukee as a total loss on September 23rd, 1892 and there is no evidence that she was ever recovered. The Milwaukee Sentinel of Thursday, May 19, 1892 carried the story of her loss:

Third Wreck of the Season
The Scow *Alma* on the Rocks at North Point

> Another wrecked vessel lies upon the shoals near North Point, and like the *Snowdrop* she will probably remain there. The third boat to be wrecked this season in sight of the Milwauke Harbor was the scow *Alma* which has been used the past season to carry gravel from the pits north of the city to the harbor. She was loaded Tuesday and that night started for the city. There was a stiff southeast breeze blowing and all night long the schooner tacked about the bay trying to make the harbor. In the meantime her hold filled with water and about 6 o'clock yesterday morning she capsized, dumping her deck load into the lake. The crew of three men scrambled onto the bottom of the boat and despite the terrible sea which was rolling clung to the hull until taken off by the fishing schooner *Prince*, which happened to be passing. Had they not been discovered at that time the men would undoubtedly have been drowned as they could not have hung to the side of the upturned scow for any great length of time. The *Alma* was the property of the roofing firm of A. Wronsted & Co., and when built cost $1,200. No tug went out to the boat yesterday, but marine men were of the opinion that the hull would not be worth the expense that would be entailed in its recovery.

The *Alma* fetched up hard on the rocks just North of present day Bradford Beach and it is likely that she was allowed to break up where she was since she would not have been a serious navigational hazard. She probably grounded in 15 to 20 ft. of water and her spines may still lie flattened on the bottom if they haven't come ashore or been buried.

The historical evidence for the *Alma's* accident comes from Arthur and Lucy Frederickson's Lake Michigan Wreck Charts, Mansfield's History of the Great Lakes, Master Vessel Enrollment Abstracts for the Port of Milwaukee, Surrendered Enrollment Documents of the *Alma*, the Herman Runge Collection of the Milwaukee Public Library, the Runge Wreck List and the Milwaukee Sentinel of May 19th, 1892.

Surrendered Enrollment Certificate for the Schooner *Alma* – National Archives

The Schooner *Monguagon* Goes to the Bottom
From WMHS Soundings

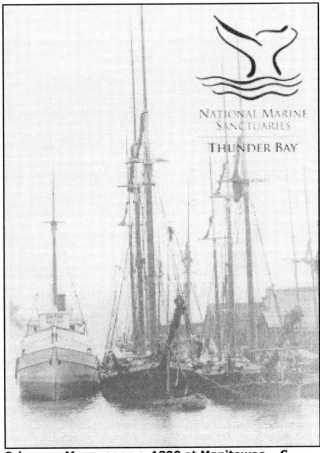

Schooner *Monguagon* c. 1890 at Manitowoc – C. Patrick Labadie Collection, TBNMS

The *Monguagon* was a three masted wooden merchant schooner of 136.5 ft. x 25.3 ft. x 11.2 ft and 301 gt., 286 nt., built at Trenton, Michigan in July of 1874 by Alvin A. Turner. Her official number was 90658. She was the victim of a serious accident in Milwaukee Harbor on May 13, 1888 when she was nearly cut in half by the steamer *Clarion*. The Milwaukee Sentinel of May 14, 1888 gave the following account of the accident.

Ran Her Down

The most serious river collision which has ever taken place in Milwaukee occurred in broad daylight yesterday. The iron propeller *Clarion* of the Anchor Line sinking the schooner *Monguagon* with a full cargo of coal. So quick did the vessel go to the bottom that the crew were obliged to leave most of their effects behind them, not even the vessel's papers being saved.

The *Monguagon* was lying outside the schooner *Montcalm* at Benjamin's lower yard at the foot of South Water street abreast of the harbor piers entrance and just opposite the lifesaving station. The *Clarion* was coming into the harbor shortly before 11 o'clock from Buffalo, closely followed by the propeller *Milwaukee*. Although the river at that point is fully twice the width of what it is at Grand Avenue bridge, the *Clarion* did not make the turn, but kept directly on the same course as she came in between the piers.

"Back her! Back her!" shouted Capt. Moore from the deck of the *Monguagon*, as he saw the *Clarion* bearing down on him. It was too late, however, and the *Clarion* struck the *Monguagon* with terrific force on the starboard side, just abaft the main rigging. Then there followed the sound of crashing timbers and plank as the *Clarion's* iron stem cut down the schooner, but just how deep cannot be determined until a diver makes an examination. From on deck it could be seen that her planksheer and several streaks of deck plank had been cut through, indicating that she has a big hole in her side. She immediately commenced to fill and in four minutes had sunk in twenty feet of water.

Of the *Monguagon's* crew, only the captain, a woman cook and one sailor were aboard when the collision occurred. Capt. Moore thought he had time to save what articles there were in the cabin and landed his own trunk and that of the cook onto the schooner *Montcalm* which lay inside the *Monguagon*, when suddenly the vessel commenced to settle and he was obliged to jump for his life. The woman cook had climbed onto the rail as the deck settled under water and, assisted by Capt. Ryan on the *Montcalm*, she walked to the forward end to the vessel and boarded the *Montcalm*, when a few moments later the *Monguagon* took a quick start and went to the bottom. The sailor was washing himself in the forecastle when the collision occurred and made his escape to the *Montcalm* without his shirt. Of all the effects on the vessel only the two trunks were saved, and one of those was emptied, the cook having most of her clothing hung up in the cabin. The sailor who escaped from the forecastle as well as the others who were ashore lost all their clothing except what they wore.

Shortly after the vessel had settled onto the bottom, a trunk floated out of the cabin. All of the vessel's hatches, too, were soon afloat as well as nearly every other loose article on deck, but all were soon recovered by the lifesaving crew, who, with the surf boat, were promptly on the scene. Amidships the *Monguagon's* deck is about eight feet under water, while her monkey rail forward and her taff rail aft are just even with the water. All her booms and canvass, too are under water, the gaffs being just out of water. While not a serious obstruction to navigation in the river, the sunken vessel is an obstruction to vessels reaching Benjamin's dock, to which several now on their way up the lakes are consigned. The *Montcalm* is squeezed in so tight between the wreck and the dock that she could not be moved yesterday, but as soon as the rest of the cargo is unloaded she can probably be pulled out by a tug.

Capt. Moore of the *Monguagon*, claims that the *Clarion* was racing into the harbor with the propeller *Milwaukee* which, he says, was lapping onto her starboard quarter. According to his theory, the *Clarion* had so much headway that she would not answer her wheel in time to make the bend in the river. Capt,. Garden of the *Clarion*, who is now serving his third season in that propeller and who has the reputation of being a careful man, denies that he was racing with the *Milwaukee*, and attributes the collision to the current. As he was coming in between the piers, a tug with a barge crossed his bows. To avoid a collision there, he was obliged to port his wheel so as to change her course until she "smelt" the bottom at the bend. Then she was caught by the current and refused to "come up." When he saw the danger, he says he gave the signal to back, and her engine was reversed, but her speed not entirely checked when the collision took place.

"Why," said Capt. Garden, "had we been racing and going at full speed we would have gone clean through the *Monguagon* and perhaps the vessel inside of her as well."

With the *Clarion* clearly at fault, Agent Brigham of the Anchor Line at once telegraphed the general manager of the company at Buffalo for instructions. The company will pay all expenses and the work of raising her will probably be commenced immediately. It will be quite a difficult job, though, and will probably take a week or more to accomplish it. The big hole in her side will have to be patched up by a diver, and a water tight box built all around her to above the water. After she is pumped out above deck, a good part of her cargo will have to be taken out before she can be floated. Just what the damage will be cannot be determined until she is raised and a survey made. With the cost of raising and repairing, besides the time and the damage to the cargo, it will be up in the thousands. The *Clarion* was not damaged and left last night for Chicago.

The *Monguagon* is owned by B. Whittaker & Son of Detroit. She measures 286 tons and was built at Trenton in 1874. She has a cargo of 600 tons of egg coal from Oswego, consigned to H. M. Benjamin & Co.

The *Monguagon* was salvaged and repaired at considerable cost following her accident. She had a long career on the lakes and was later converted to a bulk freight schooner tow barge. She was eventually lost due to old age when her seams simply opened and she foundered on the Detroit River on July 2, 1911. At 36 years old, she was no longer worth salvaging and was abandoned.

Historical information for the Monguagon comes from the Herman Runge Collection of the Milwaukee Public Library, Arthur and Lucy Frederickson's Lake Michigan Wreck Charts, Shipwreck! by David Swayze, Mansfield's History of the Great Lakes and the Milwaukee Sentinel of May 14, 1888.

The Grave of the Steamer *M.H. Stuart*

From WMM Anchor News

It is the Fall of 1981, and commercial fisherman Myril Brix of the fish tug *Butchie B.* from Milwaukee, Wisconsin has snagged his nets on a large obstruction about 8 miles off Milwaukee. The cost of a good net has never been a small matter for Great Lakes fisherman, and Brix sets out to recover his gear. Captain Jerry Guyer of Pirate's Cove Dive Shop has moored his dive boat next to the *Butchie Boy* and Brix approaches him to see if he can figure out what the nets are snagged on. Jerry makes the long cold ride out to the wreck in his dive boat the *G.J. Venture* and suits up for a cold Fall dive. Jerry makes a quick dive to the wreck on air and begins to tie a mooring line on what appears to be a large, burned schooner, when suddenly, his regulator free-flows, rapidly ejecting most of his precious air supply from his tank. Jerry makes an emergency controlled ascent and finishes the dive without getting a good look at the wreck.

At this time, visibility in Lake Michigan is about 10 ft on a good day, much less in 200 ft of water where the net lies. Jerry is none too keen to try the deep, dark dive again and approaches Great Lakes veteran John Steele to make a return dive. Steele, already in his 60s, is no stranger to the depths of Lake Michigan. He has personally found most of the historic wrecks on the western Lakes and is a pioneer deep diver. Steele makes the trip back out to the site in the Spring of 1982 and relocates it with his Klein sidescan sonar. Steele suits up and plunges into the cold, dark water, making a quick descent to the snag 200 ft below. On reaching the bottom, Steele takes a moment to get his bearing and soon he can make out the shape of an old wooden ship looming before him.

In the pitch blackness, Steele can only see a keyhole view of the massive wooden ship. It is clear that a significant portion of the ship's bow has been burned off, but the ship's cargo hatches are clearly visible in her deck. She appears to be a large schooner that has probably been burned and perhaps scuttled. Perhaps she could be the luckless schooner St. Lawrence that burned off Milwaukee in April of 1878. No name board is visible to tell the tale. Steele returns to the surface and neither he nor Guyer ever visit the site again.

Fast-forward to 2009. Zebra mussels have removed much of the zooplankton from the Lake Michigan water column and the Lake now has nearly 100 ft visibility, even at the 200 ft depth. The ambient light at 200 ft is similar to that at 20 ft prior to the invasion. Mixed gas technical diving has made the treacherous 200 foot dive much safer than the life-risking adventure it had been on air in the mid 1980s. Jerry Guyer is still running dive charters out of Milwaukee, but he concentrates on the shallower sport-diving wrecks that his customers prefer. He has published the location of the deep wreck, calling it a "burned schooner," but despite the passage of 25 years, no one has been back to the site. However, a small cadre of technical dive charter operators has grown and they are eagerly pursuing deep wrecks that were previously off limits to conventional divers.

Captain Jitka Hanakova is one of the premier technical diving charts on Lake Michigan. Having taken command from her friend and mentor, the late wreckhunter, Bill Prince, she now operates the *Molly V*, taking technical divers to some of the most pristine wrecks in the Great Lakes. Jitka has put together a team of elite technical divers including Tracy Xelowski, John Janzen and Ron Benson to visit the deep wreck and to try identifying it.

The divers suit up and splash into the water, which is not nearly as oppressive or threatening for this new breed of diver. They are no longer breathing air, but are instead breathing trimix, a combination of air, helium and nitrogen that enables them to think clearly at depth and prevents lethal oxygen toxicity. Janzen is using rebreather technology, enabling him to re-use their exhaled air which is now warm and moist compared to that breathed from a tank. All have Argon in their suits and some have suit heaters and elaborate mixed gas dive computers. The dive is now considerably more comfortable and safe than it was in 1984.

The divers can already see the full outline of the ship before they are even near its decks. The ambient light allows them to see from stem to stern on this 100 ft shipwreck. Janzen and Hanakova slowly swim the length of the ship, shooting high definition video of the entire wreck. When the divers approach the stern, they notice a detail that was easy to miss in the tense darkness 30 years earlier. A large four bladed propeller is half exposed in the clay bottom just under the ship's fantail. This vessel was not a schooner. The bow has a long metal stem stretching nearly 20 ft toward the surface, but the decking in the bow area is gone. All that remains above the hull bed of the bow is an area of metal sheathing that protected the ship's stem from ice. Further back, the decks and hatches are still present, all the way back to the stern. Amidships are two wooden posts, one on either side of the main hatch. There are no deck houses and all the machinery has clearly been removed, having been replaced by large rocks. Clearly, this ship was burned and scuttled.

Upon surfacing the team compares notes. The site is very interesting and is clearly a nice dive, with penetration possible through the holds and under the decks. However, there seems to be no way of identifying the ship. Scuttles are notoriously difficult to identify, as they were usually put to rest with little or no fanfare. Following the environmental movement of the 1960s and 70s, it became illegal to use the lake as a garbage dump and many midnight sinkings were done to avoid the cost of land-based disposal. This ship however, appears to have been sunk well before the era of environmental regulation.

I was asked to consult on the identification of the wreck immediately following the re-discovery. John Janzen emailed me a copy of the underwater video, which I watched intently. The two unusual wooden posts aside the rear hold opening caught my attention. Their shape was unusual, each flaring to a greater width at the top. Only a few hours earlier, I had been working on an article about Milwaukee's shipwrecks and had been looking at a ship photo with the same unusual posts. What are the odds?

The photo in question was of the steamer *M.H. Stuart* being towed out of Milwaukee Harbor on June 10, 1948 by a small Coast Guard motor launch. The caption states that she was towed out to deep water where she was burned and scuttled. I immediately matched up all the physical similarities between the ship on the bottom and that in the photo. Without even measuring the remains, I felt confident that we had made a positive identification. On September 19, 2009, Hanakova and Benson measured the wreck, confirming a length of 105 ft and a width of 25 ft, identical to the dimensions of the *Stuart*.

The *M.H. Stuart* was a large wooden "rabbit" steamer. So called, because of her high rear cabins and low bow with a cargo boom. Her outline resembled that of a rabbit. Many rabbit steamers were built on the Lakes, but very few have any extant remains. The *Stuart* was built in 1921 at Sturgeon Bay, Wisconsin by the Wolter & O'Boyle Shipyard for Captain Charles Anderson and Mr. Charles F. Zapf of the newly formed Traverse City Transportation Company. Captain Anderson was the patriarch of a pioneer family that settled South Manitou Island and he had captained many well-known vessels around the Lake Michigan islands. Anderson had joined forces with Zapf, who owned the Zapf Fruit Company in Traverse City. The two men formed the Traverse City Transportation Company for the sole purpose of operating the *M.H. Stuart*. During the summer and fall, the *Stuart* would haul fruit from Traverse City to the cities on the Wisconsin shore, and during the off season, she would haul lumber and other produce. The ship was named for Anderson and Zapf's friend Mr. Murray Hasgard Stuart, a wealthy Traverse City businessman who was secretary of the Wells-Higman Lumber Company of St. Joseph, Michigan. He had made his fortune in lumbering, ship chandlery and investing in Zapf's fruit orchards, which his company eventually acquired.

Captain Anderson personally supervised the construction of the *Stuart*. She was 104.5 x 25.5 x 8.7 ft. (116 ft overall length) and carried 192 gross tons. She was built to replace Captain Anderson's steamer *J.S. Crouse*, which had been lost by stranding and burning at Sleeping Bear Bay on November 15, 1919. The *Stuart* was launched with great fanfare on May 13, 1921 and marked the end of a string of hard times for the Captain:

The steamer *M.H. Stuart*, built at the Wolter & O'Boyle shipyard this last winter, slipped into the water at 11 o'clock Wednesday morning in as pretty a launching as ever witnessed. The ship slid in so nice and easily that there was scarcely any noticeable displacement of water. Miss Magdalene Anderson, daughter of Captain Charles Anderson, master and one of the owners, was sponsor and the christening was effected in the same matter as in pre-Volstead days, thirty thirsty ship carpenters and a crowd of citizens viewing the spectacle. Captain Anderson, unfortunately, is in the hospital and was unable to see his boat launched. The wife of the captain was present.

Here for the launching were C.F. Zapf, superintendent of the Wells-Higman company and M.H. Stuart, secretary of the same concern, from St. Joe, Michigan. The ship was named after the latter gentleman. Both men were greatly pleased with the job done by the Wolter & O'Boyle company. The *Stuart* is the property of the Traverse City Transportation company of which Mr. Zapf is president, Capt. Anderson, vice president, and B.T. McCalvy, secretary and treasurer. The ship is to take the place of Captain Anderson's steamer *J.C. Crouse*, which was burned two years ago. The new boat has been chartered to carry logs from the Manitou Islands to the Wells-Higman company's various plants on the west shore. The Wells-Higman company is engaged in the manufacture of packages for the fruit growers of Michigan and has a string of plants. The boat will also do freighting along the east shore and to the islands.

Work on the *Stuart* was started at the Wolter & O'Boyle plant January 10th of this year. The job complete represents an outlay of $35,000. The new boat is 110 feet long, 25 foot beam with 10 foot depth. She is equipped with fore and aft compound engines 14 by 28 by 17, built by the Manitowoc Shipbuilding company. The boiler is out of the old Goodrich steamer Atlanta and was taken out last year by the Leathem Smith company. It is a 10 by 10 ½ Scotch. The engine and boiler will be put in at the Smith yard. It will take another month to equip the boat.

The condition of Captain Charles Anderson at the Egeland Hospital has greatly improved the last few days and his recovery is now assured. Sunday his condition was so serious that the tug *Albert C. Kalmbach* was sent to South Manitou Island after Mrs. Anderson. The boat left here at noon Sunday and returned at five o'clock Monday morning. Captain Anderson was at Manitowoc last week on a business trip and was injured while there. He was riding in the rear seat of an automobile and when crossing a railroad track the jolt was so severe the captain was thrown into the top of the car his head striking a rod with such force that his scalp was cut and he was stunned. It was some time after the injury that he recovered sufficiently to return here and on the way back the pain became intense. Immediately upon his arrival here he entered the hospital where it was found that infection had set in. For the last few months, luck has been against the captain. He has a fine farm and fishing outfit on South Manitou and was reluctant to leave it to go in the steamboat business again. When he came here to have the *Stuart* built, he left his 17 year old boy and a hired man to take care of the fishing outfit and the farm. Two months ago, the boy died. The captain went to Sheboygan from here and chartered a tug to take him to the island. Not long after his return here after buying his son, he received word that the hired man was seriously ill. Now comes the accident to himself. - Door County Advocate, July 15, 1921

The *Stuart's* new engine developed 250 horsepower at 90 revolutions per minute and was built by Manitowoc Shipbuilding Co. The *Stuart* was also fitted with a single scotch boiler system with two fireboxes. The boiler measured 10 ft, 6 inches long by 10 ft, 6 inches wide with a grate surface of 27 square feet, a heating surface of 950 square feet and a working pressure of 140 lbs per square inch. The boiler was built in 1896 by John Mohr and Sons of Chicago, Illinois and had been salvaged by Leathem Smith from the Goodrich steamer Atlanta, which had burned north of Port Washington in 1906. The *Stuart* was also fitted with a steam steering gear and a complete electric light system. She was enrolled at the Grand Haven, Michigan customs house receiving registry number 221409. On July 15, 1921, after being fitted out and painted, she made her maiden voyage. She left Sturgeon Bay bound for South Manitou Island where Captain Anderson stopped to add some final personal touches. He then sailed her to Glen Haven, Michigan for a load of slabs and lumber, bound for Sheboygan, Wisconsin. On his return, he stopped in again at Sturgeon Bay for a load of hay, flour and feed for the farmers on South Manitou. By all accounts, the ship was a tremendous success, handling well and making good time.

The *Stuart* with a deckload of cordwood at South Manitou Island - Author's Collection

The *Stuart* at Sheboygan early in her career – Milwaukee Public Library Marine Collection

The *M.H. Stuart* had a long and successful career for her owners. She primarily carried fruit from Traverse City, Michigan to Sheboygan, Wisconsin, where she was a frequent visitor, but she also made runs with grapes from Benton Harbor and the other fruit growing ports on the Michigan shore. During the 1920s, she often delivered grapes for the making of prohibition era bootleg wine and would sometimes make return trips with casks of the illegal cargo hidden below decks. During the off-season, she would haul cargoes of slab wood, much of which was stripped to make fruit baskets for the next season. Although primarily a fruit boat, she also hauled deck loads of cordwood from the Lake Michigan islands to the sawmills at Traverse City and Charlevoix and occasionally hauled livestock, potatoes and other produce. She was one of the primary sources of transportation for the Lake Michigan islands during the 1920s and was well known all around the north end of the Lake. Captain Anderson would bring the *Stuart* out of layup each April when the ice thawed and would lay her up at Sheboygan each November. During the winter season, the captain would engage in commercial fishing on his tug *Grayling*, which he operated throughout the winter.

The *Stuart* weathered several notable storms and had a few close calls, including a 1924 accident in which one of the Zapf Company's deckhands was killed when the *Stuart's* deckload of cordwood shifted while the vessel was moored at the pier on South Fox Island.

In October of 1929, the stock market crash put a serious damper on Zapf's fruit business and the *Stuart's* profitability began to slip. In April of 1932, the Zapf Fruit Company agreed to formally absorb the Traverse City Transportation Company in order to remain viable and the *M.H. Stuart* was put up for sale. In April of 1933, the *Stuart* was purchased by vessel manager Chester H. Armentrout of Monroe, Michigan for $12,550. Armentrout was a vessel agent for the Roen Steamship Company and acquired the *M.H. Stuart* for Roen's Northwest Dredging subsidiary. The *Stuart* was purchased to replace the steamer *Marquis Roen*, which had burned at Bay City, Michigan in December 1932.

The *Stuart* in her Roen colors – Historical Collections of the Great Lakes

Roen spent an additional $1500 updating the *Stuart*, which he quickly recovered. He was able to put her to use promptly in September of 1933 under Captain Harold Edwardson to salvage steel from the big wrecked freighter *M.J. Bartelme*, which had stranded in October 1928 off Cana Island on Door County. In March of 1934, the *Stuart* was fitted to tow the barge *Pere Marquette 6* and in December of 1934, she was chartered to do salvage work on the wreck of the steamer *Wisconsin*, which had foundered off Kenosha in 1929. She served as a dive platform for hardhat divers and recovered some of the *Wisconsin's* cargo. The *Stuart* was also used to tow Roen's two large lumber and pulpwood barges *Interlaken* and *Transport*, making occasional runs to Lakes Huron and Superior, but primarily running on Lake Michigan.

The *Stuart* arrives at Milwaukee in 1943 – Milwaukee Public Library Marine Collection

By the end of the 1936 season, the *Stuart* was showing her age and could no longer compete with Roen's larger, newer, more powerful steamers. She was purchased on June 10, 1936 by Captain Edward J. Laway of Cheboygan, Michigan for $3000, enrolled at the Port Huron Customs House and put under the command of Captain Grant Minor. Captain Laway had planned to use the *Stuart* for salvage work, but an unusual opportunity presented itself in the fall of that year. On November 11, 1936, the big fuel tanker *J. Oswald Boyd* stranded on Simmons Reef, just north of Beaver Island. Captain Laway won a contract to recover as much of the fuel as possible and quickly had the *Stuart* converted to a tanker by installing large steel fuel tanks under her decks. In January of 1937, the *Stuart* made several runs to the stranded *Boyd*, recovering a substantial amount of her fuel and netting a healthy profit for Captain Laway. On January 1, 1937, one of the salvage vessels recovering fuel from the *Boyd* exploded while siphoning fuel. The *Marold II* was completely destroyed, killing all five of her crew. Fortunately for the *Stuart*, she was on the mainland unloading and was saved from the inferno.

The *Stuart* nearly met her end in bad weather on Saginaw Bay in Lake Huron on December 11, 1937 when she was reported as having sunk, but she was recovered and continued in service for Captain Laway. The *Stuart* disappears from most Lake vessel accounts until June 25, 1943 when she was sold to William A. Koch of the Milwaukee Diving Suit company for salvage work. Unfortunately, she was found to be in need of extensive repairs to put her in working order and she was laid up at the Washington Street slip. In 1944, she was removed from registry and abandoned at the Starke slip where she was cut down to a barge, with her rear cabins being completely removed. Over the winter of 1947, her stern settled to the bottom and she became a derelict.

The *Stuart* being towed out for scuttle – Milwaukee Public Library Marine Collection

The US Coast Guard consequently, asked her owner William Koch, to pump her out, remove her from the harbor and dispose of her. Koch loaded her hull with rocks, cut down her mast, and with the help of the Coast Guard, towed her to a point 8 miles off of Milwaukee Harbor. The old ship didn't give up without a fight. Koch poured gasoline on her and put fire to her bow, thinking the reduced weight of the bow would cause her to sink stern first. The ship however, stubbornly refused to go down. Koch then tried putting fire to the stern, but the damp wood burned slowly and the ship continued to float well into the night. Finally, the Coast Guard knocked holes in the sides of her hull and directed their prop wash at the holes to drive water into the ship. The old ship finally went down at 11:30 PM, 8 and ½ hours after Koch had first put the torch to her. She came to rest on an even keel, settling on the bottom in 200 feet of water.

The fire had consumed most of her bow, leaving only her thin, metal stem-post reaching up toward the surface, with its metal sheathing still protecting her keel shoe. The decking has been completely burned away forward of her front cargo hatch and her cargo mast and boom are long gone, having been cut down and burned when she was scuttled. The ship's railings are gone, but her mooring bits are still present along the side of her decks and two wooden posts rise from each side of her hatch amidships. These posts appear to have anchored the rear deck houses prior to their removal and were the main feature used to identify her, as they are also present in her final photo before scuttling.

The *M.H. Stuart* on fire – Milwaukee Public Library Marine Collection

The *Stuart's* fantail is still intact with her rudder-post sticking up through the deck. Her rudder and massive four bladed propeller are still present, but are partially buried in the bottom. The ship has a good deal of commercial fishing net wrapped around her stern and bow, and the *Stuart's* decking is still present over most of the hull, allowing for penetration into her cargo hold through the hatch openings.

The *M.H. Stuart's* gravesite had been lost for sixty years. This ship, once a fading memory, will now become an underwater attraction for technical divers and will join the many other historic vessels that grace the Lake bottom as one of Milwaukee's ghost fleet.

References:

Isle of View A History of South Manitou Island – Charles M. Anderson
The Fox Islands North and South – Kathleen Craker Firestone
Roen Steamship Company The Way It Was 1909-1976 – John H. Purves
Sail & Rail: A History of Transportation in Western Michigan – Lawrence & Lucille Wakefield
Namesakes 1930 – 1955 – John O. Greenwood
The Fleet Histories Series, Volume 6 – John O. Greenwood
Great Lakes Steambarges - Ships and the Sea Magazine, Vol. 2, 1952 – Kalmbach Publishing
Register of the American Bureau of Shipping, Great Lakes Department 1921 – 1935
Annual List of Merchant Vessels of the United States 1921 – 1994
Green's Marine Directory 1921 - 1948
Door County Advocate – May 1921, May 1933, September 1933
Milwaukee Public Library, Herman Runge Vessel File
C. Patrick Labadie Collection Vessel File
Personal Communication with Jerry Guyer, September 2009
Personal Communication with Jitka Hanakova, September 2009
Personal Communication with John Steele, October 1997

The Wreck of the Steamer Lady Elgin

From the Great Lakes Shipwreck Research Website

The Lady Elgin at Chicago on the morning of her departure - C. Patrick Labadie Collection, TBNMS

Introduction

One of the most significant events in Milwaukee's long history is the September 8, 1860 wreck of the steamer Lady Elgin. Although she actually lies in Illinois waters, her role in Wisconsin history is both substantial and tragic. The May 1989 discovery of some of her remains off Highwood, Illinois by Chicago salvor Harry Zych rekindled interest in the wreck and subsequent court battles over salvage rights kept the Lady Elgin in the news periodically. In the spring of 1995 the Elgin's remains were placed on the National Register of Historic Places and her notoriety continued to grow when ownership of the wreck was awarded to Mr. Zych, making her one of the only privately owned historic shipwreck sites on the Lakes. The ship's remains were subsequently removed from the National Register.

The Lady Elgin held the dubious distinction of being the worst loss of life on the Great Lakes until the steamer Eastland rolled over at her Chicago dock in 1915 killing 835, and the Elgin still ranks as the second worst wreck in the history of the Lakes. With the increasing popularity of sport diving, the Elgin's remains have now become a highly sought underwater attraction and she has been the subject of ongoing archeological investigation, although permission to access to the site is must be obtained from Mr. Zych before diving.

1854 Lady Elgin Ticket - Courtesy of Great Lakes Shipwreck Research Foundation

Political Significance

Often overlooked, is the Lady Elgin's role in Wisconsin's Civil War politics and the furor her loss produced. In 1860, Wisconsin was embroiled in the debates over states' rights fueled by the slavery question. The nation nervously awaited the results of the 1860 presidential election which would decide the country's direction on many issues.

Abraham Lincoln and Stephen Douglas were both running for president and it was widely believed that Douglas would maintain the status quo with slavery while Lincoln would abolish slavery. Many believed that if Lincoln was elected, a civil war would erupt in the south. Slavery was a very hot issue in Wisconsin. Some years earlier, an escaped slave named Joshua Glover had made his way to Wisconsin and had started a new life as a free man. Although illegal in Wisconsin, slavery was still considered legal by the Federal government. As such Joshua Glover's former owner was able to send Federal Marshals to Wisconsin to capture Glover, which they did. Glover was taken to the Milwaukee jail and held until he could be returned to the south. The citizens of Wisconsin considered Glover's arrest to be illegal and immoral, and Glover's case widely seen as an abuse of power by the Federal government. As such, over 100 Wisconsin citizens, led by abolitionist Sherman Booth, stormed the Milwaukee jail and freed Glover. Soon after this incident, Wisconsin politicians began complaining bitterly about the Federal government's trampling of Wisconsin's state rights and Wisconsin governor Alexander Randall threatened that Wisconsin might secede from the Union if slavery were not outlawed. One Wisconsin representative even placed a bill on the floor of the Wisconsin senate asking for Wisconsin to declare war against the Federal government if slavery was not abolished.

When Wisconsin secession began to look like a real possibility, Governor Randall asked all Wisconsin militias if they would support the state over the federal government in the event of secession. The Captain Garret Barry of the Union Guards responded that they considered it treasonous to take up arms against the federal government and refused to support the state. As such, Governor Randall revoked their commission as a state militia and had their weapons confiscated. In response, the Union Guards decided to re-arm themselves and made a secret arrangement with Colonel J.R. Lumsden, the editor of the New Orleans Picayune and the leader of a confederate militia in New Orleans, to have new weapons delivered to them in Chicago. The Union Guards chartered the Lady Elgin, ostensibly to attend a political rally for Stephen Douglas, but also to raise money and to pick up their weapons.

When the Elgin was sunk, many people believed it was an act of sabotage by Wisconsin abolitionists who feared that a re-armed Union Guard might fight against them. The feeling was so prevalent that there were many death threats against the crew of the Augusta, which had struck the Lady Elgin. However, there is no direct evidence that the Augusta struck the Lady Elgin on purpose. In fact, there is overwhelming evidence that it was an accident caused mostly by bad weather and poor seamanship. In the aftermath of this tragedy, there was a tremendous outpouring of sympathy for the Irish Union Guards and for the Milwaukee Irish community in general. Much of the Wisconsin secession talk died down and Governor Randall stopped checking the loyalty of Wisconsin militias. Some have speculated that had the Lady Elgin disaster not occurred, Wisconsin may have seceded from the Union before the southern states, but the disaster put a damper on the fiery rhetoric. As such, the Lady Elgin disaster had a major effect on Wisconsin's Civil War era politics and may have helped shape Civil War history. Today, most people assume that only the southern states were threatening to secede from the Union. The fact that Wisconsin came close to seceding first is not widely known and may have actually happened but for the Lady Elgin disaster.

The Wreck Event

Authentic Lady Elgin Union Guard Ticket - Reproduced here by permission of Harry Zych

The excursion left Milwaukee in the early morning hours of September 7th, 1860 and arrived at Chicago by dawn. That morning the unit went on parade before many spectators and then toured the city. In the evening, they attended a dinner-dance and heard several speeches. By 11:00 PM the Guards were ready to leave, but Captain Jack Wilson of the Lady Elgin was concerned about the weather. Wilson was a veteran lakes captain who knew the lake could be treacherous in September, but the eager passengers and pressure to maintain a federal mail schedule convinced him to get underway. Several new passenger were taken on board and around 11:30 the Elgin cleared Chicago Harbor and headed out into the open lake. Reports vary, but contemporary accounts and subsequent lists suggest that between 600 and 700 persons were aboard when the Lady Elgin departed. Many excursionists turned in for the night, exhausted from their busy day, while other guests danced and reveled in the Elgin's spacious salons. The Elgin left with little warning, reportedly departing before a number of unticketed visitors had a chance to disembark. Within a few hours the winds had increased to gale force and a high sea was running but the Elgin was weathering the storm well.

Original woodcut from Author's Collection - Frank Leslie's Illustrated September 1860

By 2:30 AM the Lady Elgin was about seven miles off Winnetka, Illinois when a tremendous jar was felt throughout the ship and she suddenly lurched onto her port side. Passengers who had been looking out the portholes reported seeing the lights of a vessel rapidly approaching the Elgin and braced for a collision. When the collision came, most of the Lady Elgin's oil lamps went out creating an air of confusion on board. Captain Wilson and First Mate George Davis had been asleep in their state rooms and dressed hurriedly. Captain Wilson went below and found a massive amount of water entering the engine room, while First Mate Davis rushed to the pilot house and ordered the Elgin turned toward shore. When Captain Wilson returned to the pilot house he privately told the mate that the Elgin would never reach shore.

The vessel that had inflicted the damage was the 129 ft., 266 ton schooner Augusta. She was a two masted vessel bound for Chicago with a deckload of lumber. Despite the gale, she was still flying most of her canvas and was sailing out of control. As she shot through the water, her deckload had shifted and she was nearly sailing on her side. The Augusta was in danger of capsizing and her crew was fighting to regain control of her. Her mate, John Vorce had sighted the Lady Elgin's lights from a considerable distance and reported it to Captain Darius Malott but in the confusion the Captain gave no orders until the Augusta was upon her. At the last minute the Captain yelled to the helmsman "Hard Up! For God's sakes, Man! Hard Up!" as the Augusta plunged into the side of the Lady Elgin just aft of her port paddlewheel.

The Lady Elgin was making good time and careened on with the Augusta's bowsprit buried deep in her side. The Augusta was pulled along with her for a short distance and pried the Elgin's sidewheel and hull planking out as she turned in the water. A few moments later the Augusta dislodged and the Elgin quickly pulled away. Captain Malott and his crew were immediately concerned for their vessel and believed that she must have sustained extensive damage below the waterline. When they looked for the Elgin, they could no longer see her, causing Capt. Malott to remark "That steamer sure got away from here in a hurry." Believing they had struck the Elgin only a glancing blow, and now fearing they might founder, the Augusta continued on for Chicago immediately.

Original woodcut from Author's Collection - Frank Leslie's Illustrated September 1860

Meanwhile, onboard the Lady Elgin, all was pandemonium. 50 head of cattle that had been in pens below deck were driven overboard in an attempt to lighten the vessel, and cargo including iron stoves was moved to the starboard side in order to raise the gaping hole in the Elgin's side out of the water. An attempt was made to launch one of the lifeboats, but it was lowered without being secured and had no oars. People watched helplessly as it drifted away from the vessel with only the First Mate and a few crew on board. Another lifeboat leaked so badly that it could not be used. Some alert coal shovelers spotted a mattress and tried to stem the flow of water by lodging it in the huge gash, but the water quickly pushed it aside. As the Elgin sank, she began to disintegrate and a split in her hull cut most passengers off from the life preservers. People began grabbing anything that would float and a crew of Irish Milwaukee firemen began chopping the hurricane deck off with axes in order to create a raft. Captain Wilson and others chopped doors down in order to rescue sleeping passengers. The Elgin sank stern first and the air rushing forward caused her upper works to explode as she broke up and sank. Within 20 minutes, the Lady Elgin had broke up and most of the vessel had gone to the bottom. Only her bow and two large sections of decking remained afloat. As the Elgin sank, a thunderstorm gathered and poured rain on the survivors with occasional flashes of lightning illuminating the horrific scene.

Rescues and Perils

From Frank Leslie's Illustrated News - Original in Author's Collection

When the light of dawn appeared over the horizon it revealed about 500 of the 700 or so passengers floating on various pieces of debris and decking. The lake was very rough and the large deck sections began to break apart almost immediately in the surging waves. Captain Wilson had taken charge of an infant and was sheltering it from the rain and surge when he handed it to another survivor in order to try and rig a sail. Just then, a large wave swept the child from the woman's arms to its death. Two large hull sections with over 100 survivors on each remained afloat for nearly five hours until they neared land. Fortunately, the water was relatively warm and most survivors that found a piece of wreckage were able to ride the 7 - 9 miles to the shallows. The First Mate's lifeboat was the first to reach shore just below the bluff at Hubbard Woods. He scaled the massive cliff and woke the Gage family who transmitted word of the disaster to Chicago via the Chicago & Milwaukee railroad station. By 8:00 AM many student volunteers from Northwestern University were on the scene as the wreckage and rafts approached the shore.

From Frank Leslie's Illustrated News - Original in Author's Collection

However, the heavy seas had generated a massive surf with a powerful undertow just off shore. When the frail rafts reached the breakers they immediately disintegrated, pounding their human cargo into the water mercilessly. Perhaps as many as 400 survivors reached the shallows, but only 160 were saved, the remainder drowning in the churning wreckage and surf. There were numerous acts of heroism on the part of both rescuers and survivors. Captain Wilson was lost trying to save two women from the surf when he was dashed on the rocks and killed just off shore. His body was not found until three days later when it came ashore at Michigan City, Indiana, some 60 miles away. Likewise, Captain Garrett Barry of the Union Guards was also lost trying to save victims. He was drowned only 100 feet from shore when he succumbed from exhaustion.

From Frank Leslie's Illustrated News - Original in Author's Collection

One of the several distinguished people lost in the disaster was Herbert Ingraham, a member of the British Parliament and owner of a London newspaper. Among the best known heroes of the Lady Elgin disaster is Northwestern University student Edward Spencer. He is said to have repeatedly charged back into the boiling surf to rescue people despite numerous injuries from floating wreckage. In all he is credited with saving 18 people after which he became delirious, repeatedly asking "Did I do my best?" He was allegedly confined to a wheelchair for the rest of his life and was the impetus for the establishment of the Evanston, Illinois US Lifesaving Station which was henceforth manned by NWU students. A plaque in his honor at a Northwestern University gymnasium commemorates his heroic effort. One survivor who reached shore did so by riding in on the carcass of a dead cow while another climbed into one of the Union Guards' bass drums and rode the waves to shore. Another man climbed into a steamer trunk which is today on display at the Wisconsin Marine Historical Society, and paddled it to shore.

From Frank Leslie's Illustrated News - Original in Author's Collection

The Aftermath

Original woodcut from author's collection - London Illustrated News September 1860

When the Augusta reached port she was leaking badly and her bow was stove in. Captain Malott was horrified to learn that the Lady Elgin had gone down. He promptly gathered his entire crew and stated his case to shipping officials. He claimed that the lighting configuration on the Elgin was incorrect and caused him to misjudge her distance. He also stated that he believed that he only damaged the Elgin's trim and feared for the safety of his struggling vesseland therefor did not stop to render assistance. Public outcry against Captain Malott was severe. The popular press attacked him as an agent of the Confederacy as well as an agent of pro-Confederacy Britain where Captain Malott had spent some time. Many felt that the ramming was deliberately planned to do away with the Union Guards. Angry mobs gathered and the crew of the Augusta went into hiding. Captain Malott was arrested and held for formal hearings. The Augusta herself was threatened with burning and had a difficult time getting crews after the incident. Her name was quietly changed to the Colonel Cook and she left the Lakes for the Atlantic. She had a long career until she returned to the Lakes and was driven ashore and wrecked near Cleveland, Ohio in 1894. Captain Malott and his crew eventually found another vessel, the bark Mojave. In a questionable coincidence, the Mojave disappeared without a trace almost four years to the day after the Lady Elgin disaster. All but one of the crew lost on the Mojave had been on the Augusta when she rammed the Lady Elgin and many though justice had been served. The Mojave was thought to have foundered in northern Lake Michigan, but it is possible that her crew was lynched in response to the Elgin disaster.

Bodies continued to wash up all around Lake Michigan well into December. Bodies were found as much as 80 miles from the wrecksite. Of the 430 or so confirmed lost, less than half were ever found. Many victims were unrecognizable and ended up in a mass grave at Winnetka. Others were returned to Milwaukee where many headstones still bear the inscription "Lost on the Lady Elgin." Because no official passenger list survived the tragedy, the exact number of passengers and victims will never be known. Many portions of the Elgin came ashore and were taken as souvenirs. A 100 ft. portion of her stern came ashore at Winnetka and was scavenged for years until it was removed and a large portion of her keel was used to construct an Evanston, Illinois barn which can still be seen. Her nameboard had been on display at the New Trier High School but disappeared some time ago. Other pieces of the Lady Elgin are still on display at historical societies around the area. The disaster was said to have orphaned over 1000 Milwaukee children and the entire city went into mourning over the tragedy. Most of the Union Guards were members of the Catholic St. John Cathedral in Milwaukee which continues to hold a memorial service for the Lady Elgin victims every September 8th to this day. Shortly after her loss, popular songwriter Henry C. Work penned the song "Lost on the Lady Elgin" which proved to be one of the most popular pieces of music over the next few years. Governor Randall of Wisconsin was cast as a villain in the Lady Elgin disaster for disarming the Union Guards and the incident created a wave of sympathy for the Milwaukee Irish. Much of the fiery states' rights rhetoric was toned down and Wisconsin cecession talk all but ceased. An official inquest into the disaster exonerated both Captains, finding the rules of lakes navigation in effect at the time to be at fault. The Lady Elgin's bow remained afloat and drifted until her anchors dragged several miles off Winnetka. The upside down hull section remained a hazard to navigation for some time after the accident until it sank.

Vessel Specifications

The Lady Elgin at Northport, MI 1858 - C. Patrick Labadie Collection, TBNMS

The Lady Elgin was a double decked wooden sidewheel steamer built at Buffalo, New York in 1851 by the well know ship chandlers Bidwell, Banta and Co. for Aaron D. Patchin and Gillman D. Appleby of Buffalo. She was named for the wife of Lord Elgin, the Governor General of Canada, and measured 252 ft. long by 33.7 ft. wide and 14.3 ft. deep. She carried 1037 gross tons beneath her decks and her steam engine sported a 54 inch cylinder with an 11 foot stroke that powered two 32 foot paddlewheels. The ship was built of white oak with frames with iron reinforcements to carry 200 cabin passengers, 100 deck passengers, 43 crew and 800 tons of freight and subsequently would have been somewhat overloaded the night of her loss. She was one of the larger steamers on the lakes and was very popular due to her luxurious accommodations and quick speed. She had been built to run between Buffalo, New York and Chicago, Illinois but had later been used to take excursionists through the new Soo Locks to the Lake Superior wilderness. The Lady Elgin was no stranger to accidents. On August 30, 1854 she was nearly lost after punching a hole in her bottom on a large rock north of Milwaukee. She was forced to run for Manitowoc, Wisconsin where she sank at the dock shortly after arriving. She was again almost lost in a June 1858 gale on Lake Superior when she was driven on the rocks while trying to enter Copper Harbor on Michigan's rugged Keweenaw Peninsula. She was abandoned to the underwriters who had insured her for $32,000. She remained high and dry until she was released on July 4, 1858. After extensive repairs totaling $8000 (a considerable sum at that time) she was put back into service. However, she was nearly lost again in early August of 1858 when she stranded on Lake Superior's Au Sable Point Reef, sustaining $1400 in damages. She remained on the reef for two days until she was pulled off by the steamer Illinois. Such was the life of an early Great Lakes steamer. When finally lost, she was owned by Gordon S. Hubbard & Co. of Chicago and was running primarily between Western Lake Michigan ports and Lake Superior.

From the London Illustrated News - Original in Author's Collection

Discovery

The Lady Elgin was forgotten by all but historical societies until the mid 1970s when salvor Harry Zych and others began to hunt for her remains, eventually finding them in 1989. Upon finding the wreck, Zych notified the Illinois Historic Preservation Agency (IHPA), that he believed he had found the Lady Elgin. The IHPA stated that they had neither the time, expertise nor the resources to examine Zych's new discovery, despite multiple requests from Mr. Zych. Soon after however, the IHPA learned of the site's significance and filed ten Felony charges against Zych, who had removed several portable artifacts for safekeeping due to the IHPA's inability to assist. In an effort to defend himself against the felony charges, Mr. Zych filed an admiralty claim against the wreck and leveraged his business relationships with the Cigna Insurance Company to secure title to the remains. Cigna had purchased the Lady Elgin's original insurer, the Aetna Insurance Company, and still had a substantial file of archival documents about the Lady Elgin in their archive.

After nearly a decade of court appearances and a great deal of hard feelings between all parties involved, ownership of the wreck was awarded to Mr. Zych on the basis that it had not been abandoned by the insurers and that Mr. Zych had legally gained title to it through the Law of Finds. From the outset, Mr. Zych's primary reasons for filing the admiralty claim were to prevent the theft of the artifacts and to defend himself against the legal charges.

Unfortunately, soon after the case went to trial, Mr. Zych and the IHPA were injuncted from visiting the site, and its location was leaked to the dive community in a dubious coincidence. A free-for-all ensued, during which most of the remaining artifacts were stolen. A great deal of Lady Elgin silverware, china, Union Guard firearms, as well as personal items of the passengers were secreted away to basement collections where they will never again see the light of day.

In the author's opinion, the Lady Elgin represents a textbook case of how not to manage the discovery of an historic wreck. It was one of the first test cases of the recently passed Abandoned Shipwreck Act and set an unfortunate adversarial tone between state preservation agencies and wreck hunters that has taken decades to overcome. The Lady Elgin's discovery was made at an unfortunate time when no precedent existed for state/private cooperation. Mr. Zych found himself in a difficult situation and chose a path that many preservation minded divers would have chosen.

Should he have left the artifacts on the bottom to be stolen? Should he have continued to wait for action from the IHPA while the artifacts disappeared? Many of us would have made the same decision that Mr. Zych made. Indeed, the only substantial artifacts that have survived from the Lady Elgin site are those which Zych was able to remove.

Had the IHPA engaged Zych in a cooperative effort from the start, the Lady Elgin might today be a centerpiece of Illinois public history. Instead, the IHPA decided to take a muscular stance with Zych, resulting in the loss of site ownership for the people of Illinois and the theft of most artifacts by unscrupulous sport divers.

Thankfully, times and conditions have changed, and the situation in which Mr. Zych found himself would be unlikely to occur today. Historic wrecksites are now routinely found by salvors and sport divers. In Wisconsin, our State Historical Society works diligently to ensure that all sites are examined and documented, and our maritime archeology staff maintain working relationships with salvors, sport divers and all persons with an enthusiasm for Great Lakes maritime history. Nearly all new wreck discoveries are now approached jointly by the discoverers and state agencies in a spirit of cooperation.

Despite his ten years of legal turmoil, Mr. Zych maintains a keen interest in the Lady Elgin and continues to research the wreck. In 2009, Mr. Zych participated with the Milwaukee Public Museum in the Lady Elgin Rediscovery Project, during which Mr. Zych hosted a group of archeologists, historians and descendents of victims who visited the wrecksite. The results of the site visit were shared via distance learning technology with school children all over the US in a series of live sessions during which Mr. Zych shared his knowledge and remembrances of the ship and her discovery.

The Lady Elgin Today

The Lady Elgin's existing remains lie today in four main wreckage fields, several miles off Highwood, Illinois. The area of greatest interest is the vessel's considerable bow section which had remained afloat for some time after the wreck. It lies mostly broken in 60 ft. of water. Numerous artifacts including the ship's anchor, chains and capstan remained in this area when the bow was discovered and some were removed for public display by Harry Zych's non profit organization, The Lady Elgin Foundation. Unfortunately, many articles were removed without permission by unscrupulous divers and will probably never be seen again. Some distance away from the bow is a debris field containing the Lady Elgin's boiler which fell through the bottom of her hull when she broke up. Another debris field reportedly contains remains of the Elgin's sidewheels, but has never been documented. Other debris fields contained machinery, tools, ship fittings and personal effects but have been largely looted. Divers are not generally welcome to visit the wreckage sites of the Lady Elgin without first obtaining permission from Harry Zych. Divers who do receive permission to dive the site should treat the site with the same respect as they would any property owned by someone else. Although the location of the Lady Elgin has been in public circulation for years, divers and charters who wish to visit the Lady Elgin should contact Harry Zych at American Diving & Salvage before planning a visit to the site.

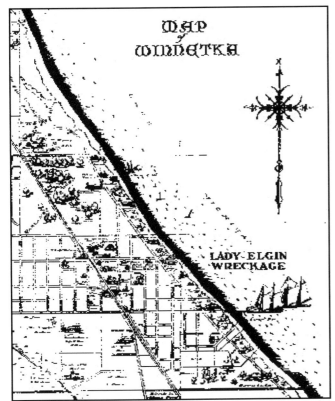
Map showing Lady Elgin Wreckage Site - The Lady Elgin Disaster, Charles M. Scanlon 1928

For the non-diver, the stretch of beach where the Elgin came ashore can be visited. Her wreckage made landfall over a five mile stretch from Winnetka to Evanston, Illinois. The main area where survivors and wreckage came ashore is shown on the inset map. Artifacts that have been retrieved by the Lady Elgin Foundation thus far include a few pre-Civil War muskets, swords, glassware, china, serving ware, a chandelier and the ship's whistle. The Chicago Historical Society, the Evanston and Winnetka Historical Societies and the Wisconsin Marine Historical Society hold many artifacts that were retrieved from shore after the wreck. Many excellent books can be purchased detailing the disaster's history. Also for the non-diver, the annual September 8th Lady Elgin Memorial Cruise from Milwaukee visits the site of her wreck and usually includes a display of artifacts as well as interesting historical presentations.

References

For further reading on the Lady Elgin Disaster the following books and resources are available and go into much greater detail:

Milwaukee Public Museum Lady Elgin Website
Brendon Baillod Lady Elgin Website
Chicago's North Shore Shipwrecks by Mark S. Braun
True Tales of the Great Lakes by Dwight Boyer
Shipwrecks of the Lakes by Dana Thomas Bowen
Ships of the Great Lakes by James P. Barry
The Lady Elgin Disaster by Charles M. Scanlan (Out of print)
The Lady Elgin is Down by Pete Ceasar (Out of print)
Great Lakes Shipwrecks and Survivals by William Ratigan
History of the Great Lakes by John Brandt Mansfield (Out of print)
The USM Lady Elgin Shipwreck 1860 by Emmett Michael Jordan (Available on the internet)
Milwaukee Public Library, Herman Runge Collection
Historical Collections of the Great Lakes, Bowling Green State University
Great Lakes Historical Society, Vermilion, Ohio
Underwater Archeology Society of Chicago
Chicago Historical Society Collection
Illinois Historic Preservation Agency
Inland Seas (Various Issues) Journal of the Great Lakes Historical Society, Vermilion, Ohio
Winnetka Historical Society, Winnetka, Illinois
Evanston Historical Society, Evanston, Illinois
Keweenaw Shipwrecks by Frederick Stonehouse
Dangerous Coast by Frederick Stonehouse & Dan Fountain

Bibliography

The following is a general list of references used in the research, compilation and preparation of this volume. The selections below fall into two main categories. Most represent material that I used to create my shipwreck database, which served as the basis of this book. However, a significant number represent material that I used for historical information on specific ports and material used to investigate the career and final disposition of area vessels wrecked elsewhere. For this bibliography, I chose to dispense with the convention of listing publisher information, as this is now readily available online for nearly every title ever printed.

A great deal of my research continues to be conducted using online sources. I have listed online resources in a separate section, but I did not list URLs, as I find that they often change or disappear. The resources should be easily findable with an online search engine using the information given. With respect to maps and charts of the area, I have specifically referenced those which came from my personal collection. However, I also made use of the amazing collection of maps and charts at the American Geographical Society Collection at UW-Milwaukee. These, I have credited where they appear.

I would also like to make an important observation about photo credits. I credited each photo to the source where I obtained it, unless I owned an archival original that I purchased from a private seller. For images that I obtained from public collections, I make no warranty about provenance. There has been a tremendous proliferation of vessel images in recent years, mostly due to the rise of electronic media. An image that was produced in 1905 by a vessel photographer such as Andrew Young or Louis Pesha may well have had hundreds of prints made at the time of creation. These prints were then collected by numerous early Lake vessel enthusiasts like Herman Runge, Dana Bowen, Father F.C. St. Clair and Edward Carus, who eventually deposited them in public collections. Latter day collectors like Ken Thro, Ralph Roberts and Pat Labadie also collected these images, sometimes from private holders, sometimes from public collections. These collectors in turn, donated their collections to public repositories. As such, most well known vessels now have the same images at every public maritime repository on the Lakes and it is possible to obtain images from the most convenient and cost effective source.

Curators of public collections sometimes naively assume that they have the only original of a given image or that their original is the one from which all extant copies were made. In practice, this is seldom the case, and it is often difficult or impossible to know definitively if a given image copy originated from a particular donor. This is especially true with the recent advances in digital image enhancement. I have tried to deal with this issue by obtaining common images equitably in order to give "equal time" to the excellent collections in our region. This is not to say that many collections don't still hold sole, uncopied originals. Nearly every public collection on the Lakes has unique vessel images not available anywhere else, and I have credited their images correctly.

Books & Publications

Andreas, A.T. History of Chicago
Arlov, Gary. Divers Guide to the Shipwrecks of Lake Michigan
Baillod, Brendon. Ghosts of the Ozaukee Coast
Barcus, Frank. Freshwater Fury
Barry, James P. Ships of the Great Lakes
Barry, James P. Wrecks & Rescues of the Great Lakes
Berman, Bruce. Encyclopedia of American Shipwrecks
Bleyer, Julius. Milwaukee's Great Industries
Board of Harbor Commissioners. The Port of Milwaukee: Historical, Descriptive, Prospective
Bogue, Margaret B. Around the Shores of Lake Michigan
Bowen, Dana Thomas. Shipwrecks of the Lakes
Bowen, Dana Thomas. Memories of the Lakes
Bowen, Dana Thomas. Lore of the Lakes
Boyer, Dwight. Great Stories of the Great Lakes

Boyer, Dwight. True Tales of the Great Lakes
Boyer, Dwight. Ghost Ships of the Great Lakes
Boyer, Dwight. Strange Adventures of the Great Lakes
Boyer, Dwight. Ships and Men of the Great Lakes
Brown, Charles E. Archeological History of Milwaukee County. The Wisconsin Archeologist, Vol. 15, No. 2
Bruce, William G. History of Milwaukee City and County, Vols. 1 & 2
Buck, James. Pioneer History of Milwaukee, Vols. 1-4
Caesar, Pete. Lake Michigan Wreck, vols. 1 - 17
Cooper, David J. and Jensen, John O. Davidson's Goliaths
Creviere, P.J. Wild Gales & Tattered Sails
Cropley, Carrie. Kenosha: From Pioneer Village to Modern City 1835-1935
Daniels, C. S. Canoe, Schooner, and Barge: Muskegon Ships & Shipwrecks
Derby, William Edward. A History of the Port of Milwaukee
Devendorf, John. Great Lakes Bulk Carriers
Donahue, James L. Schooners in Peril
Donahue, James L. Terrifying Steamboat Stories
Donahue, James L. Steaming Through Smoke and Fire: 1871
Donahue, James L. Steamboats in Ice: 1872
Elliot, James L. Red Stacks Over the Horizon
Feltner, Dr. Charles, Feltner, Jeri Baron. Shipwrecks of the Straits of Mackinac
Feltner, Dr. Charles, Feltner, Jeri Baron. Great Lakes Maritime History: Bibliography
Flower, Frank A. History of Milwaukee
Frank, Col. Michael. Early History of Kenosha. Collections of the State Historical Society of Wisconsin Vol. 3
Frederickson, Arthur & Lucy. Early History of the Ann Arbor Car Ferries
Frederickson, Arthur & Lucy. Later History of the Ann Arbor Car Ferries
Frederickson, Arthur & Lucy. History of the Ann Arbor Auto & Train Ferries
Frederickson, Arthur & Lucy. Pictorial History of the C&O Train & Auto Ferries & Pere Marquette Line Steamers
Frederickson, Arthur & Lucy. Ships & Shipwrecks in Door County, Vol. 1
Frederickson, Arthur & Lucy. Ships & Shipwrecks in Door County, Vol.2
Greenwood, John O. Namesakes, 13 vols.
Greenwood, John O. Fleet Histories, 10 vols.
Gregory, John G. History of Milwaukee, Wisconsin
Gunther, Fred. Boat Manufacturing in Racine, Wisconsin
Harold, Steve. Shipwrecks of Sleeping Bear
Harold, Steve. Shipbuilding at Manistee
Harrington, Steve. Diver's Guide to Wisconsin
Harrington, Steve. Diver's Guide to Michigan
Havighurst, Walter. The Long Ships Passing
Havighurst, Walter. The Great Lakes Reader
Heden, Karl. Great Lakes Guide to Sunken Ships
Heyl, Erik. Early American Steamers, 6 vols.
Hilton, George. Great Lakes Carferries
Hilton, George. Lake Michigan Passenger Steamers
Hirthe, Walter & Mary. Schooner Days in Door County
Hirthe, Walter. *The Marine Industry in Milwaukee*, in WMHS Soundings, Volume 22, No. 2, 1982
Holton, E.D. *Commercial History of Milwaukee*, in Collections of the State Historical Society of Wisconsin, v. 4
Jensen, Don. By Tempest Toss'd: Kenosha Maritime History
Jensen, Don. Kenosha, A History of Our Town
Johnson, Arthur F. A New Shipbuilding Enterprise in Milwaukee, in International Marine Engineering, April 1919
Karamanski, Theodore. Schooner Passage
Kellogg, Louise Phelps. The French Regime in Wisconsin and the Northwest
Kohl, Cris. 100 Best Great Lakes Shipwrecks, Vol 1 (Erie, Huron, Ontario)
Kohl, Cris. 100 Best Great Lakes Shipwrecks, Vol 2 (Michigan, Superior)
Kohl, Cris. Great Lakes Dive Guide
Kriehn, Ruth. The Fisherfolk of Jones Island
Lane, Kit. Shipwrecks of the Saugatuck Area
Lane, Kit. Lake Michigan Shipwrecks, South Haven to Grand Haven
Lane, Kit. Built on the Banks of the Kalamazoo
Mansfield, John Brandt, History of the Great Lakes, Vols. 1 & 2
Margry, Pierre. Decouvertes et etablissements des Francais dans l'ouest et dans le sud de l'Amerique septentrionale, vs. 1-3
Marine Historical Society of Detroit. Great Lakes Ships We Remember, 3 vols.
Meverden, Keith N and Thomsen, Tamara L. Wisconsin's Cross-Planked Mosquito Fleet
Meverden, Keith N and Thomsen, Tamara L. Wheat Chaff and Coal Dust
Nau Burridge, George. Green Bay Workhorses: The Nau Tug Line
Oleszewski, Wes. Stormy Seas
Oleszewski, Wes. Ice Water Museum
Oleszewski, Wes. Sounds of Disaster
Oleszewski, Wes. Ghost Ships, Gales and Forgotten Tales
Oleszewski, Wes. Great Lakes Mysteries and Histories

Oleszewski, Wes. Keepers of Valor, Lakes of Vengeance
Oleszewski, Wes. Great Lakes Lighthouses: America & Canada
Oleszewski, Wes. Lighthouse Adventures: Heroes, Haunts & Havoc on the Great Lakes
Page, H.R. & Co. History of Manistee, Mason & Oceana Counties, Michigan
Pitz, Herbert. Lake Michigan Disasters
Plumb, Ralph. Lake Michigan
Port Washington Historical Society. 1835-1985. Port Washington
Port Washington Historical Society. The Little City of Seven Hills. Port Washington
Price, Sister M. Jane Frances. The History of Port Washington, In Ozaukee County, Wisconsin
Quaife, Milo. Lake Michigan
Quaife, Milo M., Wisconsin Its Story and Biography; Vol 4; Pages 924-925
Ratigan, William. Great Lakes Shipwrecks and Survivals
Racine County Historical Museum. Grass Roots History of Racine County
Rippeth, J.L. The Lake Michigan Wreck List
Sander, Phil. Kenosha Ramblings
Schemel Jr., George W. Belle City Beacons: Lighthouses of Racine County
Sherman, Elizabeth. Beyond the Windswept Dunes: The History of Maritime Muskegon
Smith, Richard. Out of the Past: Recollections of Port Washington Maritime History, Vols. 1-3
Stanton, Samuel Ward. American Steam Vessels
Swayze, David. Shipwreck!
Swayze, David, Roberts, Ralph, Comtois, Don. Vessels Built on the Saginaw
Stabelfeldt, Kimm. Explore Great Lakes Shipwrecks, Vols 1 & 2
State Historical Society of Wisconsin. Collections of the State Historical Society of Wisconsin vols. 1-25
Stoke, Fanny S. Racine: Belle City of the Lakes and Racine County, Wisconsin, Vols. 1 & 2
Stonehouse, Frederick. Wreck Ashore: The US Lifesaving Service on the Great Lakes
Stonehouse, Frederick. Went Missing
Stonehouse, Frederick. Great Lakes Lighthouse Tales
Stonehouse, Frederick. Lighthouse Keepers & Coast Guard Cutters
Stonehouse, Frederick. Women & the Lakes: Untold Great Lakes Maritime Tales
Swearingen, Richard. *Shipbuilding in Milwaukee*, in WMHS Soundings, Volume 16, No. 2&3, 1976
Vrana, Kenneth. Harold, Steve. Inventory of Underwater Resources of the Manitou Passage Underwater Preserve
Taggart, Robert. Evolution of the Vessels Engaged in the Waterborne Commerce of the United States
Thwaites, Reuben Gold. The Jesuit Relations and Allied Documents, 71 volumes
Warnes, Kathy. *Early Milwaukee Ships*, in WMHS Soundings, Volume 23, No. 4, 1983
Wheeler, A.C. The Chronicles of Milwaukee
Werner, Ed. US Lifesaving Station Kenosha, WI 1879-1915
Weining, Paul G. Passages
Weining, Paul G. Great Lakes Ladies
Weining, Paul G. Reflections, Stories of the Great Lakes
Western Publishing Co. History of Racine & Kenosha Counties, Wisconsin
Western Historical Co. History of Washington & Ozaukee Counties, Wisconsin
Wheeler, Steve. The Boat & Yacht Designs of Fred W. Martin
Zabrowski, Ellen. The Racine Harbor

Databases

Ancestry.com – Various online Genealogical databases
Baillod, Brendon. Lake Michigan Shipwrecks: Frankfort to White Lake [Unpublished Database]
Baillod, Brendon. Lake Michigan Shipwrecks: Algoma to Kenosha [Unpublished Database]
Baillod, Brendon. Great Lakes Shipwreck List Database [Online Database]
Barron, David. Northern American Shipwrecks [on CD ROM]
Dowling, Fr. Edward. Great Lakes Vessel Database, University of Detroit-Mercy [Online Database]
Feltner, Dr. Charles. Great Lakes Vessel Enrollment Database [Online Database]
Genealogy.com – Various online Genealogical databases
Historical Collections of the Great Lakes. Online Vessel Database
Labadie, C. Patrick. Great Lakes Vessel Database [Online Database]
Leitz, Russel. Door County Advocate Marine History Database [Online Database]
Lewis, Walter. Pre-1861 Great Lakes Vessel Enrollment Database [Online Database]
Marine Museum of the Great Lakes. Online Canadian Vessel Enrollment Database
McNeil, William. Great Lakes Newspaper Transcription Marine Excerpts Database. [Unpublished Database]
McNeil, William. Great Lakes Newspaper Transcription Shipwreck Database. [Unpublished Database]
Milwaukee Public Library. Great Lakes Vessel File
Swayze, David. The Great Lakes Shipwreck File [Online Database]
Stabelfelt, Kimm. Great Lakes Shipwreck Coordinate Database [Online Database]
State Historical Society of Wisconsin. Wisconsin Shipwrecks Database.
Wisconsin Marine Historical Society. Online Great Lakes Vessel Enrollment Database

Wreck Lists

Aetna Insurance Company. Inland Marine Claims Paid 1853-1867
Buffalo Commercial Advertiser. Vessels Wrecked on the Great Lakes in 1850
Buffalo Commercial Advertiser. Vessels Wrecked on the Great Lakes in 1851
Buffalo Commercial Advertiser. Vessels Wrecked on the Great Lakes in 1852
Buffalo Commercial Advertiser. Vessels Wrecked on the Great Lakes in 1853
Buffalo Democracy. Vessels Wrecked on the Great Lakes in 1854 – February 28, 1855
Board Of Lake Underwriters. Report of Marine Disasters on the Lakes During the Year 1855
Board Of Lake Underwriters. Report of Marine Disasters on the Lakes During the Year 1856
Board Of Lake Underwriters. Marine Disasters and Loss of Life and Property on the Lakes for 1857
Board Of Lake Underwriters. Marine Disasters and Loss of Life and Property on the Lakes for 1858
Board of Lake Underwriters. Marine Disasters and Loss of Life and Property on the Lakes for 1859
Board of Lake Underwriters. Marine Disasters and Loss of Life and Property on the Lakes for 1860
Board of Lake Underwriters. Marine Disasters and Loss of Life and Property on the Lakes for 1861
Board of Lake Underwriters. Marine Disasters and Loss of Life and Property on the Lakes for 1862
Board of Lake Underwriters. Marine Disasters and Loss of Life and Property on the Lakes for 1863
Carus, Edward. Vessels Wrecked, Foundered, Burned and Abandoned on the Great Lakes, 1850 – 1930
Hall, J.W. Marine Disasters on the Western Lakes – 1871
Hall, J.W. Annual Great Lakes Shipwreck Lists – 1865 – 67, 1869 – 73
Hirthe, Walter. The Walter Hirthe Wreck list (Unpublished manuscript)
Jaeck, Robert. The Bob Jaeck Collection (Racine, Kenosha & Milwaukee)
Jetzer, James. The James Jetzer Collection – Sheboygan Falls Historical Research Center
Milwaukee Sentinel. List of Vessels Wrecked on the Great Lakes in 1849
Milwaukee Sentinel. List of Vessels Wrecked on the Great Lakes in 1848
Milwaukee Sentinel. List of Vessels Wrecked on the Great Lakes in 1843
Milwaukee Sentinel. List of Vessels Wrecked on the Great Lakes in 1868
Milwaukee Sentinel. List of Vessels Wrecked on the Great Lakes in 1895
US Weather Bureau, Report of the Chief Signal Officer – Accidents on the Great Lakes 1869 – 1883.
US Weather Bureau, Map of Casualties on the Great Lakes, 1885 – 1893
US Weather Bureau, Map of Casualties on the Great Lakes, 1894/95
US Weather Bureau, Wrecks and Casualties on the Great Lakes 1895, 1896 & 1897
Rippeth, J.L. The Lake Michigan Wreck list
Runge, Herman. Index of Disasters on the Great Lakes, 1679 – 1943 (Unpublished manuscript)
Stabelfeldt, Kimm. The Kimm Stabelfeldt Collection
US Coast Guard, Great Lakes Marine Casualties 1863-1873 [originally indexed from US Customs House Wreck Reports]
US National Archives. Wrecks and Casualties to Vessels on the Great Lakes 1863 – 1873. (Index to early Customs House Wreck Reports)
US National Archives. Wrecks & Casualties to Vessels which have occurred on Lake Michigan (Life Saving Letters Sent – Disasters to Shipping)
US National Archives. Accidents & Casualties to Vessels in the Eleventh Coast Guard District, 1908 – 1918

Vessel Registers, Catalogs & Listings

American Bureau of Shipping, Great Lakes Department. Hull Register, 1898-1935
Board of Lake Underwriters. The Inland Lloyds Vessel Register, 1856 – 1907
Board of Canadian Lake Underwriters. Canadian Inland Lloyds Register, 1854 – 1902
Beeson, Harvey C. Beeson's Inland Marine Directory, 1888 – 1921
Buffalo Democracy. List of Vessels Enrolled on the Great Lakes in 1854
Buffalo Commercial Advertiser. List of Vessels Enrolled on the Great Lakes in 1837
Buffalo City Directory. List of Vessels Enrolled on the Great Lakes in 1849
Canada Department of Marine & Fisheries. Canadian Lists of Merchant Vessels, 1868-1940
Catlin, Seth. First Annual Statement of the Trade and Commerce of Chicago, 1858
Detroit Drydock Company. Around the Lakes, 1894
Green, John B. Green's Great Lakes Marine Directory, 1909-1968
Lake Shipmasters Association. Annual Directory, 1896-1967
Lytle, William M., Holdcamper, Forrest R.: Merchant Steam Vessels of the United States
Mansfield, John, Brandt. History of the Great Lakes, vol.1 [Vessel & Wreck Index]
Marine Review. Around the Lakes – 1894 Vessel Directory
Marine Review Publishing. Blue Book of American Shipping, 1896-1915
Mears, Charles. Papers at Chicago Historical Society
Mills, John M. Canadian Coastal and Inland Steam Vessels 1809-1930
Milwaukee Public Library. Milwaukee Sentinel Index 1837 – 1890
Polk, R.L. & Co. Polk's Great Lakes Marine Directory, 1884, 1888, 1890
Runge, Herman. The Great Lakes Vessel Card File, Milwaukee Public Library
Runge, Herman. Great Lakes Vessel Build Lists, Milwaukee Public Library
Starkweather, Charles. Arrivals and Clearances from the Port of Chicago for the year 1838.
US Coast Guard. Index to Accident Investigations – Milwaukee, Wisconsin – 1924 – 1948.

US Customs House Vessel Enrollment Records (from microfilm)
US Customs House Vessel Enrollment Indexes (from microfilm)
Milwaukee Customs House Wreck Reports 1850 – 1900 (from microfilm)
US Congressional Record. Arrivals and Clearances from the Port of St. Joseph for the year 1837.
US Treasury Department, Bureau of Navigation. Annual List of US Merchant Vessels 1866 – 1989
US Lifesaving Service. Annual Report of the US Lifesaving Service, 1876 – 1914.
Wilson, Loudon S. Great Lakes Directory of Commercial Sail. Unpublished Manuscript

Maps & Charts

Ackerman, Paul. Lake Michigan Dive Chart
Caesar, Pete. Lake Michigan, Great Shipwrecks
Caesar, Pete. Lake Michigan Shipwreck Maps – I, II & III
Cook, Lynnwood. Lake Michigan Shipwreck Map
Deviney, Calvin. Flint Treasure Map Enterprises. Lake Michigan Shipwreck Maps, 1960.
Frederickson, Arthur & Lucy. Frederickson's Treasure Chart of Lost Ships and Cargoes in the Frankfort, Michigan Area
Frederickson, Arthur & Lucy. Chart of Vessels Wrecked from Michigan City, Indiana to Milwaukee, Wisconsin
Frederickson, Arthur & Lucy. Chart of Vessels Wrecked from Milwaukee to Algoma
Frederickson, Arthur & Lucy. Chart of Vessels Wrecked in the Vicinity of Door County
Guyer, Jerry. Captain Jerry's Shipwreck Charts
US Weather Bureau. Charts of Vessels Wrecked on the Great Lakes 1886–1891, 1894, 95, 96, 97

Periodicals

Anchor News – Newsletter of the Wisconsin Maritime Museum
Inland Seas – Journal of the Great Lakes Historical Society
Lake Log Chips – Historical Collections of the Great Lakes
Marine Review – Marine Review Publishing
Michigan History – Michigan Historical Center
Nor'Easter – Lake Superior Marine Museum Association
Soundings – Journal of the Wisconsin Marine Historical Society
Scanner – Toronto Marine Historical Society
Ship's Lamp – Michigan Maritime Museum
Telescope – Great Lakes Maritime Institute

Newspapers

Buffalo Daily Courier
Buffalo Daily Republic
Buffalo Commercial Advertiser
Buffalo Democracy
Buffalo Evening News
Buffalo Morning Express
Buffalo Western Star
Chicago Inter-Ocean
Chicago Democrat
Chicago Tribune
Cleveland Herald
Cleveland Plain Dealer
Cleveland Morning Leader
Cleveland Press
Collingwood Enterprise-Bulletin
Detroit Democratic Free Press
Detroit Daily Advertiser
Detroit Free Press
Detroit News
Detroit Post and Tribune
Door County Advocate
Evening Wisconsin
Evergreen City Times (Sheboygan, Wisconsin)
Green Bay Intelligencer
Kenosha American
Kenosha Telegraph
Ludington Daily News
Manitowoc Herald
Marine Review
Marine Record
Milwaukee Journal
Milwaukee News
Milwaukee Sentinel
Muskegon Chronicle
Oceana Times
Oswego Daily Commercial Times
Oswego Palladium
Pentwater News
Pultneyville, New York Commerical Press
Racine Advocate
Racine Journal
Racine Journal Times
Racine Daily Journal
Sault Ste. Marie Evening News
Southport American
South Haven Messenger
Toronto Evening Telegram
Toronto Globe
Traverse City Record-Eagle
Whitehall Forum

Public Photograph & Image Sources

Thunder Bay National Marine Sanctuary, C. Patrick Labadie Collection at the George N. Fletcher Library, Alpena, MI
Milwaukee Public Library, Great Lakes Marine Collection, Milwaukee, WI
Historical Collections of the Great Lakes at Bowling Green State University, Perrysburg, OH
Wisconsin Maritime Museum, Manitowoc, WI
Tri-Cities Historical Museum, Grand Haven, MI
Door County Maritime Museum, Sturgeon Bay, WI
State Historical Society of Wisconsin Digital Collections, Madison, WI
Kenosha County Historical Society Digital Collections, Kenosha, WI
American Geographical Society Collection, University of Wisconsin-Milwaukee

Vessel Index

The index below includes every vessel mentioned in this book as having wrecked or been built within the geographical area covered. The index includes an entry for every name that a given vessel sailed under. As such, a single vessel may have multiple entries. Each vessel is further identified either by her official number or year of build in parentheses after her name and rig. I have followed the convention of the Annual List of US Merchant Vessels in listing vessels alphabetically by the first letter of their full name. This is in keeping with the maritime tradition that unlike a person, a ship does not have a first name and last name. Rather, a ship has only one name, which may have multiple parts. As such, the propeller Alice E. Wilds will appear under the letter 'A' rather than the letter 'W'.

Numeric

#1, Scow (1895) · 123
54, Steel Dredge (172258) · 181

A

A, Barge (30189) · 80
A. P. Dutton, Schooner (376) · 87
A.A.C. Tessler, Steam Fish Tug (107409) · 177
A.B. Ward, Schooner (383) · 106
A.B.C.F.M., Schooner (12978) · 129
A.C. Tuxbury, Schooner (106706) · 145
A.E. Clifford, Steel Fish Tug (249688) · 192
A.H. Newbold, Schooner (1848) · 66
A.J. Vieau, Schooner (1847) · 165
A.P. Wright, Steamer (29894) · 47
A.V. Knickerbocker, Schooner (1840) · 37, 198
A.W. Lawrence, Tug (105948) · 119
Acacia, Mine Layer (WAGL-200) · 185
Active, Schooner (1845) · 101, 198
Active, Schooner (363) · 87
Adda, Schooner (1855) · 167
Adele, Steam Yacht (106770) · 176
Adell, Schooner (1860) · 106, 168
Adroit II, Gas Yacht (220433) · 186
Advance No. 2, Steel Tug (267897) · 192
Advance, Schooner (365) · 166, 205
Adventure, Scow (1868) · 170
Agnes W, Propeller (110724) · 175
Ahana, Gas Yacht (266250) · 90
Alert, Schooner (1847) · 165
Alexander Mitchell, Brig (1853) · 202
Algomah, Brig (1845) · 104
Alice B. Norris, Schooner (105471) · 171
Alice E. Wilds, Propeller (106170) · 121
Alice Mary III, Gas Yacht (225610) · 188
Alice, Schooner (105020) · 75
Alice, Steam Fish Tug (106005) · 172
Alkco II, Gas Launch (239246) · 188
Alleghany, Schooner (379) · 167
Alleghany, Sidewheel Steamer (1849) · 103
Allentown, Anti Sub Frigate (PF-52) · 190
Allison, Wooden Yacht (281865) · 193
Alma, Scow Schooner (106517) · 121, 175, 244

Alpena, Sidewheel Steamer (404) · 45
Alquinot, Wooden Gas Yacht (207580) · 148
Althea II, Gas Yacht (209909) · 146
Althea, Gas Yacht (215919) · 183
Alvah Eaton, Steam Fish Tug (105470) · 129, 171
Alvin Clark, Schooner (1846) · 26
Amata, Gas Yacht (222187) · 187
Amelia, Gas Launch (210628) · 180
Anacapa, Steel Tug (242999) · 189
Andaste, Propeller (1892) · 54
Andrew Jackson, Schooner · 41
Angelique, Scow Schooner (29299) · 104
Angus Smith, Schooner (105030) · 170
Ann Patrice, Wooden Yacht (285041) · 192
Anna D., Gas Yacht (220450) · 186
Anna Henry, Schooner (1801) · 70
Anna Z., Steel Yacht (547576) · 57
Annella, Gas Yacht (215477) · 90
Annie B., Steam Yacht (1895) · 88
Annie Dall Schooner (106182) · 130
Apothecariana VI, Gas Yacht (221234) · 187
Appleton, Scow Schooner (1551) · 169
Appomattox, Wooden Steamer (107236) · 131
Apprentice Boy, Schooner (29604) · 170
Aquilon, Gas Fish Tug (251025) · 188
Arab, Schooner (311) · 45
Arabella, Gas Yacht (221235) · 187
Arcadia, Propeller (106552) · 175
Archangel, Sloop · 7
Argyle, Gas Launch (232071) · 90
Ariel, Passenger Steamer (105870) · 172
Arkansas, Schooner (1849) · 38
Arrow, Gas Yacht (222818) · 187
Arthur, Steam Fish Tug (106683) · 176
Ashtabula, Schooner (367) · 118
Astor, Schooner (1847) · 165
Atlanta, Wooden Passenger Steamer (106823) · 211
Atlas, Steam Sand Scow (200815) · 179
Aubrey, Steamer (205312) · 153
August F. Janssen, Steamer (130711) · 137
Augusta, Schooner (1855) · 17

B

B.B. Jones, Steam Tug (2158) · 169
B.W. Aldrich, Steam Tug (2701) · 170

Badger State, Bark (2134) · 167
Badger, Steam Lighter (1837) · 99, 164
Badger, Steam Fish Tug (207380) · 177
Bald Head, Steel Tug (243437) · 190
Baltic, Schooner (1842) · 37
Barbarian, Schooner (2137) · 125
Barclay, Barge (166944) · 179
Barge No. 8, Barge (166944) · 179
Barney Eaton, Schooner (2142) · 167
Barney, Steam Yacht (3186) · 172
Bath, Anti Sub Frigate (PF-55) · 190
Bayforth II, Gas Yacht (221485) · 187
Beaulah Land, Gas Launch (227522) · 90
Bella Jane, Gas Yacht (210606) · 89
Belle City, Schooner (2153) · 87
Belle, Propeller (2159) · 203
Bessie, Motor Sail (111589) · 89
Beth Anne, Gas Yacht (223831) · 187
Betty D., Steel Tug (253177) · 192
Bihua, Steamer (IMO 5152195) · 55
Black Hawk, Schooner (1832) · 66
Black Hawk, Schooner (2140) · 132
Bob Richard II, Steel Fish Tug (232597) · 188
Bobtail, Wooden Yacht (285988) · 193
Bohemian, Schooner (1856) · 200
Bolivar, Schooner (1842) · 66
Boss, Gas Yacht (1921) · 186
Boston, Sidewheel Steamer (1846) · 100
Brig. Gen. John J. Hayden, Mine Layer (US Army) · 185
Brigadier General Arthur W. Yates, US Army (223693) · 185
Brigadier General William E. Horton, US Army (223692) · 184
Brilliant, Schooner (1856) · 168
Buckeye State, Bark (1852) · 101
Buena Vista, Schooner (1847) · 108
Burned Fiberglass Yacht (1981) · 56
Business, Propeller (3163) · 173

C

C. Harrison, Schooner (4569) · 167
C..J. Hutchinson, Schooner (4360) · 41
C.C. Trowbridge, Steamer (1838) · 100
C.G. Breed, Brig (4577) · 169
C.H. Hackley, Schooner (5992) · 170
C.H. Starke, Propeller (125945) · 173
C.J. Hutchinson, Brig (4360) · 165
Cacouna, Steel Steamer (C313980) · 214
Caledonia, Schooner (4384) · 80
Calumet, Steam Tug (126838) · 177
Cambria, Wooden Steamer (127100) · 212
Canuck, Gas Launch (107808) · 89
Cape Horn, Schooner (4345) · 132
Capella, Schooner (4578) · 76
Carl, Steam Tug (126575) · 176
Carolyn, Wooden Yacht (281865) · 193
Casey, Gas Launch (154779) · 177
Catharina, Gas Launch (210338) · 180
Challenge, Schooner (4574) · 106
Challenge, Schooner (4349) · 106

Challenge, Schooner (4386) · 106
Champion, Schooner (1844) · 104, 165
Charles McVea, Steamer (126517) · 54
Charlevoix, Steel Cargo Ship (246354) · 190
Chas Howard, Schooner (1845) · 67
Chatham Steel Cargo Ship (246561) · 190
Chautauqua, USCG (233306) · 184
Cheerio, Fish Tug (237885) · 55
Cherokee, Schooner (1849) · 86
Cherubusco, Bark (4329) · 165
Chicago, Steam Tug (126009) · 173
Chicago, Steam Tug (232533) · 181
Chicot, Steel Cargo Ship (246730) · 191
Chief, Steel Fish Tug (D275653) · 90
Chippewa, USCG Tug, (US Navy) · 184
Christy, Gas Fish Tug (232743) · 57
Cincinnati, Schooner (1828) · 99
City of Madison, Steamer (4350) · 43
Claiborne, Steel Cargo Ship (AK-171) · 191
Clarion, Steel Cargo Ship (AK-172) · 191
Clarissa, Sloop (1836) · 99
Cleopatra, Schooner (1880) · 57
Coddington, Steel Cargo Ship (263025) · 191
Col. Albert Todd, Mine Layer (WAGL-229) · 186
Col. Garland N. Whistler, Mine Layer (WAGL-246) · 186
Col. George F.E. Harrison, Mine Layer (US Army) · 185
Col. John V. White, Mine Layer (WAGL-245) · 186
Collingwood, Schooner (4344) · 116
Colonel Benton, Schooner (1846) · 86
Colonel Card, Mine Layer (223692) · 184
Colonel Clayton, Mine Layer (223237) · 184
Colonel M. Steeves, Steamer (1860) · 87, 168
Colonel Pond, Mine Layer (223693) · 185
Colorado, Bark (1857) · 69
Colquitt, Steel Cargo Ship (AK-174) · 191
Columbia, Steamer · 36
Comet, Gas Launch (206980) · 179
Comet, Gas Launch (212469) · 181
Commerce, Propeller (125645) · 172
Commerce, Schooner (4363) · 76
Commoner, Wooden Tug (211238) · 213
Comrade, Steam Yacht (1895) · 88
Constitution, Bark (4568) · 168
Contest, Scow Schooner (4525) · 48
Continental, Steam Tug (4352) · 169
Coquette, Sloop (5057) · 38
Cotton Blossom, Schooner (106706) · 145
Courier, USCG (WAGR-410) · 191
Craighead, Steel Cargo Ship (AK-175) · 191
Crawford, Steam Tug (125799) · 173
Cream City, Bark (1862) · 169
Cuba, Schooner (4576) · 124
Cumberland, Brig (1844) · 104
Cumberland, Scow Schooner (126476) · 174
Curlew, Schooner (4339) · 87
Cynthia, Motor Sail (107896) · 89

D

D.C. Whitney, Wooden Steamer (157075) · 210

D.O. Dickinson, Schooner (6133) · 167
Dale, Schooner (c. 1903) · 130
Dan Costello, Fish Tug (6854) · 132, 171
Daniel Slawson, Schooner (1857) · 87
Daniel Newhall, Schooner (6135) · 166
Dawn, Schooner (6127) · 120
Dawn, Scow Schooner (157211) · 176
Dawntreader, Wooden Yacht (285041) · 192
Dea Maris, Gas Yacht (220406) · 186
Dean Richmond, Schooner (1855) · 67
Deedee, Gas Yacht (221554) · 187
Defiance, Crane Dredge (165186) · 151
Dela Elisa, Steel Fish Tug (246807) · 190
Denis Sullivan, Schooner (1100209) · 193
Denver, Propeller (157268) · 177
Derry Carne, Steamer (107422) · 89
Detroit, Steamer · 35
Detroit, Steamer (1833) · 34, 36
Dewitt Clinton, Steamer (1836) · 99
Dexter, Steam Tug (6804) · 120, 171
Diamond, Schooner (1847) · 86
Dick Davis, Steam Tug (6720) · 170
Dick Somers, Schooner (6136) · 169
Doddridge, Steel Cargo Ship (248685) · 191
Dolphin, Gas Launch (206126) · 89
Dolphin, Gas yacht (223178) · 187
Dolphin, Schooner (6132) · 74
Dolphin, Schooner (6205) · 169
Doozie, Steam Yacht (157649) · 89
Dorethea III, Gas Launch (222242) · 187
Dorimar, Gas Yacht (220406) · 186
Dreadnaught, Gas Launch (222281) · 183
Dreadnaught, Scow Schooner (35270) · 78
Dredge 906, Wooden Dredge (165186) · 151
Drieka, Gas Yacht (221235) · 187
Driver, Schooner (6201) · 168
Duval, Steel Cargo Ship (248687) · 191

E

E.D. Holton, Steam Tug (135116) · 171
E.E.E.E., Wooden Gas Yacht (207580) · 148
E.G. Crosby, Steel Steamer (80861) · 54
E.M. Carrington, Schooner (8104) · 115
E.M. Ford, Steel Bulk Freighter (150786) · 153
E.M. Peck, Schooner (7490) · 40
E.M. Peck, Steamer (135983) · 82
E.R. Blake, Schooner (135812) · 194
Eagle, Scow Schooner (135158) · 75
Eagle, Steam Fish Tug (210709) · 180
Earl Cathcart, Propeller (1846) · 70
Eastern Cliff, Steamer (IMO 5152195) · 55
Edith II, Gas Yacht (SP-296) · 183
Edna May, Gas Launch (213554) · 180
Edna May, Tug (233306) · 184
Edna, Schooner (135309) · 19, 46, 238
Edna, Steam Yacht (1886) · 124, 174
Edward E. Gillen, Steel Tug (205312) · 153
Edward E. Gillen, Wooden Tug (227538) · 152
Edward E. Skeele, Schooner (76264) · 168
Edward Watkins, Steam Tug (136032) · 171
EK-10, Anti Sub Frigate (USSR) · 190

EK-11, Anti Sub Frigate (USSR) · 190
EK-8, Anti Sub Frigate (USSR) · 190
EK-9, Anti Sub Frigate (USSR) · 190
El Dorado, Barge (135117) · 170
Elbe, Schooner (7519) · 119
Elentari, Wooden Yacht (279829) · 193
Elida, Schooner (7512) · 169
Eliphalet Cramer, Schooner (1847) · 165
Eliza, Schooner (8248) · 47
Elizabeth Henderson, Schooner (1845) · 165
Elizabeth Jones, Schooner (8193) · 76
Elizabeth Pfeil, Steel Dredge (168841) · 187
Elizabeth, Gas Launch (217398) · 90
Elizabeth, Gas Launch (223751) · 187
Elizabeth, Schooner (1863) · 40, 105, 169
Elizabeth, Sloop (136004) · 175
Ella Ellinwood, Schooner (8604) · 129
Ellen, Steam Sand Scow (136358) · 139, 177
Elsie Fenimore, Gas Yacht (223717) · 187
Elsie Marie, Gas Launch (204489) · 179
Emanuel, Scow Schooner (8794) · 170
EMBA, Schooner (106706) · 145
Emily A. Roelofson, Bark (1845) · 104
Emily, Schooner (1853) · 103, 167
Emma Belle III, Gas Yacht (219538) · 184
Emma L. Coyne, Schooner (7331) · 44
Emma, Schooner (7302) · 167
Enchantress, Wooden Yacht (531813) · 193
Endeavor, Gas Launch (213601) · 179
Energy, Steel Fish Tug (233896) · 57
Enterprise, Schooner (7296) · 71
Erastus C. Knight, Steamer (205312) · 153
Erie, Schooner (1862) · 169
Esso, Gas Launch (228514) · 184
Esther, Gas Launch (212469) · 181
Esther, Steam Fish Tug (136938) · 179
Ethel Louis, Gas Yacht (217169) · 90
Eugene C. Hart, Steamer (136131) · 137
Eva Hill, Steam Yacht (1887) · 175
Eva M. Cone, Schooner (7522) · 203
Eva, Gas Yacht (220358) · 186
Evelyn C. Smith, Steel Fish Tug (226023) · 213
Evergreen, Scow Schooner (8301) · 114
Evra Fuller, Schooner (15956) · 77

F

F.C. Maxon, Steam Tug (120182) · 171, 142
F.L. Danforth, Propeller (9155) · 43
F.L. Danforth, Schooner (120018) · 47
F.W. Backus, Propeller (1846) · 70
Fair Play, Schooner (1857) · 200
Falcon, Gas Yacht (209161) · 90
Falcon, Schooner (9190) · 87
Fanny & Floy, Schooner (9309) · 167
Far West, Gas Yacht (221485) · 187
Fashion, Brig (9189) · 198
Fearless, Wooden Fish Tug (120943) · 149
Felicitous, Scow Schooner (120121) · 203
Ferdinand Schlesinger, Propeller (120841) · 177
Fire Island, Steel Tug (243531) · 190
Flash, Gas Yacht (223178) · 187

Flat Iron, sloop (1845) · 161
Flohemia II, Gas Yacht (225610) · 188
Flora Temple, Scow Schooner (9302) · 70
Flora, Passenger Steamer (120210) · 172
Flora, Scow Schooner (9301) · 169
Florence, Gas Launch (206399) · 90
Florence, Gas Launch (207494) · 89
Flying Cloud, Gas Yacht (248784) · 189
Flying Cloud, Schooner (1852) · 67, 87
Ford River, Schooner Barge (120367) · 172
Forelle, Fish Tug (205777) · 52
Frances, Gas Yacht (220433) · 186
Frank Braeger, Fish Tug (231087) · 188
Frank E. Vigor, Steamer (116732) · 213
Franklin, Steam Yacht (1888) · 88
Fred Carney, Schooner Barge (120559) · 174
Fred Engel, Steam Fish Tug (120206) · 57, 172
Fred Hill, Schooner (1854) · 167
Fred Pabst, Propeller (120794) · 176
Fred Wild, Steam Tug (120381) · 87
Freddie, Wooden Gas Fish Tug (237558) · 149
Frederick Koehn, Steam Fish Tug (120702) · 174
Free Mason, Schooner (1854) · 105
Frolic, Gas Yacht (209291) · 180
Fur Trader, Schooner (1843) · 165

G

G. Ellen, Schooner (10194) · 128
G.M.A. Herrmann, Steam Fish Tug (86171) · 177
G.R. Green, Steam Fish Tug (85390) · 171
G.W. Dole, Steamer · 36
Gallinipper, Schooner (1846) · 165
Garden City, Schooner (1854) · 18
Gargantua, Wooden Steamer (C122435) · 210
Gazelle, Schooner (10334) · 166
Gen. Absolom Baird, Mine Layer (US Army) · 185
Gen. Edmund Kirby Mine Layer (WAGL-222) · 185
Gen. J. Franklin Bell, Mine Layer (US Army) · 185
Gen. John P. Story, Mine Layer (WAGL-200) · 185
Gen. Robt. M. O'Reilly, Steel Steamer (80861) · 54
Gen. Wallace F. Randolph, Mine Layer (WAGL-230) · 185
General A.A. Humphries, Steam Tug (136032) · 171
General Gillespie, Steel Dredge (1904) · 151
General Rochester, Mine Layer (222700) · 184
General W.W. Belknap, Steam Tug (136032) · 171
Genevieve II, Gas Yacht (224671) · 188
George Barber, Schooner (10191) · 79, 168
George C. Markham, Propeller (85779) · 174
George G. Houghton, Schooner (85374) · 171
George G. Meade, Steel Dredge (1904) · 151
George H. Dyer, Propeller (86016) · 175
George Hanson, Schooner (1851) · 38
George R. West, Steam Fish Tug (85879) · 174
George T. Nelles, Steam Tug (202925) · 172
George W. Ford, Schooner (10322) · 166
George W. Westcott, Schooner (10335) · 135
Georgiana III, Gas Yacht (214160) · 54
Gertie Wing, Schooner (85665) · 206
Gilbert Knapp, Schooner (10337) · 87
Glad Tidings, Schooner Yacht (86390) · 89

Glenroy, Gas Launch (237050) · 90
Globe, Gas Launch (213448) · 89
Glynn Acor, Schooner (1849) · 86
Golden West, Bark (10199) · 168
Golden, Steam Tug (86194) · 134, 177
Goldrill 5, Drill Ship (248879) · 192
Goodwill Jr., Gas Yacht (220646) · 186
Goodwill, Gas Yacht (220646) · 186
Grace Channon, Schooner (85309) · 74
Grayling, Wooden Fish Tug (85444) · 147
Great West, Bark (10149) · 70
Greyhound, Gas Yacht (231517) · 187
Greyhound, Gas Yacht (SP-43) · 181
Greyhound, Yacht (1880) · 45
Griffon, Bark, (1679) · 7, 25
Guiding Star, Schooner (85006) · 204
Guiding Star, Schooner (85792) · 23
Gul, Gas Yacht (209909) · 146
Gusty, Steel yacht (650104) · 193

H

H. Marsh, Schooner (1838) · 99
H. Rand, Schooner (11185) · 80, 128
H.A. Root, Steamer (95885) · 51, 235
H.F. Bues, Steam Tug (95346) · 171
H.H. Sizer, Brig (1845) · 37
H.L. Whitman, Schooner (11187) · 70
H.W. Hocks, Steel Fish Tug (234604) · 189
Hannah Sullivan, Steam Tug (95475) · 172
Hanna-Kildahl, Propeller (264287) · 192
Hanover, Brig (1862) · 169
Hans Crocker, Bark (11174) · 43, 168
Harmony, Gas Yacht (220646) · 186
Harriet Farlin, Schooner (1837) · 66
Harry H., Steel Fish Tug (232597) · 188
Harushima, Mine Layer (Japanese) · 185
Hathor, Steam Yacht (1898) · 89
Hattie Taylor, Schooner (95356) · 171
Hattie, Schooner (11989) · 169
Hazel III, Gas Yacht (222187) · 187
Hazelton, Gas Yacht (SP-1770) · 181
Heartless, Schooner · 8
Helen, Scow Schooner (95651) · 173
Hennepin, Propeller (86016) · 175
Henry Clay, Schooner (1842) · 69
Henry Gust, Steam Fish Tug (96236) · 177
Henry Marshall, Tug (95759) · 134
Henry U. King, Schooner (1848) · 166
Hepburn, Steamer (C111921) · 89
High Seas Drifter, Wooden Yacht (531813) · 193
Hilda, Scow Schooner (95944) · 174
Hippogriff, Schooner (11143) · 44
Hiram Merrill, Schooner (1845) · 165
Hiram R. Bond, Wooden Steamer (95966) · 131, 175
HMS Felicity, Sloop · 7
Hoegh Cliff, Steamer (IMO 5152195) · 55
Home, Scow Schooner (42215) · 74, 170
Homer Ramsdell, Schooner (1853) · 67
Honest John, Schooner (11180) · 113, 166
HONG QI 134, Steamer (IMO 5152195) · 55

Hope, Wooden Fish Tug (207087) · 212
Hugh B, Gas Launch (220568) · 57
Huitilopochtli, Steel Tug (Mexico A-51) · 190
Hunter, Scow Schooner (11301) · 119, 239
Hurrah Boys, Scow Schooner (95341) · 87, 107

I

I.O.U., Gas Yacht (221235) · 187
Ida Caroline, Schooner (100771) · 179
Ida H. Lee, Tug (100058) · 107
Ida, Schooner (12140) · 169
Idle Hour, Gas Yacht (100738) · 89
Idler, Schooner (1893) · 51, 236
Ilex, USCG (WAGL-222) · 185
Illinois, Brig (1834) · 197
Imperial, Steam Fish Tug (207168) · 180
Indus, Schooner (1855) · 167
Irene, Gas Launch (203812) · 179
Iron Sides, Schooner (1845) · 161
Iroquois, Steam Yacht (1887) · 88
Isabella, Gas Yacht (1908) · 89
Isabella, Schooner (1845) · 161
Island City, Schooner (12084) · 123
Itasca, Gas Yacht (221124) · 179
Itasca, Schooner (100108) · 171

J

J G II, Steel Fish Tug (246807) · 190
J. & A. Stronach, Schooner (12978) · 167
J. M. Allmendinger, Wooden Steamer (76411) · 208
J. Steinhart, Schooner (1853) · 101, 167
J.A. Helfenstein, Brig (11144) · 165
J.B. Flaherty, Gas Launch (213448) · 89
J.B. Merrill, Steam Tug (75363) · 170
J.B. Prime, Scow Schooner (13749) · 209
J.C. Evans, Steam Tug (75867) · 172
J.I.C., Scow Schooner (76716) · 174
J.I.M., Gas Yacht (223831) · 187
J.M. Diver, Steam Tug (C116387) · 170
J.M. Jones, Schooner (1855) · 167
J.P. DeCoudres, Schooner (75530) · 115, 169
J.V. Taylor, Schooner (13874) · 81
J.W. Eviston, Steam Fish Tug (75723) · 171
James A. Quinn, Steam Tug (80821) · 173
James Christie, Schooner (5991) · 168
James Foley, Steam Fireboat (130654) · 145
James H. Shrigley, Propeller (76214) · 173
James McGordon, Steam Tug (75867) · 172
James Mowatt, Schooner (76518) · 174
James N. Brooks, Steam Tug (75718) · 170
Janet Virginia, Gas Launch (231862) · 188
Jennie Silkman, Steam Tug (1874) · 172
Jennifer, Steel Steamer (C313980) · 16, 214
Jesse Spaulding, Tug (95759) · 134
Jim Sherriffs, Propeller (76392) · 174
Jim, Schooner (75546) · 169
Jo Vilas, Schooner (12767) · 41, 222
Jo Ward, Schooner (1844) · 165
John B. Merrill, Schooner (75592) · 171

John D. Dewar, Steamer (76571) · 136
John Eggers, Scow Schooner (76714) · 81, 175
John Evenson, Steam Tug (76523) · 174
John F. Porter, Schooner (1842) · 103
John Mee, Schooner (76264) · 168
John Rugee, Propeller (76753) · 175
John Spry, Propeller (91998) · 175
John V. Jones, Schooner (75766) · 130
John W. Cullen, Propeller (85779) · 174
John W. Sargent, Schooner (12773) · 87
Johnny Hawkins, Steam Tug (1878) · 172
Joseph E. Rumbell, Jr., Steam Tug (6720) · 170
Joseph Goldsmith, Steam Tug (76317) · 173
Joseph Paige, Schooner (75593) · 170
Josephine Lawrence, Schooner (12976) · 167
Josephine, Propeller (76618) · 174
Josephine, Steambarge (75763) · 119, 171
Joys, Propeller (76537) · 174
Judith C., Gas Fish Tug (234935) · 57
Julia C. Hammel, Wooden Fish Tug (77076) · 211
Julia D., Schooner (77303) · 177
Juliana, Schooner (1853) · 166
Julina II, Gas Yacht (221485) · 187
Juniata Patton, Schooner (13458) · 165

K

Kama, Gas Yacht (219538) · 184
Kamloops, Freighter · 17
Kate Ellis, Steamer (14152) · 169
Kate Howard, Schooner (14169) · 132
Kate Kelly, Schooner (14031) · 78
Katherine & Mary, Trawler (235624) · 183
Kathy, Steel Fish Tug (D277442) · 90
Kearsarge, Schooner (14042) · 114
Kevin Bren, Steel Fish Tug (254619) · 192
Kewaunee, Dipper Dredge (173993) · 181
Kid, Gas Yacht (161163) · 89
Kirk White, Brig (14041) · 166
Kitty Grant, Schooner (14035) · 167
Knight Templar, Schooner (14110) · 208
Knight Templar, Steam Tug (14495) · 142, 176
Knob Knot, Steel Cargo Ship (248121) · 191
Kukui, USCG Cutter (AK-174) · 191
Kumagin, Gas Yacht (215919) · 183

L

L.A. Schultz, Steam Fish Tug (140563) · 173
L.B. Nichols, Scow Schooner (48195) · 57
L.H. Boole, Steam Tug (14809) · 168
L.R. Doty, Steamer (141272) · 16, 17, 20, 48
L.W. Perry, Schooner (15654) · 125
La Rose, Steel Yacht (612881) · 193
Lac La Belle, Propeller (15803) · 71
Lady Ann, Sloop (1849) · 37, 57
Lady Elgin, Steamer (1851) · 17, 18, 19, 253, 254, 255
Lady Lorraine, Steel Yacht (274110) · 193
Lake Serpent, Schooner (1821) · 98
Lamira, Schooner (1851) · 37

LaSalle, Schooner (1835) · 66
Laura Johnson, Scow Schooner (140527) · 77
Laurina, Scow Schooner (15875) · 122
Lavinda, Schooner (14673) · 124
Lavinia, Schooner (1847) · 201
Lawrence, Schooner (1847) · 165
Le Bote, Plastic Yacht (636151) · 193
Le Clair Bros, Steel Fish Tug (236906) · 215
Le Jean Florin, Frigate · 19
Leathem D. Smith, Steam Tug (141055) · 176
Legionnaire, Gas Launch (264162) · 189
Legionnaire, Gas Launch (279829) · 189, 193
Lem Ellsworth, Schooner (140062) · 47, 171
Lena B., Steam Yacht (1894) · 88
Lenzena, Scow Schooner (48566) · 47
Leo, Tug (140827) · 125
Leona B, Steel Tug (267897) · 192
Lester R. Rockwell, Schooner (1845) · 165
Lewis C. Irwin, Schooner (14664) · 57
Lewis Gilbert, Propeller Steamer (110672) · 207
Lexington, Sidewheel Steamer (1838) · 197
Liberty, Schooner (14672) · 113
Liberty, Schooner (14805) · 106, 165
Liberty, Steel Fish Tug (219163) · 57
Liberty, Wooden Yacht (559339) · 193
Lightship No. 57, Steamer (1891) · 139
Lillian, Steamer (1885) · 88
Lillie E., Schooner (15872) · 137
Lincoln Dall Schooner (15577) · 130
Linda E, Steel Fish Tug (236906) · 215
Little Jap, Gas Launch (121702) · 89
Lizzie L, Steam Yacht (1887) · 88
Lobo, Gas Launch (231862) · 188
Lois Pearl, Wooden Gas Propeller (92651) · 146
Loretta Mae, Steel Fish Tug (241254) · 189
Loretta, Gas Yacht (212049) · 89
Lorna P, Steel Steamer (C313980) · 214
Lorraine, Gas Fish Tug (247699) · 189
Lotus, Mine Layer (WAGL-229) · 186
Louis Meeker, Schooner (15873) · 19
Louis Pahlow, Propeller (140559) · 173
Louisa McDonald, Schooner (15872) · 137
Luckime, Gas Yacht (227790) · 151
Lulu M., Steam Yacht (1895) · 88
Lumberman, Schooner (14828) · 122
Lupine, Mine Layer (WAGL-230) · 185
Luzier II, Gas Yacht (223831) · 187
Lydia Case, Schooner (14800) · 87
Lydia, Gas Launch (209173) · 179
Lyle D., Gas Launch (206510) · 90

M

M. 2, Steel Barge (171434) · 180
M. 3, Steel Barge (171435) · 180
M. 5, Steel Scow (171436) · 180
M. Courtright, Schooner (16393) · 40
M. J. Gillen, Scow (162469) · 89
M. No. 4, Steel Scow (171438) · 180
M.C. Springer, Schooner (91936) · 121
M.F.D. No. 17, Steam Fireboat (130654) · 145
M.F.D. No. 23, Steamer (130711) · 137, 240-242

M.F.D. No. 29, Steel Steamer (203072) · 150
M.H. Stuart, Wooden Steamer (221409) · 150, 247-252
M.J. Cummings, Schooner (90592) · 123
Mabel, Steam Tug (211216) · 177
Machias, Anti Sub Frigate (PF-53) · 190
Mackinaw City, Ferry (223692) · 184
Madiera Pet, Schooner · 8
Madonna, Schooner (90717) · 170
Mae Martel, Tug (92678) · 134
Mae, Gas Yacht (93049) · 89
Maggie Thompson, Schooner (16425) · 206
Mahoning, Brig (1847) · 18, 201, 229, 230
Maine, Schooner (16402) · 119, 233
Majestic, Fish Tug (231087) · 188
Major, Steam Fish Tug (93079) · 89
Mamie Ellar, Steam Yacht (1887) · 88
Manda, Gas Fish Tug (251025) · 188
Manistique, Marquette & Northern #1, Steel Car Ferry (93363) · 143
Manitou Isle, Steel Yacht (250173) · 192
Manitowoc, Schooner (1841) · 165
Maplegreen, Propeller (C134350) · 175
Marco II, Gas Launch (C153136) · 90
Marengo, Schooner (90583) · 171
Mareuilendole, Steamer (C138274) · 183
Margaret M. II, Gas Yacht (222978) · 187
Margota, Motor Sail (122262) · 89
Marguerite, Gas Yacht (205420) · 211
Marguerite, Steam Yacht (1892) · 88
Maria, Schooner (91096) · 172
Mariner, Schooner (16401) · 167
Marion Dixon, Scow Schooner (16629) · 44
Marlen, Gas Yacht (222267) · 187
Mars, Schooner (1855) · 200
Marshall E. Ross, Gas Launch (257559) · 188
Marshall F. Butters, Propeller (91408) · 173
Martha, Steam Fish Tug (206883) · 179
Martin Treu, Steam Fish Tug (204474) · 179
Mary Ann Larned, Schooner (1846) · 67
Mary Booth, Scow Schooner (16392) · 203
Mary Ellen, Schooner (C46243) · 168
Mary G. Bonesteel< Schooner (1845) · 165
Mary II, Gas Yacht (209909) · 146
Mary Ludwig, Scow Schooner (90601) · 208
Mary Margaret, Schooner (1852) · 101
Mary S. Scott, Schooner (1856) · 69
Mary, Gas Yacht (219538) · 184
Mary, Schooner (1853) · 166
Mary, Steam Yacht (90910) · 172
Mascot, Steam Fish Tug (93302) · 179
Mate O Mine, Gas Yacht (221485) · 187
Matsu, Anti Sub Frigate (Japan PF-286) · 190
Maureen K., Aluminum Launch (1982) · 159
Max II, Wooden Yacht (290175) · 193
May B, Gas Yacht (223728) · 187
May Durr, Propeller (91998) · 175
May Queen, Schooner (1855) · 167
May Queen, Sidewheel Steamer (1853) · 105
Mayflower Jr.. Wooden Steamer (211304) · 148
Mayflower, Gas Fish Tug (213449) · 139
Mayme, Sloop Yacht (1894) · 88
McFarlane, Schooner (1840) · 66

McMartin, Dredge (C131008) · 177
Me Too, Steam Yacht (1893) · 88
Menominee, Schooner Barge (91551) · 174
Menomonee, Steam Lighter (1838) · 164
Merchant, Propeller (16332) · 73
Mesquite, Coast Guard Cutter · 18
Messenger, Gas Yacht (221554) · 187
Meteor, Schooner (1845) · 165
Michael Dousman, Schooner (1843) · 165
Michael J. Perkins, Private Boat (222700) · 184
Midge, Scow Schooner (16643) · 116
Mignon, Steam Yacht (1887) · 88
Milton, Scow Schooner (50395) · 170
Milwaukee Belle, Schooner (16642) · 167
Milwaukee, Carferry (93363) · 54
Milwaukee, Steel Car Ferry (93363) · 143
Milwaukee, Wooden Barge (51332) · 177
Milwaukie, Schooner (1840) · 161, 165
Milwaukie, Steamer (1837) · 99
Mindora, Gas Launch (222247) · 184
Minnesota, Propeller (91272) · 173
Mint, Schooner (1843) · 165
Mischief, Fish Tug (1900) · 51
Miss Duffy, Schooner (1845) · 161
Miss Liberty II, Gas Yacht (219094) · 184
Miss Liberty II, Gas Yacht (220525) · 186
Miss Liberty, Gas Yacht (219148) · 184
Miss Liberty, Gas Yacht (220525) · 186
Mistral, Gas Yacht (224671) · 188
Mistress, Wooden Fish Tug (222610) · 148, 219, 220
Mollie D., Steam Yacht (1891) · 88
Mollie Spencer, Tug (90004) · 134
Mona, Sloop (16653) · 169
Monguagon, Schooner (90658) · 245
Monitor, Propeller (90163) · 120
Montana, Gas Yacht (210911) · 90
Moonlight, Schooner (90719) · 171
Morris, Gas Yacht (1907) · 89
Mount Vernon, Schooner (17745) · 79
Muriel W., Propeller (C138505) · 175
Muskegon, Schooner (16404) · 165
My Flower, Steel Fish Tug (241254) · 189
Myosotis, Schooner (90764) · 171
Myrtle, Steam Fish Tug (213681) · 181
Mystic, Steamer (93171) · 171

N

Namaycush, Steel Yacht (250173) · 192
Nancy Ann II, Gas Yacht (219094) · 184
Nancy E., Steam Yacht (1895) · 88
Nancy Winifred, Gas Launch (228514) · 184
Nanette, Gas Yacht (222267) · 187
Naomi, Steel Steamer (80861) · 54
Napoleon, Schooner (18174) · 167
Nara, Anti Sub Frigate (Japan (PF-282) · 190
Narragansett, Schooner (18110) · 204
Nebraska, Brig (1849) · 103, 166
Nelson, Bark (18173) · 169
Nemadji, Steamer (C156861) · 90
Nena, Gas Yacht (223831) · 187

Neptune, Gas Launch (204747) · 89
Nereid, Gas Yacht (219094) · 184
Nereid, Gas Yacht (222156) · 187
Neshoto, Schooner (18104) · 87
Niagara, Sidewheel Steamer (1845) · 200
Nick II, Gas Yacht (215919) · 183
Nile, sidewheel steamer (1850) · 100
Nina, Sloop (130637) · 177
Nire, Anti Sub Frigate (Japan PF-287) · 190
No. 1, Scow (163492) · 87
No. 10, Scow (168606) · 147
No. 101, Steel Barge (171433) · 181
No. 102, Steel Barge (171434) · 180
No. 103, Steel Barge (171435) · 180
No. 104, Steel Scow (171438) · 180
No. 105, Steel Scow (171436) · 180
No. 11, Steel Scow (173490) · 188
No. 12, Wooden Scow (173491) · 187
No. 14, Wooden Scow (164058) · 177
No. 15, Wooden Scow (164059) · 179
No. 16, Steel Barge Deck Scow (1026720) · 188
No. 16, Steel Scow (173492) · 188
No. 16, Wooden Scow (164060) · 179
No. 17, Steel Scow (173493) · 188
No. 17, Wooden Scow (164061) · 179
No. 18, Steel Barge Deck Scow (1026721) · 188
No. 18, Steel Scow (173494) · 188
No. 18, Wooden Scow (164062) · 179
No. 19, Wooden Scow (164030) · 179
No. 2, Dredge (163076) · 175
No. 2, Scow (163489) · 87
No. 21, Wooden Scow (165280) · 179
No. 23, Steel Barge Deck Scow (1026722) · 188
No. 24, Steel Scow (167385) · 179
No. 3, Wooden Scow (163490) · 177
No. 4, Dredge (164057) · 177
No. 4, Wooden Scow (163491) · 177
No. 4, Wooden Scow (164215) · 177
No. 5, Wooden Scow (164216) · 177
No. 59, US Navy Tug (233306) · 184
No. 6, Dipper Dredge (173993) · 181
No. 60, USCG Tug (US Navy) · 184
No. 7. Wooden Scow (173488) · 181
No. M-1, Steel Barge (171433) · 181
Noah's Ark, Scow Schooner (13749) · 209
Nomad, Gas Yacht (209909) · 146
Norene II, Gas Yacht (220406) · 186
Norlond, Steamer (136131) · 137
Norma, Schooner (?) · 204
Norman, Schooner (130265) · 174
North Cape, Schooner (1855) · 167
North Shore, Steel Gas Launch (230121) · 145, 188
North Star, Sloop (18165) · 71
Northerner, Schooner (18176) · 202
Northwest, Bark (118102) · 43
Norway, Schooner (18105) · 167
Nucleus, Bark (18103) · 166

O

Ocean Eagle, Brig (1855) · 37
Odin, Schooner (18966) · 167

Oh Lou, Wooden Gas Yacht (207580) · 148
Olalen, Gas Yacht (220406) · 186
Ole, Fish Tug (207918) · 23, 82, 179
Olive Jeanette, Barge (155181) · 16, 20, 48
Olivette, Steam Yacht (1898) · 89
Omaha, Propeller (155146) · 175
One More, Steel Pass (567955) · 193
Onyx, Gas Yacht (220399) · 186
Opco, USN Sub Chaser, now Private Boat (?) · 183
Orleans, Brig (1846) · 101
Osceola, Brig (1839) · 8, 37
Ozaukee, Paddle Steamer (19002) · 194

P

P. Reckinger, Steam Fish Tug (150577) · 211
P.W. Arthur, Steam Fish Tug (120206) · 172
Pacific, Propeller (1853) · 87
Pacific, Schooner (1854) · 87
Palmbay, Propeller (C133922) · 177
Pam, Gas Yacht (221234) · 187
Pandour, Gas Launch (171933) · 89
Pathfinder, Scow Schooner (1888) · 175
Pathfinder, Steamer (150730) · 88
Patience, Steam Yacht (1885) · 88
Paugus, Gas Launch (239887) · 183
Paul Jones, Fishing Sloop (?) · 179
Paul Jones, Steam Fish Tug (207918) · 179
Pauline, Schooner (19674) · 168
Pearl Smith, Steam Tug (150225) · 173
Pemberwick, Steamer (1886) · 88
Penguin, Gas Yacht (211497) · 181
Penokee, Schooner (20468) · 170
Pepper, Gas Yacht (223831) · 187
Pere Marquette 18, Car Ferry · 16, 17, 18
Persia, Schooner (19672) · 77
Peshtigo, Schooner Barge (150474) · 176
Peter Doling, Schooner (1848) · 69
Philistina, Gas Yacht (206678) · 90
Photinia, Steel Cargo Ship (BR187933) · 152
Phyllis Ann, Steel Yacht (274110) · 193
Pilgrim, Steam Yacht (1889) · 88
Pilgrim, Steel Steamer (80861) · 54
Pilot, Schooner (1845) · 165
Pilot, Scow Schooner, (19667) · 204
Pilot, Steam Tug (150270) · 174
Pinta, Gas Yacht (150651) · 147
Point Arguello, Steel Tug (243245) · 190
Point Loma, Steel Tug (243000) · 189
Point Vincente, Steel Tug (243246) · 190
Polly Lee, Gas Yacht (223178) · 187
Porter, Schooner (150012) · 172
Power Scow No. 6, Steel Dredge (172258) · 181
Preceptor, Wooden Yacht (281865) · 193
Prins Willem V, Steel Freighter (1948) · 55, 151
Priscilla, Gas Yacht (225707) · 188
Progress, Schooner Barge (150205) · 143, 173
Pueblo, Propeller (150512) · 177
Puritana, Sloop Yacht (150698) · 88

Q

Quirl, Gas Yacht (224915) · 183

R

R. A. Seymour Jr., Propeller Steamer (110672) · 207
R.B. Hayes, Schooner (110338) · 47
R.G. Peters, Propeller (110424) · 116, 173
R.M & S. Dredge No. 2, Dredge (164214) · 177
Raboco, Gas Yacht (211353) · 90
Racine, Brig (21183) · 87, 198
Racine, Schooner (1851) · 86
Rainbow, Wooden Yacht (583710) · 192
Rambler, Sloop Yacht (110613) · 174
Rambler, Sloop Yacht (110705) · 57
Ramunda, Steel Yacht (579542) · 57
Ranger, Gas Yacht (218641) · 184
Ranger, Sloop (1849) · 86
Raymond, Wooden Steamer (208205) · 143
RCC-01-SPUD, Steel Barge (171434) · 180
Red Wing, Gas Launch (216324) · 180
Redfield, Steam Yacht (111420) · 88
Redick, Brig (22345) · 57
Reliable, Steamer (110435) · 133, 227
Renora II, Gas yacht (220525) · 186
Resolute, Fish Tug (237885) · 55
Restless, Gas Yacht (221261) · 187
Resumption, Schooner (110384) · 172
Rhebal, Gas Yacht (SP-1195) · 183
Richard W, Propeller (C133922) · 177
Rival, Sloop (110985) · 176
Roamer II, Gas Yacht (225610) · 188
Roamer III, Gas Yacht (220399) · 186
Roamer III, Gas Yacht (222187) · 187
Robbie Knapp, Schooner (21947) · 170
Robert Campbell, Schooner · 40
Robert Emmett, Steam Tug (21304) · 87
Rock Barge, Wooden Barge (1975) · 56
Rocky Mountain, Scow Schooner (1852) · 69
Romancing the Stone, Steel Yacht (600631) · 193
Rosa Belle, Schooner (21302) · 136, 169
Rose Dousman, Schooner (1856) · 168
Rose Marie, Gas Yacht (227790) · 151
Rosemary, Gas Yacht (223384) · 183
Roseneath, Gas Launch (C111660) · 89
Rosinco, Gas Yacht (214160) · 35, 54
Roswell P. Flower, Propeller (110724) · 175
Rough and Ready, Schooner (110686) · 130
Rouse Simmons, Schooner (110024) · 170
Rover, Schooner (1854) · 103
Roxana, Steam Yacht (200436) · 89
Rubaiyacht, Wooden Yacht (502675) · 193
Rudolph Wetzel, Steam Tug (21944) · 116

S

S.A. Irish, Bark (115597) · 45
S.S. Coe, Tug (23450) · 135
Sabot, Gas Yacht (SP-213) · 183

Sailor Boy, Scow Schooner (23105) · 118
Sails Call, Steel Yacht (600631) · 193
Saint Ignace, Scow (57924) · 123
Sainte Ignace, Ferry (223693) · 185
Sally Ann II, Gas Yacht (222187) · 187
Salmon Knot, Steel Cargo Ship (248359) · 191
Sam Hale, Brig (22345) · 57
Sandoval, Wooden Sidewheel Steamer (220423) · 146
Sandusky, Anti Sub Frigate (PF-54) · 190
Sankaty Head, Steel Tug (243387) · 190
Santa Patricia, Private Boat (WAGL-229) · 186
Sarama, Steamer (C90575) · 88
Saranac, Propeller (116318) · 48
Satisfaction, Wooden Fish Tug (116628) · 149
Savannah, Schooner (1845) · 66, 165
Saveland, Schooner (115227) · 171
Sazarac, Gas Yacht (221261) · 187
SC-328, USN Sub Chaser (235624) · 183
SC-329, USN Sub Chaser (222740) · 183
SC-419, USN Sub Chaser (US NAVY) · 183
SC-420, USN Sub Chaser (US NAVY) · 183
Schatzie, Wooden Yacht (601274) · 193
Schlitz Globe, Schooner Yacht (116747) · 88
Scorpion, Gas Yacht (116447) · 81
Scotia, Steam Yacht (1862) · 169
Scottish Chief, Scow Schooner (23744) · 40
Scow No. 4, Wooden Scow (164215) · 177
Scow No. 5, Wooden Scow (164216) · 177
Scud, Scow Schooner (1854) · 201
Sea Bee, Gas Yacht (223717) · 187
Sea Bird, Gas Launch (237429) · 90
Sea Bird, Scow schooner (23390) · 118
Sea Esta, Gas Yacht (222267) · 187
Sea Hawk, Wooden Yacht (290175) · 193
Sea Mule, Steel Fish Tug (246807) · 190
Sea Roamer, USN Sub Chaser (235624) · 183
Sea Serpent, Schooner (1821) · 98
Sea Tag, Gas Yacht (SP-505) · 183
Seafoam, Gas Launch (237699) · 189
Sebastopol, Sidewheel Steamer (1855) · 101
See Bee, Gas Yacht (223717) · 187
Seeandbee, Steel Steamer (211085) · 150
Segundo, Gas Launch (236400) · 189
Seminole, Gas Launch (221126) · 90
Senator, Schooner (22917) · 54
Senator, Steel Steamer (116725) · 212
Seneca, Gas Launch (209323) · 180
Seventy Six, Schooner (1851) · 86
Shanghai, Bark (1856) · 168
Shenandoah, Wooden Yacht (284366) · 193
Shirley K., Steel Fish Tug (255345) · 192
Sicilia, Gas Fish Tug (210226) · 180
Silver Cloud, Scow Schooner (115025) · 207
Sioux, Tug (95759) · 134
Sir William Siemens, Steamer (116732) · 213
Siren, Sloop Yacht (116721) · 88
Siwash III, Gas Yacht (222740) · 183
Skylark, Schooner (115024) · 170
Snow Drop, Schooner (22377) · 121, 237
Snug, Gas Yacht (223832) · 187
Solace III, Gas Yacht (229969) · 187
Solace, Gas Yacht (222187) · 187

Solace, Gas Yacht (225610) · 188
Solomon Juneau, schooner (1837) · 100, 164
Solomon Juneau, Tug (254619) · 192
Solon H. Johnson, Steamer (6887) · 46
Sophia Bonner, Schooner (115402) · 206
South Shore Yacht Club, Schooner (15872) · 137
South Side, Scow Schooner (57279) · 170
Southern Belle, Gas Yacht (263918) · 189
Southern Cross, Steam Yacht (116639) · 88
Souvenir, Schooner (22579) · 167
Sovereign of the Seas, Schooner (1853) · 87
SP-1195, Patrol Boat (SP-1195) · 183
Speed, Schooner (22357) · 75
Speedwell, Mine Layer (WAGL-229) · 186
Speranza, Steam yacht (1888) · 88
Spitfire II, Gas Yacht (215919) · 183
Spooner, Wooden Yacht (559339) · 193
Spruce, Mine Layer (WAGL-246) · 186
St. Albans, Propeller (23514) · 115
St. Lawrence, Schooner (22584) · 113
St. Peter, Schooner (23516) · 107
Stanley, Steamer (C112046) · 89
Starke Brothers, Tug (115226) · 120
Starke, Schooner (115474) · 172, 207
Starke, Tug (116269) · 136
Stella, Steel Fish Tug (226023) · 213
Sterling, Gas Launch (209915) · 90
Storm King, Schooner (1856) · 103
Submersion Excursion, Pleasure Boat (?) · 215
Sumatra, Schooner (115240) · 124
Sunrise, Schooner (22349) · 79
Sunrise, Scow Schooner (116219) · 175
Sunshine, Gas Yacht (221028) · 186
Sunshine, Scow Schooner (23057) · 106
Supply, Scow Schooner (23497) · 202
Surdna III, Gas Yacht (223832) · 187
Susie Chipman, Propeller (116044) · 174
Suzanne, Gas Yacht (1920) · 186
Swallow, Schooner (57280) · 113
Swan, Schooner (115352) · 87
Sylvanus Marvin, Schooner (1842) · 67, 165
Sylvia, Gas Launch (211458) · 180

T

T.P. Handy, Schooner (1849) · 35, 38
Table Rock, Scow Brig (24146) · 168
Taneek, Gas Yacht (225610) · 188
Tanner, Bark (24236) · 108, 169
Taper Splice, Steel Cargo Ship (248879) · 192
Tech Jr, Gas Yacht (223832) · 187
Telegraph, Schooner (24232) · 87
Temperance, Schooner (1847) · 69
Tempest, Schooner (24150) · 86
Tempest, Scow Schooner (1854) · 105
Tennie & Laura, Scow Schooner (145115) · 209
Terrier, Gas Launch (SP-960) · 181
Theodore W. Maurice, Brig (1831) · 66
Thetis VII, Gas Yacht (221235) · 187
Thomas A. Scott, Schooner Barge (24785) · 112, 114
Thomas C. Wilson, Schooner (24579) · 75

Thomas Clark Street, Bark (C74372) · 73
Thomas Davidson, Steamer (145482) · 176
Thomas H. Smith, Propeller (145284) · 77
Thomas Kane, Steam Yacht (1887) · 88
Three Bells, Scow Schooner (24643) · 87
Three Brothers, Propeller (91998) · 175
Thunderbird, Gas Yacht (219538) · 184
Thyra, Sloop (145551) · 174
Ting-A-Ling, Gas Yacht (231517) · 187
Toboggan, Scow (1886) · 119, 239
Toboggan, Wooden Scow (1886) · 175
Toledo, Propeller (1854) · 198
Topeka, Propeller (145510) · 176
Torsand, Steam Tug (C134245) · 176
Traffic, Sidewheel Tug (24506) · 106
Transfer, Barge (80268) · 138
Transfer, Steamer (1873) · 171
Traveller, Schooner (24148) · 165
Trial, Schooner (24233) · 169
Try Me II, Steel Fish Tug (241254) · 189
Tuna III, Wooden Gas Yacht (213207) · 142
Twin Brothers, Schooner (1848) · 104, 166
Two Brothers, Wooden Fish Tug (145600) · 148
Two Charlies, Schooner (24145) · 166
Two Henrys, Steam Scow (145521) · 176
Two Katies, Scow Schooner (24980) · 87
Two Sisters, Schooner (145340) · 207
Typo, Schooner (24981) · 171

U

Uarco, Gas yacht (222267) · 187
Ume, Anti Sub Frigate (Japan PF-289) · 190
Undine, Schooner (1855) · 167
Undine, Yacht · 75
Union, Schooner (1848) · 86, 105
Union, Schooner (25045) · 107
Union, Schooner (25046) · 119
USS SP-1770, Dispatch Boat (SP-1770) · 181
USS SP-213, Patrol Boat (SP-213) · 183
USS SP-296, Patrol Boat (SP-296) · 183
USS SP-505, Patrol Boat (SP-505) · 183
Utica, Bark (1846) · 165

V

Vagabond, Gas Yacht (225610) · 188
Valiant, Sloop Yacht (161741) · 88
Valkyrie, Steel Yacht (D283514) · 90
Vamp, Gas Yacht (218403) · 184
Vanenna, Sloop Yacht (161774) · 89
Velocipede, Schooner (25848) · 43, 225
Vencedor, Sloop Yacht (161773) · 89
Ventner, Steam Yacht (1886) · 88
Venus, Steam Yacht (1888) · 88
Vernon, Gas Fish Tug (231734) · 57
Veronica, Propeller (161560) · 175
Via-Water, Gas Yacht (227790) · 151
Viola, Steam Fish Tug (203892) · 179
Vir-Bob-O, Steel Yacht (274110) · 193
Viroling, Gas Yacht (1917) · 181
Vixen, Gas Launch (208032) · 57
Volunteer, Wooden Steamer (161592) · 133

W

W. H. Pugh, Fish Tug (213950) · 90
W.B. Hibbard, Schooner (26234) · 69
W.G. Buckner, Schooner (1837) · 197
W.H. Wolf, Steam Tug (80821) · 173
W.J. Carter, Propeller (81112) · 174
W.K. Muir, Steam Tug (26367) · 169
W.W. Brigham, Schooner (26363) · 205
W.W. Hill, Diesel Fish Tug (227094) · 57
Walk-in-the-Water, Steamer · 8
Wanda, Gas Yacht (219538) · 184
Wanda, Scow Schooner (205327) · 179
Wasp, Gas yacht (220399) · 186
Wasp, Gas Yacht (222978) · 187
Water Witch, Steamer (1862) · 23
Waucoma, Schooner (26357) · 169
Wave, Schooner (1835) · 66
Welcome, Sloop · 7
Welcome, Steam Tug (80582) · 172
Welderine No. 2, Tug (90004) · 133
Wench, Gas Fish Tug (253169) · 188
Wenona, Sloop (1837) · 99, 164
Whiponong, Gas Yacht (215919) · 183
Whirlwind, Schooner (26226) · 73, 86
White Eagle, Steel Yacht (600631) · 193
Whitemarsh, Gas Yacht (214160) · 54
Wild Goose II, Gas Yacht (219288) · 184
William B. Pilkey, Steamer (116732) · 213
William Foster, Schooner (1842) · 69
William Goodnow, Steam Tug (26251) · 169
William H. Wolf, Propeller (81164) · 175
William J. Whaling, Schooner (26364) · 168
William Lloyd Greiling, Tug, (US Navy) · 184
William McGregor, Schooner Barge (80268) · 138
William Rudolph, Steamer (80762) · 81
William Tell, Schooner (1853) · 166
Wind Song, Wooden Yacht (525970) · 189
Wisconsin, Steel Steamer (80861) · 35, 54
Wollin, Schooner (26349) · 167
Wolverine, Steel Steamer (211085) · 150
Wunx, Sloop (1851) · 87

Y

Yaquina Head, Steel Tug (243389) · 190
Yard Hitch, Steel Cargo Ship (248662) · 191
Young America, Schooner (1854) · 67

Z

Zebulon Pike, Propeller (264287) · 192
Zodiac, Gas Yacht (221261) · 187
Zouave, Steam Tug (28021) · 168

About the WUAA

The Wisconsin Underwater Archeology Association (WUAA) was founded in 1990 with the support of Wisconsin State Underwater Archeologist David Cooper as an adjunct to the Wisconsin Historical Society's Maritime Archeology program. WUAA is a not for profit group composed primarily of avocational divers, researchers and interested members of the public. Membership is open to anyone with an interest in Underwater Archeology. The WUAA's primary goals are as follows:

Provide access to information pertaining to underwater archeology statewide

WUAA's projects and events are held around the state, and incorporate training workshops. Past meetings have taken place at the Milwaukee Public Library, Door County Library, UW-Oshkosh Archaeology Lab, State Historical Society of Wisconsin, Lottie Cooper Shipwreck Exhibit in Sheboygan, and the Wisconsin Maritime Museum at Manitowoc. Here, WUAA members participated in workshops in underwater archaeological site mapping, historic ship construction methods, use of archives in conducting historical research, artifact dating and identification, and other topics. Workshop participants have an opportunity to visit various research facilities, get behind the scenes tours of facilities and collections, meet and talk with staff, learn about upcoming training and fieldwork opportunities, and just have fun meeting new people!

Provide training to perform underwater site surveys

Classroom and in-water training sessions in underwater site survey and historical research techniques have been offered at several locations around the state. WUAA and Pearl Lake have partnered to offer a PADI approved Research Diver course and WUAA offers an annual survey methods training at the Ghost Ships Festival.

Promote research and education in underwater archeology in Wisconsin and the surrounding Great Lakes

WUAA members have assisted with the following state underwater archaeological survey projects:

- Steamer Louisiana, Door County
- Steamer R.J. Hackett, Door County
- Pilot Island Wrecks, Door County
- Steamer Frank O'Connor, Door County
- Schooner-barge Adriatic, Sturgeon Bay
- Steamer Selah Chamberlain, Sheboygan
- Steamer Niagara, Port Washington
- Dyreson Fish Weir, Dane County
- Steamer Francis Hinton, Manitowoc
- Tug Arctic, Manitowoc
- Rock Lake Survey, Jefferson County
- Lac de Flambeau Survey, Vilas County
- Rest Lake Survey, Vilas County
- Roy's Point Survey, Bayfield County
- Schooner-barge Pretoria, Apostle Islands
- Clay Banks Survey, Door County
- Bailey's Harbor Wrecks, Door County
- Fireboat M.F.D. No. 23, Milwaukee County

The following projects were conducted under WUAA's direction:

- Bullhead Point Wrecks, Sturgeon Bay (barges Oak Leaf, Ida Corning, Empire State)
- Leathem and Smith Quarry Wrecks, Sturgeon Bay (former steamers Muller and J.L. Hurd)

Distribute results of research projects to members and the general public

The WUAA quarterly newsletter, Underwater Heritage, will help keep you abreast of underwater archaeological activities in the state, and contains the latest news on underwater archaeology, shipwreck preservation projects, and tips on research methods and technology. WUAA has published a report on its study of the old "stone fleet" ships wrecked near the Leathem and Smith Quarry near Sturgeon Bay, and has created a publication on the history and lore of the Madison/Four Lakes area. WUAA has also contributed to a series of studies published by the State Historical Society of Wisconsin on Great Lakes shipwrecks and the Charles E. Brown Archaeological Society's research along the Yahara River in Dane County. A report on the WUAA-assisted survey of the steamer Niagara has also been published.

Work in cooperation with organizations interested in underwater archeological resources

WUAA maintains a close working relationship with the state underwater archaeology program, is an affiliate member of the State Historical Society of Wisconsin, and is an institutional member of the Association for Great Lakes Maritime History and the Wisconsin Marine Historical Society. WUAA has also worked with many other organizations interested in the study and preservation of Wisconsin's maritime heritage, including:

- Apostle Islands National Lakeshore
- National Park Service
- Charles E. Brown Archaeological Society
- Discovery World Museum, Milwaukee
- Four Lakes Scuba Club, Madison
- Port Washington Historical Society
- Tribal Preservation Office Lac de Flambeau Band Lake Superior Chippewa
- U.S. Forest Service/State Archaeology Region 2 Center
- Wisconsin Maritime Museum at Manitowoc

Promote the conservation and preservation of underwater archeological resources and sites

WUAA fully supports the preservation of our archaeological heritage, and works with state agencies, various organizations, and the general public to promote active stewardship and protection of archaeological sites. Recent state and federal legislation has made it illegal to disturb, remove, or destroy artifacts and underwater archaeological sites, including historic shipwrecks, in Wisconsin state waters. Violators face stiff fines of up to $5,000 and possible confiscation of boats and equipment. WUAA has worked with the state on the development of sound legislation to preserve our underwater heritage, and helped with the passage of 1993 Wisconsin Act 169, which authorizes the creation of underwater preserves and provides better protection for underwater archaeological sites. WUAA members also serve on the State Submerged Resources Council, which advises the state on the management and preservation of these non-renewable resources. WUAA is an ideal way for sport divers to get involved in the fascinating study of underwater archaeology and our maritime heritage, and is also a great way to help preserve our underwater resources for present and future generations.

WUAA membership is open to the public and scuba diving is not required. Many WUAA members contribute through shallow water or surfline survey work or through historical research. Membership application may be made online at www.wuaa.org. Membership is currently only $20 per year and entitles members to WUAA's excellent quarterly publication Underwater Heritage, which always contains original research. Future volumes of this book series will be published serially in Underwater Heritage before being compiled into book form.

For further information, visit www.wuaa.org.

About the Author

Brendon Baillod has been collecting information about Great Lakes shipwrecks for over 20 years. He was born in 1967 in Madison, Wisconsin, the descendent of many generations of Wisconsinites. Brendon grew up in upper Michigan's Keweenaw Peninsula where his father taught Environmental Engineering at Michigan Technological University. He attended Calumet High School and Michigan Technological University before moving to Milwaukee. As a young man, Brendon became aware of many shipwrecks in the Keweenaw and developed an interest in scuba diving and maritime history. An early supporter of the Keweenaw Underwater Preserve, Brendon began looking for shipwrecks in the area, identifying several shipwrecks in the Keweenaw Waterway.

After moving to Milwaukee, Brendon became active in the Wisconsin Marine Historical Society and assisted in the transcription of the Herman Runge Index Card File and the creation of the WMHS Vessel Enrollment Database. While in Milwaukee, Brendon attended UW-Milwaukee, receiving Bachelor Degrees in Psychology and in Management Information Systems. Throughout the 90s, Brendon collected information on the shipwrecks of Lake Michigan, eventually building a comprehensive database of western Great Lakes shipwrecks. In 1999, Brendon co-founded the Great Lakes Shipwreck Research Foundation and the Ghost Ships Festival, now in its 11th year.

Brendon began collecting archival Great Lakes books, maps and ephemera in the early 1990s, eventually amassing a personal collection of several thousand volumes, including full runs of the Annual List of US Merchant Vessels and most 19th century Great Lakes marine directories. He is now a recognized authority on Great Lakes marine antiquities. Brendon has worked with several collections and institutions around the Lakes to digitize many valuable archival research resources and has placed several important maritime history databases online, including the Dr. Charles E. Feltner Great Lakes Vessel Enrollment Database, the WMHS Vessel Enrollment Database, the David Swayze Great Lakes Shipwreck Database and his own database of over 40,000 19th century Great Lakes vessel accidents.

Since 1995, Brendon has hosted the Great Lakes Shipwreck Research internet research portal and has been an active participant in state and regional efforts to study and preserve historic wrecks. In 2003, Brendon was elected a Director-At-Large of the Association for Great Lakes Maritime History, an umbrella organization composed of over 100 Great Lakes maritime museums, historical societies and institutions.

In 2008, Brendon was elected President of the Wisconsin Underwater Archeology Association and continues to regularly conduct and publish original research. He has written over 50 articles and papers on various Great Lakes maritime history topics and is the author of the books *Ghosts of the Ozaukee Coast* and *Ghosts of the Oceana Coast*, both dealing with Lake Michigan shipwrecks. Brendon's work has been published in numerous regional journals, magazines and newsletters, and he is frequently interviewed in local and regional media concerning Great Lakes shipwrecks. Brendon has consulted on regional and national documentaries about the Great Lakes and has been featured on the History Channel, the Discovery Channel, the Science Channel and Public Television discussing Great Lakes shipwrecks.

Brendon was recently elected to the Board of Trustees of the Wisconsin Maritime Museum and continues research, search for, and write about historic Great Lakes shipwrecks. He is married to the former Melissa Niemi of Calumet, Michigan. The Baillod family lives in Marshall, Wisconsin with their son Justin. Brendon works professionally as a senior software engineer for a large financial services corporation where he specializes in the design and development of enterprise business software systems using distributed technologies.